LONG MEMORY

LONG MEMORY

The Black Experience in America

Mary Frances Berry
John W. Blassingame

New York   Oxford
OXFORD UNIVERSITY PRESS
1982

Copyright © 1982 by Oxford University Press, Inc.

Library of Congress Cataloging in Publication Data

Berry, Mary Frances.
  Long memory.

  Bibliography: p.
  Includes index.
    1. Afro-Americans—History. 2. Afro-Americans—
Civil rights. 3. United States—Race relations.
  I. Blassingame, John W., 1940– joint author.
  II. Title.
  E185.5.B47 973'.0496073 80-24748
  ISBN 0-19-502909-7
  ISBN 0-19-502910-0 (pbk.)

Printing (last digit): 9 8 7 6 5 4 3 2

Printed in the United States of America

For
Elsie Lewis,
whose love and faith
sustained us

Preface

This book tells the story of a people wrenched from their African homeland and scattered along the inhospitable shores of the Americas. The black American was hewn from the massive rock of African civilization and sculpted into new shapes by the forces unleashed in the attempt to forge the first new nation on the continent of North America. From the black perspective, America has, throughout its history, been a country living in permanent contradiction between its ideals and its practices. Still, the oppression and exploitation the blacks endured made them the quintessential Americans. The reason for this development, Jean-Paul Sartre wrote, was that "the exploited man doesn't separate his destiny from that of others. His individual misfortune is, in fact, a collective misfortune; it is due to the economic, political, and social structures of the society in which he lives." The history of the Afro-American, as the great novelist Richard Wright observed in 1941, is the history of other citizens of the United States: "We black folk, our history and our present being, are a mirror of all the manifold experiences in America. What we want, what we represent, what we endure, is what America *is.*"

Power emanating from weakness, patience and hope in the face of overwhelming odds, and the unity of masses and elites, have at various times been characteristic of Afro-Americans. These and other traits are, however, often obscured by the mass of detail in narrative histories. Consequently, rather than follow the traditional narrative approach, we have focused on those themes and subjects most revealing of the complexities of the black experience in America. Convinced that the ideas articulated by blacks in poetry, song, folklore, novels, cartoons, plays, speeches, autobiographies, newspapers, and magazines reflected their attitudes and significantly affected their actions in the political, social, and economic arenas, we have relied heavily on such material in developing our themes. Though we have sometimes disagreed with the interpretations of many of our predecessors, we have read their works carefully, drawn upon their research, and benefited greatly from the trails they blazed.

"To visit a people who have no history," Archibald Murphy asserted, "is like going into a wilderness where there are no roads to direct a traveller. The people have nothing to which they can look back; the wisdom and acts of their forefathers are forgotten; the experience of one generation is lost to the succeeding one." *Long Memory* is an attempt to uncover roads into Afro-American history, to explore the experiences of past generations.

We set as our task the restoration of a human substance and spirit to the dry facts of history. As we delved into the race memory preserved in Afro-American literature, we were compelled to write about many subjects barely touched upon by general studies of black history. It is, for example, no accident that, with the state and their neighbors waging constant war on them, the Afro-Americans protested. While we uncovered the accommodation frequently stressed by scholars, the testimony also revealed the resistance required by the need to maintain human dignity.

Our research contradicted those scholars who have argued that the Afro-American faced the worst as a daily experience. The special remembrance of things past contained in personal memoirs and creative works encompassed much more than pain. The sources presented the Afro-American's history in its most concrete, most complex, and most classical human terms: pain, joy, love and hate.

The title we chose for this book, *Long Memory*, symbolizes our rejection of the view of Afro-Americans as an atomized, rootless people who begin each generation without any sense of what preceded them. Whatever they do, black people talk to each other. They have always done so. The searing vignettes passed on by old sages to youth made memory itself an instrument of survival. Each generation, then, built on the lessons learned by preceding ones about Africa, slavery, free Negroes, economic and political oppression and opportunity, sexual myths and exploitation, the enduring value of the family, church, and school, white proscriptions and black protest, law and injustice, black nationalism, and military service.

Historians also learn from other historians. Rayford Logan, Elsie Lewis, Harold O. Lewis, Williston Lofton, and Merze Tate made the greatest contribution to this book early in the 1960s when we were graduate students at Howard University; they undertook at that time the unenviable task of trying to teach us to think and write like historians. Whatever success we have achieved, we owe primarily to them. Genna Rae McNeil of the Schomburg Research Center gave us encouragement when our faith flagged. She and the other members of the new school of Afro-American historians—Vincent Franklin of Yale University, Darlene Hines of Purdue, Al-Tony Gilmore of the University of Maryland, Lillian Williams and T. J. Davis of Howard University, and James Anderson of the University of Illinois—challenged many of our old ideas and asked the intriguing questions. Julie S. Jones of Yale read an earlier draft of the book; we looked at it with new eyes after her critique. Mary Lang McFarland's close reading of the manuscript significantly improved it.

Minerva Hawkins and the members of our families, Teasie, John Jr., and Tia Blassingame and Frances Berry Wiggins encouraged and sustained us. They demonstrated their belief in Edward Carr's declaration that history is "a continuous process of interaction between the historian and his facts, an unending dialogue between present and the past." Betsy Dailinger, Gwen Williams, Robert Reilly, and Carolyn Johnson typed more drafts than any of us cares to remember; Linda B. Edwards and Janet Soresind made it possible for us to find the time to complete this work.

Washington, D.C.   M.F.B.
New Haven   J.W.B.
June 1981

Contents

RELEVANCE

From Luther from Inner City *by Brumsic Brandon. Copyright*
© *1969 Paul S. Erickson, Inc. Reprinted by permission of*
Paul S. Erickson, Inc.

Introduction

When slaves came to the Americas between the sixteenth and nineteenth centuries, they brought West African music, folktales, proverbs, dress, dance, medicine, language, food, architecture, art, and religion with them. In the last decades of the twentieth century the African memory of Afro-Americans permeated American folklore, speech, music, literature, cooking, and religion. Africa and the slave experience remain central to an understanding of American history.

Just as Africa and slavery left their imprint on the course of Afro-Americans' lives, the experience of free Negroes taught lessons of survival. Free Negroes lived and died within the shadow of slavery. They fought consistently against discrimination, worked to end slavery, and struggled to develop institutions within their own communities and to maintain a sense of self-esteem despite the oppression they faced. Their struggles against discrimination bore little fruit. Segregation, unemployment and unequal employment, no education or unequal education, disfranchisement, and prohibitions against bearing arms, testifying in court, or serving on juries circumscribed their lives. They constantly reminded white America of the difference between their treatment and the promises of the Declaration of Independence. The separation and unequal status they endured were the precursor of what was in store for the slaves once the Civil War ended in emancipation.

The institutions black people developed in the period before the Civil War and perpetuated thereafter provided shelter from American racism. The two most important of these institutions, the family and church, sustained blacks through slavery, segregation, violence, and oppression. Within the family and church, self-realization and a sense of community worth and pride developed. Contrary to the assertions of some scholars, the black family in America, as in Africa, was a strong institution. Slaves made every attempt to maintain family ties, adapting to disruptions by the masters by developing extended kinship networks, communal care of children, and respect for elders. Despite poverty, prejudice, and discrimination since slavery, most black families have been headed by two parents. Poor health, unemployment, and a high mortality rate among black men have contributed more to family instability than any other factors. Even in broken families, however, the traditional kinship networks have been maintained.

The black church has contributed enormously to the strength of black family networks. Founded first by free Negroes in the eighteenth century, these churches proliferated after the Civil War. Ministers became leaders in the black community, demanding the protection of black rights and providing advancement and experience in organizational development in their churches. Black clergy fueled nationalism in the black community. Many of the nineteenth-century black nationalists were ministers. In the twentieth century, nationalistic churches such as the Black Muslims became prominent. In addition, black ministers began in the 1960s to develop a systematic theology of black religion and to reinterpret Christianity in the spirit of black liberation. Ministers, beginning with Adam Clayton Powell, Jr., won election to Congress, and ministers such as Martin Luther King, Jr., also led civil rights movements.

Black people also learned that one of the guises in which the racism they confronted expressed itself was white attitudes and behavior in sexual matters. In slavery and freedom, white men regarded black women as sexual objects and treated black men as unwanted competitors for the sexual favors of white women. The exploitation and rape of a black woman by a white or black man usually went unpunished. Miscegenation, so long as it involved white men and black women, was always condoned. White men retained the privileged position of taking no responsibility for their children born of black women. The lynching of black men for allegedly raping or molesting white women flourished as a means of control and subordination. Even after bans against interracial marriages were struck down by the Supreme Court in 1967, sexual myths and fears continued to represent one manifestation of the continued racism in American society.

Blacks sought the right to vote and to hold office in a major effort to gain equality in American society. Free blacks before the Civil War and blacks after abolition were socialized to believe that the franchise held the key to gaining true citizenship. After repeated rebuffs, the right to vote was assured after 1965. Only then did blacks begin to see the limited rewards of suffrage. Blacks gained appointments and office in the local, state, and national governments, but their economic conditions did not improve. In fact, more blacks were economically deprived after than before 1965. Political participation, they discovered, did not automatically mean economic advancement. Racism, reflected in inferior education and training and lack of economic opportunity, continued to plague the black community. The capitalist economic system did not seem to have the flexibility to provide opportunity for those who had endured its burdens since slavery.

The economic and social condition of blacks had particular relevance to their fate under the criminal justice system. Blacks were underrepresented in law enforcement and overrepresented in crime and punishment. They suffered from substantive and procedural injustice in the system, incarceration of the innocent, unconscionable mistreatment of the guilty, and convictions and unfair sentencing for crimes against property in a capitalist society where the black poor lack an equal opportunity to acquire material prosperity. But black people themselves, disproportionately the victims of black crime, also worried that if conditions did not improve, the pattern would continue. They understood that so long as blacks had such an unequal chance in the economic arena, it would be difficult to separate black criminals from political prisoners in the nation's penal institutions.

Blacks fought against compulsory ignorance during slavery and unequal educational opportunities afterwards in order to gain education as a means of social and economic advancement. Blacks established their own schools during the antebellum period and, with some white support, schools, colleges, and universities after the Civil War. In their own colleges, in order to gain continued white financial support and tolerance, they had to fight to be able to teach not just industrial education but liberal arts. When desegregation of public education became the law after 1954, they were confronted with white hostility to desegregation, along with continued efforts to curb or eliminate traditionally black colleges and universities. Even when blacks were educated, they received fewer economic opportunities than whites as a result of the caste system. Compulsory ignorance for blacks has been removed as national policy, but the battle for education is far from won.

Just as they had struggled to gain the right to vote, one badge of citizenship status, blacks sought the right to serve in the military. Once they had gained the right to fight, limited economic opportunities and a desire to maintain equality caused blacks to spend an excessive amount of time and energy in military service. In the American Revolution, the War of 1812, the Civil War, the Indian wars, the Spanish-American War, and both world wars, black men and women served, fought, and sacrificed their lives while enduring unmitigated discrimination in treatment, assignment, conditions, and military employment. In Vietnam, they became a great "resource," dying out of all proportion to their numbers in the population while many young whites sought to escape military service. Their right to fight was established, based on military necessity, but the expected benefits beyond citizenship status never came.

In addition to discrimination in military service, whites used intimidation, violence, lynching, theories of racial inferiority, and segregation to keep blacks subordinated. Blacks protested against their conditions and treatment in every period of our history. They used boycotts, picketing, marching, riots, rebellions, and lawsuits, buttressed by the creative work of black artists in the struggle against racial subordination. Black artists played a significant role in reflecting and shaping the thoughts, moods, and feelings of Afro-Americans and in teaching widely scattered communities and individuals that theirs was a shared oppression. The protest took a violent turn in the late 1960s and was virtually destroyed by federal and state governments. As blacks came to realize that political participation was less viable in the 1980s, it remained to be seen whether there would be a return to protest as a means of advancement.

Some blacks have believed that instead of struggling for acceptance by white Americans, Afro-Americans should be nationalists, focusing on developing the internal strengths of the black community in America and elsewhere in the world. Black nationalist figures and movements have existed in every period of American history. Some have concentrated on black cultural differences, some on developing economic institutions, some on emigration from the United States, and others on developing ties with black African countries. Black nationalist organizations became more vocal as part of the violent protest movement of the late 1960s and saw their leadership eliminated by law enforcement officials through surveillance, wiretapping, infiltration, convictions, and incarceration. By 1980 liberation of the white-dominated countries in southern Africa became the major emphasis in black nationalist thought. However, an emphasis on black culture, pride, and black institutions persisted.

The lessons learned by succeeding generations of Afro-Americans about the condition of black people and the strategies and tactics needed for advancement taught them, above all else, that they had the strength to survive despite the odds. The lessons also emphasized the persistence of oppressive conditions and the decreased probability that equality would come without an ever-increasing emphasis on struggle.

Politics, black Americans learned, could provide access to patronage and elected officials but not economic rewards for the group. Nonviolent protest could gain the passage of laws and some enforcement. Violent protest needed to be organized in such a way that repression was expected and countermeasures planned. Economic problems, blacks discovered, were rooted in racism and were not of a different order. To nurture the struggle and the will to survive, black institutions—family, church, schools—needed to be maintained. Also, it became obvious that international problems create international opportunities for finding supporters in the struggle. All these things black Americans learned in order to survive. But from the long memory of the Afro-American past, wisdom which would provide further advancement of the race needed to be extracted.

LONG MEMORY

1

Africa, Slavery,
and the
Shaping of Black Culture

O land and soil, red soil and sweet-gum tree,
So scant of grass, so profligate of pines,
Now just before an epoch's sun declines
Thy son, in time, I have returned to thee,
Thy son, I have in time returned to thee.

In time, for though the sun is setting on
A song-lit race of slaves, it has not set;
Though late, O soil, it is not too late yet
To catch thy plaintive soul, leaving, soon gone,
Leaving, to catch thy plaintive soul soon gone.

O Negro slaves, dark purple ripened plums,
Squeezed, and bursting in the pine-wood air,
Passing, before they stripped the old tree bare
One plum was saved for me, one seed becomes

An everlasting song, a singing tree,
Caroling softly souls of slavery,
What they were, and what they are to me,
Caroling softly souls of slavery.

Jean Toomer

The Americas became an outpost of West African culture between the sixteenth and the mid-nineteenth century. That culture continued to be reflected in the United States in the last decades of the twentieth century in music, folktales, proverbs, dress, dance, medicine, language, food, architecture, art, and religion. African cultural patterns also influenced the development of American slavery as an institution.

AFRICAN SLAVERY

Before the invasion of the white man, practically all ethnic groups in Africa had some form of slavery. West African servitude among

3

those peoples who became the ancestors of American blacks such as the Ibo, Mende, Timne, Hausa, Bakongo, Ewe, Yoruba, Ibibio, Tshi, and Edo was, however, far different from European slavery in the New World. Throughout the area now constituting the nations of Ghana, Dahomey, Nigeria, Sierra Leone, Liberia, Angola, and Zaire, distinctions were always made between native-born slaves, prisoners of war, and other imported bondsmen. Native-born slaves might be children of prisoners of war, those natives enslaved for committing some crime, or those sold by their relatives. Native-born and domestic (house) slaves customarily could not be sold (except for the commission of an especially heinous crime), often inherited property from the master, married their free-born kinsmen, and occasionally became guardians of the master's minor children. The prisoner of war and the imported slave had fewer customary rights than the native-born slave and could be sold at any time.

Most men and women enslaved in West Africa were captured in the numerous civil and international wars that plagued the area. Disputes between towns, villages, or hamlets often led to war and a number of prisoners. Since these captives were frequently redeemed (in exchange for goods or money), they were treated well. Persons captured in wars between different ethnic groups faced a more uncertain future. If the captors did not execute them, they bound the prisoners and marched them to their own country; the sick, old, and lame were left to die, and anyone attempting to escape was killed. Sometimes an army attacked a village, took all of the survivors, and resettled them in the same area in the conqueror's country, usually to labor on state lands or plantations (especially among the Dahomey). Those who survived the long trek were sold in the slave marts or occasionally sacrificed to the gods. Members of victorious armies frequently took the adult women as wives or concubines and adopted the young children. For about two years, new masters watched adult male slaves closely and forced them to perform the arduous labor of collecting palm nuts and carrying heavy loads.

The liabilities faced by slaves varied from one group to another. Almost universally bondsmen and their descendants were barred from becoming priests. In a very few areas there were restrictions on slaves marrying or dressing like the freeborn, visiting the sacred places or the house of the chief, or burying their dead in the same area as the free. Masters sold slaves for laziness, stealing, murder, adultery, general misbehavior, and violation of taboos. They pawned slaves as security for, or in lieu of the payment of, debts. The greatest liability of the slaves and their descendants was that a few of them would be chosen as sacrifices to the gods or immolated upon their master's death to accompany his spirit to the afterlife.

Although the liabilities suffered by a slave were great, his rights were also extensive. The legal position of slaves among the Ashanti was typical throughout West Africa. R. S. Rattray pointed out that among the Ashanti "a slave might marry; own property; himself own a slave; swear an 'oath'; be a competent witness; and ultimately might become heir to his master." Generally a West African slave could appeal to the chief when his master abused him, occasionally obtained his freedom if mutilated by his master, and could run away if his master did not furnish him sufficient food. A slave could be killed only by the order of the chief of his village. With few exceptions, the master who killed a slave received the same punishment as for the murder of a freeman. Masters were punished for any crime (even murder) committed by their slaves.

Although slaves had to do the hardest work, they had a legal right to one day of rest and to labor in their own behalf from one to three days each week. In those areas where slaves had no days off, they labored for their masters only from sunrise until 2 P.M. Bondsmen often received a separate plot of land for their own use but had to acknowledge the master's ownership of the land at harvest time by giving him a small tribute (usually one to five yams). When prisoners of war resided on separate farms or in hamlets, they had to give their masters from one-fourth to one-half of their crops. Any property the slave acquired belonged solely to him during his lifetime. Upon the slave's death, his master inherited the property. Slaves acting as traders for their masters received a percentage of the profits from the goods they sold. Industrious slaves often earned enough to hire out their own time or to purchase slaves who worked for their masters in their stead. Most scholars agree that the West African slave enjoyed more rights and received better treatment than bondsmen in most other areas of the world. Reflecting on the institution in southern Nigeria among the Ibo, Ibibio, Yoruba, and Edo, Amaury Talbot asserted, "There is little doubt that the ordinary domestic slaves, which formed by far the most numerous class, had, as in ancient Egypt, happier lives than many of the wage slaves in modern civilized countries. They had few anxieties, lived usually as well as their masters, and their physical wants in this warm climate were not many."

Throughout West Africa the slave also had a more stable family life than New World slaves. Often when a male was sold into slavery his wife accompanied him, although she retained her freedom. An unmarried slave obtained a mate either by purchasing one, by asking his master to do so, or by marrying a woman belonging to another master. In the latter two arrangements the children belonged to the woman's owner. An industrious slave who purchased a wife could not be separated from her, and all of their children were free. Upon marriage the amount of labor a slave owed his master automatically decreased. More important, however, was the protection accorded the slave's wife from sexual abuse by his master. Among the Ashanti, for instance, a master committing adultery with his slave's wife had to make a public confession of his crime and pay a heavy fine. A chief committing the same offense could be removed from office. In addition, the slave could refuse to continue to serve his master when he violated his marriage bed.

There was a presumption in West Africa in favor of ultimate freedom. In many areas the children of slaves were considered free from birth. Masters in northern Nigeria often manumitted slaves at religious observances as an act of piety. Most slave women became free whenever they married or had children by their masters, and occasionally their closest male relative would be freed as well. The relatives of a person sold as a slave could usually redeem him at any time by paying his master what had been paid for him. An industrious slave could often purchase his own freedom.

Perhaps the most distinctive feature of servitude in West Africa was the social mobility of the slaves and their descendants. Except among the Dahomey, for example, slaves could become soldiers, often rising to command positions. Bondsmen were ubiquitous as bodyguards for chiefs and kings, served as counselors to heads of state, often obtained great wealth, and sometimes were chosen as successors to chiefs. Charles K. Meek concluded from his study of slaves among the Hausa, Fulani, Yoruba, Nupe, and Kanuri that "their lot was by no means hard. They were not usually overworked, and enjoyed a considerable measure of freedom. They could—and did, in fact—frequently rise to occupy the highest positions in the state." The condition of servitude did not follow a man or woman as doggedly in Africa as in other societies. Once a bondsman obtained his freedom, people would not publicly refer to his slave origin. Among the Ibo such a reference constituted libel, and the person making it was heavily fined. By the fourth generation most slaves were indistinguishable from freemen, even in those cultures in which slaves labored under the greatest disabilities, such as the Ashanti. R. S. Rattray contended that after a few years the rights of an Ashanti slave "seemed in many instances practically the ordinary privileges of any Ashanti free man, with whom, in many respects, his position did not seem to compare so unfavourably. . . . It seems probable that circumstances generally would have tended towards his kind treatment. An Ashanti slave, in nine cases out of ten, possibly became an adopted member of the family, and in time his descendants so merged and intermarried with the owner's kinsmen that only a few would know their origin."

The arrival of two alien groups in West Africa considerably altered the institution of slavery. First, Arab invaders penetrating the area south of the Sahara in the twelfth century began an extensive external slave trade. Wars, slave-trading expeditions, and kidnapping became more frequent. Death was an ever-present specter; millions of West Africans died on the thousand-mile march through the desert to North Africa. But because the Koran, the sacred book of the Arabs, enjoins kindly treatment to slaves and because the Moslem invaders incorporated many of the West African slave laws into their legal codes, the slaves continued to enjoy many of their customary rights. Most of these rights disappeared when the Africans fell into the hands of the second group of invaders, the Europeans. Like the Arabs before them, these new arrivals in West Africa made life more precarious in the area. Since Europeans would accept few products other than slaves ("black gold") in exchange for the European goods Africans desired, some of the rulers elevated slave raiding, kidnapping, and war from an occasional activity to a way of life.

TRANSITION TO THE AMERICAS

The first Africans arrived in the New World in 1502; by the time the slave trade ended in the 1860s, more than 100 million blacks had either been killed or transported from their homeland. Although statistics on the trade are imprecise, it appears that from 400,000 to 1 million of the 10 to 50 million Africans forcibly transported to the Americas came to North America between 1619 and 1808, when the legal slave trade ended. Thousands more, captured in wars fomented by Europeans, were smuggled in illegally until 1860. Eventually, the raids of such groups as the Ashanti and Dahomey so disrupted and depopulated West African states that rulers began to protest against the trade. In the sixteenth century, for instance, the King of the Congo, Nzenga Meremba, sent word to the Portuguese, "it is our will that in these kingdoms of Congo there should not be any trade in slaves nor any markets for slaves." African rulers, unfortunately, were powerless to stop the trade.

EVOLVING FEATURES OF AMERICAN SLAVERY

For more than 100 years, American slavery has been the subject of debate among historians. Vituperation, racial prejudice, inadequate research, guilt, apologetics, and intellectual dishonesty have been its chief hallmarks. Many of the myths about the institution are a result of these factors and the insistence of Frank Tannenbaum and Gilberto Freyre in the 1940s that slavery in Latin America was more "open" than its counterpart in North America. Subsequent research by Franklin Knight, Philip Curtin, Carl Degler, David B. Davis, Eugene Genovese, Stanley Stein, and Gwendolyn M. Hall established conclusively that throughout the Americas slaves were frequently flogged, ill housed, ruthlessly exploited for their master's profit, and sexually abused. They had few legal rights, received a meager and monotonous fare from planters, had their families separated, worked long hours, and saw religious, judicial, and military powers sanctioning their bondage.

LEGAL CONDITIONS

Legally, every African enslaved in the South and all of his or her descendants were bondsmen for life. Before 1800, however, it was relatively easy for planters to manumit slaves, and many of them did, especially among the Methodists in Maryland and the Quakers in North Carolina. Increasingly during the nineteenth century, however, southern states erected hurdles to emancipation; masters had to petition the legislature, post a bond (usually $500), and pay for transportation out of the state for any slave they liberated.

There was no protection for the slave's family; since bondsmen were legally incapable of marriage, the family was a nonentity in the law. The master could not only separate members of a slave's family at will, but could also avoid any punishment for committing adultery with his bondsman's "wife" or for the rape of the bondswoman. There was no enforceable minimum standard of labor, food, clothing, or housing for slaves.

Whites who murdered slaves were rarely tried or convicted; in the few cases in which they were, they received much lighter sentences than blacks. Blacks could not testify against whites and had to treat all of them with respect. There were dozens of crimes that, when committed by slaves, could lead to their execution, but whites generally were executed only for rape and murder of whites. A black slave who struck a white man was severely flogged and during the eighteenth century might have his ear cut off or be castrated. In order to leave his master's plantation, the slave had to have a written pass. The whites established a system of nightly patrols to keep the slaves in the quarters, and any white person had the authority to stop a slave and ask for his pass and to use force in capturing runaways. It was against the law for large crowds of slaves to congregate except when whites were present, for a bondsman to organize a secret society, to own or carry a gun, to own or ride horses, to sell agricultural produce, or to board any ship or train without his master's written permission. Slaves who conspired to rebel or who engaged in revolts were sometimes tortured to make them confess (especially during the seventeenth and eighteenth centuries) and in any case could be convicted on the flimsiest evidence. Any local or state official could call upon the state militia or the U.S. Army for aid in crushing revolts. A slave was also legally incapable of owning property.

AFRICAN RESPONSE TO SLAVERY

Coming from a land where slaves customarily had many rights, how was it possible for seventeenth- and eighteenth-century Africans to adjust to a system in which masters legally had absolute power over them? Language differences between the Europeans and the Africans complicated the whole process of adjustment. Although enslavement was at best a bewildering experience, several factors influenced the African's reaction to it. First, the blacks arriving in the Americas were among Africa's finest physical specimens; they had survived wars, a march of hundreds of miles to the seacoast, and a long sea voyage in the stinking, oven-like holds of ships, where they were stacked in racks and left in their own filth. The second factor conditioning the African's response to enslavement was his memory of African servitude. Although he could not understand the language of the Europeans, he had a behavioral guide in the numerous proverbs regarding the master-slave relationship as it had existed in West Africa. These proverbs counseled hope, perseverance, courage, patience, and an acceptance of the inevitable while preserving one's sense of self-worth. The African also knew from the proverbs and aphorisms that a slave was not to work too hard ("break everything") for his master. Among the key West African proverbs were the following: "Job-work is not the slave's first care; the master's work has the first claim on his time. . . . A dog does not bark at his master. . . . To break everything when working is not good. . . . The slave is naturally the guilty party. . . . He who waits patiently lives long. . . . If a man powerful in authority should mistreat you, smile at him. . . . A slave does not choose his master. . . . A slave's wisdom is in his master's head."

The African influenced American slavery in a number of ways. First, he extracted from American planters one of the rights he had enjoyed in West Africa: a separate plot of land for his own use. This practice developed initially because the Europeans, ignorant of African diet, had to allow their slaves to grow their own food. Second, the planters instituted the task system as a way of combining their labor requirements with the routines the blacks had known in Africa. Many features of the southern legal codes evolved as guarded reactions to the African's response to enslavement. Since drums had been the African's telegraph, the planters prohibited slaves from using them. Punishments for runaways, conspirators, and rebels, as well as the patrol laws, were a direct result of the African's resistance to enslavement.

SLAVE RESISTANCE AND SURVIVAL

According to the research of Gerald Mullin in Virginia and Daniel E. Meaders and Peter Wood in South Carolina, African-born slaves were prominent among eighteenth-century fugitives. Meaders' research is especially significant, for it shows that Africans resisted servitude more than any group of European indentured servants, who were often subjected to the same treatment as the blacks. Just as he had done while in West Africa, the African-born slave was much more likely to try to escape during his first two years of bondage than at any other time. This propensity of the Africans forced the planters to institute the patrol system.

Africans played a more important role in revolts until the 1830s than did native-born slaves. African-born conjurors usually prepared potions designed to make the slaves feel immune to injury by whites, and the rebels used drums to signal the start of uprisings in New York in 1712, in Stono, South Carolina, in 1739, and in Charleston's Denmark Vesey conspiracy in 1822. The relationship of African traditions to early slave resistance appeared in the *Maryland Gazette's* 1741 account of the execution of a black (after having his right hand cut off) for murdering his master: "The Negro Fellow that was executed here behav'd with as much Resolution and Unconcernedness as possibly could be: As he rode to the Gallows he sung all the Way . . . a Negro Song; which . . . was about War and Fighting in their own Country: And meant, I suppose, to animate him against the Fears of Death."

Inspired by their African forefathers, American-born slaves engaged almost continuously during the nineteenth century in conspiracies, rebellions, and attempts to escape from bondage. They ran away and joined Indian tribes, established small communities of runaways (maroons) in southern swamps, murdered their owners, and resisted enslavement in countless other ways. Although they were an illiterate, unarmed minority, they waged guerrilla war against their owners and risked retaliation from state militias and the U.S. Army. The most notable of the revolts occurred in 1831 when Nat Turner and his black army struck unsuccessfully for freedom in Southampton County, Virginia, and killed fifty whites in the attempt.

A number of scholars, including Ulrich B. Phillips and Stanley Elkins, have argued that slavery was so crushing for most blacks that it caused a change in their personalities, and that they worked contentedly and were loyal to their masters. This interpretation is misleading because in a totally oppressive situation, the oppressed either make some accommodations or they die. To accept survival over suicide is not, however, the same thing as being docile. After all, how many unarmed men and women would launch a frontal assault on a man pointing a loaded gun at them? The only trustworthy testimony on how the blacks felt and behaved is that of the slaves themselves. In their letters, speeches, interviews, and autobiographies, the slaves testified that they resisted bondage by every means available to them. The former Maryland slave Frederick Douglass characterized their behavior and attitudes best in an 1846 speech:

> Those who are under the yoke find themselves constantly in a state of rebellion, against the will and wishes of their masters. It cannot be otherwise. The slave has wants of his own, he has aspirations of his own, he has rights and feelings of his own, and while he remains in the condition of a slave, he finds those thoughts, feelings, and emotions all in opposition to the will of his master, and he will, on all fitting occasions, attempt to act in obedience to his own instead of his master's will. . . . Men do not go into slavery naturally—they don't go into slavery at the bidding of their fellowmen—they don't bow down their necks to the yoke merely by being entreated to do so—they don't go to the field and labour without wages, merely at the kind suggestions of some very amiable and affable slaveholder. No! Something else is necessary— the whip must be there—the chain must be there—the gag must be there—the thumb screw must be there—the fear of death must be there, in order to induce the slave to go to the field and labour for another man without wages.

No rational person could read the monotonous notations in plantation records, newspapers, or slave autobiographies of floggings, castrations, mutilations, imprisonments, and executions and argue that the bondsmen were content. Unless one contends that planters were innately sadistic, there would have been no need to punish blacks had they performed their work cheerfully and never resisted their masters. Similarly, it is inconceivable that any person who had studied the contributions the slaves made to American culture, examined the philosophy contained in their proverbs, songs, and folktales, investigated their religious beliefs, or counted the number of runaways (between

5 and 10 percent of the total slave population annually), murderers
of white masters, and arsonists could seriously maintain that the blacks
were Sambos—grinning, faithful dogs bowing and scraping at their
master's will. In spite of all the cruelty and deprivation inherent in
slavery, the blacks survived and preserved their sense of womanhood
and manhood.

The most surprising thing about southern slavery was that the blacks
not only survived, they also increased. While the death rate among
slaves in Latin America was much higher than the birth rate, the opposite was true in North America. There was a natural increase in the
slave population in the South for two reasons. First, unlike Latin American planters, North American slaveholders began at an early date importing almost as many women as men from Africa. Second, and equally
important, was the slaves' preservation of African attitudes toward
sex and procreation. The Europeans' repression of sexual desires and
glorification of celibacy were incomprehensible in traditional African
society. For the Africans, there was nothing unnatural about the sex
act. Young women received sexual training from older ones, and West
Africans placed great stress on fertility. They considered it a disgrace
for a woman not to bear a child once every three to five years. Childless-
ness was a woman's greatest calamity; contempt, ridicule, and divorce
resulted when she was barren. The slaves retained the Africans' attitude toward sex and procreation and were, as a result, freed from
the unnatural repression and guilt complexes about sex which afflicted
many American whites until the last decades of the twentieth century.

Neither the fact that the blacks managed to survive nor the romantic portrayal of slavery in such films as *Gone with the Wind* can erase
from our consciousness the hard fact that slavery was a brutal, exploitive
economic and social system. Southern planters and some historians
claim that it was a "school" designed to raise blacks from the barbarism
of Africa, civilize and christianize them. The planters insisted that
they treated the slaves ("my people") with kindness, as a father does
his children. Yet they barred slaves from schoolhouses, flogged them,
separated their families, and extracted every possible ounce of labor
from them. The institution varied, of course, from county to county
and from master to master. But its central purpose, its *raison d'être*,
was exploitation. When planters gave slaves what they described as
adequate food, clothing, and shelter, it was not because they loved
the bondsmen but because they felt that such treatment would enable
them to get more labor out of them. Considering the blacks as congeni-
tally inferior, the planters argued that they would work only when
driven by force, and that they could never be accepted as equals. If

they were emancipated, they must either be returned to Africa or exterminated.

PROFITABILITY OF SLAVERY

In spite of the debates among economists, there is considerable evidence that slavery throughout the South was profitable for individual planters. Bankruptcy was no more frequent among southern planters than among northern businessmen, and southern whites believed so firmly that the institution was profitable that they engaged in the most destructive war of the nineteenth century—the Civil War—to preserve it. Although certainly less efficient than free labor, the work of the slaves gave southern planters a standard of living which was the envy of their contemporaries. In capitalistic America, no business enterprise could have lasted from 1619 to 1865 (almost 250 years) *without* being profitable. The planters and their slaves produced enough tobacco, rice, sugar, and cotton to form the foundation for American prosperity before the Civil War.

Since most slaves lived on plantations, the pattern of the bondsmen's lives was mandated to meet the master's labor needs. Most field hands began their labor before sunrise; the overseer whipped them when they reported late for work. The plantation used slaves from childhood to death; youngsters did yard work or fanned the master, old women cooked, elderly men cared for livestock or gardens. Domestic slaves wore better clothes (the master's hand-me-downs) and ate better food (the master's leftovers) than field slaves, but they worked continuously and were always subject to punishment by the masters. Most blacks regarded floggings not as extraordinary punishments but as a central fact of slave life. Masters and overseers whipped slaves for individual acts of assumed resistance, laziness, or lack of deference.

By nineteenth-century standards, the food that planters furnished slaves was inadequate in amount and nutritional value. Although slaves constantly worked harder, they received less nourishing food as their *weekly* rations than antebellum soldiers, sailors, and prisoners received *daily*. The only way slaves avoided starvation was by raising vegetables on their own garden plots, stealing food, or hunting and fishing after they finished working for their masters.

Blacks usually thought of a master as a successful plantation owner who treated his bondsmen well, but even on the best-run plantations they knew clearly that they were slaves. Many slaveowners were moral degenerates and sadists or stupid, inefficient, uncaring businessmen. Some flogged slaves severely, shackled them, or had iron weights with bells attached placed on their necks. On some plantations, slaves suffered from overwork, abuse, and starvation. Masters took infants from mothers and raped and beat women. Other masters branded, burned, tortured, maimed, and castrated their slaves. In contrast to these outrageously victimized ones, many slaves in interviews and autobiographies testified that they sometimes had "good" masters. The good masters were those who rarely permitted physical abuse and provided slaves with sufficient food, clothing, shelter, and medical care.

Sometimes public opinion and religious belief restrained otherwise cruel and sadistic planters. As Robert Fogel and Stanley Engerman pointed out in *Time on the Cross* (1974), certain economic realities also caused some masters to manage their slaves in a relatively humane fashion. Although legally planters had absolute authority over slaves, they usually could not afford to starve, torture, or work the bondsmen to death. They required constant labor but did not try to kill the slave or reduce his capacity to perform his tasks. But it was the slave himself who placed the most important limit on the exploitation and cruelty of the master. Whites recognized that some slaves were good workers, but dangerous when pushed. They knew that others responded to pecuniary incentives, the reward of a plot for gardening, or kindly treatment. The master's interest was in profit and in an orderly, comfortable life; the slaves' interest was in as much autonomy as possible within the system. The master achieved his objectives by threats, bribery, adequate treatment, and the use of force. The reality of profit-making gave more space than might appear on the surface for the slave to lead his own social life.

Slaves often worked in factories, in construction, as skilled artisans, and in domestic service in the cities. Many owners derived a regular income from hiring out slaves, either by the year or for shorter periods. In contrast to plantation blacks, urban slaves moved about more freely, lived in houses separate from their masters' domiciles, and often worshipped in black churches free of white surveillance. They also had more opportunities for informal socializing (in illegal dram shops, dance halls, etc.) than plantation slaves had. Bondsmen employed in industry compared favorably with free workers in diligence and efficiency. The cities and factories, however, had to compete with the countryside for a limited supply of slaves. Although capitalists could substitute immigrant labor for slave labor in the cities, there were no acceptable lower-cost alternatives to it in the countryside. As a result of the competition for labor, the urban slave population generally varied with the price of slaves and with the rate of white immigration. There was, however, no one-to-one relationship between these factors. For instance, between 1820 and 1860 the percentage of slaves in the population of the ten largest southern cities declined dramatically while it increased in the second ten largest cities.

HISTORICAL IMPORTANCE OF SLAVERY

From a historical perspective, the importance of slavery lies in three areas. First, as subsequent chapters will demonstrate, it was the major determinant of American race relations. The legacy of slavery led in the nineteenth century to the institution of Jim Crow laws—laws designed to separate blacks and whites—to segregated housing and schools, to discrimination in the dispensation of justice, to myths about interracial sex, and to economic and political oppression. Second, slaves played a crucial role in the transformation of African cultural elements and the creation of a unique black culture in the Americas.

Third, although African slaves contributed much to American culture, they stood as America's accuser. As long as black people labored in chains, the Declaration of Independence and the Constitution symbolized the American's ability to lie to himself. Having lived so long with this lie, American whites found it increasingly difficult to resolve the dilemma between equality and discrimination once they had ended the conflict between slavery and freedom. Although some form of involuntary servitude had existed in all societies before the creation of the United States, in none of them did the fundamental documents and philosphies so unequivocally assert that slavery was a violation of divine and natural law. Because of the glaring contradiction between their belief in freedom and equality and their practice of enslaving and discriminating against blacks, antebellum American whites suffered from a massive guilt complex. To escape the residue of this guilt in the twentieth century, white historians tried to prove that the slaves received more advantages than white workers did, that the blacks were content as slaves, that none of the social problems afflicting Afro-Americans in the twentieth century had their roots in the "peculiar institution," and that slaves were so assimilated that their culture should be stamped "Made in America." All of these arguments were imaginary and had little relationship to the realities of bondage.

AFRICAN SURVIVALS IN AFRO-AMERICAN CULTURE

The greatest crime committed by slavery scholars in the first half of the twentieth century was their attempt to prove that blacks were inferior. The long-suffering, Christ-like, but much ridiculed Uncle Tom, the unbelievably loyal child-man Sambo, and the Mammy who loved her master more than her own family are unfounded stereotypes of incredible longevity. So many whites accepted these stereotypes and similar ones about Africans that many blacks rejected the study of slavery and Africa. Both were part of a dismal past best forgotten. But just as American whites cannot assuage their guilt by turning to myths, blacks cannot live in a present without roots in the past. The assertion by some white and Afro-American scholars that black history began in 1865 has had extremely negative results. First, since it enabled white scholars to ignore the contributions blacks made to more than 200 years of American history, it also enabled them to make blacks invisible in the rest of it. Second, such views discouraged blacks from investigating their own history. Although the ancestors of practically all white Americans were at one time slaves, twentieth-century blacks were led to believe that they were the *only* Americans who were descendants of bondsmen. One significant result of the negative feelings blacks felt over this was that for a long time most of them had less interest in history and genealogy than any other group of Americans. A third result of the denial of the slave past was the virtual destruction of many unique and functional aspects of Afro-American culture as twentieth-century blacks rushed to adopt the middle-class values of American whites. It was only in the 1960s that masses of blacks discovered that many of the values and customs of whites were less functional for the survival of an oppressed minority than those of their slave ancestors.

"It is of consequence," America's premier folklorist, William Wells Newell, declared in 1894, "for the American Negro to retain the recollection of his African origin, and of his American servitude." This was necessary, Newell said, because "for the sake of the honor of his race, he should have a clear picture of the mental condition out of which he has emerged: this picture is not now complete, nor will be made so without a record of song, tales, beliefs, which belong to the stage of culture through which he has passed." By the middle of the twentieth century, the collection of the data noted by Newell had reached the point at which scholars could begin to answer the question of the origins of black culture. There was, however, no unanimity. This debate on origins centered on the folktale.

Richard M. Dorson, in his *Negro Folktales in Michigan* (1956), argued that an overwhelming majority of Afro-American folktales came originally from Europe. Since Dorson compiled his tales in the 1950s, his theory may be correct for the second half of the twentieth century. Obviously, the spread of literacy and of radio and television sets in the twentieth century led to the diffusion of European folklore in the black community. Just as obvious, however, is the fact that the widespread illiteracy of slaves and the absence of mass communications media in the nineteenth century severely limited the spread of European immigrant folkore within the slave community. Given the degree of isolation between antebellum whites and blacks as well as differences in languages and roles, it is improbable that European sailors transporting Africans to the Americas or white plantation owners and overseers regaled the blacks with European folktales, proverbs, and riddles. Most of the diffusion of folklore in the nineteenth century involved whites borrowing from blacks. Slaves customarily entertained their master's children with tales, white folklorists regularly visited the quarters and recorded them, and large segments of the white community read the stories compiled by Joel Chandler Harris, Charles C. Jones, Jr., Alcée Fortier, and others.

Whatever the situation in the twentieth century, about 65 percent of the folktales of slaves in the nineteenth-century American South came from Africa. The 200 slave tales recorded by Abigail Christensen in South Carolina, Joel Chandler Harris and Charles C. Jones, Jr., in Georgia, Alcée Fortier in Louisiana, and the Hampton Institute's black folklorists throughout the South between 1872 and 1900 were generally identical in structure, detail, function, motif, attitudes, and thought patterns to African ones. Rarely did the slaves' tales show any trace of the sentimentality and romanticism characteristic of European folklore. The African origin of nineteenth-century black folktales has long been recognized by the collectors of African folklore. In 1892, A. Gerber compared Afro-American and African folklore and asserted that "not only the plots of the majority of the stories, but even the principal actors, are of African origin." African scholars found striking parallels between the Uncle Remus stories collected by Harris and West African folktales. According to Alta Jablow, the traditional West African animal stories "served as the prototype of the well-known Uncle Remus stories." And in 1966, Hugh Anthony Johnston, after studying more than 1,000 traditional Hausa and Fulani folktales in Nigeria, asserted: "Brer Rabbit is undoubtedly the direct descendant of the hare of African folktales. Not only are his characteristics exactly the same as those of the Hausa Zomo but the plots in at least thirteen of the Uncle Remus stories are parallels of those in Hausa stories."

A number of the nineteenth-century collectors of slave folktales also recognized their African origin. William Owen, in one of the first analyses of black folklore, wrote in 1877 that the slaves' tales were "as purely African as are their faces or their own plaintive melodies . . . the same wild stories of Buh Rabbit, Buh Wolf, and other *Buhs* . . . are to be heard to this day in Africa, differing only in the drapery necessary to the change of scene." Although Joel Chandler Harris knew very little about African folklore, one of the scholars (Herbert H. Smith) he contacted about the origin of his first series of Uncle Remus stories wrote: "One thing is certain. The animal stories told by the negroes in our Southern States and in Brazil were brought by them from Africa." Christensen pointed out that the ancestors of her South Carolina informants had "brought parts of the legends from African forests." Prince Baskins told Christensen that he had first heard the tales from his grandfather, a native African. Many of the tales even contained African words.

The folktale served some of the same functions in the slave quarters as it had in Africa. It was a means of entertainment, inculating morality in the young, teaching the value of cooperation, and explaining animal behavior. Like the Africans, the slaves had a large repertoire of "pourquoi" stories, or why animals got to be the way they were.

Among the slaves the folktale had a more specific purpose: it was also a means of training young blacks to use their cunning to overcome the strength of the master, to hide their anger behind a mask of humility, to laugh in the face of adversity, to retain hope in spite of almost insuperable odds, to create their own heroes, and to violate plantation rules and still escape punishment. In many of the tales a slave used his wits to escape from work and punishment or to trick his master into emancipating him. They also reveal the slaves' sense of humor:

> Once an old slave used to make it his practice to steal hogs. The way he would be sure of the animal was he would tie one end of a rope around his prey and the other around himself. The old Negro had been successful for many years in his occupation, but one time when he caught one of his master's hogs he met his equal in strength. He was fixing to have a big time on the next day, which was Sunday. He was thinking about it and had the old hog going along nicely, but at last as he was coming up on top of a very high hill the hog got unmanageable and broke loose from the old fellow's arms. Still the old man made sure it was all right because of the rope which tied them together, so he puffed and pulled and scuffed, till the hog got the best of him and started him to going down the steep hill. The hog carried him clear to his master's house, and the master and his family were sitting on the porch. All the Negro could say, as the hog carried him around and around the house by his master, was "Master, I come to bring your pig home!"

NAMES AND PROVERBS

Until the end of the eighteenth century the slaves retained their African names. Most of what scholars know about this phenomenon comes from ads placed in colonial newspapers by masters trying to recapture fugitive slaves. In attempting to anglicize the names, the masters distorted many of them. As they had done in Africa, the slaves continued to name their children according to the day of the week on which they were born. Although day names and their variants were most common, ninety different African names appeared in South Carolina runaway ads alone. African names, indicating a connection to the ancestral home, continued to be marks of status in the free black community throughout the nineteenth century. Significantly, many of them appeared in Carter G. Woodson's list of free blacks included in the census of 1830.

Between 5 and 10 percent of the given names of free blacks were African derivatives, with Juba, Cuffy, Abba, Cudjo, Tinah, Quashee, Chloe, Selah, Mingo, Sawney, Ferriba, Garoh, Wan, and Bena being the most popular. Occasionally the free blacks had such African-derived surnames as the following: "Quashy Baham, Wilson Africa, Edward Affricaine, Kedar Africa, Elikaim Bardor, Byer Affrica, Gadock Coffe, Pryor Biba, Alford Bim, Cuff Cawon, Ally Africa." African appellations disappeared from the lists of slaves in the nineteenth century because masters frequently chose their slaves' names. On the South Carolina Sea Islands, however, the blacks clung tenaciously to their African names. Even as late as 1940, the Sea Islanders used an anglicized name in their dealings with whites and an African name in their conversations with other blacks.

"A proverb," say the Yoruba, "is the horse of conversation." Before the arrival of the European invaders, West Africans relied on proverbs more than did any other people. They were used as greetings, played on drums, included in songs, provided the ending for folktales, and applied as nicknames. Until the last decades of the twentieth century, proverbs served as precedents in reaching judicial decisions. The scholar George Herzog, writing in the 1930s, said that in Liberian "legal proceedings it may happen that at a certain stage most of the discussion narrows down to quoting proverbs." Among the Ashanti, when a master called his slave's name, the bondsman always answered with a proverb. As a revelation of the philosophy of a people and as a way of utilizing the past to cope with a new situation, the West African proverb differed little from those found among Europeans. But West African proverbs in general had greater flexibility of imagery and application, symmetrical balance, poetic structure, and rhythmic quality than European ones. Africans used proverbs to teach modes of conduct, religious beliefs, hospitality, respect for elders, caution, bravery, humility, and cooperation by drawing on the lessons learned from history, mythology, and the observation of flora, fauna, and human behavior. The proverbs survived the coming of the Europeans primarily because they stated the moral of tales; often the proverb remained when the tale was forgotten. Through the fables of Aesop, the slave trade, and the writings of travelers, many African proverbs were incorporated in the sayings of Europeans, Arabs, and Asians. It is not surprising, therefore, to find that many of them appeared in the language of nineteenth-century slaves in the southern United States.

Largely banned from acquiring literacy, the slaves remained, like their African ancestors, a people of oral traditions, and they resorted to proverbs to teach morality and behavioral skills to their children. A comparison of the 382 proverbs contained in the folklore collections of J. Mason Brewer and the *Southern Workman* with 7,000 proverbs from West Africa shows that blacks brought 122 of them directly from Africa. As can be seen in Table I, many of the proverbs are identical in form and meaning to West African ones, but often reflect the impact of slavery and the American environment.

About 50 percent of the proverbs the slaves used reflected the plantation experience. The slaves borrowed less than 20 percent of them from their white masters. These plantation proverbs contained advice about how much labor the slave should perform, how to avoid punishment, and frequently referred to such activities as plowing and harvesting cotton, corn, and wheat, religious meetings, corn shuckings, and singing. They included such sayings as the following: "The overseer regulates the daybreak. . . . Don't fling all your power into a small job. . . . Don't say more with your mouth than your back can stand (be cautious in talking to the master). . . . You got eyes to see and wisdom not to see (don't tell the master everything). . . . Tomorrow may be the carriage driver's day for plowing (fortune changes). . . . Tired cutter in the wheat field gets sassy at the end of the row." It is a testament to the slaves' wisdom that many of their proverbs (or variants) were still being used by Americans, black and white, in the last decades of the twentieth century. They included: "The sun shines in every man's door once (fortune changes). . . . If you can't stand the hot grease, get out of the kitchen. . . . To wall eye (show anger). . . . His tongue knows no Sunday (he's too talkative). . . . Mr. Hawkins is coming (cold weather—"the Hawk"—is coming)."

WITCHCRAFT AND CONJURING

In the South hags, "ha'nts" and conjurors occupied the place the witch, ghost, and medicine man had in traditional African society. They shared many identical characteristics. Although similar in many ways to its European counterpart, the traditional African witch was a more malevolent and frightful reality. Possessing the ability to turn people into animals, to ride, kill, and eat them, the witch caused sores, incurable

TABLE I. SLAVE PROVERBS AND THEIR AFRICAN PARALLELS

Slave Proverb	African Parallel	Meaning
If you play with a puppy, he will lick your face.	If you play with a dog, you must expect it to lick your mouth. (Ashanti)	Familiarity with inferiors may cause them to lose respect for you.
Distant stovewood is good stovewood.	Distant firewood is good firewood. (Ewe)	Things look better from a distance.
"Almost kill bird" don't make soup.	"I nearly killed the bird." No one can eat "nearly" in a stew. (Yoruba) "Almost" is not eaten. (Zulu)	Literal
One rain won't make a crop.	One tree does not make a forest. (Ewe, Kpelle, Ashanti)	One part does not equal the whole.
The pitcher goes to the well every day; one day it will leave its handle.	If there is a continual going to the well, one day there will be a smashing of the pitcher. (Hausa)	One's evil deeds will one day be discovered.
A seldom visitor makes a good friend.	If you visit your fellow (friend) too often, he will not respect you. But if you make yourself scarce, he will pine for your company. (Jabo)	Literal
A scornful dog will eat dirty pudding.	When a dog is hungry, it eats mud. (Zulu)	Adversity causes one to do things he would not do in good times.
He holds with the hare (or fox) and runs with the hounds.	They forbid ram and eat sheep. (Ibo)	A deceitful person
The best swimmer is often drowned.	The expert swimmer is carried away by the water. (Zulu, Tonga)	There is no absolute certainty of anything.

Sources: Nyembezi, *Zulu;* Junod & Jacques, *Wisdom;* Brewer, *Negro;* Ellis, *Ewe;* Rattray, *Ashanti;* Herzog, *Jabo; Southern Workman,* 1872–1900

diseases, sterility, impotence, adultery, and stillbirths, and robbed a person of his money or food. Since witches were persons inhabited by demons, they could change into any animal form or become invisible and enter a dwelling through the smallest opening. The African detected witches either by spreading pepper around or through dreams. Amulets, rings, chains, and bags of powder worn on the body or placed in dwellings offered some protection, as did objects placed under pillows, the blood of fowls, effigies, and shrines. Persons proven to be witches were killed. Ghosts play a prominent role in African religions and cosmology. Viewed as the indwelling spirit or soul of a man which departs his body on his death, the ghost retains an interest in the affairs of the living and punishes or frightens them for misdeeds, aids descendants, remains in the vicinity of its grave, and sometimes inhabits the body of a newborn infant. The African's belief in ghosts is part of the process of honoring ancestors and functions to preserve social order. The medicine man or priest was a mediator between the living and the dead, a discoverer of witchcraft, and a physician. He could prepare poisons to be placed in the food of, or on a path frequented by, an intended victim. He sold powders and charms to insure success in love, war, planting, hunting, and other activities.

There were some inversions and combinations of roles in the transfer of witches, ghosts, and medicine men from Africa to America. The witch, or hag, for example, lost some of its malevolence. Even so, the slaves continued to believe that witches met as a group, took the shape of animals, and rode persons at night. They were invisible, entered a dwelling through a keyhole, and sometimes caused death. If one cut off the limb of a hag while it was in the shape of an animal, that limb would be missing when the witch returned to its human form. Protection against hags included sticks, sifters, horseshoes, and bottles of salt over the door or Bibles, forks, and needles under the pillow. Salt and pepper burned the skin of the witch. Many features of African cosmology regarding ghosts were retained in America. The slaves also believed that a person's soul remained near graveyards, communicated with and could harm or help the living, and might return to claim property which had belonged to the person. The main function of the ghost in the quarters was, as in Africa, to engender respect for the dead. The slaves universally believed, according to many nineteenth-century observers, that if "the living neglect in any way their duty to the dead, they may be haunted by them."

The conjuror, claiming to have received his power from God but believed by many to be in league with the devil, combined the malevolence of the witch with the benevolence of the African medicine man and priest. In the slave's world, the conjuror was the medium for redressing wrongs committed by his master or fellows as well as serving as druggist, physician, faith healer, psychologist, and fortune teller. Bondsmen believed the conjuror could prevent, cast, and remove spells and could cause or cure illness. He was the source of love potions, poisons, and "trick bags." Spells resulted from the ingestion of his potions or simply by walking over ground containing a trick bag. Like the Africans, slaves believed that the conjuror used items of personal property or hair and nail clippings to cast spells. In removing spells and curing illnesses, he used what was tantamount to autosuggestion or hypnotism and his knowledge of herbs. Mixing teas made from boiling sassafrass, nutmeg, asafoetida, or wild cherry, oak, dogwood, and poplar bark with vinegar, cider, whiskey, turpentine, quinine, calomel, molasses, and honey, the conjuror was remarkably successful in curing the slaves of colds, fevers, chills, and other illnesses.

MUSIC, DANCE, OMENS, AND SIGNS

It would take several volumes to describe all of the cultural elements the slaves brought with them from Africa. Some indication of the extent of the African survivals in Afro-American culture appears in a study of Georgia blacks in the 1930s, *Drums and Shadows* (1940). The Georgia investigators found seventy elements of African culture in the region. In addition to the things noted above, they included funeral rites, spirit possession, decoration of graves, taboos, wood carving, and weaving.

According to most scholars, the most obvious African retentions in black American culture were in music and dance. The melody, harmony, rhythm, form, emphasis on percussion, and aesthetics of slave music were all African. In West Africa and among blacks in the antebellum South, music was an intimate part of life—of play, religion, and work. In *Negro Folk Music, USA* (1963), Harold Courlander wrote that the black work song "particularly the kind sung by railroad gangs, roustabouts (stevedores), woodcutters, fishermen, and prison road gangs, is an old and deeply rooted tradition. Few Negro musical activities come closer than gang singing does to what we think of as an African style. . . . the overall effect instantly calls to mind the group labor songs of Jamaica, Haiti, and West Africa."

The ring games and songs of slave children also originated in Africa. A Nigerian scholar, Lazarus Ekwueme, concluded from his study of African and Afro-American forms: "A black Louisiana housewife sings to her crying baby not too differently from the way a Jamaican mother does or an Ewe woman in Ghana. The children's games, 'Ring around the Rosie' or 'Bob a needle,' each with its accompanying song, have counterparts in Africa, such as the 'Akpakolo' of Igbo children in West Africa or the funny game-song of the Kikuyu of Kenya called 'R-r-r-r-r-r-na ngubiro,' which is a special East African follow-your-leader version of 'Ring around the Rosie.'"

In contrast to the songs and ring games, few of the slaves' omens and signs appear to have come from Africa. The major reason for this was that there was a great difference in the flora, fauna, and weather in Africa and America. The correct interpretation of signs and omens was extremely important in the slave quarters. By carefully observing the habits of animals, the slaves developed (as did most rural people) skill in predicting changes in the weather. Although this was the primary function of signs, the slaves used them for many other reasons. First, they utilized them as taboos in an effort to teach good manners to children. Young slaves were taught that bad luck followed when they stepped over adults, tore their clothes, beat cats and dogs, swore, kept their hats on when entering the cabin, or made fun of a cross-eyed person. Second, the slaves insisted that slovenly housekeeping habits (sweeping the floor or cleaning the table after dark or washing in water already used by someone else) led to bad luck and death in the family. Third, they used taboos to promote good work habits: "Don't skip a row in planting or someone in your family will die." A fourth function of the signs, omens, and taboos was to inculcate morality in the young. In an effort to prevent girls from being promiscuous, for example, the slaves said: "If you kiss a boy before you marry, you'll never care much for him." One of the major functions of signs was to enable the slave to deal with the ever-present and always unpredictable specter of death. The actions of owls, killdeer, roosters, dogs, cats, hogs, and rabbits were the most frequent signs of an impending death. Every sign called for a corresponding action to prevent death. Typical ways for stopping the screeching of an owl were to put an iron poker, horseshoe, or salt in the fire or to turn one's pockets inside out.

Seeking control over a harsh world where masters and overseers were capricious and irrational, the slaves developed an unshakable belief in the infallibility of dreams and signs as predictors of future events on the plantation. Primarily an effort to determine when whippings and separations were going to occur, these signs reflect the major fears of the slaves: "If your left eye twitches, you will soon receive a whipping. . . . If you dream of your owner counting money, some slave is going to be sold. . . . If you mock an owl, you'll get a whipping. . . . Kildeer hollering, patrollers coming. . . . To mock a whippoorwill is a sure sign of a whipping. . . . To dream about dollars is a sure sign of a whipping. . . . If you mark the back of a chimney, your back will be marked the same way by a whipping. . . . If you have rice, peas, and hominy on New Year's day, you will have plenty to eat all year. . . . If a rabbit crosses your path at night, you'll soon get a whipping. . . . If you burn poplar, just as the wood pops, so will the master pop his whip on your back."

The slaves transmitted many elements of their culture to twentieth-century blacks. The clearest example of this, of course, is the spiritual; many of the religious songs of the slaves could still be heard in black churches in the last decades of the twentieth century. What is less obvious is the slaves' contribution to another distinctive genre of American music—the blues. Practically all of the motifs and patterns of the

blues were present in the nonreligious or secular songs of the slaves.
Like the twentieth-century blues singers, the slaves often sang about
their work:

> Old cotton, old corn, see you every morn,
> Old cotton, old corn, see you since I's born.
> Old cotton, old corn, hoe you till dawn,
> Old cotton, old corn, what for you born?

The oppression of whites, bouts with patrollers, floggings, and conflicts with masters and overseers represented major themes in the
slaves' secular songs. In their ironic and humorous twists, these songs
became the prototypes for similar characteristics in the blues. The
slaves approached artistry when they commented on the hypocrisy
of their owners:

> My old Mistis promised me
> dat when she died, she gwine set me free,
> But she lived so long an' got so po'
> dat she lef' me diggin' wid 'er garden ho'.

When the slaves sang of love and courting, they probably came
closest to the blues. References to unfaithful partners were frequent
in both types. According to the slave, "When I'se here you call me
honey, when I'se gone, you honies everybody." Metaphoric references
to sexual intercourse were often identical in the slave songs and in
the blues. For example, the blues singer often uses the word "rocking"
to refer to sexual intercourse. In one blues song a woman sang in
the 1920s:

> Looked at the clock, clock struck one,
> Come on, daddy, let's have some fun.
> Looked at the clock, clock struck two,
> Believe to my soul you ain't half through.
> Looked at the clock, clock struck three,
> Believe to my soul, you gonna kill poor me.
> Looked at the clock, clock struck four,
> If the bed breaks down we'll finish on the floor.
> My daddy rocks me with one steady roll,
> Dere ain't no slippin' when he once takes hold.

While revealing little of the rhythmic complexity of this song, the
slaves obviously referred to sexual intercourse when they sang:

> Down in Mobile, down in Mobile,
> How I love that pretty yellow gal,
> She rock to suit me—
> Down in Mobile, down in Mobile.

The slaves also resorted to the same double meanings and veiled messages of the blues in making other sexual references. "Cake" and "chicken" meant a woman, and "shake" and "pushing" signified sexual intercourse.

One characteristic of the blues frequently noted by musicologists is boasting. The slave singers also boasted, particularly of their ability to trick their masters:

> I fooled old Mastah seven years,
> Fooled the overseer three;
> Hand me down my banjo,
> And I'll tickle you bellee.

They emphasized their ability to fight, "to get drunk agin'," and their sexual conquests: "When I was young and in my prime, I'se a' courtin' them gals, most all de time."

Like the blues men, the slaves were always looking for a "do right" woman. They asked, "What make de young girls so deceivin', so deceivin', so deceivin'?"; warned other men, "Don't steal my sugar"; lamented, "When I got back my chicken was gone"; wondered "who's been here since I been gone?"; scorned former lovers who'd gotten pregnant by another man ("her apron strings wouldn't tie"); or observed that "many a man is rocking another man's son when he thinks he's rocking his own." The women boasted of their ability to steal someone else's lover: "You steal my partner, and I steal yours." They enjoined their mates to treat them "good" or suffer the consequences: "If you treat me good, I'll stay till de Judgment Day. But if you treat me bad, I'll sho' to run away." Another distinctive feature of the blues and old slave songs is a preoccupation with getting revenge on a lover who has "done you wrong."

Twentieth-century blacks obviously inherited what folklorists call "skill in the verbal arts" from the slaves. Precursors of those most distinctive features of twentieth-century black culture—the dozens, toasts, prayers, sermons, slang, and signifying—appear in collections of slave folklore. The slave was the quintessential folk poet. In his courtship rituals, toasts, and greetings he demonstrated those rhythmic patterns characteristic of twentieth-century black speech. The sources permit, however, only slight glimpses of some of these forms in the quarters. The practice of playing the dozens and signifying, for exam-

LANGUAGE

From Outta Sight Luther! *by Brumsic Brandon. Copyright* © *1971*
Paul S. Erickson, Inc. Reprinted by permission of
Paul S. Erickson, Inc.

ple, involves the use of so much obscenity and so many explicit references to copulation that Victorian nineteenth-century folklorists
refused to record them. Even so, some elements of signifying and
the dozens (parody, taunts, verbal dueling by indirection, allusion, and
innuendo, and metaphoric references) can be found in slave speech.

In Harlem in the 1940s, the typical answer to the greeting "Whatcha
know, ole man?" was "I'm like the bear, just ain't getting nowhere."
The formalized greetings of the slaves were similar; they would answer
the question "How do you do" or such variants as "How is all?" or
"How do you shine?" in one of the following ways: "I'm kicking, but
not high. . . . I'm barking, but I won't bite. . . . White folks calculating
to keep me behind, but I have to keep on gwine (going). . . . I'm
fat, but don't show it. . . . When you are half dead and running, I'll
be up and coming. . . . I'm hanging and dragging like an old shoe.
. . . I'm fat and fine." The verbal "put down" of a protagonist characteristic of the dozens also appeared in slave responses to verbal boasts

and threats: "You can saddle me, but you can't ride me. . . . I was never run out of a pond by a tadpole yet. . . . No use clouding up, you can't rain."

Similarities between the verbal art of the bondsmen and that of twentieth-century blacks are clearly apparent in their courtship practices. According to the folklorist William Ferris, twentieth-century blacks in the rural South have a highly formalized courtship ritual involving the propounding of a series of questions to determine one's availability as a sexual partner. Called "high pro" by the blacks, the practice is a verbal duel. The prototype of high pro was created in the slave quarters, where old men taught the young the art of courtship. In order to win a mate, a young man or woman had to "know how to talk." The courtship ritual consisted of riddles, poetic boasting, innuendos, put downs, figurative speech, repartee, circumlocution, and a test of wit. In an effort to determine whether a young lady was free to go courting, a young man would typically ask: "Are you a rag on the bush or a rag off the bush?" (Answer—If a rag on the bush, free, if off, engaged). If the lady were not married or engaged, the young man then tried to discover if she accepted him as a suitor: "Dear lady, suppose you an' I was sittin' at de table wid but one dish of soup an' but one spoon, would you be willin' to eat out ob de dish an' spoon wid me?"

Having found some one to "eat out ob de dish" with him, the young man would begin boasting of his prowess and proclaiming, through poetic allusions, his love for her: "Dear miss, ef I was starving and had jes one ginger-cake, I would give you half, an' dat would be the bigges' half." According to the former slave Frank D. Banks, "on the plantation the ability to understand and answer the figurative speeches of her lover was the test of wit and culture by which the slave girl was judged in the society of the quarters." The blacks interviewed by Ferris in the 1970s felt that through a courtship formula remarkably similar to that of the slaves, "you can test a lady out to see what she is and what she stands for and who she really are."

SLAVE RELIGION

The more religious slaves displayed their verbal skills in church. The chief medium for this was the prayer. Reduced to formulas, taught to young converts, the prayers were intoned in a musical rhythmic chant with frequent pauses for audience responses (usually moans). The power of the prayers came from their method of delivery and the vivid word pictures, fervid imagery, metaphors, and imaginative flights. The bondsman began his prayer by expressing his humility and then called on God to "come sin-killing, soul reviving" to "the low grounds of sorrow and sin" and to confront sinners and "hammer hard on their rock hearts with the hammer of Jeremiah and break their hearts in ten thousand pieces." God had to come and revive his flock because "we believe that love is growing old and sin is growing bold and Zion wheel is clogged and can't roll, neither can she put on her beautiful garments, but we ask you to come this way, seal her with love, type her with blood and send her around the hill sides clucking to her broods and bringing live sons and daughers to the marvelous light of thy glorious gospel as the bees to the honey comb and the little doves to the window of Noah's ark, I pray thee. *(Moan)"*

The slave's religious beliefs differed from those of his master in a number of ways. First, most black Christians believed in conjurors, and according to one observer, they talked "freely at their religious gatherings of 'tricking' and 'conjuring' and tell marvelous tales of the power of those endowed with supernatural gifts." Second, many of the death and burial customs differed from those of whites, with funerals held long after burials and graves being decorated with articles belonging to the deceased. Third, music was more important in black than white churches and had a more complicated rhythmic structure. The conversion experience was a long one and had to end with a definite mystical experience or sign that one had been saved. Blacks considered dreams as messages from God, signs of conversion, or calls to preach. Among other unique features of the theology of the slave was his belief that to steal from masters was no sin, that no white people went to Heaven, and that faith, not acts, was all-important. In contrast to the staid service in most white churches, the slave's service was a blur of motion with constant shouting, clapping of hands, and stamping of feet. Although the first slaves learned of Christianity from white missionaries, they quickly fused it with West African beliefs and created their own religion. The frenzied shouting frequently noted by whites was, for example, a variant of African spirit possession. So was the ring shout, the call-and-response pattern of sermons, prayers, and songs, the unrestrained joy, and the predilection for total immersion. Ekwueme asserted that religion was an "area in which Africans share a common heritage with their brothers in the New World, as evidenced in the similarity of modes of worship. . . . The music, dances, and occult rites associated with Voodoo have equivalents in most parts of Africa. The concomitant ecstasy and quasi-psychical entranced upliftment capturing the minds and physique of participants, achieved more through the medium of music than by any other means, have been adopted by black Christian churches in the United States to the point that they are now a *sine qua non* in religious worship for all black people."

The interpreter of black theology was the slave preacher. Since white ministers frequently called upon the slaves to obey their masters, the bondsmen naturally turned to those men who could discover a promise of their salvation and freedom in the Bible. Possessing a memory bordering on the photographic, the black preacher created his sermon from a few details of white church services, verses read to him by whites or, when literate, his own reading of the Bible, and close attention to the troubles and dreams of his congregation. Delivered in a musical recitation with pauses for audience response, the antebellum sermon was a model of folk poetry unmatched in its metaphors, figures of speech, and vivid word pictures. The black preacher told his flock that as with the Israelites, God was on the side of the blacks. The historian Eugene Genovese declared that the slaves, "guided by their preachers, resisted slavery's psychological assault manfully; they learned to love each other and have faith in their deliverance." In uplifting and guiding the bondsmen, the slave preacher created a style that would later be imitated in evangelical white churches and that would remain unchanged in its essential ingredients in most black churches in the twentieth century.

SOCIAL STRUCTURE IN THE SLAVE COMMUNITY

Scholars have written much more about black religion than about another important subject: slave social structure. There were three primary bases for status in the quarters. The first was occupational, but occupations translated into high social standing only if they combined two of the following features: mobility (frequently allowing the slave to leave the plantation); freedom from constant supervision by whites; opportunity to earn money; and provision of a service to other blacks. Although one's occupation was an important determinant of social standing, those blacks who performed services for other bondsmen occupied the top rungs of the social ladder in the slave community. At the bottom of the ladder were those slaves who had the most personal contact or identified most closely with masters (house servants, concubines, drivers, mulattoes). Since conjurors and physicians helped to maintain the slave's mental and physical health, they received more deference than any other black. A former slave reminiscing about the conjuror in the 1890s recalled that blacks generally bowed when meeting him and "worshipped him as if he were a priest." The slaves recognized and applauded skill in the verbal arts, singing, sewing, cooking, wood carving, gardening, hunting, and fishing.

Slaves born in the state or county or on the plantation generally ranked above those born outside these confines. The exception to the rule was native-born Africans; practically all slaves revered them as links to their ancestral home. Slaves also held educators in high esteem. Old men and women with great stores of riddles, proverbs, and folktales (creators and preservers of culture) played a crucial role in teaching morality and training youths to solve problems and to develop their memories. Literate slaves had even more status than the sources of racial lore because they could read the Bible, tell the bondsmen what was transpiring in the newspapers, and write letters and passes. John Sella Martin reported that his ability to read books and newspapers to his fellow Georgia slaves "elevated me to the judgment seat of a second young Daniel among them."

Among the slaves accorded the highest status in the quarters were the rebels, that is, the bondsmen who resisted floggings, violated the racial taboos, or ran away from the plantation. Described as "high-blooded" or "baad niggers" by their admirers, these men and women occupied a central place in slave folktales and songs. One indication of the rebel's status was that antebellum blacks often dated important events in their lives in relationship to Nat Turner's insurrection. The blacks spoke with pride of slaves who were so intractable that they frightened whites. An Alabama bondswoman said, "Dere wuz lot'ta mean 'niggers' in dem days too. Some 'niggers' so mean dat white fo'ks didn't bodder 'em much. Ever' body knowed dey wuz mean. Will Marks wuz a bad 'nigger.' . . . White fo'ks jes scaid o' him."

Physical strength, skill in outwitting whites, possession of attractive clothes, and ability to read signs and interpret dreams also contributed to a slave's social standing. Age gradations represent one of the keys to slave social structure; blacks viewed old men and women as the possessors of wisdom, the closest link to the African past, and persons who should be treated with respect. Any adult might punish a child for insulting an old person (parents usually repeated the punishment). Although no historian has systematically examined slave social structure, it is obvious that it was much more complex than the simple division of plantation blacks into a hierarchy of house servants, drivers, artisans, and field hands. An individual slave's status depended on how other blacks evaluated him and depended on his skills, job, or the provision of certain services to other blacks.

In their social structure, as in other areas of their lives, the slaves left a legacy to Americans, black and white, which was still evident in the last decades of the twentieth century. For instance, literacy and protest continued to be important keys to status in the black community long after slavery ended. Similarly, most students of black music, folklore, religion, and family life agree that Afro-Americans brought some of their unique features from Africa and preserved them for more than 200 years of bondage. However much debate there is regard-

ing the extent of African survivals, scholars accept the veracity of the
Ashanti proverb, "Ancient things remain in the ears." Although fewer
of the ancient African practices and beliefs remained in the ears of
American blacks than in the ears of those in Latin America, it was
the African memory which made the Afro-Americans a distinctive people. Without Africa and slavery, American folklore, speech, music, literature, cooking, and religion would be unimpressive replicas of
European ones, barren and somewhat sterile. Without Africa and slavery, America would not have created spirituals, blues, jazz, or rock
and roll.

In short, Africa and the slave experience are central to an understanding of the American past. The famous scholar J. Mason Brewer
clearly recognized the impression African slaves made on New World
societies when he asserted in 1968, "Probably no people have been
so completely the bearers of tradition as the African slave-immigrants.
They carried in their minds and hearts a treasure of complex musical
forms, dramatic speech, and imaginative stories, which they perpetuated through the vital art of self-expression. Wherever the slaves were
ultimately placed, they established an enclave of African culture that
flourished in spite of environmental disadvantages."

2

An Unsecure People:
Free Negroes in America

People talk of the bloody code of Draco, but . . . that code was a law of love, compared with the hellish laws and precedents that disgrace the statute-books of this modern Democratic, Christian Republic! . . . your piebald and rotten Democracy . . . talks about equal rights, and at the same time tramples one-sixth of the population of the country in the dust, and declares that they have 'no rights which a white man is bound to respect. . . .' I have no vote; I am put out of the pale of political society. . . . I am taxed to support a government which takes my money and tramples on me.

Robert Purvis

America's "marginal man" during the antebellum period was the free Negro. Living and dying in the shadow of the plantation, he shared with his fellows both the promise of America and the burden of its hypocrisy. Free Negroes were the solitary soldiers in the no-man's-land between slavery and freedom. Too often they crossed the strongly fortified border into freedom only to see the American dream still besieged. But while the dreamers themselves remained for a long time on the verge of death, while their heartbeats were faint, the dream refused to die.

The free Negro in the United States represents a nearly perfect subject for the historian. In startling contrast to free blacks in other areas in the New World, American free Negroes left a massive written record of their lives and thoughts: dozens of autobiographies, at least 32 newspapers, hundreds of speeches, sermons, and pamphlets, 9 magazines, the proceedings of more than 100 local, state, and national conventions, several volumes of poetry and hundreds of poems in contemporary journals, and thousands of letters in manuscript collections and newspapers. They also wrote a few novels, plays, and short

33

stories. Such records present a relatively full portrait of the literate free black. Since racial distinctions were so important in the United States, there is also much data on the lives of illiterate blacks in local, state, and national censuses, governmental reports, and white newspapers. Taken together, these sources provide students with a panoramic view of free blacks, their sentiments, personalities, ideologies, and place in American society.

Generally, free Negroes identified closely with the slaves. The free Negro's parents had sometimes purchased their freedom or escaped from bondage. If they had escaped soon enough, of course, they were legally fugitive slaves but had never known the overseer's lash. A number of them had been freed by their white fathers. North or South, their origin was generally identical. Free Negroes fought consistently against discrimination, enlisted in the antislavery campaign, and struggled to improve the black community, to maintain their self-esteem, and to overcome their poverty and ignorance. The most important factors which helped the free Negroes to maintain their sanity in spite of the proscriptions against them were their racial pride, occasional association with egalitarian whites, religious devotion, travel among foreigners, and their families.

LEGAL STATUS

The status of free Negroes in the United States was precarious at best. Segregation, employment discrimination, disfranchisement, and restrictions on personal freedom circumscribed their lives. They were pariahs to the white community, which generally accepted the notion that slavery rather than freedom was their natural condition.

The difference between free and unfree status was unclear. If a white person claimed that a Negro was a slave, that claim was exceedingly difficult to disprove. Some free Negroes were simply kidnapped and reduced to slavery. Several states required registration, such as Virginia, Tennessee, Georgia, and Mississippi. Florida, Georgia, and many other states required free Negroes to have white guardians. In every southern state free Negroes had to have passes or certificates of freedom in their possession at all times. Often movement from county to county without official permission was restricted. Seaboard states in the South prohibited shore leave for Negro sailors when ships arrived in port. In 1793, Virginia barred free Negroes from entering the state, and by the 1830s most southern and some northern states prohibited the entry of free Negroes. Fines and a return to slavery were the penalties exacted for violations.

Free Negroes were forbidden to bear arms without a license, and only those whose conduct was above reproach obtained permits, renewable annually. They could not hold church services without the presence of a licensed, responsible white minister and could not hold meetings without permission. They could not engage in certain occupations without a license, such as selling corn, wheat, or tobacco in Maryland or trading or peddling in South Carolina. The key to the exercise of these police powers was that licensing was used to exclude blacks from certain occupations and to reward "responsible" Negroes who supported the slave system. Although so restricted in employment, free blacks in every state were required to work and have visible means of support. Some states required blacks to post bonds as security against being public charges, continued to apprentice black children long after this practice ceased to be imposed on poor whites, and collected taxes from blacks that were not exacted from whites. In most places, however, free Negroes could own real property.

Some state constitutions written in the Revolutionary War period did not exclude free Negroes from voting, and some voted in Maryland, North Carolina, New York, and Pennsylvania for several years. But all southern states that entered the Union after 1789, except Tennessee, excluded blacks from the vote. As the nineteenth century wore on, state after state, North, South, and West, specifically denied black suffrage until by 1830 free Negroes had political influence nowhere. The exclusion of blacks from voting in the Northeast was related to the increasing political power of white workingmen, who believed that blacks would vote to support their conservative Federalist employers.

Southern free Negroes generally were not permitted to testify in cases involving whites. They did, however, often win suits for property or freedom from the appellate courts. The judges did not seem to regard decisions favorable to blacks as a threat to slavery. However, the specific social and economic circumstances of the black litigants and ties to some white protector in the community were major factors in the successful suits. On the national level, federal law excluded free Negroes from militia service and excluded blacks from carrying the U.S. mails. Federal lawmakers also authorized the citizens of Washington, D.C., to elect only white city officials and to adopt a code governing free Negroes and slaves and denied passports to free Negroes.

REGIONAL VARIATIONS AMONG FREE NEGRO COMMUNITIES

There were several different free Negro communities in the United States and therefore several different reactions to social, political, and economic conditions. In 1860 there were about 500,000 free Negroes in the country, about half of them in the slave states. There had been fewer than 60,000 in 1790 compared to a white population of 2 million and a slave population of 490,000. The mass of southern free Negroes were in the Southeast from Maryland to North Carolina, with the largest lower South contingent in Louisiana.

Unlike other societies in the New World, in the United States the social distinctions between blacks and mulattoes and between free Negroes and slaves were fluid. Mulattoes generally did not constitute a separate caste. Black and mulatto slaves worked side by side in the "big house" and in the fields. Although a mulatto elite existed in the South in a few cities—such as New Orleans, Charleston, and Mobile— they were exceptional. Free people of color constituted only about 5 percent of the total population in the South in 1840. In the 1850 U.S. Census mulattoes made up 37 percent of the free Negro population, and about 13 percent of the total Negro population in 1860. Southern free Negroes living within slave societies were largely the products of extramarital unions between white men and black women. This was especially the case in Louisiana. In 1769, when Spain gained control of Louisiana, mulattoes composed more than half of the small Negro population; by 1860, 77 percent of the free Negroes there were mulattoes and 74 percent of the slaves were black.

Because they had been subjects of France and Spain, free Negroes in the lower South initially had more legal and customary rights than those in the upper South. French and Spanish colonies were governed from European capitals, and metropolitan governments not only did not deprive free Negroes of their rights, they also regarded them as a valuable counterfoil against whites who might opt for independence. But French and Spanish creoles discriminated against free Negroes socially and imposed sumptuary laws—laws limiting private expenditure—as they did in the other colonies. Free Negroes were natural allies for whites in that they formed a large percentage of the free population in a predominantly black society. They were organized into military units and helped to police the slaves and defend the area against the Indians and foreign incursions.

The U.S. government was faced with the firmly entrenched status and privileges of free Negroes when Louisiana was purchased in 1803 and again in 1810 and 1819, when Mobile and Pensacola became American territory. Many free Negro *émigrés* from Haiti and Cuba had swelled the free Negro population. The treaty transferring Louisiana to the United States promised the inhabitants "all the rights, advantages and immunities of citizens of the United States," but the government directed its efforts toward removing the right to serve in the military and other civil rights of free Negroes. Social and political circumstances, including the need for manpower and loyalty in the War of 1812, delayed these efforts. The valor of free Negroes in the war, the wealth of some free Negroes, and the growing economic importance of those who were middle-class artisans to Louisiana's prosperity helped to preserve their rights. Louisiana free Negroes testified in court and traveled freely. The state had a large group of prosperous free Negro planters and a highly educated free Negro professional elite. In Mobile, free Negroes also maintained their rights to special privileges. When Alabama barred free Negroes from attending school in the 1830s, for example, legislators granted "free colored creoles" in Mobile the right to create their own separate school system. In 1824, when Alabama lawmakers tried to force Mobile free Negroes out of the state by the imposition of a $100 head tax, the governor vetoed the measure as an infringement of free Negro rights. Florida free Negroes who had lived in the state before it became an American territory were exempted from the requirement that free Negroes have a white guardian to supervise their affairs. In Pensacola free Negroes carried arms and sat on juries.

THE SOUTHERN FREE NEGRO ELITE

Wealthy free Negroes drew distinctions between themselves and poorer free Negroes and slaves. William Johnson, a barber in Natchez, carefully cultivated the habits of white gentility. He bred horses, hunted, provided music lessons for his daughters, subscribed to New York journals, hired a white overseer, bought a farm, and worked it with slaves, free Negro apprentices, and white tenant laborers. Andrew Durnford, a Louisiana plantation owner with seventy-five slaves, took pride in his care of his "rascally Negroes." When Norbert Rillieux, a French-trained free Negro engineer who invented a new vacuuming method of refining sugar, offered Durnford $50,000 for the use of his plantation to test the process, Durnford turned him down, not wanting to "give up control of his people."

In Louisiana, Florida, and Mobile, elite free Negroes who were of French and Spanish origin emphasized their heritage and regarded other free Negroes with disdain. They established journals, wrote poetry in French, and sent their children to France for their education. Wealth and light skin color were most often the distinguishing characteristics of the free Negro elite everywhere, although some exceptions existed. Publicly they often identified with white society and did not condemn slavery, but they did help poorer free Negroes by establishing churches, schools, and fraternal organizations.

In most areas of United States, however, there was a great deal of contact between the mass of free Negroes and slaves. They often married, worked in the same fields and workshops, and spent their spare moments in the same taverns and groceries. Free Negroes helped slaves by forging passes, loaning them money, and purchasing and freeing them. Slaves patronized free Negro shops, warned them of patrols, and fed them from their masters' kitchens. Sometimes free Negroes, like Denmark Vesey, conspired in slave revolts, but most often they refrained from doing so, knowing their own precarious "rights" could easily be taken away. A few of them, like John Chavis, a free Negro preacher and school teacher in North Carolina, demonstrated their "integrity" by opposing emancipation.

ECONOMIC CONDITIONS IN THE SOUTH

During the 1850s, a time of economic upswing in the South, southern free Negroes prospered economically. Many bought property for the first time and demanded higher wages for signing contracts because of the shortage of labor. Once they were more economically secure, many free Negroes began protesting against discrimination. In 1858 Richmond, Virginia, free Negroes petitioned the city council unsuccessfully for the repeal of the city's repressive municipal code. Free Negroes in other places began to refuse to give way on the sidewalks to whites. Competition for jobs between white and black workers became widespread. Whites became increasingly fearful of free Negro subversion of the slaves; a perceived increase in fugitive slaves was attributed to the aid of free Negroes. Deportation, colonization, and enslavement were considered; many free Negroes left the South before such steps could be taken. A number of southern states passed laws to expel all free Negroes, but they were ineffective. In the debates over expulsion, opponents argued that free Negroes were necessary, industrious, and loyal, that humanity forbade such a tactic, or that expelled free Negroes would add to the enemies of slave society in the North. Despite the refusal of many states to expel free Negroes, between 1830 and 1860 manumission was outlawed almost everywhere or permitted only with removal from the state. There were increasing attacks on free Negroes in the newspapers, police harassment, and constraints on employment. Southern free Negroes, even in the Gulf Coast states, became less free by the Civil War.

Before the influx of white immigrants into the South during the 1840s and 1850s, the labor of free Negroes was much in demand. Plantation owners employed them as casual labor in critical times during the growing season. A large minority of free Negroes, about one-third, lived in the cities and towns. In southern cities, except Savannah and Charleston, there was little competition between white and Negro workers in the colonial period. During the late antebellum period, however, significant conflict between Irish, German, and other immigrants and free Negroes pushed them out of skilled occupations.

The Arkansas and North Carolina free Negro population was overwhelmingly rural and self-supporting. Some owned farms, but most worked part time on the plantations and small farms of the whites, as common laborers, wood choppers, turpentine hands, tanners, and weavers. Some lived with white families. In Maryland and Virginia large numbers lived in Baltimore and Richmond, but most lived at the tidewater working as farmhands, unskilled laborers, tenant farmers, or sharecroppers.

Black urbanites were considerably more skilled than their rural counterparts. In Richmond 50 percent of the free Negro adult males worked as laborers in the tobacco factories, paper mills, and iron foundries that made up the industrial core of the city in 1860. Another 20 percent worked as waiters, whitewashers, and stevedores or did a variety of menial jobs as day laborers. One-third, or 3,290, performed a skilled trade.

Free people of color in the lower South port cities were considerably more successful than upper South free Negroes. In Mobile 43 percent and in Charleston 70 percent of the free Negro men worked at skilled trades in 1860. Twenty-five percent of Charleston's carpenters, nearly 40 percent of the tailors, and 75 percent of the millwrights were free Negroes. Of the 1,792 free Negro males listed in the 1850 census of New Orleans, only 9.9 percent were unskilled laborers; the overwhelming majority were skilled workers. Many upper South free Negroes had been manumitted for ideological reasons following the Revolution, but their masters had done little to prepare them for the future. Selective manumission in the lower South resembled more the personal pattern established in the Caribbean and in South America, where manumitters saw to it that freedmen knew a trade or experienced slave artisans bought their own freedom.

Most southern free Negroes were not as lucky as the artisans in the port cities. Poverty forced many free Negroes to work on two or three jobs to make a living. Some signed long-term contracts with employers for subsistence only, a practice that made them virtual slaves. In Westmoreland County, Virginia, for example, 250 blacks—a quarter of the free Negroes—lived under twenty-year contracts for labor in exchange for food, clothing, and shelter. Others there and elsewhere worked under yearly contracts. At the end of a term, the worker would usually be in debt for food, clothing, and shelter advanced during the year. Peonage was the result. The crop-lien system snared others and tied them to one master's land. Some poor whites were also caught in this system. But unlike whites, free Negroes could be forced into long terms of servitude for failure to pay fines, taxes, or jail fees. Free Negroes could also be sold into slavery for failing to pay private debts, even after imprisonment for debt was abolished for whites. Apprenticeship laws were also used to extort long periods of labor from free Negroes.

Free Negroes employed in mixed labor forces were given the worst jobs at the lowest pay. The railroads, for instance, hired blacks in labor forces with whites but used them as axemen. No blacks worked as stationmasters, agents, engineers, conductors, or watchmen.

In the decades preceding the Civil War, white artisans began complaining about wage competition from free Negroes and slaves. Planter dominated legislatures responded at first by excluding free Negroes from making drugs, selling liquor, printing, or piloting ships, but they did not limit slave hiring for jobs. As the white workers continued to protest, legislatures placed additional restrictions on free-Negro employment opportunities. The great influx of Irish and German immigrants into southern cities in the 1830s and 1840s brought additional competition for the free Negro. During the 1830s, observers in Baltimore noted "Irish and other foreigners are, to a considerable extent, taking the place of colored laborers and other domestic servants." Free Negro butchers could not work in the city market in Memphis, free Negro artisans had to have their work approved by whites in Georgia, and free Negro mechanics in Charleston and Savannah had to pay higher licensing fees than whites.

Despite systematic discrimination, some free Negroes prospered even in the South. Some made profits from operating cookshops and groceries that served free Negroes and slaves. Clinton James in Richmond ran an all-purpose store with four rooms, of which, noted a police reporter when James was arrested for running an unlicensed shop, "the first was used as a grocery, the second as a bar room, the third as a snack room, and the fourth as a kitchen." Others performed "nigger work," whatever whites did not want to do in a particular locale: running bathhouses, stables, and catering establishments and above all else barbering, servile work which drove away white competitors while it encouraged the patronage of white customers who preferred to be served by blacks. In other trades free Negroes could prosper to some degree by accepting lower wages than did whites. For example, Charleston merchants continued to hire free Negroes in the maritime trade despite the prohibition of the Negro seamen laws because "the services of colored seamen, as cooks and stewards can be more cheaply and readily procured than those of whites."

A number of southern free Negroes managed to acquire property. By 1860 in Virginia, 1,200 rural free Negroes controlled more than 60,000 acres of land worth about $370,000. At the same time, free Negroes in Tennessee counties held land worth $435,000 and $250,000 in personal property. A majority of the free Negro property owners lived in urban areas. For example, in 1800 only one-third of Virginia's free Negroes lived in urban areas, but they owned land valued at 30 percent more than that of rural free Negroes. In Tennessee the owners of almost half the black-owned real estate lived in Davidson County, the location of Nashville, the state capital. Most of the Maryland free Negroes whose property was worth more than $1,000 lived in Baltimore or its suburbs.

While most free Negroes obtained their property without the aid of whites, the largest owners had help from whites. The largest slave-holding free Negro planters were mulattoes, and in many instances so were the largest urban property owners. In New Orleans, for example, free Negroes owned $2,214,020 in real estate and Aristide Mary inherited an entire city block of Canal Street from his white father.

NORTHERN POLITICAL ECONOMY

Northern free Negroes could and did speak out against slavery as free persons in an ostensibly free society. Unlike their counterparts in the American South, who lived within a slave society, they could take advantage of the rhetorical commitment of some northern whites to the ideals of the Declaration of Independence and speak against slavery, often with more vehemence than they could afford to express against their own treatment by northern whites.

Some northern free Negroes advocated migration to the northern and western territories as a route to upward mobility. Many of them found the opportunity for economic and social advancement on the frontier. Jean Baptiste DuSable, for instance, established a trading post at the mouth of the Chicago River in 1779 and became a successful trapper and trader. He was also a miller, a cooper, and a husbandman. George Bonga, a famous fur trapper and Indian language specialist at Leech Lake, Minnesota, in the 1850s, was the son of a Chippewa tribeswoman, and a slave who belonged to a Canadian fur trapper. He attended school in Montreal and then returned to the Chippewas. He supported himself mainly by working as a voyageur for the American Fur Company. Another frontiersman, James Beckwourth, born in 1798 to black-white parentage, was an apprentice for five years to a hardbitten St. Louis blacksmith. He ran away to the West, worked for the Rocky Mountain Fur Company, was adopted into the Crow tribe, and became a Crow chief. He served as an Army scout during the third Seminole War in Florida and then later trapped and prospected for gold.

More ordinary colonies of Negroes settled in the Midwest. One of these originated when John Randolph of Roanoke freed his slaves and left them enough money to pay for their transportation to Mercer County, Ohio, for "tracts of land" amounting to from 2,000 to 4,000 acres, and for necessary cabins, clothes, and utensils. In 1832, when the 385 free people reached Mercer County by wagon and then by boat, they found they had been cheated out of their land by Randolph's relatives. They spread throughout the area but kept in touch with each other.

Numerous free Negroes lived among the Indians. A colony of Negroes settled in Hamilton County, Indiana, in 1832. Known as the Roberts Settlement, it was made up of Cherokees and Negroes who had been forced to leave Northampton County, North Carolina, during the Indian removal. In Indiana the group built log houses, a church, and a school. These blacks were not unique. An 1831 U.S. Army survey of the Choctaw tribe showed it contained 512 Negroes. Some eastern Indian tribes included so many Negroes that it was difficult to distinguish between red and black. It was, consequently, no accident that many famous nineteenth-century blacks had Indian parents. For example, Edmonia Lewis, who became the first important black sculptor in the United States, was the offspring of a Negro father and a Chippewa, and black rodeo star Bill Pickett had a Choctaw mother.

The movement of Negroes westward was met by black laws and restrictions. In the old Northwest, Negroes faced restrictions on suffrage and the requirement to post bonds. Black laws followed into Nebraska, Oregon, and the whole West. But even in California during gold rush days, Negroes contributed to the conquest of the frontier. William Leidesdorff, a wealthy San Francisco landowner in the 1840s, helped set up the first public school, introduced the first steamboat to the city, organized its first horse race, and opened its first hotel. When American troops arrived in 1846, he helped in establishing the new government and held a fancy dress ball at his home to entertain the American leaders. Biddy Mason came to California with her master, stayed behind when he returned home in 1856, got the local courts to affirm her freedom, and through hard work became a large landowner.

The small size of the free Negro population in northern cities precluded the domination of any occupation by blacks. While southern free blacks struggled to maintain their place on the occupational ladder in the 1850s, northern free blacks were trying to break into many trades and professions traditionally closed to them. The free Negroes of New York City, for instance, never more than 8.6 percent of the total population, were unable to compete successfully against whites for jobs. Discrimination limited access to employment even further. Although free Negroes constituted only 1.5 percent of the total population in New York City in 1860, they rarely obtained even that percentage of jobs in any occupation. Yet, despite fierce competition from European immigrants and virtually unyielding prejudice, the free blacks managed to obtain some jobs, concentrated in service categories. According to the 1855 manuscript census of New York State, there were also a number of black businessmen, artisans, and professionals. These included nineteen teachers, eighteen clerks, fifteen clergymen, fifteen food dealers, nine restaurateurs and caterers, eight physicians, five engineers, and one undertaker.

The free Negroes began to complain early about their relegation to the lowest rungs of the occupational ladder. Lecturing in 1832, Boston's Maria Stewart asserted that there were none who had "enriched themselves by spending their lives as house-domestics, washing windows, shaking carpets, brushing boots, or tending upon gentlemen's tables." Restricted to blacks, such labor was degrading. The path to economic uplift was in the mechanical trades. And since white artisans rarely accepted black apprentices, the free Negroes repeatedly tried to organize vocational schools. National conventions endorsed the idea of a manual labor and industrial college several times between 1831 and 1860. They were, unfortunately, never able to raise the money to endow such colleges.

The free Negro worked diligently to overcome the effects of discrimination and to prove that blacks were not indolent. When prejudiced Cleveland, Ohio, whites prevented John Malvin from working as a carpenter, he labored successively as a steamboat cook, engineer, preacher, barber, and captain of a canal boat, and later purchased land. John Levy worked as a barber, bootblack, and porter and speculated in West Indian lumber in Boston and Lowell, Massachusetts. He overcame the prejudice of whites who did not want him to live in their neighborhood by planting the best flower garden and digging a well which produced the best water in the area. James Still worked for a short time in a Philadelphia glue factory, and although the only Negro employee, he was so diligent that he was made foreman. Later, he became so proficient as a physician that he was swamped by black and white patients and earned enough money before the Civil War to purchase large tracts of land and several buildings.

Free Negro autobiographers frequently lectured to their fellows on industry and thrift. They pointed to such successful Negro businessmen as Charles Downing, James Still, Thomas Jennings, and Joseph Cassey, a wigmaker in Philadelphia with holdings worth $75,000. If one excelled at a skill which everyone needed, and if he acquired money, he would overcome discrimination. The New York minister Samuel Ringgold Ward advised the Negro in 1855: *

> Do the thing you do in the best possible manner: if you shoe a horse, do it so that no white man can improve it; if you plough a furrow, let it be ploughed to perfection's point . . . the chief, almost the *only* business of the Negro is to be a man of business. . . . Let us become of some value as customers; then, when . . . devoted men of business . . . have before them the question of treading under foot some Negro, they will conclude differently. . . . Yes, black men must seek wealth.

A number of free Negroes tried to follow Ward's advice. James Forten began in Philadelphia as an errand boy on the docks and by 1830 owned a sailmaking business which employed more than forty white and black laborers and had acquired a fortune of more than $100,000. Martin R. Delany practiced medicine. Lewis Woodson was a barber and preacher; John S. Rock practiced dentistry and law, and Frederick Douglass ran a successful newspaper. Most free Negroes, of course, were not so successful. For them, education was the crucial element in social mobility.

EDUCATIONAL STRIVINGS

Southern free Negroes desired education passionately. They educated their children largely through their own private efforts, with some support from white philanthropists. Usually the development of churches and schools was closely related. In Baltimore, Sharp Street Church's pastor doubled as schoolmaster. Many benevolent and social organizations established schools. Charleston's Brown Fellowship Society subsidized the Minor's Moralist Society for educating poor free Negro children. In New Orleans the most famous school was the Institution des Orphelins, built in 1846. The school offered courses in French and Spanish.

Whites regarded black schools as a nuisance and an unsettling influence, but free Negroes believed education offered an opportunity for economic, political, and social advancement for themselves and their children. When whites established public school systems for their own children, they generally barred free Negroes from attending or even from sharing in the public funds to support their own schools. In 1860

Baltimore free Negroes paid $500 in taxes to support schools they could not attend. Blacks risked repressive measures in an effort to keep schools open. For example, in 1811 Christopher McPherson, a wealthy free Negro, hired a white schoolmaster and opened a night school for free Negroes in Richmond. When McPherson attempted to advertise the success of his school in the local paper, his teacher was run out of town. McPherson persisted in his attempts to keep the school open. As a result, he was jailed and sent to the Williamsburg Lunatic Asylum. There were underground schools in almost every community. When a Richmond newspaper complained that black children were seen every Sunday morning marching to church with books in their hands, the police raided one black church and found the students being instructed.

The free Negro in the North never knew what to expect from public school officials. Sometimes they barred blacks altogether. On other occasions, blacks were admitted, relegated to a back seat, and then taught their lessons only after all of the white children received theirs. Various patterns of state and local law providing for black education developed. In New York an 1845 law permitted a local option on separate schools and granted the towns which established Negro schools the same state subsidies allowed for white schools. Ohio had no provision for the education of black children until a law adopted in 1847 allowed the use of state funds for separate schools, and a second law passed in 1852 made separate facilities mandatory under certain conditions. Massachusetts had a local option system permitting separate schools until 1855, when it prohibited segregated education. In Pennsylvania there was no official provision for segregated facilities until 1854, although state instructional funds after 1820 could be used for privately operated black schools.

In the early years of the nineteenth century, black schools were frequently supported by white philanthropy. In New York City the African free schools of the 1820s and 1830s were administered and subsidized by local benefactors. Boston's separate schools were funded and partially sustained by an endowment left by Abdiel Smith early in the nineteenth century after blacks had petitioned that such schools be established. In Ohio by the mid-1830s white benefactors, special subscriptions, and similar means supported scattered separate schools. The white philanthropists often struggled against great obstacles to provide segregated education for blacks. For example, Prudence Crandall's school for girls in Canterbury, Connecticut, was closed in 1834 by local hostility and a hastily passed state law prohibiting the establishment of schools for Negroes who were not residents of the state.

Northern blacks adopted a number of strategies in their campaign to obtain schools for their children. Where there were no public schools, they argued that they did not care whether schools were integrated or not, as long as schools were established for their children. In the face of white indifference, blacks joined together to finance their own schools. Several groups, including the Phoenix Society in New York City, established schools. In Cleveland, canal boat captain John Malvin solicited funds for a school, and in Pittsburgh the African Education Society served a similar purpose. Of the twenty schools that admitted blacks in Ohio in 1837, four were controlled by blacks.

Blacks' efforts to establish schools were remarkable in view of the poverty of the free Negro community and the fact that they were subjected to taxation to support white schools. Blacks petitioned legislatures to provide state support to educate their children. In 1832 Philadelphia free Negroes petitioned the state legislature unsuccessfully to admit their children to the public schools on the grounds that they, like whites, paid taxes to support public education. Twenty years later Robert Purvis, a wealthy suburban landowner, refused to pay taxes for the schools from which his children were excluded. Local officials suggested that he send them to a nearby school for blacks, but he thought this was a "flimsy and ridiculous sham" and argued that his children had a right to attend the neighborhood white school. When officials relented, he paid his taxes.

Where publicly supported schools were provided, blacks demanded integrated schooling because the approved standards and support of Negro schools were lower than those for whites. In Ohio, Pennsylvania, New York, and Massachusetts, indeed wherever there existed a sizeable free Negro community, the struggle continued. Some persons, such as Lewis Woodson, a Pittsburgh barber and preacher, asserted that blacks should continue their efforts as a matter of race pride to build up black schools "to a perfect level with their white brethren." In Rochester, New York, Frederick Douglass protested the provision of an inferior public black school in a church basement in editorials in the *North Star* in 1848. Whites ended segregated education in the 1850s because the cost of improving and running the separate black school was too high. Boston's 1849 segregation case in which Benjamin Roberts challenged the legality of excluding his daughter Sarah from the neighborhood school and forcing her to walk to a distant segregated school was the most significant of the antebellum era. Roberts lost the case, but blacks and white abolitionists continued to petition the state legislature, which ended separate schools throughout the state in 1855.

The road to education for many of the free Negroes was filled with obstacles. G. W. Offley's education was obtained through a circuitous route: a few weeks at night from an old Negro preacher, exchanging boxing and wrestling lessons with the son of a slaveholder for the ABCs or food with poor white children for reading lessons in Delaware, and then regular lessons from sympathetic whites in Hartford, Connecticut. An old slave secretly taught John Malvin to read. Many free Negro parents gave their children their first lessons. Levi Coppin's mother taught all of her children to read and write. Similarly, Samuel Ringgold Ward learned to read at his father's knee. Most of the parents could give their children only the rudiments of education. John P. Green's father was an exception. He not only could read and write, but he also collected a sizeable library and avidly read poetry.

When parents exhausted their store of knowledge, they often sent their children to private schools for blacks. John P. Green attended for two years the private school for Negroes in Newbern, North Carolina, taught by the free Negro John Stuart Stanley; Miflin W. Gibbs, until he was eight years old, attended a private school taught by an Irishman in Philadelphia; Samuel Ringgold Ward and his brother attended a Negro school in New York; and John Mercer Langston attended Negro schools in Cincinnati and Chillicothe, Ohio. Precocious Jeremiah Asher had read the Bible four or five times before he was twelve years old and later took private lessons from students at Brown University. Daniel A. Payne received one of the most thorough educations of all those trained in Negro schools. In addition to matriculating at the Minors' Moralist Society School in Charleston for two years and taking private lessons from Thomas S. Bonneau, a famous free Negro teacher, Payne also taught himself many subjects. On his own, he studied Greek, Latin, French, botany, and zoology. The last he learned by catching and dissecting animals. For six years he ran a private school in the city and wrote poetry in his spare time.

When free Negroes were admitted to white schools and mistreated, they often dropped out after a few months. On a number of occasions, however, blacks attended white schools without incident. James Still was able to go to school for only three months in Pennsylvania, but he shared equally the pleasures, sports, and sympathies of his white classmates. J. H. Magee, who had "an insatiable desire for knowledge," and his brother attended a school in Racine, Wisconsin, and although they were the only blacks there, they were well treated by students and teachers. John P. Green had "color-blind," dedicated teachers in his school in Cleveland (including the future Mrs. John D. Rockefeller) and encountered no problems with the white students. Later he studied Latin and French, read the classics, and wrote essays.

The career of John Mercer Langston reveals the hopes, successes, failures, and frustrations which were characteristic of the free Negro who tried to obtain an education. Taught by his slaveholding father in Virginia when quite young, Langston later attended private schools for Negroes in Cincinnati and Chillicothe. Inspired by his teacher in Chillicothe, George B. Vashon, a Negro student at Oberlin College, he wanted to attend college. After convincing his guardian of the value of higher education, he followed two of his brothers to Oberlin in 1844. He found that Oberlin under the presidency of Asa Mahan was an exciting place. In fact, Langston's first day on campus was an unforgettable intellectual and emotional experience: he heard the incomparable revivalist, Charles G. Finney, preach. Finney, Langston declared, delivered his sermon with "a power marvelous and indescribable. John had never heard such preaching. He had never had his soul moved by such utterance."

Langston discovered that Oberlin was a community where egalitarianism was both preached and practiced. Residing in the home of mathematics teacher George Whipple, along with one black girl and several white students, he encountered no hint of discrimination. An excellent debater and a good writer, he joined the college literary society and graduated with high honors from Oberlin in 1849.

Although all of his professors, friends, and relatives tried to convince him to go into the ministry, Langston preferred law. His disappointments in trying to obtain legal training were legion. First, a prominent New York law school refused him admittance. The president of the school did, however, offer to accept Langston if he pretended he was a Spaniard. This suggestion aroused "a deep sense of the humiliation of his manhood." He refused this offer and that of one of the professors to tutor him privately. Having studied Greek, Latin, and Hebrew at Oberlin, he decided to return to college and get a degree in theology while trying to discover a way to study law. Taught by Finney and others, he did well enough to be chosen as one of the commencement orators at the graduation exercises in 1852. Finally, in 1853 he began studying law with the abolitionist and ex-Congressman Judge Philemon Bliss of Elyria, Ohio. Years later, he looked back with fond regard on the members of the Bliss family who were "kind and cordial always" toward him. Langston made rapid progress under the scholarly Bliss and passed his bar examination in 1854.

INTERACTION WITH WHITES

There were a few occasions when the free Negro interacted with whites on cordial terms. In Newbern, North Carolina, A. H. Newton and John P. Green often played with white children, and their parents had several white friends. When John Mercer Langston went to Ohio, he lived for years with a white family who had emigrated from Virginia. These, he wrote, were "happy days" when his "cup of happiness seemed to be ever enlarging itself, and filled to its brim." There were also other cracks in the color line. John P. Green's family belonged to a white masonic lodge. Samuel Ringgold Ward served as the minister of two all-white Congregational churches in New York in the 1840s and 1850s. While free Negroes were barred from close interaction with most whites, they often knew many of the "best" whites. The list of whites they visited, dined with, invited to their homes, and knew intimately as friends or benefactors reads like a select company chosen from the *Dictionary of American Biography*. They included Gerritt Smith, Harriet Beecher Stowe, Lucretia Mott, Myrtilla Miner, Lewis Tappan, Theodore Weld, William Lloyd Garrison, Henry Wilson, Theodore Parker, Charles G. Finney, and Charles Sumner.

These small successes, however, did not materially affect the all-pervasiveness of prejudice and discrimination—soul-crushing monsters which warped every facet of the free Negro's life. Public school administrators either refused to admit them to tax-supported educational institutions or made it clear, by cold and heartless treatment, that they were not wanted. If despite these problems black children succeeded in finishing public school, their ambitions were often shattered on the almost insurmountable barriers erected to prevent them from entering law and medical schools, colleges, and seminaries. In the church they encountered the Jim Crow pew, received their Sunday school lessons after the young white seekers of Christ had received theirs, and had to stifle their desire to commune with God until the most hypocritical white had visited the communion table. Relegated to separate, incommodious, dirty, cold seats on trains, streetcars, stagecoaches, and steamboats, they were barred from hotels, restaurants, inns, bars, and white residential areas. White artisans refused to accept them as apprentices or to hire or work with them if they somehow managed to acquire a skill. In the South they were often prohibited from using the honorific titles "Mr." and "Mrs." when referring to blacks.

REACTION TO DISCRIMINATION

The free Negroes complained bitterly about their treatment. Sometimes they sank to the depths of despair. Samuel Ringgold Ward summed up the position of the American Negro in these words: "His sky is sunless, starless; deep, black clouds, admitting no ray of light envelop his horizon." Daniel A. Payne, viewing the oppression of Negroes in the South, was moved to assert: "We are killed all the day long; we are accounted as sheep for the slaughter." The sense of powerlessness was almost overwhelming. Oppression followed the free Negro every-where. Law was nonexistent for blacks. Miflin W. Gibbs, on arriving in the California gold fields to seek his fortune, was immediately struck by "the disheartening consciousness that while our existence was toler-ated, we were powerless to appeal to law for the protection of life or property when assailed."

Free Negro autobiographers wrote at great length on the all-perva-siveness of prejudice and discrimination against blacks. The most crush-ing aspect of the whole process was the feeling that a man could do nothing to avoid the snares, for regardless of his conduct, education, culture, and wealth, discrimination dogged his heels and gnawed away at his vitals. Payne, lamenting the exclusion of blacks from the seminar-ies, concluded that "neither beauty of person nor grandeur of intellect nor varied culture can exempt any man or woman from the ostracism of Americans if he or she be tainted with one drop of blood of Noah's second son." Prejudice and discrimination blunted the free Negro's ambition, crushed his hopes, embittered his heart, and threatened his psychic security. Samuel Ringgold Ward articulated the baneful effects of prejudice better than any other free Negro. For the Negro, he wrote, there was always "the ever-present, ever-crushing Negro-hate, which hedges up his path, discourages his efforts, dampens his ardour, blasts his hopes, and embitters his spirit."

Whether in New York, Boston, or Charleston, the free Negro found himself a virtual outcast among his fellow citizens. He was an untoucha-ble who could not aspire to the things readily given to the most de-graded white man. Jeremiah Asher wrote that in Philadelphia, "no colored persons, except almost white, are allowed a right enjoyed by the lowest dregs of society, if only white, thus encouraging deception and hypocrisy, and practically offering a reward to amalgamation, if not to licentiousness." Samuel Ringgold Ward felt the same way about New York. It was impossible, he declared, for one to escape "the thou-sand snares and the ten thousand forms of cruelty and injustice which the unspeakable cruel prejudice of the whites visits upon the head and heart of every black young man, in New York." Upon her return from Europe to Boston, Nancy Prince reported that "the weight of prejudice has again oppressed me, and were it not for the promises of God one's heart would fail."

From early childhood to old age, the autobiographers frequently encountered discrimination and prejudice. They sat in pews parti-tioned off as though for untouchables and took jobs as bootblacks be-cause white artisans refused to accept them in any other position. They were forced to ride, even in the dead of winter, on the outside seat of stagecoaches. They were thrown off streetcars and railroads to make room for whites and taxed without representation. Their personal contacts with whites represented continual assaults on their humanity and self-respect. One white minister, for instance, told Samuel Ringgold Ward that even Jesus Christ would sell his house if a Negro moved next door. The autobiographers often described their daily and lifelong travail. Ward spoke eloquently for all of them when he wrote that throughout his life, prejudice

> was ever at my elbow. As a servant, it denied me a seat at the table with my white fellow servants; in the sports of childhood and youth, it was ever disparagingly reminding me of my colour and origin; along the street it ever pursued, ever ridiculed, ever abused me. If I sought redress, the very complexion I wore was pointed out as the best reason for my seeking it in vain; if I desired to turn to account a little learning, in the way of earning a living by it, the idea of employing a black clerk was preposterous—too absurd to be seriously entertained. . . . So, if I sought a trade, white apprentices would leave if I were admitted; and when I went to the house of God, as it was called, I found all the Negro-hating usages and sentiments of general society there encouraged and embodied in the Negro pew, and in the disallowing Negroes to commune until all the whites, however poor, low, and degraded, had done.

The free Negro reacted in various ways to prejudice and discrimination. The violent outbursts of whites, the rabid mobs which formed when the free Negro violated some local custom, often forced him to tread across the mountain of discrimination with caution and fear lest he plunge down its precipices. John Mercer Langston discovered how flimsy the foundation of Negro rights was as he dodged through the streets of Cincinnati in 1840 while a wild mob of white men wreaked vengeance on every black they found. While the burning homes and clatter of gunfire were exciting to the young school boy, he was severely shaken at the sight of five black men huddled in his brother's barbershop: "All found there were agitated, disturbed and anxious about their safety." Samuel Ringgold Ward complained that many of the Negroes, "wanting in manliness," cowered before white demagogues.

Many of the autobiographers were often heartbroken by the cruelty of whites. Decades after a New England driver had forced her to sit on the outside of a stagecoach in midwinter, Nancy Prince asserted: "his inhumanity grieves me even now." John Mercer Langston recalled that as a young man he was denied a seat inside a stagecoach and then refused admittance to a hotel in Columbus, Ohio, where he felt like "an outcast, heartbroken, not knowing what to do, nor where to go." This experience, he said, "was absolutely more deadly in fact to

John's feelings than the quickest poison could have been to his body."
Given such treatment as this, Samuel Ringgold Ward was amazed,
when considering the free Negroes, that "the mass of us are not either
depressed into idiocy or excited into demons."

Oppressed by pious, God-fearing whites, many free Negroes rejected Christianity as hypocritical cant. Those who remained in the
church had ambivalent feelings toward the Supreme Being. On the
one hand, they prayed for God to smite their oppressors. On the other
hand, they were sometimes so oppressed that they doubted the very
existence of God. For example, when whites closed the Negro schools
in Charleston, Daniel A. Payne wondered if God existed and asked,
"If so, why does he suffer one race to oppress and enslave another,
to rob them by unrighteous enactments of rights, which they hold
most dear and sacred."

Regardless of their religious beliefs, many free Negroes developed
a deep and abiding hatred of whites. They could not forget the insults,
derision, or physical abuse they had suffered from whites. Sometimes,
especially violent treatment brought out the thinly veiled hatred. John
Mercer Langston declared that the white attacks on blacks during
the Cincinnati riot of 1840 "drove every feeling of love and veneration
out of the hearts of those who had thus been outraged and terrified."
Samuel Ringgold Ward understood clearly the reasons for the hatred:
"I very well know, from painful experience, that the black people
were goaded into a constant temptation to hate their white fellow-
citizens. I know, too, how natural such hatred is in such circumstances."

Many of the stronger free Negroes refused to be warped by hatred.
Remembering the sufferings of Christ, they tried to be forgiving rather
than be dragged down to the level of whites in mutual hatred. Daniel
H. Peterson, for example, after observing that many Negroes viewed
all whites as enemies, asserted, "That is not true, for I declare that
from a child unto this day I have found all my best friends among
the white people." Other blacks tried to perform personally satisfying
acts when their anger threatened to erupt. When Daniel A. Payne's
school was closed in Charleston, for instance, he wrote a long poem
which he declared "was the safety valve which let out the super-abun-
dant grief."

RACE PRIDE

The stronger free Negroes refused to sink into despair because of discrimination. Instead, they turned inward, emphasizing individual reliance, race pride, and their own humanity. James Still learned early
in life that prejudice left him "nothing to depend on but my own

energy." He determined that no act of his would bring discredit on Negroes as a race: "I have tried to live so as to prove that the race is capable of a great many things." Every Negro, in his own life, had to vindicate the race. As he struggled against oppression, Samuel Ringgold Ward felt he had a right to complain against "any black man who throws discredit upon our people." The free Negroes were proud of their race. When someone suggested that John Mercer Langston pretend to be white, he retorted, "I am a colored American; and I shall not prove false to myself, nor neglect the obligation I owe to the Negro race!" Oppression did not decrease the Negro's sense of humanity. Instead, his survival in the face of white oppression convinced him that he was their equal. All the prejudice and discrimination which Samuel Ringgold Ward faced, for instance, did not make him feel less than a man: "No, I always felt that; however wronged, maltreated, outraged—still, a man. Indeed, the very bitterness of what I had suffered . . . consisted chiefly in the consciousness I always carried with me of being an equal man to any of those who trampled upon me."

Writing in *Frederick Douglass' Paper* in 1853, New York's William J. Wilson described the problems facing the self-conscious black: "At present, what we find around us, either in art or literature, is made so to press upon us, that we deprecate, we despise, we almost hate ourselves, and all that favors us. Well may we scoff at black skins and woolly heads, since every model set before us for admiration, has pallid face and flaxen head, or emanations thereof." Seeking to counter such feelings, black lecturers frequently discussed the theme of black pride. John S. Rock, a Boston dentist and lawyer, gave a typical exegesis of the theme in an 1858 speech. Declaring that "I not only love my race, but am pleased with my color," Rock asserted, "White men may despise, ridicule, slander and abuse us; and make us feel degraded; but no man shall cause me to turn my back upon my race. With it I will sink or swim." Rock followed by delivering a blow to white claims to superior beauty.

> The prejudice which some white men have, or affect to have, against my color gives me no pain. If any man does not fancy my color, that is his business, and I shall not meddle with it. I shall give myself no trouble because he lacks good taste. If he judges my intellectual capacity by my color, he certainly cannot expect much profundity, for it is only skin deep, and is really of no very great importance to any one but myself. I will not deny that I admire the talents and noble characters of many white men. But I cannot say that I am particularly pleased with their physical appearance. If old mother nature had held out as well as she commenced, we should, probably, have had fewer varieties

in the races. When I contrast the fine tough muscular system, the beautiful, rich color, the full broad features, and the gracefully frizzled hair of the negro, with the delicate physical organization, wan color, sharp features and lank hair of the Caucasian, I am inclined to believe that when the white man was created, nature was pretty well exhausted—but determined to keep up appearances, she pinched up his features, and did the best she could under the circumstances.

Other free Negroes joined Rock in dismissing claims that they were inferior to whites. In fact, in light of the white man's denial of human brotherhood, of democracy, and of Christian principles, he could lay no claim to moral equality with blacks. Samuel Ringgold Ward asserted that he could not "degrade myself by arguing the equality of the Negro with the white; my private opinion is, that to say the Negro is equal morally to the white man is to say but very little."

The extension of social equality was accepted as an individual right by the free Negroes. They reasoned that there was no social equality among whites; upper-class whites did not associate on equal terms with lower-class whites. Still, the free Negro refused to accept his social rejection by whites as a mark of his inferiority. John Mercer Langston felt that social equality "was a matter dependent upon individual choice, favor or otherwise." But when Ohio whites inveighed against his intimate associations with white girls, he chided them by asserting that any white man would do his sister or daughter a favor by introducing them to John Langston. Samuel Ringgold Ward, who was often entertained by wealthy whites, felt that the lower-class whites were most prejudiced against Negroes. For him, the specter of social equality was a moot question: "Now, far be it from me to complain of any white man's denying any Negro a seat at his table or the association of his family. I am free to confess that, so far as a majority of them are concerned, *that* would be, to me, no honour—in many cases I could not reciprocate it, consistently with my own self-respect."

Many of the Negro autobiographers insisted that American Negroes had to study the record of famous blacks in the ancient world in order to counter the white man's argument that blacks were naturally indolent, stupid, savage, and inferior to whites. American Negroes contended that Africa was the seat of ancient civilization. Peter Randolph's attitude was typical: "Ethiopia was once the most civilized nation upon earth, and . . . the enlightened nations of the present day are indebted to her for many of the arts of civilization." The exploits of ancient Africans and of blacks like Frederick Douglass and Henry Highland Garnet showed that the intellect of Negroes was equal to that of whites. In this regard, free Negroes pointed to the injustice, hypocrisy, and cowardice of whites in barring them from educational institutions and then citing their ignorance as proof of their inequality.

One of the major historical motifs in black autobiographies, pamphlets, and lectures was the citation of the 5,000 blacks who had fought in the war for American independence. July 4 became a symbol of black pride in the exploits of black Revolutionary War soldiers and of American hypocrisy in enslaving and proscribing their descendants. For much of the eighteenth and nineteenth centuries, however, blacks celebrated Independence Day before or after July 4. Whenever they tried to join with other Americans, they were waylaid by drunken white mobs.

Despite their pride in black heroes of the Revolution, blacks recognized that Independence Day was the day above all others when they were reminded that they were enslaved, proscribed, and oppressed in a land which boasted of its dedication to freedom and equality. After 1816, when the American Colonization Society was organized in the U.S. House of Representatives and included among its founders a descendant of George Washington and Francis Scott Key, the author of the U.S. national anthem, July 4 became a day of mockery for blacks. The Colonization Society, arguing that blacks would never receive equal treatment in the United States, adopted July 4 as the day to raise funds to transport all free blacks back to Africa and thus harden the grip of slavery on the land.

Even before this, blacks had seen the ironies, contradictions, and hypocrisy in the American Revolution. As the American colonists increased their protests against British tyranny in the 1770s, five groups of slaves petitioned the Massachusetts legislature for freedom. In 1774 a black man addressed the Sons of Liberty in these words: "You are taxed without your consent, because you are not represented in parliament . . . and have petitioned for relief and cannot get any . . . are the Britons' hearts harder than yours? Are not your hearts also hard, when you hold them in slavery who are entitled to liberty, by the law of nature, equal as yourselves? If it be so, pray, sir, pull the beam out of thine eye." In February of that same year, one of America's first black poets, Phillis Wheatley, complained of the contradiction between the colonists' "Cry for Liberty, and the reverse Disposition for the Exercise of oppressive Power over others." Wheatley believed that "in every human Breast, God has implanted a Principle, which we call Love of Freedom."

But the American colonists rejected this principle. As their descendants would continue to do after them, they were willing to use black men to get rights which they would then deny to the blacks. Even Thomas Jefferson, the author of the Declaration of Independence, refused to free his slaves when he died on July 4, 1826. Nat Turner, the slave, had a better understanding of the Declaration than his fellow Virginia patriot Jefferson. Significantly, the day he initially chose to begin his slave revolt was July 4, 1831. Free blacks also saw clearly the inverse relationship between the Declaration of Independence and the continuation of slavery and oppression. The black abolitionist William Wells Brown spoke for most of them in 1847 when he asserted, "I know that upon 4th of July, our 4th of July orators talk of Liberty, Democracy, and Republicanism. . . . This is called the 'land of the free, and the home of the brave;' it is called the 'Asylum of the oppressed;' and some have been foolish enough to call it the 'Cradle of Liberty.' If it is the 'cradle of liberty,' they have rocked the child to death."

One of the alternative days blacks chose to commemorate the American Revolution was March 5, the day in 1770 a runaway slave, Crispus Attucks, shed his blood in the cause of freedom at the Boston Massacre. Attucks, owned by William Browne in Framingham, Massachusetts, was born around 1723. He early developed a desire for freedom and in 1750 ran away from his owner, who placed an ad in the Boston *Gazette* describing him as "a mulatto fellow, about 27 years of age, name Crispus, 6 feet 2 inches high." Going to Boston, Attucks led a relatively quiet life until March 1770, when he joined a group of men taunting British soldiers. On March 5 the soldiers fired on the men, killing five of them, including Attucks. The first bloodshed in what was to become the American Revolution was caused, according to John Quincy Adams, by Crispus Attucks. Adams, later President of the United States, said that the Americans were led by Attucks, "whose very look was enough to terrify any person. Attucks appears to have undertaken to be the hero of the night; and to lead this army with banners, to form them in the first place in Dock Square, and march them up to King Street with their clubs. . . the dreadful carnage of that night is chiefly to be ascribed" to Crispus Attucks. Three days after the massacre, thousands of Bostonians gathered to honor the men who had given their lives on the altar of British tyranny. In 1858 the black community in Boston revived the practice of honoring Crispus Attucks with a public lecture on March 5.

INSTITUTIONS, CLASS, AND PROTEST

The free Negro found some respite from prejudice, some sense of social structure, self-fulfillment, and status, in his relations with other blacks. Free Negroes organized all-black churches and debating, literary, and library societies, and wrote essays and poems which they read to black audiences. A number of the autobiographers were members of the black upper class. Admission to this class was based on education, wealth, and how long an individual's family had been free. Color was apparently of little significance. Some of the autobiographers befriended such black leaders as Morris Brown, Charles Reason, Charles B. Ray, Samuel Cornish, Thomas Jennings, and David Ruggles. Generally, upper-class Negroes married into other upper-class families. John Mercer Langston, for example, married Caroline Wall, the daughter of a white planter in North Carolina and the sister of O. B. S. Wall, who was an officer of Negro troops during the Civil War. Similarly, A. H. Newton married the daughter of Robert Hamilton, editor of the New York *Anglo-African.*

Drawing on community and individual resources, the free Negroes refused to be crushed by prejudice. Often they started fighting against it in childhood. Jeremiah Asher wrote that as a result of the teachings of his grandfather, a Revolutionary War veteran, "whenever I was insulted, I would always resist it. Neither my father nor mother could persuade me that white boys were allowed to insult me because I was colored. I invariably felt justified in defending myself."

Barred from or discriminated against in white organizations, the free Negroes either organized their own or fought within white institutions to bring about change. White Christians were continually upbraided for their contemptuous treatment of blacks. John Malvin spoke out against the black pew in the predominantly white Baptist church he attended in Ohio every Sunday until the trustees dropped the segregated seating arrangement. Jeremiah Asher led a Negro boycott of the predominantly white First Baptist Church in Hartford, Connecticut, until the congregation voted to end the Jim Crow seating arrangement. By then, it was too late to reconcile the communicants, and Asher helped to establish an all-Negro church. Increasingly, other Negroes followed his example. Despairing of ever reforming white churches, believing that they were the only real Christians in the land, they withdrew from white congregations and formed their own religious organizations. Richard Allen, Morris Brown, and Daniel A. Payne led the way in this movement. They simplified the liturgy of the white denominations and called for an educated ministry to uplift the race.

Many free Negroes in the South took the lead in maintaining institutions where slaves and free Negroes could experience a communal life. Churches were formed in the late eighteenth century and became important meeting places feared by whites. After Nat Turner's rebellion in Virginia in 1831, in which fifty whites were killed, black churches were increasingly outlawed and black ministers prohibited from preaching. Blacks still continued to congregate in secret, and in the late 1840s whites permitted their churches to operate openly again. Churches thrived in the cities and in areas where large numbers of poor and working-class free Negroes lived. Churches provided education, insurance, spiritual comfort, social activities, and the opportunity to exercise leadership. Many schools operated within the churches even while schooling for Negroes was outlawed. Burial associations and fraternal organizations frequently were formed from the base of church membership.

The free Negroes struggled against a massive wall of indifference, prejudice, and discrimination. They petitioned the state legislatures against discriminatory laws and disfranchisement. In California, Miflin W. Gibbs refused to pay the state poll tax even when his property was auctioned off to collect it. In 1851 he helped to establish a Negro newspaper and in 1854, 1855, and 1857 organized state conventions of black men to protest disfranchisement. Individual free Negroes tried to crack the color line in travel and sometimes succeeded. After one cold day of riding on the outside of an Ohio stagecoach, John Mercer Langston demanded that he be given the seat to which his ticket entitled him. When the white passengers refused to take their seats unless Langston was also seated, the driver relented. Jeremiah Asher charged boldly into a first-class cabin, locked the door, and refused to open it until he reached his destination when he learned that the captain of a steamboat wanted to relegate him to the deck in spite of the first-class ticket he held. When a steamboat captain tried to prevent another Negro from eating at a table with other passengers, he knocked the captain down and sat at the table anyway. Philadelphia blacks, contrary to law, sat in the streetcars reserved for whites and then organized a competing line.

Frederick Douglass, who spent his first twenty years as a slave in Maryland, was one of the leaders in nonviolent resistance to segregation. Refusing, he said, "to be proscribed when I can possibly help it," Douglass argued that as a man, he was "entitled to the rights and privileges of a man." Douglass faced his sternest test as he traveled through the Northeast lecturing. Despite threats, he demanded equal treatment on Massachusetts trains in the 1840s. Of this period he wrote:

> My treatment in the use of public conveyances about these times was extremely rough, especially on the Eastern Railroad, from Boston to Portland. On that road, as on many others, there was a mean, dirty, and uncomfortable car set apart for colored travelers called the Jim Crow car. Regarding this as the fruit of slaveholding prejudice and being determined to fight the spirit of slavery wherever I might find it, I resolved to avoid this car, though it sometimes required some courage to do so. . . . I . . . sometimes was soundly beaten by the conductor

and brakeman. On one occasion six of these "fellows of the baser sort," under the direction of the conductor, set out to eject me from my seat. As usual, I had purchased a first-class ticket and paid the required sum for it, and on the requirement of the conductor to leave, refused to do so. . . . They . . . found me much attached to my seat, and in removing me I tore away two or three of the surrounding ones, on which I held with a firm grasp, and did the car no service in some other respects. . . . The result was that Stephen A. Chase, superintendent of the road, ordered all passenger trains to pass through Lynn, where I then lived, without stopping.

There were times, of course, when the free Negro met physical abuse with violence. John Mercer Langston saw black men, frightened as they were, take up arms to defend themselves from white mobs in Cincinnati in 1840. Free Negroes often assailed the ears of whites and appealed to their conscience. But they refused to fawn upon whites or to beg for the rights to which they were entitled. Samuel Ringgold Ward, who often lectured to whites, typified their attitude. In his speeches, he asserted, "I never so compromised my own self-respect, nor ever consented to so deep a degradation of my own people, as to ask pity for them at the hands of their oppressors. . . . Justice, 'even-handed justice,' for the Negro—that which, according to American profession, is every man's birthright—*that* I claimed, nothing less."

EUROPEAN TRAVEL

One of the most important events in the life of many of the autobiographers was their travel outside the United States. As they emerged from the shadow cast by the American eagle, they escaped for a while the talons fastened irrevocably to their hearts and the horrifying tearing of their flesh. They fled from the republic which had "Liberty" engraved on its banners, to the "decadent" Old World to find "freedom" and "equality" engraved in the hearts of men. It was an experience they rarely forgot. Foreign travel elevated the Negro's sense of self-respect and increased his racial pride.

The favored resort of the antebellum blacks, whether free Negroes or fugitive slaves, was England. If they crossed the Atlantic in an English ship, they were immediately struck, as they left the dock in New York, with the contrast between American and English attitudes. Generally they had no trouble obtaining cabins and were not refused seats at the dining tables. Many of the autobiographers began to breathe free air, they asserted, for the first time in England. While they had been relegated to Jim Crow benches in churches and barred from intimate social interaction with whites in America, they spoke before large and sympathetic congregations and dined with aristocrats in England.

Although the autobiographers found a few proslavery Europeans, they encountered no discrimination. Henry Watson asserted that in England, "wherever I went, I was treated like a man. They looked not at the color of my skin, but judged me from my internal qualifications." Nancy Prince, whose husband was one of Czar Alexander I's Negro doormen, had a similar experience in Russia in the 1820s: "It is well known that the color of one's skin does not prohibit one from any place or station that he or she may be capable of occupying." Frederick Douglass spent almost two years in England and was entertained frequently by English aristocrats. He traveled throughout the United Kingdom and lectured to enthusiastic audiences. His views were characteristic of those of many black travelers:

> I can truly say, I have spent some of the happiest moments of my life since landing in this country. I seem to have undergone a transformation. I live a new life . . . the kind hospitality constantly proffered to me by persons of the highest rank in society; the spirit of freedom that seems to animate all with whom I come in contact, and the entire absence of everything that looked like prejudice against me, on account of the color of my skin—contrasted so strongly with my long and bitter experience in the United States, that I look with amazement on the transition. . . . I meet nothing to remind me of my complexion. . . . Thank heaven for the respite I now enjoy!

Foreign travel frequently increased the Negro's pride in being an American and in being black. In spite of egalitarian treatment in England, the trappings of royalty made Jeremiah Asher "rejoice in the simplicity of the form of government practically adopted in my own country, not withstanding that I might think that she seems to have forgotten its true spirit and design." Travel to Africa proved to American blacks the Negro's capacity for civilization. Daniel H. Peterson was overjoyed when he visited Liberia, which he felt was a veritable Garden of Eden, to find black men running their own government.

ANTISLAVERY ACTIVITIES

Foreign travel gave a respite from, but did not end the free black's fight against, discrimination. While fighting against discrimination, the free Negro enlisted in the crusade against slavery. Often the solitary knight in a sea of infidels, he fought in many ways to free his brethren. Reasoning that he himself could not be free as long as any black people were enslaved, remembering the horror stories about slavery recounted by his parents, or having witnessed the cruel treatment of the bondsmen, he enthusiastically served as an agent on the Underground Railroad, as an abolitionist lecturer, and as a political canvasser.

Organized black antislavery activities began in the eighteenth century when blacks petitioned state legislatures and Congress to abolish slavery. In the 1790s, Prince Hall, Benjamin Banneker, Absalom Jones, and Richard Allen wrote pamphlets denouncing slavery. Between 1800 and 1830 such blacks as Peter Williams of New York and William Whipper of Philadelphia delivered antislavery lectures and organized more than fifty antislavery societies. In 1827 Samuel E. Cornish and John B. Russwurm began one of the earliest northern anti-slavery newspapers, New York's *Freedom's Journal*.

The free blacks radicalized the American antislavery movement. It was, for example, after a debate with free blacks that William Lloyd Garrison abandoned his support of gradual emancipation and colonization. In 1831 Garrison began publishing the *Liberator* and in 1832 joined with eleven other white men in organizing the New England Anti-Slavery Society in a school room under Boston's African Baptist Church. When a new national organization, the American Anti-Slavery Society, met in Philadelphia in 1833, three free Negroes, James McCrummell, Robert Purvis, and James G. Barbadoes, were among the delegates. George B. Vashon, Peter Williams of New York, and Abraham D. Shadd of Chester County, Pennsylvania, were named to the board of managers of the new society. Within three days after the meeting ended, a young black woman, "Ada," wrote:

> Their works shall live when other deeds
> which mark a nation's fame,
> Have sunk beneath times whelming wave
> unhonored and unnamed.

Black women participated in the founding of women's auxiliaries to these organizations. Sarah M. Douglass, the Quaker principal of the preparatory department of the Institute for Colored Youth, Harriet Purvis, and Sarah and Margaretta Forten, the daughters of James Forten, were charter members of the Female Anti-Slavery Society of Philadelphia.

After the antislavery campaign became an integrated movement in the 1830s, blacks complained that though the white abolitionists were among the most egalitarian of Caucasians, they were sometimes prejudiced and paternalistic. Blacks contended that they were often used as soldiers (lecturers and agents of the abolition societies) in the war against slavery but were rarely given command positions. They had no policymaking power, and some local societies excluded blacks. Some white abolitionists refused to admit blacks to their schools or to employ blacks in their businesses except in menial capacities.

Black and white abolitionists clashed repeatedly over differences in ideology. Many white abolitionists, with their emphasis on moral suasion or political action as modes of abolishing slavery, were initially too conservative for the more militant blacks. While, for instance, William Lloyd Garrison was still supporting gradual emancipation, the Boston Negro David Walker was writing a seventy-six-page pamphlet calling for the abolition of slavery by violent means. In *David Walker's Appeal* (1829), he wrote:

> The man who would not fight under our Lord and Master Jesus Christ, in the glorious and heavenly cause of freedom and of God—to be delivered from the most wretched, abject and servile slavery, that ever a people was afflicted with since the foundation of the world, to the present day—ought to be kept with all of his children or family, in slavery, or in chains, to be butchered by his *cruel enemies*.

Blacks became increasingly militant after 1840. Their sentiments were summed up best by the Rev. Henry Highland Garnet in his 1843 address to the slaves:

> Brethren, arise, arise! Strike for your lives and liberties. Now is the day and the hour. Let every slave throughout the land do this and the days of slavery are numbered. Rather die freemen than live to be slaves. . . . Awake, Awake, millions of voices are calling you! Let your motto be resistance; no oppressed people have secured their liberty without resistance.

In 1844 the Rev. Jermain W. Loguen echoed Garnet's sentiments: "If our rights are withheld any longer, then come war—let blood flow without measure—until our rights are acknowledged or we perish from the earth. White men fight—all men fight for their freedom, and we are men and will fight for ours. Nothing can stop the current of blood but justice to our people."

The passage of the Fugitive Slave Law of 1850 produced a sharp upsurge in calls for violence. "Death to Tyrants" became the rallying cry of the free blacks. Since the law facilitated the recapture of fugitive slaves, blacks threatened anyone trying to enforce it with death. A convention of free Negroes in Portland, Maine, expressed the typical view in 1850 when they resolved, "There is no remedy left us but to solemnly warn our fellow citizens that, being left without legal and governmental protection for our liberties, we shall as God may help us, protect our own right to freedom at whatever cost or risk." Four years later, a free Negro convention adopted a resolution that "those who, without crime, are outlawed by any Government can owe no allegiance to its enactments . . . we advise all oppressed to adopt the motto, 'Liberty or Death.' "

Shocking as such sentiments were to some free Negroes, they produced even greater consternation in the camps of the white abolitionists. Even so, increasingly after 1830 there was greater cooperation between white and black abolitionists as they were able to reach compromises.

Because of the fragmentation of the abolition movement into several competing societies and the free Negroes' fears of abolition paternalism, the blacks never gave up their separate antislavery organs. Although free Negroes gave great support to William Lloyd Garrison's *Liberator*—James Forten supplied the money to buy the first ream of paper for it, and a majority of the initial subscribers and agents were black—they did not depend solely on abolition editors to protect their interests. Beginning in 1827 and sometimes over the protests of white abolitionist editors who feared the loss of black subscribers, antebellum free Negroes established thirty-two newspapers in the North and one periodical in the South (the New Orleans *L'Album Littéraire*).

The golden age of the antebellum black press was the period between 1840 and 1860. The prince among the black journalists was Frederick Douglass, who decided in the fall of 1847 to move to Rochester, New York, and publish the *North Star*. Douglass wrote that he hoped the paper would help dispel the notion of the blacks' inferiority and be the means of "making them acquainted with their own latent powers, by enkindling their hope of a future and developing their moral force." On December 2, 1847, the first issue of the *North Star* appeared, with the motto "Right is of no sex—Truth is of no color—God is the father of us all, and we are all Brethren." From 1847 to 1863 Douglass published the journal (or variants), changing its name to *Frederick Douglass' Paper* in 1851 and beginning *Douglass' Monthly Magazine* in 1858. The subscribers, black and white, varied between 3,000 and 4,500 and were located in eighteen states and two foreign countries. In spite of financial difficulties, Douglass was able to publish his newspaper continuously for thirteen years.

Several other important black newspapers were published between 1847 and 1860. Samuel Ringgold Ward edited the *Impartial Citizen* in Syracuse, New York, in 1848. Louis H. Putnam edited the *Colored Man's Journal* in New York City from 1851 to 1861; W. H. Day, a graduate of Oberlin College, published the *Aliened American* in Cleveland, Ohio, from 1852 to 1856. Miflin W. Gibbs, a Philadelphia free Negro who had emigrated to California, edited the *Mirror of the Times* in San Francisco from 1855 to 1862, and in 1854 the Rev. Jabez Campbell began publishing the long-running journal of the African Methodist Episcopal Church, the *Christian Recorder*. These able editors battled valiantly in the cause of abolition and equality for free blacks.

Trying to define the black man's place in American society, the antebellum black journalists concentrated on his African heritage, stressed the need for racial unity and cohesion, urged resistance to degradation and oppression, and suggested various self-help schemes. The thirty-two papers published before 1860 represent the most complete record of what blacks thought between 1827 and the Civil War. The *raison d'être* of the black press appeared in the March 16, 1827, edition of *Freedom's Journal:*

> We wish to plead our own cause. Too long have others spoken for us. Too long has the publick been deceived by misrepresentations, in things which concern us dearly. . . . The civil rights of a people being of the greatest value, it shall ever be our duty to vindicate our brethren, when oppressed; and to lay the case before the public. . . . Useful knowledge of every kind, and everything that relates to Africa, shall find a ready admission into our columns; . . . From the press and the pulpit we have suffered much by being incorrectly represented . . . we intend by a simple representation of facts to lay our case before the public, with a view to arrest the progress of prejudice, and to shield ourselves against the consequent evils.

Although devoted to the interests of Afro-Americans, the press supported many of the general reforms of the nineteenth century (temperance, women's rights, penal reform, peace). Advocating universal suffrage and protection for the laboring classes, the black press placed a special value on education as a vehicle for liberating Afro-Americans. Practically all nineteenth-century newspapers were national in scope, containing letters from black correspondents and reports of meetings throughout the country. Sketches of great black historic figures found a prominent place in these journals, and frequently the first publications of black poets and novelists appeared in them. The journals were universalistic in their advocacy. For instance, the *Aliened American* in its April 9, 1853, editorial asserted, "We speak not for ourselves alone. We speak for Humanity. . . . If Humanity be a unit, wherever it is cloven down, whenever the rights common to human beings are infringed, there do we sympathize; . . . Our humble advocacy does not rest upon the accident of color. We claim for all and especially for all Americans, equal justice before American law." The major preoccupation of black journalists was, however, the black community. Conventions of free Negroes frequently called for the establishment of black journals to represent their interests and those of the slaves.

In contrast to their lack of power in the abolition societies, blacks played a major role in the Underground Railroad. Whites participated, but blacks were the major actors. Such stalwarts as Harriet Tubman and Josiah Henson made repeated trips into the South to lead blacks out to freedom. When blacks escaped from the South, they were taken over by free Negroes like David Ruggles, printer, bookseller, and secretary of the New York Vigilance Committee, who aided Frederick Douglass in his flight. Ruggles and Charles B. Ray collected pennies and nickels, mainly from blacks, to help runaways.

Since whites denied any capacity to the Negro, many free Negroes argued that individual progress was a blow against the slaveholder. Samuel Ringgold Ward, who spent years on the abolitionist lecture tour, echoed this sentiment: "all the upright demeanour, gentlemanly bearing, Christian character, social progress, and material prosperity of every coloured man . . . [is] in its kind, anti-slavery labour." Many free Negroes, of course, went beyond this. They provided room and board to abolitionist lecturers when no one else would. Negro barbers distributed copies of the *Liberator* and pleaded the slaves' case with their white customers. The free Negro joined the political canvass for any antislavery candidate. The demands for emancipation of the slaves were linked, in the mind of the free Negro, with the hope of improving his own position. Success in the one campaign spurred on the troops in the other. Miflin W. Gibbs felt that the battle for the abolition of slavery enlarged the free Negroes' sense of liberty and "spirit of determination to defend our homes and churches from infuriated mobs and to contend for civil and political justice."

Feeling that there was no chance of breaking the grip of the slaveholders on American institutions, unwilling to appeal to an unjust law, and sharing vicariously the overseer's lash, the free Negro was sometimes willing to go to great lengths to promote the cause of liberty. A. H. Newton asserted, "I was born under the curse of slavery, surrounded by the thorns and briars of prejudice, hatred, persecution and the suffering incident to this fearful regime. . . . in my family, I learned what slavery was, I felt its curse in my bones and I longed for an opportunity and the power to play the part of Moses in behalf of my people."

Samuel Ringgold Ward indicated the empathy many free Negroes felt for the slaves after he conversed with a fugitive slave, Jerry, in a Syracuse, New York, jail: "I have heard a speech from Jerry. I feel for him, as for a brother. . . . I feel oppressed. . . . Yonder is my brother in chains, those chains press upon my limbs." Later, he joined a mob of free Negroes and abolitionists who took Jerry from the jail and gave Ward the pleasure of helping to file off those chains. John Malvin paid the bonds for imprisoned free Negroes, led mobs to prevent their return to slavery, helped to disguise them to aid them in eluding their pursuers, and once stole five slaves from a boat tied up at Cincinnati. His attitude was typical of that of many free Negroes: "So great was my abhorrence of slavery, that I was willing to run any risk to accomplish the liberation of a slave." John Mercer Langston said that Lewis Sheridan Leary, one of the free Negroes who accompanied John Brown on his 1859 raid on Harpers Ferry, had similar ideas. He had

> learned those lessons of freedom by experience, observation and parental instruction which made him at once intelligent with respect to the condition of the American slave, and which inspired him with the manly resolution to do whatever he might in the use of any means which he could control and wield, to overthrow the institution which so thoroughly wronged and ruined the class with which he and his kin were identified.

LITERARY EXPRESSION

Remarkably, while heavily engaged in antislavery activities, free blacks contributed to American literature. In addition to their autobiographies and newspapers, free Negroes wrote poetry, novels, and plays. Most of the early literature lamented the existence of slavery and appealed to religion and morality as a basis for abolition. The eighteenth-century poetry of Jupiter Hammon and Phillis Wheatley infrequently mentioned slavery or black oppression. The picture changed dramatically in the nineteenth century.

Family separations, bloodhounds, chains, coffles, fear, crushed hopes, helplessness, sadness, and prayers to God for freedom were among the primary images in antebellum black poetry. Many of the major images appeared in Frances Watkins Harper's famous 1858 poem, "Bury Me in a Free Land." The poet wanted no slaves around her grave, she wrote, because

> I could not rest if I heard the tread
> Of a coffle-gang to the shambles led,
> And the mother's shriek of wild despair
> Rise like a curse on the trembling air.
>
> I could not rest if I heard the lash
> Drinking her blood at each fearful gash,

And I saw her babes torn from her breast,
Like trembling doves from their parent nest.

I'd shudder and start, if I heard the bay
Of the blood-hounds seizing their human prey:
If I heard the captive plead in vain,
As they tightened afresh his galling chain.

Black fiction published in the late antebellum period expressed the strongest hostility toward slavery and white oppression. During the early 1850s Frederick Douglass wrote *The Heroic Slave,* a fictional narrative based on the 1841 mutiny on board the slave ship *Creole.* In writing about Madison Washington, the leader of the slave rebellion, Douglass places violence by slaves within the tradition and context of the American Revolution. Washington tells a white sailor, "We have struck for our freedom . . . we have done that which you applaud your fathers for doing, and if we are murderers, so were they." The mate of the ship, explaining later his reaction to Washington's bold explanation of his action, said, "It was not that his principles were wrong in the abstract, for they are the principles of 1776. But I could not bring myself to recognize their application to one whom I deemed my inferior." In placing black violence within the tradition of the American Revolution, Douglass confirmed the identity of blacks as Americans and underscored his belief in the rightness of resistance to oppression.

Martin R. Delany's novel *Blake; or, The Huts of America* (1859–62) brought together the two important themes of black emigration to Africa and black violence against whites. In the novel Henry Blake, "a black—a pure Negro—handsome and intelligent . . . a man of literary attainments," born in Cuba, the son of a merchant, had "been decoyed as a young man" and sold to a Mississippi planter. Blake married Maggie and had a son whom they named Little Joe. In the opening of the story, the relationship between Blake and Maggie is cruelly broken by Colonel Franks, who sells Maggie to Cuba. Blake runs away and organizes slave insurrections in the South and in Cuba.

Blake knows that racism is too widespread in the United States and even in Canada for blacks to realize freedom from oppression and discrimination. Only in Africa can redemption be found. As Blake explains to his followers, black redemption requires economic enterprise, the accumulation of money and skills, and revolutionary violence against whites. But Blake is ambivalent toward violence. He does not kill Franks when he has the opportunity. He thinks of it but decides instead to leave, taking as many blacks as he can induce to go. Maturer reflection leads him "to the expedient of avenging the general wrongs of our people, by inducing the slave, in his might, to scatter red ruin throughout the region of the South." But still he cannot find it in his "heart to injure an individual, except in personal conflict." Violence for Delany's Blake is an expression of rage and alienation toward America and a hope that Africa will provide relief from the anguish he has suffered.

William Wells Brown, author of a slave autobiography, published his novel *Clotel: or the President's Daughter* in 1853 and his play *The Escape, or a Leap for Freedom,* in 1858. In *Clotel* he expressed the anxieties of mulattoes about their marginality to both the black and white worlds. Isabella is a victim of white male sexual manipulation and has a daughter, Clotel, who is despised for her whiteness by blacks. She grows up, escapes to Europe, and marries a man of "pure African origin," an act which unifies mulattoes and blacks at the same time as it affirms her acceptance of her husband's endorsement of revolutionary violence. In the end she is reconciled with her white father, who accepts her husband and begins to overcome his racism.

In *The Escape,* Glen and Melinda run away when the master decides to sell Melinda for refusing his sexual advances. In their escape to Canada, Glen knocks down the white overseer and boasts later to Melinda, "I made the wine flow freely." He "pounded his old skillet well for him, and then jumped out of the window. It was a leap for freedom." As a slave, Brown, a mulatto, had experienced the mulatto's travail. He had also heard a slaveowner offer a slave woman the chance of becoming his mistress or being sold to the deep South. Brown, unlike his fictional hero, did not defend her but only gave her words of comfort, though he "foresaw but too well what the result must be." She became the white man's mistress. Years later, after Brown escaped to the North, he learned that when the slaveowner married, he, "as a previous measure, sold poor Cynthia and her four children . . . into hopeless bondage." Brown had a cowardly fear of punishment and of white men. He experienced the pain of seeing his sister sold to the deep South and heard stories of how his mother had been whipped for leaving the field to nurse him when he was small. He attempted to flee to Canada with his mother after his sister had been taken to Mississippi. They were captured and returned to Missouri, and his mother was sent to the New Orleans slave market as punishment for running away. Brown's literary creativity helped to relieve the pain of his personal sufferings. But the reconciliation between the races and the end of prejudice that he hoped for never occurred. He saw the violence in which blacks participated in the Civil War as a precursor to the end of oppression. But in the end he recognized in *My Southern*

Home, published in 1884, four years before he died, that whites were as vicious and violent as they had always been. No real revolution had occurred. His final solution was: "Black men, emigrate."

The literature, press, speeches, and autobiographies of the free Negroes reflected their continuous search for freedom and equality for themselves and their enslaved brothers and sisters. They sought to fulfill the promises of the Declaration of Independence by pointing to the gap between American creeds and American practices. Treated as pariahs by American whites, free Negroes emphasized moral uplift, education, and economic mobility in the face of unremitting discrimination, insecurity, and violence.

3

Family and Church:
Enduring Institutions

But a step from slavery, its darkness still infolding us, who now is fitted to face the journey's end, to guide and to warn, to SHIELD US FROM OURSELVES against VAIN GLORYING, IMPROVIDENCE, LICENSE, the "DUNCE STOOL," the "CAP AND BELLS"?

W. Allison Sweeney

The family and the church enabled blacks to endure American racism, slavery, segregation, violence, and oppression. Indeed, these institutions provided the foundation for personal identity, communal strength, individual triumphs in the face of overwhelming odds, creative and rewarding lives, and pride. The autonomous black community drew much of its ideology from and created much of its distinctive culture in the institutions nurturing the young, sustaining the spirit, and arming against caste and prejudice. Heroic and tragic in its dimensions, the history of black institutions is a story of a struggle that began in the family.

GENERAL OUTLINE OF FAMILY LIFE

The history of the black family is a largely uncharted field. The signposts, where they exist, frequently lead the researcher down false trails. Consequently, in order to understand the family life of blacks, the outline of American family life in general must be sketched. Much of the confusion over the nature of the black family is a direct result of myths about the white family that historians and sociologists have all too often accepted.

The first of these myths is that the nineteenth-century white American family was a close-knit, patriarchal institution that was the exact replica of the seventeenth-century European family. In operating on this assumption (usually unstated), scholars ignored the differences in the demographic features of American and European life. Women in frontier areas, for example, undoubtedly had a much stronger voice in family affairs than scholars have realized, simply because there was such a shortage of women. In spite of the laws that discriminated against them, women exercised a great deal of authority in the family. Whatever can be said against European travelers as trustworthy witnesses, it is difficult to discount their almost completely unanimous report that the American husband had far less authority in his family than his European counterpart. In the cities, where the family had little importance as an economic unit and the father was at work so much, the rearing of children was primarily the responsibility of the mother. The more time the American father spent away from home, the more voice American women and children gained in the family. By 1880, the American family was more democratic than patriarchal or matriarchal.

After the second half of the nineteenth century, some amazing changes occurred in the nature and functions of the family. Industrialization, improvements in transportation, the weakening of religious bonds, and increased knowledge of birth control led to more working wives and more premarital sex and downgraded the economic importance of the family. Relaxed divorce laws and a greater emphasis on romantic love increased the number of divorces. By the 1970s one in every three marriages ended in divorce, the failure rate for new marriages was 30 percent, 9 million people were divorced or separated, and 12.5 million single individuals were heading households with children. In fact, there were so many divorces in the United States that it could be said that a significant number of whites were practicing serial monogamy—one person having only one spouse at a time, but more than one in his or her lifetime.

In studies of the family, blacks have been hurt by their overzealous white friends. Frequently researchers speak of the pathological disorganization of the black family and imply that all black families are matriarchal. The most dangerous part of this myth was popularized by Daniel P. Moynihan, who asserted in 1965 that the pathological weakness of the black family was "capable of perpetuating itself without assistance from the white world." The weaknesses of the twentieth-century black family may be seen instead as a direct result of centuries of white oppression of blacks and not as inherent and immutable.

The black family grew out of a complex combination of African traditions, Christian beliefs, and adjustments made to slavery. In Africa the family was a strong communal institution stressing the dominance of males, the importance of children, and extended kinship networks.

African societies generally forbade extramarital sex yet regarded sexual intercourse as a healthy, natural act unconnected with sin. The enslavement of the African led to the evolution of new familial practices in the quarters. Men were forced to share authority with women and parents no longer completely shaped the destiny of their children. However, monogamy remained the norm; although the law did not recognize slave unions, most bondsmen lived in two-parent households. Because its members could be separated at any time by heartless masters, the slave family was a relatively powerless institution. Slaves consistently lamented their separation from mates, parents, and children, and the sexual exploitation of black women.

WHITE CHURCH SUPPORT FOR THE SLAVE FAMILY

The slave family received its primary institutional support from southern white churches. In numerous sermons and catechisms prepared especially for the slaves, ministers stressed biblical prohibitions against premarital sexual intercourse, adultery, fornication, and the separation of mates. Typical of the lessons thousands of slaves learned was the section in the 1837 catechism published by South Carolina Episcopalians where young blacks memorized such passages as "Thou shalt not commit adultery. . . . Our Saviour saith, He who looketh on a woman, to lust after her, hath committed adultery with her already in his heart. . . . St. Paul saith, Fornication and all uncleanness, let it not be once named among you, as becometh saints; neither filthiness, nor foolish talking, nor jesting, which are not convenient. . . . St. Paul saith, Let every man have his own wife, and every woman her own husband." The catechumens also learned that they should avoid "impure thoughts" and "lewd and filthy words," that fornication was "a great sin," a disgrace, "a sin against God," leading to "falsehoods, and jealousies, and murders, and loss of health." God would punish adulterers in "everlasting Hell" or, like the people of Sodom and Gomorrah, destroy them.

Southern clergymen considered the family second only to the church as a force that insured morality in a community. Consequently, they gave a great deal of thought to family life in the slave quarters. Having largely abandoned attempts to abolish slavery in the first decades of the nineteenth century, clergymen were forced to determine the relationship between bondage, marriage, property, and Christianity. Lacking the wisdom of Solomon or legislative power, the ministers often took a long time to develop a consistent policy. In all probability, the agony of the churches represented as much fear of moral contamination of whites because of their proximity to the slaves as it did a desire to preserve Christian practices in the quarters. A group of South Carolina ministers made the point succinctly in 1837 when they wrote: "The influence of the negroes upon the moral and religous interests of the whites is destructive in the extreme. . . . We are chained to a putrid carcase; it sickens and destroys us. We have a millstone hanging about the neck of our society, to sink us deep in the sea of vice."

Because of their concern with morality, the churches began in the 1740s to insist that the slaves be married in Christian ceremonies; many denominations required ministers to perform slave weddings. Thousands of slaves were married in southern churches between 1800 and 1860, and white churches exercised moral oversight over the slaves after their weddings. The churches frequently investigated charges of adultery and fornication and tried to promote the development of Christian familial practices in the quarters. They often excommunicated or publicly criticized slaves for abandoning their mates, premarital pregnancies, and engaging in extramarital sex.

Frequently confronted with masters who separated mates, ministers called for the passage of laws prohibiting this practice and appealed to slaveholders to recognize the inviolability of slave marriages. A Mississippi minister in 1859 sent a pastoral letter to the members of his church telling them that in regard to their slaves they should "be careful to protect them in the enjoyment of the rights, and encourage them in the discharge of the duties of the family. The chiefest of these rights is that of marriage. . . . so sacred are these rights to your servants, and so debasing must be any denial of them, that we feel it our duty to put you on your guard, and renewedly to invoke your dilligence, exhorting you rather to suffer pecuniary damage yourself, than to allow moral wrong to accrue to your servants." In that same year a committee of the South Carolina Episcopal Church asserted that "every Christian master should so regulate the sale or disposal of a married slave, as not to infringe the Divine injunction forbidding the separation of man and wife." Despite the efforts of the churches, about 30 percent of all slave unions were broken by masters.

PREMARITAL AND EXTRAMARITAL RELATIONS

Slaves adapted to the frequent disruptions of their families by developing extended kinship networks, communal care of and responsibility for children, and great respect for elders. Though they adopted some of the Christian ambivalence toward sex, slaves considered abstinence by the young a human impossibility. Premarital pregnancy did not lead to permanent loss of status for women or bar them from marriage. Indeed, a woman having a child out of wedlock usually later married the father of her child.

Marital fidelity was apparently the norm in the quarters, with adultery usually leading to separation of mates. As among whites, the double standard prevailed; women lost more status because of extramarital affairs than men. Beginning sexual experimentation and marrying at an earlier age than their masters, slaves placed greater emphasis on love and affection in choosing mates than did whites. The historian Eugene Genovese concluded in his study of slavery that the female slaves "did not demand premarital chastity; that they freely experimented before marriage; that they would drop one husband for another if he proved unsatisfactory; and that, relative to their white mistresses at least, they enjoyed a relaxed attitude toward their own sexuality." Although no laws prevented their divorce, slaves often preserved their unions for decades. The Rev. R. Q. Mallard, for instance, asserted that slave marriages "were, by the slaves themselves and their masters, generally regarded quite as sacred as marriages solemnized with legal license of the courts; and the obligations as commonly observed as among the same class anywhere. There were as many faithful husbands and wives, we believe, as are to be found among the working white population in any land."

ROLES OF MEN, WOMEN, AND MASTERS

The marriage of slaves meant the sharing of responsibility and authority among men, women, and masters. Labor, food, housing, and treatment of family members were dependent on masters. Almost inevitably, the intervention of whites led to an oppressive distortion of familial roles. Under the plantation regime, for example, the economic function of slave women was often comparable to that of men. At the same time that it enlarged the woman's sphere, the plantation severely limited that of the slave man. Always, there was an external power greater than the slave husband's. Genovese characterized the restraints on black males perfectly when he wrote, "The slaveholders deprived black men of the role of provider; refused to dignify their marriages or legitimize their issue; compelled them to submit to physical abuse in the presence of their women and children; made them choose between remaining silent while their wives and daughters were raped or seduced and risking death; and threatened them with separation from their family at any moment." Black women often performed the same labor as men and had limited time to care for their children or to perform domestic chores. Because of the love they shared, parents supported each other in times of tribulation and tried to protect their children. Often they provided positive images. A South Carolina slave, for example, said: "My mammy she work in de field all day and piece and quilt all night. . . . I never see how my mammy stand such hard work. She stand up for her chillen though. De old overseer he hate my mammy, 'cause she fought him for beatin' her chillen."

In his relations with whites, the black man was generally submissive. But he taught his children the difference between fear and capitulation to overwhelming force. Whatever his behavior when interacting with a threatening white world, in the quarters the black man played the roles of father and husband. Black children never forgot the oppression their fathers endured, yet they also remembered those times when, in the privacy of their cabins, these fathers demonstrated their strength and love. One ex-slave illustrated the character of such homes when he spoke of his boyhood on the plantation:

> I loved my father. He was such a good man. He was a good carpenter and could do anything. My mother just rejoiced in him. Whenever he sat down to talk she just sat and looked and listened. She would never cross him for anything. If they went to church together she always waited for him to interpret what the preacher had said or what he thought was the will of God. I was small but I noticed all these things. I sometimes think I learned more in my early childhood about how to live than I have learned since.

NAMING PATTERNS AMONG THE SLAVES

Central to the slave's personal and family identity was the selection of names. Most black parents named their children, but occasionally masters did so or ordered young blacks to adopt new ones. The slaves often refused to change their names. Ordered to change his name, William Wells Brown recalled, "This at the time, I thought to be one of the most cruel acts that could be committed upon my rights; and I received several severe whippings for telling people my name was William, after orders were given to change it." Planters usually cared little for the names of their slaves, treating them all as an undifferentiated mass. On such plantations a name was a very fragile link in a kinship network or base for identity. Speaking in 1853, the former slave David Holmes said: "slaves never have any name. I'm called David, now; I used to be called Tom, sometimes; but I'm not, I'm Jack. It didn't much matter what name I was called by. If master was looking at any one of us, and call us Tom, or Jack, or anything else, whoever he looked at was forced to answer."

Slaves rarely used surnames. Indeed, in common parlance a slave's name was inverted; usually the master's name appeared first, with blacks being referred to as "Bentley's George." Although some planters forbade blacks to use surnames, they frequently did so surreptitiously. According to historian Herbert G. Gutman, the blacks often chose the name of the whites who owned the first member of the family line. To preserve the link with their past, blacks generally took the name of their former owners after the Civil War. Occasionally, they merged African and American traditions, as did William Jackson, who reported:

> The master's name was usually adopted by a slave after he was set free. This was done more because it was the logical thing to do and the easiest way to be identified than it was through affection for the master. Also, the government seemed to be in a almighty hurry to have us get names. We had to register as someone, so we could be citizens. Well, I got to thinking about all us slaves that was going to take the name Fitzpatrick. I made up my mind I'd find me a different one. One of my grandfathers in Africa was called Jeaceo, and so I decided to be Jackson.

Frequently naming children after their grandparents, the slaves tried to inculcate respect for ancestors in spite of the breaks in the family chain. Slaves found companionship and love in the family circle, preserved some traditions, and trained children to survive an oppressive institution. The internal belief system of the slaves, buttressed by religious teachings, strongly supported the concept of a close-knit family. Although many slave families were separated, the tradition of monogamous unions and extended kinship networks had taken deep roots in the quarters before the Civil War.

FREE NEGRO FAMILIES

One of the most important sources of black family tradition was the antebellum free Negro community. Although haunted by poverty, the free black family was nevertheless strong. It was especially crucial in the socialization of children. Black children imbibed important lessons from their parents. As industrious and earnest Christians, parents stressed morality, the value of labor and education, and racial uplift. They held family devotional services and regularly took their children to church. If they were skilled craftsmen, they taught their trade to their sons. If not, black boys were frequently apprenticed to black or white artisans. Finally, and most important, black parents exemplified, in their own lives, the character traits they wanted their children to learn.

Parents were frequently very strict with children. Black fathers insisted that boys work hard in order for the family to rise from the level of poverty. As a result of this strictness, girls married early and boys frequently left home around the age of sixteen. Sometimes children were put to work at an early age to pay for rent or to keep away the pangs of hunger. Still, the respect blacks had for their parents was almost unlimited. Amanda Smith's attitude toward her father was typical of that expressed in many autobiographies: "I loved my father, and thought he was the grandest man that ever lived."

Free Negro women were strong and important members of the family. Their industry, economy, and cheerful dispositions were heavily relied upon by the men. They not only worked to add to family funds but also tried to prevent their husbands from squandering the family resources. Many families were clearly matriarchal. The women gave advice to the men and often acted contrary to their wishes. These black women were strong, industrious, pious, and loved by their children. The high mortality rate of black men enhanced the position of black women. The father of practically every nineteenth-century autobiographer died before his mate. Not all black women, however, were domineering. They were particularly submissive to their husbands when their mates had purchased their freedom. Generally, however, the free Negro family was patriarchal.

THE POSTEMANCIPATION FAMILY

Family life of blacks, while unrestricted by law after the Civil War, was hedged in by poverty and bludgeoned by prejudice and discrimination. Even so, there was greater variety in family types and more chances for the development of strong family ties than in the antebellum period. Many blacks remained with mates they had had in slavery. Otherwise, they married while quite young. Freed of the restraints of slavery, black parents struggled against the constricting tentacles of poverty and their own ignorance to build a meaningful family life. Black males began to assert their authority over their families after the war, but their efforts were often undermined by their inability to provide even the barest living. Sharecropping on southern plantations, often with his antebellum master, illiterate and penniless, year after year the black ended up deeper in debt. Seeking to elude the persistent hunger that nagged at his children's stomachs, he often was forced to move annually, trying to find a planter who would treat him fairly. William Pickens' family, for example, moved twenty times in a fifteen-year span. Sometimes the black male gave up the struggle and deserted his family. The incessant labor and the unremitting struggle against poverty frequently killed strong black men long before they reached the haven of old age.

"Bootsie, you ever read the statistics? Man, they say that bachelors
who ain't married don't live no time at all, so I'm real worried
about you, Baby!"

COURTSHIP

From Bootsie and Others *by Ollie Harrington. Copyright © 1958 The
New Pittsburgh Courier Publishing Company. Reprinted by permission of the New Pittsburgh Courier Publishing Company.*

   Contributing significantly to the family larder, rearing large families, and often less ignorant than their husbands, recently emancipated
black women did not relinquish the roles they had played in the slave
family. Often this was simply a result of the mental and physical superiority of the female partner that one often finds in the marriage relationship. Black women who were physically robust, strong, and courageous
made decisions for their husbands and managed families in the same
way that some white women related to their mates. As a farm worker,

the black woman contributed to the economic well-being of the family. If she worked as a domestic servant, she was often in a better position to keep her children from starving than her husband was. Many black autobiographers testified that the food their mothers brought them from the "big house" saved them from starvation. Black women constantly pushed their men to greater exertions. Lawrence C. Jones' mother, for instance, rejected his father's satisfaction with his porter's job and easygoing philosophy: "That one should be supinely content in whatever place he chanced to fall was something that she simply could not understand." William Holtzclaw's father was patient and long-suffering, but his mother "was a woman with considerable fire in her make-up." Both the authority and responsibility of emancipated black women, like their free antebellum counterparts, were enhanced as a result of the early death of their mates. Because of this and dire poverty, they often worked such long hours that they had little time to spend with their children.

In spite of the lack of time, intensely religious parents taught moral lessons to their children by example. They inculcated respect for elders and the dignity of work, and stressed the importance of obtaining property and of education. The rod was applied religiously. William Holtzclaw's parents always gave him a second whipping whenever he was flogged at school. Lawrence C. Jones wrote that his father was a devotee of the rod. "My father, plain, strict and practical, was a valorous, verbal supporter of the rod." Poor and inadequately educated themselves, black parents were nonetheless ambitious for their children. Booker T. Washington's mother, he wrote, "had high ambitions for her children, and a large fund of good, hard, common sense which seemed to enable her to meet and master every situation." Black parents moved to new areas, gave up their claims to their children's labor, or hid them from unsympathetic planters so that the children could go to school.

Many autobiographers were reared by grandparents and other relatives. In spite of their own poverty, relatives enthusiastically tried to provide for orphaned children. William Edwards' experience was typical of that of many blacks. After his mother died in 1870 and his father deserted the children, he moved in with his grandparents. When his grandfather died, young William went to school for three months of the year, worked the farm with his grandmother, and then read the Bible to her for hours at a time. Upon her death in 1880, his father returned and took the children to Selma, Alabama. Shiftless and improvident, he left the children on the verge of starvation for days, and when William got sick the father took the children to his sister's cabin. Living in indescribable poverty, sometimes begging for food from almost equally poor black neighbors or existing for days on a scrap of bread and the juice left over from boiling vegetables, William helped his aunt farm. She urged him to continue his schooling and when everyone else spoke against his going to college, she encouraged him to try. Of all his adult relatives, his aunt made the greatest impact on his life.

PATRIARCHAL MIDDLE-CLASS FAMILIES

Despite poverty, discrimination, and oppression, the postemancipation rural black family was a strong institution contributing significantly to Afro-American survival. After 1865 the male-headed household predominated in the rural South and the relatively small urban communities throughout the United States.

Although economic deprivation led to increases in female-headed households, since emancipation a majority of all black families in the United States have been headed by males. In 1960 about 74 percent of these families were headed by males; in 1970 the figure was 69.7 percent; in 1976, it was 67 percent. Several studies showed that blacks had the same ideals regarding the family as whites. Tests conducted in 1951, 1960, and 1965 revealed that blacks and whites were practically identical when it came to control of the family. Among both groups, the egalitarian or democratic family prevailed. There was, however, no one family type that predominated in all classes, geographical areas, or times.

As the statistics reveal, Afro-Americans were battered, but not destroyed by slavery and oppression. An overwhelming majority of black families in every historical era were headed by males. According to a series of studies published in the *Negro History Bulletin*, it was the stable, male-headed families that produced Afro-American social, political, economic, cultural, and intellectual leaders between the 1800s and the 1980s. Within a single family tree extending over two hundred years might be found Revolutionary War soldiers, leaders of slave revolts, founders of black colleges, poets, physicians, architects, engineers, businessmen, and scientists. Persistent efforts to acquire land, upward social mobility, political activism, and pride of race were characteristic of the stable, male-headed Afro-American families.

Measured solely by the indicators of social class within the Afro-American community, most blacks were born and grew up in "middle-class" families. Indeed, one measure of a male's status in the black community historically was his ability to provide for his family, to educate his children, and to support his church. It mattered not, for example, that barbers, mailmen, carpenters, or porters were considered "lower class" by whites, they were ascribed "middle-class" status if they held steady jobs enabling them to provide for their families. Thus defined, the large black middle class contributed significantly to the predominance of the male-headed family among Afro-Americans.

Like their white American counterparts, middle-class Afro-Americans have been geographically mobile, especially in the twentieth century. Because of their strong roots, middle-class black families survived migration from the South to northern cities. In fact, the family survival rate of blacks was greater than that of the European immigrants with whom they have often been compared. For example, Herbert Gutman discovered that the percentage of male-headed households was consistently higher among black than European migrants to New York between 1855 and 1925.

Whether of slave or free. ancestry, middle-class blacks often had one or more white men or women in their family trees, and generally rose from low estates. Over several generations the middle-class black family played a prominent role in military affairs, promoted or sustained interest in Africa, led protest movements against white proscriptions, and fought consistently for Afro-American economic and political rights. For such families, genealogy was important. Stories of sagacious and aggressive male progenitors were constantly recounted in family circles in the middle of the twentieth century. The dominant males in middle-class families often took on heroic dimensions as the stories of their escapes from slavery, service in the Revolutionary and Civil Wars, confrontations with white mobs, and successes in business and politics were recounted. Historians would agree that some of these men, such as the Civil War naval captain, Robert Smalls, were, indeed, heroes. The twentieth-century descendants of Robert Smalls were fond of repeating an anecdote that buttressed the historical assessment. According to the story, two admirers of Smalls were standing on a street corner one day, when one said to the other, "I tell you Smalls is the greatest man in the world." The other said, "Yes, he's great, but not the greatest man." "Pshaw man," inquired the enthusiastic admirer, "who's greater than Smalls?" To which came the reply, "Why, Jesus Christ." "Oh," said the laudator, "Smalls is young yet."

Since most middle-class black families were descended from slaves, great difficulty was encountered in establishing origins. Even so, some blacks could trace their families back to the 1730s, especially if a progenitor obtained freedom at an early date. Typical of such families were the Colsons of Petersburg, Virginia, whose genealogy was published in the *Negro History Bulletin* in 1946.

In the black community most families had histories similar to the Colsons once they obtained freedom. Before and after freedom, middle-class families fought for economic, social, and moral respectability.

THE PATERNAL ANCESTRY OF JEANNE AND
WILLIAM NELSON COLSON
CHILDREN OF CORTLANDT AND ELSIE DURHAM COLSON

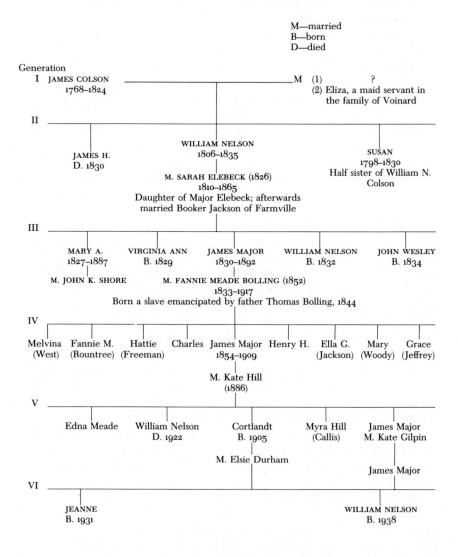

M—married
B—born
D—died

Generation

I JAMES COLSON ————————————————— M (1)   ?
   1768–1824   (2) Eliza, a maid servant in
                                                       the family of Voinard

II ——

                         WILLIAM NELSON
   JAMES H.   1806–1835   SUSAN
   D. 1830   1798–1830
                     M. SARAH ELEBECK (1826)   Half sister of William N.
                            1810–1865   Colson
                   Daughter of Major Elebeck; afterwards
                   married Booker Jackson of Farmville

III ——

   MARY A.   VIRGINIA ANN   JAMES MAJOR   WILLIAM NELSON   JOHN WESLEY
   1827–1887   B. 1829   1830–1892   B. 1832   B. 1834

   M. JOHN K. SHORE   M. FANNIE MEADE BOLLING (1852)
                                 1833–1917
                   Born a slave emancipated by father Thomas Bolling, 1844

IV ——

Melvina Fannie M.   Hattie   Charles James Major Henry H.   Ella G.   Mary   Grace
(West)   (Rountree) (Freeman)   1854–1909   (Jackson) (Woody)   (Jeffrey)

                                      M. Kate Hill
                                        (1886)

V ——

   Edna Meade   William Nelson   Cortlandt   Myra Hill   James Major
                    D. 1922   B. 1905   (Callis)   M. Kate Gilpin

                                 M. Elsie Durham

                                                                 James Major

VI ——

   JEANNE   WILLIAM NELSON
   B. 1931   B. 1938

Almost always their efforts were dogged by prejudice and discrimination, especially in the South between 1865 and the early years of the twentieth century. Searching for a better life for their wives and children, large numbers of Southern black men eventually concluded that they had to migrate to the North.

THE TWENTIETH-CENTURY URBAN FAMILY

The rapid migration of blacks to northern urban centers in the twentieth century sometimes had a disorganizing effect on family life. Although often exaggerated by scholars, it is clear that migration had the same impact on blacks as it did on European immigrants. Since black males were the first to leave, there was an increase in desertion rates in the rural South. The receiving community was also often adversely affected because it had to absorb so many people in a short time. From 1910 to 1920, for instance, the black population of Detroit increased 611 percent, Chicago 148 percent, and the borough of Manhattan in New York, 80 percent. Millions of young, unattached black males and females were freed of parental or societal restraints. Partially as a result of the loosening of restraints, there was an increase in black illegitimacy and desertion rates in a number of northern cities.

For the most part, scholars have been too quick to generalize about the urban black family in the first decades of the twentieth century. Although there is much evidence of the disorganizing effects of urban migration on familial patterns, there was, however, no one family type that predominated in any city. For example, the sociologist E. Franklin Frazier discovered several family types in Chicago in the 1930s. He found that the blacks nearest the center of the city were poorer and had more broken families; a lower percentage of the population married, and there was a higher percentage of single men than in any of the areas lying outside the city center. As education, occupational skill, and wealth went up in different strata of the black population, the percentage of stable families increased accordingly. In Frazier's study, the highest percentage of female-headed families was found among those earning $3,000 or less annually. Several factors helped to account for this condition. The most important was economic discrimination. All too many black males were paid so low a wage for the unskilled labor they performed that they could not support a family. The high unemployment rate among this group meant that a man's authority and self-respect were both undermined because of his inability to provide for his family. The structural nature of the economy added to this frustration because it provided many more low-paying unskilled jobs for black women than for black men. Haunted by low wages, unemployment, and the fact that white America would let only the black woman be a steady provider, many black men gave up and deserted their families. For example, in 1964 the U.S. Bureau of Labor Statistics reported: "the percent of nonwhite women separated from their husbands has a significant correlation . . . with the unemployment rate *for the preceding year.*"

In the twentieth century there was a systematic, institutionalized attack by federal, state, and local governments on low-income families. Throughout most of this century, welfare regulations prohibited payments to indigent women and children when a husband was present. It is ironic that some black males thus had to desert their families in order to feed them. The impact of such regulations on family stability is obvious. Between 1961 and 1971 about 30 percent of the 690,000 black women applying for aid to dependent children had been separated from or deserted by their husbands. It seemed as though the social system of white America, watching with such sleepless vigilance to prevent blacks from acting the roles of men, frequently caused insurmountable tensions in the black family it allegedly wished to preserve. Dorothy Height, president of the National Council of Negro Women, noted this in 1963 when she wrote, "A Negro woman has the same kind of problems as other women, but she can't take the same things for granted. For instance, she has to raise children who seldom have the same sense of security that white children have when they see their father accepted as a successful member of the community. A Negro child's father is ignored as though he didn't exist." The result of this systematic oppression was a steady increase in the percentage of female-headed families: 22.4 percent in 1960 and 33 percent in 1976 (among whites, 10.8 percent of families were headed by females in 1976).

One of the most important causes of family disorganization is generally overlooked by students. Poor health in the black community and the extremely high death rate among black males probably accounted for more family disorganization than any other factor except economic oppression. In New Orleans, for example, 81 percent of the female heads of black families were widows in 1880. If widows are excluded from the statistics, the percentage of male-headed families in New Orleans was more than 90 percent. As the black mortality rate fell in the twentieth century, its impact on family instability declined. Even so, the death of husbands consistently accounted for about one-half of the broken families in the black community. In 1950 roughly 52 percent of the female heads of black families were widows; in 1976 the figure was about 50 percent.

LOWER-CLASS FAMILY LIFE

Although it does not by any means represent the majority of black families, the lower-class matriarchal family is an example of the remarkable adaptation black institutions have made to oppressive conditions in America. This family, created by the social and economic proscriptions against the black community, was disturbingly weak in certain areas and surprisingly strong in others. One of the major functions of the lower-class black family was to toughen its members to a world of systematic brutalization by the police, by businessmen, and by other facets of white caste restrictions. Lower-class culture helped to minimize the pain this involved. Within the family, as in no other area of life, white America freed the black man to work out his response to systematic oppression. One mode of adaptation was the extended family.

After slavery, the extended family was prevalent in the black community. Generally, black households had twice as many relatives outside the immediate family as did white ones. Egalitarian in nature, the family was marked by flexibility of roles, informal adoption of children, and care for the aged. Blacks seemed to have greater abhorrence of institutionalizing the aged than whites did. When aged blacks did not live with their children, several other members of the local community took responsibility for them.

Since many had done so historically, black women who had to head households did not seem as intimidated by the role as white women were. Sometimes several generations of a family lived in a household headed by a grandmother. Control over children in such households was lax, and new illegitimate children might be added with each generation. On occasion boyfriends contributed to family finances. In the lower-class community the self-sufficiency of the black woman was stressed from childhood on. Children were taught not to give up completely in the face of verbal and physical aggression from others and learned strategies of survival: manipulating or persuading others, using violence, and keeping one's physical needs at a bare minimum.

The lower-class family was strong in many respects. Since it was an extended family, it had a closeness of kin missing among whites. Consider illegitimacy, for example. An illegitimate birth among blacks brought the family closer together to care for the infant; among whites, it tended to pull the family apart. In New York City in 1930, while 73 percent of black illegitimate children were in a home with the mother and her relatives, only 34 percent of white illegitimate children were in this position. Studies in the 1930s also showed that black fathers of illegitimate children were more likely to contribute to their support than white fathers of the same class. The black women who headed these families were the true heroines of America. Although when they worked they received considerably less money than white women did, they tended to provide better care for their children than did white women heading families. Consistently white children were more likely to be abused or neglected than blacks in these families. In 1960, for example, only 8.4 percent of all children in institutions for dependent and neglected children in America were black. One study in 1967 showed that while 63 percent of white welfare families neglected or abused their children, only 43 percent of black welfare families did.

While aid to and from friends was important in lower-class family life, the black woman had the chief responsibility for holding the matriarchal family together. Josephine Carson gave a perfect description of the matriarch in her 1969 study of the black woman, *Silent Voices:* "The impression left is of a formidable woman: a worker, a believer; one who is patient, enduring, full of wit. A fortress. A matriarch by default. Someone had to mother that estranged white South and try to bind the sundered black family. Negro society is no more matriarchal, no more addicted to her healing power than the South itself."

LITERARY TREATMENT OF THE BLACK WOMAN'S ROLE

Some sense of the historic role of the black woman in the family emerges from an examination of her treatment in novels. First, there is the view of her as emasculator. She tries to repress the rage in black boys, to prevent them from striking back at whites and risking death. Richard Wright reported that after he fought with a group of white boys:

> I sat brooding on my front steps, nursing my wound and waiting for my mother to come home from work. . . . When night fell, my mother came from the white folks' kitchen. I raced down the street to meet her. I could just feel in my bones that she would understand. I knew she would tell me exactly what to do next time. I grabbed her hand and babbled out the whole story. She examined my wound, then slapped me.
>
> "How come yuh didn't hide?" she asked me. "How come yuh always fightin'?"
>
> I was outraged, and bawled. Between sobs I told her that I didn't have any trees or hedges to hide behind. . . .
>
> She grabbed a barrel stave, dragged me home, stripped me naked, and beat me till I had a fever of one hundred and two. She would smack my rump with the stave, and, while the skin was still smarting, impart to me gems of Jim Crow wisdom. I was never to throw cinders any more. I was never to fight any more wars. I was never, never, under any conditions, to fight *white* folks again. And they were absolutely right in clouting me with the broken milk bottle. Didn't I know she was working hard every day in the hot kitchens of the white folks to make money to take care of me? When was I ever going to learn to be a good boy? She couldn't be bothered with my fights. She finished by telling me that I ought to be thankful to God as long as I lived that they didn't kill me.

John O. Killens described a similar scene in *Youngblood* (1954). Trying to teach her children the caution mandatory for their survival, the black mother often incurred their hostility. Yet, they often understood later that she was only doing what white America forced upon her.

The heroines of early black novels usually stressed respectability and were mulattoes. They struggled against sexual exploitation by black and white men and found their chief security in marriage with dominant husbands. During the black renaissance of the 1920s and 1930s, fictional Afro-American women began to reject white family values. By the 1960s, black novelists were treating black women as symbols of the race's struggle for freedom. Vryy, the strong black woman in Margaret Walker's *Jubilee* (1966), and Jane in Ernest Gaines' *The Autobiography of Miss Jane Pittman* (1971) faithfully portray the quiet persistence, courage, adaptability, and endurance of the black woman. Perhaps the writer Maya Angelou said it best when she observed: "There is a kind of strength that is almost frightening in Black women. It's as if a steel rod runs right through the head down to the feet. And I believe that we have to thank Black women not only for keeping the Black family alive, but [also] the white family. . . . Because Black women have nursed a nation of strangers. For hundreds of years, they literally nursed babies at their breasts who they knew, when they grew up, would rape their daughters and kill their sons."

The most revealing portrait of the black woman as lover, wife, mother, and person appears in poetry. In their love poems black men described the Afro-American woman as a graceful, rhythmic, proud, alluring, and enchanting reflection of the myriad colors of "rainbow-sweet thrill." One of the "goddesses of happiness," the black woman was a honey-mouthed flower, a divine melody inviting man to a love feast where no crumb could be left. The black man grew taller in her presence, as Paul Laurence Dunbar wrote in "Lover's Lane" in 1899:

> White folks wo'k all done up gran'—
> Me an' Mandy han'-in-han'
> Struttin' lak we owned de lan'
> 'Long de lovah's lane.

The black woman was a troubled, defiant fighter. Though oppressed, she could still laugh. William L. Morrison spoke of the complexity of the Afro-American woman's life in his 1943 poem, "Eternal Desire":

> You have known what love can be:
> Some joy, some tears and misery. . . .

"Say Rev., before you asks 'Is there anybody here objects to this
man and this woman bein' wed in holy wedlock, step forth now
or forever hold your peace' . . . well you better look around first
and *dig these well-wishers!*"

MARRIAGE

From Bootsie and Others *by Ollie Harrington. Copyright* © *1958 The
New Pittsburgh Courier Publishing Company. Reprinted by permission of the New Pittsburgh Courier Publishing Company.*

While celebrating her beauty, the poets admitted it was often unsung.
Many of them repeated the 1925 message of Waring Cuney's poem,
"No Image":

> She does not know her beauty.
> She thinks her brown body has no glory.
> If she could dance naked under palm trees
> And see her image in the river
> She would know.
> But there are no palm trees on the street,
> And dish water gives back no images.

Langston Hughes' 1925 *Opportunity* offering, "Troubled Women,"
showed the black woman confronting life:

> She stands
> In the quiet darkness,
> This troubled woman,
> Bowed by
> Weariness and pain,
> Like an
> Autumn flower
> In the frozen rain,
> Like a
> Wind-blown autumn flower
> That never lifts its head
> Again.

Lewis Alexander presented similar views in his 1929 *Opportunity*
poem, "Negro Woman":

> The stars twinkle to-night
> Like the glaze in a Negro woman's eyes
> Drinking the tears set flowing by an aging hurt
> Gnawing at her heart.
>
> The earth trembles to-night
> Like the quiver of a Negro woman's eyelids cupping tears.

The black woman lived with and conquered pain. Through her
tears she gave the love that sustained the black man. Jon Eckels, in
Our Business in the Streets (1971), summarized a century of black poetry
when he dedicated "You Are Not, to Me, a 'Queen'" to beautiful
black women:

> Radiant with reality,
> You walk this vile
> deathland
> hating-loving; waiting
> suffering, working, wishing
> for the real
> beyond the screams
> or need of garish
> crowns . . .
> surrounded by death
> you are life's living
> witness,

the essential rhythm
of my interrupted
soul love song—
symmetrical
spirit force
woman,
here is my hand,
we are all
we need

The poets were alternately reverent and humorous when they looked at wives. On the one hand, the black man's chief glory was the wife whose sorrows and joys he shared, and to whom he was ever faithful; on the other, she was the one from whom he tried to hide his peccadillos. In "Kinfolks," Paul Laurence Dunbar portrays an unfaithful husband and a wife who gets revenge. After Melindy twice announces her intention to marry, only to be told by her father that her fiancés were her half brothers,

Melindy, she forgot her oath,
And blurted out to mother,
"Pop say I cain't marry Rufus Brown,
"For he be my half brother.

"An' den I tuhns to Sonny Smif,
"Although it seem like treason;
"Pop, he say I can't marry him
"On account ob de same reason."

Ma said, "Now honey chile, don't you cry.
"Put on yo' weddin' cap
"An' marry either one you likes,
" 'Cause you ain't no kin to Pap!"

"Tribute" in James F. Ragland's *Lyrics and Laughter* (1939) united the reverent and humorous strands:

A fellow owes a lot, to the girl he calls his wife,
Whether he makes good or not, she will follow him through
    life.
She helps to bear his sorrow, share his troubles big and small,

To her there's no tomorrow, if she does not hear his call.
She makes him think he's boss
When it's she who holds the reins,
She pets him when he's cross
To get bawled out for her pains.
She will lift his waning powers, make his battles thrice as strong,
By his side she toils by hours, if the way grows tough and
   long.
When the whole world seems to shun him, and he's weakened
   and forlorn,
She will gird her strength upon him, and will make him carry
   on.

In poetry the black woman was Everyman's mother and more. Added to those traits universally ascribed to mothers, the black woman armed her child against racial hatred and the misery of segregation and discrimination. Her wise counsel prepared her children to struggle against all the forces designed to crush them. She was, as Langston Hughes wrote in *The Weary Blues* (1926), the personification of courage, endurance, and the indomitability of the human spirit. Hughes' "Mother to Son" captured these qualities:

> Well, son, I'll tell you:
> Life for me ain't been no crystal stair.
> It's had tacks in it,
> And splinters.
> And boards torn up,
> And places with no carpets on the floor—
> Bare.
> But all the time
> I's been climbin' on,
> And reachin' landin's,
> And turnin' corners,
> And sometimes goin' in the dark
> Where there ain't been no light.
> So, boy, don't you turn back.
> Don't you set down on the steps
> 'Cause you finds it's kinder hard.
> Don't you fall now—
> For I's still goin', honey,
> I's still climbin',
> And life for me ain't been no crystal stair.

THE IMPORTANCE OF THE DEVELOPMENT OF AN INDEPENDENT
BLACK CHURCH

Much of the strength of the black woman and the Afro-American family can be attributed to their roots in the black church. From slavery to emancipation, embattled blacks found comfort in the biblical injunction to "refrain thy voice from weeping, and thine eyes from tears: for thy work shall be rewarded . . . and they shall come again from the land of the enemy" (Jeremiah 31.16). What distinguished the black church from its white counterpart was its adherence to a nationalistic theology of liberation, reform, and uplift. The black church came to fulfill the prophecy of Isaiah: "The spirit of the Lord is upon me, because he hath anointed me to preach the gospel to the poor; he hath sent me to heal the broken-hearted, to preach deliverance to the captives, and recovering of sight to the blind, to set at liberty them that are bruised." However, before blacks could preach deliverance to the captives, they had to establish independent churches.

The first independent black church had its beginning in 1787 when Philadelphia blacks, led by Richard Allen and Absalom Jones, formed a benevolent organization, the Free African Society. After the St. George Methodist Church inaugurated a policy of separating black members in November 1787, the blacks withdrew and conducted religious services as a part of the activities of the Free African Society. In 1794 Philadelphia blacks opened the Bethel African Methodist Episcopal Church and the St. Thomas Protestant Episcopal Church. Throughout the North, free blacks rejected segregated seating arrangements and formed many all-black congregations between 1790 and the 1830s. By and large the blacks retained the liturgy of the white denominations and sought to affiliate their churches with the white ones, but in those churches that gave blacks no voice in the state and national associations, blacks began to establish separate and independent denominations. Led by Richard Allen, Daniel Coker, and Stephen Hall, black Methodists met in Philadelphia in 1816 and founded the African Methodist Episcopal Church as an independent national association. The first African Methodist Episcopal Zion Church was built in New York City in 1800; in 1821 several churches organized as an independent denomination. The year 1809 saw the building of the First African Baptist Church in Philadelphia, the African Baptist Church of Boston, and the Abyssinian Baptist Church in New York City. By 1840 there were more than 300 separate northern black churches, including 6 Episcopal, 3 Presbyterian, 1 Congregational, and 1 Lutheran.

In their calls for moral improvement, Christian virtues, education, temperance, charity, and benevolence, nineteenth-century black churches differed little from white ones. Nor did they differ significantly in the belief that Christianity offered hope for the downtrodden and the afflicted. Like the white churches, black denominations supported home and foreign missions in an effort to spread the Gospel. However, blacks did place greater stress on christianizing Africa and the West Indies than did whites. The black clergy felt that Afro-Americans had a special duty to regenerate the land of their fathers. The African Methodist Episcopal (AME) Church established a mission in Haiti in 1827, for instance, to "aid in making the Haytian nationality and government strong, powerful and commanding among the civilized nations of the earth."

THE BLACK CHURCH IN THE ANTISLAVERY MOVEMENT

The antebellum black church was in the forefront of the religious campaign against slavery and discrimination. The black clergy contended that slavery was a sin and chided proslavery white churches. In 1838 the Rev. Samuel Cornish argued that until the white church spoke out "against oppression and slavery, and against persecution and caste, the church in America will barely live in name, a corrupt and corrupting, putrifying body—an offence in the eye of God, and a curse to the nations of the earth." The 1856 conference of the AME Church resolved to do all in its power to aid the bondsman, because slavery was "a sin of the first degree, and the greatest known catalogue of crimes—the highest violation of God's law—a shameful abuse of God's creatures, and shocking to enlightened humanity." To those ministers who tried to find biblical sanctions for slavery, the black clergy quoted the verse, "All things whatsoever ye would that men should do to you, do ye even so to them; for this is the law and the prophets."

The clergy contended that discrimination against one made in the image of God was a sin inviting divine retribution. Since "God has made of one blood all the nations that dwell on the face of the earth," equality was universal. The black clergy condemned American Christians because, as Reverend Cornish declared in 1839, "they seem to forget that the colored man is made in the same image of God and of the same blood. They seem to forget that God has commanded them to treat him as a brother beloved. They seem to forget that he has a soul like their own, capable of the same cultivation, and endowed with the same tender sensibilities. They seem wholly insensible or wholly regardless of offending Christ in their neglect and abuse of his proscribed and ignored brethren."

Though criticized by such antebellum spokesmen as Frederick Douglass, black ministers played prominent roles in the abolition movement and used their churches to hide fugitive slaves. The black clergy also dominated the early black conventions, the first of which was organized by Richard Allen in 1830, and were often the most revolutionary delegates. The Rev. Henry Highland Garnet, for instance, tried unsuccessfully in the 1843 Buffalo convention to convince the delegates to adopt an address calling upon slaves to rebel. Garnet urged the slaves to confront their masters:

> Tell them in language which they cannot misunderstand of the exceeding sinfulness of slavery, and of a future judgment, and of the righteous retributions of an indignant God. Inform them that all you desire is FREEDOM, and that nothing else will suffice. Do this, and forever after cease to toil for the heartless tyrants, who give you no other reward but stripes and abuse. If they then commence the work of death, they, and not you, will be responsible for the consequences. You had far better all die—*die immediately,* than live slaves, and entail your wretchedness upon your posterity. If you would be free in this generation, here is your only hope. However much you and all of us may desire it, there is not much hope of redemption without the shedding of blood. If you must bleed, let it all come at once—rather *die freemen than live to be the slaves.* It is impossible, like the children of Israel, to make a grand exodus from the land of bondage. The Pharaohs are on both sides of the blood-red waters.

For much of its history, the church militant was a distinctly northern phenomenon. The black church in the South was watched so closely by whites that its leaders made few *public* calls for resistance. Like the early Christian church, the black church in the South was oppressed. When, for instance, Andrew Byran established the First African Baptist Church in Savannah, Georgia, in 1788, he was arrested and flogged several times. Only after his master intervened was Byran allowed to continue his services. In Georgia and throughout the South, when blacks were allowed to form separate churches, they were under the control of whites. Still, blacks began forming churches at an early date. In 1776 at Petersburg, Virginia, blacks formed the Harrison Street Baptist Church, and in 1785 a Baptist church in Williamsburg, Virginia. The expansion of independent black churches was limited after 1800 because slaveholders suspected that they fostered insurrection. Until the Civil War, most southern blacks worshipped in churches with their masters. Secret meetings were held on the plantations, while separate churches were generally found only in southern cities.

THE POST-EMANCIPATION EXPANSION OF BLACK CHURCHES

After the Civil War separate black churches proliferated as Afro-Americans sought to exercise autonomy over their religious lives. Soon, sepa-

"IT WASN'T ANYTHING LIKE THE BOOK"

BIBLICAL CRITICISM

From God is Groovy *by Morrie Turner. Copyright © 1972, New American Library, Inc., 1981, Field Newspaper Synd. Reprinted by permission of Morrie Turner.*

rate denominations appeared as southern and northern churches united. In 1867 Baptists organized the Consolidated American Baptist Convention, which was absorbed by the National Baptist Convention in 1880. The representatives of 3 million members met in Atlanta, Georgia, in 1895 and formed the National Baptist Convention of the United States. Southern Methodists formed a new denomination in 1870, the Colored Methodist Episcopal Church. As new denominations were formed, the older ones spread into the South. Most of the congregations, especially rural ones, were small and could rarely pay adequate ministerial salaries. Consequently, black ministers not only held full-time nonministerial jobs but usually served two or more churches.

According to their autobiographies, postbellum southern ministers often faced discrimination and violence. In the Rev. Levi Coppin's neighborhood in the 1860s, for example, a white mob broke up a religious service when a white minister delivered a sermon to the black congregation. The Ku Klux Klan killed a member of the Rev. A. H. Newton's congregation in Pulaski, Tennessee, in the 1870s. "These were," Newton declared, "dreadful times." M. F. Jamison recalled that in Alabama during the same period, "there was scarcely any safety for anyone." Many of the ministers recounted tales of the white terror during the presidential campaign of 1876. When William H. Heard led a successful campaign for the legislature in Abbeyville, South Carolina, in 1876, the local Democrats kidnapped him, took him to Georgia, beat him unmercifully, and left him for dead. Newton asserted that the outrages perpetrated by whites on blacks in 1876 were "not easily forgotten." When Coppin looked back on a lifetime of abuse from whites, he asserted in 1919 that prejudice was a leech sucking the life-blood of all Americans, black and white alike: "Prejudice is an awful thing. It is more far reaching in its effects than we are wont to give it credit of being. The man who indulges in the feeling, is fostering a bitterness of soul that is like a hissing serpent in the bosom. The one who is victim of it, may have a feeling of vindictiveness that keeps him so constantly on the alert that often innocent persons are accused. Color prejudice, of all kinds, seems the most shallow and unreasonable."

MINISTERS IN THE POSTBELLUM STRUGGLE FOR BLACK RIGHTS

Black ministers in both North and South frequently expressed pride in their race. The Rev. M. L. Latta of North Carolina asserted in 1903, "We, as a race ought to be proud of our color." Robert Anderson agreed, declaring, "I belong to the black race and am not ashamed of it." Such men reveled in blackness. They appealed to Afro-Americans to be proud of their God-given beauty. In his speeches the Rev. Thomas Fuller of North Carolina often lectured on this theme in the 1890s: "I express the hope that for all time to come and until the volume of human history shall be sealed and delivered to the Omnipotent Judge, there shall always be among the people of the earth a race known as the Negro race. I hope and pray that the Anti-Kink and Anti-Black which wily schemers of the country are dumping upon the market, will fail to destroy the identity of the race or make us ashamed that we are Negroes. . . . I rejoice tonight that I am a Negro." Early in the twentieth century, an exuberant black minister in Savannah, Georgia, expressed a similar view when he told his congregation that if he caught his wife "bleaching her black skin or straightening her kinky hair I would sue her for divorce and my allegation would be immorality."

Many ministers refused to be "Jim Crowed." In the 1880s Daniel A. Payne got off a Florida train and walked to the church conference he was going to attend in Jacksonville rather than move to the Jim Crow car. The convention protested to railroad officials, and blacks in Jacksonville held an indignation meeting.

Most of the ministers rejected a one-dimensional approach to race problems in the United States. Since they supported several different avenues to racial uplift, they rarely attacked the proponents of any single approach. The Rev. Henry Proctor of Atlanta provides one of the best examples of a man who advocated a multifaceted attack on discrimination. Often harking back to the cordial relations he enjoyed with whites, he believed in the possibility of racial cooperation. In spite of southern oppression of blacks, he urged Afro-Americans to stay in the South, save their money, educate themselves, promote racial cooperation, appeal to the deeply religious nature of southern whites, denounce discrimination, and agitate for equal treatment. Having met Booker T. Washington when he delivered his famous address in Atlanta, Proctor admired him greatly. He was also an intimate friend of W. E. B. Du Bois and saw no conflict between the ideologies of the two men. In fact, Washington and Du Bois often conferred at his home. There was a place, Proctor argued in 1925, for all shades of opinion in the Afro-American's campaign for equality: "Just as a bird must have both wings for successful flight, so must any movement have the radical and conservative wings."

Appealing to the American sense of fair play by emphasizing the Afro-American's role in building the country's civilization, ministers demanded that black rights be protected. They called upon Americans to live up to their creed, to abide by their laws, and to enforce the law impartially. Alexander Walters insisted in 1917 that fair administration of the law would end racial strife: "What some of the white people of this country need is for those in authority to give them to understand that they are going to accord to every man his rights, whether he be white or black. Let those who administer the laws impress upon the people that they must obey the laws, and all this trouble which we are having because of race prejudice, etc., will soon pass away." Thomas Fuller said essentially the same thing. The Afro-American, he contended in 1910, wanted a fair chance, freedom from fear, and the equal application of the laws:

We ask nothing extraordinary, but simply to enjoy "life, liberty and the pursuit of happiness." Life needs to be free from mob violence; political rights should be guarded by the law as laid down in the statute books, founded upon the Constitution; and we should be given a free field to earn a legitimate support for our families, unmolested by white

cappers and hoodlums. We do not object to stringent laws. All we ask
is that the power that makes them acknowledge their majesty and obey
them as well as execute them upon the weak and defenceless.

America, the ministers prophesied, would never be at rest until
it gave the black man his full manhood rights. Speaking in 1895, Proctor
asserted that southern whites should either reconsider segregation ordi-
nances or "better beware or they would find firebrands under their
houses and poison in their coffee." More often, the black minister saw
divine retribution for America's treatment of blacks. In a characteristic
exposition, the Rev. Francis J. Grimke of Washington, D.C., asserted
in 1902: "God is not dead,—nor is He an indifferent onlooker at what
is going on in this world. One day He will make requisition for blood;
He will call the oppressors to account. Justice may sleep, but it never
dies. The individual, race, or nation which does wrong, which sets at
defiance God's great law, especially God's great law of love, of brotherhood, will be sure, sooner or later, to pay the penalty. We reap as
we sow. With what measure we mete, it shall be measured to us again."

Explicitly rejecting the advice that Afro-Americans eschew politics
and agitation, Alexander Walters urged blacks in 1898 to "organize
for self-protection." Calling upon blacks to enter industry and to obtain
all forms of education, Walters argued that it was the duty of the
federal government to educate ignorant blacks. The chief responsibility
for ending specific forms of oppression, however, rested squarely upon
blacks. He insisted that blacks had to organize "to resist the tyrannical
uses of railroads, steamboats and other corporations, and the violent
and insulting conduct of their employees." Walters was emphatic in
his belief that blacks should never withdraw from politics:

> Because of the antagonism of the Southern whites toward the Negro
> it has been suggested by some of our leaders as well as some of the
> whites, that the Negroes in that section withdraw from politics alto-
> gether. In my opinion this would be a very unwise step. The Negro is
> a citizen and interested in the welfare of his country; therefore it is
> his duty to vote. . . .
> It is unreasonable and unchristian to debar the Negro from holding
> office on account of his color; therefore it would be unwise to yield to
> the prejudice of our enemies by giving up all offices to white men. . . .

RELIGIOUS SERVICES AND SERMONS

With its members enslaved, powerless, poverty-stricken, and oppressed, the southern black church concentrated on buttressing the
spirit with an emotional and often otherworldly religion. Since emanci-

pation did little more than change the shape of that oppression, rural black churches continued many antebellum practices. Growing out of the black's longing for spiritual salvation and escape from his earthly hell, and from the African tradition of the shout, the lower-class black church put a premium on emotionalism. Nineteenth-century blacks had a strong belief in the presence and power of God in everyday life and emphasized revelation, visions, dreams, and inward expressions of the divine presence. Their services, a mixture of grief and gladness about their weary life on earth, provided an emotional release for them. The sermons and songs about their oppression and the passionate prayers for divine aid gave their services a reality, a vividness, and an emotionalism which created a sense of shared suffering and hope, causing the congregations to shout, cry, and raise "a joyful noise to God." David Macrae, an Englishman who traveled through the South in 1867 and 1868, asserted that he was struck by the black man's "devoutness and recognition of God's hand in everything." Most observers were impressed by the emotional services in black churches. Macrae wrote:

> All of their religious exercises partake of this exciting character; and in some of their churches a service seems to be regarded as a kind of failure unless the audience gets itself worked up to a frenzy. I remember, at an evening service in Savannah, where a dimly-lighted church swarmed with a black audience of nearly a thousand people, a little excitable-looking negro, who turned out to be a revival preacher . . . [addressed] frantic appeals to the people, under which they began to sway, and cry, and groan in the most extraordinary manner. Presently a shriek was heard, and a young woman sprang into the air near one corner of the church, and fell back amongst her friends, writhing and shrieking as if in a fit . . . . the preacher . . . [held] on to his appeal, which was a constant repetition of the same words, uttered with interjected gasps at the top of his voice, the audience swaying and groaning, the three convicted sinners struggling and shrieking, while their friends, crying "Glory to God! Glory to God!," were trying to hold them down.

An important facet of black religious life was the folk sermon. James Weldon Johnson committed many of these sermons to verse in the early part of the twentieth century. One of the most famous is based on Ezekiel's story of the resurrection of the bones (Ezekiel 37). In 1970, a folklorist found that many of these sermons were still being delivered in storefront churches in the cities. Recited without the aid of notes, parts of the sermon are chanted or sung. The sermon is often punctuated by responses from the congregation, and certain phrases are frequently repeated.

Clearly the most famous folk sermon was John Jasper's "The Sun Do Move." Thousands of people, black and white, gathered at Jasper's church in Richmond, Virginia, whenever he delivered the sermon in the 1870s. After discussing his experience as a slave, Jasper told his congregation:

> I goin' to take you all dis afternoon on an excursion to a great battle-field. Most folks like to see fights—some is mighty fond of gittin' into fights and some is mighty quick to run down de back alley when dere is a battle goin' on for de right. Dis time I'll 'scort you to a scene where you shall witness a curious battle. It took place soon after Israel got de Promise Land. You 'member de people of Gideon make friends with God's people when dey first entered Canaan and dey was monstrous smart to do it. But, just de same, it got 'em in to an awful fuss. De cities 'round'bout dere flared up at dat and dey all joined dere forces and say dey gwine to mop de Hebrew people off the ground, and dey bunched all dere armies together and went up for to do it. When dey come up so bold and brave, de Gideonites was scared outen dere senses and dey sent word to Joshua dat dey was in trouble and he must run up dere and git 'em out. Joshua had de heart of a lion and he was up dere directly. Dey has an awful fight, sharp and bitter, but you might know dat General Joshua was not dere to get whipped. He prayed and he fought and de hours got away too fast for him, and so he asked de Lord to issue a special order dat de sun hold up awhile and dat de moon furnish plenty of moonshine down on de lowest part of the fightin' grounds. As a fact, Joshua was so drunk with de battle, so thirsty for de blood of de enemies of de Lord, and so wild with de victory dat he tell de sun to stand still till he could finish his job.
>
> What did de sun do? Did he glare down in fiery wrath and say, "What you talkin' 'bout my stoppin' for, Joshua? I ain't never started yet. Been here all de time and it would smash up everything if I was to start." No, he ain't say dat. But what de Bible say? Dat's what I ask to know. It say dat it was at de voice of Joshua dat it stopped. I don't say it stopped; 'tain't for Jasper to say dat, but de Bible, *de Book of God*, say so. But I say dis: nothin' can stop until it has first started. So I knows what I'm talkin' 'bout.

Having proven that "the sun do move," Reverend Jasper proceeded to turn more of nineteenth-century science on its head. Like many southern black clergy, Reverend Jasper was a fundamentalist. He rejected the Darwinian theory of evolution and the view of astronomers that the earth was round. Scientific theories carried little weight when confronted with biblical revelations. Pursuing the scientists, Reverend Jasper asserted:

But I ain't done with you yet. As de song says, dere's more to follow. I invite you to hear de first verse in de seventh chapter of de Book of Revelations. What do John under de powers of de Spirit say? He says he saw four angels standin' on de four corners of de earth, holdin' de four winds of de earth and so forth. 'Low me to ask, if de earth is round, where do it keep its corners? A flat square thing has corners, but tell me, where is de corner of an apple or a marble or a cannon ball or a silver dollar? If dere is anyone of dem philosophers what's been takin' so many cracks at my old head 'bout here, he is cordially invited to step forward and square up dis vexin' business. I hear tell dat you can't square a circle but it looks like dese great scholars done learned how to circle a square. If dey can do it, let 'em step to de front and do de trick. But, my brothren, in my poor judgment, dey can't do it; 'tain't in 'em to do it. Dey is on de wrong side of the Bible— dat's on de out-side of de Bible, and dere's where de trouble comes in with 'em. Dey done got out of de breastworks of de truth and as long as dey stay dere de light of de Lord will not shine on dere path.

When southern blacks began migrating in large numbers to northern cities during the First World War, they tried to retain their links to their folk religion. Uncomfortable with the relatively staid services of the established black churches, the migrants turned to Holiness and Pentecostal sects. Small congregations, located in abandoned stores, these storefront churches brought comfort to blacks disappointed in their search for the promised land. The migrants had come to the North in search of economic opportunity and racial equality. After a few years' residence there, most were repeating the lament of Jeremiah: "The harvest is past, the summer is ended, and we are not saved." Searching for salvation, the migrants eagerly followed Daddy Grace and Father Divine (who claimed he was God). The House of Prayer for All People, the Church of God in Christ, the Apostolic Overcoming Holy Church of God, the Christian's Church of the Living God, and dozens of smaller sects had attracted more than 4 million members by 1970. How can one account for the strength of the more emotional sects in the black community? The Rev. Will Jackson of Sedalia, Missouri, gave the most convincing answer in 1902. Arguing that religious emotionalism had enabled blacks to keep "alive the principles and aspirations of true manhood," Reverend Jackson contended, "Had it not been for this irrepressible and ever-assertive element of his character, the Negro would have degenerated into the depths of a hopeless and irretrievable infidelity. It has kept him in touch with his God, and that means also in touch with the possibilities of his moral, religious and intellectual resurrections."

BLACK CRITICISM OF THE BLACK CHURCHES

As the central institution in the black community, the church was often a target of criticism leveled by black humorists, novelists, intellectuals, and nationalists. A typical story ran thus: visiting the farm of one of his members, a black minister asserted, "You and the Lord have certainly done a fine job out here." After hearing this remark several times, the farmer responded: "Yes, Parson, what you say is true. But I wish you could have seen this here farm about five years ago, when the Lord had it all by Himself." Many jokes scored the worldly living of ministers and questioned the depth of their faith. One of the most popular jokes recounts the story of a minister and his son who encounter a bear while walking through the woods. The son asks his father to pray. But the minister starts running as he says, "Son, prayers is all right in prayer meetin' but they ain't no good in bear meetin'." Folk singers often castigated ministers. The blues singer Frank Stokes gave a characteristic portrait when he sang:

> Well some folks say 'bout a preacher wouldn't steal
> I caught about eleven in the watermelon field
> I dont like 'em
> They'll rob you
> Steal your daughter
> Take your wife from you
>   Yeah
> Eat your chicken
> Take your money
>   Yeah.

In the twentieth century, ministers and Christianity were anathema to the leaders of black nationalist churches. For them, Christianity had been used by whites to deflect black protest. In a typical harangue, the Black Muslim minister Malcolm X asserted:

My brothers and sisters, our white slavemasters' Christian religion has taught us black people here in the wilderness of North America that we will sprout wings when we die and fly up into the sky where God will have for us a special place called heaven. This is white man's Christian religion used to *brainwash* us black people! We have *accepted* it! We have *believed* it! We have *practiced* it! And while we are doing all of that, for himself, this blue-eyed devil has *twisted* his Christianity, to keep his foot on our backs . . . to keep our eyes fixed on the pie in the sky and heaven in the hereafter . . . while *he* enjoys *his* heaven right *here* . . . on *this* earth . . . in *this* life.

Novelists were among the most consistent critics of the church. Often the characters in black novels are portrayed trying to escape the constricting tentacles of religion. A character in James Baldwin's *Go Tell It on the Mountain* (1953), for instance, says of her friends: "Not one of them ever went to Church—one might scarcely have imagined that they knew that churches existed—they all hourly, daily, in their speech, in their lives, and in their hearts, cursed God. They all seemed to be saying, as Richard, when she once timidly mentioned the love of Jesus, said: 'You can tell that puking bastard to kiss my big black ass.' "

Until the 1960s scholars regularly lamented the emotionalism of the black church, the illiteracy of its ministers (in 1960 only 33 percent of the black clergy had college degrees), and claimed that the church was primarily otherworldly in its concern. Since, by its very nature, the church is a conservative institution overwhelmingly concerned with the hereafter, scholars highlighting these traits in the black church tortured the truth. Ignoring similar features of white evangelical churches, grossly overestimating the potential power of the black church, and forgetting the nature of religion, critics were frequently misled. The famous lawyer Clarence Darrow repeated a familiar refrain in the 1930s in his critique of black churches: "Prayers won't do you any good. Your race has accomplished a great deal by the methods of education and organization, but nothing by prayer, reliance on preachers, and naive trust in the Deity. If there is a Lord Who governs everything, be sure He knows all about your troubles before you ever tell them to him. And He has done nothing about them."

Acquainted with more of their history than such critics as Darrow, the mass of Afro-Americans knew that the black church did no more or less than its members demanded. It did no more or less than it could. It must never be forgotten that the black church represented a relatively powerless people. Its vaunted wealth was relative. In a poverty-stricken community the black church seemed fabulously wealthy. But compared to other institutions in capitalistic America, the black church's holdings were minuscule. Given the paucity of their resources, the secular programs of black churches were extremely impressive: orphanages, day-care centers, employment bureaus, literary societies, schools, burial societies, insurance companies, and colleges.

LITERARY PRAISE FOR THE BLACK CHURCH

Black poets, less critical of black religion than novelists, captured more of the essential spirit of the church than most scholars could. While occasionally complaining about the excessive humility of black Christians, the poets used the rhythm and message of sermons, prayers, and services in celebration of God's love and promise of deliverance. James Edwin Campbell's "When Ol' Sis Judy pray" is an example:

> When Ol' Sis Judy pray,
> De whole house, hit des rock an' moan
> Ter see huh tears an' hyah huh groan;
> Dar's somepin' in Sis' Judy's tone
> Dat melt all ha'ts, dough med ur stone
> When Ol' Sis' Judy pray.

The black minister, portrayed sympathetically, was also a favorite subject of black poets. Like James Weldon Johnson, many of the poets reproduced the cadences and messages of the folk sermon. They portrayed the minister's beautiful word pictures. Among the best of them was Paul Laurence Dunbar's 1896 poem "An Antebellum Sermon," which demonstrates the black preacher's attempt to correlate biblical messages with his flock's hopes of earthly rewards:

> We is gathahed hyeah, my brothahs,
>   In dis howlin' wildaness,
> Fu' to speak some words of comfo't
>   To each othah in distress. . . .
>
> Now ole Pher'oh, down in Egypt,
>   Was de wuss man evah bo'n,
> An' he had de Hebrew chillun
>   Down dah wukin' in his co'n;
> 'T well de Lawd got tiahed o' his foolin',
>   An' sez he: "I'll let him know—
> Look hyeah, Moses, go tell Pher'oh
>   Fu' to let dem chillun go. . . ."
>
> But fu' feah some one mistakes me,
>   I will pause right hyeah to say,
> Dat I'm still a-preachin' ancient,
>   I ain't talkin' 'bout to-day.
> But I tell you, fellah christuns,
>   Things'll happen mighty strange;
> Now, de Lawd done dis fu' Isrul,
>   An' his ways don't nevah change,
> An' de love he showed to Isrul
>   Wasn't all on Isrul spent;
> Now don't run an tell yo' mastahs
>   Dat I's preachin' discontent.

'Cause I isn't; I'se a-judgin'
  Bible people by deir ac's;
I'se a-givin' you de Scriptuah,
  I'se a-handin' you de fac's.
Cose ole Pher'oh b'lieved in slav'ry,
  But de Lawd he let him see,
Dat de people he put bref in,—
  Evah mothah's son was free. . . .

But when Moses wifh his powah
  Comes an' sets us chillun free,
We will praise de gracious Mastah
  Dat has gin us liberty;
An' we'll shout ouah halleluyahs,
—On dat mighty reck'nin' day,
When we'se reco'nized ez citiz'—
  Huh uh! Chillun, let us pray!

The poets recognized that the black church clearly fulfilled many of the needs of Afro-Americans. Historically, it was the blacks' major primary association, and they customarily joined the church at a higher rate than did whites. Between 1951 and 1973 there were more than 2.5 million Methodists and an equal number of members of the National Baptist Convention. Blacks clung steadfastly to the church partially because it combined many secular and sacred concerns.

SECULAR CONCERNS OF THE BLACK CHURCH

One of the most outstanding features of the black church is that historically it has been multifaceted in its functions. W. E. B. Du Bois, in his classic study *The Philadelphia Negro* (1899), recognized the many secular concerns of the church when he wrote, "all movements for social betterment are apt to centre in the churches. Beneficial societies in endless number are formed here; secret societies keep in touch; co-operative and building associations have lately sprung up; the minister often acts as an employment agent; considerable charitable and relief work is done and special meetings held to aid special projects. The race problem in all its phases is continually being discussed, and, indeed, from this forum many a youth goes forth inspired to work." No other American institution did so much with so little as the black church.

The black clergy in the 1950s pushed the largest mass-based assault on racial oppression in the nation's history. Spurred on by the Rev.

PRAYER

From God is Groovy *by Morrie Turner. Copyright © 1972, New American Library, Inc., 1981 Field Newspaper Synd. Reprinted by permission of Morrie Turner.*

Martin Luther King, Jr., black ministers led boycotts and nonviolent disobedience campaigns throughout the country from 1955 until the 1970s. Reporting on this campaign in 1963, William Brink and Louis Harris asserted, "Long dependent on the word of God because he had nothing else, the Negro is today utterly convinced that his cause is just because it is just before God, and that he must ultimately win because that is God's word and will. In a literal sense, his revolution is thus a holy war."

The seeds of a twentieth-century civil rights revolution led by the clergy had been planted earlier in two features of the black church: its nationalistic and political orientation. In antislavery societies, national conventions of blacks, and church associations the black clergy received its training in politics. Because they were among the most highly educated group in the black community, ministers frequently served as both religious and political leaders. When the Civil War ended slavery, the blacks moved to establish independent denominations in the South and then used them as springboards to political power. Henry McNeal Turner of Georgia, R. H. Cain of South Carolina, and Mansfield Tyler of Alabama took this route to legislative seats during Reconstruction. The disproportionate representation of the clergy among political leaders can be seen by looking at South Carolina. Of the 190 blacks who served in the South Carolina legislature between 1868 and 1876, at least 43 were ministers.

The historian Philip A. Bruce aptly characterized the nineteenth-century preacher-politician when he wrote:

> The preachers of the negroes are their most active politicans, as a rule, but even when they are not they have much political influence, for they constitute, individually, the natural leaders of their race. . . . The two parts of minister and orator are played so skilfully at one and the same time that it is impossible to distinguish them; and the affairs of the Hereafter and a contemporary political canvass are mixed in inextricable confusion. His church is thus converted into a political organization that is consolidated by the religious fervour that pervades it, and propelled towards a single political end by a religious enthusiasm that expects to be rewarded spiritually for the performance of partisan duties. The preacher playing alternately upon both at once, excites an emotional responsiveness that is prepared to obey his slightest injunctions; and he does not hesitate to turn this exalted state of feeling to the most useful account.

The pattern continued well into the twentieth century. In 1944 the Rev. Adam Clayton Powell, Jr., of New York City's Abyssinian Baptist Church was elected to Congress, as was the Rev. Andrew Young of Atlanta, Georgia, in 1972. In 1972 the Walter Fauntroy was elected to fill the post of nonvoting delegate for the District of Columbia, and in 1978 the Rev. William H. Gray was elected to the seat long held by Congressman Robert Nix of Philadelphia.

BLACK NATIONALIST CLERGY

Many of the major nineteenth-century black nationalists were ministers: James T. Holly, Henry McNeal Turner, Alexander Crummell,

Edward Wilmot Blyden, and Henry Highland Garnet. Turner was the father of black religious nationalism. A leader in the spread of AME missions to Africa, he began in the 1890s to espouse the belief that God was black. Lambasted by white theologians for his views, he responded in 1898:

> We have as much right biblically and otherwise to believe that God is a Negro, as you buckra or white people have to believe that God is a fine looking, symmetrical and ornamented white man. For the bulk of you and all the fool Negroes of the country believe that God is a white-skinned, blue-eyed, straight-haired, projecting nosed, compressed lipped and finely robed *white* gentleman, sitting upon a throne somewhere in the heavens. Every race of people since time began who have attempted to describe their God by words, or by paintings, or by carvings, or by any other form or figure, have conveyed the idea that the God who made them and shaped their destinies was symbolized in themselves, and why should not the Negro believe that he resembles God as much so as other people? . . . This is one of the reasons we favor African emigration, or Negro naturalization, wherever we can find a domain, for, as long as we remain among the whites the Negro will believe that the devil is black and that he (the Negro) favors the devil, and that God is white and that he (the Negro) bears no resemblance to him, and the effect of such a sentiment is contemptuous and degrading, and one-half of the Negro race will be trying to get white and the other half will spend their days in trying to be white men's scullions in order to please the whites.

Black Pentecostal churches echoed Turner's sentiments. For example, the Church of the Living God, founded by Arkansan William Christian in 1889, depicted Christianity as a black religion. The catechism of the church clearly revealed this belief:

Was Jesus a member of the black race?
Yes. Matthew 1.

How do you know?
Because He was in the line of Abraham and David the King. . . .

Should we make a difference in people because they are black?
No. Jer. 13:23.

Why?
Because it is as natural to be black as the leopard to be spotted.
     Jer. 13:23

The widespread migration of blacks to northern urban centers after 1910 spawned a number of black religious nationalists. Increasingly,

Afro-Americans adopted the view Claude McKay expressed in "Outcast" in 1922:

> But the great western world holds me in fee
> And I may never hope for full release
> While to its alien Gods, I bend my knee.

Sometime before World War I, F. S. Cherry founded the Church of God or Black Jews sect. Claiming to be a prophet, taking as his sacred text the Talmud, Cherry preached that blacks were the original Jews, the first inhabitants of the earth, and that God and Jesus were black. Believing that God intended men to drink intoxicating drinks, the Black Jews sang, testified, and used drums, castanets, rattles, and guitars during their services. The scholar Arthur Huff Fauset described a sermon by Cherry in the 1930s:

> He castigates preachers, calls them "dumb dogs," asserts that one policeman is worth twenty-five preachers because a policeman will give up his life to save you or your property, but preachers want to keep everything good from you, your money, your women, your wine. . . . He bewails the fact that the Gentiles (whites) have taken from the black folk their land, their money, their names, and cursed them with the title "Negro." . . . He will prove that black folk are not Negroes, coons, niggers, or shines, and he calls out to "all 'niggers' to get the hell out of the place!" He traces the genealogy of black folk, going back to Noah, Shem, Japheth, Ham, Lot, Abraham, Isaac and Jacob. He rails at the Gentiles who "have not left you a spoonful of dirt for yourselves, have taken your name, your religion and your government." Yet he preaches love for all mankind, asserting that he could not be a child of God if he did not love everybody. He makes fun of a picture of Jesus, embarrassing a Baptist preacher who is seated on the rostrum by making him get the picture from behind his chair and holding it up to the congregation while he calls out, "I'll give anybody one thousand dollars tomorrow night who can tell me who the hell that is!" Thus he goes on for an hour or more. . . .

Another nationalistic church organized during this period was the Moorish Science Temple of America. Established in 1913 by North Carolinian Timothy Drew, the first temple of the church appeared in Newark, New Jersey. It soon spread to many northern and southern cities. Proclaiming himself the prophet of Allah, Drew taught that blacks could find salvation only when they realized they were Asiatics or Moorish Americans. Fauset briefly summarized their beliefs:

> The charter of the Moorish Science Temple came from the great capital empire of Egypt. Before you can have a God, you must have a

nationality. Noble Drew Ali gave his people a nation (Morocco). There is no Negro, black, colored, or Ethiopian—only "Asiatic" or Moorish-American. Ethiopian signifies a division. Negro (black) signifies death. "Colored"signifies something that is painted. . . . The name means everything; by taking the Asiatic's name from him, and calling him Negro, black, colored, or Ethiopian, the European stripped the Moor of his power, his authority, his God, and every other worth-while possession. Christianity is for the European (paleface); Moslemism is for the Asiatic (olive-skinned). When each group has its own peculiar religion, there will be peace on earth. Noble Drew Ali is a kindred personage and spirit to Confucius, Jesus, Buddha, and Zoroaster.

In 1930 the most influential nationalist religion, the Black Muslims, was established. W. D. Fard, who organized the Black Muslims, defined his mission as the preparation of blacks for the day when the white forces of evil and the black forces of good would join in final battle. He contended that the word "Negro" was invented by whites to separate blacks from their African and Asian brothers. Since Christianity was a religion the white man used to enslave blacks, only in Islam could Afro-Americans obtain justice. Civilization began with blacks, the chosen people of Allah. According to Fard, on the continent of Afro-Asia, "black civilizations flourished long before the white man stood up on his hind legs and crept out of the caves of Europe." Further, the prophet said, the white man was a devil by nature, the physical embodiment of evil and incapable of doing good. According to Fard, blacks had been enslaved, robbed of their names and language and given Christian ones, and forced to learn the English language, all badges of slavery. Brainwashed by white teachers and lulled into submissiveness by Christianity, blacks were taught to hate themselves and worship a blue-eyed, blond Jesus as their God.

The Muslims believed that as the lost nation of Islam in the wilderness of North America, blacks were destined to throw off the last remnants of the manacles of slavery. Stressing the study of African and Afro-American history in an effort to instill self-respect in blacks, they insisted that Arabic be taught in their schools and that black children have black teachers. They preached frugality, hard work, the right of self-defense, and obedience to the laws of the land. When Fard disappeared in 1934, there were already about 8,000 identifiable Muslims. Their new leader, Elijah Poole, the son of a Georgia Baptist preacher, had come to Detroit with his family in the 1920s. Disillusioned by northern discrimination (even against blacks who had fought in the U.S. Army), Poole eagerly followed the tenets of Fard. As Elijah Muhammad, he succeeded Fard and expanded the movement so that by the mid-1960s it had adherents in every major city in the United

You know, some primitive people actually think he's white.

DEITIES

From Black Humor *by Charles R. Johnson. Copyright © 1970 Johnson Publishing Co. Reprinted by permission of Johnson Publishing Co.*

States; in 1960 there were about eighty temples. The blatant racism evident in law enforcement and the efforts of the Muslims to rehabilitate black prisoners brought many converts to the sect by the time of Muhammad's death in 1975. One of the most famous of the Muslim ex-convicts was Malcolm X, who was assassinated in 1965.

The Muslims emphasized economic independence, and most large American cities contained Muslim restaurants, bakeries, and laundries by 1960. After 1960 the Muslims purchased several large cattle farms in the South, began importing and selling fish from Peru, and published the most impressive publication of a black religous sect, *Muhammad Speaks*. The Muslims demanded equal treatment of blacks in America, the release of all black prisoners, the end of police brutality, and a federal guarantee of jobs for blacks. They also contended that blacks should be exempt from taxation and military service and called for the prohibition of racial intermarriage. Since Muslims believed that there could be no justice for blacks in America, they demanded that the U.S. government grant a separate territory to blacks as payment for decades of slavery. Much of the Muslim ideology reflected the late nineteenth- and early twentieth-century Protestant ethic of Booker T. Washington with its emphasis on economic uplift, puritan values, racial pride, and the realities of American life. Elijah Muhammad's program for the deliverance of the lost colonies of Islam in the wilderness of North America contained twelve points: separate yourselves from the slave master; pool your resources, education, and qualifications for independence; stop forcing yourselves into places where you are not wanted; make your own neighborhood a decent place to live; rid yourselves of the lust for wine and drink; learn to love self and kind before loving others; unite to create a future for yourselves; build your own homes, schools, hospitals, and factories; do not seek to mix your blood through racial integration; stop buying expensive cars, fine clothes, and shoes before being able to live in a fine home; spend your money among yourselves; build an economic system among yourselves; and protect your women.

Radical changes occurred in ideology and tactics after the death of Elijah Muhammad in February 1975, when the Black Muslims, under the leadership of his son Wallace D. Muhammad, began to modify their tenets. They no longer referred to whites as devils and conceded that some whites could be good members of the Nation of Islam. Rejecting the goal of a separate state, the Muslims began promoting and recruiting women and disclosed their membership and assets. According to Wallace D. Muhammad, physical white flesh was not the enemy, and "whiteness" was a mental falsehood. Establishing mosques in Africa and the Caribbean, he moved closer to orthodox Islamic doctrines, called upon Afro-Americans to adopt the name "Bilalians," and urged the hitherto apolitical Muslims to register and vote. By 1977 Muhammad had changed the name of the Muslims to the World Community of Islam in the West, or Bilalians (because Mohammad's first black convert was Bilal), rejected the divinity of Fard, abolished the paramilitary temple guards, the Fruit of Islam, permitted Muslims to serve in the military, and announced, "Our purpose is the revival and restoration of pure Islam. . . . The Prophet Mohammad is the seal of the prophets, and the Koran is the last book." Though there was some dissent from the new policies and doctrines, the Bilalians claimed a membership of 70,000 in 1977 (some said 1.5 million).

Before the revolutionary changes in Muslim ideology, black ministers began in the 1960s to develop a systematic theology of black religion. Although frequently ahistorical, the theological writings often reflected trends begun in the antebellum period. Shaken by the tardy response of their churches to black protest movements in the 1960s, black clergy in predominantly white churches (Episcopalians, Presbyterians, and Unitarians) began forming separate caucuses and holding conferences to determine the nature of black religion. Led by Joseph R. Washington, Albert Cleage, and James Cone, the black clergy contended that the black church had to confront the reality of black oppression. The National Committee of Black Churchmen defined the essential character of the black church in its 1969 declaration that "Black Theology is a theology of black liberation. It seeks to plumb the black condition in the light of God's revelation in Jesus Christ, so that the black community can see that the gospel is commensurate with the achievement of black humanity. . . . The message of liberation is the revelation of God as revealed in the incarnation of Jesus Christ. Freedom IS the gospel. Jesus is the Liberator!"

4

Sex and Racism

My old man's a white old man
And my old mother's black,
If I ever cursed my white old man
I take my curses back.

If I ever cursed my black old mother
And wished she were in hell,
I am sorry for that evil wish
And now I wish her well.

My old man died in a fine big house,
My ma died in a shack,
I wonder where I'm gonna die,
Being neither white nor black?

Langston Hughes

Throughout American history, one important indicator of the unequal status of blacks was the taboo against interracial sexual contact and the legal prohibition of interracial marriage. The sexual fear and curiosity about blacks that white males exhibited reflected their desire to subordinate and exploit blacks and was in itself a significant barrier to black progress in America. Some white men seemed to fear that if a black earned a living wage, received a better education, or moved into a white neighborhood, he would then succeed in obtaining a white wife. The white man's fear was as persistent as it was unfounded, for it was fueled by myths instead of by reality.

One expression of sexual fears, the penis envy of whites, for example, is revealed clearly in the treatment of blacks in pornographic literature. When two psychologists, Eberhard and Phyllis Kornhauser, studied this literature, they found in scenes describing sexual relations between black males and white females that the males always had a massive penis and were lovers *par excellence*. The books they examined illustrated the popular belief of whites that blacks "are extraordinarily virile, sensuous, and given to all kinds of perversions." Believing that black males had more physical prowess, fewer inhibitions, inexhaustible sexual appetites, and uncontrollable passions, many white males naturally were afraid to compete with them for sexual favors. In life and literature, it might be said without much exaggeration that the black male was America's phallic symbol.

SEXUAL ATTITUDES TOWARD WOMEN

Until the last decades of the twentieth century white men, often suffering from puritanical and psychological inhibitions and taught that sex was somehow sinful and unnatural, put up many barriers to interracial sexual contacts. Yet, blacks fascinated them. Many of the white man's sexual fantasies, dreams, and desires that he considered sinful were projected onto blacks. The fantasies appeared most clearly in the myths about black women. The image of the black woman was that she was the most sensuous, exotic, mysterious, and voluptuous female in the world—the embodiment of passion. In the traditional sexual and racial mythology of the United States, the white woman was just the opposite. By creating a mythological black Venus and a white Virgin Mary, the white man dehumanized both. In myth, considered frail, cold, and concerned only with the ennobling aspects of life, the white woman was not expected to show passion or erotic interests. In effect, as the sociologist John Dollard observed in *Caste and Class in a Southern Town* in 1949, "the idealization of the white woman . . . especially in the South . . . made her sexually untouchable." But not the black woman. Obviously, if the black Venus was as passionate as the white man's image of her suggested, then she had to be exploited for the sexual pleasure of the white man. Similarly, if the black male was the Apollo white men said that he was, white women might be seduced by him. To prevent this from happening the middle- and upper-class white man cloistered his women, sheltering them from contact with black men. Contrary to the evidence and his own fears, he argued that the white woman was too angelic, too concerned with preserving the purity of the superior race, to have sexual relations with black men. And just to be on the safe side, he passed laws banning interracial marriage.

Tragically, blacks were victimized in many ways by the white man's centuries-old mythology. Given the belief in the ungovernable passion of blacks, the rape of a black woman by a white man was a legal *non sequitur*. She stood defenseless before the bar of justice because it was always assumed that she had been the seducer. The South Carolina demagogue Senator Cole Blease once declared that there was a "serious doubt as to whether the crime of rape can be committed upon a negro." That such beliefs were still prevalent in the United States in the 1970s was indicated by the case of Joanne Little. When Ms. Little killed a white policeman who was allegedly raping her in 1975, the state of North Carolina tried her for murder—in spite of the fact that the man was naked, had obviously used a weapon to force her to submit, and had dried semen on his leg. Reflecting on similar cases in *Crisis* magazine in 1913, W. E. B. Du Bois pointed to the operation of myths and laws that left black women "absolutely helpless before the lust of white men." The legal system had created a population of black women "the ownership of whose bodies no one is bound to respect."

INTERRACIAL MARRIAGE BANS

Although leaving all avenues open to his exploitation of black women, the white man consistently tried to ban interracial marriage. Because prohibitions against interracial sex were so important to whites, they generally represented an almost impassable barrier to the equal treatment of blacks. The Swedish scholar Gunnar Myrdal pointed out in his classic, *The American Dilemma* (1944), that American whites were most fearful of sexual contacts with blacks and felt that desire for interracial sex was what lay behind all black demands for equality. Blacks, on the other hand, had the least desire for interracial sexual contacts. White males were rarely able to separate sexual from other kinds of equality. For them, forbidding contacts between black men and white women while making black women freely available to them was another expression of the unequal condition of blacks in the society. It was still possible in the last quarter of the twentieth century to stop practically any discussion of black rights with the query, "Would you want your daughter to marry one?" The relationship between this and other forms of oppression was stated succinctly by race-baiting William Pickett in 1909: "Forbidden matrimonial equality . . . [the Negro] cannot obtain social privileges. Denied social equality, his political status becomes that of an inferior. Refused political equality, his progress in business is hampered, his education retarded, and his industrial subordination assured." The 1910 Oklahoma law banning interracial marriage was consciously designed to promote the kind of subordination that Pickett supported. Oklahoma whites, desiring to obtain Indian lands, banned not only black-white marriages but black-Indian unions as well. In this regard, one of the primary reasons for twentieth-century opposition to integrated schools was the white man's fears of fostering interracial sex contact. In Louisiana, for example, there were proposals in 1969 to segregate the schools by sex if they were racially integrated.

PRE–CIVIL WAR INTERRACIAL SEXUAL CONTACTS

Despite the existence of legal bans, there was a great deal of interracial sex contact. Miscegenation was, during the antebellum period, part of the "southern way of life." Although there was considerable sexual exploitation of black women by white males in the South, it is impossible to determine precisely how extensive it was. Statistics on the question are unbelievably treacherous. Many categories of literary sources, on the other hand, are very suggestive. Southerners, black and white, commented on the pervasiveness of miscegenation.

When asked whether the planters in South Carolina had sexual intercourse with their slave women, ex-slave Harry McMillan declared in 1863: "There was a good deal of it. They often kept one girl steady and sometimes two on different places; men who had wives did it too sometimes, if they could get it on their own place it was easier but they would go wherever they could get it." Frederick Douglass echoed McMillan's claim and asserted that the planter, "in cases not a few, sustains to his slaves the double relation of master and father." After living thirty-two years in North Carolina, Hiram White wrote, "Amalgamation was common. There was scarce a family of slaves that had females of mature age where there were not some mulatto children."

The sexual exploitation of black women began in African slave castles when the European soldiers and slave traders raped captured African women. European and American sailors and traders continued the practice during the Middle Passage. Zephaniah Kingsley, a wealthy Florida planter and slave trader, is a good example of the transfer of racial mixing from Africa to America. When Kingsley came to Florida in 1803 he brought his wife Anna Jai, the daughter of an African prince, with him. One of the South's most famous polygamous miscegenators, Kingsley chose other mistresses from among his slaves during the next twenty years and had several children by them.

The scarcity of white women in most of the early European colonies in the New World guaranteed miscegenation a prominent role in the new societies. Eleven years after the first blacks landed at Jamestown, one Hugh Davis was accused of "defiling his body in lying with a negro," and in 1640 Robert Sweet had to do penance "for getting a negro woman with child."

The slave woman was at the mercy of her master, his sons, the overseer, and most other white men. John Thompson, a slave, reported that his master "was the father of about one-fourth of the slaves on his plantation" and that none of the black women "could escape" the planter's "licentious passion." Another bondsman, William Anderson, claimed that the sexual exploitation of slave women "was carried on to an alarming extent in the far South." An overwhelming majority of these women submitted to white males because of their fear of punishment for refusing. Others did so for material rewards, in hopes of being freed at a later date, or because they loved the white men. Occasionally, slave women became the concubines of white planters and maintained a liaison with them extending over several years. In *The Peculiar Institution* (1956), Kenneth Stampp, quoting from court cases, noted several such relationships: A South Carolinian "lived for many years in a state of illicit intercourse" with a slave woman "who assumed the position of a wife"; another permitted a female slave "to act as the mistress of his house" and control his domestic affairs. A Kentuckian owned a woman who was his concubine and "possessed considerable influence over him." And a Virginian, his colored mistress, and their mulatto children lived "as a family upon terms of equality, and not as a master with his slaves." Most slave women were caught on the horns of a dilemma. If they rejected the advances of the planter, they would be flogged until they submitted. If they submitted and the planter's wife discovered the relationship, the mistress would flog or sometimes try to kill them or their mulatto children.

In southern cities, miscegenation was institutionalized in brothels where black women consorted with white men and in quasi- or common-law marriages in which they were concubines of middle- and upper-class white males. There was so much interracial mixing in New Orleans that weekly dances were held at which white men met the nearly white quadroons. Even that staunch defender of slavery, Gov. James H. Hammond of South Carolina, felt that interracial mixing was "perpetrated for the most part in cities." A northern white visiting Mobile in 1850 found "few southern boys who would not sleep with Negresses." Writing from New Orleans, a Virginia white drew a similar conclusion: "The fair skin and the Quadroon here intermingle promiscuously." Sometimes the white man deserted his black concubine when he married a white woman; on other occasions he maintained two families. Practically all classes of white males made such alliances. One result of this practice was that almost 50 percent of the antebellum nonwhite population in such cities as New Orleans, Baltimore, and St. Louis consisted of mulattoes. Even if some of the mulattoes were children of mulatto parents, interracial contacts were a part of their lineage. Another consequence was the humiliation of white women, who knew they had been rejected as sexual partners by white males. This was certainly the case of the white women in New Orleans, who often complained that their husbands "deposited" them at white socials and then rushed to attend quadroon balls.

WHITE WOMEN AND BLACK MEN

White women bitterly resented the white man's philandering and some of them chose black lovers. A Virginia white woman symbolized their defiance in 1815 when she admitted that she had given birth to a mulatto and asserted that "she had not been the first nor would she be the last guilty of such conduct, and that she saw no more harm in a white woman's having been the mother of a black child than in a white man's having one, though the latter was more frequent." Although the white woman's role in miscegenation has been repeatedly denied by southern romantics, the number of mixed couples listed in the manuscript census returns, public records of white women giving birth to mulatto children, court cases, and the research of such scholars as Letitia Brown, Richard Wade, and James Hugo Johnston refute such denials. And, however extravagant some of his claims, Joel A. Rogers unearthed an impressive amount of evidence on the white woman's role in miscegenation.

Though not as numerous as their black counterparts, white concubines of black men were not unknown in the South. One Louisiana free black, described by a white contemporary as a handsome man with "a body of Hercules and with eyes as black as the moonless nights of Africa," had two white concubines simultaneously in Lafayette Parish. He had nineteen children by them. The daughters of planters were sometimes the lovers of the black men they had associated with since childhood. For instance, a Kentucky minister, John Rankin, wrote in 1837 that he knew of several cases of slaves "actually seducing the daughters of their masters. Such seductions sometimes happened in the most respectable families." Several white men divorced their wives when they had mulatto children, ran off with, or publicly consorted with black men. Many indiscretions of white women went undetected until they became pregnant. But in innumerable cases (and especially when the father was a mulatto), the children of black men and white women were light-skinned enough to be accepted as white.

Sexual contacts between black men and white women were most visible in southern cities. For example, between October 15 and November 13, 1859, the police in Mobile, Alabama, arrested five white women on charges of "amalgamation." In one of the cases a policeman discovered two black males and two white females in a bedroom with "only one garment on apiece." The police caught another white woman "laying on the same bed with a well known negro driver of a baggage wagon." Journals reported similar incidents in Richmond, Memphis,

Charleston, Nashville, and New Orleans. Morris Helpler found in his investigation of crime in New Orleans that "each year during the 1850s police arrested several white women for taking up with slave men."

In addition to the casual sexual contacts between black men and white women, there were many long-term unions. David Dodge, a white native of North Carolina, recalled in 1866 that in his state "hardly a neighborhood was free from low white women who married or cohabited with free negroes." The U.S. census for Nansemond County, Virginia, in 1830 included eight white women listed as the "wives" of free blacks.

Few blacks lived in the antebellum North; consequently, there was less miscegenation there than in the South. However, considerable sexual contact between the races in northern cities did take place. In Philadelphia, Thomas Branagan wrote in 1805, "I solemnly declare, I have seen more white women married to, and deluded through the arts of seduction by negroes in one year in Philadelphia than for the eight years I was visiting [in the West Indies and in the South]. . . . There are perhaps hundreds of white women thus fascinated by black men in this city, and there are thousands of black children by them at present."

In 1821 a group of whites from Greene County, Pennsylvania, agreed with Branagan, for they declared that many of the blacks settling in the state had "been able to seduce into marriage the minor children of white inhabitants." Similarly, in 1857 a committee of the New York State legislature found, upon visiting one tenement house in New York City, that "in answer to inquiries, and in fact by ocular demonstration, it was ascertained that nearly all the inhabitants were practical amalgamationists—black husbands and white (generally Irish) wives making up the heads of constantly increasing families." The same patterns prevailed in New England. Rhode Island's colonial historian, William Weeden, asserted that "illicit intercourse between white men and colored women in Rhode Island marked a numerous progeny." The high percentage of mulattoes in the black population of northern cities confirmed the impressionistic data. Prostitution houses which had both an integrated staff and clientele, the exploitation of black women by slaveholders, the intermingling of indentured servants and slaves, and the keeping of black mistresses by upper-class white males accounted for a large number of these mulattoes.

MISCEGENATION AFTER THE CIVIL WAR

Many historians contend that miscegenation decreased in the South after the Civil War. All indications are that it simply changed in character. First, many white men who had had black concubines before the war married them in those states that abolished bans against intermarriage. Second, because of the breakdown of customary antebellum societal restraints and the dislocation attendant to war, the number of white women who had sexual intercourse with black men increased. Slave patrols disappeared with the end of the war, and when blacks joined southern law enforcement agencies the police were less effective in preventing miscegenation. As a result of the civil rights acts of 1866 and 1875, the poverty of white women, the refusal of many Reconstruction governments to ban interracial marriage, and the loss of many white males in the war, white southerners saw an increase in "promiscuous mixing." Black soldiers, as the members of victorious armies have always done, found love and sexual gratification in the arms of the women of the vanquished. For instance, the Freedmen's Bureau noted in 1866 that there were six white women married to black soldiers in Jacksonville, Florida.

Whatever the reasons, miscegenation continued in the South after 1865. Even after Reconstruction ended and many states and municipalities enacted antimiscegenation laws, interracial sexual intimacy was still prevalent in the South. For example, historian Howard Rabinowitz, in *Race Relations in the Urban South, 1865–1890* (1978), observed, "In Nashville during the 1880s the annual number of arrests for interracial cohabitation never dropped below thirteen couples. One year it reached a total of fifty-seven individuals, some charged with more than one offense. . . . Couples brought to trial ranged from those who were married or in love to those who had a single sexual liaison." Contemporary observers often noted the continuation of interracial sexual contact after the Civil War. In 1887 the editor of the Montgomery *Herald* asked, "Why is it that white women attract Negro men now more than in former days? There was a time when such a thing was unheard of. There is a secret to this thing, and we greatly suspect it is the growing appreciation of white Juliets for colored Romeos." The editor was run out of town, but he had touched an essential truth. Speaking on January 31, 1887, a black minister in Baltimore, P. H. A. Braxton, observed, "In sight of the capitol at Richmond, white men, and not a few, cohabit with colored women daily; they build fine houses for them, and stay with them, and get children by them. It is said that there are hundreds of colored women in Richmond, saying nothing of the other part of the state, who are kept and supported by white men for their lascivious purposes. . . . Go where you may in this country, and especially in the South, and you will find that two-thirds of the so-called Negroes are Negroes only in name; many of them are as white as the children of their father by his white wife."

Frederick Hoffman, a prominent statistician, declared in 1896, "It is my firm conviction that unlawful intercourse between the sexes is excessively prevalent at the present time in the large cities as well as in the rural sections of the country." In 1910 John James Holm, an Alabama anthropologist, asserted that 25 percent of the white males of the South had sexual intercourse with black women. There were numerous interracial couples in Florida, Louisiana, and most southern cities during this period. All of the statistical indices support the observations of Holm and Hoffman. There was, for instance, a phenomenal increase in the number of mulattoes in the South after the Civil War. While the number of blacks increased by 129 percent between 1850 and 1920, the number of mulattoes increased by 498 percent.

THE ATTACK ON RACE MIXING

Reflecting on the evil of the "promiscuous mixing" that occurred during Reconstruction, the white South developed a monolithic assault on miscegenation. It began as part of the campaign to wrest control of the political structure from blacks, but the ideology did not emerge in its final form until the 1880s. First, the whites convinced themselves that interracial sex was unnatural, that whites had an "instinctive repugnance" to mating with blacks. Writing in *Century Magazine* in 1885, T. U. Dudley, Protestant Episcopal bishop of Kentucky, said, "Instinct and reason, history and philosophy, science and revelation, all alike cry out against the degradation of the race by the free commingling of the tribe which is highest with that which is lowest in the scale of development." Drawing on the concepts of Social Darwinism, whites expressed great fear that miscegenation would lead to an irrevocable degradation of the superior white race. There were those who disagreed, of course, but generally most whites believed that blacks were so far down on the scale of humanity that the descendants of white-black unions would be low in intelligence, capacity for self-government, self-control, and morality—as well as weak, short-lived, and sterile. In short, miscegenation threatened to destroy civilization.

This destruction, they contended, had begun during Reconstruction, when all of the "false" rhetoric about equality had undermined the instinctive aversion of whites to blacks and the laws permitting interracial marriage had encouraged black men to rape white women. The trend could be reversed only by rigid separation of the races and the prevention, by any means, of the pollution of white women, in whom rested all hope of preserving racial purity. As one Texas editor screamed in 1897, "If the South is ever to rid herself of the Negro rape-fiend, she must take a day off and kill every member of

the accursed race that declines to leave the country." The antimiscegenation rhetoric of white politicians and editors so inflamed the popular imagination that the anti-intermarriage laws and subsequent
constitutional bans were not considered sufficient to prevent race mixing and especially rape.

The southern white man's sense of manhood and chivalry, so battered by his defeat in the Civil War and by his subjection to "black
rule" during Reconstruction, demanded that he avenge the "honor"
of white women by resorting to the rope and faggot. One of the major
reasons for the lynching campaign was the postwar increase in voluntary sexual contact between black men and white women (who often
claimed that they had been raped when the liaisons were discovered).
The number of lynchings was also closely correlated with the disfranchisement of blacks, greater segregation, and the enlarged role of the
poor white in southern politics.

The heyday of these trends, the 1890s, also represented the high
point in the yearly average of lynchings for rape-related "crimes."
Between 1882 and 1936, allegations of rape accounted for the lynching
of 1,093 blacks and 97 whites. Of the 3,383 blacks lynched during
this period, 32.3 percent were accused of raping white women.

By the 1890s, copulation between a black man and a white woman
had become synonymous with rape in the white mind. But the antimiscegenation proponents were frustrated time and time again when
white women who had mulatto children refused to identify their "rap-
ist." The frustration was revealed clearly in a story appearing in the
Memphis *Ledger* on June 8, 1892:

> If Lillie Bailey, a rather pretty white girl seventeen years of age who
> is now at the City Hospital would be somewhat less reserved about
> her disgrace there would be some very nauseating details in the story
> of her life. She is the mother of a little coon. The truth might reveal
> fearful depravity or it might reveal the evidence of a rank outrage.
> She will not divulge the name of the man who has left such black evi-
> dence of her disgrace, and, in fact, says it is a matter in which there
> can be no interest to the outside world. . . . She is a country girl. She
> came to Memphis from her father's farm, a short distance from Her-
> nando, Miss. . . . When the child was born an attempt was made to
> get the girl to reveal the name of the Negro who had disgraced her,
> she obstinately refused and it was impossible to elicit any information
> from her on the subject.

The fact that most interracial sexual contact was voluntary and
not a proper subject for control through the lynching bee eventually
became evident to thoughtful observers. In examining the southern

rape complex in 1941, Wilbur J. Cash concluded the obvious when he asserted in *The Mind of the South* that the chance of a white woman being raped by a black man was "much less, for instance, than the chance that she would be struck by lightning." Realizing this, noting the frequent occasions on which white men raped black women with impunity, and angered by the continuation of clandestine sexual relations between white men and black women, southern white women rebelled. Between 1900 and 1932 southern women denied that there was any need to resort to lynching to protect them and publicly deplored the practice. The declaration of the Georgia Women's Interracial Commission was typical: "We believe no falser appeal can be made to Southern manhood than that mob violence is necessary for the protection of womanhood, or that the brutal practice of lynching and burning of human beings is an expression of chivalry."

In spite of the appeal of white women, white males insisted on preserving their racial purity through violent means. Two twentieth-century cases illustrated so obviously the barbaric insanity of such violence prevalent in white America that they made news throughout the world. In 1951 a black sharecropper in Yanceyville, North Carolina, was convicted and sentenced to prison for the "rape by leer" of a white girl. Although he was seventy-five feet away from the woman, Matt Ingram was convicted of assault because of the way he allegedly looked at her. He obtained his freedom only after two and a half years of court maneuvers. Emmett Till, a fourteen-year-old boy, was kidnapped and killed in Money, Mississippi, in 1955 because he allegedly whistled at a white woman.

The American rape complex was productive of much injustice. Because of the social taboos associated with interracial sex, even the habitual white prostitute could assure a black man of death or imprisonment by shouting that vile four-letter word. The fact that two promiscuous Alabama white girls who consented to have sexual relations with nine black boys in Scottsboro, Alabama, in 1931 could cause a long incarceration for them was simply one famous case that proved the point.

In his reaction to reports of interracial sex contacts, the white man sometimes transformed himself into a primitive savage. When a black man was accused of raping a white woman in the second half of the nineteenth century and early part of the twentieth, southern whites usually castrated him, lynched him, riddled his body with bullets, and then burned it. In fact, any crime involving interracial sex seemed to plunge the white man into the very depths of antediluvian barbarism. The 1934 case of Claude Neal, a black man arrested in Marianna, Florida, for the murder of his white mistress, is an example. After an enraged mob kidnapped him from an Alabama jail (where he had been placed for his "safety"), they traveled toward the Florida state line as fifteen southern newspapers announced the date of the coming lynching and the route and progress of the mob. The white men tortured Neal for twelve hours. They hung him until he was almost dead, forced him to eat his own penis, burned him with red-hot irons, slashed his side and stomach, and cut off his fingers and toes before they murdered him and hung his body in the Marianna courthouse square.

The number of such lynchings decreased dramatically after 1940 as American whites depended more and more on the police to harass, beat, and imprison black men caught dating or having sexual relations with white women. Closely related to this was another development: judicial lynching for alleged rape. A black lawyer, Haywood Burn, described this process perfectly in 1970:

> White America still reserves special penalties for blacks convicted of sex crimes—especially interracial sex crimes. National Prison Statistics show that of the 19 jurisdictions that have executed men for rape since 1930, almost one-third of them—six states—have executed *only* blacks. There have been some years in which everyone who was executed for rape in this country was black. Detailed state-by-state analysis has shown that the discrepancy in death sentences for rape is related to the race of the victim. . . . For example, in Florida between 1960 and 1964, of the 125 white males who raped white females, six—or about 5 percent—received death sentences. Of the 68 black males in the same period who were convicted in Florida of raping black females, three— or about 4 percent—received death sentences; and this when in two cases the victims were children. However, of the 84 blacks convicted of raping white women, 45—or 54 percent—received the death sentence. *None* of the eight white men who raped black women were sentenced to death.

The injustice revealed in the statistics is compounded by studies of criminologists suggesting that in more than 80 percent of all allegations of rape, the woman lies. Yet until the 1970s scores of black men were executed every year for allegedly raping white women. Obviously, as the imposition of the death penalty shows, rape was, for all practical purposes, a "Negro crime." Of the 455 men executed for rape between 1930 and 1969 in the United States, 405 or 89 percent were black.

DEFINING THE RACES

Throughout American history the great problem faced by the foes of miscegenation was to define who was black and who was white. By the first decades of the nineteenth century it had become virtually impossible in many instances to designate southerners by race. Fugitive slaves, for example, were frequently described as having "straight hair and complexion so nearly white that a stranger would suppose there was no negro blood in him," or as having "light sandy hair, blue eyes, ruddy complexion; he is so nearly white as to easily pass for a white man." So many mulattoes succeeded in concealing their black ancestors and intermarrying with "pure whites" that many southerners found themselves in the position of the Virginia woman who declared in 1831 that she "did not know whether she was entirely white or not."

Southern racial patterns were so complicated that they sometimes defied description. The racial admixture that designated a person "Negro" varied from place to place. Often a combination of wealth and light skin color was enough for a mulatto to be defined legally as "white." As a South Carolina jurist ruled in 1835, "The condition [of mixed ancestry] . . . is not to be determined solely by . . . visible mixture . . . but by reputation . . . and it may be . . . proper, that a man of worth . . . should have the rank of a white man, while a vagabond of the same degree of blood should be confined to the inferior caste." Such judicial and social attitudes enabled many descendants of blacks to be absorbed by whites. One of the clearest cases of this occurred in Sumter County, South Carolina. In 1790, a group of mulattoes successfully petitioned the legislature to be relieved from acts discriminating against blacks. By the 1860s they were accepted as whites, and many of them fought as "white men" in the rebel army.

The legal definitions of race that evolved in the United States were nothing short of bizarre; for foreigners they were incomprehensible. But if law is to ban interracial marriage, then it has to define race. In 1967, a person was considered black in Alabama, Arkansas, Georgia, Oklahoma, and Texas if he had in his "veins any negro blood whatever" or any black ancestors. One-third "negro-blood" made one black in Maryland, North Carolina, and Tennessee; one-fourth in Florida; one-eighth in Mississippi and Missouri. Georgia and South Carolina complicated matters further. In the nineteenth century they defined anyone with "one-eighth negro blood" as black; in the twentieth century they changed the definition to "any ascertainable trace" of black ancestors. Between 1919 and 1930, the Virginia legislature annually considered, passed, amended, and repealed several acts defining a black person. In applying for school admission in some states "one drop of Negro blood" made one a black, while in applying for a marriage license seven-eighths "white blood" made one "white."

In the final analysis, visibility and reputation appeared to be the most important factors in determining racial identity. Both methods were fallible. Some blacks were not only legally white in several southern states, they appeared so to any observer. This was certainly the case with the families of Walter White, the Hunts, Westmorelands, and Millers. Poppy Cannon, a rather dark brunette white woman from South Africa, indicated how bewildering the whole phenomenon was when she and her black husband, Walter White, went to India in 1949:

> We were guests of the Calcutta Association for the United Nations, a meeting hurriedly arranged. The president of the Association turned to me. "I have read in the journals," he said, "that you are white." He pointed to his snow-white cuff. "And your husband," pointing now to his coat sleeve, "is black."
> Both of us looked across the table at Walter. "Obviously," I answered. And the whole table, up to the moment formal and solemn, broke into a roar of laughter. "These mad Americans."

The southerner's preoccupation with racial definitions indicated his well-founded paranoia about "passing." The incredible geographical mobility of the American people defeated all attempts to prevent passing. In the 1890s, for example, W. E. B. Du Bois found several "white" families in Philadelphia who were descendants of mulattoes: "Between 1820 and 1860 many natural children were sent from the South and in a few cases their parents followed and were legally married here. Descendants of such children in many cases forsook the mother's [black] race; one became principal of a city school, one a prominent sister in a Catholic church, one a bishop, and one or two officers in the Confederate Army." In Louisiana and other southern states, mulatto women and their white lovers often bribed officials to register their newborn children as white; baptismal records of mulattoes were regularly destroyed. They were mutilated so often in New Orleans that one observer thought the baptismal books looked as though a rat had eaten his way through them with a pair of shears. Even without the records in such places, Ohio State University sociologist Robert Struckert estimated in a 1958 article in the *Ohio Journal of Science* that one out of every five American whites had some Afro-American ancestors. It is no wonder, then, that twentieth-century America added a new genre to the world's literature, "the passing novel and autobiography." James Weldon Johnson began it in 1912 when he published the *Autobiography of an Ex-Coloured Man,* Sinclair Lewis explored a similar phenomenon in *Kingsblood Royal* (1947) and Reba Lee wrote *I Passed for White* in 1955.

OPPOSING INTERRACIAL MARRIAGE

Unable as they were to determine with any precision who was "white" and who was "black," American whites nevertheless consistently op-

WALTER WHITE AND POPPY CANNON

From Ebony *8:46 (July 1952). Copyright © 1952 Johnson Publishing Co.*
Reprinted by permission of Johnson Publishing Co.

posed racial intermarriage. Prohibition laws began appearing in the colonial period: Virginia and Maryland, 1662; Massachusetts, 1705; North Carolina, 1715; Delaware, 1721; and Pennsylvania, 1725. Most of these laws were reenacted after the American Revolution. During the nineteenth century thirty-eight states banned interracial marriage, though seven repealed such laws: Pennsylvania, 1780; Massachusetts, 1843; Rhode Island, 1881; Maine and Michigan, 1883, New Mexico, 1886, and Ohio, 1887. Most of the laws fined the minister performing the ceremony (sometimes as much as $10,000), imprisoned the black involved (for up to twenty years), and fined or imprisoned the white partner in the union. According to the colonial Pennsylvania law, a free black marrying a white person was to be sold into slavery for life. In several southern colonies the mulatto children of a white woman were taken away from her and indentured for between eighteen and thirty years, and the woman herself was bound to service for seven years.

Generally, antebellum whites expressed their opposition to mixed marriage by resorting to violence whenever such unions occurred. When whites found that a black man had married a white girl in Indianapolis in 1840, a mob gathered at the house where they were spending their wedding night, dragged them outside, rode the bride on a rail, and chased the groom out of town (the couple was eventually reunited in Cincinnati). A similar case occurred in New York in 1853 when William G. Allen, a black professor at the integrated New York Central College, proposed to one of his white students, Mary King. On January 30, the couple met at the house of friends in Mary's hometown, Phillipsville. Mary's white townsmen, on hearing about the intended match, decided then and there to prevent such a "foul connection." A mob gathered in front of the house, forced Mary to return to her home, and threatened to kill Allen if he did not leave the village. Mary was placed under virtual house arrest, and some of the townsmen and her enraged relatives pursued Allen to Syracuse. He soon found refuge with friends in Pennsylvania. In March, Allen wrote to Mary renewing his proposal and asking if she would go to England with him. Mary answered, "Yes; gladly and joyfully will I hasten with you to a land where unmolested, we can be happy in the consciousness of the love which we cherish for each other." Through subterfuge Mary escaped from her family and married William Allen in New York City on March 30, 1853. The Liberty Party of New York, Harriet Beecher Stowe, Gerrit Smith, Frederick Douglass, and Sarah D. Porter expressed their indignation over the mob attack and their approval of the marriage. On April 9, the Allens sailed to England, where they were received cordially by such abolitionists as Joseph Sturge and George Thompson.

ABOLITION SUPPORT FOR INTERRACIAL MARRIAGE

Although most abolitionists opposed intermarriage, a few of them spoke out against the marriage restriction. One of them, the editor of Indiana's *Free Labor Advocate,* wrote in 1842, "Such legislation is not only pitiably contemptible, but it is wicked and tyrannical; tending directly to increase that abominable prejudice which is crushing to earth the free people of color in the professedly free states." The most successful attack on a law banning intermarriage was led by William Lloyd Garrison in Massachusetts. Garrison contended in January, 1831, that a 1786 Massachusetts law banning interracial marriage was "an invasion of one of the inalienable rights of man, namely, 'the pursuit of happiness'—disgraceful to the state—inconsistent with every principle of justice—and utterly absurd and preposterous." The next month Garrison asked, "Does a man derive or lose his right to choose his wife from his color? Yes, say our sapient legislators. Why, then, let us have a law prohibiting tall people from marrying short ones. Here is a more palpable and unpardonable distinction than the other!" When the opponents charged the abolitionists with being consumed with a passionate desire to marry blacks and declared that repeal of the law would lead to a spate of interracial marriages, Garrison retorted, "The blacks are not so enamored of white skins as some of our editors imagine. The courtship, the wooing, the embrace, the inter-mixture—in nine cases out of ten—will be proposed on the part of the whites, and not of the opposite color."

Though the Massachusetts legislators refused to be prodded into action between 1831 and 1832, they did respond to an avalanche of abolitionists' petitions between 1839 and 1843. The campaign began when white women in Lynn, Rehoboth, and Dorchester petitioned for a repeal of all the state's laws discriminating against blacks. George Bradburn of Nantucket supported the petitions and contended that the 1786 law violated the first article of the Massachusetts Declaration of Human Rights and encouraged "vicious connections between the races," led to licentiousness, and "legalized prostitution of the marriage covenant." In March, 1839, the Massachusetts Anti-Slavery Society gave its support to the movement for repeal. Among the prominent abolitionists who supported the repeal campaign were Edmund Quincy, Caroline Chase, John Greenleaf Whittier, Lydia Maria Child, Maria Weston Chapman, Henry B. Stanton, Charles Francis Adams, Henry Wilson, John A. Collins, Wendell Phillips, James Birney, and William E. Channing. By the spring of 1840 the legislature had received ninety-two different petitions with 8,700 signatures for repeal of the law.

Three years later an overwhelming majority of the legislators voted to repeal the anti-intermarriage law.

Some abolitionists were unequivocal in their support of interracial marriage. Theodore Tilton felt that "when a man and woman want to be married it is *their* business, not mine nor anybody else's. . . . So far from denouncing the marriage of blacks and whites, I would be glad if the banns of a hundred thousand such marriages could be published next Sunday." The Virginia-born abolitionist Moncure D. Conway espoused one of the most extreme positions when he asserted in 1864, "I, for one, am firmly persuaded that the mixture of the blacks and whites is good; that the person so produced is, under ordinarily favourable circumstances, healthy, handsome, and intelligent. Under the best circumstances, I believe that such a combination would evolve a more complete character than the unmitigated Anglo-Saxon. . . . Every race has a genius in some sort, to be unfolded by proper culture; and so long as that of the African, or any other race, however lowly, is excluded, some function will be absent from every brain, some flaw will be in every heart."

Regardless of the well-publicized views of the abolitionists, whites continued to react hysterically whenever an interracial union took place. When Frederick Douglass took as his second wife a white clerk in his office in Washington, D.C., in 1884, there was a storm of protest, and Congress received several petitions to prohibit such marriages. Douglass, who said his father had been white, answered the protesters in characteristic fashion. He allegedly said that when he married his first wife he honored his mother's people, the blacks, and when he married his second wife, he honored his father's.

The black who caused more nightmares for white America than any other was bullet-headed, braggadocious heavyweight boxing champion Jack Johnson. Publicly consorting with white prostitutes, Johnson married five times; four of his wives were white. His first marriage to a white woman in 1911 caused such a sensation that anti-intermarriage bills were introduced in ten of the states which did not at that time have them. Georgia Congressman Seaborn A. Roddenberry proposed a constitutional amendment to ban such unions and said that Johnson's action was "more revolting than white slavery. . . . No brutality, no infamy, no degradation in all the years of southern slavery possessed such villainous character and such atrocious qualities as the provisions of laws . . . which allow the marriage of the negro Jack Johnson to a woman of the caucasian strain." Newspapers throughout the country were whipped into a mad frenzy by Johnson's marriage. Eventually, the U.S. government launched a vendetta against the world champion

and convicted him in 1913 of violating the Mann Act, that is, of transporting a woman across state lines for purposes of prostitution. Primarily as a result of Johnson's sexual exploits, twenty-one anti-intermarriage
bills were introduced in Congress between 1909 and 1921. Between
1925 and 1930, attempts were made to ban racial intermarriage in
eleven states (Connecticut, Illinois, Iowa, Maine, Massachusetts, Michigan, New Jersey, Ohio, Pennsylvania, Rhode Island, and Wisconsin).

FEATURES OF INTERRACIAL MARRIAGES

Statistics on interracial marriages are so difficult to obtain and so frequently contradictory that we can only draw tentative conclusions
about the nature and extent of such marriages. Because of legal prohibitions, most of our statistics are for a few places in the North. In
Michigan, Rhode Island, and Connecticut, between 1874 and 1893 there
were an average of 5.6 black-white marriages annually.

It is obvious that even in states permitting interracial marriage,
these unions were rare. Only 27 of them occurred in Philadelphia
between 1900 and 1904. The 6 consummated in 1900 represented less
than 1 percent of the 633 marriages in the city that year. In Boston
from 1914 to 1938 only 276, or 3.9 percent, of all marriages involving
blacks were interracial. In Connecticut between 1953 and 1959, there
were 285 black-white marriages. Only 11 out of every 1,000 marriages
in New York State between 1924 and 1933 were interracial. As for
the total number of interracial families in America by the 1960s, the
best estimate we have was made by an N.A.A.C.P. lawyer in 1967:
550,000.

Some features of the interracial marriage emerge clearly from an
examination of the statistics. First of all, these marriages occurred primarily in cities. For example, 90 percent of the black-white marriages
that occurred in Rhode Island from 1881 to 1940 were in Providence.
Second, in the North a black male was far more likely to marry a
white woman than a black woman a white male. About 70 percent
of the interracial marriages in Rhode Island between 1900 and 1916
were between black males and white females. In the 1890s W. E. B.
Du Bois found that 29 of the 33 blacks married to whites in one ward
in Philadelphia were men, or 87 percent. The percentage was even
higher in Boston; 210 of the 227 interracial marriages between 1900
and 1907, or 92 percent, were between black males and white females.
In southern states that permitted interracial marriage in the nineteenth
century, the pattern was just the reverse. For example, there were
255 black-white marriages in New Orleans between 1868 and 1880.
In 176, or 78 percent, of these unions the husband was white.

Most whites insisted that only poor whites who were either debased or criminal married or engaged in sexual relations with blacks. As one southern historian, Philip A. Bruce, asserted in 1889, "The few white women who have given birth to mulattoes have always been regarded as monstrosities, and without exception they have belonged to the most impoverished and degraded caste of whites. . . ." Much of the evidence, however, suggests just the opposite.

Many of the white women in these unions were clearly upper class. In 1938, wealthy Mary B. Dawes, a descendant of the man who rode with Paul Revere on his famous ride, married a black. Similarly, in 1951 steel heiress Ann Mather, a descendant of the Puritan divine Cotton Mather, married a black. Studies of the occupations of interracial couples in Boston indicate that the black groom tended to be superior in status to the general black population. In other words, upper-class black males were more likely to choose white brides than were lower-class blacks. While in the nineteenth century the white bride in such marriages was generally lower on the occupational scale than the general white population, the reverse was true by the 1960s. The partners in an interracial marriage after 1960 were generally superior in education and economic status to the general population.

Numerically, black-white marriages were insignificant. In regard to race relations, however, they were very important. At first glance, for instance, the predominance of the black male-white female union between the 1870s and the 1950s seemed to substantiate the white man's fear that all black men were secretly lusting after white females. In actuality, this pattern developed because the number of black males exceeded the number of black females in northern cities in the first part of the twentieth century, while the number of white females often exceeded the number of white males.

THE NATURE OF INTERRACIAL MARRIAGES

Given the violent opposition to such unions, several questions emerge when interracial marriages are considered. Why did whites and blacks intermarry? What was the nature of the interracial family? What pressures did interracial couples face? And finally, what adjustment problems confronted the children of interracial couples, and how did the parents help them to overcome them? When one cuts through the mythology, the reasons for interracial marriages are not difficult to fathom. The myth that the partners in interracial marriages had deep psychological problems must be rejected. In spite of social taboos, love and passion are "color-blind." Some factors which seem to facilitate interracial marriages are mutual interests, shared values, geographical propinquity, physical attraction, curiosity, and desire for forbidden fruit.

Generally, interracial sex contacts occur where there is social and spatial proximity and similarities of culture between different races. Joel A. Rogers, the famous black student of miscegenation, for instance, concluded that "propinquity and personality are more than a match for prejudice." Integrated housing and the anonymity that city life afforded created many opportunities for interracial sexual contacts and the softening of racial antipathies. Another important factor in facilitating interracial marriages is a large foreign-born population. With far less antipathy to blacks than native-born whites, especially Anglo-Saxons, immigrants are much more willing to have sexual relations with and to marry them. This fact is reflected in the relatively high percentage of the foreign-born among white partners in interracial marriages in many cities.

Most scholars also believe that blacks seek out white partners as a way of raising their status and achieving equality. This was especially true, they argue, in the case of the black male. The Martinican psychiatrist Frantz Fanon asserted that the black male in these unions unconsciously says, "I wish to be acknowledged not as *black* but as *white*. Now . . . who but a white woman can do this for me? By loving me she proves that I am worthy of white love. I am loved like a white man. Her love takes me onto the noble road that leads to total realization. . . . I marry white culture, white beauty, white whiteness. When my restless hands caress those white breasts, they grasp white civilization and dignity and make them mine." While there may be an element of truth in Fanon's poetically expressed theory, sociologists and psychologists appear to have exaggerated the black male's desire to obtain status by marrying a white woman. Status seeking seemed to play a lesser role in interracial marriages than in conventional ones. On the other hand, it was a very strong factor in casual interracial sex contacts. In these liaisons, the black male frequently felt that he was enhancing his status by violating one of the strongest taboos of white America.

The most important factor in promoting interracial marriage was not the dream life of the black male. The opportunity for social contact and childhood experiences were the keys. Josephine, the white wife of journalist George Schuyler, gave the following among the reasons for her marriage:

The fact that he was dark and I fair gave an added fillip to our association. This was not surprising for I, as the daughter of a Midwest Texas cattleman and banker, had been pleasantly associated with Negroes all my life. As a child, the activities of the Negroes fascinated me. They were always doing something interesting. . . . Goodnaturedly, they let us white children follow them as they went about their work. Thus I had much pleasant association with Negroes from the very beginning. I also knew of such association, in the reverse, among the grown-ups. Early I had found out that the deacon of a local Baptist church, a most respectable man, had had a colored companion for twenty years with everyone aware of the intimacy. I knew, too, that an important family there had numerous colored "cousins" whom they privately acknowledged and visited. I knew, besides, that the same system existed in my own family, with my father drawing no color line in his love life, and that my eldest brother, publicly thought to be childless, had a colored daughter attending school outside the state. So interracial love was not unknown in my environment.

Although there are few statistics on the matter, there is little evidence to support the popular belief that interracial marriages were less stable than other marriages. In fact, when we consider that one in every three marriages in America ended in divorce in the 1970s, the interracial family seemed remarkably stable. The most revealing study of black-white marriages was conducted by Eugene Cash in Philadelphia in the 1950s. Based on questionnaires and intensive interviews of seventeen interracial couples, the study showed that a surprisingly high percentage of the white partners were attracted to their black spouses (76 percent of whom were males) because they had discovered that their parents had consistently lied to them about the character of black people. More than 90 percent of the marriages were stable, and the spouses were psychologically well-adjusted individuals. Their intelligence was far above the average of the general population, and they had completed an average of two years in college. The women had been attracted to the males, white or black, because they were aggressive, poised, forceful, and considerate. The general psychological profile of the partners in these seventeen interracial marriages showed that they were unusually confident, independent, individualistic, emotionally mature persons who had broad intellectual and cultural interests. The courtship preceding most of the marriages was a long one, and the opposition raised by the relatives of the whites tended to cement the relationships. Often the relatives relented and accepted the marriages after their initial opposition.

These unions survived in spite of being subjected to every weapon in the arsenal of the oppressive American system. Parents frequently disowned the white partners, and so-called friends ostracized them. White divorcees who won custody of their children suddenly had them taken away by the courts when they married black men. People stared at interracial couples on the streets as if they were circus curiosities.

The police harassed them, sometimes arresting the women as prostitutes. The F.B.I. occasionally investigated them. Sick people wrote the couples vulgar, obscene letters and sick employers fired them upon learning of their union. Banks refused to give them loans. When Walter White and his white wife, Poppy Cannon, tried to buy a house in 1951, for instance, no bank in New York City would finance it.

Mixed couples found it almost impossible to rent apartments. After 1950 they adopted a subterfuge in their efforts to obtain housing; the white partner applied to white realtors and the black partner to black ones. When the white partner in the union was male the couple usually resided in a white neighborhood. If the husband was white, the mixed couple suffered far less harassment from white neighbors than when the husband was black. The experience of Tamara and her black husband, Vincent Wright, was typical. When the Wrights moved into a predominantly white middle-class neighborhood in East Meadow, Long Island, in 1963 they were "plagued by anonymous 'hate' phone calls, obscene letters, and . . . a cross-burning on their front lawn and a firecracker blast through their living room windows." After the cross-burning, the Wrights received an avalanche of scurrilous letters. Generally, there was considerably more opposition to mixed couples than to black families moving into predominantly white neighborhoods.

White America's opposition to mixed marriages was sometimes maddening in its intensity and led to personal tragedy. Helen Lee Worthing, for example, the "Golden Girl" of the 1920s, was the star of the Ziegfeld Follies and considered one of the five most beautiful women in the world. She was frequently a cover girl on American magazines and became a co-star in movies with John Barrymore and Adolf Menjou. Then Helen met and fell in love with a wealthy black California doctor. She married him because, as she asserted, "I thought then that our love was strong enough to whip a thousand dragons." She had, unfortunately, underestimated white America. Her marriage ended her movie career, and she found she could not bear the stares of strangers and the snubs of her friends. After a few weeks of marriage, Helen wrote, "We continued to go out to night clubs and theaters as I thought that surely my friends would come at last to accept him as my husband. But it wasn't easy to bear the snubs, the surreptitious glances and the whispers. I began carrying a small flask of liquor in my bag and when I couldn't bear it any longer, I would go to the powder room and take a drink. It helped a lot and only thus was I able to face the cold scrutiny of the eyes that looked at me." Eventually she was committed to a sanitarium, her paranoia deepened, once she tried to kill her husband, and frequently she attempted suicide. After separating from her husband, she became a dope addict and an inhabitant of skid row. Helen Worthing died in Los Angeles in 1948.

Frequently inner-directed individuals who were deeply in love, the partners of an interracial marriage insisted that although society might oppress them, love would enable them to survive. Still, before the 1960s the oppression often led interracial couples into a strange way of life. Their activities sometimes took on a secretive air. Frequently they did not go out together. Generally the white woman in such unions was excluded from white society and had to find all of her friends among blacks. On occasion, interracial couples organized in an effort to fight oppression and lead meaningful social lives. One of the first clubs of interracial couples, the Manassah Society, was founded in Chicago in 1890, and one of the great social events in the early part of the twentieth century was its annual ball. At one point the club had 700 members. A similar organization, the Penguin Club, was organized in New York City in 1936 with 100 couples. There were nine of these clubs in Washington, D.C., Los Angeles, and Detroit in 1950. Among middle- and upper-income mixed couples, a different pattern of life prevailed after 1950 in the North. Growing toleration, the broad social and intellectual interests of the partners, and the steadfastness of former friends led to wide social contacts for the couples.

However mixed couples were able to make adjustments in their social lives, they often faced a crisis in rearing their children. Indeed, they were often urged not to have any. White relatives frequently recommended that the wives have abortions when they became pregnant. The birth of the child added to the long line of insults the couple received. The question of the racial identity of the children and the inevitable discrimination they would face perplexed many of the mixed couples, especially the white partner. Most of them, however, rejected the suggestions of white friends that the children "pass for white." The child-rearing credos of the mixed couples were remarkably similar: teach the children to have pride in being black, give them plenty of love, affection, and solid values, and instill self-confidence.

BLACK REACTIONS TO INTERRACIAL MARRIAGE

Crucial to the problems faced by an interracial couple was the reaction of blacks to the union. Unfortunately, most studies of sex and racism ignore the attitudes of blacks to interracial marriage. But these attitudes can be traced from the pre-Civil War era to the last decades of the twentieth century by a careful reading of primary sources. Fearing a violent backlash from whites, blacks rarely expressed a desire to abolish the restrictions on interracial marriage during the antebellum period. Samuel E. Cornish, David Ruggles, and Henry Highland Garnet argued the inevitability of miscegenation and found nothing inherently wrong with racial intermarriage. There were so many circumlocutions in their arguments, however, that they seemed to come down on both sides of the fence simultaneously. Even during the campaign to repeal the 1786 Massachusetts anti-intermarriage law, blacks were largely silent. The greatest public display occurred in 1843 when a group of Boston black males called for the abolition of all discriminatory laws and especially the 1786 act which "we rejoice to believe . . . will soon be wiped away." William Wells Brown, a novelist, playwright, and fugitive slave who had frequently written about Thomas Jefferson's mulatto children, was an uncompromising exponent of miscegenation. Writing in the *Anglo-African* newspaper in February, 1864, Brown contended that "the blending of races is requisite to peace, good feeling and the moral, mental, and physical development of mankind. It breaks down caste and teaches the brotherhood of man."

Spurred on by the optimism of Reconstruction, more confident of their own strength, and less fearful of reprisals, the stance black leaders took on racial intermarriage after the Civil War starkly contrasted to their silence before 1865. North and South, they demanded the removal of bans against intermarriage and fought against their adoption in states where they did not exist. Black newspapers in New Orleans led a campaign against such bans in the 1860s and 1870s. On March 7, 1872, the New Orleans *Louisianian* questioned whether it was "anybody's business whether a white man chooses to [marry] a colored woman, or vice versa? Is it not one of those transactions in which individuals should preeminently consult their own tastes?" Such attitudes continued to be expressed by black opinion leaders until the end of the nineteenth century. For instance, a state convention of Indiana blacks petitioned the legislature to remove the "invidious distinctions" in the marriage laws in 1875.

One of the foremost black champions of unrestricted marriage laws in the nineteenth century was T. Thomas Fortune, editor of the New York *Globe*. Fortune argued against the anti-intermarriage laws because they encouraged immorality, left the black woman defenseless, and represented the white man's belief in the inferiority of blacks. The Indianapolis *Journal*, Cleveland *Gazette*, New York *Freeman*, the black historian and Ohio legislator George Washington Williams, Ida Wells Barnett, and South Carolina Congressman Robert Smalls expressed similar views between 1880 and 1900. There was near unanimity among black leaders regarding bans on intermarriage after 1900. The editorial position of New York's *Messenger Magazine* was typical:

We favor the intermarriage between any sane, grown persons who desire to marry—whatever their race or color. . . . We therefore demand the repeal of all laws against intermarriage as being inimical to the interests of both races. We further call attention to the fact that there is no desire to check the association of white men with colored women, colored women with white men, nor to serve any interests of Negro men. And inasmuch as no law requires any woman under any circumstances to marry a man whom she does not will or want to marry, these laws narrow themselves down to the prevention of *white women marrying colored men* whom they desire to marry.

Traditionally, the major opposition to intermarriage in the black community was expressed by black women. A group of twenty black women in Boston set the tone for the debate in 1843 when they appealed to the Massachusetts legislature to retain the 1786 ban on interracial marriage. Repeal of the law would, the women felt:

exert a most pernicious influence on the condition of colored women. If the proposed change of the laws takes place, we shall be deserted by our natural protectors . . . and thrown upon the world friendless and despised, and forced to get our bread by any vile means that may be proposed to us by others, or that despair may teach us to invent. . . . If this request be granted . . . Colored husbands will regret that they married before the change of the law, and will wish their wives out of the way. The least evil that we can expect . . . is the utter destruction of domestic happiness. The petition of the colored men show that we are despised. . . . we . . . beg that you will not, by a legislative act, plunge us into an abyss of wretchedness, temptation and ruin. . . .

Middle-class black women led the campaigns against intermarriage because of the propensity of middle- and upper-class black males to marry white women. One black woman argued in 1947 that every black man "who has changing clothes is looking for a near-white or white woman for his mate." Since traditionally more black women obtained college degrees than black males and the American economy did not permit many black males to rise to middle-class status, there were generally not enough men to go around in this class. Obviously, when these men began to marry white women the supply of eligible bachelors declined further. Writing to *Ebony* magazine in 1970, a black woman asserted, "I am not a racist but white women are a threat to black women. In the near future there aren't going to be enough black men around for us to marry."

The psychological burden of rejection was heightened by the constant emphasis in the press on the famous black males who married white women. Many of the black women propounded the same views

as whites regarding mixed marriages. Some of them felt that only degenerate poor whites married blacks. One black minister, Nannie Burroughs, argued in 1904 that such unions indicated that the black man
had no self-respect or racial pride. Besides, she claimed, interracial
marriages violated God's divine plan: "The Negro has native charm,
spirit and endurance. Amending a race by the infusion of fresh blood
from another race tends to modify to some degree the divinely-be-
stowed characteristics of that race. It also tends to pass on into offspring
weaknesses of each and little of the strength, if there, by such commingling of blood. The white man has sent oceans of blood into the Negro
race by the back door and the race is no better off by his gratuitous
contribution."

Historically, however, and in spite of such feelings, many Afro-
Americans viewed mixed marriages as signs of racial progress, as indications of the acceptance of blacks on equal terms by whites. At the
same time, more cautious blacks frowned on such unions because they
might increase the white man's fears and make progress in other areas
of life more difficult. As blacks became increasingly more revolutionary
in the 1960s, their attitudes toward mixed marriages became increasingly complex. Their emphasis on black being beautiful and on black
manhood made blacks more desirable as sex objects and as marriage
partners for whites. Greater desirability, coupled with the decline in
legal barriers to interracial contacts, led to a rise in mixed marriages.
Conversely, the growing emphasis on racial pride and repudiation of
integration as an end in itself led to an absolute rejection of mixed
marriages by many blacks.

By the 1970s, even though the nexus between racial oppression
and sex was still painfully obvious, there was less concern with prohibiting free association among individuals. Public opinion polls showed a
sharp decline in white opposition to interracial marriages after 1950,
and after 1967 the U.S. Supreme Court systematically and consistently
ruled that anti-intermarriage laws were unconstitutional. Progress in
this area was revealed in the fact that by 1967 only seventeen states
prohibited interracial marriage. One state, Maryland, repealed its anti-
intermarriage law in 1969, and there were no violent outbursts over
the 566 black-white marriages that took place in the first nineteen
months after the law was stricken from the books.

Despite this progress, however, sexual myths and fears and the
oppression they reflected and perpetuated still represented one of the
greatest barriers to a democratic society in America. These barriers
will be broken down only when most Americans agree with the declaration made by William Lloyd Garrison in the May 7, 1831, edition of
the *Liberator:*

The pursuit of happiness is among the inalienable rights of man: it is inseparable from his existence, and no legislative body has a right to deprive him of it. . . . A union of the sexes is a matter of choice, as well as duty. To limit this choice to a particular family, neighborhood or people, is to impoverish and circumscribe human happiness, and to create an odious aristocracy. These propositions we conceive to be reasonable, plain undeniable, self-evident. . . . The standard of matrimony is erected by affection and purity, and does not depend upon the height, or bulk, or color, or wealth, or poverty, of individuals. Water will seek its level; nature will have free course; and heart will answer to heart. To attempt to force or obstruct the flow of the affections, is ridiculous and cruel.

5

Blacks and the Politics of Redemption

We
worship
different heroes
now.
We stop
bowing to Uncle Tom
baseball players
and phony politicians
who drive long shiny cars
and attend 25 dollar a plate
luncheons for the United Appeal.
We now listen
to our bushy head
brother
standing on the corner
rapping out the side of his mouth
about the man.
2 . . .
We
worship different heroes
now.
Since we
stop reading the newspaper.

Norman Jordan

Jeffersonian Democracy, Jacksonian Democracy, Progressivism, and many of the other labels frequently used in describing American politics had virtually no meaning for blacks. For long periods of time, white men excluded Afro-Americans from the body politic. Throughout most of their sojourn in America, blacks confronted the unshakeable white belief that Chief Justice Rogert B. Taney expressed succinctly

142

in his 1857 decision in the Dred Scott case. According to Taney, American blacks "had for more than a century been regarded as beings of an inferior order . . . so far inferior that they had no rights which the white man was bound to respect."

Confronting such white supremacists as Taney, blacks argued that both the Declaration of Independence and the Constitution had been perverted. Until white men lived up to the ideals embodied in these documents, they would be cursed by the prophecy of Isaiah:

> Wherefore hear the word of the Lord, ye scornful men, that rule this people which is in Jerusalem. Because ye have said, we have made a covenant with death, and with hell are we at agreement. Your covenant with death shall be disannulled, and your agreement with hell shall not stand; when the overflowing scrouge shall pass through, then ye shall be trodden down by it.

Outside of abolitionists, there were few whites who placed any stock in the prophecy until expediency and moral concerns led to the formation of the nation's first antislavery political parties.

With a passion born of denial, blacks struggled consistently to obtain the right to hold office as a means of gaining freedom and equality in American society. Whites just as consistently denied blacks the right to vote or to hold office in order to guarantee the economic and social subordination of Afro-Americans. Free Negroes before the Civil War and blacks after emancipation believed, however, that the franchise held the key to gaining true citizenship. Blacks wanted political power because they believed it would end racial discrimination and ultimately result in improved economic and social conditions in the black community. Beyond the usual rewards of political action in a democratic system—patronage, influence on domestic and foreign policy, and access to decision makers—they expected better jobs, better education, and ultimately equal status with whites in the society. They believed political participation would free white Americans from bondage to the practices of racism and inequality and would liberate blacks from their oppression.

Throughout most of American history the efforts to gain some of the traditional rewards from political participation failed, with some major exceptions—Reconstruction after the Civil War, machine politics in Chicago in the twentieth century, the post-1965 period in the South, and the election of Jimmy Carter to the presidency in 1976. But when the exceptions arose, blacks saw that the rewards of political participation had limits. They saw that voting and holding office alone could lead to the end of overt racial discrimination but did not solve the social and economic problems facing the black community. The legacy of slavery and racism required more radical solutions than the normal business of politics. Protest was perceived as an essential element. But before this truth became evident, blacks had to win the battle to participate in politics.

POLITICAL PARTICIPATION BEFORE THE CIVIL WAR

The masses of black people were slaves who were not permitted to participate in American politics in the period before slavery's abolition, the enactment of the Reconstruction Act of March, 1867, and the Fifteenth Amendment. Free Negroes before the Civil War believed political participation would provide the leverage for ending their unequal status. But by 1830, free Negroes had been excluded from voting state by state. They had little political influence.

The political powerlessness of the free blacks led to numerous systematic attempts to win or regain the franchise. Despite overwhelming and repeated rejections of their claims by white voters, judges, and legislators, the free blacks persisted. Elaborating their political philosophy in petitions, periodicals, and state and national conventions, the free Negroes demonstrated their deeply held belief in the redemptive power of the ballot. In Rhode Island, free Negroes petitioned in 1831 for full voting rights or an exemption from taxes, and the 1834 Negro National Convention proposed a committee to investigate voting rights in the various states. In August, 1840, the New York State Convention of Colored Men met in Albany and resolved that the absence of respect for Negroes stemmed "from the want of the elective franchise." The New York *Colored American* of October 10 that same year insisted that the "possession of political rights," was the essential power needed to destroy caste. "The reason the colored population of this country are not socially and morally elevated is because they are almost universally, as they ever have been, disarmed of this power for their own, and the good of others. . . ."

The Pennsylvania decision to disfranchise blacks in 1838 stirred new efforts on the part of free Negroes to gain the vote. In the fall elections of 1837, Bucks County Democrats had been defeated, they claimed, by black votes. The Democrats obtained a county court decision that blacks were not "freemen" as defined by the 1790 Constitution and therefore could no longer vote. The second session of the state constitutional convention incorporated this ruling into the state constitution. Blacks responded by campaigning unsuccessfully against ratification of the new constitution through "an appeal of forty thousand citizens threatened with disfranchisement to the people of Pennsylvania." The Pennsylvania developments alarmed New York blacks, who expanded the suffrage campaign started earlier by Henry Highland Garnet and Charles Reason. The target of the campaign was the provision in New York's constitution permitting blacks to vote only if they could prove they held at least $250 worth of property. Since white voters did not have to meet a property requirement, blacks appealed to the legislature to repeal the discriminatory constitutional provisions. In county and state meetings blacks passed condemnatory resolutions, wrote addresses to white voters and state officials, and drafted petitions demanding an unrestricted ballot.

After the Albany convention, Garnet and others repeatedly pressed their petitions for suffrage before the New York legislature. They failed each time. The repeated defeats when the issue was put to a vote, according to Frederick Douglass, resulted from "unmitigated pride and prejudice"; whites intended to continue to "depress and degrade" blacks. In Pennsylvania and Connecticut repeated efforts to obtain the vote could not overcome white prejudice. Rhode Island blacks, however, took advantage of the revolt by Thomas Dorr and his followers in 1841 to gain the vote. The Dorrites demanded universal manhood suffrage, but for whites only. Blacks openly supported the conservative government and volunteered to fight when violence was threatened. The anti-Dorrite constitutional convention eliminated all restrictions on the franchise in 1842.

Blacks lost the right to vote in most northern states in the years prior to the Civil War. In New Jersey they were disfranchised in 1844. In the Northwest Territory states, black laws denied them the vote. As new western states came into the Union, black suffrage was prohibited. By the time of the Civil War, except in five New England states, blacks either could not vote or, as in New York, had to meet special qualifications. Despite their struggles, nowhere had blacks gained the vote, except in Rhode Island. In New York and northern and central New England, where some blacks could vote, their numbers were too small to be politically significant.

Although their small numbers reduced the political influence they had at the polls, free Negroes clearly recognized that they had to establish their right to vote if they were ever to improve their unequal status. They were left out of a political process which was of enormous interest to the general public. Unlike the twentieth century, mass participation in politics was pronounced in the antebellum period. Voter turnouts ran as high as 84 percent for the North in 1860, for example. Local political rallies in 1856 easily mobilized from 20,000 to 50,000 persons. Politics was, in part, mass entertainment, and leading politi-

cians served as a focus for popular interests, aspirations, and values.
Politics was both fun and a serious business from which blacks were
largely excluded.

In pressing for suffrage in the 1840s, blacks were caught up in the
general debate in abolitionist circles over whether slavery should be
attacked by organizing an antislavery party, by moral suasion, or by
noninvolvement in politics. Most blacks supported the political action
group among the abolitionists.

Denied their natural, God-given rights, and perceiving themselves
as descendants of men who had fought and died in the American
Revolution, blacks held firmly to the view that the Declaration of Independence and the Constitution guaranteed their citizenship. Any laws
denying them the right to vote were negated by God's laws. Disfranchisement, blacks contended, was immoral, undemocratic, and tyrannical. It subjected blacks to taxation without representation. Believing
with the abolitionists that "politics rightly conducted are properly a
branch of morals," blacks tried to convince American whites to vote
for men of principles, free the slaves, enfranchise blacks, and to see
clearly the distinction between political and social equality.

White politicians and voters were not convinced by the appeals
of blacks. When, for example, the Liberty Party ran on a platform
calling for the abolition of slavery in 1840, its presidential candidate
James G. Birney only received a total of 7,000 votes out of the 2,500,000
cast. Running on the Free Soil ticket in 1848, former President Martin
Van Buren received only 14 percent of the votes cast in the North.
Given a choice between an antislavery or a proslavery presidential
candidate, whites consistently voted for the proslavery one. In fact,
between 1789 and 1852, southern slaveholders held a virtual monopoly
on the White House.

The bleakness of the antebellum political horizon was relieved for
blacks with the rise of the Republican party, the nomination of John
C. Frémont as its first presidential candidate in 1856, and the adoption
of its heavily symbolic slogan, "Free Speech, Free Press, Free Men,
Free Labor, Free Territory and Frémont." Despite its large reservoir
of antislavery sentiment, the Republican party initially had a very limited conception of the citizenship rights of blacks. Even so, the Republicans were considerably more sympathetic to Afro-Americans than were
the Democrats. Their differences appear in sharp relief in the words
of two Illinois politicians, Democrat Stephen A. Douglas and Republican Abraham Lincoln.

Basing his assessment partially on the Declaration of Independence,
Lincoln opposed the Dred Scott decision in 1857 and urged his fellow
Republicans to preach "with whatever ability they can, that the negro

is a man; that his bondage is cruelly wrong, and that the field of his oppression ought not to be enlarged." Unlike Lincoln, Stephen Douglas did not believe slavery was a moral issue. Supporting the Dred Scott decision and insisting repeatedly that the Negro was an "inferior being," Senator Douglas asserted in 1858 that

> I believe that this government of ours was founded, and wisely founded, upon the white basis. It was made by white men, for the benefit of white men and their posterity, to be executed and managed by white men. . . . I am utterly opposed to any amalgamation on this contingent. . . . The Negro is not a citizen, cannot be a citizen, and ought not to be a citizen.

CIVIL WAR DEVELOPMENTS

On the eve of the Civil War, blacks confronted a Democratic party that denied rights of any kind to Negroes, slave or free, and a Republican party that denied them all political rights. Republican leaders asserted that free Negroes were human beings with civil rights to life, liberty, and property, but without the right to participate in politics. Women, children, unnaturalized foreigners, and Negroes had natural rights but not political rights. Even the Republican position was unacceptable to H. Ford Douglass, a runaway slave and an abolitionist orator, who told a Massachusetts audience in July, 1860, that no party deserved their votes "unless that party is willing to extend to the black man all the rights of a citizen." But other blacks, like Frederick Douglass and John Rock, supported the Republicans, and black conventions throughout the North endorsed Republican candidates. When choosing between the Republicans and Democrats, the Republicans were the only logical alternative.

When the Civil War started, free blacks believed that general abolition would be one step on the road to political and civil rights. They also knew that enlisting blacks into the military service was the fastest route to abolition. They encouraged the enlistment of blacks in the service and exerted every effort to convert what began as a war to save the Union into a war to free the slaves. They urged the War Department to accept black troops and organized volunteer black regiments in their own states. As the war continued and a great movement of slaves away from their masters ensued, they opposed any effort to solve the black problem short of abolition.

Free Negroes disagreed with most of Lincoln's early plans for the disposition of blacks, including his plan for compensated emancipation and colonization elsewhere. A joint resolution of April 10, 1862, provided that the United States would cooperate with any state adopting a plan of gradual emancipation together with satisfactory compensation for the owners. A law passed in April, 1862, provided for the emancipation of slaves in the District of Columbia, with compensation not in excess of $300 paid to the owner of each slave. The law provided $100,000 to support voluntary emigration of freedmen to Haiti and Liberia. Lincoln called a prominent group of free blacks to the White House in August, 1862, and urged them to support colonization, and he instructed the State Department to inquire if various South American and African governments would be willing to accept blacks. Two places were regarded favorably by Lincoln: Panama and the Isle à Vache in the Caribbean. But most blacks knew that the Civil War offered the best opportunity for gaining equality in America. They continued to oppose colonization and, in fact, denounced such suggestions as stridently as they had earlier proposals. As Isaiah Wears, a prominent black Philadelphian, asserted, "To be asked, after so many years of oppression and wrong have been inflicted in a land and by a people who have been so largely enriched by the black man's toil, to pull up stakes in a civilized and Christian nation, and to go to an uncivilized and barbarous nation, simply to gratify an unnatural wicked prejudice emanating from slavery, is unreasonable and anti-Christian in the extreme."

Free blacks encouraged and supported Lincoln, however, in the antislavery aspects of his policy. They were thrilled when on June 19, 1862, he signed a bill abolishing slavery in the territories and on July 17 signed the Confiscation Act, setting free all slaves of disloyal masters who were found or fled into Union-held territory. As he prepared an Emancipation Proclamation to free all slaves in states in rebellion on January 1, 1863, antislavery delegations including blacks encouraged him to issue it. When Lincoln issued the proclamation on September 22, 1862, with a reminder of the availability of compensated emancipation and of the benefits of voluntary colonization, there was jubilation. The document was not all it could be, but it was a stride toward freedom and was eagerly embraced by blacks. As the *Christian Recorder*, official organ of the AME Church, announced, "It will be said that the President only makes provision for the emancipation of a *part* of an injured race, and that the Border states and certain parts of the rebel states are exempted from the relief offered to others by this most important document. We believe those who are not immediately liberated will be ultimately benefitted by this act, and that Congress will do something for those poor souls who will still remain in degradation. But we thank God and President Lincoln for what has been done, and take courage." The proclamation provided that "all persons held as slaves within any state, or designated part of the state, the people whereof shall be in rebellion against the United States, shall be then, thenceforward, and forever free." On December 31, 1862, blacks held watch meetings to see in not only the New Year but also emancipation. Emancipation, as Lincoln said, was "a fit and necessary war measure"; it helped to save the Union but it also had political consequences.

Black politicians worked to shape the politics of black people in the new atmosphere of freedom. They focused on general abolition and the enactment of measures giving some recognition of black citizenship during the war as a precondition for black political participation. The State Department issued a passport to Henry Highland Garnet in August, 1861, which stated that he was a "citizen of the United States." In response to a request as to whether a black could legitmately command a ship flying an American flag, since only citizens were permitted such commands, Attorney General Edward Bates advised Secretary of the Treasury Salmon P. Chase in 1862 that every free person born in the United States was "at the moment of birth prima facie a citizen." A measure providing for the acceptance of the testimony of black witnesses in federal courts was passed in 1864, and in March, 1865, a bill permitting blacks to carry the mails became national law. Congress admitted blacks to its visitors' galleries during the Civil War, public lectures at the Smithsonian Institution were opened to blacks for the first time, blacks were invited to public receptions at the White House, and in February, 1865, John Rock was admitted to the bar of the U.S. Supreme Court. But as Frederick Douglass said in December, 1863, "Our work will not be done until the colored man is admitted as a full member in good and regular standing in the American body politic."

In Louisiana, where Union victories came early, the suffrage question did not wait until the end of the war. Free men of color in New Orleans insisted on obtaining the right to vote as a condition of the restoration of Louisiana to the Union. They submitted a petition to President Lincoln in March, 1864, reminding the nation of their service in the War of 1812 and the Civil War and asking that "the right of suffrage may be extended not only to natives of Louisiana of African descent, but also to all others, whether born slave or free, especially those who have vindicated their right to vote by bearing arms, subject only to such qualifications as shall equally affect the white and colored citizens." In response, Lincoln wrote to Louisiana Governor Michael Hahn, "I barely suggest for your private consideration whether some of the colored people may not be let in as, for instance the very intelligent, and especially those who have fought gallantly in our ranks."

Northern free Negroes also actively pushed the suffrage issue. In October, 1864, 144 blacks from eighteen states, meeting in Syracuse, New York, in a National Convention of Colored Citizens of the United States, issued an address to the people of the United States, written by Frederick Douglass, which asserted, "We want the elective franchise in all the states now in the union, and the same in all such states as may come into the union hereafter. . . . The position of that right is the keystone to the arch of human liberty; and without that the whole may at any moment fall to the ground; while, with it, that liberty may stand forever. . . ."

POLITICAL POWER DURING RECONSTRUCTION

The leadership for blacks in their struggle for political power would come, at first, largely from that articulate class of leaders before the war led by Frederick Douglass, the most prominent black political leader until his death in 1895. These leaders understood that the true meaning of freedom was not automatically encompassed by the Thirteenth Amendment's declaration that neither slavery nor involuntary servitude shall exist in the United States. Slavery could be defined narrowly, and merely lifting the shackles could be enough; slavery could be defined broadly, and political enfranchisement might be one result of the amendment. But as the Nashville *Colored Tennessean* asserted in August, 1865, blacks expected whites to

> Deal with us justly. Tell us not that we will not work, when it was our toil that enriched the South. Talk not to us of a war of races, for that is to say you intend commencing to butcher us, whenever you can do so with impunity. All we want is the rights of men. Give us that and we shall not molest you. We do not intend leaving this country. No land can be fairer in our eyes, than the sunny one beneath whose skies we have lived. We were born here. Most of us will die here. We are Americans and prouder of the fact than ever. Deal justly with us. That's all we want. That we mean to have, come what may!

Despite the views of blacks, abolition was narrowly defined by southern whites, who enacted legislation designed to insure the continued exploitation of blacks as a permanent underclass. No southern state provided for black suffrage or office holding, and many of the same whites who were bulwarks of the Confederacy were picked to lead this new Old South. The Lincoln and Johnson plans of Reconstruction did not require black suffrage. The only national concession to the needs of blacks seemed to be a relief agency, the Freedmen's Bureau.

Douglass and other black leaders objected strongly to what they regarded as the reestablishment of slavery. Practical Republicans became concerned that their party could never grow and hold power with an unreconstructed Democratic party in control in the South. Northern industrialists were eager to exploit the cheap labor and markets of the South—to modernize the southern economy—and were not interested in the mere reestablishment of the old plantation system. By the time Congress met in December, 1865, it was ready to create a Joint Committee on Reconstruction to inquire into the condition of the southern states and to make recommendations for a new policy.

Two major pieces of legislation, the Freedmen's Bureau Extension Bill and the Civil Rights Act of 1866, were vetoed by President Andrew Johnson, who also condemned a proposed Fourteenth Amendment which provided for civil equality. The resulting fight between Johnson and Congress, including the overriding of his vetoes and the enactment of the Fourteenth Amendment, paved the way for congressional control of Reconstruction. Congress passed its own Reconstruction Act in 1867, disfranchising participants in the rebellion and enfranchising blacks, with elections held under the supervision of the Union Army. The beginning of congressional Reconstruction presented the opportunity for blacks to become elected political officials.

Congressional Reconstruction established martial law in the South and provided that, on the basis of universal male suffrage, a convention in each state was to draw up a new constitution acceptable to Congress. No state would be readmitted to the Union until it ratified the Fourteenth Amendment. Former rebels who could not take the iron-clad oath of allegiance were disfranchised after Congress overrode Johnson's veto of the legislation.

Each of the constitutional conventions called in the southern states had black members, but blacks were in a majority only in South Carolina and Louisiana. In most states, blacks constituted a small minority. In six states, native whites were in the majority. Some black members were slaves and others free, some were emigrants from the North, and many were veterans of the Union Army. The blacks who spoke in the conventions took a moderate conciliatory position toward white Confederates, even supporting their enfranchisement.

In South Carolina's constitutional convention the subject of political rights of former Confederates stimulated heated debate. True to their affection for the principles of the Declaration of Independence, blacks refused to vote to disfranchise whites. Black delegate R. C. DeLarge offered a resolution to petition Congress to remove all political disabilities from citizens of the state. Francis Cardozo thought this was an opportunity for blacks to show that "although our people have been oppressed and have every inducement to seek revenge, although deprived of education and learning," they could rise above "all selfishness and exhibit a Christian universality of spirit." The Charleston *Advocate* explained in May, 1867, that "in the great work of reconstruction we should scorn the idea of the white or black man's party. . . . All should be admitted to equal rights and privileges in church and state whatever may be their race or color. . . . we should all live together in peace and harmony. . . ."

The state constitutions approved by the Reconstruction conventions were much more progressive than the constitutions of antebellum days. They abolished property qualifications for voting and holding office; some abolished imprisonment for debt. Slavery was abolished formally in all constitutions, and some eliminated race distinctions in real property law. In every constitution universal male suffrage was enacted, except for certain classes of former Confederates. Public school systems and modernized local government administrative machinery were also included. These constitutions were apparently so highly regarded that even when Reconstruction was overthrown by white supremacists, their basic provisions were maintained.

During congressional Reconstruction, blacks obtained the traditional fruits of political participation. They held public office and wielded some political power and influence in each state, although they were never in control in any, even where they constituted a majority of the population. In South Carolina whites always had a majority in the senate and there was always a white governor, but there were eighty-seven blacks and forty whites in the first legislature. There were two black lieutenant governors, Alonzo J. Ransier in 1870 and Richard Gleaves in 1872, and two black speakers of the house, Samuel J. Lee in 1872 and Robert B. Elliott in 1874. Francis L. Cardozo, who had been educated at the University of Glasgow, was secretary of state from 1868 to 1872 and treasurer from 1872 to 1876.

In Louisiana between 1868 and 1896, there were 133 black members of the legislature, 38 senators, and 95 representatives. Most who served between 1868 and 1877 were veterans of the Union Army and educated free men of color before the war. But some were former slaves. John W. Menard was elected to Congress but denied a seat. Oscar Dunn, P. B. S. Pinchback, and C. C. Antoine served as lieutenant governors. Pinchback was acting governor for forty-three days in 1873 when Governor Henry C. Warmoth was impeached.

In national politics between 1869 and 1901, two blacks served in the U.S. Senate and twenty in the House of Representatives. The two senators were Hiram R. Revels and Blanche K. Bruce, both of whom represented Mississippi. Revels was born free in North Carolina in

1822. He migrated to Indiana, Ohio, and Illinois, receiving his education at a Quaker seminary in Indiana, a black seminary in Ohio, and Knox College in Illinois. While living in Illinois, he was ordained a minister in the AME Church at Baltimore in 1845. Revels was in Baltimore when the Civil War began and assisted in organizing the first two Maryland black regmients. In 1863 he moved to St. Louis, founded a school for freedmen, and helped recruit a black regiment there. He went to Vicksburg, Mississippi, in 1864 to work with the Freedmen's Bureau provost marshal in managing the affairs of freedmen. Revels also served as pastor of the Bethel AME Church in Vicksburg. He was elected as a compromise candidate to the state senate in 1869 and was elected by the state senate to fill the seat previously occupied by Jefferson Davis in the U.S. Senate. He served one year in the Senate in 1870, during which he supported the removal of all political disabilities from former Confederates, appointed a black to West Point, and obtained the admission of black mechanics to work in the U.S. Navy Yard. At the end of his term, Revels became president of Alcorn A & M University, established as a segregated institution of higher education for blacks.

Blanche K. Bruce, elected to the U.S. Senate in 1874, was the only black who served a full term in the Senate until the election of Edward Brooke from Massachusetts in 1966. Unlike Revels, Bruce was born a slave in Virginia. He escaped from his master in St. Louis when the Civil War came. He studied for several years and in 1869 went to Mississippi, where he entered politics. He served as tax collector, sheriff, and superintendent of schools. In the Senate he took an interest in both race-related matters and matters of general interest. He spoke in support of P. B. S. Pinchback when Pinchback was denied a seat in the Senate in a contest over irregularities in his election. He worked diligently with the Manufactures, Education, and Labor Committee and the Pensions Committee and chaired a committee that conducted a careful investigation into the causes for failure of the Freedmen's Bank.

The first of the twenty blacks to serve in the U.S. House of Representatives were seated in 1869. There were eight from South Carolina, four from North Carolina, three from Alabama, and one each from Georgia, Mississippi, Florida, Louisiana, and Virginia. James H. Rainey and Robert Smalls, both of South Carolina, each served five consecutive terms. John R. Lynch of Mississippi and J. T. Walls of Florida both served three terms. Their activities in Congress did not differ substantially from those of white congressmen. Most of them had served in some state political capacity before being elected to the House. They fought for such local issues as rivers and harbors legislation, as well as civil rights and education measures. Overall, ten of the blacks who served in Congress between 1869 and 1900 were drawn from the old free Negro caste. On the local level, 43 of the 102 who held office in Virginia between 1867 and 1890 had been free before the war. Of the 59 black delegates in the 1868 South Carolina constitutional convention, at least 18 were former free Negroes; another 14 had been born free in other parts of the nation. All but 20 of the 111 black delegates to the Louisiana Republican Convention in 1865 were freeborn. But the most influential and successful black Reconstruction politician in South Carolina, Robert Smalls, was born and lived out his antebellum life as a slave, and Oscar Dunn, a former Louisiana slave, was as significant a figure in politics as P. B. S. Pinchback.

Most blacks who were influential during Reconstruction had been urban slaves, blacksmiths, carpenters, clerks, or waiters in hotels and boarding houses. A few of them had been favored body servants of influential whites. Some had been preachers, lawyers, or teachers in the free states or in Canada. Others were self-educated free men like Robert Carlos DeLarge, the tailor from Charleston who was the best parliamentarian in the South Carolina convention. P. B. S. Pinchback had only a common school education, and Oscar James Dunn was a plasterer.

Black politicians learned a very significant lesson during Reconstruction: the limits of coalition politics and the limits of the officeholders they elected. Northern politicians who enacted Reconstruction measures wanted black participation in the state governments but not black control. They wanted reform but not an economic revolution. They were not prepared to sanction the expropriation of white-owned property in order to give property to blacks. Northerners wanted middle-class, white-dominated governments operated on business principles, not an overthrow of capitalism and white control. Generally, black politicians were in accord with these views. Some, such as James T. Rapier of Alabama, were separated from the black masses by their own interests. Others, such as Francis Cardozo, who kept reminding his colleagues of the necessity of not "impairing the obligations of contracts," were prisoners of their own education. Men such as Beverly Nash of South Carolina spoke eloquently in the defense of voting and officeholding privileges for the very Confederates who were at that moment preparing for the destruction of blacks who dared participate in the political process.

There were dissenters from the black political strategy of coalition politics. The Pure Radicals in Louisiana urged blacks to take power into their own hands. But forty-six-year-old Oscar James Dunn, a former slave who managed to manipulate power for the Pure Radicals for three years as lieutenant governor, died a month before a crucial effort to impeach the incumbent governor in November, 1871.

THE OVERTHROW OF RECONSTRUCTION

By the time Reconstruction was overthrown completely in 1877, blacks had voted, held office, and wielded some influence in the political system. In addition, the Fourteenth and Fifteenth Amendments gave permanent legal recognition to black citizenship and outlawed denial of the right to vote for racial reasons. But the continued enfranchisement of whites meant that if they could by force or fraud prevent blacks from voting in opposition to them, they would regain power. The Republican party discovered that it could maintain power in national affairs even while letting the Democrats regain power in the South. Through duplicity, bloodshed, riot, and murder, whites forced blacks out of the political arena while the national government acquiesced. Reconstruction unraveled even as it began; by 1877 it was at an end.

The three enforcement acts passed by Congress in 1870–71, under the authority of the Fifteenth Amendment, seemed to ensure protection for blacks in the enjoyment of their political rights. The laws provided for extensive enforcement machinery, including authority for the president to call out the Army and Navy and to suspend the writ of habeas corpus if necessary. The acts permitted states to restrict suffrage on any basis except race or color. But between 1870 and 1896, when the bulk of this legislation was repealed, 7,372 cases were tried and hundreds of offenders, who were never brought to trial, were arrested. Despite this pre-1896 activity, the disfranchisement of blacks proceeded successfully. After 1874, enforcement efforts gradually declined altogether. The white South remained opposed, the white North was not interested, and the Supreme Court soon decided that most of the federal efforts to punish individual violations of voting rights were unconstitutional. Local officials arrested and punished blacks, who complained to harassed federal officials. The few federal troops who were stationed in the South were not used to enforce the law. Additionally, Congress failed to provide adequate funds to finance the federal courts and officials refused to undertake serious enforcement. Many federal officials disagreed with the effort and were not willing to attempt enforcement. The protection of black voting rights in the South was not a national priority.

As the federal government continued to ignore white terrorism in the South, blacks spoke out against the perfidy of the Republican party. The *Colored Citizen* of Fort Scott, Kansas, in October, 1878, said, "The Democrats of the South are determined that the colored voters shall either be Democrats or not vote at all." T. Thomas Fortune in the New York *Globe* in October, 1883, expressed the view that "we have the ballot without any law to protect us in the enjoyment of it. . . . The Democratic Party is a fraud—a narrowminded, corrupt, bloody fraud; the Republican Party has grown to be little better."

Political participation by blacks became increasingly fraught with dangerous consequences. A variety of so-called legal measures, including gerrymandering, poll tax requirements, and elaborate election procedures, applied in fact only to blacks, were instituted to keep most blacks permanently disfranchised. By 1889, blacks had been practically eliminated from Southern politics. Rather than a temporary setback, the overthrow of Reconstruction marked a long-term withdrawal from political power.

BLACK RECONSTRUCTION FAILS IN SOUTH CAROLINA

A closer look at the Reconstruction experiences of blacks and their political leadership in South Carolina provides an example of the successes and failures of political participation. If black political participation during Reconstruction could succeed at all in improving social and economic conditions for blacks, it should have succeeded in South Carolina. Blacks were a distinct majority of the population and their political leadership was stronger in both numbers and influence than in any other state, but they were not able to maintain political power. As Thomas Holt explains in his *Black Over White, Negro Political Leadership in South Carolina During Reconstruction,* one reason for the failure lay in the origins of black leadership. Divisions between the freeborn mulatto *petit bourgeoisie* and slave-born blacks and mulattoes emerged quickly in the leadership group. Out of a total of 255 Negroes elected to state and federal offices between 1868 and 1876, one in four had been free before the war and one of every three was a mulatto. Almost one in three owned some real estate, and 46 percent possessed some form of wealth, real or personal. One-fifth had combined property holdings in excess of $1,000; 11 percent had more than $1,000 in real property alone. Only 15 percent had no property at all. Sixty-five percent were literate, and 10 percent were professionally or college trained. Ministers and teachers predominated among the professionals, but ten of these lawmakers were or became lawyers during their terms of office. Those engaged in agriculture were the next largest group, and more of these appear to have been landowners than field hands.

Although it might appear that intraracial color prejudices between mulattoes and blacks were the basis for the divisions which inhibited political power, the divisions were in fact due to class differences. The free Negro class before the war, although hedged about with restrictions, was in a better economic position than was the slave class. Free Negroes were wealthier, better educated, and in many ways better prepared for political competition than were slaves. Slaves manumitted before the war were often provided with cattle, land, or other property, and many of them were the mulatto products of unions between white planters and slave women. Therefore, those with greater resources happened to be mulattoes, and some of the hostility between blacks and mulattoes resulted from their different class positions. Many of the black leaders freed during the war had served in the Army and had acquired enough financial resources to gain economic ground on the old free Negro class. In any event, all black legislators of whatever color had a constituency consisting largely of illiterate ex-slaves, upon whom they relied for continued power and who expected some improvement in their condition in return for bestowing that power.

Another significant factor which prevented the exercise of black power was the way in which blacks became politicians. The new politicians, black and white, were novices, but blacks had absolutely no experience in partisan politics. Most of the antebellum history of blacks had been spent trying to gain access to politics. The Freedmen's Bureau, the Army, and the missionary societies and churches provided whatever political experience they had gained in establishing a constituency. What these three institutions provided was a job, an opportunity for developing leadership qualities, and a pattern of public contacts, but these opportunities fell far short of the kind of local experience required for quick, effective action as a state or national political official.

These particular black officials were not able to convert a base of 60 percent of the population into political control in South Carolina. The population base was quickly converted into a majority in the legislature and control of the offices of secretary of state, lieutenant governor, adjutant general, secretary of the treasury, speaker of the house, and president pro tem of the state senate. But blacks never held the offices of governor, U.S. senator, comptroller general, attorney general, and superintendent of education, or more than one of the three positions on the state supreme court. In the legislature blacks were very successful in controlling some of the key committees in the general assembly until 1874. When it came to executive branch appointments, however, blacks early adopted the policy of supporting whites, because they had real or presumed contacts in the North and because of the urgings of their northern white supporters. This was one reason why black leaders never even considered pushing a black for governor, a position that required contacts with northern centers of power. "We don't want a colored Governor," Martin Delany insisted in the June 25, 1870, *Daily Republican.* "Our good sense tells us differently."

Not until the spring of 1870 did blacks in South Carolina fully realize that they had to have a larger portion of the appointed positions and of those elected by the legislature before they could develop a strong political organization. The *Daily Republican* reported on June 24, 1870, that Robert DeLarge had announced at a celebration in Charleston that blacks were thankful to the Republican party, but "some impudent scoundrels in the party now say, 'You want too much; you want everything.' We placed them in position, we elected them and by our votes we made them our masters. We now propose to change this thing a little, and let them vote for us." He was followed by Alonzo Ransier and Martin Delany, who expressed their support for this new approach. The result was an increase in political offices for blacks.

The failure to control the governorship was a significant problem for blacks. The governor appointed most local officeholders, including county treasurer, auditor, jury commissioner, and trial justices. The economic insecurity of many Republicans, which led even professional men to need part-time political appointments, increased the power of the governor. Even local newspapers, dependent on contracts to publish laws and governmental announcements, could be manipulated by the governor.

Although blacks normally dominated the apparatus for running the election campaigns, their control was tenuous. The largely black state central committee, the party convention, the county chairmen, and the union leagues organized the freedmen. The party central committee was responsible for raising and distributing campaign funds. But when black leaders ignored the policy of not electing blacks to conspicuously high offices and elected a black chairman to the state central committee, an agent of the Republican National Committee who was in South Carolina in 1868 simply advised the national party to bypass the central committee. The funds should instead be sent directly to the four congressional district campaign committees.

Federal patronage for local offices was controlled by the senior U.S. Senator and the local Congressman. The collector of the port of Charleston was the most important post, because the collector could hire a number of workers. Blacks were never able to gain control of the custom house patronage, because no black was ever elected Senator. Overall, blacks failed to control another avenue for developing a political machine and lost one of the most important traditional fruits of political participation.

On issues that could have crippled their white opponents, black members of the legislature showed a lack of resolve. They rejected confiscation of land and redistribution to the freedmen. They also withheld support from a measure that would have used tax collection as a measure for ending white control of land, even though Richard H. Cain explained that if the large landowners "are obliged to sell their lands the poor man will have a chance to buy."

The weaknesses of origins, interests, experience, and reliance on northern Republicans created conditions in which the Republicans and blacks lost power to the Democrats in South Carolina in 1876. President Rutherford B. Hayes' decision to withdraw federal troops in April, 1877, merely ratified a result that had already taken place. The Democrats had, through violence, intimidation, and the aid of certain Republicans including the governor, undermined the Reconstruction regime and taken control of the state. The Republicans' division over legislative policy and patronage was the very ingredient needed to consolidate political power. Daniel Chamberlain, elected Republican governor in 1874, consciously adopted a policy of destroying existing Republican alliances and forming a Democratic-Republican coalition which he could control. Chamberlain asserted that he was merely bent on decreasing corruption in government. Even so, the cuts in programs and budgets made by Chamberlain undermined Republican political support and his insistence on appointing Democrats to many local offices further destroyed the party. Chamberlain became the darling of the Democrats.

In July, 1876, the Hamburg massacre of a black militia company during an attack by whites on a barracks in which the militia was barricaded ushered in more violence and marked the end of Republican rule in South Carolina. Wade Hampton was the Democratic gubernatorial candidate and his militia, called the "Red Shirts," forced Republican officials to resign their offices and took over effective control of local government. In a similar situation in 1870, Governor Robert K. Scott had mobilized the black militia long enough to carry the election. But under Chamberlain's policies, the militia, a constant irritant to whites, had been unused and practically disarmed. Indeed, there is some evidence that the white clubs obtained guns from the state arsenal. By the time the disputed election was settled in favor of Hampton and federal troops were removed, the result was a foregone conclusion.

It can be argued that greater unity among the Republicans would have prevented the overthrow of Reconstruction. The preconditions for such unity at that time, however, are difficult to find. To expect more experienced black politicians is a self-evident contradiction, and to expect stronger northern white support of black control of politics is to expect more radical views than even the most radical Republicans then espoused. Not only did black politicians fail significantly to improve the conditions of their black constituency, they did not even receive all of the patronage and influence that are the usual concomitants of political power. However, given the general inexperience of black politicians, the perfidy of white Republicans like Chamberlain in the South, and the unwillingness of northern Republicans to support black control, it is phenomenal that blacks were as successful as they were.

POST-RECONSTRUCTION DECLINE IN POLITICAL PARTICIPATION

Once Reconstruction was over and black voters were largely driven from politics in the South, their absence exacerbated the problem of class divisions among white voters. In the 1880s depressed economic conditions for poor farmers led them to join radical agrarian organizations. The Southern Farmers' Alliance of whites was joined by a Colored Farmers' National Alliance and Cooperation Union in 1886. Radical leaders such as Tom Watson in Georgia began preaching solidarity for poor black and white farmers. The Populist party tried in 1892 to protect blacks in the exercise of the franchise, to insure equal application of voting procedures, and to gain the black vote. The Democrats retaliated first by trying and failing to make an alliance with the Populists and then by forcing blacks who worked for them to vote Democratic. The Democrats also resorted to riots and murder.

Facing such violence, Populists and Republicans gained control of the North Carolina legislature in 1894, and blacks were able to vote and hold office in the eastern black belt of the state. Blacks served as deputy sheriffs, policemen, and aldermen. This resurgence of black power was temporary. Democrats complained that even when they controlled black voters, this made for corruption in politics. The Populists feared that they would not always be able to control blacks if blacks were permitted to behave as allies, and they equally feared Democratic control of black voters and efforts to disfranchise poor whites. Even Tom Watson supported a constitutional amendment excluding blacks from the franchise. Poor whites, the planter class, and industrialists joined in forcing blacks out of the political arena in the 1890s. State after state formally disfranchised blacks by the discriminatory use of "reading and understanding clauses," by writing rigid educational and property tests into their constitutions, and by enacting "grandfather clauses" which enfranchised only those whose fathers and grandfathers were qualified to vote on January 1, 1867—that is, whites only. The disfranchisement of blacks was regarded by whites as necessary. White Democratic primaries and legalized racial segregation became the rule. The last black member of Congress in the nineteenth century, George H. White of North Carolina, was elected in 1896. Not until the 1960s would black political participation again become a significant factor in southern politics.

Despite the disfranchisement of blacks in the South, a few blacks were appointed to "Negro jobs" in the government in exchange for their support of the Republican party in national nominating conventions. Frederick Douglass, for example, was appointed marshal of the District of Columbia (1877), recorder of deeds (1881), and minister to Haiti (1889–91). Attempted black rebellion against the legal structure which resulted in political powerlessness and Jim Crow rule was quickly suppressed, with military force when necessary. Black organizations such as the Afro-American League and the Niagara Movement, which drew their membership from leading black newspapermen, ministers, educators, and former politicians, protested against this continued oppression, but the white majority did not regard alleviating the plight of blacks as a high-priority.

Most blacks who clung to the hope of political participation as a solution to racial discrimination and as a route to equal social and economic opportunity continued to support the party of Lincoln, the Republicans, between 1877 and the New Deal. As a group of Wisconsin blacks said in 1892, they knew the Republicans did not protect them but they were "yet unfailing in their devotion to this party and its principles." There was, essentially, no place else to go. Some Republicans continued to believe that the party had something to gain from the large black population that lived in the South until the turn of the century, but the party, in fact, did very little to enable blacks to vote. In every presidential election in the late nineteenth century, the GOP platform reiterated the wrongs of the defeated South and Republican support for ending the oppression of blacks. But these rhetorical flourishes, along with the "Negro jobs" in the government, were about all the Republicans were willing to do. In 1890 the House of Representatives passed its last serious effort to legislate protection of voting rights—the Lodge Federal Elections Bill. The measure was, however, abandoned in the Senate by the Republicans, who wished to gain Democratic support for high tariff and silver legislation. Southern black Republicans could exercise influence only in the national nominating conventions, when they were permitted to become delegates, which depended upon their support for the preferred candidate, usually the incumbent.

BOOKER T. WASHINGTON'S INFLUENCE

Blacks who had so eagerly rushed to vote in the elections during Reconstruction soon developed habits of nonparticipation in its aftermath. In states where blacks could vote and where they existed in sufficient numbers, black political participation achieved some limited results. In the northern states, after the Supreme Court declared the Civil Rights Act of 1875 unconstitutional in 1883, blacks succeeded in obtaining the passage of state civil rights laws. But most blacks were in the South, and it was in the South that their efforts to vote were extinguished. The government in Washington, D.C., seemed very distant and no longer interested in their plight. There were few opportunities to develop a tradition of voting and amassing other political resources such as income, wealth, status, knowledge, and military prowess. Schools for black children in the South taught the basic symbols and rituals of the nation, including loyalty, but they were poor places to learn the role of political participant. This situation was one in which Booker T. Washington, who said he did not believe in political involvement, could practice his particular brand of politics. His politics included loyalty to the nation, a belief that blacks were passive figures who were inactive in political affairs and for whom such affairs had little importance.

Washington believed that political rights for blacks could be obtained only after wealth and hard work had gained the respect of whites and that political rights were not a precondition for economic advancement. Washington's reputation grew until he became the power broker between blacks and whites. His position with whites was threatened temporarily when they learned that he had accepted an invitation to have dinner at the White House with President Theodore Roosevelt. Washington was, however, ensconced solidly as the black patronage dispenser. Any black who wanted a federal appointment had to obtain his stamp of approval.

Washington's influence was obvious. President William McKinley spoke at Tuskegee Institute in 1898 during a visit scheduled for the purpose of addressing the Alabama legislature. President Theodore Roosevelt openly relied on Washington's advice in appointing both blacks and whites to southern posts. He wrote to a friend in 1903 that his black appointees "were all recommended to me by Booker T. Washington." Washington's influence, however, seemed to result overall in only a small number of black appointees. Roosevelt appointed T. Thomas Fortune, editor of the New York *Age*, to a special commission to investigate conditions in U.S. insular possessions. He also selected William Henry Lewis, a graduate of the Harvard Law School, to be assistant U.S. attorney for Massachusetts. When Theodore Roosevelt, on one of his southern tours in the fall of 1905, spoke at Tuskegee, he echoed Booker T. Washington's philosophy of self-help and emphasized the duty of blacks to make war against all crime, especially that committed by other blacks.

Booker T. Washington enjoyed the same close relationship with Roosevelt's successor, President William Howard Taft. He helped Taft persuade Dr. William D. Crum, whose appointment as collector of customs at Charleston in 1903 had been opposed by whites and had never been permanently confirmed by the Senate, to resign in March, 1909. Upon Washington's advice, Taft appointed Whitefield McKinlay collector of customs for Georgetown, D.C., in 1910 and promoted William H. Lewis to be Assistant Attorney General in March, 1911, the highest post held by a black to that date.

Washington, a complex personality, covertly supported efforts to prevent disfranchisement while espousing his public philosophy of economics first, politics second. He provided financial support for court cases attacking disfranchisement provisions in Louisiana's constitution. He contributed money to the political cause in Alabama and Maryland. In 1903 and 1904 he "spent at least four thousand dollars in cash, out of my own pocket . . . in advancing the rights of the black man." He believed it was best to keep these activities secret in order to maintain the confidence of whites in his leadership role, but he made sure that his behind-the-scenes activities were known by black leaders. Washington wanted to keep the support of blacks while he maintained the confidence of whites, so that he could be unchallenged leader of the black community in all quarters. His behavior was consistent in that he wanted to mitigate legal discrimination if he could but did not believe it would end until economic self-sufficiency and black assimilation to white standards had been achieved.

Some black spokesmen and organizations, in the spirit of the antebellum convention movement, still pushed for the right to vote. They continued to believe that political power was necessary for economic and social advancement and for ending racial discrimination. It was not just that the black leaders had already achieved economic status and wanted political rights for themselves; they saw politics as a way for the masses of blacks to vote themselves into equality of economic opportunity. From opportunity would flow an improvement in status. They saw Washington as an "Uncle Tom" who sold their political rights in exchange for power for himself.

The convention movement soon became a vehicle for vocal opposition to Booker T. Washington. In 1890 three major conventions were held and in January, 1890, T. Thomas Fortune founded the Afro-American League in Chicago. Fortune, a native of Florida, came North to undertake a career as editor in 1880. He was the leading black journalist from the mid-1880s until he sold the New York *Age* to Fred R. Moore and Booker T. Washington in 1907.

In February, 1890, J. C. Price, the president of Livingstone College in Salisbury, North Carolina, who had just been elected vice president of the Afro-American League, chaired a convention in Washington, D.C., which organized a Citizens Equal Rights Association. Both groups were beset with internal rivalry and friction and became inactive. The Afro-American League, however, was resumed in 1898 as the Afro-American Council and met annually for ten years thereafter until its membership dispersed into the Niagara Movement and the National Association for the Advancement of Colored People (NAACP). Through these various groups the convention movement was extended from its antebellum origins.

Booker T. Washington soon gained control of the Afro-American Council, which therefore became "conservative in all of its actions" insofar as political rights were concerned. Washington worked aggressively behind the scenes, using money and influence to gain control of the council so that, by the 1902 convention, Washington's secretary, Emmett J. Scott, could say in truth, "We control the council now." But their control was short-lived. William Monroe Trotter, editor of the *Boston Guardian,* provided effective newspaper criticism of Washington's leadership. Other influential critics of Washington, including W. E. B. Du Bois, soon emerged openly. In the spring of 1903 Du Bois' *The Souls of Black Folk* appeared, including the essay on "Mr. Booker T. Washington and Others," which provided a rallying point for the opposition.

Blacks in leadership roles in this period emphasized political rights as a means of achieving an end to Jim Crow and lynching. They paid little attention to the economic issues that the black masses faced. Perhaps Booker T. Washington's insistence that economic advancement could be made in the absence of political rights led the advocates of political rights to insist the reverse: that political rights were supreme and that economic equality would result when the political cause was won. T. Thomas Fortune reiterated his 1887 position on the Negro in politics in December, 1905, in the *Colored American Magazine*— that blacks should be independent voters. If northern blacks voted without adhering specifically to a particular party, "the vast body of disfranchising and separation laws which now cumber the statute books of the Southern states would never have been adopted." He thought,

"In a democracy a citizen without a vote would have every other civil and political right denied him."

Despite Washington's "dirty tricks," including depriving critics of jobs, arranging to have some of them sued for libel, placing spies in their midst, and subsidizing the black press to prevent attacks on him, some of his critics formed the Niagara Movement in 1905. Their Declaration of Principles publicized the duty of blacks to engage in self-improvement efforts but indicated, "We believe in manhood suffrage and believe that no man is so good, intelligent or wealthy as to be entrusted wholly with the welfare of his neighbors." The movement, organized in response to a call issued by Du Bois to combat Washington's policy, successfully penetrated the Afro-American Council, which became by October, 1906, a protest voice against ballot restrictions, Jim Crow, and violence. Bishop Alexander Walters, who as president of the group in 1898 was preaching conciliation ("Let us improve our morals, educate ourselves, work, agitate and wait on the Lord") was asserting in 1906, "It is nonsense for us to say peace! peace! where there is no peace. . . . We use diplomatic language and all kinds of subterfuges; but the fact remains that the enemy is trying to keep us down and we are determined to rise or die in the attempt."

However, the victory of the Niagara Movement in taking over the Afro-American Council led to the decline of both. Washington effectively cut his opponents off from sources of support and publicity. But the black radicals took advantage of the support of a small group of prominent white progressives, who provided the backing for the founding of the NAACP in 1910. Oswald Garrison Villard, John Milholland, and other white progressives backed the organization of the NAACP, which had only one black official at first, W. E. B. Du Bois, who edited *Crisis,* but the membership was chiefly composed of educated blacks. Villard had long been friendly with Washington and had raised $150,000 for the Tuskegee endowment, but he believed more aggressive efforts were needed to advance the cause of blacks. He invited Washington to the conference that led to the founding of the NAACP, but Washington declined. With the beginning of the NAACP the torch of the convention movement had been effectively passed to an organization determined to gain black civil and political rights in the courts and in Congress.

SUPPORTING THE DEMOCRATIC PARTY

Blacks had threatened time and time again to become independent voters, which would mean abandoning the Republican party, but no viable alternative appeared. Some southern conservative blacks supported the Democratic party, and northern blacks sometimes advocated cooperation with them. The Populist movement resulted in large numbers of blacks voting Democratic as whites applied economic pressure, fraud, and intimidation. Sometimes the support was willingly given. During the 1880s and 1890s in the black counties of Mississippi and South Carolina, fusion—dividing offices between black Republicans and white Democrats, giving blacks a few legislative seats and unimportant local posts—was widely practiced. In Georgia, AME Bishop Henry M. Turner sided with the Cleveland Democrats in 1889 and was rewarded when Hoke Smith, Secretary of the Interior, appointed three of Turner's close relatives to office.

Some northern blacks supported the Democrats. Peter H. Clark, a high school principal in Cincinnati, supported them because, as he said in 1885, he did not think blacks should have their vote "concentrated in one party." They must indicate a willingness to be flexible on political issues. George Downing, one of the best-known black workers in the struggle for citizenship rights of the period, broke with the Republicans in 1883 because he wanted "more than one party anxious, concerned, and cherishing the hope that at least part of that vote may be obtained."

In 1883 President Chester Alan Arthur's policy of siding with white independents and southern liberal white Republicans caused considerable black dissatisfaction with the Republican party and renewed interest in the Democrats. At the 1883 Negro convention in Louisville, so much concern was expressed that Frederick Douglass defended the party's position but called himself "an uneasy Republican," saying, "If the Republican Party cannot stand the demand for justice and fair play it ought to go down." In Massachusetts, James M. Trotter repudiated the party and resigned his political appointment as assistant superintendent of the registered letter department in the Boston post office. Later President Grover Cleveland appointed him recorder of deeds for the District of Columbia. Massachusetts Democratic Governor Benjamin F. Butler, in return for a substantial black vote, appointed Harvard Law School graduate and former member of the state legislature George L. Ruffin judge of the Charleston City Court, the first black judge in the North.

There were sizeable groups of black Democrats in New York, Cleveland, and other cities, all advising a split of the black vote or independence of black voters as the best political policy. But by the early 1890s most of those who had joined the Democrats had returned to the Republican fold. George Downing had become critical of the Democrats by 1891. T. McCants Stewart, a Charlestonian, graduate of the

University of South Carolina and its law school during Reconstruction, and now a resident of New York, returned to the Republicans in 1895 after being frozen out of a job by objecting Democrats.

In the December, 1905, issue of the *Colored American Magazine*, T. Thomas Fortune argued that black voters were needed by the Republicans in the northern and western states, but since blacks always voted Republican they were taken for granted. Afro-American persistence got "nothing but crumbs from party success. A few offices of the lowest grade are here and there given to it, for the most part such offices as white partisans do not want. Afro-Americans have the strength of a giant and use it as a child."

J. Milton Waldron, Alexander Walters, and William Monroe Trotter supported the Democrats in 1908. In 1912 there was increasing discussion of the possibility of defection to the Progressive party or the Democrats. Woodrow Wilson met with Trotter and Waldron, and eventually a letter to Walters containing views conciliatory toward blacks but without specifics was circulated as Wilson's position on the race question.

W. E. B. Du Bois, then editor of *Crisis*, insisted in December, 1910, that blacks should vote, but independently: "No intelligent man should vote one way from habit." In August, 1912, he recommended Woodrow Wilson to the 500,000 blacks who could vote in the North. He asserted, "You could easily sell your votes for an Assistant Attorney General, a Register of the Treasury, a Recorder of Deeds, and a few other black wooden men whose duty it is to look pleasant, say nothing, and have no opinions that a white man is bound to respect. Do not do it." Blacks should ask for the abolition of interstate Jim Crow transportation, an end to peonage, the enforcement of the Fourteenth Amendment, "cutting down the representation in Congress of the rotten boroughs of the South," and national financial aid for all elementary public schools without regard to race. He knew Wilson was a southerner, but Taft was "utterly lacking in initiatives or ideals" and had done nothing on race issues. Wilson, "a cultured scholar," would do better "if he became President by grace of the black man's vote." The best choice was Eugene Debs, who "stands squarely on a platform of human rights regardless of race or class," but he could not be elected. Therefore, voting for Wilson was the best option. Many more blacks voted against the GOP, although there is controversy about the number of defectors.

As President, however, Wilson proved to be extremely hostile to black interests. He even expanded racial segregation among federal employees in several government departments, including the Bureau of Engraving and Printing, the Treasury Department, and the Post

Office. Strong and prolonged protests ensued, but Wilson, conferring with a delegation led by Trotter in November, 1914, defended segregation as in the best interest of both races and said it would continue. Wilson, in following the usual patronage policy, dismissed or accepted the resignations of black officeholders including William H. Lewis, but he only reluctantly appointed other blacks to office. He did reappoint Robert H. Terrell judge of the District of Columbia Municipal Court in February, 1914, and he appointed James J. Curtis as minister to Liberia in 1915. These were the only two black appointments made during his first term.

The experience with Wilson confirmed the unattractiveness of a Democratic alternative, but the election results in 1920 made the Republican option even worse. The Republicans picked up support in the border states, even carrying Tennessee. Party leaders, focusing on attracting southerners, made strong efforts to purge the party of the stigma of association with blacks. When Warren Harding was elected, James Weldon Johnson of the NAACP discussed the issues of disfranchisement, the Ku Klux Klan, lynching, and the necessity for black appointments with him, but it did not seem to have beneficial results. Harding, who was rumored to have black ancestry, knew little and cared less about the race question. For example, he had never heard of Tuskegee or Booker T. Washington. He finally did send a message to Congress asking them to outlaw lynching, but he never really pressed for the passage of such legislation, which would have been doubtful even with his support.

EFFORTS TO GAIN VOTING RIGHTS IN THE SOUTH

Black voters in the South continued to fight to gain the right to vote. Succeeding in having grandfather clauses outlawed in 1915, the NAACP carried the legal burden. In 1925 blacks united in making a test of the southern white primary law, beginning with Texas. The Supreme Court unanimously declared the white primary laws unconstitutional in March, 1927. Texas and other states responded by enacting new evasive legislation which was eventually declared illegal. Meanwhile, the black citizen in the South faced, as James Weldon Johnson described it in 1929, "the grim determination of the Southern politicians never to allow him to take part in politics—his education, economic progress and moral fitness, notwithstanding—and the specter of force, violence and murder lurks not far behind." Not only plebeian demagogues like Senators J. Thomas Heflin of Alabama and Cole Blease of South Carolina but such aristocratic statesmen as Senator Carter Glass of Virginia expressed the southern determination to disfranchise blacks. Glass was quoted as saying, "The people of the original thirteen Southern states curse and spit upon the Fifteenth Amendment—and have no intention of letting the Negro vote." Southerners obeyed the letter of the law, "but we frankly evade the spirit thereof—and propose to continue doing so. White supremacy is too precious a thing to surrender for the sake of a theoretical justice that would let a brutish African deem himself the equal of white men and women in Dixie."

ADJUSTMENTS AFTER THE NORTHERN MIGRATION

As black oppression and disfranchisement persisted in the South, large numbers of blacks migrated to the North after the turn of the century. Greater economic opportunity and the possibility of political participation seemed in the offing. But the opportunities to advance through politics were not as available as they seemed. When blacks migrated North they, like the earlier immigrants from Europe, were confronted with established political organizations. They had to compete for political power with other groups who still insisted on their share of the fruits. In return for votes, black newcomers, like groups before them, received political favors, material assistance, and low-paying jobs.

Blacks in the cities expressed strong interest in politics at the grass roots level. Very quickly a large number of associations and organizations, including the Urban League and the NAACP, evolved. But the issues the masses of blacks faced—discrimination in jobs, services, and housing, for example—did not dissipate even when blacks became an increasingly large portion of the electorate.

Blacks had to attempt to gain power in the cities within the context that already existed. If there was no white boss or white machine, there could be no black machine. In Chicago blacks gained the greatest immediate success because there was a machine. Blacks moved into a concentrated area of the city where, led by black political boss Edward Wright, they became a major cog in the Republican machine of Mayor Bill Thompson. In order to consolidate Republican power in the ward, the Republicans backed Oscar DePriest, who was elected in 1915 to the city council. Blacks were served by Thompson's machine. Jobs, intervention with the police, and payoffs on election day worked to consolidate machine support in the black wards. By 1928 DePriest had been elected to Congress. Black political power developed in Chicago because blacks were concentrated residentially in one or two wards, and because Mayor Thompson saw the importance of bringing blacks into politics, as another group in a city of ethnic groups, to support his machine.

During the ten years after Thompson's election, blacks gained increasing power in city politics. Black assistant corporation counsels, city prosecutors, and one assistant state's attorney were appointed. Aldermen and members of the state legislature, in addition to DePriest's elevation to Congress, were elected. Blacks took over the second and third ward machines. DePriest got involved in politics while he was earning a living by painting and decorating and a friend asked him to attend a political meeting one night. As the vote remained evenly divided for rival candidates, he approached one of the candidates and suggested that he would give him two additional votes if he supported DePriest for secretary. After the man refused, DePriest made the same offer to his rival, who accepted.

DePriest learned that the ward organization, with its committeeman at the top dispensing campaign funds and responsible to the county organization for delivering the vote and its precinct captains at the bottom, was the most important political organization in Chicago. The machine protected illegal businesses, arranged licenses and zoning exceptions for votes, and provided small services—Christmas baskets, picnics, parties, and jobs for the voters. DePriest organized a group of precinct captains for bargaining with Martin B. Madden, the white committeeman of the second ward. He began to make money from real estate and kept close ties with Madden. Three times when blacks ran for alderman, he supported Madden's white candidate for the same office. Then Madden supported him for his 1914 election as alderman. After DePriest won, he began organizing his own people's movement to sponsor him as an independent candidate. After his candidates lost in four tries at office, he supported Bill Thompson in the 1928 election. Thompson made him committeeman of the now black-dominated third ward. DePriest used his power to support his longtime crony Madden in his bid for reelection to Congress, even though a young black lawyer, college graduate and World War I veteran William L. Dawson, was running against him in the primary.

Dawson made the election, in part, an issue of race, pointing out that Madden did not even live in the district, and "he is a white man." Thompson was denounced when he went into the black community to support Madden. As he spoke, "the stomping became deafening." DePriest, pleading party regularity, continued to support Madden, who was successfully nominated. When Madden died between his nomination and the general election, DePriest ran for the seat himself. He won with the support of Mayor Thompson, who asserted:

When he died there came some Judas from Washington and said to me, "We don't want a Negro Congressman. You're the man that can keep a Negro out of Congress." I said, "If I'm the one man who can keep a Negro out of Congress, then, by God, there'll be one there."

DePriest became the first black Congressman since George H. White of North Carolina left in 1901, and he remained in Congress for three terms.

When the Depression made it possible for the Democratic organization in Chicago to elect a mayor, blacks were already a significant factor in politics and the Democratic machine wanted their support. Edward Kelly, who was elected mayor by the city council upon the death of Anton Cermak, began to build a strong permanent Democratic organization. William L. Dawson, a black maverick Republican still active in the city council, wanted to advance politically; he switched to the Democratic party. Kelly gave him control of all patronage in the second ward and Dawson began to build a black machine, with himself as undisputed leader, to deal with the white citywide machine. Dawson, a shrewd politician, began with his second ward base and by 1949 was boss of the entire South Side. What Dawson did was to take over the black voters already organized by Thompson, DePriest, and Madden and to turn them into a black Democratic machine. The machine elected Arthur Mitchell to Congress in 1934 and then Dawson himself in 1942.

Blacks found it more difficult to gain a share of political power in other cities. New York had even more blacks than Chicago and had a machine system, even though it was weaker than the one in Chicago. But there was no black district leader in Tammany Hall until 1935. In 1917 blacks had elected Edward A. Johnson to the state assembly, but a larger share of offices came slowly. New York districts were larger than Chicago wards, and there was less opportunity for a concentration of black voters. A district could have significant numbers of blacks, Italians, and Jews all competing for offices and power. The single vote possessed by the district in Tammany Hall would have to be split into three one-third votes. When blacks began to enter the Tammany organization at the district level in the 1930s, the city machine was under heavy attack. Mayor Fiorello LaGuardia, elected in 1933, led a successful movement that displaced the power in Tammany Hall with control by the mayor and the board of estimate. Blacks, then, entered Tammany Hall just when the posts there were decreasing in value. No strong black leader emerged; blacks were used by other factions one against the other. When a strong black leader, Adam Clayton Powell, Jr., ran for the twenty-second congressional district seat, created in 1944 specifically for a black, the Democratic district leader was so weak that he was overruled in the central party organization's decision to support Powell. But by the 1950s, Powell and his followers were even able to defeat regular organization candidates in the Democratic congressional primary and in three district leaders' contests.

INFLUENCE IN NATIONAL POLITICS IN THE 1920s

While blacks in New York and Chicago tried to gain a share of local power, at the national level blacks had little influence in the South or in the Republican party in the North. Blacks continued to recognize appointive office as a political resource, but they wanted more than "Negro jobs" in the government.

Some blacks continued to be critical of even the patronage rewards of party loyalty. Among the most consistent of the critics was the Socialist editor of the *Messenger*, A. Philip Randolph, who wrote repeatedly during the 1920s explaining the "causes for the political backwardness of the Negro." Reviewing these causes in November 1917, Randolph wrote words that he would reiterate in the 1920s:

> One of the most prominent of . . . [the causes] is his slavish and foolish worship of the Republican Party, which has pursued a policy of giving "big Negro leaders," the proverbial "job." . . . The Negro has not realized that, while a few leaders rode into jobs by pledging the support of the Negro voter to cunning, conniving, deceptive, and reactionary Republican politicians, the masses of colored voters and people were without civil protection and that they were growing lean and hungry, while the little Negro peanut politicians grew sleek and fat. . . . Fleas don't protect dogs, nor will big Negro leaders or white politicians protect the defenceless Negro.

W. E. B. Du Bois agreed with Randolph.

Du Bois despaired of any possible President making a difference and began admonishing blacks in 1920 to focus on local and congressional elections. In January, 1921, in *Crisis*, he advised of the necessity for disregarding the "chronic colored office seeker." He knew that after Harding's inauguration "he will be besieged by black men who want to be Recorder of Deeds, Register of the Treasury, Assistant Attorneys General and Fifteenth Auditor." These people would assert that "recognition of the Negro is the aim and object of the Negro vote." He wanted blacks to make it clear that voting was not for the purpose of providing "bread and butter for a few unemployed politicians who have been vociferous during the campaign." Instead, blacks should tell Harding that they wanted an end to lynchings, disfranchisement in the South, and Jim Crow everywhere.

But the Bronx and Manhattan Non-Partisan League wanted to expand the traditional pattern. They asked President Harding in February, 1921, to appoint a black Attorney General. Even though some might think their request paradoxical, they believed that "today the 12,000,000 colored citizens of this country are represented in no position of honor or emolument in this Government." James C. Waters, Jr., of Hyattsville, Maryland, was even more explicit when on March 1, 1925, he wrote in a letter to the editor of the New York *Times* that blacks needed a different type of federal appointee. "All we have," he asserted, "is one appointee 5,000 miles away in a fever infested section of Africa, a Recorder of Deeds in the District of Columbia, a customs officer at New Orleans, and a Collector of Revenue at New York. . . ." He thought blacks should be appointed to powerful jobs like those on the Interstate Commerce Commission, the Federal Trade Commission, and the like. He asked, "Is the colored man to be used only when there's need for cannon fodder and his sister only when there's need for a scrubwoman?"

As the 1920s wore on, some blacks became increasingly critical of party loyalty. A group called the National Democratic Negro Conference Committee, represented by Oscar H. Waters, P. Hampton White, Harvey E. B. Davis, Bishop George A. McGuire, the Right Rev. E. B. Robinson, Alexander Manning, William Bailey, and Perry Brown, announced in Washington on January 17, 1924, that blacks should give "careful consideration" to their vote in the upcoming campaign. The Republican party "has used the Negro as the great football of our American politics." The party was "brazenly, openly, defiantly, trafficking in and traducing the Negro's civic and civil rights as one of the means of retaining control of the government." As the Republican party remained unresponsive to pleas for black patronage and support for civil rights, blacks continued to discuss the best approach to political participation and the role black voters should play in the conservative politics of the 1920s. *Opportunity,* the official publication of the Urban League, noted in February, 1924, that "the tendency appears to be to take more and more interest in local politics." Blacks could see "the civic advantages which come largely through politics such as better educational facilities, police protection, better sanitary conditions, etc." W. E. B. Du Bois in February, 1922, used the absence of schools, sidewalks, and public facilities in Mississippi communities as an example of the discrimination which proceeded from the absence of political power. He therefore lamented the fact that "some persons continue to admonish the Negro that political power is not omnipotent and that without it much may be done to uplift the people; while with it much may be left undone." In July, 1924, he advised blacks, "You don't really care a rap who is president. Republican presidents are just about as bad as Democratic and Democratic presidents are little better than nothing." But he told them that they should carefully select Congressmen and local officials without regard to party.

In January, 1926, S. L. Corrothers, pastor of Roosevelt Memorial Temple and president of the National Independent Voter Association of America, maintained that blacks had derived little benefit from their loyalty to Republicans over the years. A few "menial jobs" and a mention of civil rights were "given to the Negro to make him believe he was receiving some attention." He was convinced that there would be "a halt in this unqualified support of Republican policies." The shift Corrothers saw was only gradual.

As Republicans openly bid for white support in the South, they removed the little influence which prominent blacks had possessed in national nominating conventions by recognizing local white leaders in their stead. The Republican party in the South had been a federal officeholding oligarchy. The bosses carried handpicked delegations to Republican national conventions and used them as pawns in securing continued federal patronage in the South. The states were controlled by the Democrats and the federal offices by the Republican bosses. Now blacks were being excluded from even that minimal share of power. The stage was set for increasing defections from the GOP.

In 1928, Herbert Hoover carried Florida, Kentucky, North Carolina, Tennessee, Texas, Virginia, and West Virginia, capitalizing on southern antipathy toward Roman Catholic, "wet" or anti-prohibition Al Smith. Some black voters defected to Smith, but to no avail. After Hoover's victory, he began to discuss publicly the desire to build up the Republican party in the South, which meant catering to whites at the expense of black aspirations for equal treatment.

However, black voters in the North began to rely upon their strength to lobby for black causes. Their opposition, added to that of labor groups, tipped the vote against Circuit Court Judge John J. Parker, which resulted in the rejection of his nomination to the Supreme Court by the Senate in 1930. Blacks organized to help defeat those senators who had voted for Parker's confirmation, including Henry J. Allen of Kansas, Roscoe McCulloch of Ohio, and Samuel Shortridge of California, when they ran for reelection in 1932. In the defeat of Parker, the NAACP reported in April, 1931, "the bench was kept free of a

man who had publicly flouted the wartime constitutional amendment
. . . expressing opposition to the Negro's participation in politics." Beyond the constitutional issues, "a body blow was struck at the lily white
policy, by which the Hoover administration proposed to conciliate
southern white sentiment by sacrificing the Negro and his rights."
Franklin D. Roosevelt's candidacy in the midst of the Depression offered an opportunity for many blacks to desert the Republican party,
although many stayed with the party of Lincoln until the 1936 election.

During the 1920s and early 1930s the Communist party actively
attempted to mobilize blacks. The party sent black visitors, such as
Claude McKay, to Russia, where they were warmly welcomed. The
Communists called for revolutionary action by black and white workers, applying their theory of nationalism for ethnic minorities in the
Soviet Union to a proposal for "self-determination for the Black Belt."
They also ran candidates for local and national offices, helped to organize boycotts of businesses which refused to hire blacks in Harlem,
and took every opportunity to champion the cause of blacks. A black
man, James W. Ford, was the vice presidential candidate on the Communist party ticket in 1932, 1936, and 1940, but not many blacks took
the symbolic step of voting for him. The Communist party organizers
worked assiduously to gain black adherents during the 1930s and some
blacks, including Angelo Herndon, a young Birmingham, Alabama,
coal miner, joined the cause. Herndon became a party organizer and
was convicted and sentenced to eighteen to twenty years on a chain
gang for allegedly inciting blacks in Georgia to insurrection in 1932.
Until he was freed by the Supreme Court, the Communists made an
international issue not only of his conviction but also of the convictions
of nine young blacks for allegedly raping two white women on a freight
train near Scottsboro, Alabama, in 1931. New trials were ordered for
the Scottsboro boys, but they were convicted again and sentenced
to up to ninety-nine years.

The Communists in the 1930s developed a tactic which they utilized
persistently throughout the twentieth century—that of attempting to
combine with black organizations in a united front against racism.
After the National Negro Congress was organized in 1936, they worked
to gain some control over its activities, and worked with the congress'
president, A. Philip Randolph. Black opposition to the Communist
party was based on pragmatism. As James Weldon Johnson said, "Placing our stake on the chance of solving our problem by gaining security
through a communistic revolution is taking odds that are infinitely
long." Marcus Garvey, holding similar views, wrote in the *Blackman*
in 1933: "We would prefer the Communists carrying out their pro-
gramme by themselves, and then in their success admit the Negro

to the right of partaking in the benefits of the new system which they seek to establish, rather than placing the onus on the Negro at this early stage, making him a target of an organized political opposition. . . . The whole world is in arms against Communism. For the Negro, therefore, to lead in the crusade against the present order . . . [is] placing a terrible handicap on his head."

SHIFTING TO THE DEMOCRATIC PARTY IN THE 1930s AND 1940s

Herbert Hoover tried hard to inspire black voters to stick with his party in the 1932 presidential election by using traditional tactics. He sent a message to the May, 1932, NAACP convention lauding the continued progress of blacks since the Civil War. He met with 200 loyal black voters in Washington, who pledged their loyalty to him and he to the cause of civil rights. But after Senator Robert LaFollette, in a long speech at the convention, criticized Hoover for not doing enough to relieve unemployment, Walter White predicted that the black vote would be balanced in November. White insisted that "the old practice of handing out a few dollars to a group of discredited and powerless white and Negro politicians is futile." Unfortunately, "neither of the likely candidates of the major political parties stirred his blood."

The Republicans had to answer for Judge Parker and their silence on lynching and unemployment. Blacks would remember Roosevelt's "boast" that he wrote the constitution of Haiti when it was invaded by American marines, and they would be "suspicious to the extreme" of his support by the South. Increasingly, according to White, blacks understood "that the inequalities which made possible the concentration of enormous wealth in the hands of a few while the vast majority of the world are on the ragged edge of starvation has many of its roots in the exploitation of the brown and yellow people in Africa, India, the Far East, the United States." Black voters would be interested not only in the presidency but also in electing "an intelligent and liberal" Congress and state and local officials who would consider their welfare.

Blacks did not shift quickly to support Democrats, despite the Republican party's failure to protect their interests. Franklin D. Roosevelt was little known outside New York, and his service in the staunchly segregationist Wilson administration did not speak well for him. Also, having John Nance Garner of Texas as his running mate did not help in the black wards. In Chicago, only 23 percent of the black vote was for Democrats in the 1932 election. Blacks in the most depressed areas changed party allegiance the slowest. Personal loyalty to Republican precinct captains and officials whose machine had delivered in the past, and the influx of new migrants from the South who brought their long-held fondness for Republicans with them, seemed to influence the poorer black voters to remain Republican longer.

Throughout the 1930s more and more black leaders called for Afro-American voters to support the Democratic Party. Among them was Marcus Garvey, who declared in August 1936:

> The Republicanism of America is too cunning, too crafty, to be of real beneficial use to the Negro. It only uses the Negro for convenience. Its philosophy is poor, its humanity is poorer. In fact, it has nothing today to recommend it to a people who are seeking a way out from the oppression of those who are seated in power. . . . Sooner or later the American Negro will declare himself. In that event it will need a man with the philosophy and humanity of Roosevelt to bridge the great gulf between crackerdom and real democracy. American Negroes, therefore, should support solidly the democratic standard bearer and send him back to the White House with flying colors.

Black voters responded to the pleas of Garvey and other leaders as well as the "philosophy and humanity" of Roosevelt. By 1936 Roosevelt, in Chicago, for example, received 49 percent of the black vote and by 1940, 52 percent. Blacks were grateful for Roosevelt's programs to alleviate unemployment. Franklin and Eleanor Roosevelt, aware of the growing importance of the black vote, invited blacks to social events at the White House and let it be known that Robert L. Vann of the Pittsburgh *Courier* and other blacks were frequently sought after for advice. Mrs. Roosevelt, who was an intimate friend of Mary McLeod Bethune, was often photographed with her and other blacks.

The long-standing practice of having at least one black adviser and appointing blacks to patronage positions—the "Negro jobs"—in the government was expanded and modified. Roosevelt had an enlarged group of black advisers on racial matters in governmental departments, who constituted a black cabinet: Mary McLeod Bethune as director of the Negro Affairs Division of the National Youth Administration, Robert L. Vann as special assistant to the Attorney General, and Robert Weaver as adviser in the Department of the Interior. Weaver served in a variety of governmental posts and in 1966 he became the first black official cabinet member when the Housing and Home Finance Agency became the Department of Housing and Urban Development. In addition to the black advisers, the number of blacks in the Civil Service increased substantially, although even until the 1980s the majority of blacks were in the lowest skilled and unskilled brackets, with a few in the top grades of government service.

In the 1940s black legislators and local judges, both Democratic and Republican, became commonplace in northern communities where there were large numbers of blacks. However, a large percentage of black officeholders and voters were Democrats.

While the number of blacks holding office grew along with the increase in black voters, certain political changes in cities where there were large numbers of blacks dimmed their future political prospects. In Chicago, where the Dawson machine seemed safely empowered, the Democrats elected a reform mayor, Martin Kennelly, in 1947. Kennelly gave up control of the machine and began using the Civil Service Commission to make appointments. The machine deteriorated to the extent that by 1951 Democratic votes fell off sharply. By 1955, Dawson and the party leaders dumped Kennelly in favor of Richard J. Daley, a party man and a regular member of the inner circle of the county central committee. After Daley won, patronage positions increased somewhat, but Daley decided that he would develop a new political style. His machine would rule, but he would appoint "blue ribbon" newspaper-endorsed candidates for major offices. This meant a diminution of power for Dawson's machine, which was thoroughly disliked by the major papers. Also, Daley's new civic projects such as urban renewal and crime reduction through police harassment affected the black wards most harshly. Dawson found that the few blacks appointed to prestigious boards and commissions were not often his machine-backed candidates.

Blacks fared much worse politically in Detroit and Los Angeles than in Chicago. In both cities politics was nonpartisan. In Detroit, black voters were organized by the United Automobile Workers Union, to which most of the black workers belonged. Most workers learned to vote the union ticket and to vote across racial lines. In addition, city council members were elected at large, which meant that not until 1957 was a black candidate found who could get enough votes citywide to be elected. The possibility of a black mayor and council majority had to await the decline of white population and votes in the city.

Blacks persisted in their loyalty to the Democratic party, but the payoff in terms of appointments was disproportionately small. Blacks had helped the Democrats to destroy the Republican machines, but they did not react to these new events by changing their allegiance again to the Republicans.

Black support for Roosevelt did not prevent racial discrimination in the administration of relief programs, in employment opportunities in the defense industry, and segregation in the armed forces during Roosevelt's presidency. A. Philip Randolph, in calling for a march on Washington in 1941, began to emphasize the need for protest to complement political participation. He asserted, "In this period of power politics, nothing counts but pressure, more pressure, and still more pressure, through the tactic of broad, organized, aggressive mass action behind the vital and important issues of the Negro." If blacks would march, the President would be forced to respond politically. Roosevelt's response in issuing Executive Order 8802 in June, 1941, providing for equal employment in defense industries, proved the efficacy of Randolph's approach.

As the NAACP began to win a large number of cases involving unconstitutional discrimination in education, housing, and voting, the organization increasingly emphasized the importance of actually voting on Election Day to achieve civil rights objectives. In celebrating the drift of blacks from devotion to the Republican party into the Democratic camp, the NAACP in December, 1943, asserted, "The Negro knows that his voting strength in seventeen or more states with 281 or more votes in the electoral college gives him the potential balance of power in any reasonably close national election and in many state and local elections his vote no longer belongs to any one party." David Cartwright, in applauding the black shift to Roosevelt in 1936 as a sign of "greater political maturity," had warned in the pages of *Crisis* that blacks should not become tied to the Democratic party. Continued support of the Democrats would only result in "creation of another Negro political caste whose members will serve as perpetual decoys of the Negro masses." But his warning was ignored, and soon the black vote was as firmly tied to the Democratic party as it had been to the Republicans earlier.

President Harry S. Truman, continuing the trend developed by Roosevelt, seemed to respond to his black constituency. He appointed a committee in 1946 to inquire into the condition of civil rights and make recommendations. Their report, "To Secure These Rights," called for positive programs to provide for legal equality. Truman ordered the desegregation of the armed forces and issued an order in 1948 requiring fair employment in the federal service.

The events surrounding World War II had accelerated the trend toward black participation in political and governmental affairs. By 1948, more than 2,500,000 blacks in the North and West voted and more than 600,000 blacks were registered to vote in twelve southern states. In 1948 there were six black members of city councils in the nation and thirty-three members of state legislatures, including two senators. More than a dozen black judges and magistrates presided over courts, and there were two black Congressmen. As another recognition of his black constituency, Truman affirmed Roosevelt's appointment of Mary McCleod Bethune, Mordecai W. Johnson, president of Howard University, and W. E. B. Du Bois and Walter White of the NAACP as delegates to the United Nations. Ralph Bunche went as a member of the official State Department staff. Bunche became director of the UN Trusteeship Council and won the Nobel Peace Prize in 1950 for his service as UN mediator in the Palestine dispute. He served as Deputy Secretary General of the UN until his death in 1971. Although it became evident very quickly that the UN would not intervene in U.S. race relations or even in cases of colonialist and neocolonialist oppression in Africa, blacks were usually a part of the American UN delegation.

The formation of the Dixiecrat party to oppose Truman in the 1948 election did not deter Truman from his civil rights policy, and he kept the Progressive party nominee, former Vice President Henry A. Wallace, from making inroads into the black vote. At the NAACP annual meeting in Kansas City in June, Loren Miller suggested that blacks were "pro-Truman" but they would be "pro-Wallace" if Wallace were a factor. At the same meeting, Henry Lee Moon, director of research for the NAACP, predicted an "influential" black vote in several southern states in the fall elections. James Herman of Atlanta pleaded passionately for the black vote to go to Wallace, but Dowdal H. Davis, editor of the Kansas City *Call,* insisted that blacks could not "solve their problems by looking to Russia," and Austin T. Walden, an Atlanta lawyer, stated that "the Negro belongs" in the Democratic party "for practical reasons." When the votes were counted, Wallace carried not one state and black voters were strongly in the Truman column. By the 1952 election, a majority of black voters voted for Adlai Stevenson even while Dwight D. Eisenhower was being elected President.

THE EFFECT OF THE 1950s AND 1960s CIVIL RIGHTS MOVEMENTS

In 1954, William L. Dawson was elected to Congress from Illinois for his seventh term, and Adam Clayton Powell Jr., was serving his sixth term. That year Charles Diggs was elected from Detroit. By 1964, there were six blacks in the House of Representatives; by 1974 there were seventeen. Blacks were increasingly appointed to posts other than the "Negro jobs" in the government. In 1949 William H. Hastie was appointed to the U.S. Court of Appeals, Third Circuit. Thurgood Marshall was appointed to Circuit Court in 1961, resigned in 1965 to become Solicitor General, and was appointed to the Supreme Court in 1966. The environment in which these advances in political participation took place included Supreme Court decisions protecting voting rights and promoting school desegregation, the Montgomery bus boycott and the emergence of the Rev. Martin Luther King, Jr., the passage of the Civil Rights Act of 1957, the rise of nation-states in Africa, and the sit-ins and civil rights marches of the 1960s.

The boycott and arrests in Montgomery, Alabama, and resistance to the Supreme Court school desegregation decision in *Brown* v. *Board of Education* became issues in the 1956 presidential campaign. When Adlai Stevenson made what seemed to be a weak civil rights statement in February, Roy Wilkins of the NAACP criticized him for not insisting on immediate integration. Stevenson, in clarifying his statement, said he supported integration but "no child can be properly educated in a hostile environment." He thought too rapid government interference might "delay progress." He still received strong support from black voters while Eisenhower was being reelected. In 1957 President Eisenhower sent federal troops to Little Rock, Arkansas, to enforce a desegregation decision at Central High School and to keep order when faced with Governor Orville Faubus' opposition. The first civil rights bill to be enacted by Congress since 1875 was proposed by President Eisenhower in 1957. The act authorized the federal government to bring a civil suit in its own name to obtain injunctive relief when a person was denied or threatened in his right to vote and created a civil rights division under an Assistant Attorney General in the Department of Justice. It also created the U.S. Commission on Civil Rights from its forerunner, President Truman's Committee on Civil Rights, authorized to investigate denials of the right to vote, to study and collect information concerning legal developments constituting a denial of equal protection of the laws, and to appraise the laws and policies of the federal government with respect to equal protection. The Civil Rights Commission held hearings on black voting in several cities, North and South, and found that blacks were being regularly denied the right to vote by certain white southern registrars. In 1960 another civil rights bill was passed to strengthen voting rights enforcement.

The 1960 presidential nominating conventions and election took place in the midst of the direct action ferment. Roy Wilkins warned both parties before their conventions that they should adopt a civil rights posture "without equivocation." For "equivocation will insure the equivocation of Negro voters in the choosing of party designees in the November election." During the Democratic Convention, the NAACP organized a civil rights rally in which about 6,000 blacks booed

Lyndon B. Johnson when Oscar Chapman, who came to represent him, tried to speak, and then they barely let John F. Kennedy speak for himself.

When Chapman mentioned former President Harry S. Truman, who had said that the nonviolent sit-ins in the South were "Communist inspired," loud booing erupted again. But the booing was soon transformed into support. Mordecai Johnson was a voice crying in the wilderness when he told the National Colored Women's Club shortly before the election that "we still do not have a political party that we as a group can trust." Neither party had done anything, according to Johnson, to "give the American Negro an Equal Right to Work."

In the 1960 election, John F. Kennedy won the presidency with significant support from blacks. In the crucial states of Illinois and Michigan, black voters held the balance of power. Kennedy consolidated support in the campaign by interceding when Martin Luther King, Jr., was jailed after a sit-in in a restaurant in an Atlanta, Georgia, department store. He campaigned openly for black votes, criticizing his opponent for inaction. When the returns were in, black voters received some of the traditional rewards for their support. As President, Kennedy appeased Senators from the South by appointing a number of white racist federal judges, but he also appointed large numbers of blacks to federal jobs, including Thurgood Marshall to the Second Circuit and Wade McCree to the District Court for Eastern Michigan. He appointed Carl T. Rowan as Deputy Assistant Secretary of State and later Ambassador to Finland, and Clifton R. Wharton as Ambassador to Norway and Mercer Cook as Ambassador to Niger. He appointed two black U.S. Attorneys and several blacks to presidential commissions. Overall, the percentage of blacks in federal employment increased, but some agencies still had no blacks at all, and the majority of blacks were still in the lowest ratings.

As the sit-ins, marches, demonstrations, and violent opposition to them continued in 1963, President Kennedy proposed a civil rights bill to Congress in March which became bogged down and seemed likely not to pass. A march for jobs and freedom on August 28, 1963, drew 200,000 people to Washington, but Congress did not move on the bill until after Kennedy's assassination on November 22, 1963, when Lyndon B. Johnson made it "must" legislation. The act, passed early in 1964, gave the Attorney General additional power to protect citizens against discrimination and segregation in voting, education, and the use of public facilities. It established an Equal Employment Opportunity Commission (EEOC). and extended the life of the Commission on Civil Rights. It forbade discrimination in federally assisted programs, with the termination of assistance for failure to comply. The lesson blacks learned reinforced A. Philip Randolph's view at the time of the proposed 1941 march on Washington: protest is an essential ingredient of political success.

President Kennedy and his brother, Attorney General Robert Kennedy, strongly favored a massive voter registration campaign, believing that until blacks became voters, southern Congressmen would not vote for significant civil rights legislation. They also wanted to dissuade blacks from protesting by focusing their attention more directly on political participation. Also, they knew the importance of black voters to Kennedy's election and wanted to create a massive increase of black Democratic voters before the 1964 election. With White House support, CORE, SNCC, SCLC, the NAACP, and the Urban League embarked on a Voter Education Project (VEP) in April, 1962. Designed to last two and one-half years, it cost $870,000, nearly all of which came from the Taconic and Field foundations and the Stern Family Fund. Wiley Branton, the attorney from Pine Bluff, Arkansas, who had been counsel in the Little Rock cases, was appointed to head the project. The VEP was hampered from the start by a Kennedy policy of urging voter registration but failing to protect civil rights activists and blacks attempting to register in order to appease southern whites.

In Mississippi the Council of Federated Organizations (CORE and the NAACP), led by Aaron Henry, Robert Moses, and David Dennis, worked to register blacks. They did so despite the withdrawal of VEP assistance in 1963, when it became evident that few blacks would be able to register. In 1964 the Mississippi effort focused on making a challenge to the regular Mississippi delegation at the 1964 Democratic Convention. The idea was to dramatize the illegal exclusion of blacks from politics by running black candidates for Congress in the Democratic primaries. Blacks tried to participate in precinct and county conventions and run independent candidates in the general election with the notion of unseating the all-white delegation at the National Convention. Late in April a statewide Mississippi Freedom Democratic party (MFDP) convention was held, and Aaron Henry was elected chairman. Four party candidates ran for Congress in the June primaries but were defeated, since few blacks could vote. Blacks who were registered were turned away when they tried to participate in precinct meetings. In August delegates were elected by the MFDP to the National Convention with Henry as chairman. At the convention, Lyndon B. Johnson and Hubert Humphrey arranged a compromise in which the credentials committee seated the regulars, and decided that the two MFDP delegates could be seated as delegates at large. Henry, moved by claims by King, Joseph Rauh, and Bayard Rustin that it was a symbolic victory, wanted to accept. But the entire delegation rejected the compromise and walked out. To them it was just one more failure of the national party to protect them in the South. Fannie Lou Hamer, a Mississippi sharecropper and one of the delegates of the MFDP to the National Convention who had earlier run as one of the four congressional candidates, believed that the experience would make blacks work harder in politics in Mississippi. The people would support the decision not to compromise "because we didn't have anything to compromise for. . . ." She was disconcerted by the lack of support of "other leaders of the Movement." She attended one meeting, where she said she "wouldn't dare think of" accepting a compromise. Thereafter she "wasn't allowed to attend the other meetings. It was *quite* an experience." With nowhere else to go, those blacks who voted still voted for Lyndon Johnson in the 1964 election.

White hostility to civil rights enforcement did not end after Johnson's overwhelming victory over Barry Goldwater, and the marches and violence continued. The murder of black and white civil rights workers continued in some areas of the South. President Johnson federalized the Alabama National Guard to protect the demonstrators on a march from Selma to Montgomery to push for additional voting rights legislation. Local civil rights workers were faced with strong opposition, economic sanctions, and murder. After the march itself, a white woman from Detroit, Viola Liuzzo, was killed as she transported passengers from Montgomery back to Selma. Lyndon Johnson sent Congress a proposal for a voting rights act which Congress passed quickly in 1965. The act authorized the Attorney General to use federal examiners to register voters, and it suspended literacy tests and other devices in states and counties where less than 50 percent of the adults had voted in 1964. Alabama, Georgia, Louisiana, Mississippi, South Carolina, Virginia, parts of North Carolina, Alaska, and some counties in Arizona, Idaho, and Hawaii were covered by the act. By year's end, nearly 250,000 new black voters had registered, and blacks won seats in the Georgia legislature and in several southern city councils.

President Johnson expanded the policy of appointing blacks to federal posts as a reward for black political support. He appointed Mercer Cook to Senegal, Hugh Smythe to Syria, Franklin Williams to Ghana, Elliott Skinner to Upper Volta, and Patricia Harris to Luxembourg as ambassadors. He appointed Wade McCree to the Circuit Court and Thurgood Marshall to be Solicitor General and then Justice of the Supreme Court; Robert C. Weaver as Secretary of the new Housing and Urban Development Department; Hobart Taylor to the board of the Export-Import Bank; Andrew Brimmer to the Federal Reserve Board; and Walter Washington as Mayor of Washington, D.C.

SENSING THE LIMITS OF POLITICAL PARTICIPATION IN THE 1970s

Somewhere along the way, many blacks became bitter about the possibility of achieving equality even though there was more political participation than ever before. When did this pessimism become endemic? Perhaps the bitterness began when, a month after the march on Washington, four black children were killed in a church bombing in Birmingham. Or it could have been when the protest movement moved North and northern whites who had loved and supported blacks while they protested in the South began to draw careful distinctions between de facto segregation in the North, which was legal because unintended, and de jure segregation in the South, which was bad, to protect their own race and class interests. Or it could have been that blacks had heard too many whites warning them that to demand affirmative action for blacks would be to betray the American principles of democracy and to engage in reverse discrimination against whites. Perhaps it was the repeated warnings of Malcolm X that all of America was the South, or the assassination of the Kennedys and Martin Luther King, Jr., or seeing white people kill not only black rebels in the riots of the 1960s but also their own children in antiwar demonstrations. The net effect was to heighten the sense of the contradictions in American society; blacks sensed the limits of political participation.

By 1966, even as blacks in the South began to vote and participate in.politics in large numbers, they began to recognize the limited rewards of suffrage. The problem of overcrowded housing in the cities in the North, a black unemployment rate twice as high as that of whites, and the segregation of black children in inferior schools seemed not to change much as a result of voting and office holding.

Some blacks reacted by turning against police and property in a veritable rash of riots in the 1960s, beginning with the violence in the Watts area of Los Angeles in August, 1965. The move of Martin Luther King, Jr., North in 1965 in order, as he put it, to halt "the increasing segregation in the North" met with hostility from whites and criticism from some blacks who did not believe the social and economic problems they faced would be solved by Christian charity and peaceful demonstration. The assassination of King on April 4, 1968, set off a series of riots and lootings in more than 100 cities by blacks who had seen King's efforts as at least promising some resolution to their plight.

Malcolm X, a year before his death in February, 1965, predicted that the events of the 1960s and the civil rights movement were making blacks "more politically mature." In echoing views expressed earlier by W. E. B. Du Bois, Walter White, and others, he said blacks saw that they could hold the balance of power in certain elections, as in the Kennedy-Nixon 1960 election, "yet when the Negro helps that person get in office the Negro gets nothing in return. All he gets is a few appointments. A few handpicked Uncle Tom handkerchief head Negroes are given big jobs in Washington, D.C., and then those Negroes come back and try and make us think that that administration is going to lead us to the promised land of integration. And the only ones whose problems have been solved have been those handpicked Negroes. A few big Negroes got jobs who didn't even need the jobs. They already were working. But the masses of black people are still unemployed."

Blacks in the civil rights movement who had been closely involved with registering voters had become more and more disillusioned after full equality seemed beyond their reach. They believed that public officials would not enforce laws even after they were passed. They began to believe that blacks must reject coalitions with whites and find some other way to gain equality. Black leadership in black organizations became the watchword.

When Stokely Carmichael became Chairman of the Student Nonviolent Coordinating Committee (SNCC), he had an answer for the politically mature blacks Malcolm had described. Carmichael explained, "traditionally, for each new ethnic group, the route to social and political integration into America's pluralistic society, has been through the organization of their own institutions with which to represent their communal needs within the larger society." The oldest civil rights organizations both disavowed partisan political activity and relied on coalitions with liberal whites to make gains. Carmichael asserted that this approach would not work because "the political and social rights of Negroes have been and always will be negotiable and expendable the moment they conflict with the interests of our 'allies.'" The result of such coalition policies was that a few "qualified assimilated blacks could get good jobs." If blacks followed his advice and organized in their own communities to control them, their "chief antagonists" would be in the South, the overtly racist Democratic party, and in the North the equally corrupt big city machines. He pointed out that when Kennedy and Johnson embarked upon registering black voters, what they really wanted to do was "to register Democrats." The black leaders enlisted in the cause were told to "go home and organize your people into the local Democratic party—*then* we'll see about poverty money and appointments." One result was that blacks were more closely tied to the Democratic party than ever for fear of losing poverty money, and black leaders knew they were "vote deliverers, more responsible to the white machine and the white power structure, than to the community they allegedly represent."

Some blacks continued to be "vote deliverers," while others cast deciding votes in local and national elections and the Democratic party responded to the black voting bloc by significantly increasing the number of black delegates to the 1972 Democratic National Convention. Some supported black Congresswoman Shirley Chisholm in her unsuccessful campaign for the Democratic presidential nomination in 1972. Others responded to the call for black political organization by participating in the National black Political Convention in Gary, Indiana, in March, 1972. Congressman Charles L. Diggs of Michigan, Mayor Richard Hatcher of Gary, and black poet LeRoi Jones (Imamu Amiri Baraka) issued the official call for the convention of more than 2,700 delegates and 4,000 alternates and observers. The black political agenda released by the leaders of the convention in May, 1972, contained a poor peoples' platform, model pledges for black and nonblack candidates who wanted black support, the outline of a voter registration bill, and a bill for community self-determination. Its provisions opposing school busing and United States support of Israel were denounced by Hatcher and Diggs, who feared appearing to approve continued segregation and the loss of Jewish political support. Black politicians saw supporting an independent party as a means of gaining leverage within the Republican and Democratic parties and not as a real alternative. By the 1972 elections, most blacks who ran for office and voted were still in the Democratic column as Richard Nixon swamped George McGovern at the polls.

Despite the ascendancy of Richard Nixon and his active southern policy and disinterest in civil rights, black concentration in urban districts and continued black voting in the South led to some gains. The numbers of black elected officials increased year by year. By 1974 more than 200 blacks sat in 37 state legislatures and 17 in Congress—one Senator from Massachusetts, Edward Brooke (the only Republican), and four women, Shirley Chisholm of New York, Barbara Jordan of Texas, Yvonne Braithwaite Burke of California, and Cardiss Collins of Illinois. In 1966 there was no black mayor of any major American city, but by 1974 blacks had served as mayors of a number of small southern towns as well as Cleveland, Los Angeles, Gary, Newark, and Washington, D.C. After Nixon was forced to resign for the crimes of

Watergate, in January, 1975, Gerald Ford appointed William T. Coleman, Jr., a distinguished Philadelphia lawyer, as Secretary of Transportation, the second black cabinet Secretary in the nation's history.

In May, 1975, there were 3,503 blacks in elective offices, but there were more than 500,000 elected officials in the United States—287 elected officials for every 100,000 people—and the 3,503 black elected officials added up to only 16 for every 100,000 people. The South, which had 53 percent of the total black population, had 55 percent of the black elected officials. Blacks saw that litigation, political participation, and the protest movement had helped to remove legal racial discrimination, but they began to believe that 11 or 15 percent of the total population could not, even with a few white allies, vote the nation into a benevolent democracy. Even white liberals were opposed to the fundamental changes in the economic system required to improve the lot of the black masses. Blacks celebrated the number of black mayors until they noticed that the economic power of the cities was controlled by whites and that whites who could afford to moved to the suburbs and then began establishing metropolitan governments to prevent black political control of additional cities. But, of course, it took the experiences of the 1960s and 1970s to make black people realize the limits of political participation to change the predicament of the masses. Even the Congressional Black Caucus soon confessed the limits of its effectiveness. The theme of their fifth anniversary dinner in 1975 was "from changing institutions to using institutions." Time, the crush of routine congressional business, the need to tend to problems in their own widely differing districts, and the task of trying to make gains for blacks in the face of a declining economy and what they saw as a hostile Ford administration and an indifferent Congress all contributed to making them "more realistic," the members said.

As the political campaign leading to the 1976 presidential election proceeded, some blacks were determined this time to make their political participation result in substantial benefits to the black community. The Democrats seemed sure to defeat the Republicans in the presidential election after Watergate. Andrew Young, Congressman from Georgia, bet early on Jimmy Carter, reconstructed Governor of Georgia, and provided crucial support for him in the Florida Democratic primary and thereafter. After Carter was nominated, blacks gave him critical votes accounting for his margin of victory over President Gerald Ford in the November election. Carter responded as no President had before in distributing the traditional rewards of political support to his black constituency. He named Andrew Young as Ambassador to the UN, Patricia Harris as HUD Secretary, (and later Health and

Human Services Secretary), Wade McCree as Solicitor General, Drew Days as Assistant Attorney General for Civil Rights, Eleanor Holmes Norton as Chair of the EEOC, at least one black to a subcabinet post in each of the cabinet departments, and a record number of black federal judges. Andrew Young quickly succeeded in refurbishing America's image in black Africa and extending Henry Kissinger's policy of appearing to support black opposition to the white Rhodesian government. Kissinger's policy and Congressional opposition to United States support of the new regime in Angola, even though it was pro-Communist, was designed to contain Communist influences among the guerillas fighting in Southern Africa.

Soon the blacks' enchantment with President Carter began to dissipate. They saw more clearly than ever before that the traditional rewards for political support did not solve their economic problems. Black unemployment remained twice as high as for whites, and unemployment among black youth was at an all-time high. In addition, President Carter's National Security Advisor, Zbigniew Brzezinski, attacked Andrew Young's support of guerrilla movements in southern Africa as being supportive of Russian expansion in the continent. Young was quickly reined in by Secretary of State Cyrus Vance and the President.

Hard times for blacks seemed marked by a plethora of reverse discrimination cases in which whites struck out against affirmative action programs that were only beginning to bear fruit. When the case of *Bakke* v. *University of California* brought the issue before the U.S. Supreme Court, blacks strenuously pushed the effort to have the Justice Department in the person of Wade McCree, the black Solicitor General, file an *amicus curiae* brief in support of affirmative action. After weeks of behind-the-scenes struggle, the administration took a pro-affirmative action position. As one White House staffer put it, "The President could not solve the economic problems of blacks cheaply, but the brief did not cost anything."

The first black Assistant Attorney General for Civil Rights, Drew S. Days, and the black chair of the EEOC, Eleanor Holmes Norton, asserted that they did not believe affirmative action programs would be deterred by the *Bakke* decision. Significantly, President Carter issued no statement on the subject at first. At an already scheduled meeting of black political appointees on the day of the decision, Andrew Young, as the most senior official present, was urged to ask the President to issue a strong statement of support for affirmative action efforts directed toward blacks. Young refused and advised that none of those present should urge such an action on the President since "it is not our role to tell the President what to do." Black White House staffers announced that their recommendations that the President issue a statement were overruled by Stuart Eizenstat, the President's Assistant for Domestic Policy, and his deputy, Bert Carp. They reported that Carp explained to them that "white people have rights also" and that the President needed to worry about alienating Jews and other white voters who would be displeased by a presidential statement supporting strong affirmative action efforts for blacks.

A few days later Drew S. Days, in answer to a press question, did express concern about the absence of a statement from the President. Shortly thereafter the President responded to the demands of his black constituency. He issued a memorandum to heads of executive departments and agencies that "the recent decision by the Supreme Court in *Bakke* enables us to continue these efforts [affirmative action] without interruptions." He wanted "to make certain that, in the aftermath of *Bakke* you continue to develop, implement and enforce vigorously affirmative action programs." Ralph Perotta, executive director of the National Italian-American Foundation, saw in the *Bakke* decision that "affirmative action will be opened up to a lot of other groups that have not benefitted before." He planned to ask that the federal civil rights laws be refocused to conform to his view of the decision.

When the Supreme Court decided the *Weber* case in 1979, upholding the right of an employer to train blacks for higher positions to achieve affirmative action goals even if it meant bypassing a white with greater seniority, civil rights advocates were gleeful. They had feared the Court would impose limitations on employment efforts just as the *Bakke* case had limited affirmative action in higher education admissions policy. At least the court left the door open for novel solutions to the employment problems of blacks.

Toward the end of the 1970s, blacks were having great difficulty in reaping the benefits of political participation, in particular their crucial support of President Carter in the 1976 election. The President had trouble convincing Congress to accept his urban employment and social services programs designed to help blacks concentrated in the cities. Congress seemed more concerned with the complaints of their constituents about high taxes and waste in federal programs and by 1980 became obsessed with the need to balance the budget while increasing support for Defense Department programs.

Surely voting had some beneficial effects. In several southern states, enforcement of the Voting Rights Act of 1965 made blacks a significant factor in state and local politics. A fall 1978 Gallup poll reported that blacks had made considerable progress in American society in the fifteen years since the march on Washington. Prejudice toward a black presidential candidate had declined substantially. Seventy-seven percent of Americans, as opposed to 43 percent fifteen years before, were willing to vote for "a qualified black" for President.

The benefits of black political participation were still mixed. In 1976 about 57 percent of whites of voting age voted, but only 45 percent of blacks did so. Of the estimated 9,024,800 blacks registered to vote on November 7, 1976, about 64.1 percent voted. The 1976 results showed that in the presidential election, black voters were safely locked in the Democratic columns but not automatically so in congressional, state, and local races. Prognosticators who had labeled American voters, particularly black voters, apathetic before the election were surprised. There was a steady decline of black voter participation from 1968 through the presidential primaries in 1976, but several factors worked to change apathy to involvement again. Blacks who had become completely disenchanted about achieving social and economic gains through the political system came to believe during Richard Nixon's two terms that, in the absence of a revolution, some political influence was to be preferred to none at all. In the aftermath of the 1960s rebellions and the suppression of black revolutionary movements by the federal government, a revolution seemed entirely beyond reach.

As early as May, 1976, a group of black leaders who represented major national, civic, religious, fraternal, labor, and civil rights organizations, convinced that the time was right to use voting for social and economic gains, met in Washington, D.C., to devise a strategy to combat voter apathy. They created the Nonpartisan National Coalition on Black Voter Participation. As the summer progressed, labor unions, civil rights groups, and the Atlanta-based VEP linked to mobilize the black vote. Registrations increased, and one result was that for Jimmy Carter, as the Joint Center for Political Studies reported, "the bottom line was black votes." The structure of the electoral college and the concentration of black voters in key states provided opportunities for blacks to exercise leverage in a presidential election.

While the long struggle to gain the right to vote resulted in the traditional benefits of political participation, blacks registered disappointment with their status, and their social and economic problems appeared intractable. Black members of Congress reported that constituents often did not feel that their representatives were solving housing and unemployment problems. Black mayors reported that not enough was being done to provide economic support in their cities. The continued complaints underscored the limits of political participation. Increased black participation in politics did result in more black officeholders, some increase in government contracts to blacks and black institutions, more public service job programs, and more obvious enforcement of civil rights. But no amount of participation seemed to precipitate a redistribution of national income or jobs or other changes that would solve the problems the masses of blacks face in their lives.

As the public increasingly focused on the politics of the 1980 presidential election, black prospects for reaping the benefits of political participation worsened. By September, 1979, Andrew Young was no longer with the Carter administration, although at the 1978 Black Caucus dinner the President had announced that Young would be in his administration as long as he wanted to stay. Young resigned after Israeli protests over his meeting with Palestine Liberation Organization (PLO) representatives to try to influence the course of a UN vote on the Middle East.

Young's violation of the government's prohibition against meetings with the PLO, maintained since the Nixon administration, led to his departure. Black reaction was fierce and fast. The Congressional Black Caucus, chaired by Cardiss Collins of Illinois, informed President Carter that he was not invited to speak at their annual dinner in September, 1979. The Rev. Joseph Lowery, president of the Southern Christian Leadership Conference (SCLC) Walter Fauntroy, Congressman from Washington, D.C., and other SCLC members accepted an invitation to visit Yasir Arafat and the PLO in Lebanon, as did the Rev. Jesse Jackson, national president of Operation People United to Save Humanity (PUSH), on a separate mission. In doing so, Lowery, Fauntroy, and Jackson incurred the wrath of American Jews and Jackson, who had seemed to become President Carter's favorite black leader, suddenly found himself to be persona non grata at the White House. Benjamin Hooks and Vernon Jordan tested the waters and then withdrew into silence or lamentations regarding the excursions by their brothers into the Palestinian issue, which could be better left to the State Department. Although Lowery, Fauntroy, and Jackson asked to see Prime Minister Menachim Begin of Israel and Jackson stopped off in Israel for a visit before visiting the Palestinians, their requests were denied. Andrew Young and Jesse Jackson pointed out that if Begin could meet with Prime Minister John Vorster of South Africa, he could certainly find reasons to meet with them.

Suddenly on October 13, 1979, after Bayard Rustin wrote several pieces denouncing his brethren for visiting the Palestinian terrorists without mentioning that Begin himself was a terrorist, and after Hooks announced that blacks should not meddle in foreign policy, Begin decided to receive a group of black civil rights leaders, including Rustin and representatives of the National Urban League, the NAACP, and various labor unions. Rustin said, "We owe it to the people of Israel to show that there are a variety of views in the U.S. and that ours is the major one."

After Vernon Jordan added fuel to the fire by publicly criticizing the leaders who had visited the PLO, a hastily called meeting of the Black Leadership Forum on Wednesday night, October 24, criticized Jordan and Rustin for attacking other black leaders and issued a statement denouncing attacks by Jews and others on blacks who criticized the failure of Israel to make peace with the Palestinian Arabs. Throughout the controversy, President Carter stood on the sidelines and did not explain the "resignation" of Andrew Young.

The opening of Senator Edward Kennedy's official challenge to President Carter for the Democratic party nomination could have been the signal for blacks to join the Kennedy bandwagon. But the leadership in the Congressional Black Caucus and the civil rights groups was hesitant to take the risk of supporting a challenge to an incumbent President. Some supported President Carter, a few opted for Kennedy, and others organized a black political convention in Richmond, Virginia, in late February, 1980, to update an agenda reiterating the economic and social needs of the black community. In an increasingly conservative political climate, so disinterested were the presidential candidates in the influence of black leadership over the black vote that none of them appeared when invited to speak before the convention.

Despite their economic concerns, blacks supported Carter after his nomination because Republican nominee Ronald Reagan offered no economic program to meet the unemployment crisis directly and promised weaker civil rights enforcement. Ronald Reagan, dubbed a "racist" by Carter, won by a landslide, while about 85 percent of the black vote went to Carter. When Republicans won not only the presidency but control of the Senate, the Congress could not be expected, as in the Nixon era, to reject cuts in the budgets of social programs for which blacks were major beneficiaries. Also, long-time civil rights opponent Senator Strom Thurmond replaced Edward Kennedy as Chairman of the Senate Judiciary Committee, which controls the confirmation of federal judges. Senator Orrin Hatch of Utah replaced Harrison Williams as Chairman of the Subcommittee on Labor and Human Resources, which controls many social programs and the confirmation of the officials who manage them. Furthermore, Hatch, a strong opponent of civil rights, succeeded Birch Bayh as chairman of the Judiciary Subcommittee on the Constitution, which controls civil rights agencies and legislation.

As blacks reflected on the strategies they might use to address the political changes, they saw increasingly that direct action, protest, whether violent or nonviolent, was an essential ingredient of successful political action. But the political action did not improve the overall black condition. Even the new coalition-building politics had worked in the economic arena only to the extent that the goals did not require inordinate sacrifices on the part of any other members of the coalition. Unfortunately, the goals sought by the masses of blacks would require economic and status sacrifices on the part of whites.

6

The Economics of Hope and Despair

Wealth is the man; if you have nothing, no one loves you.

Hausa proverb

The economic history of blacks proves conclusively that America failed on practically all fronts to guarantee them a right to life and the pursuit of happiness. The historic economic plight of blacks is inexplicable without referring to the racial caste system which prevailed in the United States. Most important, after 1865 blacks were viewed as social inferiors as a result of their enslavement. Consequently, whites systematically fought against any effort to assure them economic equality. Several forces combined to lock blacks in an airtight cage of poverty after the Civil War.

FROM SLAVERY TO PEONAGE AFTER THE CIVIL WAR

At the beginning of emancipation blacks were left virtually helpless before the monstrous forces of capitalism. Freed without land, the poverty and ignorance of the black left him at the mercy of the southern planter in spite of the efforts of the Freedmen's Bureau from 1865 to 1872. Almost immediately after the war the planters turned to share-cropping arrangements with black farmers. Through the mechanism of the plantation store, which charged exorbitant prices for goods, planters kept their black tenants in perpetual debt. Later this system was augmented by the convict lease system, in which planters either paid the fines of black prisoners or were permitted to work them until their sentences were served.

After the Civil War southern blacks moved quickly from slavery to virtual peonage. Under the aegis of the Freedmen's Bureau, large numbers of black peasants signed annual contracts with white planters. Generally penniless, they obtained advances on their wages or shares

195

of the crop. Since they were illiterate, the planters often overcharged and cheated them. The result was perpetual debt, compulsion, violence, oppression, and de facto slavery. The murder of black peons was a frequent occurrence in the South until the 1940s. Writing in the *Voice of the Negro* in 1906, T. H. Malone declared:

> there is in truth but little difference between the peonage of today and the actual slavery of the past. . . . the peon is worked from dawn until night under the strict espionage of a merciless foreman, . . . identical in duties and prerogatives with the "overseer" of the old system. . . . [If the black man] makes a railroad trip . . . he must report where he is going and how long he will be gone. If he overstays his time, he is liable to be brought back handcuffed. At all stages of his existence he is subject to be whipped. . . . Nobody is spared the lash. . . . The old grayhaired man or woman and the child of tender years are alike subject to its stings.

Reflecting on peonage in 1907, a white resident of Florida argued, "Slavery is just as much an 'institution' *now* as it was before the war." The Georgia Baptist Convention agreed with this view in 1939: "There are more negroes held by these debt slavers than were actually owned as slaves before the War between the States."

Although black peons appealed by the thousands to the Justice Department in an effort to escape from their bondage, there was little change in their situation until the American Communist party started defending their interests. In 1930 Otto E. Huiswood, a black member of the party, pointed out that after 1865,

> the Southern Negro was practically completely re-enslaved on the plantations. The courts enacted innumerable laws which served to keep the Negro under the complete domination of the landowners. Every instrument at its disposal was used by the ruling class to shackle the Negro workers and bind them to the plantations. . . . The Negro tenant farmer, share cropper, and farm workers are virtually slaves on the land. The poor farmer and share cropper can never hope to own the land he tills, due to a credit and mortgage system which chains him to the land and makes him the serf of the merchants, landholders and bankers. Not only the land, but even the implements, crops—everything is mortgaged, placing them under complete domination of the white ruling class. . . . Peonage, debt and convict slavery, vagrancy laws, disfranchisements, segregation, lynching and mob violence are the methods used to mercilessly exploit and oppress the Negroes in the South. These are the methods of double exploitation of the Negro used by the capitalist class in order to extract super profits from their labor.

In an effort to bring a halt to this super exploitation, the Communists launched a massive effort to organize southern tenant farmers and sharecroppers into unions. Despite lynching, harassment by and shoot-outs with police, they had helped to organize more than 50,000 rural laborers in the South by 1940.

Acting through an affiliate, the Communists organized the first agency dedicated to fighting peonage, the Abolish Peonage Committee, in 1940. The committee, with the help of such people as the young Marxist historian Herbert Aptheker, investigated complaints of peonage and constantly pressed the Justice Department and Congress to abolish America's twentieth-century "peculiar institution." Beginning in 1945, another Communist organization, the Workers Defense League, sued state and local officials for their part in peonage and set up commissions to compile data on the practice and to rouse public indignation. Primarily as a result of the assaults of the Communists and of the NAACP, the Supreme Court definitively struck down the legal underpinnings of peonage in the 1940s, and the Justice Department, armed with federal antipeonage laws (passed in 1948), finally began a campaign against peonage. Even so, cases of peonage were still being occasionally reported in American newspapers in the 1970s; the Justice Department received fifty-four complaints in 1973.

EARLY EFFORTS TO AMASS CAPITAL

In spite of peonage, there were a few auspicious beginnings for blacks in the second half of the nineteenth century. Congress chartered the Freedmans's Savings and Trust Company in 1865, and thousands of blacks had deposited money in it by 1874. That year deposits totaled more than $3 million. The bank was so haphazardly run, however, that when Frederick Douglass became president in 1874, he declared it bankrupt. Though Congress had chartered the bank, it steadfastly refused to reimburse the depositors. The bank's failure created a deep suspicion of all financial institutions in the black community and contributed significantly to the development of spendthrift attitudes which long afterward plagued blacks.

A more hopeful development was the acquisition of land by blacks. Blacks in Georgia, for example, had acquired more than 350,000 acres of land by 1874. The total amount of land held by blacks increased dramatically until the early part of the twentieth century. By 1910 blacks had acquired more than 42 million acres of land. Generally, however, black farms were too small to survive twentieth-century mechanization of agriculture and periodic depressions. In 1930, when the average black farm contained 42 acres, the average white farm contained 165 acres. Between 1910 and 1930, the land held by blacks declined by almost 5 million acres, and by 1930 79 percent of all black farmers were tenants. The number of black farm owners declined from 240,221 in 1910 to 194,046 in 1960.

BECOMING INDUSTRIAL WORKERS IN THE NORTH

The twentieth-century economic progress of blacks was tied irrevocably to emigration from the South and to war. The first great improvement came during the First World War, when blacks migrated in large numbers to northern industrial centers. The sharp drop in European immigration, increased demand for war matériel, and the abandonment of jobs by whites enlisting in the army created a vacuum for unskilled industrial workers which was filled by black migrants from 1915 to 1920. Spurred on by editorials in northern black newspapers such as the Chicago *Defender,* the activities of labor agents, and the depression in agriculture caused by the rampages of the boll weevil, blacks abandoned their tenant farms in the South for economic opportunity in the North. As a result of the migration, the percentage of blacks employed as farm workers declined by 10 percent and the number of black males employed as unskilled industrial workers rose from 25 percent to 30 percent from 1910 to 1920. While some blacks were displaced in the 1920s, generally they held on to their jobs until the Depression.

Largely unskilled workers, blacks were especially hard hit by the Depression and 50 percent of skilled blacks lost their jobs between 1930 and 1936. Paradoxically, there were many gains for blacks during this period as a result of the policies of the administration of President Franklin D. Roosevelt. First of all, black government employees increased substantially from 50,000 in 1937 to 200,000 in 1946. More important, Roosevelt appointed several black intellectuals to subcabinet posts. This so-called black cabinet, including later Secretary of Housing and Urban Development Robert Weaver, and William Hastie, who became Governor of the Virgin Islands in 1946, was influential in protecting the economic interests of blacks. Several New Deal policies benefitted blacks. The first minimum wage law, passed in 1938, insured some degree of equality between black and white workers. The Public Works Administration and the National Relief Act gave jobs and relief to large numbers of blacks. Throughout the 1930s, however, blacks complained that these agencies discriminated against them in the South. Blacks probably gained more from the Civilian Conservation Corps and the National Youth Administration than from any other agencies. In the construction of public housing, Robert Weaver was able to get federal officials to support a policy which called for the hiring of a quota of skilled blacks equal to their percentage in the local labor force.

The greatest economic gains for blacks came during the period from 1940 to 1950 as a result of the Second World War. At the beginning of the war, however, blacks were largely excluded from skilled jobs in the defense industry. Consequently, while there was a 16 percent decline in the white unemployment rate from 1940 to 1942, the black rate remained stationary at 22 percent of the black labor force. In one period in 1941 only 17 of the nearly 9,000 new aircraft workers, 245 of the 35,000 metal workers, and 1.7 percent of the new shipbuilding workers hired were black. Labor-starved plants in Connecticut, Baltimore, and Los Angeles imported unskilled white workers from other parts of the country rather than hire local blacks. Charleston, South Carolina, defense contractors made plans in September, 1942, to import 9,000 white workers while 4,000 blacks in the city were unemployed. Connecticut's Pratt and Whitney and Colt companies became national disgraces by such practices.

The federal government complicated matters by agreeing to closed shops in many defense industries. Since most of the craft unions excluded blacks, it was virtually impossible for them to get jobs. The vocal opposition of blacks to discrimination and the inability of the United States to meet its defense needs led to some changes in this situation. The most important development in this regard was the plan of A. Philip Randolph to stage a march on Washington of 50,000 blacks in 1941. As a result of this threat, Roosevelt issued Executive Order 8802 banning discrimination in employment by companies filling defense contracts and created the Fair Employment Practices Commission to oversee this order. The role of defense needs in decreasing discrimination was illustrated in the Detroit auto plants. With the exception of the Ford plants, where there were 11,000 black workers who constituted 12 percent of the total labor force, in 1940 few blacks were employed in the automobile plants and most of those were unskilled workers. When blacks were first upgraded to skilled jobs, there were numerous wildcat strikes in spite of the admonitions of the leaders of the United Automobile Workers. Blacks were accepted in these new positions only after the Navy Department designated striking workers as disloyal to the government and ordered them fired. Labor competition led to a number of riots during the war; the worst was in Detroit in 1943.

In spite of riots and discrimination, there was greater diversification in black occupations between 1940 and 1944 than there had been during the previous seventy-five years. The percentage of skilled black males nearly doubled, from 4.4 percent in 1940 to 7.3 percent in 1944. There was, however, little change in clerical, sales, and professional occupations. At the end of the war, 95 percent of all professional jobs were held by whites. In the South the color caste occupational structure changed little during the war. There was little change comparable to the 1940s in later decades.

BLACK BUSINESS AFTER 1865

From a broad perspective, it is possible to discern considerable progress in the field of business by blacks after 1865. Lack of capital and experience and economic fluctuations were the greatest barriers for blacks in this area. It was demonstrably easier for blacks, like whites, to get consumer loans and mortgages from banks than to get commercial loans. While consumer loans can be secured by the property being purchased, commercial loans are based largely on the managerial skills of the borrower. Blacks have so few opportunities to develop such skills that it would be difficult for them to obtain loans even if white bankers were not prejudiced. As a result of these factors, black businesses were generally concentrated in those areas needing the smallest initial amount of capital. They also operated, in a sense, in protected markets, offering goods and services not supplied by whites to the segregated black community.

Although there have been few formal studies of black businesses, they may be described generally as small, one-owner concerns which lasted only a short time. W. E. B. Du Bois' first survey of black businesses in 1898 revealed that the average capital invested was only $4,600. A study of almost 4,000 black businesses in twelve cities in 1944 showed that the average annual volume of business done was only $3,260. In many respects, the black businessman steadily lost ground during the twentieth century. Although in 1929 blacks operated 25,000 stores with sales of $101 million, in 1939 they operated nearly 30,000 retail stores with sales of only $71.5 million and employed only 13,778 persons. By 1950 the number of black businessmen had risen to 42,500. Then came the debacle. From 1950 to 1960 the number of black businessmen declined by almost one-fourth to 32,400. In 1960, blacks constituted only 2.5 percent of all self-employed businessmen.

The major achievements of the black in business were in banking, insurance, and publishing. The first banks began as depositories for black benevolent societies in the last decades of the nineteenth century. Between 1888 and 1934, blacks organized 134 banks. Few of these survived more than a few years. In 1911 there were fifty-six black banks in the United States; by 1951 the number had declined to fourteen, with total assets of $32 million and total deposits of $29 million. All but two of them were located in the South. By 1963 there were twenty black banks and forty savings and loan associations with total assets of $422 million. In 1977 there were forty-seven banks and forty savings and loan associations with 2,175 employees and assets of $1.4 billion. Only twenty of these institutions had been established before 1940 and twenty-one or 24 percent, were located in the South. Blacks owned a tiny 0.03 percent of the 14,541 banks in the United States in 1977 and had only 0.001 percent of total bank assets.

The rise of black businessmen was partially a consequence of a long campaign begun in the late 1860s by opinion leaders to encourage self-help and racial solidarity. The leaders contended that the only way that blacks could protect their freedom was to engage in business pursuits and accumulate wealth. Facing unremitting discrimination, they had to create a firm economic foundation to foster racial uplift. Colonel James Lewis of New Orleans took this position in 1875 when he said, "Our labor and our crops bring us money; we need banks wherein we have an interest in which to deposit. We like to insure our houses and our furniture, we then need insurance companies. The fact is we need to enter all the branches of trade." Conferences held at Tuskegee Institute, Atlanta University, and Hampton Institute in the 1890s constantly restated the view that blacks had to enter business in order to insure their economic survival. In 1893 John Hope of Atlanta Baptist College told a group of blacks that "the white man has converted and reconverted the Negro's labor and the Negro's money into capital. . . . We must take in some, if not all, of the wages, turn it into capital, hold it, increase it. . . . Employment must be had, and this employment will have to give an opportunity to Negro workmen who will be crowded out by white competition. . . . There is not much race independence for the race that cannot speak its mind through men whose capital can help or harm those who would bring oppression."

The chief exponent of the business ethic in the twentieth century was the National Negro Business League, organized by Booker T. Washington in 1900. The annual conventions of the league, often attended by more than 1,200 delegates, urged blacks to take advantage of their segregation and contended that Afro-Americans should have enough racial solidarity to patronize their own businesses. Business was, they preached, power; it created respect for blacks and decreased discrimination. An agent of the league, Fred R. Moore, expressed its central creed in 1904: "All business enterprises should be supported, how else can we expect to be respected . . . if we do not begin to practice what a great many of us preach? How can we otherwise succeed?

Some would say that this was drawing the color line. I do not believe it. Jews support Jews; Germans support Germans; Italians support Italians until they get strong enough to compete with their brothers in the professions and trades; and Negroes should now begin to support Negroes." Practically all black newspapers published after 1865 took the same stance as the league. The 1927 assertion of the Pittsburgh *Courier* was characteristic: "It is the duty of American Negroes to support Negro business, *Because It Is Negro Business.*" This sense of patronage as moral obligation permeated the ideology of the National Negro Business League.

Among the earliest exemplars of the racial solidarity preached by the league were black insurance companies. Traditionally the largest enterprises among blacks, the insurance companies were begun in the 1880s because white companies would not insure blacks. Although the earliest companies were so haphazardly run that they rarely lasted more than twenty years, by 1945 there were forty-four black insurance companies, with a total of 4 million policies in force, an annual income of $42 million, and an average of 24.4 employees. In 1960 there were fifty companies, with the twenty largest having $311 million in assets. By 1977 the number of black insurance companies had fallen to thirty-nine with an average of 196 employees, total assets of $614 million, and $11.2 billion in policies in force. Thirty-two of these companies, or 82 percent, were located in the South.

Immediately after the Civil War, blacks established hundreds of newspapers, mostly in the South. The most successful of those in the nineteenth century were the *Weekly Louisianian,* the New York *Age,* and the Savannah *Tribune.* Because of the precariousness of publishing ventures, the number of black newspapers perhaps fluctuated more than any other business. From 1948 to 1956 the number of black newspapers rose from 169 to 350. By 1965 the number had fallen to 156. Generally black newspapers were weeklies of small circulation; the Atlanta *World* was the only daily in 1956. The most important publishing houses have been those of the AME and Baptist churches and the giant of them all, the Johnson Publishing Company. Johnson's *Jet, Black World, Hue, Bronze Thrills,* and numerous books in the 1970s made it one of the most successful publishing ventures. *Ebony* magazine, begun by Johnson in 1946, reached a circulation figure of 1 million by 1965. In 1977 the Johnson Publishing Company had 395 employees and gross sales of $50 million.

Blacks did not participate in great numbers in manufacturing. Easily the most important black enterprises were in cosmetics. Madame C. J. Walker began the first of these businesses in the 1890s and allegedly made $1 million before her death. While few black cosmetic firms equaled Madame Walker's until the 1960s, they were generally more important as a source of employment for blacks than any other business. In 1945 the average number of employees for such businesses was thirty-seven. Two other concerns, the multi-million-dollar S. B. Fuller Brush Company and the Parker House Meat Company of Chicago were the largest black manufacturing concerns until the 1960s. They were joined by a Baltimore meat processor, H. G. Parks, who founded his company in 1951 and by 1974 had 300 employees and sales of $15 million.

Diversification marked the growth of black-owned concerns in the 1970s. They expanded to the manufacturing of electronic, office, petroleum, and communications products. In 1977, the 100 largest black companies had sales of $886.7 million and employed 11,962 persons. Taken at face value, the 1970s diversification of black business hid some of the endemic problems faced by the mass of Afro-Americans. The problems appear in sharp relief, however, when the focus shifts to employment patterns.

THE IMPACT OF COLOR CASTE ON BLACK OCCUPATIONS

The color caste system in the United States was the main determinant of the rate and direction of economic progress or retardation for black workers. Whites readily conceded the heaviest, dirtiest, and lowest-paid unskilled jobs to blacks. Consequently, as long as there was a heavy demand for unskilled workers, blacks were able to garner a disproportionate number of these jobs during times of labor scarcity. The much-heralded shift of black workers from farm to factory labor has been blown out of proportion. Although it is true that the percentage of black male farm laborers declined from 60 percent in 1890 to 40 percent in 1930 and 11 percent in 1960, these workers largely became concentrated in unskilled and service jobs. In 1890 more than 21 percent of the black males were in domestic service, and by 1960 more than 33 percent of them were either domestic servants or unskilled workers.

Relegation to unskilled jobs in industry had a depressing effect on blacks because of the increasingly high rate of automation, an effect that reached crisis proportions in the 1960s. It was estimated, for example, that in 1964 alone automation wiped out 40,000 unskilled jobs weekly.

Blacks were especially susceptible to displacement by technological innovations because of the color caste nexus in occupations. Traditionally in the United States, and almost universally in the South, any job requiring the running of a machine or which was not dirty was a white man's job. A few cases will illustrate the impact of this tradition on blacks. There were a large number of black coal miners between 1910 and 1920. Coal mining was so arduous and dangerous that even when the total number of miners declined by 14 percent between 1920 and 1930, the number of black miners *increased* by 5 percent. But when the mines introduced machinery to load coal in the 1930s, the number of black miners fell drastically. The case of black railroad firemen illustrates this process even more clearly. As long as the coal-burning locomotive was king in America, railroad companies reserved the hot, heavy job of stoker for black firemen in spite of the opposition of white unions. Contrary to the practice with the few white firemen, blacks were ineligible for promotion to engineers and conductors. When diesel engines with mechanical stokers began to replace coal engines in the 1930s, white unions and railroad managers entered into agreements which excluded black firemen. The result was a steady decline in the number of black firemen. While in 1930 blacks consti-tuted almost 7 percent of all locomotive firemen, in 1960 they repre-sented only 2.4 percent of them. The same was true of the teamsters. Throughout the nineteenth century when teamsters drove wagons, blacks were overrepresented in this occupation. When trucks replaced wagons in the twentieth century, blacks almost disappeared from this category. For example, the number of blacks in the teamsters union in New York City fell from 6,000 in 1910 to 313 in 1928. In southern textile and tobacco plants, blacks were barred from operating machines almost from the beginning.

By the 1970s, white capitalists controlled the hiring and firing of more than 70 percent of all wage and salaried employees in the United States. Therefore, they were the chief exploiters of blacks. Among capitalists, it was generally the largest corporations and public utilities which were most guilty of discrimination. For instance, the EEOC investigated the communications industry and reported in 1972: "From the earliest times Black workers were almost completely excluded from employment in the telecommunications industry. In 1930, when Blacks constituted 9.7 percent of the total population in the United States, they represented only 0.7 percent of the workers in the telecommuni-cations industry and were exclusively concentrated in the service worker and laborer jobs." The chief culprit in this area was the giant monopoly, the American Telephone and Telegraph Company (AT&T). Traditionally, AT&T imported workers from other parts of the country rather than hire local blacks. Even when, under government pressure, AT&T increased the number of its black employees until they repre-sented 9.8 percent of its total labor force in 1970, they were heavily concentrated in the lowest-paid, least desirable jobs. Since all telephone company employees are *trained on the job*, blatant racism and not lack of qualifications was the explanation for discrimination against blacks. The gas and electric utility companies were worse than AT&T. In 1970 the EEOC reported that one-third of all utility companies in the United States had no black employees and that the utilities ranked last among the twenty-three largest industries in the employment of blacks. The relative contribution of white capitalists and white laborers to the economic oppression of blacks was revealed in 1972, when 86 percent of the complaints received by the EEOC were against employers while only 5 percent were against unions.

Capitalists appealed to racism in an effort to lower the cost of production. In the South, where the income of blacks was only 47 percent of that of whites in 1969, the income of southern whites was also considerably lower than that of northern whites (23 percent less in the case of factory workers). Significantly, southern whites earned less than northern blacks in many occupations: 4 percent less for craftsmen, 18 percent less for factory workers, and $3,500 less for bus drivers. Capitalists discriminated against blacks in an effort to lower *all* wages.

The clearest example of the capitalists' exploitation of blacks appears when inventions are examined. By the 1970s, there were numerous manufacturing enterprises in the United States which owed their existence to a black person's invention but excluded blacks from employment. The total number of patents filed by blacks for new inventions is not clear. According to an early survey, however, blacks filed more than 1,000 patents between 1834 and 1900. Unlike other inventors, blacks gained little wealth or recognition. Garret Morgan, the creator of the gas mask and other firefighting equipment, received only $40,000 from the General Electric Corporation when it purchased the patent for the automated traffic light he invented in 1923. The black inventor of portable refrigeration units for trucks (McKinley Jones), the mechanical shoe-lasting machine (Jan Matzeliger), automatic lubricators for machines (Elijah McCoy), and automatic air brakes (Granville T. Woods) fared little better than Morgan when their patents were purchased by such corporate giants as the United Shoe Machinery Company, Bell Telephone, Westinghouse, and General Electric.

After exploitation by capitalists, the second greatest barrier to black economic progress was European immigration. While capitalists encouraged immigration in an effort to enlarge the labor supply and depress all wages, the chief sufferers were black. The immediate result of the large-scale immigration in the nineteenth century was to reduce the percentage of blacks in the labor force. On their way to the top of the economic ladder, European immigrants competed with blacks for the lowest-paying jobs. And as long as the industrialist had an abundant supply of cheap white labor, he made no effort to employ blacks.

Successive waves of European immigrants climbed over blacks on their way up the economic ladder. The consequence was that by 1971, every immigrant group had a higher median income than blacks, who were forced to come to the United States first.

UNION DISCRIMINATION AGAINST BLACKS

The third greatest barrier to black economic survival was the union. From their beginning in the second half of the eighteenth century until the 1980s, unions excluded blacks in several ways. Some unions restricted their membership to whites either by constitutional provision or by the initiation ritual. Others refused to accept blacks as apprentices. The exclusion was greatest in the craft unions, which always tried to limit the number of skilled workers in order to keep wages high. The occupational mobility of blacks was also blocked because early craft unions were quasi-fraternal organizations with numerous social functions. Most whites felt that if blacks were admitted to these functions, it would be a recognition of their social equality. As a result, none of the thirty-two unions formed before 1860 accepted blacks.

On the surface, there appeared to be a surprising change in the sentiment of organized labor toward black workers after the Civil War. Practically all of the leaders of nationwide labor organizations favored cooperation with black workers. For example, the leaders of the National Labor Union (NLU), formed in 1866, tried for three years to get the affiliated unions to accept blacks and finally in 1869 urged blacks to form separate unions to be affiliated with the NLU. As a result of the failure of the integration movement, the Colored National Labor Union was formed in 1869. For the most part, it was ineffectual, and under the leadership of Frederick Douglass it became an arm of the Republican party in 1872. The enduring problems of labor were apparent in the short history of the NLU. In spite of the pronouncements of the leaders, the locals of the national unions refused to accept blacks. In fact, one of the major catalysts in the formation of the Colored National Labor Union was the refusal of the Washington, D.C., local of the typographers union to accept Lewis H. Douglass, Frederick's son, as a member.

Only two national unions formed before 1920 fostered racial cooperation. The first of these was the Knights of Labor, active from 1869 to 1887. Black Knights belonged to both separate and mixed locals, held union offices, and attended integrated social functions and conventions. Blacks supported the Knights because it organized all workers in an industry rather than just those in crafts. This meant that many unskilled blacks could join and were actively recruited. The Knights also appealed to blacks because it stressed land reform and the improvement of education and because of its willingness to support the demands of black workers. It supported, for example, the successful 1883 strike of 3,000 black tobacco workers in Lynchburg, Virginia, for higher wages. In 1887, in spite of threats and some lynchings, the Knights were prominent in the unsuccessful strike of black farm workers in the Louisiana sugar fields. As a result of the union's policies, there were about 400 separate black locals and 90,000 blacks among the 700,000 Knights in 1887. The inheritor of the ideals of the Knights was the interracial union, the Industrial Workers of the World (IWW). From its organization in 1905 until its destruction in the 1920s, the IWW made a special effort to recruit blacks. It was especially successful in creating solidarity between black and white timber and dock workers in the South and probably had 30,000 black members by 1914.

The most powerful national union after 1880 was the American Federation of Labor (AFL). Led in its first decades by a Jewish immigrant, Samuel Gompers, the AFL took an advanced position in regard to black workers. From 1886 to 1895 the AFL required a nondiscrimination pledge from all unions seeking a charter, threatened to establish rival unions to those practicing discrimination, and set up all-black locals as a temporary expedient when blacks were not organized. From the beginning, however, Gompers retreated from this position. Even while he insisted on integrated unions, Gompers appointed only two black organizers in the 1890s. Many of the affiliates of the AFL did not have constitutional bans against blacks but had bans in their rituals. Seeking opportunistic gains for skilled workers, the AFL automatically excluded the mass of unskilled blacks.

In actuality, the only reason that AFL leaders were concerned about blacks was the fear that they would endanger white workers. Gompers stated this clearly when he wrote in 1893, "If our fellow white wage worker will not allow the colored workers to co-operate with him, he will necessarily cling to the other hand (that of the employer) who also smites him, but at least recognizes his right to work. If we do not make friends of the colored men they will of necessity be justified in proving themselves our enemies, and they will be utilized upon every occasion to frustrate our every effort for economic, social and political improvement." From 1896 on, the AFL made few efforts to organize blacks. In fact, it capitulated completely to the rising tide of Jim Crowism and became one of the major agencies for preserving white supremacy. After 1896, unions with lily-white constitutions were given charters, most blacks were organized in separate locals, and the constitution of the AFL was amended to permit white workers to control black locals. When black spokesman Booker T. Washington charged in 1897 that the AFL was blocking the economic advance of blacks, there were vehement denials but little action.

After 1896 Gompers became an outspoken opponent of black workers. While in 1893 he had charged that the black would be an enemy of labor only if white workers refused to cooperate with him, he now began to insist that the major barrier to cooperation was that blacks were prone to strikebreaking. In 1899 Gompers claimed that the only reason the unions discriminated against blacks was that they had "so conducted themselves as to be a continuous whip placed in the hands of employers to cow the white men and to compel them to accept abject conditions of labor." After unorganized blacks broke a strike in the Chicago stockyards in 1904, Gompers described them as "hordes of ignorant blacks . . . possessing but few of those attributes we have learned to revere and love . . . huge, strapping fellows, ignorant and vicious, whose predominating trait was animalism." The impact of such attitudes was obvious. W. E. B. Du Bois found in 1902 that forty-three national unions had no black members, and there were only 40,000 blacks among the 1 million members of the AFL. Gompers ignored black protests and in 1910 virtually read blacks out of the labor movement because, he asserted, they were only a few years removed from slavery and did not think like white workers.

In the twentieth century the AFL craft unions tried to control black skilled workers through separate locals and auxiliaries. Under this scheme the unions ignored seniority, and blacks were relegated to the lowest-paying jobs and hired only after all whites were employed. This was especially true of the building trades and longshoremen. In the nineteenth century so many blacks had learned painting, bricklaying, and carpentry as slaves that it was impossible to have unions which excluded them, especially in the South. Utilizing separate locals, white unions usually restricted blacks to work in certain areas of cities, to work with black contractors, and to handle small projects. This had a depressing effect on blacks because as large-scale building ventures became dominant in the twentieth century, they were unable to develop the new skills demanded for such jobs as pipe fitting, electrical work, and welding. Then, to solidify their control of jobs, the unions utilized the apprenticeship system to restrict the number of new members. For example, in the 1960s the Washington, D.C., electrical union admitted only sixty new apprentices annually with one-third of the openings reserved for relatives of union members. Some programs in New York accepted only twenty apprentices each year, who had to obtain the recommendations of two union members. If he somehow got through the apprenticeship program, a black man still might not obtain employment, for as a journeyman, he often had to have the recommendation of two union members to get a job. The impact of these practices on blacks was devastating. For example, in 1960 there were no blacks in the ironworkers, steam fitters, plumbers, electrical, or sheet metal unions in Baltimore, Maryland. Of the 10,000 members of thirteen Baltimore skilled craft unions in building trades, only 400 were blacks. Although the percentage of black carpenters, bricklayers, painters, and plasterers increased between 1890 and 1960, their share of the most lucrative jobs declined as a result of union practices. Black Local 1888 of the carpenters union in New York, organized after World War I, was still largely restricted to working in Harlem for black contractors in the 1960s.

The same pattern was true among longshoremen. The loading and unloading of ships was such arduous, dangerous, and irregular labor that the percentage of blacks rose from about 29 percent in 1910 to 38 percent in 1960. Whites generally obtained the best jobs by establishing separate locals where most of the hiring was done.

Blacks were uncompromising in their opposition to white-only unions. If, they argued, the unions monopolized skilled jobs, blacks would be permanently frozen into the "lumpenproletariat," to be perpetual hewers of wood and drawers of water. The actions of white organized labor placed the people who were the living symbols of the working class in the anomalous position of warring against their fellow workers. Until the 1960s an overwhelming majority of blacks opposed the organization of unions. Whenever an industry was unionized, blacks campaigned against closed shops which restricted jobs to union members. Chandler Owen, co-editor of the *Messenger* magazine, succinctly characterized this phenomenon in 1923:

> In all parts of the United States the Negroes are generally opposed to labor unions. They favor the open shop. It is not facetious to state that many Negroes understand the term "closed shop" to mean "closed to Negroes." . . . It is obvious the Negroes could not secure or retain confidence in white unions so long as everything—from pretext, ruse and evasion to brutal frankness—excluded them from labor unions. Naturally and properly the *man of color decided: "What care I how fair she be, if she is not fair to me?"* It is better to have *low wages than no wages!* The Negro quite sanely prefers a *lower standard of living* in the open shop, to starvation, or no standard of living, as a result of the closed shop!

A year later a convention of fifty-two editors of black newspapers passed a resolution "condemning all forms of Unionism."

From 1865 to the 1930s black workers made many of their most important advances as "scabs," that is, strikebreakers. Most black leaders condoned this practice. They contended that the more active blacks were in breaking strikes called by white-only unions, the more pressure would be put on organized labor to admit blacks. With unassailable logic, W. E. B. Du Bois declared in 1912 that white unionists "beat or starve the Negro out of his job. . . . What then must be the attitude of the black man in the event of a strike . . . ? The mass of them must most naturally regard the union white man as their enemy. . . . So long as union labor fights for humanity, its mission is divine; but when it fights for a clique of Americans, . . . they deserve themselves the starvation which they plan for their darker and poorer fellows." The instinct for self-preservation and a desire for revenge on their enemy made blacks, along with the police, the most potent instrument for breaking strikes. As a result of racial exclusion, Chandler Owen argued, "Negro workers were and are ever ready to take the place of union strikers. . . . The labor unions of America have frequently felt this blow. Negroes have participated as strike breakers in most great American strikes. They have been a thorn in the strikers' side." Since every man wanted to improve his condition, it was, A. Philip Randolph contended, "idle and vain to hope or expect Negro workers, out of work and who receive less wages when at work than white workers, to refuse to scab upon white workers when an opportunity presents itself."

By excluding blacks, white labor was insuring its own oppression by the capitalist class. Exclusion allowed capital to pose as a friend of the blacks. Traditionally, businessmen were more effective in bringing blacks into industry and eventually forcing them into the unions than was organized labor. Black labor was played off against white labor by the capitalists in an effort to exploit both more systematically. The Communist party saw this clearly. In 1930 the party declared:

> The low standard of living of Negro workers is made use of by the capitalists to reduce the wages of the white workers. The mis-leaders of labor, the heads of the reformist and reactionary trade union organizations are refusing to organize Negro workers and thereby are helping the capitalist masters to drive a wedge between the white and colored proletarians. This anti-Negro attitude of the reactionary labor leaders helps to split the ranks of labor, allows the employers to carry out their policy of "divide and rule," frustrates the efforts of the working class to emancipate itself from the yoke of capitalism, and dims the class-consciousness of the white workers as well as of the Negro workers. . . .

M. C. Work, a black Communist, felt that it was mandatory for white labor to march in the vanguard of those working for black liberation.

LABOR AND CAPITAL

From Messenger Magazine 2 (Aug. 1919). Copyright © 1919 Messenger Magazine.

"Unity among the toiling masses," he claimed in the 1930s, was "absolutely necessary in the revolutionary struggle against American capitalism." Whether they were Communists or not, most blacks agreed with Work.

The Socialist-oriented black magazine, the *Messenger,* called repeatedly for unity between black and white workers and in 1919 demanded the dissolution of the AFL because it was "the most wicked machine for the propagation of race prejudice in the country." Dubbing the AFL the "American Separation of Labor," the *Messenger* fought for unity among black and white workers as a way of achieving their common goals of more wages, shorter hours, and improved working conditions. Without unity, the bargaining power of each group was dissipated:

> The history of the labor movement in America proves that the employing class recognizes no race lines. They will exploit a white man as readily as a black man. They will exploit women as readily as men. They will even go to the extent of coining the labor, blood and suffering of children into dollars. The introduction of women and children into

the factories proves that capitalists are only concerned with profits and that they will exploit any race or class in order to make profits, . . . if the employers can keep the white and black dogs, on account of race prejudice, fighting over a bone, the yellow capitalist dog will get away with the bone—the bone of profits. No union man's standard of living is safe so long as there is a group of men and women who may be used as scabs and whose standard of living is lower.

Much of the black's progress in organized labor was a result of such protests and of the policies of the United Mine Workers (UMW). Founded in the 1890s, the UMW followed a nondiscrimination policy primarily because unorganized blacks had successfully broken several strikes in the 1880s. To prevent this, the UMW used black organizers in the 1890s but was unable to organize many of the mines in Alabama and West Virginia until 1933 because of management's use of the race issue. The Congress of Industrial Organizations (CIO), an assembly of industrywide unions like the UMW, constantly prodded the exclusivist AFL on the racial issue. Primarily as a result of the CIO, the number of blacks in trade unions rose from 60,000 in 1930 to 700,000 in 1945.

On a very limited and primarily moral basis, the AFL made some progress in the twentieth century. For example, A. Philip Randolph formed the 9,000-man union of Pullman porters in 1925 and eventually received a charter from the AFL. While in 1940 there were 26 affiliates of the AFL whose constitutions banned blacks from membership, there was only 1 in 1960—the Brotherhood of Locomotive Firemen and Engineers. Under pressure from government and black leaders, 116 of the AFL-CIO affiliates signed voluntary antidiscrimination agreements in the 1960s and labor leaders were prominent in their support of the civil rights movement. Such support was largely meaningless, because the AFL was powerless to enforce the antidiscrimination agreements. For example, in the 1960s the home local of George Meany (president of the AFL) in New York steadfastly refused to accept black plumbers.

The merging of the AFL and the CIO in 1956 revitalized egalitarianism in organized labor. A civil rights department was established in the AFL-CIO, and there was a steady increase in black unionists; in 1970 there were 2 million blacks in trade unions, or 10 percent of the total. Union membership was one of the key factors in the movement toward the equalization of black and white incomes. The United Automobile Workers had the best record of equality of treatment of workers and the teamsters, construction, communications, and railway engineers unions had the worst. In 1973 alone the Justice Department filed 349 suits against the teamsters union and trucking companies because of their discrimination against blacks.

EXPLOITATION IN GOVERNMENT EMPLOYMENT

The federal, state, and local governments did little beyond giving rhetorical support to the black man's right to make a living. On paper, however, the record is impressive. In 1933 the Unemployment Relief Act banned racial discrimination, and the Fair Employment Practices Commission created by Roosevelt banned it in defense contracts. President Truman established a Fair Employment Board to oversee Civil Service employment in 1948, and President Eisenhower later created a committee on government contracts to prevent discrimination. The most effective effort in this regard was launched in 1961 with President Kennedy's creation of the Committee on Equal Employment Opportunity. In spite of all of these committees and of the fact that after 1943 all government contracts banned discrimination, there were relatively few actual benefits for blacks. The 10 million workers on the payrolls of the 100 largest defense contractors in 1960 included few blacks. This was primarily a result of the weaknesses of federal compliance procedures—the Fair Employment Commissions were always understaffed and without the power of enforcement.

The worst record of the federal government was in preventing discrimination in state and local projects financed by federal grants-in-aid, which totaled $7.5 billion in 1960. These grants covered highway, hospital, school, and airport construction. Similarly, the requirement that the number of black skilled workers on public housing and slum clearance projects equal their percentage in these occupations in local areas was rarely enforced. In many ways, the government was an active participant in the restrictive activities of the craft unions. An example is the federal support of vocational training that began with the Smith-Hughes Act of 1917. Although discrimination in the program was banned in 1948, little of the money went to blacks and then only for understaffed, underequipped schools. Discrimination in this area increased with the passage of the National Defense Education Act in 1958. Although the federal government did not finance apprenticeship programs, it did provide technical assistance to them. This assistance was given in 1960 to about 8,000 such programs which excluded blacks. For example, only 14 blacks were among the 4,000 apprentices in the state of New Jersey in 1960. The U.S. Employment Service, which provided funds for state-operated employment bureaus, acted contrary to the interests of blacks. It encouraged skilled blacks to register for unskilled jobs, established separate black employment agencies, accepted requests from lily-white employers, and made no effort to get employers to accept black workers.

It must be admitted, however, that federal jobs were easier for

blacks to obtain than jobs in any area of private industry. Although
representing only 10 percent of the labor force in 1960, blacks held
13 percent of the 6 million federal jobs. In the Government Printing
Office, Veterans Administration, General Services Administration,
Health, Education and Welfare Department, and Post Office, blacks
represented 20 to 40 percent of the labor force in the 1970s. Unfortunately, most of the black federal employees were in the lowest-paid
jobs. In 1960 more than 90 percent of all black federal employees
earned less than $6,500 annually. One reflection of the gross economic
exploitation of blacks by the federal government was the fact that
their per capita income in the District of Columbia was only 39 percent
of that of whites in 1969.

Title VII of the Civil Rights Act of 1964 and the Equal Employment
Act of 1972 banned discrimination by employers with more than 100
workers and empowered the EEOC to investigate complaints, to bring
suits, and to call for the cancellation of federal contracts held by offending companies. In spite of frequent documentation of discrimination,
few government contracts were cancelled. The federal government
was never serious about ending discrimination. In 1975 less than one-
tenth of 1 percent of the federal budget was devoted to ending discrimination in employment. The U.S. Commission on Civil Rights concluded
in 1973 that "executive branch enforcement of civil rights mandates
was so inadequate as to render the laws practically meaningless." Since
approximately 40 percent of the civilian workers in the United States
were employed by companies receiving more than $100 billion in fed-
eral contracts annually by the 1970s, the government was directly subsidizing discrimination.

Although 28 percent of all blacks held local, state, or federal jobs
in 1970, they were still concentrated in the lowest-paying occupations.
In the federal government, blacks were rarely employed in policymaking positions. The U.S. Commission on Civil Rights reported in 1973,
"Minorities at the highest policy levels (GS-16-18) remain below 3%.
Many agencies, including CSC (Civil Service Commission) have no
minorities in such positions. None of the regulatory agencies have any
minorities among their 418 GS-16-18 positions. Less than 1% of the
982 such positions in the Department of Defense are held by minorities.
The Atomic Energy Commission and the National Aeronautics and
Space Administration each have one minority person at the GS-16-
18 level, out of 640 such positions." So many corporate executives
from businesses notorious for discriminating against blacks were appointed to high-level positions that there was little likelihood that this
pattern would change in subsequent years. When the New York *Times*

reported in December, 1973, that twenty members of Congress speci-
fied "whites only" in advertising for staff workers, any hope that help
might come from that branch of government virtually disappeared.

PERSISTENT POVERTY AND ECONOMIC EXPLOITATION
IN THE 1960S AND 1970S

The black worker was so victimized by the American caste system
that it became a truism among economists that while whites generally
fluctuate between prosperity and recession, blacks fluctuate between
depression and great depression. As a result of economic deprivation,
blacks suffered from greater mortality, lower life expectancy, lower
income, and greater unemployment than did whites. In 1965, while
only 12 percent of the white families lived in poverty, 43 percent of
all black families earned less than $3,000 yearly. In other words, blacks
were more than three times as likely as whites to live in poverty.

After World War II, the black lived in a state of constant depression.
His unemployment rate was always double that of whites and after
1954 rarely fell below 7.5 percent. During slack times, the black unemployment rate skyrocketed. For example, in 1960 when blacks constituted only 19 percent of the labor force in Detroit, they were 61 percent
of the unemployed. In 1973 the unemployment rate for black adults
was 12.5 percent (compared to 6.2 percent for whites), and for black-
teenagers it was 38.3 percent. Dismal as they are, unemployment figures are only a small reflection of the plight of black workers. In 1963
when 10.9 percent of all black workers were unemployed, 9.5 percent
of them had only part-time jobs. Then, too, blacks tended to be unemployed about two months longer on the average than whites.

In the twentieth century, blacks lost ground in many areas, and
in others their progress was exaggerated. By 1960, blacks had reached
the level whites had attained in 1940 in education, income, death rate,
and life expectancy, and were thirty-five years behind whites in college
education and sixty years behind in their share of white-collar jobs.
While the number of poor families in the United States declined by
30 percent between 1947 and 1963, the number of poor black families
increased by 2 percent. Similarly, the movement toward equalization
of family income frequently lost ground after 1945. Black families
earned 55 percent of the income of whites in 1945; by 1965 they were
earning only 53 percent of white incomes. The high point came in
1970, when the median income of black families was 61.3 percent of
that for white families. The gap widened after 1970; in 1973 the median
family income of blacks fell to 57.5 percent of that of whites. The

figure was below 60 percent for all except four of the years between 1945 and 1973. Since black families were larger than white families, the disparities in income were understated.

Although there were many sharp increases in the family incomes of blacks, few of the increases were sustained. The 1973 figure indicates that black income as a proportion of white median income increased at an abysmally low rate of about 1.2 percent every fifteen years after 1954. If this rate of progress continues, the family income of blacks will equal that of whites in 2393 A.D.

Economic discrimination and the systematic emasculation of the black male are revealed clearly in statistics on occupation, education, and income. Since six out of every ten black families earned less than $4,000 in 1961, more black than white wives had to contribute to the family income. The discrimination against the black male is shown in the fact that from 1949 to 1965 black women were able to narrow the gap between their income and that of white women, but black males lost ground to white males. At the 1970s rate, it will take twice as long for black males as for black females to equal whites in income. In 1964 black women earned 70 percent of the income of white women, but black males earned only 56 percent as much as white males. Then, too, the black male was much more likely to be unemployed than the black female. The black female was also more likely to obtain a high-status job than was the black male. In 1960 only 6 percent of black males had white-collar jobs, as opposed to 10 percent of black females. Similarly, only 3.9 percent of black males held professional jobs, while 7.5 percent of black females held them. All of these factors, of course, undermined black family stability.

The economic oppression of the black male continued in the 1970s. A black man had to have three more years of education than a white man to earn as much as he did. At the same time, the more favorable position of the black female was a function of the general oppression of females (even the most highly educated white females earned less than 50 percent as much as white males with the same amount of education).

In actuality, the black woman was triply oppressed: as a worker, as a black, and as a female. The much-heralded movement toward the equalization of the income of black and white women between 1952 and 1972 was deceptive. An overwhelming majority of black women in the labor force worked *full time,* while a majority of the white women worked part time. In spite of this, black women generally earned *less* than white women. Consequently, although it appeared that education led to greater equalization of income for black women, it might, in fact, have caused greater discrimination. As a despised sexual and racial minority, even when the most highly educated black women earned more than equally educated white women, they earned only 68 percent as much as black men and 48 percent as much as white men at the same educational level in 1971.

Before the depression which began in 1972, there was much talk of the economic progress which had been made by blacks. Viewed in terms of black folklore, however, black Americans had been making progress at a snail's pace. For example, between 1964 and 1972, the median family income of blacks increased from 54 to 59 percent of the white family income. The "progress" made by blacks in this area was confined almost entirely to black females. Between 1952 and 1972, the income of black females rose from 49 to 96 percent of the income of white females. During that same twenty-year period, the income of black males increased at a painfully slow rate, rising from 55 to 62 percent of the income of white males. While all of the progress of blacks was being hailed in the press, 7.7 million blacks were still living in poverty in 1972. Compared to the rest of the nation, blacks had been steadily losing the race against poverty. While blacks constituted only 25.1 percent of all persons living in poverty in 1959, they constituted 31.5 percent of the poverty-stricken in 1972.

After 1950, blacks in the United States lost between $30 and $40 billion in personal income annually as a direct consequence of discrimination. Added together, the losses exceeded the total personal income earned in the United States in 1972 ($715.3). In all age and educational groups and in all regions, blacks earned less than whites. With 10.8 percent of the population in 1965, blacks earned only 5 percent of the country's income, about $27 billion. The picture improved little after 1965; in 1971 blacks earned $53.3 billion, or 6.9 percent of the total income in the United States.

While being grossly exploited, blacks were perceived by whites as primarily welfare recipients. Yet, in spite of the fact that one-third of the black population lived in poverty in 1972, only 5.6 percent of their total income came from public assistance. Stereotypes notwithstanding, most welfare recipients were neither black, Puerto Rican, nor Mexican-Americans. The poor, black and white, received fewer subsidies while paying a higher rate of taxation than any other class. People earning less than $2,000 paid out 44 percent of their income in state, federal, local, and sales taxes in the 1970s. Middle- and upper-income families rarely paid more than 20 percent of their income in taxes. The rich not only received annual subsidies which dwarfed welfare payments, they did not have the subsidies consumed by a nonfunctional bureaucracy. For every dollar received by a welfare recipient, more than one dollar was absorbed by the bureaucrats who gave the

POVERTY

From Luther Raps *by Brumsic Brandon. Copyright © 1971, Paul S. Erickson, Inc. Reprinted by permission of Paul S. Erickson, Inc.*

money to him. More of the money of the poor went to subsidize the rich than the contrary. Federal tax laws exempting mortgage interest from taxable income of middle-class families often amounted to a 30 percent monthly subsidy in the 1970s. The billions of dollars of direct federal subsidies to the maritime and aviation industries alone far exceeded welfare payments. Until the mid-1970s, the oil depletion allowance frequently amounted to a 46 percent subsidy to multi-billion-dollar oil corporations, while thousands of farmers received more than $20,000 annually *not* to grow crops.

BLACK CAPITALISM CAMPAIGN

If the black share of public assistance, wages, and federal subsidies was abysmally low, the picture in business was even worse. In 1960, blacks made up only 2.5 percent of all self-employed businessmen and earned a median income of only $3,368. Blacks remained concentrated in service categories and were restricted to a small segregated market.

Their share of the most important financial institutions was insignificant. In 1960 blacks represented only 0.2 percent of the bankers in the United States and had less than 1 percent of the assets in all banks. Similarly, black companies had only 0.23 percent of the $133 billion in assets in the insurance field. Not only were black businessmen restricted to a segregated market, they were losing out in competition to whites for even that business. More than 90 percent of all money spent in black communities in the 1960s went into the pockets of whites.

After more than 350 years of oppression, blacks had no stake in the capitalist system. In 1969 there were only 4,807 black families with incomes of $50,000 or more (in most cases both the husband and wife worked). For all practical purposes there were no capitalists among blacks, and the petit bourgeoisie (managers, administrators, self-employed) constituted only 3.2 percent of all gainfully employed blacks in 1970. The number of black-owned businesses was always minuscule; in 1969 there were 163,000 of them, with total annual receipts of $4.4 billion. An overwhelming majority (125,000) were operated by one person. All of the black-owned businesses combined had a total of 277,000 workers. The black share in business was trivial. The 347 largest black business firms had total sales of only $877 million and employed only 17,687 employees in 1969. The largest black firm in 1977, Motown Industries, had 300 employees and total sales of $61 million. Only five companies had more than 500 employees, and the $886 million in sales of the 100 largest black companies in 1977 was smaller than the earnings of a medium-sized white corporation.

President Richard Nixon launched a campaign in 1969, "Black Capitalism," to give blacks a greater stake in the economy. Inaugurated during an era when ownership of capitalist enterprises was being increasingly concentrated in the hands of a smaller and smaller white elite, the Nixon campaign was doomed to failure. Neither the business establishment nor the government committed substantial funds to the movement. While extending $26 billion in credits to white corporations in 1973, the government granted less than $1 billion to black-owned businesses. According to the publicity releases of the Nixon administration, a special effort was to be made to increase the assets of black-owned banks. Yet, the thirty-five black banks received an average of only $3 million. The result was that by 1973 the largest black bank, the Independence Bank of Chicago, had assets of only $56 million. The "Black Capitalism" campaign was a colossal hoax. It was never intended to be anything more than propaganda to attract black voters to the Republican party. The New York *Times* concluded in 1973, "The Nixon administration's program to provide funds and other aid to minority businessmen was turned in 1972 into the vehicle by which the president's re-election effort sought nonwhite support. Not only were minority businessmen under intense pressure from the White House and the president's campaign staff to support him . . . but few minorities were awarded contracts last year without at least an attempted political quid pro quo. . . . Besides political misuse of the program, there were instances of money set aside for minorities ending up with whites."

Even before its seamy side came to light, many blacks rejected the Nixon approach to black economic development. It was, they felt, too slow. Julian Bond, a Georgia legislator, argued in 1971 that it was "a pitifully underfinanced public relations gimmick. . . . What we need is not Black capitalism but something more properly called 'community socialism,' that we may have profit for the many instead of the few." James Boggs, in his book *Racism and the Class Struggle* (1970), asserted, "Capitalism, regardless of its color, is a system of exploitation of one set of people by another set of people. . . . Black capitalism is a dream and a delusion. Blacks have no one under them to exploit. So Black capitalism would have to exploit a Black labor force which is already at the bottom of the ladder and in no mood to change from one exploiter to another just because he is of the same color."

Based on the rate of progress of the 50 years from 1925 to 1975, it will take blacks 150 years to obtain their fair share of businesses and more than 900 years in the case of banking and insurance. In regard to occupations, even if blacks progressed at the relatively rapid rate seen in the period between 1940 and 1970, it will take 270 years for them to be fairly represented as sales workers, 415 years in the area of managers, officials, and proprietors, and 530 years for fair representation as professionals. Increasingly after 1960, blacks let America know they would not wait that long. A number of specific plans were articulated to improve the black's plight; some things were seen as absolutely essential in this regard.

Considering the underdeveloped nature of black communities and the perpetual depression blacks face, drastic measures had to be taken to insure their economic survival. First, many economists argued that there should be preferential treatment for blacks in business, apprenticeship, employment, and educational programs. This, they claimed, was not a new concept. For decades whites had received preferential treatment in segregated schools and in employment. Universities traditionally admitted less qualified sons of alumni, athletes, and band members. The federal government gave tax exemptions for interest on state bonds, provided subsidies to railroads, airlines, ship companies and farmers, and insured companies engaged in foreign trade. Second, since employment opportunities were greater for blacks in government service, all apprenticeship programs should be operated by the government; skilled craftsmen should be licensed by state agencies on a nondiscriminatory basis; local building codes requiring that no construction work be approved by housing inspectors unless completed by union workers should be revised; and building inspectors should be required to include at least the same percentage of blacks as they represent in the total population.

CONSIDERING ALTERNATIVES TO CAPITALISM

Because the economic problems faced by blacks were endemic, they began to see that they would have to deal systematically with ideas to reform the economy as a whole. Beginning in the 1870s, a few black intellectuals saw some hope in socialism. As early as 1878, Ohio's Peter H. Clark ran for Congress on the Socialist Labor party ticket. New York journalist T. Thomas Fortune supported socialist ideas in the 1880s in his editorials and in his book *Black and White: Land, Labor and Politics in the South* (1884). Criticizing monopolies, land grants to railroads, and capital's exploitation of labor, Fortune called for "restrictions on the power and extent of monopoly and corporate extortion" and taxation of large incomes to redistribute wealth. Other socialist sympathizers during this period were the journalist T. McCants Stewart and D. A. Straker. Since socialism stressed equality and was nearest to "the teachings of Jesus," Reverdy C. Ransom called upon blacks in 1905 to become socialists because "socialism is begirt with the spirit of righteousness and seeks to establish itself on the foundation of justice." In that same year the *Colored American Magazine* carried a series of articles on socialism in which the author argued that private ownership of the means of production had led to the degradation and poverty of blacks. Since socialism's "beneficence shall be for all races," blacks would accept it "when once they grasp the truth and see the criminality, the brutality of Capitalism in its nakedness."

An Atlanta black accepted these views and wrote in November, 1905, that he had "faith that the Socialist Labor Party will emancipate the Negro on the political and industrial field. The Negro being of the proletariat class, how can he expect the relief he seeks from the Republican-Democratic—Democratic-Republican parties—both capitalistic and non-humanitarian. . . . Socialism is going to save the Negro and nothing else." A year earlier, a black socialist from New Orleans insisted that "Socialism will settle the industrial problem for blacks and whites, for the *human race,* and for all time. . . . the Socialist protests and is going to abolish 'wage slavery,' an advanced and ingenious method of a small minority fleecing a great majority of the human race, whether white, black or intermediate shades." As editor of the *Horizon*, W. E. B. Du Bois aligned himself with socialism and asserted in 1907 that it was

> the one great hope of the Negro American. We have been thrown by strange historic reasons into the hands of the capitalists hitherto. We have been objects of dole and charity, and despised accordingly. We have been made tools of oppression against the workingman's cause— the puppets and playthings of the idle rich. Fools! We must awake! Not in a renaissance among ourselves of the evils of Get and Grab— not in private hoarding, squeezing and cheating, lies our salvation, but rather in that larger ideal of human brotherhood, equality of opportunity and work not for wealth but for Weal—here lies our shining goal. This goal the Socialists with all their extravagance and occasional foolishness have more stoutly followed than any other class and thus far we must follow them. Our natural friends are not the rich but the poor, not the great but the masses, not the employers but the employees. Our good is not wealth, power, oppression and snobbishness, but helpfulness, efficiency, service and self-respect.

Between 1918 and 1923 the major black supporters of socialism were the editors of the *Messenger* magazine, A. Philip Randolph and Chandler Owen. Contending that a small capitalist minority was exploiting and robbing the workers, the *Messenger* called upon blacks to replace the "greed, selfishness, oppression, murder" of capitalism with collective ownership of the means of production, railroads, and utilities. The *Messenger* pushed the socialist program with relentless logic: "Most Negro families are upon the brink of poverty. They are not striving to live but they are struggling to keep from dying. . . . Capitalism or the private ownership of the social tools of production and exchange is the mother of poverty . . . ignorance, crime, prostitution, race prejudice, etc." The editors favored free food and medical care for school children, consumer and farmer cooperatives, the worker receiving the full value of what his labor produced, job security, guaranteed incomes during sickness, old age, unemployment, and maternity leave, and equal pay regardless of race and sex.

Blacks would especially benefit from the new regime because it would abolish high rents and landlord exploitation and guarantee "equal opportunity for all men to improve their talents, and to advance according to their ability, and not according to the arbitrary will, pleasure or favor of persons in power." Finally, socialism would raise blacks from the base of the industrial world and lower the cost of living. According to the *Messenger:*

The Socialists would abolish the high cost of living, by taking the mills, coal mines, factories and land which labor uses to produce life's necessities, also warehouses, meat packing industries, etc., out of the hands of private individuals, whose only desire is to make profits, and would make them public properties and conduct them for the public's good.

The social ownership of social tools which produce necessities for social use, is the only solution to the problem of the high cost of living.

Today both the producer and the consumer are robbed. The farmer gets little or nothing for what he produces. He is told that the market is bad, that the demand for his products is low, [and] thereby is induced to accept a price below the market price. The consumer, on the other hand, is told that crops are bad, that goods are scarce and is thereby forced to pay an extortionate price for life's necessities.

Almost as soon as the Socialist party began to receive serious attention in the black community, however, it was eclipsed by the rise of a more revolutionary ideology, communism.

Blacks greeted the Communist party, the moral and intellectual inheritor of nineteenth-century abolitionists, with ambivalence. Increasingly after its organization in 1919, the Communist party U.S.A. was in the vanguard of American whites demanding equality of economic opportunity for blacks. Both Lenin and Leon Trotsky urged their American comrades to lead in the campaign to liberate blacks, and Karl Marx had declared emphatically that white labor could not be free as long as black labor was enslaved. Between 1919 and 1940, Communists pressed for the inclusion of blacks in organized labor and called upon them to join in overthrowing capitalism and establishing a dictatorship of the proletariat. The Communists played prominent roles in rent strikes led by black tenants and protests against evictions in northern cities. In the South they fought against peonage and led in the formation of unions of black sharecroppers and tenant farmers. In addition to its struggles for the economic liberation of blacks, the Communist party took the most uncompromising egalitarian stance on civil rights of any white organization in the twentieth century.

In spite of their consistent and often courageous egalitarian ideals and practices, relatively few blacks joined either the Socialist or Communist parties. The high point of Afro-American support came in 1917, when 25 percent of the blacks in Harlem cast their votes for the Socialist Morris Hillquist for mayor. The Socialists paid so little attention to blacks that they had little chance of attracting the masses. The refusal of blacks to join the Communist party has, however, perplexed historians.

Blacks remained cool to the Communists primarily for three reasons. First, like whites, they found it impossible to obtain accurate information on developments in the Soviet Union. Subjected to a massive barrage of propaganda from the American news media, few of them knew about Russia's constitutional safeguards for minorities, the extent of the equality of opportunity, or the equal provision of social services to its citizens. Closely allied with this was the fact that blacks, like most other Americans, generally did not understand Marxism. Claude McKay, the black poet, claimed in 1922 that "Karl Marx's economic theories are hard to digest, and the Negroes, like many other lazy minded workers, may find it easier to put their faith in . . . that other Jew, Jesus." Second, blacks distrusted white workers and felt that blacks would be the major losers in a state and an economy ruled by them.

Third, many blacks did not publicly acknowledge their belief in communism or join the Communist party because they feared reprisals from whites who had always doubted their loyalty to America. For blacks to advocate taking the property of whites would be to make their position in America even more precarious than it was. Many blacks, observing the brutal repression of the radical labor unions or thinking about the lynching bee against Afro-Americans, felt that the whole armed might undergirding capitalism would be turned on them if they joined a Communist revolution. W. E. B. Du Bois articulated the feelings of many blacks in 1931:

> American Negroes do not propose to be the shock troops of the Communist Revolution, driven out in the front to death, cruelty and humiliation in order to win victories for white workers. They are picking no chestnuts from the fire, neither for capital nor white labor.
>
> Negroes know perfectly well that whenever they try to lead revolution in America, the nation will unite as one fist to crush them and them alone. There is no conceivable idea that seems to the present overwhelming majority of Americans higher than keeping Negroes "in their place."
>
> Negroes perceive clearly that the real interests of the white worker are identical with the interests of the black worker; but until the white worker recognizes this, the black worker is compelled in sheer self-defense to refuse to be made the sacrificial goat.

In spite of these factors, many blacks responded positively to Marxism. Most black newspapers applauded when the Russian Revolution occurred in 1917 because they viewed it as a triumph of democracy over tyranny. Black journals often expressed their views of American capitalism in the same way as the Marxists did, speaking of capitalist rule, Wall Street domination, and the like. Socialists such as Eugene Debs were described as "sincere friends" of blacks, while Lenin was lionized as a man of "gigantic intellect" and "undaunted courage." Black creative artists received so much encouragement from the Communist party that it was natural for many of them to become Marxists (including Claude Mckay and Richard Wright).

In the Baltimore *Afro-American,* William Jones consistently supported the Marxists in the 1920s. Arguing the necessity for revolution when change was slow, he asserted in 1929, "The fact is the fate of the colored races of the world is wrapped up in the success of Russia and Russian propaganda which sets forth the proposition that all working groups of all races should merge their economic and social forces to overthrow class slavery." The intellectuals, believing firmly in the vision held out by Marxists, felt that blacks, as the most oppressed group in society, would be the chief beneficiaries of a Communist revolution. Angelo Herndon, a Birmingham coal miner, explained in 1934 why he joined the Communist party:

> All my life I'd been sweated and stepped on and Jim-Crowed. I lay on my belly in the mines for a few dollars a week, and saw my pay stolen and slashed, and my buddies killed. I lived in the worst section of town, and rode behind the "Colored" signs of streetcars, as though there was something disgusting about me? I heard myself called "nigger" and "darky" and I had to say "Yes, sir" to every white man, . . . I had always detested it, but I had never known that anything could be done about it. And here, all of a sudden, I had found organizations . . . that weren't scared to come out for equality for the Negro people, and for the rights of the workers. The Jim-Crow system, the wage-slave system, weren't everlasting after all! It was like all of a sudden turning a corner on a dirty, old street and finding yourself facing a broad, shining highway. . . . I felt then, and I know now, that the Communist program is the only program that the Southern workers—whites and Negroes both—can possibly accept in the long run. It's the only program that does justice to the southern worker's ideas that everybody ought to have an equal chance, and that every man has rights that must be respected. . . .

Blacks shared so many of the economic goals of the Communists that many of them might be described as fellow travelers without an organizational affiliation. For instance, when *Crisis* magazine questioned the editors of black newspapers in 1932 about their attitudes towards communism, an overwhelming majority of them accepted the ideology. P. B. Young of the Norfolk *Journal and Guide* contended that communism was a movement "to improve the conditions of the underprivileged, to make government more the servant of all the people, to give the rank and file of those who labor a larger share in the fruits of production, and to afford to all men equality before the law, and equal opportunity to work and live." While Frank M. Davis of the Atlanta *World* was less enthusiastic, he reported that it was "a fact that the Negro, getting the dirty end of the economic, social and political stick, finds in Communistic ideals those panaceas he seeks." An increasing number of blacks embraced Marxism after 1930. The ideological continuity is best indicated by a reading of the 1967 platform of the Black Panther party: "We believe that if the white American businessmen will not give full employment, then the means of production should be taken from the businessmen and placed in the community so that the people of the community can organize and employ all of its people and give . . . high standards of living." James M. Boggs, one of the more articulate black Marxists, argued in 1970 that at "the bottom of *every* ladder in American society is a Black man. His place there is a direct result of capitalism supporting racism and racism supporting capitalism." Since capitalism had caused "decay, decline, and dilapidation" in black communities, economic development must proceed at a revolutionary rate to prevent further deterioration. According to Boggs, that development could occur only by "getting rid of the exploiters" and introducing large-scale social ownership of the means of production.

According to most observers in the 1980s, whether blacks would answer the clarion call of the oppressed and rise up and break the chains of economic bondage depended, in part, on the success of more conservative solutions to their plight. If in economic recession and inflation white workers demand a reform of the economy, black workers could benefit. Most blacks remained unemployed or employed in the lowest-paying occupations, unable to escape the poverty resulting from the persistence of racial discrimination. Whatever the solutions, it seemed highly unlikely that the majority of blacks could advance in the United States by continuing to play the economic game as long as whites were using loaded dice.

7

American Archipelago:
Blacks and Criminal Justice

The mood and temper of the public with regard to the treatment of crime and criminals is one of the unfailing tests of the civilization of any country. . . . An unfaltering faith that there is a treasure, if you can only find it, in the heart of every man—these are the symbols which in the treatment of crime and criminals mark and measure the stored up strength of a nation, and are the sign and proof of the living virtue in it.

Winston Churchill

The American criminal justice system has put blacks and other minorities behind bars out of all proportion to their numbers in the general population. The celebrated acquittals of Angela Davis, Bobby Seale, Huey P. Newton, Joanne Little, and others in the 1970s changed neither the fact of discrimination against blacks nor the system itself. The system remained rotted through with two centuries of substantive and procedural injustice, incarceration of the innocent, and unconscionable mistreatment of the guilty. Even the meaning of "guilt" in a system run by and for white people was distorted for blacks. On April 6, 1970, *Time* magazine stated the essential facts:

Whites often assume that civil rights acts and court decisions made law the black man's redeemer. In practice, many blacks see the law as something different: a white weapon that white policemen, white judges and white juries use against black people. Indeed, blacks are clearly under-represented in law enforcement and over-represented in crime and punishment. . . . Blacks are arrested between three and four times more than whites, partly because police stop and search blacks far more frequently than they do whites. . . . Most of the victims

LAW ENFORCEMENT

From Outta Sight Luther *by Brumsic Brandon. Copyright © 1971
Paul S. Erickson, Inc. Reprinted by permission of
Paul S. Erickson, Inc.*

of black crimes are black. Example: black women are 18 times more
likely to be raped than white women, and usually by black assailants.

Once caught, black suspects are more likely than whites to be convicted than acquitted, and more likely to receive stiff sentences. . . .
According to many experts, one factor in this disproportion is poverty:
few black defendants can afford skilled lawyers.

RACIAL DISPARITIES IN PUNISHMENT FOR CRIMES AGAINST PROPERTY

From the beginning of their history in the United States, blacks raised
critical issues concerning the criminal justice system: procedural fairness in trials of blacks, the inequities in administration of justice (from
arrest to sentencing after trial to postconviction remedies), the punishment of whites for mistreatment of blacks, and the sentences blacks
and whites received for the same offense. They questioned whether
economic conditions were more important than race in determining

treatment and whether black-on-black crime was punished. In addition, blacks raised serious questions about whether the entire legal system had any legitimate role to play when so-called crimes were perpetrated against private property in a capitalist society where the poor did not have equal opportunity to acquire material possessions. In such a setting, crimes aimed directly or indirectly at acquiring equal access to property take place primarily because private property exists. Poor black criminals, according to this analysis, were slaves of a capitalist system, without other means of accumulating capital.

The criminal justice system punished and harassed black political prisoners whose crimes might have been ostensibly against property but whose basic offense to the system was their race. Racism imprisoned small-time thieves, among whom blacks were disproportionally represented but released white-collar swindlers or political operatives with a reprimand. And the system has come under fire despite the fact that a black and a white might be given the same sentences for similar crimes in some cases, for the deeper realities are: (1) that blacks suffered measurable oppression as defendants, as prison inmates, as victims of official mistreatment, and even as crime victims for whom there was often no legal redress; and (2) that the oppression of blacks was facilitated by the legal definition of what is a criminal offense and what is not. How many blacks have been in a position to swindle huge fortunes from their corporations in the past century? The severe penalties for crimes against property were reserved for just those offenses which black people were in the best position to commit most often.

When a corporate executive received a $1,000 fine for evading $60,000 in income taxes and a poor black man was sentenced to jail for four years for stealing a Social Security check from the mails, serious questions were raised about the equity of treatment within the criminal justice system. For example, in 1969 in a federal court in New York City, a stockbroker pleaded guilty to an indictment charging him with $20 million in illegal trading with Swiss banks. He hired a prestigious lawyer who described the offense in court as comparable to breaking a traffic law. Judge Irving Cooper gave the stockbroker a tongue lashing, a $30,000 fine, and a suspended sentence. A few days later, the same judge sentenced an unemployed black shipping clerk who pleaded guilty to stealing a television set worth $100 to one year in jail.

An analysis of sentencing in the southern district of New York from May 1, 1972, to October 31, 1972, indicates that white-collar defendants, predominantly white, received more lenient treatment as a general rule than defendants charged with common crimes, largely unemployed and undereducated blacks, who were more likely to receive prison sentences. There was little differentiation in sentencing between blacks and whites charged with the same offense. However, most whites were charged with white-collar crime, and the only certain punishment even after conviction was a suspended sentence or a very short prison term. The same criminal justice system mandates certain incarceration for the so-called common crimes, with which most blacks were charged.

In fact, some judges seemed not to believe that white-collar offenders were criminals. A prime example is the famous electrical equipment price-rigging case of 1961. The defendants, including several vice presidents of General Electric and Westinghouse, had committed flagrant criminal offenses in conspiring to fix prices. They even employed secret codes. General Electric alone set aside $225 million to settle damage claims that resulted from the conspiracy. In court after they pleaded no contest, the defendants were fined and sentenced to thirty days in jail. Even this short period of incarceration offended one defense attorney, who said he could not understand why his client should be put "behind bars with common criminals who have been convicted of embezzlement and other serious crimes."

As a holdover from the period when a certain amount of brigandage, as typified in the expression "robber baron," was accepted as the price of economic growth, a lack of integrity and fair dealing in business, even when it cheated the government, consumers, or shareholders, seemed to be expected. The perpetrator of white-collar crimes such as tax evasion or fraud was likely to be winked at or confined to plush quarters in a minimum security Allenwood prison for a short period. The black numbers operator, dope dealer, or other successful criminal was cited as an example that blacks were just naturally criminal or preferred to pursue a criminal way of life, instead of as an example of an entrepreneur in the best tradition of American economic development.

The ruling classes defined crime in such a way that they themselves usually escaped scrutiny and punishment. For example, in compiling the Uniform Crime Statistics, the Federal Bureau of Investigation (FBI) had no categories for white-collar crimes (embezzlement, bribery, price fixing, and consumer fraud). The Uniform Crime Statistics misled the public by highlighting the least costly crimes. The crimes with which blacks were usually associated accounted, according to a 1974 *U.S. News and World Report* study, for less than 10 percent of the cost of crime. Organized crime (gambling, narcotics, hijacking, and loan sharking) accounted for $37.2 billion, white-collar crimes (embezzlement, fraud, forgery, kickbacks, and business thefts) accounted for $17 billion, and drunken driving accounted for $6.5 billion, but the crimes commonly associated with blacks (robbery, burglary, theft, shoplifting, homicide, and assault) accounted for only $6.0 billion, or less than 10 percent of the estimated total of $66.7 billion for crime. When one adds the $20.6 billion for law enforcement to the total, the black percentage falls even lower. Consistent with the economic history of blacks, one would expect the crime rate for blacks to be higher than the measured rate for whites. So long as economic oppression and racial prejudice thwarted black potential and ambitions, it would be extraordinary indeed if the black crime rate did not exceed that for whites who, whatever their economic condition, did not have to overcome the burden of racial oppression.

THE LEGACY OF SLAVERY

Twentieth-century blacks caught in the criminal justice system were scarred as a group by instruments of oppression derived from punitive laws that buttressed slavery in the South and continued to oppress blacks, North and South, after emancipation. After the Civil War the criminal justice system was corrupted in that it assumed the controlling role formerly played by the institution of slavery. Many blacks walked away from the chains of slavery only to become ensnared in the faceless and, in many respects, more horrible oppression of courts, executions, prisons, poverty, and despair.

In the period before the Civil War, each of the slave states had elaborate and severe laws dealing with black criminals. Blacks, free and slave, were not permitted to testify against whites and were punished for failure to accord them respect. The statutory punishment for most crimes was much more severe for slaves than for whites. Whites were executed for rape and murder alone, but slaves could be executed for stealing; a slave who struck a white person was flogged and, during the eighteenth century, often maimed or castrated. Slaves conspiring to rebel or engaging in revolts were sometimes tortured to extract a confession and could be convicted on the flimsiest evidence. There were a small number of reported trials of slaves, but often trials were held only to determine the compensation to be provided to a master when his slave was convicted of killing the slave of another slaveowner or of killing a white person.

Laws restrained the movement and conduct of free blacks as they attempted to maintain a semblance of freedom. They were forced to give bond or register in local communities upon penalty of deportation, forbidden to assemble in groups for fear of slave insurrections, and punished more severely than whites for teaching slaves to read and write, "the use of figures excepted."

Laws also forbade or regulated the use of firearms and "any ardent spirits" by free blacks. Because the lack of facilities for criminals made imprisonment unpopular, fines and whippings were the punishments of choice as alternatives to all or part of a sentence. A free black found guilty of threatening a white man with a deadly weapon in North Carolina was "sentenced to three months imprisonment, to stand two hours in the stocks on two different days and to give bond, with good security, in the sum of 18 pounds."

The impoverished state of most free blacks made fines an unrealistic proposed punishment. Some of the laws which imposed fines on free blacks stated that an alternative of whipping or imprisonment could be meted out at the discretion of the court. In response to this problem the North Carolina assembly in 1831 enacted a measure providing that "when any free Negro or free person of color should be hereafter connected in any offense against the criminal laws of the state and sentenced to pay a fine, and it shall appear to the satisfaction of the court that the free Negro . . . so convicted is unable to pay the fine imposed, the court shall direct the sheriff . . . to hire out the free Negro . . . so convicted to any person who will pay the fine for his services for the shortest space of time."

CONTROLLING FREED BLACKS THROUGH THE
CRIMINAL JUSTICE SYSTEM, 1865–1920

After emancipation, the statistics reported by the U.S. Census Bureau indicated an increase in black criminality. This was predictable. No longer valuable property, the former slaves became despised free blacks. The criminal law was used to control and harass them. For example, in the state of Georgia, there were only 183 prisoners confined in the penitentiary in 1858, all of whom were white. In 1870 there were 393 persons confined, of whom 59 were white and 334 were black. According to the U.S. census, the total number of blacks confined in southern federal and state prisons in 1870 was 6,031; ten years later the number had increased to 12,973; twenty years later there were 14,244; and in 1904 there were 18,550. The commitment rate for blacks in 1904 was higher than that for whites; the rate for whites was 187 per 100,000 population and for blacks 268 per 100,000 population. However, for certain immigrants, the rate was higher than that for blacks. While Poles had the same commitment rate as blacks (2.6), Russians (2.8), Canadians (3.0), French (3.4), Austrians (3.6), Italians (4.4), and Mexicans (4.7) had more prison commitments per 1,000 inhabitants than Afro-Americans. The commitment rate for immigrants declined as they became absorbed into American life. But blacks remained unassimilated and with a higher commitment rate.

In the criminal court system in the South after emancipation, case loads increased substantially, with the major part of the courts' time taken up with trying cases involving blacks. Increasingly, the law was used to restrain or punish blacks as a substitute for the constraints of slavery. Many blacks became familiar with the courts not as protective institutions but rather as places where labor contracts which reduced them to peonage were enforced. Many observers and participants in the process believed that blacks usually received procedural fairness but that whites would often be acquitted for offenses which when committed by blacks brought certain conviction. After ten years as a trial judge in Montgomery, Alabama, Judge W. H. Thomas told the Southern Sociological Congress at Nashville, in 1912, "It is not that the Negro fails to get justice before the courts, . . . but too often it is that the native white man escapes it." The judge went on to point out that minority groups would not accept this uneven status before the law as fair, and that a distrust of the law would be the result.

With the failure of Reconstruction, penal systems picked up the oppression of blacks where slavery left off, except that the prisons made no provision for handling black female offenders. The prisons were transformed surreptitiously into a far-flung routing system—imitating that of the slave trade—through which poor blacks passed on their way to serving as the property of whites in need of cheap labor. There were large numbers of able-bodied blacks in prisons, there was a great demand for labor throughout the South, and maintaining a prison system was a great financial burden for the state. By leasing prisoners to contractors, the state was relieved of the responsibility of supporting the prisoners and acquired a source of profit for the state treasury. Some planters paid the fines of black prisoners directly to state officials and were permitted to work them until their sentences expired. Each state soon had an interest in increasing the number of convicts in order to lease them. Futhermore, many of the convicts were mistreated by the lessors, who were interested only in profits and not in the health and welfare of their charges. Indeed, the lessors had even less concern for the convicts than the master had had for slaves who were, after all, his valuable property.

The pardoning power of executives in the southern states was also utilized inequitably. A 1901 study reported that "the last reports of Virginia and Louisiana show: In the former, one out of every 3½ white men receives a pardon, while only one out of every 14 Negroes obtained such clemency. In the latter, for the whites it is one to every 4½ white men, and one to every 49 Negroes." Furthermore, the study showed that the complete absence of white women in prisons was

the result of judges who deemed prison conditions unfit for them.
There were, however, sixty black women in the prisons of the two
states at that time.

The criminal justice system reinforced the oppression of blacks
in other ways. Large numbers of black workers signed contracts to
work for white planters who underpaid, overcharged, and cheated
them and then prosecuted them for contract violations when they
attempted to leave the plantation. Many black peons appealed to the
Justice Department to protect them. Despite the federal antipeonage
law of 1867, the Justice Department failed to abolish debt slavery,
which continued to flourish until the 1940s.

During the later years of the nineteenth century and throughout
the twentieth century, many Afro-Americans agreed with the black
historian John Henrik Clarke when he wrote in his poem *Love* (1964):

> Who is Justice? I would like to know,
> Whoever she is, I could love her so.
> I could love her, though my race
> So seldom looks upon her face.

Between 1898 and 1913 conferences of black leaders at Hampton Institute, Tuskegee Institute, and Atlanta University protested the inequities blacks faced in criminal proceedings. In a typical listing of the
reasons for the high crime rate among blacks, the Atlanta University
Conference for the Study of Negro Problems of 1904 included:

> Laws as to vagrancy, disorder, contracts for work, chattel mortgages
> and cropliens are so drawn as to involve in the coils of the law the
> ignorant, unfortunate and careless Negroes, and lead to their degrada-
> tion and undue punishment, when their real need is inspiration, knowl-
> edge and opportunity. . . . Courts usually administer two distinct sorts
> of justice: one for whites and one for Negroes; and this custom, together
> with the fact that judge and court officials are invariably white and
> elected to office by the influence of white votes alone, makes it very
> difficult for a Negro to secure justice in court when his opponent is
> white. . . . The methods of punishment of Negro criminals is calculated
> to breed crime rather than stop it. Lynching spreads among Black folk
> the firmly fixed idea that few accused Negroes are really guilty; the
> leasing of convicts, even the present system of state control makes the
> state traffic in crime for the sake of revenue instead of seeking to reform
> criminals for the sake of moral regeneration; and finally the punishment
> of Negro criminals is usually unintelligent; they are punished according
> to their criminal record; little discrimination is made between old and
> young, male and female, hardened thug and careless mischief-maker;
> and the result is that a single sentence to the chain-gang for a trivial
> misdemeanor usually makes the victim a confirmed criminal for life.

DISPARITIES IN ARREST AND SENTENCING, 1920–50

Despite the protests of Afro-American leaders, the reported black crime rate continued to be higher than that of whites. For instance, in the first half of 1924 in Philadelphia, blacks, who made up 7.4 percent of the population, accounted for 24.4 percent of the arrests. During the first six months of 1926 in Detroit, the black crime rate was 3.9 per 10,000 as opposed to 1 per 10,000 for whites. In the superior courts of North Carolina in 1922–25, there were 4.65 indictments per 1,000 for whites and 8.71 per 1,000 for blacks. Nationwide, the U.S. Census Bureau reported in 1923 that blacks formed 31.3 percent of the total prison population and 23.3 percent of the commitments, contrasted to only 9.3 percent of the total adult population. Racism—pure and simple—generated these statistics.

The Jackson, Mississippi, *Daily News* reported in 1916, "We allow petty officers of the law to harass and oppress our Negro labor, deprive them of their wages, assessing stiff fines on trivial charges and often they are convicted on charges which if preferred against a white man would result in prompt acquittal." The Chicago Commission on Race Relations reported in 1922, "The testimony is practically unanimous that Negroes are much more liable to arrest than whites, since police officers share in the general public opinion that Negroes are more criminal than whites." Studies of criminal trials of blacks confirm the observation that when blacks were arrested, their conviction rate was higher than that of whites. In Alabama, the percentage of acquittals based on cases brought to trial in 1920–22 was much lower for blacks than for whites for all serious crimes except robbery. A 1926 Detroit study found that the rate of conviction of blacks for burglary, armed robbery, simple larceny, assault and battery, disturbing the peace, accosting and soliciting, prostitution, sex crimes, offenses against the state and prohibition laws, embezzling, and forgery was much higher than the rate for whites.

Sentencing patterns gave even stronger evidence of racial discrimination. In the Detroit study 48.6 percent of the black defendants compared with 43.8 percent of the whites were convicted of felonies. Of the blacks, only 7.1 percent were given the alternative of a fine or prison sentence, compared with 13.5 percent of the whites. Only 7.2 percent of blacks were given probation, while 12.2 percent of the whites received it. Altogether, 30.9 percent of the blacks and 15.5 percent of the whites were sentenced to imprisonment. Of course, it could be argued that fewer blacks had opportunities for proper probation work, also a result of discrimination, or that blacks committed offenses calling for heavier penalties.

PERCEPTION

From Outta Sight Luther *by Brumsic Brandon. Copyright © 1971
Paul S. Erickson, Inc. Reprinted by permission of
Paul S. Erickson, Inc.*

Blacks were not only convicted more often than whites but also
received longer sentences. For example, a 1927 study of 1,521 chain
gang prisoners in North Carolina found that 7 percent of the white
prisoners and 11 percent of the blacks were serving sentences shorter
than three months. On the other hand, 6 percent of the white prisoners
and 11 percent of the blacks were serving sentences of three years.
It may be argued that blacks had committed more serious offenses,
but that is not evident from the statistics.

By the 1940s it was well established that the black crime rate was
consistently higher than that for whites, and more emphasis was placed
on studying the causes of crime and the relationship of blacks to criminal justice agencies. Scholars theorized that one cause of black crime
was that "slavery in a sense dehumanized the Negro." Furthermore,
"slavery nurtured a set of habits and attitudes which still affect many

thousands of Negroes." Among these were lack of self-respect, lack of self-confidence, a distaste for hard work, a habit of dependence upon white friends, lack of regard for the property of others, a feeling that "the white folks owe us a living," disdain for the white man's law, and a tendency to "let tomorrow take care of itself." Scholars agreed that after slavery blacks were subjected to continuous social and economic deprivation which made them large contributors to crime. Since ecological studies had demonstrated the relationship among socially disordered neighborhoods, vice, and crime, it was easy to extrapolate from the fact that 90 percent of all blacks in the North and West in 1940 were urban dwellers, and that about 90 percent of these lived in or adjacent to disorganized areas, the assumption that consistent criminality would result.

In the South, violation of segregation customs could result in arrest: "recklessly eyeballing" a white woman, disputing a white man's word, or refusing to leave a public place when asked. Furthermore, blacks were useful targets for scapegoating and frame-ups. A white person could commit a crime with his face blackened or arrange a situation so that a particular black would appear to be guilty. If the hapless black escaped lynching, he would go to prison. Whites murdered blacks and successfully pinned a serious crime—actually committed by the murderer—on the dead victim.

Even more significant than scapegoating and frame-ups was the differential punishment of blacks whose victims were white. M. D. Richardson described the process in the Atlanta *World* in 1933: "When a Negro is arrested for a crime and brought to trial, the first question is against whom it was committed, white or colored. If against a white, the sentence is severe, usually far severer than it deserves. . . . If against a Negro, however, the whole complexion of the case is different. A meager sentence is very likely imposed, and in some cases no sentence at all." A 1941 study of Richmond, Virginia, five counties in North Carolina, and one county in Georgia pointed out the disparity of conviction and sentencing in homicide cases when blacks allegedly killed other blacks and when blacks allegedly killed whites. There were few interracial murders, but the conviction rate was higher and the sentences more severe in cases where blacks allegedly killed whites.

Five blacks were indicted in Richmond for murdering whites; all 5 were convicted and sentenced to life. In the five North Carolina counties, 19 blacks were indicted for murdering whites; 17 were convicted; 6 of these were sentenced to death, 2 to life imprisonment, 4 to 20 years to life, and 5 to less than 10 years in prison. Of the 194 Richmond blacks who were indicted for murdering other blacks in Richmond, 141 were convicted; 8 of these were sentenced to life, 31

to 20 years to life, 43 to 10 to 19 years, and 59 to less than 10 years.
Of the 247 blacks who were indicted for killing other blacks in the
North Carolina counties, 201 were convicted; of these 11 were sentenced
to death, 1 to life imprisonment, 38 to 20 years to life, 46 to 10 to 19
years, and 105 to less than 10 years.

The data indicated that blacks who killed other blacks literally got
away with murder. This effect helped to make blacks even more contemptuous of the law. They knew how little whites cared for black
life and property. The Chief of the Atlanta Police Department put it
best in 1933: "One reason for the high percentage of killings among
Negroes is that few of them are electrocuted for slaying members of
their own race. We bring them before the courts charged with murder,
and the verdict is usually manslaughter. This does not serve as a sufficient deterrent."

Black folklore reflected the consistent discrimination against Afro-
Americans in the courts. The prejudiced judge frequently appeared
in jokes and folk songs. There was, for example, the early-twentieth-
century joke about the judge who interrupted a lynch mob with the
plea: "We've always been considered a progressive community and I
think we're progressive enough so's we can give this boy a fair trial
and then lynch him." Expressing the view of the masses that whites
frequently arrested, convicted, and sentenced blacks to long terms
in prison in an effort to crush them, the folk singers saw little justice
in the system:

> Standin' on de corner, weren't doin' no hahm,
> Up come a 'liceman an' he grab me by de ahm.
> Blow a little whistle an' ring a little bell
> Heah come patrol wagon runnin' like hell.
>
> Judge he call me up an' ast mah name
> Ah tole him fo' sho' Ah weren't to blame.
> He wink at 'liceman, 'liceman wink too;
> Judge say, "Nigger, you got some work to do."
>
> Workin' on ol' road bank, shackle boun'.
> Long, long time 'fo' six months roll aroun'.
> Miserin' fo' my honey, she miserin' fo' me,
> But, Lawd, white folks won't let go holdin' me.

While describing the oppressiveness of the law, the singers often voiced
their hatred of the system:

> If I got to hate somebody, rather it would be
> Judge and Jury and mean bossman, not
> Poor Black Man like me.

Blacks were still decidedly ill-treated in prisons in the 1940s. In the South, black women, juvenile offenders, hardened criminals, and the criminally insane were often imprisoned together. The chain gang system was still in use for highway work, and it led to terrible accidents, such as the burning of twenty men in a truck cage because they were trying to warm themselves by setting fire to some gasoline. In another incident, convicts had their feet amputated after they were frostbitten during solitary confinement in a cage on a cold night.

Most black prisoners served out their time and did not receive the benefit of pardon or parole. Blacks generally lacked the influence to obtain pardons, and the disposition of many parole cases followed the example in which the butler for a white man murdered a black woman who spurned his attentions. He was defended by his employer, received a light sentence, and then was paroled to his employer. The major factor in the release of blacks was the interest of some white person in using them. Letters such as these were received by parole officials in Alabama: "I can use a Negro full time . . . will see that he has something to eat, and keep him at work all the time clearing land, cutting wood, and helping cultivate the land. . . . I am in need of a Negro farm hand and I am depending on one from you and if you have one for me, you may write what prison I can get him and when. . . . I understand that the state is letting out prisoners on parole, if so I would like to get a Negro named G——— W———."

EXPLORING THE CLASS BASIS OF BLACK CRIME IN THE 1950s

By the mid-1950s social scientists had reached a consensus that crime statistics had more to do with class than with race. The existing significant difference was still attributed to such variables as police discrimination toward blacks, discrimination in the sentencing process, differences in treatment inside prison, differences in education and job opportunities, and the effect of migratory patterns on criminal behavior. Any of the social and economic indicators used by experts showed that the black condition was not expected to improve to any substantial degree so long as racism and an unwillingness to provide opportunities to relieve the effects of past discrimination existed among the white majority. Unlike white immigrants of an earlier day or even more recent immigrants, blacks could scarcely hope that the majority of their numbers would be provided opportunities for advancement based solely on merit. White liberals were patronizing more often than helpful. A 1958 *Time* editorial is typical: "This pervasive discrimination holds down capable Negroes at the top of the social ladder, dims their voices among their own people, builds up tensions and resentments inside the Negro Society, and keeps great masses of Negroes segregated in ghettos where the standards of personal morality, discipline and responsibility are lower than those in the white world outside." San Francisco's black deputy city attorney, R. J. Reynolds, put it best when he said, "Slam enough doors in a man's face, and he may break one of them down." Despite the increased awareness, little was done to ameliorate social and economic conditions among blacks so as to reduce criminal actions against white persons and rising crime rates against the property of blacks. Blacks remained largely a people without capital, property, or jobs in a capitalist system and were often driven to prey on those just as disadvantaged who lived in close proximity to them.

INCREASED PUBLIC ATTENTION TO BLACK CRIME IN THE 1960s AND 1970s

Several events occurred in the criminal justice system to focus increased public concern on black crime rates in the 1960s. First, the Supreme Court rendered a series of decisions which served to apply most of the due process requirements of federal criminal procedures to state criminal justice systems. Since the Tenth Amendment to the Constitution left the punishment of crimes to the states, enjoining federal constitutional procedures in the state criminal justice system was a matter of great controversy. The Court had held earlier that the Fourteenth Amendment did not make all of the provisions of the U.S. Bill of Rights applicable to the states' legal systems. But the Court had recognized that some of the rights safeguarded in the Bill of Rights might be protected against state infringement because to deny them might be a denial of due process of law.

By 1969 the specific earlier rulings had been overruled, but the Court still rejected the total incorporation theory. However, in a series of separate decisions, most of the Bill of Rights had been selectively incorporated to apply to the states. The Fourth Amendment right to be free from unreasonable searches and seizures and to have excluded from criminal trials any evidence illegally seized was applied to the state investigation procedures. The Fifth Amendment right to be free from self-incrimination was applied, as well as the Sixth Amendment right to counsel, the right to a speedy and public trial, the right to confront opposing witnesses, the right to compulsory process for obtaining witnesses, and the right to trial by jury. The Court went on to extend the right to counsel during the interrogation stage and to rule out the use of a confession obtained in the absence of the opportunity to counsel and on effective waivers of the right.

The climate in which abuse of law enforcement in the streets of Selma, Montgomery, Bogalusa, and other cities was blatantly obvious and in which there was continuous controversy over police brutality, dragnet arrests, and discriminatory official conduct in the North possibly accelerated the Court's willingness to enlarge due process protections. Liberal lawyers and the Court succeeded in restraining the power of the police to treat suspects arbitrarily and in enlarging the scope of due process protection. Policemen viewed liberal efforts to restrain their discretion as an unconscionable effort to make their jobs more difficult and to increase the physical danger to which they were exposed in enforcing the law.

The 1960s rebellions, riots, and insurrections in the cities, carried out by blacks in reaction to the failure of both the legal civil rights changes and the Johnson administration's War on Poverty to improve their social and economic condition, erupted usually in response to perceived police brutality. As defenders of the social order, police were in the most exposed position among blacks in the cities and were thus more likely to have their activities become the precipitating cause of any rebellion. In Detroit, police efforts to close a "blind pig," an illegal after-hours drinking establishment, resulted in a large-scale riot; in Watts, it was the arrest of a black man in the midst of a crowd and in other cities the shooting of black suspected criminals. During the rebellions, blacks destroyed and appropriated the property of businessmen and store owners in what many whites regarded as needless, irrational rage. The spectacle reinforced the notion that blacks were likely to be criminals, violators of law and order.

Blacks viewed the police in the 1960s and 1970s as a white alien army occupying their neighborhoods. Statistics supported their characterization. For example, in 1970 blacks made up between 27 and 63 percent of the total population of Detroit, Atlanta, Chicago, and Washington, D.C., but represented only between 5 and 21 percent of the police forces in those cities. An overwhelming majority of the policemen lived in the suburbs. The novelist James Baldwin correctly described black attitudes toward the police in *Nobody Knows My Name* (1962):

> The only way to police a ghetto is to be oppressive. None of the Police Commissioner's men, even with the best will in the world, have any way of understanding the lives led by the people they swagger about in twos and threes controlling. Their very presence is an insult, and it would be, even if they spent their entire day feeding gumdrops to children. They represent the force of the white world, and that world's criminal profit and ease, to keep the Black man corralled up here, in his place. The badge, the gun in the holster, and the swinging club make vivid what will happen should his rebellion become overt. . . .
> He moves through Harlem, therefore, like an occupying soldier in a

bitterly hostile country, which is precisely what, and where he is, and is the reason he walks in twos and threes.

Speaking in 1973, Benjamin Ward, deputy commissioner of the New York City Police Department, echoed Baldwin's sentiments: "Blacks in America are jailed first and bailed last. The police discretionary power is used least in the ghettos. Police there are viewed as an army of invaders, and, in turn, the police often view black people as inferiors."

White police not only viewed blacks as inferiors, they also frequently beat and killed them. During the 1920s, according to historian Arthur Raper, 50 percent of the blacks killed by whites were murdered by policemen. A Department of Justice study of reported cases of police brutality against private citizens from January 1, 1958, through June, 1960, found that out of 1,328 incidents, 461 or 34 percent were against blacks. Afro-Americans found little redress for their grievances from either the police or the few police review boards. Without regard to class, blacks were mistreated by the police with impunity.

During this period, scholars and the public became more aware of the problem of urban poverty and the need for law enforcement to reckon with the consequences of continued social and economic injustice. But many white Americans opposed or betrayed the War on Poverty and began asserting that the new measures were not working even before they were really tried. Significantly, the liberal economic solutions of the War on Poverty were not designed to redistribute the wealth and overturn the existing structure, but merely to provide blacks with better education to enable them to compete within the existing system. Even this change was more than many white Americans would support, especially when it became apparent that the provision of better education and social welfare was costly and that when blacks became competitors for a wide variety of opportunities they would be competing with whites who already had such opportunities. The whites were just not willing to provide justice for blacks if it led to greater competition for jobs.

Increasingly, some whites began to assert that it was the inadequacy of punitive measures that caused the high black crime rate, not continued oppression by the white majority. Predictably, law and order became a pungent issue in the 1968 presidential campaign. American party candidate George Wallace in his campaign preached incessantly about a high black crime rate. Democrat Hubert Humphrey talked about black crime but was careful to stress that most of the victims were blacks. Republican Richard Nixon tried "law and order with justice" in his speeches as a compromise, but the phrase "with justice" got lost in the final weeks of his campaign.

"Now look, Baby, don't come tellin' me I'm crazy. I'm just gettin'
tired of the way these big fat ofay policemens is breakin' down
folks's doors and jumping in all snarlin' and growlin'!"

BREAKING AND ENTERING

From Bootsie and Others *by Ollie Harrington. Copyright © 1958 The
New Pittsburgh Courier Publishing Company. Reprinted by permission of the New Pittsburgh Courier Publishing Company.*

Even before the campaign, federal officials began to emphasize
crime control. President Johnson had created a Commission of Law
Enforcement and the Administration of Justice in July, 1965, which
published many volumes of reports in the spring of 1967. In March
and June, 1967, respectively, the First International Congress on Crime
Control and the National Conference on Juvenile Delinquency were
convened to determine what the next steps should be. These conferences concluded that support should be provided to individual states
to implement the recommendations of the President's Commission.
Congress enacted the omnibus Crime Control and Safe Streets Act
of 1968, authorizing unprecedented federal funding, and established

the Law Enforcement Assistance Administration (LEAA) as a key instrument for the national response to the crime problem. The LEAA distributed $870 million to state and local police for fiscal year 1975.

In mid-September, 1968, when the election campaign was at its height, Attorney General Ramsey Clark, testifying before the National Commission on the Causes and Prevention of Violence, pointed out that blacks, 12 percent of the population, were involved in 59 percent of the arrests for murder. Fifty-four percent of the victims were black; nearly 50 percent of the persons arrested for aggravated assault were black, and blacks were the primary victims; 47 percent of those arrested for rape were blacks, and again blacks were the primary victims; 61 percent of those arrested for robbery were black, but less than 33 percent of the persons arrested for other property crimes such as embezzlement were black. The picture was that of a crime-ridden black community with blacks striking out at those closest to them—other blacks. The arrest rate among blacks for murder, robbery, carrying concealed weapons, prostitution, and gambling was about five times that for whites. Most of the data on black crime had been analyzed by scholars for years, but it began to penetrate the white community only when whites noticed blacks coming out of their communities to attack whites or attacking white persons and their property in the black community. Clark, unlike the winner in the presidential campaign, emphasized that the reasons for black crime could be found in the economic and social deprivation perpetuated in communities where they lived.

Racism accounted, in part, for what occurred thereafter. Instead of focusing on efforts to improve the conditions and prospects of blacks in order to stop breeding crime, politicians focused on efforts to stamp out the criminal behavior involved and to punish the criminals. "Law and order" should be enforced by courts, more police officers, and stronger punitive measures adopted in prisons. As the LEAA poured more and more money into the training and education of police and prison officials, the crime rate continued to increase.

THE BLACK FOCUS ON PRISONER RIGHTS IN THE 1960s AND 1970s

The black focus in the 1970s shifted to correctional institutions and the rights of prisoners. Some of the most influential leaders of the black community in the 1960s had been prisoners or had served time in jail: Malcolm X, Eldridge Cleaver, Huey P. Newton, and the Rev. Martin Luther King, Jr., as well as some of the leaders of the past—Marcus Garvey and Elijah Muhammad. Blacks became increasingly aware that young blacks in the cities were more likely to spend some time in prison than not, and that any militant who advocated black nationalist programs was likely to be convicted of some offense requiring imprisonment as a natural outcome of leadership. Increasingly, Malcolm X, Cleaver, Newton, the Black Panther party, and the Muslims focused on the issue of political prisoners. The Black Panther party insisted that "we want freedom for all black men held in federal, state, county, and city prisons and jails" and that all blacks on trial should be judged "by a jury of their peer group or people from the black communities." At the same time, scholarly research indicating that continued deprivation seemed to be the cause of black crime reinforced the notion that the criminal justice system was engaged in a multitude of injustices.

Prisoners began to see themselves as objects of genuine public concern rather than scorn. They began to rebel against ill treatment and to insist on the right to self-realization inside the walls. Others saw their detention as the result of basic defects in the system itself. They saw the beginning of the oppressive criminal justice system in pretrial detention, which in discriminating against the poor necessarily discriminated against a disproportionately large number of blacks. As Attorney General Robert Kennedy said in 1964, only one factor determined whether a defendant stayed in jail before trial—"the factor is simple, money." When bond was unavailable a prisoner immediately became more likely to be convicted, because he was less able to locate witnesses and to assist in his defense. Some observers asserted that prisoners preferred long periods of pretrial detention because it decreased the likelihood that prosecution witnesses would be available, increased the chances for acquittal, and provided the opportunity for a longer stay in residential areas near families, whereas once convicted the offender would be sent to a long-term penal institution in an isolated, more inaccessible area. This observation presumed, of course, that persons charged were in fact guilty, or would be convicted whether they were guilty or not. This observation also assumed that prisoners preferred conditions such as those existing in the Manhattan House of Detention, "The Tombs," where in 1970, 4,000 men were housed in an area designed to house 1,000 and noise levels were often high enough to prohibit normal conversation. During the summer months the temperatures inside often rose above 110 degrees, and inmates spent fourteen hours of every day confined to a six-by-eight-foot cell. U.S. District Court Judge Morris Lasker ruled in 1974, in a suit by and on behalf of Tombs inmates, that confinement there represented unconstitutional "cruel and unusual punishment."

Courts usually had inadequate resources to handle the many criminal cases before them. Plea bargaining—negotiation between prosecutor and defendant whereby the defendant agrees to plead guilty to a criminal charge in return for the dismissal of other charges of a multi-count charge or the reduction of charges to offenses carrying lesser penalties—was constitutionally sanctioned by the Supreme Court as an appropriate way of relieving court congestion.

Some prisoners complained that by encouraging them to plead guilty, the court system effectively short-circuited their opportunity to remain free after a trial. Most of these evils were unmitigated by the Supreme Court's order that counsel must be provided to indigents, no matter what the offense, if imprisonment was a possible penalty. In reality, the great mass of criminal cases continued to be disposed of in a perfunctory way by an overcrowded court system including overburdened appointed counsel. The poor defendant emerged consistently worse off than the prisoner of means with privately retained counsel. A shortage of judges to handle the case load became worse year by year, as poor salaries and almost intolerable work conditions made all but the most dedicated abandon the bench for private practice. The impact of plea bargaining on blacks was summed up in 1973 by Judge Harry T. Alexander of the Superior Court of the District of Columbia, who contended that

> judges ought to be concerned about plea bargaining. The American system of justice ought not have to depend upon plea bargaining to eradicate case loads. Our country, with all its creeds, all of which now belong to the Black people because of the 14th Amendment, should pave the way for quality administration of justice. Plea bargaining has the great tendency to deny people their constitutional right to a fair trial. Plea bargaining is *always* accompanied by over-charging. For example, possession of a prohibitive weapon is usually accompanied by several other charges—possession of a dangerous weapon, possession of unregistered firearms, or possession of unregistered ammunition. A person can then plead guilty to carrying a pistol without a license, for which you can get a year. The other two things are minor misdemeanors.

Studies indicate that poor defendants with appointed counsel pleaded guilty more frequently, received fewer dismissals, and received suspended sentences or probation less frequently than defendants who were able to hire counsel. The "mockery of justice" test, under which representation is considered "ineffective" only when it is so inadequate as to "reduce the trial to a farce" or to render it a "mockery of justice," according to Chief Judge David Bazelon of the U.S. Circuit Court of Appeals for the D.C. Circuit, "requires such a minimal level of performance from counsel that it is itself a mockery of the Sixth Amendment." As Margaret Burnham, co-counsel for Angela Davis in her trial, explained, "He who can pay for a good lawyer, gets one, he who cannot gets a lousy P.D." The public defender typically "is an overworked, harassed cog in the wheels of the Court apparatus." Therefore, "with good reason, blacks have come to view the P.D. as a worse enemy than the prosecution. The image of the defender as a man, in cahoots with the prosecutor and the judge, whose sole function is to pave the way for the conviction of the defendant and to mask the inequity and brutality of the criminal process, has become more and more commonplace." The Public Defender's major contribution is to "help the judge 'move the case.' "

THE ROLE OF BLACK LAWYERS, JUDGES, AND JURORS

Historically, the Afro-American's best chance for fair treatment at the bar of justice hinged on the presence of black lawyers, judges, and jurors. Statistically, his chances were never good. For example, only 3,000 or 1 percent of the nation's 300,000 lawyers in 1970 were black. The numbers in the judiciary were not much better. Only 22 of the 459 federal judges were black, and there were only 178 blacks among the 12,000 state and city judges in 1970. Such statistics were disturbing even to some white jurists. Judge Bazelon told a group of black jurists in 1972:

> We have been forced to preside over a grim parade of pain and social injustice that has, I think, scarred each one of us. All of us who carry the scar have a responsibility to speak out. But you, as Black judges, have a special sensitivity to the problem. You have to speak first, because your attitude has exceptional importance to the public. I don't pretend that our social institutions will be improved as soon as you speak out. But if you swallow your pride and suppress your anger, pretending that you cannot see or hear the suffering in the street, the conscience of the public will be soothed. If you remain silent, you will unwittingly lend comfort to the champions of the status quo, the enemies of social and economic change who will point to your silence as a sign that nothing is really wrong. If you, above all people, remain silent, none of us should be surprised that the real problems remain completely unsolved.

Black lawyers had a particular commitment to serving blacks. They were almost wholly dependent on black clients if not employed by government agencies. In terms of income and clientele, most black lawyers were poverty lawyers; they served poor blacks. In the criminal justice system, a black prosecutor, defense counsel, or judge could have an ameliorating effect on poor blacks ensnared by law enforcement agencies. Although the very discrimination which traps the black offender prevented a sufficient number of blacks from becoming trained and educated as lawyers, those who existed demonstrated their commitment to blacks. Through public defender systems, the National Conference of Black Lawyers, and as private practitioners, black lawyers strived to insure procedural fairness and to facilitate acquittal of their clients, not only because every lawyer wants to win his case, but also because they recognized the substantive unfairness of the system. In celebrated cases Howard Moore, Haywood Burns, and other black lawyers proved their ability to manipulate and combat the intricacies of a system dedicated to conviction. These cases, however, remain exceptional.

For over 100 years the philosophy of law expounded by black lawyers and jurists centered on the racism inherent in the system. Judge Raymond Pace Alexander spoke for most of them when he declared in 1975:

> Those who hold power in the Criminal Justice System are primarily white, primarily male, well-educated people from the middle and upper income backgrounds or if you will, middle or upper middle class backgrounds. Those upon whom the power is exercised are primarily non-white, male, uneducated or undereducated, and from poverty-stricken backgrounds. Thus, we have a system where the decision-makers are primarily from one race and class, and the victims of the decision-making are primarily from another race and class. It is from this inherent, systematic conflict and contradiction that insensitivity and injustice arise in our system making our present system more criminal than just.

Within the matrix of discrimination, black lawyers complained about the systematic exclusion of blacks from juries. As late as 1970, a New York City lawyer demonstrated that a federal grand jury list (drawn from voting rolls) included only 1.1 of every 10,000 voters in Harlem while containing 62.6 of every 10,000 voters from the predominantly white East Side. The statistical probability of such ratios emerging from a random selection of jurors was smaller than the probability of being dealt twenty-four consecutive royal flushes in a game of five-card stud.

Discrimination in jury selection most often manifested itself in cases in which blacks were accused of crimes against whites. The expectation that an all-white jury would convict a black defendant was the primary motivation for the discrimination. Except in well-publicized cases, the Supreme Court hesitated to face the issue directly. The Court from the 1880s held to the standard that black defendants were entitled to be tried by juries from which members of their race were not systematically excluded. While theoretically available to every defendant, that right was usually granted only when the defendant was involved in controversial activities, such as civil rights, or in widely publicized rape or murder cases. The defense won reversals and new trials in southern states when the discrimination was blatantly obvious and provided federal courts with a means to ameliorate or at least delay punishment in cases where the issue of rape, for example, was raised when in fact only a seduction had occurred. A leading case of this type was the Scottsboro case, in which nine black youths in Alabama were convicted of raping two white women by an all-white jury from which blacks had been excluded. William Pickens demonstrated in 1933 how the cards were stacked against blacks in such cases:

> For generations in this country when a Negro came into court facing a white opponent, he had to settle not only the question involved in the charge against him as an individual, but also all the traditional charges against his race—in fact the whole "race question." Like Socrates before his accusers, he had to face a jury which was influenced not only by the evidence just presented, but also by the "evidence" that had been taught to them in their infancy, in their growing up, in literature, taverns, shops, and from a million other sources.

The Supreme Court did not agree with Pickens.

The Court made it manifestly more difficult to win jury discrimination cases as a result of a 1965 decision in Alabama in which the court declined to accept mathematical evidence that the percentage of black males in the population was much larger than the percentage of black males who had been drawn for the grand and petit jury panel since 1953, and that no black had actively served on a petit jury panel since 1950, as a basis for finding discrimination. Furthermore, the Court refused to find the prosecutor's use of the peremptory challenge to remove the blacks who remained in the jury panel discriminatory unless the defendant could show that over an indefinite period of time the prosecutor's use of the challenge had in fact been responsible for the complete exclusion of blacks. This would, of course, be difficult to prove, but it would be easier to force the prosecutor to show that he had not in fact contributed to the discrimination.

Underrepresentation of blacks on juries remained a problem in the second half of the twentieth century. But even in jurisdictions where blacks were selected for jury service, the problem of tokenism and the selection of blacks who reflected as much as possible the views of the majority were problems. A writer in the *Yale Law Journal* in 1970 observed that "the basic difference between white jury commissioners purposefully including Uncle Toms on a jury, and a system which, taking race into account, seeks an automatic black representation in meaningful numbers is that of control." The writer suggested that jury districts be redrawn so that every black community would

constitute a jury district providing all-black juries. In mixed neighborhoods every jury should be proportionately representative of the population of the district. Of course, black defendants who committed
offenses against other blacks might prefer white juries who might care
little for the vicitm, but "no defendant has the right to profit by discrimination against his race."

Studies in the deep South, where blacks were long excluded from
juries, indicate that inclusion did not result in substantial changes in
verdicts. One civil rights attorney in Mississippi counties where blacks
constituted as much as 75 percent of the population reported that
juries regularly contained seven to twelve blacks and were as likely
to convict as all-white juries. In Jackson, Mississippi, where members
of the Republic of New Africa (RNA) were indicted for the murder
of a policeman in August, 1971, during an early morning raid on RNA
headquarters, juries in the first of these trials had two, four, and three
blacks. In each case, the defendants were found guilty and given life
sentences. Lawyers reported that black jurors were anxious to show
they were opposed to crime, relied heavily on the prosecutor, and
seemed to bend over backward to prove their fairness and ability to
be good jurors. As the *Yale Law Journal* writer pointed out in 1970,
more was involved than jury selection so long as "black people are
under complete political and economic control, in many, if not most
parts of the country." It was difficult for black jurors to act without
fear, tension, or outside pressure.

SURVIVING THE PRISON SYSTEM

What were the effects of all these factors conspiring against the black
person caught in the criminal justice system? Public defenders were
unreliable or hostile, juries were too often uncaring or prejudiced altogether, judges were frequently contemptibly racist, and prisons run
by white guards were hostile to the mostly black population. How
did a black person survive all this?

Prisons, as Richard W. Velde, administrator of the Law Enforcement Assistance Administration, put it in 1970, "are, without question,
brutal filthy cesspools of crime—institutions which seem to brutalize
and embitter men to prevent them from returning to a useful role
in society." The 1970 National Jail census noted that 52 percent of
160,000 jail inmates were pretrial detainees, but the jails in which they
sat overwhelmingly lacked recreational or educational facilities and
one-half had no medical services. Prisons were cesspools, and the indeterminate sentence was the millstone that increasingly dragged prisoners permanently into its morass.

The indeterminate sentence originated in the 1840s as a liberal reform measure by which a prisoner could serve one day or for life depending upon his performance and the extent of his rehabilitation. In fact, this rehabilitation was a myth. Treatment was scarce, staff was inadequate, and most prisoners did not want or need psychotherapy. The system served only to take offenders off the street, permitting society to ignore the social causes of crime, and to punish political beliefs and unpopular views by incarceration and then more extended incarceration for failure to respond to "treatment." Inmates were forced to play a therapy game if they wished to be released. For black prisoners especially, who were arrested on phoney charges because of their political beliefs and activities, or who were arrested on legitimate charges but who attributed their plight to social conditions they could not control, incarceration and the indeterminate sentence were particularly oppressive. One black prisoner described his fate; he was given an indeterminate sentence in 1968 for robbery with a deadly weapon. He was twenty-three years old and "a revolutionary, nothing big nothing small, a revolutionary that's all." Therapy was mandatory once a week for two or three hours. "Now put this jig-saw together and tricky nick might make you his advisor to Negroes." How did he survive? He "escaped these manacles twice," once for five hours and once for four nights. He wrote poems, one for every day of fifteen days he was in solitary confinement. One poem, "In Communicado," read:

> The best years of my life
> have vanished right before my eyes.
> Where have they gone
> I can't remember
>
> . . .
>
> They shot George Jackson down,
> They shot at intrepid me,
> but the bullets hit the ground.
> Now the repercussions got to come,
> but I'll feel no pain because
> my body is numb.

He also wrote that it was "mandatory to protect one's masculinity" because of the separation of the sexes in prison. The denial of access to women broke up families on the outside and created problems in prisons. Young prisoners were harassed, attacked, raped, and forced into homosexuality for sexual gratification. Some prisoners lied, stole, and killed over bed partners. Prisoners complained of mandatory therapy provided because they were assumed to have some psychological problem. They objected that they were psychologically healthy if psychological health meant being in touch with outside reality; "If I can't work and make it, I'll steal and take it."

In addition to physical surroundings that were often unfit for human habitation and the rehabilitation game, prisoners were subjected to the most risky types of experimental drugs and medical devices. Medical experimenters claimed that prisoners volunteered in order to earn good time, serve humanity, and earn pay for their services. Since blacks constituted a disproportionate percentage of the prison population, they were especially subjected to the experimentation hazard. Studies indicate that volunteerism is related to the type of prison and the values of the prisoner. Federal prisons were more tightly controlled and orderly than state, and state prisons more orderly than county and city jails. In the city and county jails, boredom, uncertainty, and idleness made medical research appear as a constructive use of time for prisoners. Prisoners who volunteered often referred to this time-use factor. They also minimized the degree of risk when talking to their families, spoke rarely of the long-term adverse effects, and viewed the research teams and physicians as protectors who would not subject them to unjustified risks. Money earned allowed them to purchase more commodities, to send money home to families, and to bargain with other inmates for favors and influence.

Some black prisoners survived the system by constant agitation. They engaged in prison uprisings to raise the consciousness of prison officials and the public, in hope of improving living quarters, food, parole, and visiting hours. They thereby focused attention on conditions and influenced concerned representatives to introduce legislation designed to improve prison life. They and their families and friends hired lawyers to bring suits to improve treatment. They wrote letters, articles, and books to inform the world of their plight. They viewed their incarceration in political terms. Joanne Chesimard, imprisoned member of the Black Liberation Army, wrote in 1973:

> I am a black revolutionary and, by definition, that makes me part of the Black Liberation Army. The pigs have used their newspapers and TV's to paint the Black Liberation Army to be vicious, brutal mad dog criminals. They have called us gangsters and gun molls and have compared us to such characters as John Dillinger and Ma Barker. It should be clear, it must be clear to anyone who can think, see or hear, that we are the victims. The victims are not the criminals. . . . as was proven by the Watergate, the top law enforcement officials in this country are a lying bunch of criminals. The president, two attorney generals,

the head of the FBI, the head of the CIA, and half the White House staff have been implicated in the Watergate crimes. . . .

They call us thieves and bandits. They say we steal. But it was not us who stole millions of black people from the continent of Africa. We were robbed of our language, of our gods, of our culture, of our human dignity, of our labor and of our lives. They call us thieves yet it is not us who rip off billions of dollars every year through tax evasions, illegal price fixing, embezzlement, consumer fraud, bribes, kickbacks and swindles. They call us bandits, yet every time we walk into a store in our neighborhood we are being held up. And every time we pay our rent the landlord sticks a gun in our ribs.

INCREASING BLACK DISTRUST OF THE LAW

Several events in the 1970s deepened blacks' distrust of the law and increased their feeling that differentials in punishment depended on class and race. In 1973 Vice President Spiro Agnew pleaded no contest when charged with accepting bribes and income tax evasion; the judge sentencing Agnew placed him on probation. Under threat of impeachment for "high crimes and misdemeanors" committed during the course of an attempt to cover up White House involvement in the 1972 break-in at the Democratic National Committee offices in the Watergate Hotel, President Richard M. Nixon resigned on August 9, 1974. A few days later his successor, Gerald Ford, granted Nixon a pardon for federal crimes that "he committed or may have committed or taken part in" while in office. A host of Nixon's aides (including former Attorney General John Mitchell and F.B.I. Director L. Patrick Gray) were indicted or served short sentences in minimum security prisons for Watergate-related crimes.

By early 1977 it appeared that jurists had dropped all pretense that wealthy, well-known whites were subject to the penalty of the law. When actress Claudine Longet was convicted in January, 1977, of killing her lover, for instance, the trial judge sentenced her to thirty days in jail, two years probation, and fined her $25. Afro-Americans were incensed at the contrast between such cases, which represented a mockery of justice for most lower-class blacks and whites, and official governmental concern for the human rights of political dissidents in foreign countries.

Although historically blacks had shown great sympathy for the oppressed of other lands, they reacted negatively to official American criticism of police state tactics and alleged violations of human rights in the Soviet Union, Brazil, and Argentina in the 1970s. American deification of the great Russian novelist Aleksandr Solzhenitsyn after his exile from the Soviet Union and critical acclaim for his books denouncing the criminal justice system in the Soviet Union (*One Day in the Life of Ivan Denisovich* and *Gulag Archipelago*) appeared especially hypocritical to blacks. They contrasted the frequent congressional receptions for dissidents exiled from the Soviet Union with official indifference to the incarceration of the Rev. Ben Chavis for his civil rights activities in North Carolina.

Increasingly, blacks began to view the prisons as places designed to scoop up their leaders and to demoralize and dehumanize them. John O. Boone, commissioner, Massachusetts Department of Corrections, spoke characteristically in 1973:

> And our leaders are where? . . . strong men, chased down by police, labeled sociopaths and antisocial, and put in prison because they had guts enough to try to survive. Bad, yes. Some of them did some bad things, but many have grown in prison. I think I know what happened to George Jackson, for example. He looked out one day and he said, "What am I doing in this prison?" And he said I stole $70 or $75 and I'm on my way to ten years for $75. What am I doing here? I'm smart. I can read many books and all of that. And I can write. He started thinking. Yes, I'm guilty of stealing. I was a thief and then he started looking at the forces that led him toward that $75. In a sense, he became a revolutionary when he started writing and when he started learning.

Black prisoners learned first to analyze the system that had trapped them. They became practical legal scholars, economists, sociologists, and historians. Included among the most prominent of them were George Jackson, Joanne Chesimard, and Eldridge Cleaver. Looking at the broad spectrum of criminality in American society, they saw themselves and many of their fellow inmates more as victims than as criminals. Chesimard, writing from New York's Riker's Island in 1978, analyzed this phenomenon:

> There are no criminals here at Riker's Island Correctional Institution for Women (New York), only victims. Most of the women (over 95%) are black and Puerto Rican. Many were abused children. Most have been abused by men and all have been abused by "the system."
>
> There are no big time gangsters here, no premeditated mass murderers, no godmothers. There are no big time dope dealers, no kidnappers, no Watergate women. There are virtually no women here charged with white collar crimes like embezzling or fraud. Most of the women have drug related cases. Many are charged as accessories to crimes committed by men. The major crimes that women here are charged with are prostitution, pickpocketing, shop lifting, robbery and drugs. Women who have prostitution cases or who are doing "fine" time make up a substantial part of the short term population. The women see stealing or hustling

as necessary for the survival of themselves or their children because jobs are scarce and welfare is impossible to live on. One thing is clear: amerikan capitalism is in no way threatened by the women in prison on Riker's Island.

The writings of black prisoners, recidivism, mounting crime rates, the expense of attempting to develop rehabilitative mechanisms, and public disgust with reformers in general led to increasing expressions of skepticism in the black community about the value of correctional treatment of offenders and great uncertainty about community-based treatment and the steps that should be taken to punish convicted criminals. But in the mid-1970s there were still some 400,000 sentenced inmates behind bars, and most of them were black. The National Advisory Committee on Criminal Justice Standards and Goals (1973) noted that in many large and Central Atlantic cities, "the jail inmates are reported to be black, poor and without jobs." Nationally, 58 percent of the inmates in federal and state correctional institutions in 1970 were white, compared to 41 percent black and 1 percent native American.

DISCRIMINATION IN EMPLOYMENT OF CORRECTIONAL PERSONNEL

Geography, policies of recruitment, remuneration, and standards of employment created a white prison work force overseeing a largely nonwhite prison population. The racial composition of the employees is important. In Attica Prison, where from September 9 through 13, 1971, forty-three died and hundreds of others were seriously injured during riots, there was one Puerto Rican and no black employee among 540, but the prison population of 2,200 was at least 55 percent black and 8 percent Puerto Rican. Forty-three percent of the inmates were from New York City, an eight-hour bus ride plus a $15 cab ride away. As the executive director of Cook County Department of Corrections, Winston E. Moore, explained in 1971, "If we stop to analyze Attica and all other prison eruptions we will find that the underlying cause in each case was racism—plain and simple white racism aimed at blacks."

Individual racism, including beatings, murders, slurs, harassment, and other violent and dehumanizing behavior have long been noted by observers of prison systems. One scholar noted, "If a white prisoner is openly anti-racist he is immediately considered a radical by the prison and is likely to be harassed by the guards as well as by other white prisoners. Since the approval and support of the guards is important for gaining one's freedom, racism has positive survival value for the individual white prisoner." The Attica Report stated that fear, hostility, and mistrust nurtured by racism characterized relationships between officers and inmates. The relationship was probably inevitable when predominantly poor, urban, black and Spanish-speaking inmates were placed under the supervision of white officers from rural areas who were equipped with only three weeks of training.

In the 1960s criminal justice and correctional officials noted the need for minority personnel in prisons, but the number of minority employees remained low. Blacks made up only about 12 percent of the correctional work force and only 3 percent of top- and middle-level administrators. LEAA provided funding for the recruitment of minorities into training programs, but the numbers did not substantially improve. Like the ghetto, barrio, and reservation, the prison was largely a nonwhite colony, occupied and controlled by whites.

Cultural diversity in prison populations was increasingly permitted by enlightened prison officials in the 1970s. Attempts to maintain rigid homogeneous standards regarding lifestyle, speech, and group organization create disruption when prisoners are as ethnically, socially, and politically conscious as the outside society from which they came and to which some of them return. The National Advisory Commission on Criminal Justice Standards and Goals (1973) expressed ambivalence toward such notions in view of the traditional discretion exercised by prison officials in controlling their prisons: "cultural groups, strengthening the individual's awareness of his group identity and raising questions of discrimination are potential sources of discord. But they are nonetheless vital links to the self-help potential of such groups on the outside."

The Black Muslims were instrumental in creating the possibility for diverse behavior in prison. They started organizing prisoners to counter official prison ideology with an activist consciousness of racial oppression. They united black prisoners for the immediate goal of legitimization of Black Muslim worship and cultural expression in prison. They used two major tactics—lawsuits and strikes—which became commonplace in the late 1960s and early 1970s.

INCREASED POLITICIZATION OF PRISONERS

The general politicization of prisoners can be understood within the context of attempts to reform most institutions in American society in the 1960s. The civil rights movement, poor people's movement, welfare rights movement, and antiwar movement all seemed to increase consciousness of the inequality and oppression in major American institutions. Even universities, traditionally characterized as apolitical, became the battlegrounds of the social reformist conflicts of the 1960s. Youth, nonwhites, and other powerless groups increasingly became politically sensitized. Since the powerless were the primary candidates for imprisonment, they brought their political sensitivity to the prisons with them.

Richard Clark, a twenty-five-year-old former inmate of Attica and a Black Muslim, helped save the lives of the guard hostages during the riot at Attica. Paroled as a first offender after serving a thirty-two-month sentence for armed robbery, he described the basis of black incarceration quite well. As he explained, some people "in prison did not commit a crime. They're in there because they did not understand the bureaucracy of the judicial system." Others are there because they are poor. In order to change that, "you would have to set up programs in the community so that black and poor and white people can educate themselves and then you would have to set up a system so that we can possibly earn wages and support ourselves instead of having to resort to the fact that we have to pick up guns." When the society is revamped, "then you wouldn't have 90 percent of the people committing crimes to get money, you would have 10 percent, 10 percent that are committing crimes, and then you wouldn't have the large over-abundance of the prisoners."

As Russell G. Oswald, commissioner of Correctional Services in New York, said after Attica, the prison movement was an interracial militant attack upon the structure of American society. "The new revolutionaries in the prison wanted no improvement in living conditions. They wanted and sought to provoke the kind of repression that would put the clock back and serve their purposes. . . . The last thing the radicals wanted was meaningful prison reform. Instead, they wanted to polarize the people of the United States against—and for—the prisons as the *paramount* oppressive instruments of the power structure."

So long as the myth of treatment and rehabilitation was accepted by prison reformers, the deprivation of civil and human rights of prisoners was accepted. But many offenders regarded rehabilitation as a myth used by correctional officials as propaganda. They also had a clear idea of the systemic basis of their incarceration. Prisoners won some judicial recognition of their constitutional rights to minimally decent living conditions, freedom from brutality, freedom to a limited degree of political expression, unimpeded access to the courts and, religious, racial, and sexual equality. However, efforts to gain relief for prisoners were in basic conflict with the duty of judges, wardens, and other correctional personnel to protect society through the sanction of criminal law.

Prisoners seeking reform first faced the court-formulated rule designated as the "hands-off doctrine": that in the interest of states' rights, federal interference against state administrators, even to enforce the Bill of Rights, was prohibited. In cases involving federal prisons, many feared that judicial review would subvert the authority of prison officials and that discipline would become increasingly difficult. In general, once a judge determined that a person was legally incarcerated, any review of grievances was beyond the court's jurisdiction. Nevertheless, by the mid-1960s, the scope of the court's jurisdiction began to expand. The Arkansas practice of inflicting corporal punishment was held in 1968 to be a violation of the Eighth Amendment's ban against cruel and unusual punishment. In New York, Martin Sostre's case is one example of the development of procedural law on this issue.

In 1965, Sostre opened a bookstore in Buffalo, New York, where he sold black literature. During the June, 1969, riots, he became unpopular with the police for providing a refuge for young blacks. Two weeks later he was arrested on a narcotics charge. Unable to raise bail ($25,000 property bond or $12,000 cash), he spent eight months in jail prior to trial. He refused representation by a public defender and represented himself at trial. After he refused to recognize the legitimacy of the trial and asked no questions, he was found guilty and sentenced to thirty to forty-one years. While serving this sentence in New York, he won a district court case against prison officials for their mistreatment of him during his imprisonment. Sostre charged that he was kept illegally in punitive segregation for 124⅓ days, punished for political beliefs and activities, subjected to cruel and unusual punishment, and given disciplinary action without the opportunity for procedural due process. In reversing Judge Constance Motley's decision in favor of Sostre, Circuit Judge Irving Kaufman repeatedly emphasized the necessity for courts to defer to prison administration officials and other agencies of government. In concluding he noted, "We disclaim any intent in this decision to condone, ignore or discount the deplorable conditions of many of this county's jails and prisons. . . . Nevertheless, we would forget at our peril and at the peril of a free governmental process, that we are federal judges reviewing decisions made in due course by officers of a sovereign state. We have interpreted and applied the law as it appears to us in the light of circumstance and principle." Sostre might have wondered if the white-dominated criminal justice system would ever rise above its "principles" to provide justice for all. Even Judge Kaufman, however, restrained prison officials from interfering with some of Sostre's oral and written communications.

The death blow to the "hands-off" doctrine was struck by the Supreme Court in January, 1972. The Court, in considering a prisoner's complaint for damages for injuries, for the aggravation of a preexisting ailment caused by cell conditions, and for the deprivation of rights, said that however inartfully they plead, such defendants have the right to offer evidence and claim relief without having their claims dismissed out of hand. The recognition that prisoners are not deprived of all rights with their incarceration and, further, that they will forfeit only such rights as are necessary to ensure the orderly administration of an institution, transformed, in a relatively few years, correctional case law by focusing attention on the treatment of prisoners, conditions of prison facilities, educational and vocational programs, medical treatment, and numerous other problems that had been hidden from public view.

The rebellions by prisoners in Attica, Soledad, Raiford, San Quentin, and other prisons caused Congress to hold hearings in 1972 and to investigate the entire field of corrections. Congress learned that in Attica Prison men were sold ground coffee in the commissary but had no means to cook it. "You need a coffee pot to make it on a stove. They lock you up for making a stove." Prisoners at Attica could take only one shower a week because of lack of facilities. In the Florida system no rehabilitation, which prisoners expected and the public believed existed, was taking place because "the money is not available for the kind of rehabilitation that is being touted." Judge Richard Kelly of the Florida Circuit Court testified that if "you start down this tunnel of rehabilitating prisoners, it is going to take so much money to accomplish it in any real sense that the question of whether the trip is practical at all will be raised. You are going to meet coming back through the tunnel citizens saying, well, why are you spending so much money training these people when my son is honest and he is untrained." When Judge Kelly visited Raiford Prison he described the evening meal as tasting and smelling like "five cent dog food." He did not stay in one place very long because "the minute I would stop a small group would gather and they would start asking me about the inequities that exist in life. . . ." In this prison "there was a high percentage of blacks, . . . and they had a great many questions of this kind." Arthur Adams, Jr., an inmate of the Santa Fe Correctional Farm, indicated that "we are never going to be feeling we are fairly treated until there are black officials." Adams had been transferred from Raiford and was permitted his liberty in the daytime, going back to a minimum security institution at night. Even in death row at Raiford, whites were placed in front cells and blacks in the rear. A guard testified that he "was told immediately you shower from front to rear," and "never shower a nigger before you shower a white man."

In Florida prisons, more than 50 percent of the inmates were black, only 4 of 598 guards were black, and there were no black parole or probation commissioners. In South Carolina a system of furlough existed—two times a month for trusted prisoners—but only a small percentage of the inmates enjoyed this possibility and few of these were black.

The black community knew the source of the black offenders' frustration and the abysmal conditions in the prisons. But they launched few effective movements to insure the prisoners' human rights and contributed sparingly to defense funds raised for blacks arrested on phoney charges. Misled by the communications media in specific instances, Afro-Americans in general thought long about how the sickness generated by white America spread a crime plague through their communities. But even though they were most sympathetic to the demand for prisoner rights, they could not forget that the major victims of black criminals were themselves black. Or, as the black novelist Ishmael Reed asked in 1974, "What are you going to do with somebody who comes into your house, rips off your stuff and hits your mama on the head with a blackjack?"

Long before scholars Marvin Wolfgang and Bernard Cohen conducted their study of the criminal justice system, blacks uniformly accepted the conclusion they reached in 1970: "Arrests, convictions and punishments have been reserved principally for the lower economic and social classes. . . . These facts suggest that the man who steals a wallet lands in jail; but if he steals a railroad he may become not only wealthy . . . but politically powerful." If the unequal chances blacks have in the economic and political arenas were equalized, prisons would still exist to punish offenders, but it would be less difficult to separate black criminals from political prisoners in the nation's penal institutions.

8

The Battle for Education

On sour cream walls, donations. Shakespeare's head,
Cloudless at dawn, civilized dome riding all cities.
Belled, flowery, Tyrolese valley. Open-handed map
Awarding the world its world. And yet, for these
Children, these windows, not this world, are world
Where all their future's painted with a fog,
A narrow street sealed in with a lead sky,
Far far from rivers, capes, and stars of words.

Surely, Shakespeare is wicked, the map a bad example
With ships and sun and love tempting them to steal—
For lives that slyly turn in their cramped holes
From fog to endless night? On their slag heap, these children
Wear skins peeped through by bones and spectacles of steel
With mended glass, like bottle bits on stones.
All of their time and space are foggy slum.
So blot their maps with slums as big as doom.

Unless, governor, teacher, inspector, visitor,
This map becomes their window and these windows
That shut upon their lives like catacombs,
Break O break open till they break the town
And show the children to green fields, and make their world
Run azure on gold sands, and let their tongues
Run naked into books, the white and green leaves open
History theirs whose language is the sun.

Stephen Spender

The nineteenth-century schoolhouse was a battleground where European immigrants, lower-class whites, and blacks fought for intellectual, social, economic, and political advancement. Unlike the other warriors, however, the Afro-American was disarmed before the battle began. Beginning in the colonial period, whites insisted on the compulsory ignorance of blacks to insure the continuation of slavery and caste distinctions. South Carolina early instituted the pattern of deprivation when it enacted a law in 1740: "That all and every person and persons whatsoever, who shall hereafter teach, or cause any slave or slaves to be taught to write, or shall use or employ any slave as a scribe in any manner of writing whatsoever, hereafter taught to write; every such person or persons shall, for every offense, forfeit the sum of one hundred pounds current money." Throughout the antebellum period state laws forbade the education of slaves and law and custom severely limited the education of free Negroes.

EDUCATION DURING THE CIVIL WAR AND RECONSTRUCTION

Beginning in the Civil War and continuing through Reconstruction, black education became a national public policy issue. As the Union Army swept through the South, it accomplished, long before even Lincoln desired, the emancipation of blacks. Blacks abandoned the plantations and followed the Union Army, and they came under the military category of "contraband of war." Northerners, both black and white, were moved by the plight of these newly freed slaves, and the first activities on their behalf were usually private and charitable. The Sea Islands off the coast of South Carolina fell to the Union Navy in November, 1861, and were the first plantation territory to come completely under Union control. That small group of islands, where masters had fled leaving their slaves behind, became the first area for which the North had to develop a plan of action to deal with the freed slaves. In the confusion of an uncertain federal policy, many philanthropic agencies were formed in the North to send teachers to educate the newly freed blacks. With the arrival of the "Yankee schoolmarms," a new chapter of education for the blacks opened.

Despite the efforts of the courageous teachers on the Sea Islands and elsewhere, it was only after the Civil War that a national educational policy could be implemented throughout the defeated South. Through national Reconstruction legislation and the activities of the local Reconstruction governments, the patterns of black education were established. By 1869, there were seventy-nine northern aid societies supporting black schools in the South. The Freedmen's Bureau, established in 1865, had spent more than $5 million on black education by 1871. In 1870 the bureau was operating 4,239 schools with 9,300 teachers and 247,000 pupils.

Blacks did not wait for the federal government to guarantee their education. Although it took the former slaves some time to learn all the painful lessons necessary to survive as free persons, almost immediately they recognized the need for and sought an education. They built schools and paid teachers; both children and adults enthusiastically thronged the schools. On his travels among freedmen in the South in 1865, John Mercer Langston found that "their thoughts were easily directed and their purposes aroused to those duties which respected their education, the accumulation of property, the cultivation of all those virtues and habits which are indispensable in a country and under a government where they must build their homes and win their standing, commingling in ordinary enterprises of business, trade and labor, with the native and foreign elements which compose the population of the country."

Barred from white schools in the South, and having few schools of their own in the 1860s, black youngsters clutched at any morsel of education. According to black autobiographers, bondsmen who had learned to read while in slavery taught their own children and sometimes taught other blacks in their little cabins at night. When schools existed, they were likely to have very short terms. Even these could only be attended infrequently. Kindly southern whites sometimes taught black youngsters. Robert Russa Moton was taught by the white members of the family for whom he worked and by an ex-Confederate soldier. William H. Heard hired a poor white man to teach him when no schools were opened in his neighborhood. Blacks sometimes forced planters to establish schools, organized their own, or refused to vote for politicians who would not support black schools. A number of the autobiographers attended small private schools taught by blacks. Inspired by a desire to learn to read the Bible or spurred on by parents, young blacks enthusiastically walked long miles to the schoolhouses or borrowed books and engaged in arduous self-study. Booker T. Washington's view was characteristic of the autobiographers: "There was never a time in my youth, no matter how dark and discouraging the days might be, when one resolve did not continually remain with me, and that was a determination to secure an education at any cost."

Apt scholars, young blacks made the most of the educational opportunities opened to them, North or South. James Corrothers, the only black boy in his Michigan school, soon led his class and later avidly read history, the Bible, and books in the library of a man for whom he worked. Studious Alexander Walters had little schooling as a child but later took private lessons in physics, rhetoric, and divinity from white teachers in Louisville, Kentucky. William Pickens worked before and after school in Arkansas and yet graduated as valedictorian of his class. Lawrence Jones' grandfather had built a school in antebellum Michigan, and the boy was an enthusiastic Latin scholar, regular visitor to the public library, reporter for the school newspaper, and the first black graduate of his Iowa high school in 1905. In spite of their poverty, in spite of the teachers' frequent resort to the rod, young blacks loved school. William Holtzclaw recalled his great disappointment over being taken out of school. He "became morose, disheartened, and pulled away from all social life, except the monthly religious meetings at the cabin church."

The blacks' passion for education in the 1860s was equaled by the whites' desire to deny or limit the education they received. During the early years of Reconstruction, southern whites burned schools (thirty-seven in Tennessee in 1869) and regularly insulted and whipped white teachers of blacks. In a typical case, white college students in Lexington, Virginia, regularly greeted one white woman as that "damned Yankee bitch of a nigger teacher." What southern whites feared most was that the education of blacks would destroy white supremacy. In spite of such fears, black legislators led in the establishment of the South's first publicly supported common school system in the 1860s.

By the 1870s, southern whites had grudgingly accepted the education of blacks as long as it prepared them to assume their "place" in society. Wanting a contented, reliable work force, southern whites began to view education as a barrier to attacks on property and a way of training blacks to be industrious, honest, and well behaved. In order to guarantee this kind of education for blacks, southern whites had to bring an end to the northern "interference" with their laborers which had begun in the Sea Islands. Southern white leaders appealed to northern industrialists who shared their view of black laborers, gradually incorporated the aid society schools into the public system, and continually railed against integration and the specter of miscegenation it created. When blacks lost their effective political influence in 1877, white politicians were profuse in their promises to maintain "separate but equal" school facilities. Still, the end of Reconstruction represented the end of attempts to provide equal educational opportunities for blacks and whites.

From the 1870s to the first decades of the twentieth century, southern white leaders contended that blacks were incapable of benefiting from the same education whites received. Since blacks, they claimed, were intellectually inferior to whites, and were fit only for manual labor, to expose Afro-Americans to the same education as whites was dangerous. Writing in the *Educational Review* in 1894, southern educator Lawton B. Evans expressed the white fear that similarity of education would obliterate caste distinctions between blacks and whites: "Being taught as a Negro child the same things and in the same way as the white child, when he becomes a Negro man he will want the same things and demand them in the same way as a white man."

Southern whites wanted to limit black education to elementary schools where the chief focus would be on industrial education, teaching trades and manual skills. The black schools should be organized around the labor needs of southern planters and consequently close during planting and harvesting times. The schools should turn out well-trained domestic servants and farm laborers. High schools and colleges would be wasted on blacks. Allen D. Chandler, former governor of Georgia, defined the rudimentary education southern whites wanted for blacks when he wrote in 1901, "I do not believe in the higher education of the darky. He should be taught the trades, but when he is taught the fine arts he gets educated above his caste and it makes him unhappy." The views of Atlanta newspaper editor Clark Howell were similar. Complaining that black Greek and Latin graduates did "not want domestic work," Howell called for schools "dedicated to turning out well-equipped household servants, coachmen, gardeners, farm laborers and the like."

Because of such views, black public schools in the South rapidly turned into disaster areas after 1877. Native-born whites were placed in charge of black schools, and the funding for such institutions was drastically reduced in the 1880s. The process of guaranteeing separate and unequal schooling in the South was completed in the 1890s. While blacks constituted 31.6 percent of the school-age population in the South in 1899, they received only 12.9 percent of public school funds. That same year, black parents contributed $3,712,617 or 79.4 percent of the funds used to educate black children in the South. South Carolina and Georgia illustrate the typical downward spiral which continued well into the twentieth century. In 1895, South Carolina was spending $3.11 per white pupil and $1.05 per black pupil annually. The gap continued to widen, so that by 1930 South Carolina was expending $52.89 per white pupil and $5.20 per black pupil. During this period black teachers received one-third the salary of white teachers, and the school term for blacks was fifty-nine days shorter than for whites.

According to historian John Dittmer, the story was essentially the same in Georgia. By the early years of the twentieth century, in counties where blacks constituted 75 percent of the total population, the per capita expenditure for black children was only 7 percent of that for whites. In 1905 white teachers received a monthly salary of $42.85, while black teachers received only $19.85. County school boards owned fewer school buildings for black students (208) in 1915 than blacks owned privately (1,544). There were few state or municipally supported high schools for blacks. The first black high school in Atlanta, the state capital, did not open until 1924.

Throughout the twentieth century, whites fought for separate black schools so that they could appropriate less money for them. In 1900, for example, while blacks constituted 31.6 percent of the school-age population in the South, they received only 12.8 percent of the school appropriations. This disparity was consistent throughout the twentieth century. In 1930 the South spent an average of $44 per white pupil and only $12 per black pupil annually. The southern states also deliberately used education as a device to make blacks submissive. Mississippi's policies were indicative of this practice. In 1940 Mississippi decreed that black and white children would use different textbooks. All books used in black schools had to delete all references to voting, elections, and democracy.

Educational inequality was guaranteed through several other devices. Black teachers were paid lower salaries than whites until the 1940s. In the early part of the twentieth century there were few southern high schools (64 in 1916) for blacks. As late as 1938, only 610 or about 10 percent of the 6,059 accredited high schools in the South were open to blacks. In fact, had it not been for the efforts of blacks and northern philanthropists, there would have been no advance in black education in the twentieth century. Between 1913 and 1932, for instance, the Julius Rosenwald Fund helped to construct 5,000 school buildings for southern blacks who contributed 17 percent of the money for them. The intellectual advance of blacks was also hampered by the general educational deprivation of the South and discrimination in auxiliary services. Most blacks, for instance, were unable to augment their already meager public education because public libraries were closed to them. In 1935 blacks could use only 83 of the 565 public libraries in the South.

The relentless opposition of whites to the extension of educational opportunities to blacks led to a spirited debate among Afro-Americans. As long as they had any hope of aid from northerners, blacks campaigned for integrated schools and a federally financed national educational system. The New Orleans *Tribune* set the tone in 1867 when it declared, "Separation is not equality. The very assignment of certain schools to certain children on the ground of color, is a distinction violative of the first principles of equality." While this refrain would continue in the black community until the 1970s, nineteenth-century blacks rarely attended schools with whites. Afro-Americans had little more success in their campaign for a national education system. Led by Alabama Congressman James T. Rapier, the delegates at the 1871 convention of the National Negro Labor Union called on Congress to establish a national educational system. Rapier asserted: "We want a government school house, with the letters U.S. marked thereon in every township in the State. We want a national series of textbooks which will teach the child that to respect the government is the first duty of a citizen."

Thirteen years after Rapier's plea, Republican Senator Henry W. Blair of New Hampshire introduced a bill providing for federal assistance to the states for public schools, with the amount based on the number of illiterate persons. States with separate school systems were required to apportion the money to blacks and whites on the basis of the proportion of illiterates in each race between the ages of ten and twenty-one. Passed by the Senate in 1884, 1886, and 1888, the Blair Bill was defeated each time in the House of Representatives. Blacks constantly appealed for passage of the bill. When Blair resurrected his bill in 1890, Frederick Douglass wrote:

> To me it is a Bill in the interest of both races, and is of a tendency to do away with the spirit of caste and of sectionalism and to promote the general welfare by diffusing knowledge . . . in the darkest corners of the Republic where it is most needed and where the people are the least able to secure such knowledge for themselves. . . . It will be at least a recognition of a great national duty towards a people to whom an immeasurable debt is due. . . . If the national Government had the power to put down Slave Insurrections, hunt fugitive slaves over state lines, protect slavery in the states while Slavery existed, it has the right to assist in the education and improvement of the newly emancipated and enfranchised citizens, now that Liberty has become the base line of the Republic and the fundamental law of the land.

The Senate refused to pass Blair's bill in 1890. Southern white fears of integration largely defeated the nineteenth-century attempts to obtain federal support for public schools.

SEARCHING FOR HIGHER EDUCATION OPPORTUNITIES, 1865–1910

Despairing of federal aid, blacks and whites began soon after the Civil War to develop institutions of higher learning for blacks. In 1865 the American Missionary Association (AMA) founded Atlanta University, and the American Baptist Home Mission Society helped establish Virginia Union University and Shaw University. The Methodist Episcopal Church founded what later became Morgan State University, and the AMA founded Fisk University in 1866. A year later the AMA founded Emerson and Talladega colleges, and the American Baptist Home Mission Society founded Morehouse. In 1867 the federal government also added to the growing list of higher educational institutions for blacks by establishing Howard University in Washington, D.C. And in 1868, the AMA founded one of the most influential schools in the history of black education, Hampton Institute. Most of the colleges and universities deserved the name only out of politeness. They were engaged primarily in college preparatory work, and the number of students actually graduating from their college divisions was small. Yet, many of the schools endured, gradually abolished their secondary curricula, and early in the twentieth century became regularly accredited colleges.

Two pieces of legislation also contributed to the development of black institutions of higher learning. The Morrill acts of 1862 and 1890 established the basis for the development of land-grant colleges. Though the first act had no specific provisions for black education, Mississippi took advantage of that legislation and founded Alcorn Agricultural and Mechanical College. The college had a series of distinguished presidents starting with Hiram Revels, who had also served the state as a U.S. Senator. Succeeding Revels was John H. Burris. Burris, along with his brother, James Burris, who also taught at Alcorn, were graduates of Fisk University, a liberal arts college. Having heard that if a black man could master either Greek or mathematics his equality would be proved, each brother set out to master and become proficient in one of the skills. They were firmly committed to a liberal education, and when they came to Alcorn they began a program of development that transformed the school into a liberal arts college with high standards of scholarship. The result of the second Morrill Act was the growth of a number of black land-grant colleges, including Florida Agricultural and Mechanical and Tennessee Agricultural and Industrial.

The establishment of black colleges and the acceptance of black students at Oberlin, Berea, and a number of northern white institutions were the first steps in ending antebellum proscriptions against the acquisition of higher education by Afro-Americans. Still, the individual quest for collegiate instruction, frequently described in black autobiographies, was an arduous one. Although it was difficult for blacks to obtain a common school education, it was practically impossible for most of them to obtain a college degree. Still, they persevered. The obstacles they faced were legion. First, they were almost penniless. Henry Proctor went to Fisk with $25 in 1884; Thomas Burton arrived at Berea in 1881 with $9 in his pockets; William Holtzclaw had to borrow clothes to wear to Tuskegee; Booker T. Washington had 50 cents when he reached Hampton; and M. L. Latta arrived at Shaw University with 10 cents and lived on saltine crackers and cheese for one semester. Second, they were almost unbelievably ignorant. William J. Edwards knew no grammar when he arrived at Tuskegee and had to watch the other students in order to learn how to use knives and forks. When William Holtzclaw reached Tuskegee in 1890, he did not know what state or country he lived in and slept between sheets for the first time in his life. Most of the students worked part time on the college campus and then farmed, taught school, and waited on tables during vacations to pay for their college educations.

Inspired by Tuskegee, Hampton, or Fisk graduates and sometimes helped by sympathetic whites, blacks were often remarkably successful in their attempts to obtain a higher education. Sometimes they went beyond the black college. J. Vance Lewis attended Lincoln University for two years, graduated from the University of Michigan law school in 1894 and the Chicago School of Law in 1897, and then studied law in England in 1903. Lawrence Jones attended a business school and later the University of Iowa. Henry Proctor attended Central Tennessee College, graduated from Fisk after seven years, and then graduated from Yale. William Pickens followed him in 1902 from Talladega to Yale, where, supported by William Dodge, he won the literary prize and was elected to Phi Beta Kappa.

College education made a great impact on black youth. Otis M. Shackleford reported that the eight years he spent at Lincoln Institute (Missouri) were especially rewarding: "The new life of books, music, oratory, debate and general intelligence was the source of much inspiration to me." Whether at Tuskegee, Fisk, Hampton, Talladega, Shaw, or Yale, young blacks were impressed by their dedicated teachers and especially by their college presidents. Booker T. Washington amazed Holtzclaw and Edwards with his grasp of details, regularity, concentration, fastidious dress, kindness, and consideration. Samuel C. Armstrong at Hampton Institute and Erastus Milo Cravath at Fisk made similar impressions on black youth.

The youth imbibed deeply of the advice to return home and to uplift their race. For many, college shattered forever their acceptance of the white man's characterization of the black as an inferior being. Robert Moton was ashamed when he heard educated blacks singing plantation melodies at Hampton until Armstrong urged the students to have race pride and to preserve their songs and folklore. Such advice was like a flash of light to Moton: "This . . . was the first time in my life that I had begun to think that there was anything that the Negro had that was deserving of particular consideration." Similarly, Henry Proctor's Yale thesis on slave songs, he wrote, "gave me a new insight into the heart and life of my people."

The occupations chosen most often by the graduates were teaching and the ministry, and often these professions were combined. Most of them concluded that the best way to uplift the mass of blacks was through education. Ignorant and poverty-stricken, few rural black communities in the South were able to wrangle school appropriations from reluctant state legislatures.

EXPERIENCES OF BLACK TEACHERS IN ESTABLISHING SCHOOLS FOR BLACKS, 1877-1920

Many of the college graduates tried to establish black schools. It was not an easy task. Often unknown in the community they had selected for a school, equipped only with enthusiasm, they set out first to compile information about their new community. Walking or riding through the back country on a bicycle, they lectured the blacks on personal hygiene, farming techniques, thrift, self-help, and the value of land ownership. The blacks often looked upon them as charlatans, and the whites viewed them as rabble rousers. William Holtzclaw discovered this early in his efforts to organize a school in Mississippi: "It is so easy to be misunderstood by both whites and blacks."

Upon selecting a community for his school, the zealous pioneer thus had to allay the fears and suspicions of both groups. Neither was easy. First, he had to identify the relatively prosperous black farmers who were the leaders in the black community. However illiterate they might be, if they accepted the " 'fessor," his battle was half won. The real struggle came, however, with the black preachers. A power unto themselves as leaders of the most important social institution in the black community, they could destroy a school caught in the cross fire of bitter denominational feuds. Holtzclaw succeeded in his effort to organize a school in Utica, Mississippi, largely because of his long campaign to woo a hostile Baptist minister. Reflecting on his struggle, he wrote: "If you cannot get on with the colored preachers in a place, your chances of success are slim in that community."

Once the influential blacks were won over (and this might take two or three years), the black teacher had to start trying to allay the fears of the whites in the community. He stressed the importance of having educated laborers, the moderating effects of education on the (alleged) vices afflicting the mass of blacks, and the economic importance of an educational institution to a community. He discounted the idea that the school would threaten any of the cherished customs of the whites. Instead, he argued, it would make the black less prone to steal or to rape white women. As the whites weakened, the black teachers orated at great length on the cordial relations which existed between the races during slavery, the bondsman's loyalty during the Civil War, and the way he protected his master's property and guarded his wife from rampaging Union soldiers.

Often, the teacher's appeals were successful. Still, while trying to win friends among blacks and whites, the teacher frequently lived in poverty and taught modest-sized classes. Lawrence Jones, for instance, began his school at Braxton, Mississippi, under a tree. Impressed by such sacrifice, members of the community began to offer aid. The first material help Jones received was from an old black man who gave $50 toward the establishment of the school and deeded forty acres of land to it. The aid of local whites was often crucial in establishing a school. In Utica, Mississippi, a woman sold the prospective school twenty acres of land on very easy terms, and a white-owned lumber company gave lumber on the word of several prominent blacks. The first 100 acres of land for William Edwards' industrial school in Snow Hill, Alabama, were donated by his former master. But black farmers were the steadiest and most indispensable supporters of the schools at the outset. They cleared the land, cut lumber, and actually constructed the buildings. The wives of black trustees gave fairs and picnics to raise money.

Even with the cooperation of community leaders, the teachers lived primarily on enthusiasm for the first few years. The students were dreadfully ignorant. Tuition payments were slow, inadequate, and often in the form of farm produce. Salaries were nonexistent. With too few blankets, too little fuel, and too much ventilation in ill-constructed cabins, students and teachers almost froze when the temperature fell and almost drowned when it rained. But sustained by hope and cheered by grateful farmers, the teachers persevered. Influential blacks wrangled appropriations from the county school superintendent, Booker T. Washington dropped a few words in the right places, a few northern philanthropists began to give money, and the school would become an ongoing concern.

Yet the demands on the founder were almost unbelievable. He had to superintend every aspect of the administration and also teach several classes. As soon as the school term ended, he began his northern tour to raise funds. Often he would take a few students or the school quartet along on the tour. The first sorties into the North were always disappointing. Diligence, however, created its own rewards. Helped by Booker T. Washington, William J. Edwards eventually convinced Anna T. Jeanes to give $5,000 to Snow Hill in 1902 and Andrew Carnegie to give $10,000 in 1906. Beginning with a gift of $500 from F. B. Guinn of the Guinn Publishing House, William Holtzclaw had built up a $32,000 endowment fund for the Utica institute by 1915. In spite of the gifts, the black schools were always on the verge of bankruptcy. Lawrence Jones, who had received several gifts from Emily Howland, still had to raise $25,000 for his school in 1922.

The work done by the schools was impressive. They published newspapers, organized agricultural extension services, established rural improvement societies, held annual farmers' conferences, initiated educational societies, and sought to promote the acquisition of land by blacks. Holtzclaw established one of the most successful community organizations in Utica, Mississippi. The Black Belt Improvement Society he founded held conferences, urged blacks to be thrifty and acquire homes and education, established a community court of justice, was eventually incorporated with $30,000 in capital, and sold land to blacks on easy terms. Accepting the philosophy of Booker T. Washington, these schools stressed industrial education. They taught everything from the ABCs to brick making and printing. While there were some white teachers, Tuskegee graduates made up the bulk of the faculties.

A great part of the credit for the success of these schools goes to the black men and women who taught in them. From the Reconstruction period to the early 1970s, the majority of blacks who received a college education received it at a black college. It was the responsibility of these institutions, often poorly financed, dominated by white boards of trustees, and dependent on philanthropy and state aid, to train each generation of black leaders and professionals, especially school teachers.

THE INFLUENCE OF BOOKER T. WASHINGTON

From the post-Reconstruction period and until the death of Booker T. Washington in 1915, there were two conflicting types of schools that vied for dominance: the industrial arts school and the liberal arts school. And from 1900 to 1910 the major arguments among racial leaders centered on which type of education would be the most beneficial to blacks. Booker T. Washington was the leader of the group that favored industrial education and W. E. B. Du Bois the leader of the group that favored liberal education. Both men were in many ways products of the type of school they espoused and represented the conflicting educational philosophies not only in their ideas but also in personality.

Washington, the son of a slave mother and an unidentified white father, was a graduate of the premier industrial school in the South, Hampton Institute. The institute, run by General Samuel Chapman Armstrong, the son of a missionary, was built as an effective compromise between those who wanted blacks to have no education and those who wanted blacks to have an equal education. Hampton was designed to teach its students the rudiments of learning skills, but its main emphasis was on training students to have a useful trade. This type of education was a departure from what was then usually considered higher education. In fact, until the development of the white industrial and agricultural schools in the South, and the development of elite technical schools in the North like the Massachusetts Institute of Technology and the Sheffield Scientific School at Yale University, a college education rarely trained one for a specific trade. A college education was supposed to give persons general culture and knowledge that would benefit them in any endeavor they cared to undertake. It was, and in part has remained, the symbol of a cultured elite. It was into this exclusive club that most white southerners were unwilling to admit blacks. The kind of education that southern whites preferred for blacks was one which stressed a trade and economic usefulness.

Booker T. Washington at Hampton was one of Armstrong's most apt pupils. Among his other distinctions, he was put in charge of the division of that school that trained Indians. When Armstrong was asked to recommend a person to start a school similar to his own in Alabama, he recommended Washington without hesitation. Washington's call to Tuskegee, Alabama, was the beginning of a career that would make him one of the most influential leaders of the race. He found that he was not summoned to take over an existing school, but was presented only with a site upon which one could be built. Through his ingenuity and the dedication of his students, he managed (mostly with student labor) to build a school. Tuskegee Institute was in a sense a product as well as a demonstration of the practical benefits of industrial education. His students were taught, of course, reading, writing, and mathematics, but the emphasis was on carpentry, brickmasonry, and other crafts for the men and domestic arts for the women. Washington believed strongly in the Protestant ethic, and he encouraged his own students to work hard, save their money, invest in property (particularly a home), and have a strong moral character. His teachings were the essence of middle-class values. This to him was a mission, to make blacks who were used to a semi-peasant existence strong and virtuous middle-class citizens.

Washington's philosophy had a wide appeal. He was pragmatic and tried to achieve all he could in the situation in which he found himself. He stuck to the idea of the benefits of an education that taught a man how to make a living and to be a useful member of the community. In his autobiography, *Up from Slavery* (1900–1901), Washington wrote, "there is something in nature which always makes an individual recognize and reward merit, no matter what colour of skin merit is found. I have found, too, that it is the visible, the tangible, that goes a long ways in softening prejudices. The actual sight of a first-class house that a Negro has built is ten times more potent than pages of discussion about a house that he ought to build, or perhaps could build." He believed in the concrete, and the dignity of working with one's hands. Ultimately he felt that as the black person became a useful part of the southern economy, political and personal freedom would follow. He managed in this approach to please white southerners and northern philanthropists. Both looked to Washington as having the best solution for the race problem. In 1895 Washington delivered his now famous Atlanta Exposition speech, in which he distilled his philosophy. After this speech he received nationwide attention and became, at least in the minds of whites, the leading spokesman of the race.

The vision of education held by most blacks was much broader than Washington's. From the 1870s to the 1920s Afro-American newspapers, conventions, and autobiographers railed against any proposal to limit blacks to industrial education. The Washington (D.C.) *New National Era,* pointing to the exclusion of blacks from most trades, asserted in 1873 that the advocacy of industrial education for Afro-Americans was "like telling a man in the water with his hands and legs heavily ironed, to strike out manfully for the shore." The growing hegemony of Washington over the southern educational establishment in the last decades of the nineteenth century led to even sharper denunciations of industrial education. The Texas Colored Teachers' Association reacted typically in 1900 when it rejected Washington's focus as "unjust, illogical, spurious, and antagonistic to American peace and prosperity, and entirely out of harmony with the soundest philosophy of the age. We disagree with those who hold that conditions force us to take the lower order of occupations exclusively." Black autobiographers writing between 1865 and 1920 saw education not so much as preparation for the jobs whites were willing to allow blacks to hold but as a vehicle for acquiring the tools to fight against oppression. J. H. Magee, for instance, felt that blacks needed education in order to determine their own destiny: "Therefore let us educate, educate, educate, until our people can take the helm and thus guide the ship of destiny among our own people, until we shall have reached that true eminence to which all greatness tends—the moral and intellectual development of true manhood and womanhood." John Mercer Langston argued that education could be used to build a ram to batter down the walls of prejudice and discrimination. He was always interested, he asserted, "in a high intellectual, moral Christian training for colored youth as the only means by which they might be brought to a wise, comprehensive understanding of their situation and duty as American citizens, and thus enabled to free themselves from prejudices which exist against them and brought, educated, cultured and refined, to take their places in general society."

It was mandatory, many Afro-Americans felt, for blacks to know more about themselves and to acquaint whites with the historical greatness of the race. When blacks wrote about their struggles, their triumphs, and their contributions to civilization, the opinions of whites would change. Furthermore, the more blacks knew of their past, the more pride they would have and the more willing they would be to fight for their rights in America. Otis M. Shackleford argued that blacks had to "have poets to sing of our deeds, and we must have historians to record them. It is unfair and unreasonable for us to expect men of the other race to do this. . . . We are left alone to tell our own tales of woe and to sing our own songs of gladness. We cannot longer afford to neglect or to set aside the cultivation of literature."

The past, rather than being used by whites to discredit blacks, could be used to illustrate the merits of the race. Miflin W. Gibbs insisted that a study of the white man's history would help the black because "it might assuage the pang of deprivation and stimulate opportunity did he fully know the stages of savagery, slavery, and oceans of blood through which the Anglo-Saxon passed to attain the exalted position he now occupies." The past could also provide models for black youth to emulate. Lamenting the propensity of whites to bury the black man's heroic deeds in the past, Levi Coppin asserted, "Unless we, as a people, do some writing of a historical nature, we may but expect that much that would be inspiring and educative to our youth, will be buried in the past, while much that is unfavorable, and hence depressing, will be exhibited as true history."

Because of such views, it was the liberal arts colleges that dominated in the actual education of blacks. Even Tuskegee, overshadowing Hampton, by the 1890s, had to draw on the liberal arts colleges for much of its teaching staff. Many colleges, seeing that money was going to industrial education, added mechanical and agricultural courses to their curricula in the 1890s, but these industrial divisions were hastily conceived and were often merely contrivances to tap much needed resources. The majority of black colleges remained, in fact if not in name, liberal arts colleges, and from schools like Fisk, Atlanta University, Lincoln, and Howard University came the majority of the black leaders and writers between 1870 and 1970.

These early black colleges were originally staffed and administered by teachers from Oberlin, Harvard, and Yale, who tried to make black colleges the counterparts in every detail to the most elite New England colleges. They were sincere in their missionary zeal, and if anything they were often overwhelming in their sense of mission. As one reads the autobiographies of blacks who went to these schools, one gets little sense that there was the type of undergraduate fun that is associated with the education of their white counterparts. Education was serious business, and the teachers made the students aware that they were being trained to uplift their race. James Weldon Johnson, who went to Atlanta University, remembered that in his education "the central idea embraced a term that is now almost a butt for laughter—'service.' We were never allowed to entertain any thought of being educated as 'go-getters.' Most of us knew that we were being educated for life work as underpaid teachers. The ideal constantly held up to us was of education as a means of living, not of making a living. It was impressed upon us that taking a classical course would have an effect of making us better and nobler, and of higher value to those we should have to serve."

In Johnson's observation lies the core of the difference between industrial education and liberal education. Washington felt that he could be of no better service to his race than teaching blacks how to make a living. The New England school teachers, and the blacks who in time succeeded them, felt that they were spreading a civilization. Education was to give a person a sense of values, a sense of ideals, and a way of life. As Washington emphasized the dignity of labor, the liberal arts colleges emphasized the dignity of the mind and the importance of rationality and intellect in human affairs. The differences were, however, mostly matters of emphasis. Washington was adamant about his students meeting certain standards of behavior and conforming to middle-class ideals, and the liberal arts teachers emphasized the importance of sacrifice and dignity in work.

THE INFLUENCE OF W. E. B. DU BOIS

There was no better product of the liberal arts college than W. E. B. Du Bois. Born in Great Barrington, Massachusetts, he was by upbringing as much a New Englander as were his white counterparts. He attended Fisk University and noted that "all of the teachers but one were white, from New England or from the New Englandized Middle West. My own culture background thus suffered no change or hiatus." At Fisk he studied Greek and Latin, chemistry and physics, German, and philosophy and ethics. From Fisk he went to Harvard and later to the University of Berlin. Du Bois finally got his Ph.D. in history from Harvard in 1895. By the time he had received this degree, he was not only one of the best educated blacks, he was also one of the best educated men in the country. More than anyone else, he epitomized the potential of the liberally educated person.

Du Bois was bound to come into conflict with Booker T. Washington, and the major break between them came in 1903 when Du Bois published *The Souls of Black Folk*. Washington, after the publication of *Up from Slavery*, had become something of an American folk hero. His philosophy of industrial education won wide backing, and Washington became powerful as a broker and adviser to philanthropists and politicians. In this position he overshadowed much of his opposition. With the publication of *The Souls of Black Folk*, with its forthright and direct criticism of Washington, Du Bois became a center around whom anti-Washington leaders coalesced.

The Souls of Black Folk was a pivotal point both in the history of Afro-American education and in Afro-American thought. Du Bois criticized Washington's emphasis on industrial education as unrealistic, since he thought it impossible for black artisans to become businessmen and property owners "under modern competitive methods" without civil rights, including the right to vote. He also summarized and embodied in his book the argument for a liberal education. Du Bois believed that morality was absolute, that there was a knowable difference between right and wrong, and that once aware of the right course a person was morally obligated to pursue it. The race problem to him was a matter of national morality. He advocated the education of blacks so that they would be able to teach and to inculcate these principles in their fellows, and he called for the education of whites so that they would be able to see their oppression of blacks. Education for him was humanistic. It acquainted men with the broad range of human knowledge, taught them to be critical, and provided them with the basis to live and develop as thinking beings. He did not dismiss training men to make a living, but he emphasized the training to understand life and to develop intellectually. His philosophy is best summed up in his often repeated dicta, "education makes men, not workers."

THE STRUGGLE FOR BLACK CONTROL OF BLACK EDUCATIONAL INSTITUTIONS

Black intellectuals found it difficult to "make" men and women because whites dominated so many of the black colleges, making up a majority of the faculty, trustees, and presidents. By the early years of the twentieth century, many of these whites had lost the missionary zeal characteristic of their predecessors in the Reconstruction period. Instead, they were often domineering and paternalistic. The northern financiers who controlled the boards of trustees of many of the black colleges were often dictatorial and sometimes withheld money from institutions dedicated to protest. For example, after Du Bois began publicly attacking Booker T. Washington, the secretary of the General Education Board wrote the president of Atlanta University that no funds had

been given to the school because the board "feels that Du Bois unconsciously is conveying to his students a feeling of unrest, which is not
helpful to them."

Because of such attitudes, blacks began at an early date to call for
Afro-American control of black educational institutions. In a typical
appeal, the Fort Scott (Kansas) *Colored Citizen* editorialized in 1878:

> While we believe it is an outrage upon the civilization of the age to
> carry on the caste schools, yet if they must be forced upon us and if
> our children are always to be reminded by them that they are not
> entitled to the privilege of going to the same school that every other
> class of Americans are permitted to attend, then we shall insist upon
> it, that our educated sons and daughters are placed in them as teachers
> and not always content with sending them to some poor white man
> or woman who would not be permitted to teach in the white schools,
> but are put off on the colored people.

A year later, the New Orleans *Louisianian* expressed similar views
about collegiate education. The black, the *Louisianian* argued, could
"only be thoroughly educated, in part, by his own color; for education
does not consist in simply mastering what is learned from books. To
know and to *feel* that he is a man, the Negro should have the black
professor side by side with his white brother. This manhood education
can never come from white teachers alone, however competent."

Black protest against white control of educational institutions
reached a crescendo in the 1920s. Precipitated by the wholesale dismissal of "radical" students and professors, the demeaning remarks
made by white presidents James E. Gregg, J. Stanley Durkee and Fayette McKenzie and the segregation policies practiced by these presidents, student riots and strikes occurred on the campuses of Hampton
Institute and Howard and Fisk universities between 1925 and 1927.
Throughout the twenties black intellectuals increased their demand
for black leaders for such institutions. Kelly Miller of Howard University
spoke for many of them in 1926 when he asserted, "The Negro race
is developing a number of men who are qualified by every test of
efficiency and experience to man and manage their own institutions.
The foreign overlord never feels that the time has come for his erst-
while wards to assume self-government." Black journalists and editors
were generous in their praise of the student protesters. Reflecting
on the riot at his alma mater, Du Bois wrote in *Crisis*, "I am uplifted
by the student martyrs at Fisk. . . . Here is the real radical, the man
who hits power in high places, white power, power backed by unlimited
wealth; hits it and hits it openly and between the eyes; talks face to
face and not down 'at the big gate,' God speed the breed! . . . *Men*

and women of Black America: Let no decent Negro send his child to Fisk until Fayette McKenzie goes." By 1926, Fayette McKenzie had resigned as president of Fisk and J. Stanley Durkee had followed suit at Howard. In that year, Mordecai Johnson became the first black president of Howard University.

ATTACKING SEGREGATION IN PUBLIC SCHOOLS AFTER 1930

As blacks extended their control over institutions of higher learning for blacks in the 1930s, they began a massive assault on segregated education in public schools and colleges. The assault was led by the NAACP, which began its campaign against educational inequality in 1934. At first the concentration was on graduate and professional schools, because the fact that most southern states did not provide such training for blacks was *prima facie* evidence that facilities were not equal. Using this argument, with NAACP briefs and the rulings of the Supreme Court, Donald Murray desegregated the University of Maryland law school in 1935 and in 1938 the Supreme Court decided in favor of Lloyd Gaines in his suit to desegregate the University of Missouri law school.

The southern states reacted quickly to this threat by providing tuition grants for black students to study in institutions outside the state. In 1938 the Supreme Court ruled that these grants notwithstanding, each state had to make all forms of education equally accessible to all regardless of race. The southern states, however, continued these grants and quickly began building graduate facilities for blacks. In 1950, in *Sweatt* v. *Painter,* the Court struck at this subterfuge when it ordered Sweatt admitted to the University of Texas Law School because the hastily organized black law school at Texas Southern University was not substantially equal to that for whites. By 1950, it was becoming increasingly clear to the Court that separate facilities were almost inherently unequal in practice. One of the most important cases in this regard had occurred in 1949, when the Court ordered black student G. W. McLaurin admitted to the University of Oklahoma. While complying with the court order, the university forced McLaurin to live and study totally isolated from whites; when he attended lectures he had to sit in a chair outside the classrooms. In 1950 the court prohibited racial segregation within institutions of higher education once blacks were admitted. The result of these rulings was that by 1956 only South Carolina, Georgia, and Mississippi flatly refused to admit blacks to institutions of higher learning.

In an attempt to preserve segregated institutions, southern states began frantically in the late 1940s to improve public education for

"Sisters! Sisters, please! Remember, our delegation came up here
only to *discuss* the segregated schools issue with the good Brother
Commissioner!"

DISCUSSION

From Bootsie and Others *by Ollie Harrington. Copyright © 1958 The
New Pittsburgh Courier Publishing Company. Reprinted by permission of the New Pittsburgh Courier Publishing Company.*

blacks. Yet by 1950 it was becoming increasingly clear that separation
meant discrimination. In 1954 the NAACP tackled the problem head
on in a masterful brief in *Brown* v. *Topeka Board of Education.* In
this case, the Supreme Court completely reversed the 1896 *Plessy* v.
Ferguson decision, which had approved separate but equal public accommodations, and ordered the integration of public education. Although Delaware, Kansas, and Washington, D.C., immediately
desegregated the schools, the Court's call for "all deliberate speed"
rather than immediate compliance gave time for massive resistance
and evasive maneuvers in the South. While the Court ruled in 1956
that all deliberate speed was inapplicable in higher education, it still

had not moved very far from its 1955 position in regard to public education as late as the 1970s.

After the Brown decision, several states adopted the policy of interposition, white citizens' councils were organized and supported by state appropriations, Alabama paid a psychologist to "prove" that blacks had a lower IQ than whites, and in 1956 a Southern Manifesto urging resistance to integration was signed by nineteen Senators and eighty-one Representatives. Blacks whose children integrated the schools often lost their jobs, and public schools were closed in Little Rock, Arkansas, in 1957 and in Prince Edward County, Virginia, in 1959. Often private schools for whites were opened with state support. Between 1954 and 1963 there were nine instances in which southern whites rioted over school integration or bombed school houses. Some states planned a very deliberate integration scheme, generally at the rate of a grade a year. At the same time they began systematically firing or downgrading black teachers. There was so much delay in implementing the court order that by 1962 only 7.6 percent of the black students in the South were attending integrated schools.

The picture differed little in the North. The continual migration of blacks to northern urban centers and the flight of middle-class whites to the suburbs led to the creation of public school systems in the nation's largest cities where an overwhelming majority of the students were black. Predictably, as the tax base eroded, the cities devoted smaller and smaller shares of their revenues to education. Increasingly in the 1960s black children in the nation's central cities were taught by white teachers who lived in the suburbs or who sent their own children to urban private schools. By the 1970s the small black upper and middle classes had joined the exodus from the cities or were also placing their children in private schools as the quality of education in the central cities continued to deteriorate. During this same period, middle-class voters in the cities began a massive resistance to new bond issues and taxes needed to maintain and upgrade the quality of education. There was a collision between teachers (who had become heavily unionized in the 1960s) and cost-conscious voters over the educators' demands for salary increases. In effect, both groups were being victimized by rampant inflation.

The greatest victims, however, were black children. Though there was no legal segregation after 1954, blacks discovered that integration was costly and often ineffective. The first to feel the brunt of integration were black teachers and principals in the South. When states and cities abandoned dual systems, they often downgraded black school personnel or refused to hire black teachers. Black students in newly integrated school systems were suspended, expelled, and placed in the lowest

"Goodness, gracious, Gaither. You reckon these fools expect us
to run through this hassle every day an' *do our homework too?*"

SCHOOL DESEGREGATION

From Bootsie and Others *by Ollie Harrington. Copyright © 1958 The*
New Pittsburgh Courier Publishing Company. Reprinted by permis-
sion of the New Pittsburgh Courier Publishing Company.

educational tracks at far higher rates than whites. Black parents found
that they had little voice in the staffing, curriculum, or goals of the
schools their children attended. For blacks, statistical indices were chill-
ing. Black students suffered greatly from the "tracking" system introduced in many school districts in the 1950s. For example, among
Washington, D.C.'s, 3,940 tenth graders in 1956, blacks represented
13.7 percent of those in the college preparatory course, 69.3 percent
of those in the terminal course, and 89.3 percent of those in the basic

course. Black teachers could offer little assistance to the students because they were increasingly losing their supervisory and policymaking positions. In Florida, Georgia, Louisiana, and Mississippi, for instance, the number of black principals between 1968 and 1970 declined by 233, or 20 percent.

North and South, the "career counseling" black students received was abysmal. Recalling his high school experiences in his autobiography, *The Making of Black Revolutionaries: A Personal Account* (1972), James Forman described the typical experience of black youth:

> The whole argument about *us* being Negroes and all the implications of this, and *our* not being able to get jobs and *we* must prepare for the future and *we* have to live and *we* should get some security and four years of shop would give *us* some basis for getting a job if *we* do not go to college and *we* might well not go to college because *we* don't have much money—all those arguments were too much for me. At no point in this debate did anyone consider my personal aptitudes.

The 1960s and 1970s saw a concentration of blacks in the nation's largest and oldest school districts. By 1970, half of the 3.4 million black children in the United States lived in the 100 largest school districts. An overwhelming majority of the black students were attending schools where the enrollment was predominantly black. By 1980 two-thirds of black school children were in racially isolated schools. The worst schools were concentrated in black neighborhoods. Once a school became more than 50 percent black, it was ignored by public officials. For example, most of the fifty-three black schools in Los Angeles were on double sessions in 1963. Almost twice as many black as white children attended schools which were more than forty years old. Overcrowded and understaffed, the schools often did more harm than good. Kenneth Clark's characterization of Harlem schools and their effect on black students holds for most urban communities during this period. In 1965 he wrote of the students, "Little is expected of them; they are rewarded for mediocre performance, and consequently accomplish increasingly less than pupils at their grade level should accomplish. It is an ironic and tragic inversion of the purpose of education that Negro children in ghetto schools tend to lose ground in I.Q. as they proceed through the schools and to fall further and further behind the standard for their grade level in academic performance. The schools are presently damaging the children they exist to help."

The deterioration of the urban schools led in the mid-1960s to demands for administrative decentralization, parental participation in children's education, and local "community control" of the schools.

The struggle was centered in New York City in 1967 and 1968. Alvin Poussaint, a black psychiatrist, expressed the common view of Afro-Americans when he declared: "The Negro should have the say in selection of teachers for schools that are all black because of white segregation. Further, the black community should be able to keep out a teacher who is a racist. The black community should have a significant voice in the development of curriculum, selection of textbooks, the style of teaching in all-black schools, and perhaps even in how the teachers are trained for schools in the black community." Opponents of community control, especially the teachers, reacted vehemently. Albert Shanker, president of the American Federation of Teachers, rejected the decentralization plan because, he said, "we don't like little districts. Little districts can be taken over by little Hitlers." Well-publicized confrontations between parents in Brooklyn's Ocean Hill-Brownsville district and the school board ended, for all practical purposes, the possibility of effective community control of urban school systems in 1968.

Community control was wrecked because of white fears that it would increase black power and liberal fears that it would increase racial segregation. Taking cognizance of such fears, Mario Fantini, an advocate of community control, wrote in the *Harvard Educational Review* in 1968:

> the goals of integration . . . must be broadened to restore a quality that has been sidetracked in the emphasis on the educational achievement goal of desegregation. That is, we must reaffirm our commitment to connect with each other as human beings. We must recognize that viewing diversity and differences as assets rather than unfortunate barriers to homogeneity has as positive an effect on human growth and development as the teaching of academic skills. All of which is to suggest that militant Negro demands for participation in control is actually a means of greater *connection* to society, precisely opposite from the connotations of separatism usually associated with "black power."

During this period the judiciary continued its attempt to insure diversity in the nation's urban schools by insisting on integration. Because of the continuation of residential segregation, the federal courts began to adopt several expedients to bring about integration of the schools in the 1960s. Accepting the argument that "racial balance" increased the quality of education received by both black and white students, the courts paired black and white schools, redrew school district lines, and ordered students bussed across districts and neighborhoods in serpentine patterns. Although the school bus had become an institutionalized feature of American life by 1960, it quickly became

INTEGRATION

From Luther Raps *by Brumsic Brandon. Copyright © 1971 Paul S. Erickson, Inc. Reprinted by permission of Paul S. Erickson, Inc.*

the focus of those whites resisting integration. Responding to political pressure, Congress passed several bills in the 1970s to prevent the use of federal funds in any attempts to achieve racial balance. School bussing in the North became as emotional an issue as desegregation had once been in the South. There were, for example, several riots in Boston after the courts ordered students from black neighborhoods bussed into the predominantly white schools in South Boston. Eventually, the courts began to emphasize the development of quality education in predominantly black schools along with the need for desegregation.

THE STRUGGLE TO DESEGREGATE HIGHER EDUCATION

Just as blacks encountered difficulties with court-sanctioned integration of the public schools, they faced obstacles in meaningfully integrating white colleges and universities. One of the major impulses in the black campaign to integrate institutions of higher learning was the limited curricular offerings in most black colleges. Most of the black colleges in 1955, for example, still concentrated on teacher training to the virtual exclusion of professional training. For the most part, as a result of segregation blacks had to go outside the South for professional training. Although most white colleges barred blacks, a few of them began to admit a small quota of Afro-Americans in the last decade of the nineteenth century. From 1826 (when the first blacks graduated from Bowdoin and Amherst colleges) to 1890, about 80 blacks graduated from northern white colleges. By 1910, some 693 blacks had graduated from predominantly white colleges (Oberlin 149, Kansas 60, Harvard 41, Yale 37, Penn 29, and Dartmouth 13). As the twentieth century progressed, such institutions as Princeton dropped their ban against admitting black students, while others increased the quota of Afro-Americans they would accept (many colleges controlled the number of blacks admitted by requiring a photograph with all applications). By 1954, approximately 1 percent of the 480,000 freshmen entering predominantly white colleges were Afro-Americans.

It was standard practice, however, for black students to be segregated when they attended many northern white colleges. For example, in 1923 the president of Harvard University wrote to a black parent who was trying to reserve a room for his son in the freshman dormitory, "I am sorry to have to tell you that in the freshmen halls we have felt from the beginning the necessity of excluding Negroes. I am sure you will understand why we have thought it impossible to compel the two races to live together." The board of overseers of Harvard voted unanimously in April, 1923, that "men of the white and Negro races shall not be compelled to live together."

Segregated living arrangements represented only one of many assaults on the black student's ego. Many of the white colleges had quotas on the number of blacks who could participate in collegiate sports or join bands. Because of the opposition of southern colleges, a number of northern schools barred blacks from intercollegiate sports altogether until the 1950s.

Upon entering the classroom on predominantly white campuses, the black student sometimes faced prejudiced teachers and had to use racially demeaning books. In one widely used book, William A. Dunning's *Reconstruction: Political and Economic* (1907), the student read that Reconstruction was a period "dominated by a mass of barbarous freedmen." The typical view of American historians appeared in Columbia University's celebrated John W. Burgess' assertion that "a black skin means membership in a race of men which had never of itself succeeded in subjecting passion to reason; has never, therefore, created any civilization of any kind." Sociologists, political scientists, anthropologists, and others followed the lead of the historians.

Buffeted by prejudiced white administrators, faculty, and students, the Afro-American at white colleges led a strained existence. Even as late as the 1970s, his white fellow students sometimes donned Ku Klux Klan robes when he came on campus. The result was often intense alienation and schizophrenia among black students. The prominent black scholar J. Saunders Redding, for instance, recalled in 1942 that during the time he attended Brown University, "I hated and feared the whites. I hated and feared and was ashamed of Negroes. (The memory of it even now is painful to me.)" Ordinarily, the black students found some relief from their ordeal by leaving the white campus and immersing themselves in nearby black communities. A number of mulattoes passed for white. Beginning with the founding of Alpha Phi Alpha at Cornell University in 1906, black collegians established a number of secret societies as refuges from discrimination and training centers for leadership.

However black students tried to adjust, they generally looked in vain for black professors. Before 1960 black faces among the ranks of the faculty on white college campuses were rare. However, a few blacks had served on the faculties of white colleges during the nineteenth century. In the 1850s William Allen taught at New York's Central College, from 1873 to 1882 Patrick Francis Healy served as president of Georgetown University, and in 1884 George Grant became an instructor at the Harvard School of Dentistry. By and large, however, black graduates of prestigious northern white colleges and universities found no employment in them regardless of their scholarly achievement. In 1915, Harvard broke a decades'-long pattern when its Medical School hired William H. Hinton as an instructor (Hinton retired in 1950). Few institutions followed the Medical School's example; in 1940 none of the 330 black Ph.D.s in the United States taught at predominantly white colleges. Between 1941 (when the University of Chicago appointed Allison Davis as professor) and 1960 (when about 200 blacks were serving on the faculties of white colleges) there was some movement toward integration. Still, in 1968 blacks constituted only 0.13 percent of the faculties at such institutions.

Caught up in the spirit of the civil rights movement of the sixties, predominantly white colleges rapidly integrated their student bodies. By 1978, more than 50 percent of all black students were attending white colleges. As the percentage of black students rose to between 5 and 10 percent of the total on many campuses in the 1960s, the students began a campaign to force the colleges to expand the number of black faculty members and Afro-Americans admitted to graduate schools. Since they had spearheaded the civil rights movement, it was natural that black collegians would lead the campaign to revolutionize institutions of higher education. In 1967 and 1968 students at Howard, Fisk, Tennessee A & I, Southern University, South Carolina State College, and Jackson State College protested against administrative policies, occupied campus buildings, held trustees hostage, and demanded a focus on Afro-American issues in black institutions. Violent confrontations with the police and the National Guard caused the movement to spread to white campuses, where black students demanded an end to institutional racism: quotas on black faculty and students, flying the Confederate flag over college buildings, the irrelevance of curricula for blacks. A Northwestern University committee accepted such arguments when it wrote:

> Northwestern University recognizes that throughout its history it has been a university of the white establishment. This is not to gainsay that many members of its administration, its faculty and its student body have engaged themselves in activities directed to the righting of racial wrongs. It is also true that for many years a few blacks have been members of its administration, faculty and student body. But the fact remains that the university in its overwhelming character has been a white institution. This it has had in common with virtually all institutions of higher learning in the United States. Its members have also had in common with the white community in America, in greater or lesser degree, the racist attitudes that have prevailed in this society and which continue to constitute the most important social problem of our times. This university with other institutions must share responsibility for the continuance over many past years of these racist attitudes.

One of the central demands of black students attending white colleges was that the institutions recognize the historic Afro-American presence in the United States by instituting courses, programs, and departments of black studies. They wanted their education to be more relevant to their concerns. The black students at San Francisco State College, in their 1968 prospectus for a black studies program, expressed the common view:

> We have begun to say that perhaps colleges and universities as they now exist are, at least irrelevant, sometimes even destructive, to Black Students in terms of the recognition of new needs in the Black community. We have begun to define the concept which is called "Black Consciousness." We have begun to say that perhaps the recognition of oneself in terms of one's historical presence is the primary interest of Black students today, or should be. That is, Black people did not come from the West, they came from Africa. We came here not as immigrants,

but as slaves. We exist here not as first-class citizens, but as a domestic colony. In schools, when allowed to go to school, we learn little or nothing about African history or our own history in this country, the literature of Black people, of African languages, of black art and music, of the development of our culture.

We are saying that in our own college experiences that if a college's political purpose is to make students more productive members of the society, then those colleges must mean for the *entire* society, including the Black community. This means that in some way the concept of education for students might change so that the information received by the students becomes more relevant to a larger number.

When officials greeted demands for black studies with delaying tactics, black students disrupted classes, locked themselves in administration buildings, and at Cornell marched on campus with guns. By 1970, hundreds of predominantly white colleges had established Afro-American Studies programs.

AFFIRMATIVE ACTION IN THE 1960s AND 1970s

While the white colleges were able to accommodate or deflect student demands rather easily, they faced a potentially more formidable opponent in the Department of Health, Education and Welfare (HEW). In 1967 HEW began requiring colleges and universities to adopt affirmative action plans setting goals for hiring women and minorities. Almost immediately, white males started complaining about "reverse discrimination" and claiming that less qualified women and blacks were being hired simply to meet a quota. The university, they contended, was a meritocracy where there was no place for goals and quotas. Although academics had long applauded affirmative action programs to force unions and employers to accept a certain number of blacks, they rejected the application of similar procedures in higher education.

The greatest conflict over affirmative action developed between three oppressed groups and former allies. Jews, recalling that quotas had once been used to keep them out of colleges, vehemently opposed affirmative action programs. Blacks and women vociferously supported affirmative action. One critic, Paul Seabury, argued in 1972 that the universities "now are required to redress national social injustices within their walls at their own expense. Compliance with demands from the federal government to do this would compel a stark remodeling of their criteria of recruitment, their ethos of professionalism, and their standards of excellence. Refusal to comply satisfactorily would risk their destruction." Having reached the millennium in the 1950s when they attained "an egalitarianism of excellence, a democracy of performance . . . an authentic cosmopolitanism of scholarship" in which "the quest for professional excellence . . . militated against group parities," the universities, Seabury contended, were being required to commit themselves "to abstract preferential goals without regard to the issue of individual merit." Given all of the progress which had been made, so the argument ran, it was reprehensible to return to a system reminiscent of the *numerus clausus,* or quotas used widely until the 1950s to restrict the number of Jews admitted to professional schools.

An impartial review of the law, executive orders, and federal compliance procedures reveals the absurdity of the charges against HEW. The universities were simply being required, as long as they had government contracts, to insure equal employment opportunities. This entailed a number of innovations which were long overdue. First, HEW required that the college president inform all department and division heads that it was the institution's policy to guarantee equal employment opportunity in recruitment, hiring, promotion, and compensation. Second, it required the appointment of a university official to check periodically to see that all divisions were complying with university policy. Third, there was to be constant review of recruitment practices to make sure that minorities and women were apprised of job openings, encouraged to apply, and that all ources of referrals were notified in writing that the college intended to recruit and hire on an equal opportunity basis. Fourth, where no women or minorities were employed or where their numbers were well below the apparent potential in the work force, the university had to take corrective action. Usually this involved the university establishing a goal based on its analysis of a number of variables: the skill levels of women and minorities, the resources of the university, and the number of trained women and minorities in the job market. Finally, there were periodic reviews of these procedures by HEW compliance officers to determine that they went beyond mere nondiscrimination and that the university had taken whatever steps were necessary to assure equal opportunity in all aspects of employment. When the compliance officers found that a university had either discriminatory hiring policies or no affirmative action plan, they were authorized to implement procedures to halt payment under federal contracts. The procedures were not arbitrary; full opportunities were given the offending institutions to answer the charges.

The hysteria generated by affirmative action was unfounded; by 1980, no university or college had lost any federal funds because of noncompliance. College faculties remained what they had always been: the bastions of white males. Since HEW guidelines left essentially untouched the pre-1967 institutional frameworks of colleges and universities, less than 1 percent of the faculties at most colleges were black. A high-ranking government bureaucrat underscored the inherent racism in a letter in the October 6, 1972, issue of the Washington *Post.* He wrote:

> we *do* hire, promote, etc., on "merit"—but the opportunity to achieve that "merit" is systematically denied to minority groups, and even the definition of "merit" is biased to reward the elite. . . .
>
> Unless all people have an equal opportunity in education and other hiring procedures, unless qualifying tests are not culturally biased (which they are), and unless the selection panel consists of people from various backgrounds (which they are not), there is no way in hell for members of racial and ethnic minorities of this country to attain "merit."
>
> The fundamental reason for these contributory elements of gaining "merit" being so biased is that they too, just like the federal government, do not have enough minority group representatives in their decision-making processes to eliminate the inherent racism. This elitist racism pervades the system, and the implications within the context of the federal government are tragic.

Within the university community, the bias against women and minorities had even more tragic consequences. Every advance they made was challenged by Jewish groups in the 1970s. For example, when the faculty of the California state college system was "revolutionized" by reaching the "staggering" figures of 2.6 percent black, 2.4 percent Mexican-American, and 19.4 percent women, the Anti-Defamation League of B'nai B'rith charged that the colleges were guilty of blatant discrimination against white males. For the most part, college faculties, traditionally among the most conservative of groups, refused to budge. The problem HEW faced was summed up by Reece McGee, author of *Academic Janus* (1971), when he asserted:

> resistance to change on the part of faculty members of all kinds of institutions is so widespread and so camouflaged by faculty politics and ideologies that it is very difficult even to convince men that it exists. My own experience (in administration at two huge universities and with faculty committees and politics at institutions of all sizes) has been so consistent that I once formulated McGee's Law of Faculty Conservatism: Any faculty, given the choice between the admission of an unpleasant truth about themselves or the institution with which they are affiliated, the recognition of which will make possible a universally desired progressive change, or the abandonment of a self-congratulatory myth the adherence to which will make the desired change impossible, will invariably elect to maintain the myth.

After more than a decade, affirmative action programs had not produced equal educational opportunity. In 1977 there were 1,062,000 blacks attending postsecondary institutions. Sixty percent of these youths were studying in two-year community and junior colleges or technical and vocational schools. While 34 percent of whites in the eighteen to twenty-one age group were attending college in 1977, only 26 percent of blacks were enrolled. Blacks were severely underrepresented in law, medicine, dentistry, pharmacology, engineering, and the sciences. One-half of the approximately 400,000 blacks attending four-year colleges and universities were in black institutions in 1977. Only about 5 percent of the students at predominantly white colleges were black. Given these statistics, Afro-Americans were understandably shaken when Allan Bakke argued before the Supreme Court that he had been denied admission to a California medical school while less qualified blacks had been admitted. Bakke's charge that the medical school's affirmative action program led to reverse discrimination against whites was decided by the Supreme Court in the summer of 1978.

The Court ruled that the University of California Medical School at Davis, by setting aside a number of places for minorities in a class, had violated the rights of Bakke, and the Court ordered him admitted. The Court also ruled that universities could, but need not, consider race as one factor in determining admissions policy in order to diversify student bodies and to redress past discrimination. When the Court in subsequent cases involving the use of quotas in employment rejected the claims of white employees that the quotas resulted in reverse discrimination, it signaled the limited applicability of the Bakke decision.

Considered from any vantage point, the Bakke decision was unsettling for blacks. After more than 100 years of fighting on the educational battlefield, Afro-Americans were still losing many campaigns. Although 378,000 blacks were attending predominantly white colleges in 1970 (mostly junior colleges), Afro-Americans still received fewer economic rewards from education than did whites. The poet Frank Marshall Davis characterized the dilemma many Afro-Americans faced in "Giles Johnson, Ph.D."

> Giles Johnson
> had four college degrees
> knew the whyfore of this
> the wherefore of that
> could orate in Latin
> or cuss in Greek
> and, having learned such things

> he died of starvation
> because he wouldn't teach
> and he couldn't porter.

THE ECONOMIC RESULTS OF RACIAL DISCRIMINATION IN EDUCATION

As a result of the caste system, blacks gained less from education in economic terms than whites did. In fact, there was an inverse relationship between the amount of education a black man had and the likelihood that his income would equal that of a white man with the same degree of education. In 1963, while a black with a college education earned only 60 percent of the income of his white counterpart, it was 68 percent for those completing high school and 73 percent for those who attended only elementary school. Even when blacks had more education than whites, they frequently earned less. A black who had completed five or more years of college in 1965 was projected to earn less in his lifetime than a white man who had finished only high school.

By the 1970s, the Afro-American battle for equal educational opportunity still had not been won. As national test scores on reading and mathematics revealed a precipitous decline for students in the central cities, the number of blacks who dropped out of school continued to rise, and white academics led massive assaults on affirmative action and recently established Afro-American studies programs, blacks began to search for new solutions. Many Afro-Americans urged a return to earlier nineteenth-century practices when black social and benevolent organizations laid heavy stress on education.

Many black leaders tried to turn the battle for education into a moral crusade. The most vocal of them was the Rev. Jesse L. Jackson, head of PUSH (People United to Save Humanity). In the mid-1970s Jackson urged black parents to keep their children in school. He contended that the new generation of black youth had to excel in their intellectual pursuits. Writing in *Ebony* in 1978, Jackson asserted:

> The challenge of this generation is to protect the gains of the past and close the education and economic gaps in our society.
> This generation must run faster in order to catch up. It must *excel* because we are behind. There is one White attorney for every 680 Whites, one Black attorney for every 4,000 Blacks; one White physician for every 649 Whites, one Black physician for every 5,000 Blacks; one White dentist for every 1,900 Whites, one Black dentist for every 8,400 Blacks. Less than one percent of all engineers are Black. Blacks make up less than one percent of all practicing chemists.

The New Generation must excel because resistance to our upward mobility has increased. Bakke and "Bakkeism" has convinced White America, erroneously, that Blacks are making progress at the expense of Whites. The mass media has conveyed to White America that Blacks have gained too much, too fast and have come too far in their quest for equality. There is resistance to our upward mobility.

The New Generation must excel because the sickness of racism, in too many instances, forces us to be superior in order to be considered average. A White high school dropout still has greater job opportunities than a Black high school graduate. . . . Our goal is educational and economic equity and parity.

Federal policies in the 1970s seemed destined to defeat all efforts to provide educational parity for Afro-Americans. In the mid-1970s HEW began demanding that states desegregate separate black colleges by merging them with white ones or by increasing the number of white faculty and students. The HEW campaign posed a dilemma for those black leaders who had been fighting for integration. Most black educators countered by insisting that wherever legally possible they had hired white faculty and admitted white students. Indeed, the percentage of white students and faculty in black colleges far exceeded the percentage of blacks in white colleges. Having seen such historically black institutions as Lincoln University (Missouri) and West Virginia State College turned into predominantly white institutions, blacks feared that the abolition of black colleges would severely limit their opportunities to obtain higher education. The issue was primarily economic and ideological. The median income of black families was so low that the only colleges their children could attend were the black ones, which traditionally had far lower tuition than white institutions. Where, Afro-Americans asked, could one find an institution concentrating its intellectual energies on the special concerns of blacks outside the black college? Where would black students go if white colleges barred them?

Affirmative action programs leading to agonizingly slow change, a clear recognition of the need for more effective public education, and frustration over defeats in the integration campaign marked the Afro-American educational scene. While compulsory ignorance of blacks was no longer national policy by the 1980s, many Afro-Americans felt that they were still being lightly armed for the battle for education.

9

Military Service
and the Paradox of Loyalty

*I've had white people tell me, "This is white man's country,
white man's country." They don't sing that to the colored man
when it comes to war. Then its all our country, go fight for
the country. Go over there and risk his life for the country
and come back, he aint a bit more thought of than he was
before he left.*

Nate Shaw

Military service historically was a critical test and major barometer
of the status of blacks in American society. Blacks were the only Americans who continually fought to serve in the military to prove their
humanity. Ironically, they had to die in order to live. Hypocritical
white officials consistently promised blacks better treatment only to
discriminate against them during and oppress them after their military
service. Despite repeated disappointments, blacks became cannon fodder again and again to prove their loyalty to a nation which disowned
them. The history of black military service is filled with paradoxes.
Whites, insisting on the inferiority and natural cowardice of blacks,
usually entered wars by prohibiting or limiting black participation.
As the patriotic ardor of whites waned with mounting casualties, they
turned to blacks to fill the ranks. Quick to praise blacks for their bravery
in the heat of battle, whites discovered that the same men were cowards the day after peace was declared. Generally anti-imperialistic and
opposed to American oppression of colored peoples, blacks often found
themselves being called upon to crush the legitimate aspirations of
native Americans and Asians for freedom. Afro-Americans greeted such
tasks with ambivalence.

It was the rare period in American history when the black man
had enough of a stake in the society to justify his fighting for its survival.

Unlike whites, blacks fought because of their dreams of future rewards and recognition. Their present was all too often marked by slavery, oppression, high unemployment, disfranchisement, forced ignorance, and deprivation. Military service only highlighted how long the dream of equality was deferred. W. E. B. Du Bois noted many of the Afro-American's paradoxes in 1924 when he wrote in *The Gift of Black Folk* that the black soldier "used his own judgment and fought because he believed that by fighting for America he would gain the respect of the land and personal and spiritual freedom. His problem as a soldier was always peculiar: no matter for what America fought, the American Negro always fought for his own freedom and for the self-respect of his race. Whatever the cause of war, therefore, his cause was peculiarly just. He appears, therefore, in American wars always with double motive—the desire to oppose the so-called enemy of his country along with his fellow white citizens, and before that, the motive of deserving well of those citizens and securing justice for his folk."

PRE–CIVIL WAR SERVICE

In the Revolution, the War of 1812, the Civil War, wars against native Americans, the Spanish-American War, and both world wars, black men and women served, fought, and sacrificed their lives while enduring unmitigated discrimination in treatment, assignment, conditions, and military employment. After every war until Vietnam, laws or (later) military directives ordered the strict exclusion of blacks from whatever important work the war had thrust upon them. In peace and war, significant service rankings and posts were denied to blacks. Until the 1970s, they were restricted in their roles to the dangerous infantry or to menial tasks.

During the colonial period, blacks fought against Indians and encroaching Europeans, but they were generally excluded from bearing arms in areas where large numbers of slaves were held. When crises occurred in the Middle and New England colonies, however, blacks fought. In the French and Indian War, blacks served as soldiers, scouts, wagoners, laborers, and servants, and some slaves were freed for their service. Blacks also manned fishing vessels, freighters, and privateers. Some slaves gained their freedom by running away to join crews of privateers.

In the Revolutionary War, blacks were among the minutemen at the Battle of Lexington and Concord. Salem Poor enlisted in the Fifth Massachusetts Regiment and Lemuel Haynes became one of Ethan Allen's Green Mountain Boys. Salem Poor fought so bravely at Bunker Hill that fourteen Massachusetts officers signed a petition addressed to the Massachusetts legislature asking for official recognition of Poor. "In the person of this Negro," said the petition, "centers a brave and gallant soldier." Peter Salem reportedly fired the shot that mortally wounded Major John Pitcairn, the leader of the British forces at Bunker Hill.

Soon, however, the Continental Army issued an order not to accept any more blacks, and when Lord Dunmore, the royal governor of Virginia, issued a proclamation promising freedom to slaves who enlisted in the British forces, hundreds of blacks joined the British. This, coupled with patriot manpower problems, led the Continental Army to issue a new order in January, 1776, accepting blacks again. Early in 1778, with two-thirds of the state occupied, Rhode Island raised a black militia of 226 officers and men by offering freedom to slaves who enlisted for the duration of the war and compensating their masters for the value of the slaves up to $400. The preamble to the act authorizing the regiment stated that "history affords us frequent precedents of the wisest, freest and bravest nations having liberated their slaves and enlisted them as soldiers to fight in defence of their country." Governor William Cooke, notifying General George Washington of the legislature's favorable action, added that the measure had been adopted because it was "impossible to recruit our battalions in any other way." Connecticut organized a black company of fifty-two men which was later dispersed among the white companies.

Maryland was the only southern state that officially permitted slave enlistments. In October, 1780, the legislature authorized the recruitment of slaves with the consent of their masters and later subjected free blacks to the draft. A contingent of 545 free colored men and some slaves from the French West Indies fought for the Americans in the Allied French forces during the unsuccessful 1779 siege of Savannah. Henri Christophe and others who later played important roles in the liberation of Haiti were a part of these forces. When Spain joined France as an ally of the American cause, black troops from Louisiana saw service in the war. The Spanish organized militia companies of free blacks and slaves commanded by black line officers. In 1779, Governor Bernardo Galvez of Louisiana led "a half-white and half-black army" in a successful drive to remove the British from Louisiana and the Mississippi Valley. Later that year, "with more slaves and free colored added to his force," Galvez took possession of Mobile and Pensacola. Six black officers received medals of honor for bravery from the King of Spain.

About 5,000 blacks served in integrated units in the patriot services, and approximately 1,000 blacks bore arms for the British. On both sides blacks served as guides, spies, informers, and pilots. Some slaves were freed for their efforts in the war, but others were reenslaved and the British carried away about 20,000 after the war.

From the Revolution to the Civil War, blacks were legally excluded from militia service by law, except in Louisiana. The militia was a social and military organization to which all white male citizens belonged; blacks were not seen as being capable of citizenship status. The Regular Army statutes, however, contained no racial exclusion clause. The congressional acts of 1811, 1812, and 1814 referred to "able-bodied, effective men" or "free, effective, able-bodied men." But despite the absence of congressional prohibition, when blacks tried to volunteer during the first two years of the War of 1812 they were rejected. Secretary of War John Armstrong received several appeals urging the recruitment of black units, but the appeals were unavailing. The first significant break came in October, 1814, when the New York legislature authorized the enlistment of 2,000 black troops, including slaves whose masters would receive their pay and bounty while the blacks would receive their freedom. The second opportunity for black service came as a result of the U.S. inheritance of "an organized and disciplined colored militia," composed of free Negroes, with the Louisiana Purchase in 1803. In 1814 members of the Free Negro Battalion offered their services against the British. Andrew Jackson used them, announcing in a proclamation that he would give blacks the same pay, rations, clothing, bounty, and 160 acres of land received by white soldiers. When on the morning of January 8, 1815, the British attacked New Orleans, at least 600 black troops aided in their defeat. They were praised and received their pay and bounties but soon were ignored and denied recognition.

Blacks played a significant role in the first and second Seminole wars, but in fighting against federal troops. Slaves who had escaped from South Carolina and Georgia into Florida found refuge among the Seminoles for many years. They intermarried and lived in peace together. The blacks and Seminoles fought in the First Seminole War to prevent the federal government from wiping out the slave haven in Florida and returning fugitive slaves and their offspring to slavery. After the U.S. purchase of Florida in 1819, President Monroe ordered the removal of the Seminoles and blacks to the Oklahoma Territory. The battle began again. The Second Seminole War lasted from 1835 to 1842. Federal troops finally defeated the blacks and Indians at a cost of 1,500 lives and $40 million. Throughout the war the blacks liberated hundreds of slaves from Florida plantations, and at the war's conclusion, Army officers sold hundreds of black Seminoles into slavery.

The valor of black soldiers, both as allies and as enemies, was soon forgotten. Concerted efforts began in the 1820s to exclude them from military service. In 1820 the Army issued a general order that read, "No Negro or mulatto will be received as a recruit." A year later the General Regulation of 1821 limited enlistments to "all free white male persons."

Free blacks petitioned and protested unsuccessfully their exclusion from the militia in New York, Ohio, Massachusetts, and other states. They viewed the restriction of militia service to "able-bodied white" men as a violation of the Declaration of Independence and as cruel payment for their services during the Revolution. Blacks demanding to be included in the militia, William Watkins of Massachusetts asserted, were "the descendants of Revolution sires, and Revolution mothers; the descendants of those, who, in those times that tried men's souls, counted not their lives dear unto them, but their blood flowed freely in defense of their country; they fought, they bled, they conquered— aye, they died, that we might live as free men. And shall we be excluded from the pale of humanity, denied those rights, left to us as a legacy by our fathers? Shall we be driven from the festive board, when all the world has been invited to come, and sit around the table? . . . Our fathers were not able-bodied white male citizens; but they were able enough to face British cannon in 1776 and 1812." The arguments of blacks were ineffectual because the peacetime militia was often more of a social than a military organization. To accept blacks, whites contended, was to promote social equality.

The long exclusion of Afro-Americans from the militia led to ambivalence in the black community about future military service. The Boston dentist John S. Rock symbolized the ambivalence. In 1860 he testified, "I am not yet ready to idolize the actions of Crispus Attucks, who was a leader among those who resorted to forcible measures to create a new government which has used every means in its power to outrage and degrade his race and posterity. . . . I do not mean to imply that should our country be situated as it was then, we would be willing to re-commit the errors of our Revolutionary fathers." Two years earlier, however, Rock spoke differently: "Sooner or later, the clashing of arms will be heard in this country, and the black man's services will be needed: 150,000 freemen capable of bearing arms, and not all cowards and fools, and three quarters of a million slaves, wild with the enthusiasm caused by the dawn of the glorious opportunity of being able to strike a genuine blow for freedom, will be a power which white men will be 'bound to respect.' Will the blacks fight? Of course they will. The black man will never be neutral. He could not if he would and would not if he could."

SERVICE IN THE CIVIL WAR

Rock's 1858 prediction was correct on all counts. When South Carolina troops fired on Fort Sumter in April, 1861, they began a four-year rebellion which would be the costliest war in the nineteenth century. At the war's end in April, 1865, more than 600,000 men had been killed. Viewing the conflict as an abolition war, free blacks began volunteering their services in 1861. Union officials, thinking they would defeat the rebels in a few months, rejected black volunteers. There could be no thought of enlisting blacks, an Ohio Congressman asserted, because "this is a government of white men, made by white men, for white men, to be protected, defended and maintained by white men." In the first year of the war, most Union commanders even sent fugitive slaves back to their masters for fear of inciting a slave insurrection against rebellious whites.

As the war dragged on into the summer of 1862, heavy casualties and growing white resistance to Army service led to a change in the sentiments of many northern whites. They began to sing one of the war's most popular tunes, "Sambo's Right to be Kilt." Lincoln's issuance of the Emancipation Proclamation on January 1, 1863, and the passage of the nation's first draft bill on March 1, 1863, accelerated white demands that blacks be recruited. White workers, afraid that if they were drafted blacks would take their jobs, participated in riots in several northern cities, the bloodiest of them occurring in New York City in July, 1863.

From the outset black leaders viewed the attempt to crush the rebellion as a war of liberation. Frederick Douglass argued that though the Emancipation Proclamation was issued as a "military necessity," it marked the beginning of "a struggle between the beautiful truth and the ugly wrong." Douglass, Martin R. Delany, Henry Highland Garnet, and other leaders urged blacks to enlist when the Union began accepting black troops in large numbers in 1863. They contended, as Douglass said, that there was "nothing more certain than that the speediest and best possible way to open to us manhood, equal rights, and elevation is that we enter this service." Black men responded enthusiastically to such calls. A. H. Newton joined the 29th Connecticut Volunteers (Colored) because his "bosom burned with the fire of patriotism for the salvation of my country and the freedom of my people."

By the middle of 1863, black soldiers had proved their mettle in battle at Port Hudson, Milliken's Bend, and Fort Wagner. As one newspaper put it, they "had given the lie to those who would sneer at the abilities of black soldiers." Their bravery notwithstanding, throughout most of the war black soldiers were paid less than white troops.

Finally in March, 1865, a bill was passed granting full pay retroactively to black soldiers. Black soldiers, subjected to unequal pay and often given worn-out muskets and equipment, were often compelled to perform fatigue duty as well as combat. They were frequently abused and insulted by white soldiers and officers.

Very few blacks ever became officers. General Benjamin Butler commissioned more than seventy-five blacks from among Louisiana free people of color for the Louisiana Native Guard Regiments. However, General Nathaniel Banks, who succeeded him, dismissed all but one of them from service as having a bad influence on the soldiers and because white officers objected to their presence. Perhaps the command thought that the light-skinned Louis Snaer who remained was white.

According to Lincoln, black soldiers were "the heaviest blow . . . dealt the rebellion." Some 186,000 blacks fought in 449 engagements, 39 of which were major battles. Sixteen black soldiers earned the Congressional Medal of Honor for bravery. A few, including Stephen Swails of the 54th Massachusetts Regiment, were commissioned from enlisted status for bravery on the battlefield.

Black women also provided valuable support to the Union war effort. Some, including Lucy Carter and Elizabeth Bowser, provided valuable military intelligence to the Union. Bowser, a former Richmond slave, spied for the Union while working as Jefferson Davis's servant in Richmond. Susie King Taylor was one of the many black nurses who worked with Clara Barton tending the sick and wounded. Sojourner Truth and Harriet Tubman, famous abolitionists, also served. Truth acted as a spy and nurse and Tubman as a nurse and scout.

As early as September 20, 1861, a black enlistment policy was adopted by the Navy because of a manpower deficit. Of 118,044 enlistments in the Navy, 30,000 were blacks. Many of them were Massachusetts men. Blacks were in the lowest ranks and were discriminated against and segregated by commanders. None were petty officers. Four blacks received the Medal of Honor for their service. Robert Smalls, a South Carolina slave, had been impressed by the Confederates to serve on the naval craft *Planter*. Early on the morning of May 13, 1862, while the vessel's officers were asleep ashore, Smalls and a crew of seven slaves, accompanied by their wives and children, piloted the craft out of Charleston Harbor and surrendered it to the blockading Union forces. Smalls was rewarded by an appointment in the Union Navy. After the War, he became the political leader in South Carolina and served in Congress until the 1880s.

The Civil War soldier became a hero in the black community, inspiring songs and poetry. Afro-Americans, as Paul Laurence Dunbar wrote in "The Colored Soldiers" in 1896, felt that military service should guarantee their rights:

> In the early days you scorned them,
>   And with many a flip and flout
> Said "These battles are the white man's,
>   And the whites will fight them out."
> Up the hills you fought and faltered,
>   In the vales you strove and bled,
> While your ears still heard the thunder
>   Of the foes' advancing tread.
>
> Then distress fell on the nation,
>   And the flag was drooping low;
> Should the dust pollute your banner?
>   No! the nation shouted, No!
> So when War, in savage triumph,
>   Spread abroad his funeral pall—
> Then you called the colored soldiers,
>   And they answered to your call.
>
> They were comrades then and brothers,
>   Are they more or less to-day?
> They were good to stop a bullet
>   And to front the fearful fray.
> They were citizens and soldiers,
>   When rebellion raised its head;
> And the traits that made them worthy,—
>   Ah! those virtues are not dead.

At first, Congress agreed with Dunbar. Black contributions to the war effort stimulated the passage of the Thirteenth Amendment abolishing slavery in 1865, the Civil Rights Act of 1866, and the Fourteenth Amendment.

SERVICE FROM RECONSTRUCTION TO THE SPANISH-AMERICAN WAR

When the Civil War was over, Congress in 1866 authorized six regiments of black soldiers, two of cavalry and four of infantry; the infantry regiments were consolidated into two in 1869. The 9th and 10th Cavalries and the 24th and 25th Infantries became prominent black regiments. Black soldiers were utilized between 1869 and 1890 in fighting the Indians on the frontier; they won fourteen Medals of Honor and were almost the only national heroes the black community had. Black troops, called "buffalo soldiers" by the Indians, guarded the mails, protected railroads, and mapped water holes and roads in addition to fighting Indians. They suppressed wars between cattle ranchers and farmers in Wyoming, strikes, and the army of jobless men marching on Washington in 1894.

Because of the limited opportunities in civilian life, blacks viewed military service as a desirable career guaranteeing a steady income and a chance to obtain an education in post schools. Despite the literacy they gained, black troops faced much discrimination. Away from their posts, they were frequently unable to buy food or drink and had little redress when attacked by police. The discrimination in the larger society also appeared in the Army.

Military academies generally barred blacks. Only three blacks graduated from West Point between 1870 and 1889—Henry Ossian Flipper in 1877, John Hanks Alexander in 1887, and Charles Young in 1889. Not until 1936 was another black, Benjamin O. Davis, graduated from West Point. Flipper was court-martialed and dismissed from the service in 1882 as a result of alleged irregularities in his accounts as commissioning officer of Fort Davis, Texas. Alexander died on duty as a second lieutenant in 1894, leaving Young as the only black line officer and graduate of West Point still on active duty at the beginning of the Spanish-American War. Young became a military instructor for Wilberforce University in Ohio.

During the long period between 1869 and the 1890s, black soldiers were denied the comfort of stations east of the Mississippi. Since white citizens North and South and even on the frontier objected to the presence of black soldiers, they were almost always garrisoned in the most dangerous isolated western areas. As one Army officer who opposed the policy explained, "New Englanders have always peculiarly loved the Negro, but they do not love him in their midsts; they prefer him away in Georgia or Louisiana, whither they can send him their sympathy by mail."

In the Navy a few blacks were integrated aboard ship but were limited to service as regular seamen, gunners, or gunner's mates. They slept and lived together with whites in the crowded quarters of the ships. But white officers still meted out discriminatory punishment to blacks, and white sailors complained about sharing meals and quarters with blacks. When Frederick Douglass was appointed Minister to Haiti, three commanders found a reason not to captain a vessel to take him to his new post, because that would have required eating with him at the captain's table. One commander resigned, the second declared his ship unfit for service, and the third requested transfer to a new command. Between 1872 and 1897, five blacks were appointed to the U.S. Naval Academy in Annapolis, Maryland. Three of those appointed passed the entrance examination, but not one graduated. All three were faced with social ostracism and harassment like that faced by black cadets at West Point. Not until 1936 did another black male go to Annapolis, and the first black graduated from the academy in 1949.

Insofar as the militia or National Guard was concerned, the word "white," which had been taken out of the Militia Act in 1862 for the duration of the Civil War, was struck from the recruiting regulations of the Federal Militia Law for peacetime on March 2, 1867. Many southern Republican governments during Reconstruction organized black militia units, although many of the so-called black units contained whites. The militia units were designed to maintain Reconstruction governments in the South and to protect them from the hostility of unreconstructed southerners and conservatives and the Ku Klux Klan. The local whites were just as opposed to the so-called black militia units as they had been to black soldiers being stationed in their areas, and only in a few cases did southern Republican governors even use militia. Most of them hesitated to do so because, as they put it, they were afraid of racial conflict. Often different Republican factions in the reconstructed states used the militia to fight to keep themselves in power, rather than using them against the conservative whites.

After the end of Reconstruction, blacks were almost entirely excluded from militias or national guards in the South and from an increasing number of those in the northern states. By the time of the Spanish-American War, it was as difficult for blacks to serve in the militia as it had been in the period before the Civil War.

The Army still followed its general policy of stationing black regulars on the frontier. But on April 28, 1891, the Secretary of War issued an order assigning Troop K of the 9th Cavalry to Fort Myer, Virginia, outside the nation's capital as a reward for their service in Indian campaigns. During the same period, a correspondent in the Army and Naval Journal urged that black soldiers receive like recognition, such as transfer to less isolated stations, that were awarded to their more fortunate white comrades-in-arms. Such recognition finally came to the members of the 24th Infantry Regiment on September 18, 1896, when the Secretary of War announced their transfer to Fort Douglas, Utah, removing the regiment from the frontier of Arizona and New Mexico for the first time in twenty-two years. The soldiers regarded this as a promotion, although citizens in Salt Lake City, Utah, seemed to be opposed. The Salt Lake City Tribune published an editorial describing apprehension among "the best people of the city" that they would be faced with "direct contact with drunken colored soldiers on the way home from the city to Fort Douglas."

BLACK TROOPS IN THE SPANISH-AMERICAN WAR

At the beginning of the Spanish-American War blacks hoped that in responding to the call to defeat the Spanish and to liberate Cuba, they might help to eliminate racism in America. When the *U.S.S. Maine* was sunk in Havana harbor on February 15, 1898, there were 22 black sailors among the 250 persons killed. Many blacks felt that it was their duty to destroy Spanish tyranny, avenge the blacks who were killed aboard the *Maine,* and free Cuba. There were many, however, who argued that black soldiers should not fight in Cuba until the constitutional rights of black citizens at home had been guaranteed. Others, like AME Bishop Henry McNeal Turner, Charles Baylor, Clifford Plummer, and Lewis Douglass, opposed the war as an imperialistic venture. Baylor denounced the war in the July 30, 1898, issue of the Richmond *Planet* "because the American Negro cannot become the ally of Imperialism without enslaving his own race." The editors of the Des Moines *Iowa State Bystander* objected to black participation in the war because they could see little difference between Spanish and American barbarism:

> The American white man's rule in dealing with the American Negro . . . in times of peace and prosperity [relegates] him to the rear, deprives him of his rights as an American citizen, cuts off his opportunities of existence, outrages colored women, burns down his home over his wife and children . . . and now they . . . have the audacity to talk about the cruelty of Spain toward the Cubans. There is no half-civilized nation on earth that needs a good hard war more than the United States, and it is high time if there is any such being as an omnipotent just God, for Him to rise and show His hand in behalf of the American Negro.

Booker T. Washington, one of the earliest and most persistent advocates of black participation in the Spanish-American War, spoke for most blacks when he announced from the beginning that "the Negro . . . will be no less patriotic this time than in former periods of storm and stress." During the war in Cuba, black soldiers, who were called "smoked Yankees" by the Spaniards, were in the forefront of the fighting. And after the war was over, black regulars and volunteers participated in many of the operations in the Philippines. Some black soldiers became regular correspondents, sending reports to the black press reflecting the high hopes of black military personnel that their valor and loyalty would earn the appreciation of whites and lead to an easing of the oppression of blacks.

On Cuban soil, black units participated in all the engagements of the short campaign and performed creditably on the field of battle. The 10th Cavalry won considerable praise for courage in the Battle of Las Guásimas and distinguished themselves at El Caney, where after a costly battle the 25th Infantry, along with the 12th Infantry, captured the village. The 24th Infantry played a major role in the famous assault on San Juan Hill. After this engagement, the Rough Rider and future Secretary of the Navy, Frank Knox, wrote to his parents that he never saw braver men anywhere. The Army awarded five Medals of Honor and twenty-six Certificates of Merit to blacks for their heroism in the Cuban campaign. When black soldiers came back from the war they were showered with gifts, special luncheons, and victory parades at first. Theodore Roosevelt spoke of the black regulars as brave men worthy of respect: "I don't think any Rough Rider will ever forget the tie that binds us to the 9th and 10th Cavalry." In many black homes, prints of the charge up San Juan Hill could be found hanging on the wall.

Afro-Americans optimistically asserted that the recognition of the achievements of blacks in the Spanish-American War foreshadowed an improved status for black soldiers and citizens. These expectations were, however, soon shattered. There was a renewed upsurge of racial hostility in the postwar period, and some white southerners resented the way newspapers and the public played up the role of black soldiers. They believed that blacks had developed an exaggerated sense of their own importance. There was a new wave of disfranchisement, mob action, and brutal lynchings, several of which culminated in burnings at the stake. In Wilmington, North Carolina, there was a reign of terror directed against local blacks. Estimates of the number of blacks killed range from 12 to 100.

Enthusiasm for the black soldiers cooled quickly and noticeably. Late in November, 1898, when whites in Little Rock, Arkansas, learned that the War Department had ordered part of the 25th Infantry to nearby Fort Logan H. Roots, they begged Washington officials not to implement the assignment because it would have disruptive effects on race relations. On November 20, the order was canceled, and a white infantry regiment was sent to the post. Even Theodore Roosevelt began to minimize the accomplishments of black soldiers. He went so far as to say that at the Battle of San Juan Hill none of the white regulars or the Rough Riders had weakened but that he had to draw his revolver to stop a group of black infantrymen from fleeing to the rear. According to Sergeant Presley Holliday of the 10th Cavalry, Roosevelt came up to them when they were obeying an order from an officer to move to the rear to bring up ammunition and he stopped them. The next day, Roosevelt, informed of his error by the officer, had come to the black troops and said he "found them to be far different than he had supposed." Still the story was perpetuated.

Two thousand blacks served in the Navy during the Spanish-American War. One of them was the man who fired the first shot at Manila Bay—John Jordan, chief gunner's mate on Admiral George Dewey's flagship. Another black sailor, Robert Penn, won the Congressional Medal of Honor for saving a shipmate's life while the fleet lay off the Cuban coast. After the war there were about 500 black men in the enlisted forces of the Navy serving on the same ships as white men and eating in the same messes. However, they had little chance for advancement.

In addition to the four black regular regiments that served during the Spanish-American War, some 8,000 to 10,000 blacks entered the volunteer Army. When Congress passed a bill calling for several units of volunteers who were supposedly immune to yellow fever and malaria, four of the ten regiments were to be made up of black enlisted men. The President had the power to appoint their officers. Many blacks insisted that some black officers be appointed. As a result of the clamor, John R. Lynch, a prominent black Republican from Mississippi, was appointed temporarily as paymaster of the volunteers with the rank of major. Another black paymaster was Major R. R. Wright of Georgia. Subsequently, ninety-nine blacks received temporary commissions as first or second lieutenants in the line companies of these new regiments. Approximately thirty of them were soldiers from the Regular Army. Several were commissioned in recognition of their service in the war.

But of the more than 200,000 volunteers called up during the Spanish-American War, no more than 35,000 ever left the country or were even assigned to expeditions before the armistice in August, 1898. The only black volunteer unit sent into combat was Company L of the 6th Massachusetts Regiment, which took part in the invasion of Puerto Rico. Late in August after the armistice, three black volunteer regiments were selected by the War Department to perform garrison duty in Cuba. Beginning early in 1899, the troops were mustered out of the volunteer service.

When the black volunteer regiments were disbanded, the black officers lost their commissions and returned to their units as enlisted men. The other black volunteers, after being officially discharged, returned to their homes by troop train. A number of them were assaulted on the way home. An officer in charge of the 10th Cavalry, which was fired upon several times while traveling from Huntsville to San Antonio, Texas, requested aid from the War Department for his troops to "pass an area which they were supposed to protect without danger from hidden assassins." When the train carrying the 3rd North Carolina Infantry Regiment from Macon, Georgia, reached Atlanta, members of the police force climbed on board and clubbed the soldiers, and the train pulled out of Atlanta for Raleigh carrying many bloody heads. There was another assault on black troops in Tennessee when the train carrying the 8th United States Volunteer Infantry reached Nashville; the black soldiers were asleep in the coaches. About 75 policemen and 200 citizens entered the cars armed with pistols and clubs and proceeded to beat the men. The idea was to teach them that their status was not changed because they were in the Army or had served in the Army.

Some black soldiers were well known for responding to real and imagined insults from locals with violence. In 1899, while on the way to the Philippines, the 25th Infantry stopped for a meal in Winnemuca, Nevada. They took possession of the saloons, shot a barkeeper, and "terrorized the town." While awaiting the sailing of General William R. Shafter's army to Santiago, a corporal and an enlisted man of the regiment were jailed in Key West, Florida, by city police and charged with assault with intent to kill. Men of the regiment believed the charges resulted from police harassment. Forty soldiers, armed and in uniform, surrounded the jail, overpowered the sheriff, and "liberated their comrades and after smashing up the jail, departed."

FIGHTING AGAINST THE FILIPINOS, 1899

When the Spanish-American War was over, some black regulars and volunteers were sent to battle the Filipinos. The American forces that had landed on the islands turned out, to the dismay of the Filipinos, to be an army of occupation. On February 6, 1899, the Senate gave its consent to a treaty to annex the Philippines. Two days before, the shooting of a Filipino soldier by an American soldier had set off the spark for the mass insurrection of the Filipino people against American rule. On March 2, 1899, Congress authorized the President to enlist 35,000 volunteers to serve until July 1, 1901. From the beginning of the war on February 4, 1899, to March 10, 1901, when the U.S. forces suppressed the insurrection with the capture of its leader, Emilio Aguinaldo, the Filipinos fought against American annexation by conventional and guerrilla warfare. The two years of the war claimed the lives of at least 4,000 Americans.

There was a great deal of concern in the black community about the morality of blacks fighting against Filipinos, another people of color, who were seeking their independence. The black press led the opposition. For example, W. A. Holmes of the Helena (Arkansas) *Reporter* called upon blacks to reject service in the Philippines:

> Every colored soldier who leaves the United States and goes out to the Philippine Islands to fight the brave men there who are struggling and dying for their liberty is simply fighting to curse the country with color-phobia, jim-crow cars, disfranchisement, and lynchers and everything that prejudice can do to blight the manhood of the darker races, and as the Filipinos belong to the darker human variety, [it is] the Negro fighting against himself. Any Negro soldier that will cross the ocean to help subjugate the Filipinos is a fool or a villain, more fool, however, than villain, we trust. May every one of them get ball-stung is our sincere prayer.

A large number of journals expressed similar views, and in 1900 Afro-American leaders formed the National Negro Anti-Imperialism and Anti-Trust League.

Opposition became so vocal and widespread that the War Department questioned the wisdom of sending black volunteers to the Philippines. Black regulars, though, were considered reliable, and in the spring of 1899 companies of the 24th and 25th infantries were dispatched to the Philippines, arriving in Manila in mid-July. They were joined during the next two years by other units of these regiments, as well as by those of the 9th and 10th Cavalry.

In August, 1899, the Army decided to organize two black volunteer regiments for service in the Philippines and to staff these units with black officers below the grade of major, to be chosen from among black regulars who had distinguished themselves in the Cuban campaign. While blacks were pleased that they could now become captains, it did not escape their notice that their assignments were to be temporary and in the volunteer regiments rather than in the four black regular units. The two regiments of black volunteers, known as the 48th and 49th Infantry, with an aggregate of seventy-five officers, arrived in the Philippines in 1900 and stayed there until their service ended eighteen months later.

During the skirmishes and campaigns against the Filipino freedom fighters, black regulars and volunteers were active throughout the islands and were used for scouting, garrison, and reconnoitering activities as well as actual warfare. The troops associated on terms of equality with the local population, and when peace was restored more than 1,000 blacks remained, married Filipino women, and made the Spanish-speaking islands their permanent home. One observer reported that "the black soldiers got on much too well with the little brown brothers, and particularly to the little brown sisters, they became united in the tenderest of ties."

When the insurrection was suppressed, none of the volunteer black officers were able to acquire commissions in the regular service. However, John R. Lynch was appointed a captain in the Paymaster Department of the Regular Army to become the first and only black regular paymaster, and Benjamin O. Davis, who had served during the Spanish-American War as a first lieutenant in volunteers, passed the examination for a commission in the Regular Army. Upon his discharge, he enlisted in the 9th Cavalry with the aim of qualifying for a commission, and went with that unit to the Philippines. Sergeant Davis would be the first black to rise from the ranks to a commission in the Regular Army. He made lieutenant, was assigned to the 10th Cavalry, and remained with that unit when he returned from the Philippines. In July, 1901, Corporal John A. Green of the 24th Infantry passed the examination and was appointed second lieutenant. Years went by, though, before there were additional promotions of black soldiers.

There were, however, some victories in the campaign to improve the lot of blacks in the service. In 1908, Booker T. Washington and his associates persuaded President Theodore Roosevelt to order the replacement of the white regimental chief musicians of the four black regiments with blacks. But the War Department resisted efforts to open the artillery branch to blacks. Many officers continued to say that blacks were inferior in intelligence and could not handle the guns. White officers still refused to come to the aid of black soldiers or to defend them when they came into conflict with local white citizens.

THE BROWNSVILLE INCIDENT, 1906

In November, 1906, a widely publicized incident involving the deprivation of fair trial by court martial of a battalion of blacks took place. When the First Battalion of the 25th Infantry was ordered from Nebraska to Fort Brown just outside Brownsville, Texas, white residents were outraged that they were coming to replace a white regiment. From the time that they arrived, there were strained relationships between the citizens and the soldiers. The soldiers resented the segregation and discrimination that prevailed in most of the town, as well as the abuse they received (a sign in the park read "No Niggers and No Dogs Allowed"). Black soldiers were pushed and knocked down for allegedly jostling or speaking disrespectfully to whites. On August 13, a rumor spread that a black soldier had attempted to rape a white woman. That night some sixteen to twenty armed men moved through the streets of Brownsville, shooting at random, killing a bartender, and wounding a policeman. The garrison was aroused and roll was called; all the soldiers were present. Shortly thereafter, several cartridge cases were picked up along the garrison road by the mayor of Brownsville. On inspection the next morning, the battalion rifles were found to be clean, and their ammunition was accounted for. On the same day a Brownsville citizens committee, which had already concluded that the shots were fired by soldiers, quickly found them guilty of the assault upon the town. The same presumption of guilt was made by the several government investigators sent by President Roosevelt to search for the parties responsible for the shooting.

After two days of inquiry, the officers in charge reported that the shots were fired by soldiers and recommended the removal of the black battalion. They were transferred to Fort Reno, Oklahoma Territory. Meanwhile, twelve soldiers had been confined to the post stockade on warrants issued by the state of Texas, charging them with murder and conspiracy to murder. Before leaving Brownsville, officers were instructed to transfer the suspects to Fort Sam Houston, near San Antonio. The prisoners were held in confinement, and on August 29 the military submitted a final report repeating that the soldiers stationed at Fort Brown had been found guilty of raiding the town. Since every soldier disclaimed any knowledge, the commander concluded that there was "a conspiracy of silence," and unless the guilty ones confessed, all the enlisted men of the battalion should be discharged without honor and barred from reenlistment. The report concluded that black soldiers were "much more aggressive" than they used to be "on the social equality question."

President Roosevelt, after ordering an additional investigation, instructed Secretary of War William Howard Taft to dismiss the enlisted men of three companies because of their conspiracy of silence. But the decision was not made public until the day after the 1906 congressional elections, for fear of its effect on black voters.

From November 16 to the 26th, 167 black soldiers, 1 of whom had served twenty-seven years and twenty-five who had served more than ten, were discharged from the service without honor, denied all back pay, allowances and benefits, declared ineligible for pension, barred from reenlisting, and excluded from civil service employment. Six of the blacks dismissed were Medal of Honor winners, and thirteen had citations for bravery in the Spanish-American War. One newspaper said, "whatever may be the value of black troops in wartime, in peacetime they are a curse to the country."

Black leaders, including Booker T. Washington, "were hurt and disappointed and outraged." The Constitution League of the United States, an interracial civil rights organization, conducted an independent investigation and on December 10, 1906, submitted to Congress a report that accused all of the investigating agencies of presuming the guilt of the soldiers and of not giving them a fair hearing. The report called for a congressional investigation.

Senator Joseph B. Foraker of Ohio championed the cause of the blacks and introduced a bill calling for an investigation by the Senate Committee on Military Affairs. As the committee was beginning its hearings, both the commanding officer of the black battalion and the officer of the day, on the day in question, were court-martialed for neglect of duty. They were found not guilty. The Senate Committee conducted hearings and submitted majority and minority reports. The majority found that the shooting had been done by the soldiers, but was not able to identify anyone specifically. The minority said that neither a motive for the raid nor any convincing evidence to indicate the soldiers had done the shooting had been presented. Two members of the committee, including Foraker, went even further, and in a separate section attempted to prove the soldiers' innocence. Foraker then proposed a bill enabling the soldiers to reenlist. A board of inquiry set up by statute still ruled that the blacks were guilty, but that 14 of the 167 were eligible for reenlistment. No reason was given as to why the others were ineligible. Within a year, 11 of the 14 eligibles had reenlisted and received pay for the time they had been out of the service.

On September 28, 1972, more than sixty years after the incident, the Army finally cleared the records of the 167 black soldiers discharged for the shooting incident in Brownsville, declaring the original action a gross injustice. The Army ordered the discharges changed to honorable, but ruled out back pay for survivors or allowances for their descendants. A Minneapolis man, Dorsey Willis, eighty-six years old, was the sole remaining survivor. Late in 1973, Congress passed a bill granting him $25,000 in compensation and providing him with medical care at a Veterans Hospital.

RESTRICTING OPPORTUNITIES FOR SERVICE, 1890–1916

Black sailors found no redress comparable to that of the soldiers involved in the Brownsville incident. In the Navy in the 1890s, there was a deterioration in the already unpleasant status of black sailors. Gradually the Navy began to restrict blacks to the mess men's branch established on April 1, 1893. In time, black men were no longer eligible for other ratings. They were permitted to enlist only as mess men and could be promoted only to the position of officer's cook or steward. The Navy explained that it adopted its policy because of hostility of the whites toward serving with blacks, and that the alternative would be not to admit blacks into the Navy at all.

As the Great White Fleet assembled at Hampton Roads, Virginia, in preparation for its round-the-world cruise in 1907 and 1908, there was tension between the United States and Japan over discrimination against Japanese on the Pacific Coast. There were a number of Japanese stewards in the Navy, and it was feared that they might act as spies and saboteurs. As a consequence, they were discharged and blacks who were in the Navy were placed in the mess branch in their places. In February, 1909, when the fleet returned, black petty officers were transferred to shore duty. After that it was virtually impossible for a black to become a seaman other than a mess man.

Efforts to remove blacks from the Army were considered several times by ranking officers. Black newspapers and spokesmen protested and pointed to the splendid record of blacks during wartime. In January, 1912, a bill was introduced in the House of Representatives calling for the repeal of the statutes authorizing formation of the four black regiments. But the measure never came to a vote. A bill was introduced which prohibited blacks from serving as commissioned and noncommissioned officers in the Army and Navy in 1914, but it did not come to a vote.

When Pancho Villa crossed from Mexico into New Mexico and attacked the town of Columbus in March, 1916, General John J. Pershing led a punitive expedition across the border in pursuit, and the 10th Cavalry formed part of one of the two invading columns. They engaged in a skirmish in June, 1916, in which ten black soldiers were killed and a number of others were captured.

While black troops were engaged in the Mexican expedition, Congress in June, 1916, passed the National Defense Act, increasing the size of the Regular Army. In spite of appeals from the NAACP, the measure made no provision for additional black units. At the same time, southern Congressmen sponsored a bill to eliminate black soldiers and sailors from the armed forces by preventing the enlistment or reenlistment of "any person of the Negro or Colored race" in the military service in the United States. The new Secretary of War, Newton Baker, spoke out strongly against the proposal, noting that black soldiers had performed "brave and often conspicuously gallant service" as part of the American forces since the Revolution. The measure was defeated.

THE FIRST WORLD WAR

When war broke out with Germany on April 6, 1917, the black component of the Regular Army still consisted of four regiments of enlisted
men and three black line officers, Colonel Charles Young, First Lieutenant Benjamin O. Davis, and First Lieutenant John E. Green. In addition
to the regular regiments, there were a number of black National Guard
units, constituting about 5,500 men and 175 officers. These included
the 8th Illinois Regiment, the 15th New York Regiment, and single
companies from the District of Columbia, Maryland, Ohio, Tennessee,
and Massachusetts. The 8th Illinois alone had a complete roster of
black officers. The 15th New York had a famous regimental band, led
by Lieutenant James Europe, and with Sergeant Noble Sissle as its
drum major. At the beginning of the war, approximately 20,000 of
the 750,000 men in the Regular Army and National Guard were black.
Military leaders revived the old canard that ability to serve in combat
was largely a matter of race and that blacks were not suited for such
a role. They also asserted that the service of blacks should be limited
to that of labor and menials in the Navy. Blacks would be used in
the war to help fight, but in ways that reinforced the conception of
them as different, inferior, and not fit to serve as equals.

In World War I, black leaders responded to the Democratic rhetoric
of President Woodrow Wilson, as well as to promises of significant
improvement in racial affairs, and urged blacks to join the country's
effort. W. E. B. Du Bois declared in June, 1918, that out of the Allied
victory would arise the right to vote, work, and live without insult.
Though Du Bois had at first opposed blacks' joining the war effort,
he then called upon them to close ranks and put aside their special
grievances for the duration of the war. Some black radicals, including
A. Philip Randolph and Chandler Owen, dissented; they were active
socialists at the time who edited the *Messenger* magazine. They conducted a vigorous campaign against black participation in the war,
saying that if disfranchisement, lynching, and discrimination continued
at home, it didn't make sense to fight in a foreign war; blacks had
fought in every other war and ended up without the rights and privileges of full citizenship status. In the January, 1918, issue of the *Messenger*, Owen wrote: "Since when has the subject race come out of a
war with its rights and privileges accorded for such participation? . . .
Did not the Negro fight in the Revolutionary War with Crispus Attucks
dying first . . . and come out to be a miserable chattel slave in this
country for nearly one hundred years after? Did not the Negro take
part in the Spanish-American War . . . and have not prejudice and
race hate grown in this country since 1898?" However, black sentiment

seemed overwhelmingly in favor of serving, and there was a fear that if blacks were excluded, any claim to improved civil rights enforcement would be diminished.

The U.S. involvement in World War I soon required the rapid recruitment of a massive Army. Congress passed a Selective Service Act, which required all able-bodied American male citizens between twenty-one and thirty-one to register with the draft board. There was no racial exclusion clause in the act. Approximately 2,291,000 black men registered for the draft and by the end of the war, 367,710 had been inducted, at a rate of 31.4 percent accepted as opposed to 24.4 percent for whites. Although blacks were 9 percent of those registered for the draft, they were 13 percent of the persons drafted. In fact, a number of blacks who, had they been white, would have been found physically unfit or eligible for deferment of some kind were inducted into the Army.

In May, 1917, the Army announced that Colonel Charles Young, the only black West Point graduate on active duty, had been retired for medical reasons. He was sixth in line for promotion to brigadier general, and accelerated wartime promotion would have given him the rank. The examining board, saying that he was unfit for service because of high blood pressure, ordered his retirement. To prove his fitness, Young rode horseback several hundred miles from his home in Ohio to Washington, D.C., but to no avail. On June 30, 1917, he was retired from active service with the rank of colonel. Most blacks did not believe the medical reasons that were given. Young was called back to active duty five days before the armistice (Nov. 11, 1918) and was ordered to take charge of trainees at Camp Grant in Illinois. After the war he went to Liberia to help organize that country's army and, while on furlough in Nigeria, contracted fever and died in 1922.

There were numerous serious racial incidents during the training for the war and in the war itself. In the summer of 1917, fighting developed between black regulars and white policemen and civilians in Houston, Texas. A reaction similar to that which had occurred in Brownsville occurred in Houston among the white citizenry. Racial insults and epithets were hurled at black troops, and they were denied access to recreational facilities that had been opened to whites. On August 23, a black soldier who saw two policemen cursing and beating a black woman asked the officers to release her. They turned upon him, beat him to the ground with their revolvers, and then arrested him. Later that day, when one of the black corporals asked the officers about the arrest, they responded by striking him over the head with their revolvers. When he tried to flee, they beat and arrested him. When the word reached camp, together with rumors that a mob had killed a black soldier and was about to attack the camp, one company seized rifles and ammunition and marched to Houston seeking revenge. They exchanged fire with policemen and a posse and returned to camp. In the short but bloody confrontations sixteen whites, including four policemen, and four black soldiers died. The next day, the entire battalion was disarmed and transferred to New Mexico. Between mid-October and late November, 1917, sixty-four black soldiers were court-martialed at Fort Sam Houston for murder and mutiny, thirteen were sentenced to death, forty-two received life sentences, four were given long prison terms, and five were acquitted. Details of the court-martial and the verdict were not made public until after the thirteen men sentenced to death were secretly hanged, without a review of the sentence by either President Wilson or the War Department. White journalists justified the executions, but black Americans were furious.

In two additional trials, sixteen more of the men were condemned to death and twelve received life sentences. Black organizations, especially the NAACP, worked to mitigate the sentences imposed. The NAACP presented a petition with 12,000 names to President Wilson asking for clemency. Wilson agreed to review the trial record and commuted ten of the death sentences to life in prison. The other six men were hanged. In 1921, after receiving a petition of 50,000 names, President Warren Harding reduced the sentences of those still in prison. By 1924 a majority had been released from prison, but not until 1938 was the last soldier freed. As a result of this case, Congress passed a law providing appellate review at the War Department level before death sentences could be implemented.

The Army at first refused to admit blacks to officer training schools, but after protest on the part of the NAACP and other groups, a separate training camp for black officers was set up in Des Moines, Iowa. Many blacks regarded NAACP support of separate training camps as reactionary. But W. E. B. Du Bois wrote in *Crisis* that if black officers were wanted, "we cannot get them by admission to the regular training camps because the law of the land or its official interpretation wickedly prevents it. Therefore give us a separate training camp for Negro officers." Of the 1,250 candidates who were trained at the Iowa camp, one-third came from civilian life. The remaining two-thirds had been noncommissioned officers in the four regular Army regiments. In October, 1917, the first group of 639 captains and lieutenants were graduated. All told, 1,200 blacks received commissions, or about 0.7 percent of the officers in the Army, although 13 percent of the enlisted men were black. Black officers above the rank of major were few and were found in volunteer regiments, not in the regular regiments.

Black officers were treated with disrespect by white officers and in many cases were removed from command and replaced by whites.

In asking permission to replace the black officers of the 372nd Infantry Regiment with whites, Colonel Herschel Tupes argued, "The racial distinctions which are recognized in civilian life naturally continue to be recognized in military life and present a formidable barrier to the existence of that feeling of comradeship which is essential to mutual confidence and esprit de corps." His request was granted.

Only about 42,000 out of about 380,000 black troops were actually in combat; most, regardless of qualifications, were assigned to noncombat service in labor and stevedore battalions, and not even provided military training. Civilian agencies serving the Army discriminated against black troops in numerous ways. Nearly all the YMCA facilities, both in the United States and abroad, were segregated. Canteens were reserved for white personnel. Even the five buildings located in the black troop sections of one camp were for whites only.

Black soldiers who suffered the least discomfort were those who joined French regiments in France. The French treated them like men. So freely did black soldiers associate with French soldiers and civilians that the American military authorities issued orders prohibiting them from conversing or associating with French women, attending social functions, or visiting French homes. The military authorities also distributed to French military and civilian officials a document entitled "Secret Information Concerning Black American Troops," warning the French that Americans resented their attitudes of "indulgence" and "familiarity" with blacks and that they might create serious complications with the U.S. government. The French were asked to understand that the vices of blacks were "a constant menace to the Americans who had to repress them sternly." Therefore, the French should not eat with blacks or "shake hands with them or seek to talk or meet with them outside the requirements of military service."

During the entire period of World War I, the Marine Corps accepted no blacks and the Navy accepted them only as mess men and servants. An exception was made for a group of about thirty black women who enlisted as yeomenettes and worked in a segregated office in the Navy Department. On June 30, 1918, there were only 5,328 blacks among the 435,398 men in the Navy. The rank and file of blacks were mess men or attached to the fireroom as coal passers, although they often performed duties as yeomen on detail. A very limited number of black seamen were in the petty officer grades with assignments as water tender, electrician, or gunner's mate.

DISCRIMINATION BETWEEN THE WORLD WARS

When black Americans returned from military service after World War I, they were greeted with the now traditional abuse from white civilians. In the South, black servicemen attracted special abuse. A number of people thought they should immediately be reminded that they were not in France and that they could not expect to be treated equally. Returning black soldiers were insulted, stripped of their uniforms, and beaten by white ruffians and police. In 1919, seventy-seven blacks were lynched; ten of the victims were war veterans, several of them still in uniform. The purpose was to terrorize the whole black population. During the bloody months from June to December, 1919, twenty-six incidents of serious racial violence erupted in American towns and cities, and police authorities gave little or no protection to black citizens. The most serious riots occurred in Washington, D.C., Longview, Texas, Chicago, Illinois, Knoxville, Tennessee, and Omaha, Nebraska. In many of these riots, black veterans armed themselves and fought back against white mobs.

As soon as peace was established, a campaign was launched to discredit the role played by black officers and enlisted men in the war. Commanders of the two combat divisions submitted reports to the War Department and the Army War College on the performance of black troops. Blacks, they insisted, were inferiors, biologically and intellectually, and could not adapt to modern combat conditions "because of certain racial characteristics." Black officers were described as inefficient and weak in character and as distrusted inherently by blacks when they were in leadership roles. Blacks were "second class material" who should be eliminated from the Army. The Army should use blacks only in segregated units, and as few black organizations as possible should be established. These should be noncombatant, confined to labor and service duties.

Under the terms of the National Defense Act of June, 1920, the four Regular Army black units were retained in the service, largely because it was generally considered within the Army and among the black public that such units were required by law and could not be abolished. Also a number of commanders were aware that if they kept blacks out altogether and losses in combat were confined to white troops, "there would be resentment from families of white enlisted men." There was no increase in the number of black units. Black soldiers were confined to infantry and cavalry and barred from the specialized ranks of military service. The Air Corps totally rejected blacks. There were no new black line officers; the total number remained at two. The exclusion of blacks from the Marine Corps remained complete. Not only were they unacceptable in uniform, but the Marine Corps headquarters in Washington, D.C., refused to employ blacks even as messengers. Black Americans were enlisted in the Coast Guard only as menials, and from 1919 to 1932 the Navy closed its door to black enlistments. Blacks already in the service were permitted to remain, but were limited to labor and housekeeping branches.

The 1930s marked a change in several discriminatory practices. In June, 1936, Benjamin O. Davis, Jr., whose father was a Regular Army colonel, became the first black cadet to graduate from West Point since 1889. And on June 15, 1936, for the first time in sixty-one years, a black, James Lee Johnson, Jr. of Illinois was admitted to the Naval Academy. Johnson resigned in 1937 because of academic deficiency, but blacks were sure that his resignation was related to the environment of ostracism and racism.

While some of the barriers to equality were falling, all service branches moved more and more slowly against the remaining ones. The Army in 1938 adopted a policy requiring that black military manpower be maintained at a ratio approximating the reported proportion of blacks in the national population, that is, from 9 to 10 percent. But at no time until late in World War II did the percentage of blacks in the service reach that quota. Indeed, the strength of the four black units was reduced so that by 1939 the number of black enlisted men had declined to less than 4,000, far fewer than the total of American blacks in uniform in 1900. The total number of black Regular Army officers in 1939 was five. Three were chaplains and two were line officers, Colonel Benjamin O. Davis and his son, Lieutenant Benjamin O. Davis, Jr. Colonel Davis received his first major command in the National Guard unit in Harlem in 1939. Lieutenant Davis commanded the ROTC at Tuskegee Institute. In addition, there were 353 black officers in the Army Reserve. Seven states and the District of Columbia had black National Guard units, all but two staffed by white reserve officers. A shortage of Filipinos resulted in the reopening of enlistments for the mess men's branch of the naval service to blacks in December, 1932. The 2,807 black enlisted men in the Navy in June, 1939, had no opportunity to learn any of the regular trades. They were permitted service only as mess attendants, and they were paid less than other naval servicemen. There were 19,477 naval commissioned and warrant officers; not one of them was black.

During the 1930s blacks reflected on the continuing discrimination in military service. As they had done on many occasions before, black leaders threatened that never again would Afro-Americans risk their lives to defend a nation which did not guarantee their rights. In a typical outburst, the *Louisiana Weekly* editorialized in 1933:

> The Negro of today is not patriotic in the strict sense of the word. He couldn't be, and we should not expect the same love for this country that Crispus Attucks demonstrated on Boston Commons. The Negro

in America is the underdog, the handy man for all occasions and the door mat for all other races and nationalities who flock here seeking refuge from the oppressor elsewhere. Irrespective of nationality, the newcomers are taught the principles of citizenship in America, and they immediately rise to be potential political factors in their respective environments. The Negro sings the "Star Spangled Banner" and stands at attention when Old Glory is unfurled to the breeze, as an outgrowth of custom. . . . It is a difficult thing to teach a man citizenship in a country where he is also taught that the members of his race have no rights that a white man is bound to respect. You could no more expect that man to conscientiously leave his plow to go look after someone else's business than you can expect him to be sympathetic with a government that holds him in scorn.

The test of the *Weekly*'s views would come during the Second World War.

SERVICE IN THE SECOND WORLD WAR

The long history of discrimination led to black ambivalence toward participation in the Second World War. On the one hand, Benito Mussolini's conquest of Ethiopia in the 1930s, Charles A. Lindbergh's deification of Adolf Hitler as the champion of the white race, and Hitler's race theories combined to make blacks defenders of the Allies. Even those blacks who initially viewed the conflict as a white man's war retained little sympathy for Germany upon learning that Hitler had written in *Mein Kampf:* "In each Negro, in one of the kindest disposition, is the latent brute and primitive man who can be tamed neither by slavery or extreme varnish of civilization. All assimilation, all education is bound to fail on account of the racial inborn features of the blood." Since the Japanese were colored people, Afro-Americans were sympathetic to them. But with the Japanese attack on Pearl Harbor in December, 1941, the pendulum swung; thereafter, blacks would close ranks with white Americans. Mary McLeod Bethune expressed the sentiments of many blacks after the Pearl Harbor attack: "No blood more red, nor more loyal penetrates the veins of mankind; America can depend upon us. I know that at a time like this, every Negro man, woman and child will stand straight up without reservations to his responsibility to his country."

Despite their loyalty, however, blacks did have reservations about fighting in a war in which they would be second-class warriors. A January, 1942, conference of black leaders in New York adopted a statement: "We believe the Negro today is not unreservedly, whole-heartedly, all-out in support of this war." Throughout the conflict, the black press campaigned for the "Double V": victory abroad and victory over racism at home. The editor of the New York *Age*, on June 27, 1942, took a position repeated by many black newspapers during the following three years: "The Negro can less afford to keep silent at this time than at any time in his history. For the record shows that we only get what we are willing to fight and die for. At the same time we are fighting to repel an invading foe, we must insist that our neighbors here at home realize and recognize us as and give us all the rights and privileges of Americans too."

During the World War II struggle against Fascism and racism, black men were used in the service and willingly sacrificed their lives while being discriminated against and segregated. At first the Navy accepted a few blacks only as mess attendants, and the Army was as selective as possible. But as the war continued, more than 1 million black men and women, half of whom served overseas, entered the armed forces. Furthermore, they participated in more branches and services and in higher capacities than previously. They were admitted into the Air Force, flew as pilots, and served as commissioned officers in the Navy. The Army integrated its officer training schools, and the Marines broke a long tradition and inducted blacks. As late as July, 1940, the Navy insisted that it would still use blacks only as mess attendants, cooks, and stewards, and blacks were permitted to enlist in the Army only in the two infantry and cavalry regiments provided by law. Once these were filled, recruiting stations turned away black volunteers seeking enlistment.

As Congress prepared to pass a conscription measure in the summer of 1940, the Committee on Participation of Negroes in the National Defense Program, founded by a number of black organizations and the black press, launched a vigorous campaign to make sure that if blacks were conscripted, they would be used in more branches of the service than labor battalions. Judge William H. Hastie, dean of the Howard University Law School and the first black to be appointed a federal judge, said that if blacks were going to be soldiers they would have to be aviators, laborers, and included in every program, "but we won't be black auxiliaries." When the draft bill was passed in September as the first peacetime draft in American history, it included a provision that there be no discrimination against any person on account of race or color.

There was growing pressure about the issue in the black community as the 1940 presidential election approached. A meeting was arranged by Eleanor Roosevelt between the President and Walter White of the NAACP, A. Philip Randolph, and T. Arnold Hill, adviser on Negro affairs for the National Youth Administration, to discuss the matter of black participation in the armed services. Finally a statement was issued by Roosevelt that the number of blacks in the Army would correspond to the proportion of blacks in the total population. There would be combat and noncombat units, and blacks would be admitted to the officer candidate schools, but except for the three established black National Guard units, black units would be commanded by whites. Black pilots would also be trained. The policy of not integrating blacks and whites would be continued. The NAACP immediately organized its branches to protest this policy of not using black officers. Since there was considerable concern in Democratic ranks about the black vote, Roosevelt partly repudiated his statement. Colonel Benjamin O. Davis, Jr., was made a brigadier general, the first black to obtain that rank in the U.S. Army. Most blacks applauded the appointment, but still thought it was a political device to allay black pressure. But black support for Roosevelt in the presidential election was overwhelming. There was no alternative.

Despite cosmetic changes in some official policies, blacks continued to have their egos assaulted by equally pernicious policies that remained or were invented anew. For instance, during the war the Red Cross, in response to pressure from the Army and Navy, refused to accept blood plasma from blacks for blood banks. "White men in the service would refuse blood plasma if they knew it came from Negro veins." The irony was that Dr. Charles Drew, the pioneer researcher in blood preservation and medical director of the Red Cross Blood Program, was black. Drew resigned from the Red Cross upon learning that the Army refused to accept blacks' blood.

Again, as in World War I, blacks did not receive a proportionate share of the occupational dependency and similar types of deferment within the law. There were practically no blacks among public officials deferred by law. In contrast to World War I, when blacks were overrepresented in the draft, the rejection rate in World War II was substantially higher than that of whites. Mental deficiency was often cited as a cause of black rejections. The effort in World War II seemed to be to accept blacks for some roles in the service, but to limit the numbers of blacks and the kinds of service in which they would be permitted to engage. As the war continued, however, the policy gradually changed and more and more black soldiers were inducted. During the last years of the war, the number of black inductees steadily increased. The percentage by August 1, 1945, was 9 percent of all draftees. This was still below the announced goal of 10.6 percent of total military strength, the percentage of blacks in the general population.

Galling discrimination in the armed services took its toll on the loyalty and patriotism of blacks. In World War II a number of blacks refused to serve in the armed forces for reasons of conscience. Some protested against segregation and discrimination in the service. Some resisted on religious grounds. Members of religious groups recognized by the Selective Service, such as Quakers or Mennonites, were assigned to civilian public service camps. Others who refused to serve on religious grounds were imprisoned. By the end of 1943, there were 219 blacks classified as conscientious objectors. But draft officials denied deferment to disciples of the Nation of Islam, or Black Muslims. Elijah Muhammad was sentenced to five years in prison, and fifty of his followers were sentenced to three years for refusing to register for the draft. On February 3, 1943, the general messenger of a group of black Hebrews in New Orleans was sentenced to fifteen years for persuading members of his group to avoid military service on religious grounds. This was probably the most severe sentence given to a draft law violator during World War II.

The tendency to concentrate black soldiers in the service branches intensified during the war, increasing from 48 percent in 1942 to 75 percent by 1945. Primary functions of the service troops were road building, stevedoring, laundering, and fumigating. The Army justified its assignments by pointing to low test scores registered by black enlisted men on the Army General Classification Test (AGCT), which really reflected the extent and ability of schooling, but which the Army viewed as indicators of native intelligence and ability to function.

As in previous wars, there were numerous insults and acts of violence directed toward black soldiers in towns surrounding southern Army camps. A black sergeant was killed in March 1943 by city policemen on the streets of Little Rock, Arkansas. On Memorial Day of that year, the town sheriff of Centerville, Mississippi, intervened in a fight between a white military policeman (MP) and a black soldier. When the MP began getting the worst of it, he yelled, "Shoot the nigger." The sheriff fired point blank at the soldier's chest and then asked the MP, "Any more niggers you want killed?"

Black soldiers everywhere responded to such treatment by fighting back. There were serious eruptions of violence as black soldiers fought against white soldiers and police at many bases in the United States, Australia, the South Pacific, and England. Similar unrest occurred in the civilian community; riots and pogroms took place in Los Angeles, Detroit, New York, and Beaumont, Texas. One riot that same summer in New York was triggered by a rumor that a black soldier had been killed by a white policeman.

Many blacks were pessimistic about the war. "The Army Jim-Crows us. The Navy lets us serve only as mess men. The Red Cross refuses our blood. Employers and labor unions shut us out. Lynchings continue.

We are disfranchised, Jim-Crowed, spat upon. What more could Hitler do than that?" a black college student asserted. Judge William H. Hastie resigned in January 1943 as civilian aid to the Secretary of War to protest War Department policies affecting blacks.

Pessimism, protest, and the insatiable German and Japanese war machines that decimated the ranks of all-white units caused some rethinking of the Army's segregation policies as the war progressed. Finally a black unit—the 92nd Infantry Division—was put into combat. There were reports that they had not been efficient, had low morale, and that their activities supported the view that blacks should not be used to fight. But demand for infantry replacements sharply increased following the Battle of the Bulge, and it was decided to draw men from supply and service units, retrain them as riflemen, and place them in the line. Black enlisted men from service units were permitted to volunteer for duty as infantrymen to fight on a fully integrated basis. General Dwight D. Eisenhower decided, though, that black volunteers would be organized in platoons assigned to white units. Many blacks volunteered for service and fought side by side with white platoons as they moved across Germany from the end of March to VE Day; the experiment was generally successful.

The Air Corps wanted no black inductees, but when forced to enlist some, created ten "Aviation Squadrons (Separate)" which served as a manual labor force. The Corps began by training blacks for combat aviation in only one branch—pursuit flying at a segregated base near Tuskegee. Advanced training was at Selfridge Field. As one observer noted, the Air Corps knew that "pursuit flying is the most difficult type of combat aviation. Perhaps the Air Corps was paying tribute to the Negro; possibly it was trying to discourage him." The black pilots succeeded. Six hundred black airmen, trained at Tuskegee as pilots, saw combat in Africa, France, Italy, Poland, Rumania, and Germany. In more than 200 missions in Europe, not one U.S. bomber escorted by the black 99th Pursuit Squadron was lost to enemy fighters. In 1943 schools for bombardiers and navigators were opened to blacks.

Black units received presidential citations and many individuals won commendations, the Silver Star, the Legion of Merit, the Distinguished Flying Cross, and the Air Medal. Several black GIs won foreign decorations from the Croix de Guerre to the Order of the Soviet Union. But just as in World War I, no black received a Congressional Medal of Honor.

Every auxiliary service but the Women's Army Corps excluded blacks, and black women were subjected to the same racial oppression suffered by black men. The WAC, started in 1942, opened its first officer training center in Des Moines, Iowa; 39 of the 440 women enrolled were black. The black women ate at separate tables, were lodged in separate quarters, and had different swimming pool hours. After they graduated, the black officers were assigned to command black troops or to serve in administrative capacities on so-called colored posts. Two exceptions were Major Charity Adams, who became supervisor of Plans and Training at the Des Moines Training Center, and Major Harriet West, who was chief of the Planning Bureau Control Division at WAC headquarters in Washington, D.C. By the summer of 1945, there were 120 black officers and 3,961 black enlisted women on duty with the Corps. Thirty black units were sent to the Army Services Forces and thirteen to the Army Air Forces.

WACs made the same charge of discrimination in assignments as those made by blacks in other branches of the Army. Black women were being sent to cooks' and bakers' schools instead of being assigned to higher technical jobs. Some black WACs who were well educated were assigned to sweep warehouses or to work in service clubs or in laundries. In March, 1945, black WACs engaged in a sit-down strike at Lovell General Hospital at Fort Devens, Massachusetts, where they charged that only white WACs were assigned to technical duties while they were restricted to kitchen police. They declared that the commander of the hospital wanted black WACs to mop walls, scrub floors, and do all the dirty work, and would not use them as ambulance drivers or medical technicians. Four of the blacks were court-martialed on charges of having disobeyed a superior officer, found guilty, and sentenced to dishonorable discharges and one year at hard labor. The conviction was reversed by the Judge Advocate General, who ruled that the court had been improperly convened, and the women were released and restored to duty. The colonel in charge of the hospital was removed from his post.

The Army Nurse Corps accepted black nurses, but they were assigned to hospitals that served only black troops. As late as March, 1944, the Army, while calling for thousands of nurses, held the quota of black nurses to about 200. In July, 1944, the Army removed all limitations on black nurses, but by VJ Day a total of only 479 black nurses had been accepted by the Army, constituting 1 percent of the Army Nurse Corps.

In the period before World War II, blacks had been "the chambermaids of the Navy," chefs, stewards, and mess men. The Navy opened enlistments for general service to blacks during the war. But the Secretary of the Navy made it clear that these volunteers would receive basic and advanced training in separate camps and schools and would be grouped in separate units. They would not be stationed on seagoing combat vessels, but would be assigned to shore installations and harbor craft and to construction crews and labor battalions based outside the continental United States. White petty officers would command them until black petty officers could be trained, and there would be no black commissioned officers. The whole enterprise would be experimental. Actual recruiting began in June 1942, at Great Lakes Naval Training Center in Illinois. Advancement for blacks was still very slow, and few blacks were assigned to sea duty except as stewards.

A number a widely publicized incidents occurred involving black Navy personnel who sought to remedy the conditions under which they served. On July 17, 1944, there was a huge ammunition explosion on two ships at the Port Chicago Ammunition Depot in California, in which about 250 black seamen engaged in loading ships were killed and several hundred were wounded. Subsequently 258 of the survivors, assigned to resume the loading, expressed extreme reluctance to return to work, claiming inadequate training and safety provisions for the job. After the chaplain urged them to proceed, all but forty-four resumed the loading. These, plus six others who balked after working a few days, were charged with mutiny and tried by court-martial. They were found guilty, sentenced to long prison terms at hard labor, and given dishonorable discharges. In January, 1946, after numerous petitions and appeals for clemency, the convictions were set aside and the men were restored to duty on probation.

At the end of the war, after continuing pressure from black organizations and protests from black seamen, a number of actions led to improved status for blacks in the Navy. The number of blacks to be assigned to ammunition depots was limited to 30 percent of the black men in the Navy, and a special training camp was set up for black illiterate recruits at Camp Robert Smalls. Fifteen thousand men passed through the school. In 1944, the Navy issued a special order requiring that individual performance, not race, be the basis for employment. The Navy announced that two ships, a destroyer and a patrol craft, would be manned with predominantly black crews under white officers. As soon as blacks reached a level of competence at sea, the white petty officers in charge would be transferred and replaced by blacks. The Navy announced that some blacks would be trained for officer commissions.

On January 1, 1944, 16 men were selected from the enlisted ranks of the 160,000 blacks in the Navy and began their officer training on a segregated basis at a special class at Great Lakes. After ten weeks of training, twelve of the original sixteen were commissioned as ensigns.

None were assigned to duty outside the United States. Six were stationed in Boston, New York harbor, and Treasure Island, San Francisco, aboard patrol craft or tug boats, and six were kept at Great Lakes. They were kept segregated and were strictly forbidden to use the station's officers' club. The commander claimed that there would be racial tension if they socialized with white officers.

In time other line officers graduated from the Navy's officer candidate schools, where they were trained in mixed groups and were assigned to the Navy Department in Washington, D.C., or to small craft. When integration finally spread, a black officer, Ensign Samuel Gravely, Jr., was assigned to the first submarine chaser commissioned with a crew of blacks. Ensign Gravely was promoted to the rank of rear admiral in 1971 to become the Navy's first black flag officer. By September, 1945, the number of black male commissioned officers had increased from 12 to 52, 15 line and 37 staff officers, as compared to more than 70,000 white officers.

Even with all the changes that took place in the Navy at the end of the war, more than 90 percent of the blacks were still mess men and all the blacks who received the Navy Cross and other awards for gallantry were members of the mess men's branch. On December 7, 1941, the day Pearl Harbor was attacked, Dorie Miller, a mess attendant, second class, on the *U.S.S. West Virginia*, ran to the bridge to help drag the seriously wounded captain out of the direct line of fire to a more sheltered spot. Then, although he had no battle training and was unfamiliar with heavy weapons, Miller took a machine gun from a sailor and brought down at least four attacking Japanese planes before the ship had to be abandoned. His identity was not disclosed until several weeks later, and it was not until nearly a year later, on the stubborn insistence of various civil rights groups, that the Navy awarded the sharecropper's son from Texas the Navy Cross, the first ever received by a black. Then they promoted him to mess attendant, first class. Three years later, still a mess man, he was lost at sea when his ship, a light air craft carrier, was attacked by a Japanese submarine.

Conditions in the Marines and the Coast Guard differed little from those in the Navy. The Marines began training black enlistees in August, 1942. About 17,000 blacks served in the Marine Corps, 12,000 of them overseas during World War II, but there were no black Marine officers. The main duty of black Marines was to unload ammunition onto beaches and move it inland to the front lines and to carry out the wounded as they returned.

Almost 4,000 blacks served in the Coast Guard during the War. The Guard's first black officer, Ensign Joseph Jenkins, was commissioned in April, 1942, and assigned as an engineering officer in Boston, where he directed a mixed unit of seamen. In August, 1945, the Coast Guard had four black commissioned officers.

POST–WORLD WAR II DISCRIMINATION

In a war in which propaganda made much of America's moral superiority over racist Fascism and Nazism, segregation, discrimination, mistreatment, and abuse characterized the black experience in the armed forces. Immediately after the war, black veterans perceived that the same discrimination and economic depression that beset them in the service and before the war was continuing. The Army adopted a policy of recruiting people into the regular service and giving them a choice of branch of service and theater of occupation if they would reenlist or enlist for a three-year period. Faced with little opportunity for jobs or training—since vocational schools, for example, were closed to blacks—many black soldiers reenlisted. Army officials became frightened about the large number of blacks in the service and decided to discourage black enlistments in the Army by banning shipment of black troops to the European theater and then, in 1946, by restricting enlistments to blacks who scored 99 on the AGCT, although whites were accepted with a score of 70. When these restrictions failed to reduce black enlistments, in the summer of 1946 the Army halted all further enlistments. Its black quota had been reached. A number of black organizations protested, recognizing that for many black males the Army offered the only available opportunity for economic security and was especially attractive during peacetime. But the policy continued until the end of 1947, when the reduction of the proportion of blacks in the Army to 10 percent permitted the discriminatory restriction to be lifted.

In the Navy, most blacks remained confined to the mess and related services immediately after the war. The Marine Corps announced that it would utilize black troops as antiaircraft specialists, garrison forces, service troops, and stewards, but in early 1947, the Corps switched its policy and offered black Marines a choice between transfer to the steward's branch or discharge. Consequently, during the immediate postwar years, the majority of blacks were still largely excluded from professional and technical careers and stuck in menial occupations in the service.

The familiar pattern of racial violence that had greeted veterans of World War I now greeted many veterans of World War II in the South. The Ku Klux Klan and other southern white groups took steps immediately to intimidate blacks. Several shocking murders took place, one near Monroe, Georgia, where two black veterans and their wives were shot at a lonely spot by a white mob, including a white employer, with whom one of the blacks had had a fight because he had not been paid for his work.

DESEGREGATION OF THE ARMED FORCES

In the 1946 elections, many alienated black voters in the North voted for Republicans or did not vote at all, contributing to the off-year election defeat of the Democratic party. President Harry S. Truman, after assessing the election results, issued an executive order creating a presidential committee to investigate and to make recommendations to him on all aspects of racial discrimination. The committee report denounced discrimination and segregation in the armed forces and called for immediate legislation or administrative action to end discrimination and segregation by race, color, or creed. President Truman was advised by strategists, including special counsel Clark P. Clifford, that the Democratic chances in the 1948 presidential election depended in part on the bloc of black voters, which held the balance of power, and that they might either sit on their hands and not vote or go Republican. Since the white South was already safely Democratic, he could ignore it and make some concessions to blacks. Truman acted on this advice and sent a special message to Congress asking for the end of racial discrimination in a number of areas, based on the Civil Rights Committee Report. He also announced that he had instructed the Secretary of Defense to eliminate discrimination in the armed forces as soon as possible. After a civil rights plank was adopted at the Democratic Convention and the Dixiecrats (southern wing of the party) bolted the party, Truman became very concerned about the appeal of Henry Wallace's Progressive party to black voters. He issued an order that the military service would immediately start providing equality of treatment and opportunity without regard to race, color, religion, and national origin.

The period between World War II and the Korean War marked a major transition in the long history of blacks in the military. Perhaps because of the emergence of the United States as a great power in the world—with the large modern war establishment this role entailed—events conspired in this interim to bring an end to the long tradition of frank, overt segregation and discrimination against blacks in the military.

After a great deal of discussion and controversy and after Truman had won the election of 1948, Secretary of Defense Lewis Johnson issued a directive to the service secretaries in April, 1949, declaring that the policy of his department was to provide equality of treatment and opportunity for everyone in the services. Blacks must be allowed to fill any type of position without regard to race. The three service secretaries were ordered to submit plans for furthering these objectives. Plans were submitted and limited steps toward desegregation were taken, but it was not until the coming of the Korean War that integration was expanded to include training units in the United States and to combat units. The rate of desegregation accelerated rapidly in Army units during the Korean War (June 25, 1950, to July 27, 1953). All-black units dating from the Civil War, such as the 24th and 25th Infantries, fought for the last time in Korea. They were deactivated before the war ended. Others were converted, like the 9th and 10th Cavalry, which became the 509th and 510th Tank Battalions, and their ranks were mixed with whites. In a final chapter of the unit's long history, the 24th Infantry seized the important city of Yech'on and won the first significant U. S. victory of the war. Two of its men, Private William Thompson and Sergeant Cornelius Charlton, died and won the Medal of Honor, becoming the first black winners of the award since the Spanish-American War. By 1954, full integration of black soldiers in previously all-white units was completed, and the last segregated unit had to be disbanded.

As early as June, 1950, there were a few blacks in most of the general ratings in the Navy, and a large number were being trained because racial quotas had been eradicated in technical schools. Also a few blacks were petty officers and junior officers. However, not until March, 1954, did the Navy discontinue its separate recruitment of stewards, who were almost solely black, and open every specialty group to all seamen. In the same year, the Defense Department desegregated civilian facilities at southern Army and Navy bases and eliminated segregation at post-operated schools for dependents of military and civilian personnel. Of course, at some bases commanders still insisted on attempting to segregate facilities, like NCO clubs and enlisted men's clubs and buses. Surrounding communities were largely segregated. And there were problems with the education of black children in school systems and the use of public facilities. In 1954, 7 percent of the soldiers in the U.S. Army were black. During the post-Korean reduction of Army strength, black personnel declined more rapidly than white, but ten years later, blacks constituted 12 percent of total Army personnel, which approximated the reported percentage of blacks in the total population. In 1965, the Vietnam War escalated and draft calls began to increase rapidly. Blacks were drafted out of proportion to their numbers in the total civilian population, as they had been during the Korean War. After 1966, blacks constituted almost 16 percent of all draftees.

The primary cause of this discrepancy was the difficulty blacks had in qualifying for deferments. Deferments were granted to undergraduate and graduate students and to those engaged in critical occupations. In almost every instance, these criteria benefited whites. In addition, in order to avoid the draft, more white youths than blacks applied for and were accepted in officer training programs in the Army Reserve or in the service of the National Guard. In many places local National Guard units refused to induct blacks, who were told that the quotas were filled.

On several occasions after 1965 the armed forces' educational requirements were lowered to induct previously rejected black enlistees, and late in August, 1966, the Pentagon launched Project 100,000 to induct men who had previously been rejected. Defense Secretary Robert McNamara said that this project was intended to assist educationally disadvantaged young men and that they would be given special training programs. Later on, Defense Department officials conceded that they had started the program simply because they needed to enlarge the military manpower pool. Most whites were not willing to fight in Vietnam, so the Army was left with poor whites and blacks. As in World War II, blacks were not as able to take advantage of conscientious objector status as many whites were. Most of the traditional pacifist churches were white, and there was almost a complete lack of draft counseling facilities for blacks. Few black students had the opportunity or knowledge to develop the philosophical and procedural sophistication required to gain the conscientious objector status. There were some black religious objectors, but they experienced great difficulty in obtaining conscientious objector status. The most widely publicized case was that of Muhammad Ali, world heavyweight boxing champion. Ali contended that since he was a Black Muslim, Army service would violate his religious beliefs. His refusal to be inducted and his subsequent indictment led the World Boxing Association in April, 1967, to announce that he was no longer the heavyweight champion. In June, 1967, he was convicted and sentenced to five years in prison and received a $10,000 fine for refusing to be inducted into the armed forces. After he had been deposed as world heavyweight champion and was out of boxing for three years, his case was reversed on appeal. He had to fight and defeat George Foreman, acknowledged as champion, in order to regain his title.

In the service, blacks were still assigned disproportionately to combat units—in most cases to those in Vietnam—and remained in large numbers in the lower ranks. As of December, 1965, almost 27 percent of black soldiers were in the infantry compared to less than 18 percent of whites. Military service was still attractive as a career, and the services needed black soldiers. The continuing economic depression for blacks meant that there was little opportunity for young black males and some females except to go into the service. The black unemployment rate in 1967 was 7.3 percent, while for the white population it was 3.4 percent. Some 10 percent of black males age twenty to twenty-four were unemployed. In the service, large numbers of blacks volunteered for front-line combat and hazardous duty, because they received more money and believed they could improve their status and get promoted for doing so. As a result, blacks suffered nearly 16.3 percent of the combat deaths among enlisted men. As a black sergeant explained, he volunteered for hazardous paratrooper jump duty "because of the extra $55 and because it was the elite part of the service. . . ." He reenlisted "because the job opportunities outside just weren't that good. The Army is taking care of me and my family."

BLACK POWER AND ANTIWAR PROTESTS IN THE ARMED FORCES DURING THE VIETNAM WAR

As the civil rights movement became one of protest, sit-downs, and strikes in the 1960s, the Student Non-Violent Coordinating Committee, the Congress of Racial Equality, and the Rev. Martin Luther King, Jr.'s Southern Christian Leadership Conference joined the antiwar movement to denounce the war in Vietnam as United States oppression of the Vietnamese people. But many blacks who were in the service agreed with Clyde Brown, selected by *Time Magazine* for the cover portrait of its "Negro in Viet Nam" story, who said Ali "gave up being a man when he decided against getting inducted and I don't want him as no Negro either." But by mid-1968, the comrades of Clyde Brown burned a cross before his tent and privates like Floyd Herbert wondered aloud, "How many Negroes has communism cattle prodded, lynched and sicked dogs on?" And a young black poet, Norman Jordan, wrote:

> Hell.
> We are on
> to you whitey
> trying to off
> yellow power
> with black power
> (killing two birds
> with one stone) . . .

The black power and black protest movements of the 1960s had wide-ranging effects in the armed forces. Black soldiers became more insistent about demanding their rights; they began to point out that they were being used as cannon fodder and were in the service because there was no opportunity for them in society at large. They became immersed in black awareness, black pride, and black cultural nationalism. They began to demand the right to wear Afro hairstyles and to listen to soul music instead of country music in mess halls and clubs. They read militant black literature and articulated the views of Eldridge Cleaver and Malcolm X on the racism in American society. They began to use black handshakes and to wear amulets and medallions to symbolize their pride and culture, and they increasingly disregarded many black military career personnel whom they believed wanted them to be subservient and docile "Uncle Toms" and "Oreos." As one black soldier explained, "I just don't trust a black dude who stays in the Army. . . . I don't see why a brother would live with this prejudice for more than two or three years." Increasingly they questioned whether they should be fighting in Vietnam at all. Black reenlistments dropped severely from 66.5 percent of those whose tours were ending in 1966 to 31.7 percent in 1967, while white soldiers' reenlistment dropped during the same period from 20 percent to 12.8 percent.

Blacks and poor whites became more aware that the kind of training they received and the jobs they held in the service did little to prepare them for civilian life after discharge. Blacks complained that they were either expected to stay in the service forever or to go back into society and remain unemployed. The training they received in combat specialties was totally inapplicable to civilian life. They also complained about the military justice system, which, since the first use of black soldiers, had been used to impose discriminatory sentences on black offenders. They pointed out that when they were charged with an offense, they would usually get more severe punishment than whites did and that they ended up being court-martialed for offenses when whites received warnings for similar behavior. This meant that a disproportionately large number of blacks ended up in stockades and brigs, where, besides outmoded facilities and severe overcrowding, they found poor food, short rations, defective sanitation, and inhumane treatment rampant.

Blacks in the service also pointed out that nonjudicial punishment, so-called Article 15s, were administered much more often to blacks than to whites. This meant that the serviceman would get a record of being an offender without a court-martial or any opportunity to defend himself. And the more Article 15s a soldier had on his record, the more difficult it was to get an honorable discharge. During the

Vietnam War, so-called administrative discharges were widely used to eliminate servicemen considered unsuitable or undesirable prior to the end of their service, a disproportionately large number of whom were blacks.

There were discharges for unsuitability and for unfitness. The unsuitability discharges were general discharges under honorable conditions which entitled the recipient to the regular medical, educational, and other veteran's benefits available to those who received honorable discharges. However, a general discharge was not officially accepted as honorable, and sometimes it had harmful effects on the veteran's ability to gain employment. Usually discharges for unfitness were classified as undesirable discharges. This meant that a veteran so discharged had to have his case considered on an individual basis by the Veterans Administration in order to receive any veteran's benefits. He had practically no chance of obtaining private employment, since many people thought an undesirable discharge was the same as a bad-conduct or dishonorable discharge. Black militants and activists were labeled troublemakers or misfits as a basis for an administrative discharge procedure.

During the Vietnam War, there was a scarcity of black officers. In 1967, although blacks were 12.6 percent of the enlisted men in the Army, they comprised only 3.3 percent of the officers. In the Navy, blacks were 5 percent of the enlisted ranks and 0.4 percent of the officers; in the Air Force, 10.2 percent of the enlisted men, 1.8 percent of the officers; in the Marines, 11.5 percent of the enlisted men, 0.9 percent of the officers. There were only 2 black generals among 1,346 generals and admirals, 1 in the Army and 1 in the Air Force. The Marines had no black colonels. On the battlefield only 2 battalion commanders out of 380 were black. Of the 9,800 students in the service academies 81 were black, and there were only 84 blacks among 9,285 Naval ROTC students. By 1969 there were 116 black cadets in the service academies, and 2.1 percent of all officers in the services were black.

The assassination of the Rev. Martin Luther King, Jr., in April, 1968, accentuated racial tensions and controversies at home and abroad, particularly in Vietnam. Those black soldiers who had criticized King's opposition to the war now felt betrayed. As Barry Wright, a black seabee, explained, "It took my spirit away from wanting to do anything." At one Navy installation, whites wore makeshift Klan costumes to celebrate the leader's death, and at DaNang, Confederate flags were raised. When news of the assassination reached Cam Ranh Bay, a group of whites laughed at a black whose tear-stained face was buried in his hands. One told him, "they should have got Carmichael and that whole bunch of Niggers." At the same post, on the day of national mourning for Dr. King, whites burned a cross and hoisted a Confederate flag in front of Navy headquarters. Because of the growing tension, an order was issued for the removal of all flags carrying the symbol of the Confederacy from above the men's bunks, including state flags with this symbol. However, when one southern Congressman objected, the Pentagon responded by saying that the order would be rescinded.

Black soldiers mounted a number of protests and antiwar activities in the 1960s that attracted national attention. In the summer of 1968, more than 100 black soldiers at Fort Hood, Texas, staged an all-night demonstration to protest reassignment to Chicago for possible riot control duty at the Democratic National Convention. They feared they might be used against Chicago blacks. Many of those involved were faced with trials by special courts-martial with the maximum sentence of six months, and those who were considered leaders underwent general courts-martial.

By the summer of 1969 there was open warfare between black and white troops. In Newfoundland at Goose Bay, white security police arrested "white women dating black airmen," and black airmen stabbed several whites. In Vietnam "fraggings"—grenade attacks against officers—became so common that commanders feared their own men; officers and sergeants nightly swapped beds in a grotesque game of survival. The Army counted nearly 100 fraggings in 1969. In the Marine Corps racist incidents climbed from seventeen in 1969 to eighty-one in 1972.

In January, 1971, black soldiers at Tuy Hoa attacked a Ranger unit. When MPs tried to break it up, a fragmentation grenade was exploded, hurling bodies into the air; twenty-seven men were injured. At An Loc whites raised a Confederate flag over the camp, blacks complained that the first sergeant called them "Nigras," and a gas grenade was hurled into an all-black barracks. One morning James Taylor, a black private, asked that the new company commander, a West Pointer, tell the Inspector General that the racial situation was out of hand. The captain refused, and Taylor killed him before several witnesses. He was sentenced to Leavenworth for fifteen years. That same month at Quang Tri, one white officer was killed and another critically injured after they ordered five blacks to turn down their stereo tape recorder, yanking out the plug simultaneously. A five-officer general court-martial found a black enlisted man who had a good record and was in his second voluntary enlistment guilty of the offenses. In March, two more white officers were killed when a grenade rigged to their barracks window screen at Bien Hoa exploded. A black private from the Watts area of Los Angeles was charged with the offense, jailed for twenty months, and given a bad-conduct discharge for kicking and spitting on the MPs who had come to arrest him.

At one camp in Japan, black and white Marines battled with rocks, bottles, and beer cans after the whites loudly derided the black power greetings. One black crushed the skull of a white Marine with a four-foot-long tent pole. Eleven blacks were arrested in 1972 after assaulting four white crewmen from the Navy oiler *Hassayampa* at Subic Bay in the Philippines. In 1973 at Naho in Okinawa, six black Marines tied up a white sailor and cut off his left hand. The incident grew out of a fight between black and white servicemen on an air transport en route from the United States.

The same pattern of violence erupted in the European theater. In early spring 1970, the corpse of a long-missing black soldier was found beneath a sheet of ice in a trench behind the motor pool at Heilbronn, West Germany. Angry black soldiers marched on the enlisted men's club and wrecked it. A white soldier died after a fist fight with a black soldier. The attorney representing the black GIs told reporters, "A bunch of brothers just declared war." At a training post in eastern Bavaria, a grenade exploded in the mess hall, wounding ten; a black sergeant was charged with the attack. At Mannheim, blacks forced a black sergeant they considered an Uncle Tom out of the third floor of their barracks. In Friedberg, three whites were hospitalized after two dozen club-swinging blacks roamed through town bars, terrorizing Germans and white soldiers alike. In Naples, Italy, three white Marines from the *U.S.S. Kennedy* were stabbed by two black Marines from the *U.S.S. Guam* after one white kicked one black in the head. In England, three black airmen jumped a white airman they considered a racist and carved the letters "KKK" on his chest.

The revolt surfaced on the high seas in October, 1972, when the warship *Kitty Hawk* sailed from the Philippines to a station off Vietnam. Black soldiers complained that forty whites had jumped a lone black seaman at Subic Bay. Some blacks believed that a white sailor had killed a black. At the evening meal aboard ship, after a white dropped his tray, a black seaman began to clean up; black onlookers shouted their opposition. Fights began, and a Marine detachment was used to suppress the disorder. In the early morning, blacks appeared on the hangar deck armed with chains; forty whites and six blacks were engaged in battling about the decks. Twenty-seven sailors, all black, were arrested. In November, while the aircraft carrier *Constellation* was ashore at San Diego, about 130 men who had complained of discrimination were discharged or transferred to shore duty. At about the same time, after fighting broke out on the aircraft carrier *Intrepid*, sailing in the Mediterranean, a white sailor was fined and reduced a rank for striking a black, and four blacks were confined for assaulting two white sailors. In November, 1973, ten black and two white sailors were charged with rioting and assault aboard the *Little Rock.*

Back in the United States, in July, 1969, after black and white Marines battled at Camp Lejeune, North Carolina, a white Marine died of his injuries. The riot started when a black Marine tried to cut in on a black woman dancing with a white man. Racial tension on the base had been accelerated by right-wing literature mailed to the troops promising blacks "one-way boat tickets to Africa" with "chicken coops and watermelons on deck" and "free barrels of axle-grease for hair, delicately scented with nigger sweat." Fighting spread from the club throughout the base. The white Marine who was killed was innocently returning to his barracks from a motion picture theater when he was assaulted with other whites by thirty or more black Marines. Two other whites were stabbed. One black was convicted of involuntary manslaughter and thirteen others were convicted of riot, disobedience, or assault. Brawls broke out between black and white Marines at Camp Pendleton, California, and at Jacksonville, North Carolina, outside Camp Lejeune. At Fort Ord, California, a black man refused to perform kitchen duty because "we've been waiting on white people all our lives."

The Air Force was not immune to the violence. In May, 1971, during three days of disorder at Travis Air Force Base, outside Fairfield, California, some 600 black airmen fought whites and vandalized their quarters. Five persons were treated for injuries, including a white officer who was attacked as he sat in his car. And a civilian fireman died of a heart attack fighting a blaze set at a transient officers' quarters. At least 135 airmen, including 25 whites, were arrested. A dispute between black and white WAFs over the volume of a record player seemed to be the precipitating cause, although blacks complained of long-standing problems of discrimination in off-base housing and on-base job assignments.

Deep, persistent racism contributed to this violence. It did not erupt without effect. A military harassed at home and abroad for the role it played in implementing U.S. policy in Vietnam could ill afford the sagging morale and dissension engendered by racial discrimination. The time had come for meaningful change.

After continued protests, fragging, and disorder on military posts throughout the world, Defense Secretary Melvin Laird established "human goals" for the Defense Department and for all services: "opportunity, for everyone, military and civilian, to use as high a level of responsibility as his talent and diligence will take him." He wanted to make the department "a model of equal opportunity for all, regardless of race." Every one of the services responded to the racial disturbances with a positive program for action. Military commanders conceded that blacks could have Afro haircuts and that the Army would not bar the black power clenched-fist salute as an expression of unity in the Army, Air Force, and Marines. Also, blacks were successful in having the services order that in servicemen's clubs on bases there would be some soul music along with the usual programs of country music and pop tunes. The Army, Marines, and Air Force began a series of interracial human relations seminars and appointed human relations officers. And in 1970 the Army and Air Force Exchange Service started a million-dollar program to train 6,000 barbers and 1,100 beauticians in the technique of cutting and styling the hair of black people; also the shelves of the 3,300 Army and Air Force post exchanges were stocked with black-oriented products and supplies. In March, 1970, Air Force Colonel Daniel "Chappie" James, Jr., became the fourth black general in the history of the armed forces and the highest-ranking black in the Air Force. He had been called the "Black Panther" in Korea for his combat sorties. From Thailand he led a sweep which destroyed seven MIGs in a single day. Laird made him a three-star general. James was immediately appointed Deputy Assistant Secretary of Defense for Public Affairs, a position in which he could provide a service for the Secretary of Defense that his white counterparts could not. James expressed the opinion that "this was the first time we had a Secretary of Defense with a moral commitment."

In the service academies there was an increase in black enrollment. For example, there were forty-five black cadets at West Point in 1969, compared to nine in 1968; in 1973 the first-year class included seventy-nine blacks, or 5.7 percent. Each new class of the Air Force Academy had an average of twenty-four black cadets; in the 1973 first-year class there were forty-six blacks, or 3.1 percent, whereas, prior to 1963 there were none. The number of blacks also increased at the Naval Academy. In 1973, Annapolis counted 150 black midshipmen.

In August 1970, President Richard Nixon sent a special team to review race relations in military installations in Germany, Spain, and Italy. They listened to black soldiers and visited community restaurants and bars to see how soldiers were being treated. The Army started a general policy of placing off limits all places where discrimination was practiced. The group that had gone through Europe to make the investigation found that there was overwhelming discrimination in military justice, police, work assignments, promotions, the management of clubs and housing, and off base. The team recommended that equal opportunity or human relations officers and counselors be appointed in all major units and that mechanisms be developed to end discriminatory activities. The team also visited the Pacific; in Japan, Korea, Okinawa, and the Philippines they found similar racial problems.

In late June, 1971, General Michael S. Davison, one of the youngest four-star generals, took over as the Army's commander in Europe. Then Major General Frederick E. Davison, the Army's highest-ranking black officer, was appointed Chief of Staff for Enlisted Personnel of the Seventh Army. Both Davisons gave top priority to resolving the Army's racial and morale problems. In some Seventh Army units a soldier was given the right to appeal at any time to his battalion commander against an unreasonable order or unfair or discriminatory treatment. The Army improved morale in one fell swoop in 1969 when twenty-seven blacks were promoted to full colonel. By 1974 there were twelve black generals on active duty.

Admiral Elmo R. Zumwalt, Jr., became Chief of Naval Operations, the youngest chief in naval history, in June, 1970. Immediately he instituted programs to improve service life for enlisted men, both black and white. He posted these orders in a series of directives known as "Z-grams," personal messages from him to the entire Navy. He liberalized hair and dress regulations, permitted enlisted men to wear beards, sideburns, mustaches, and civilian clothes on post, and started a series of study groups for black officers, enlisted men, and their wives, who met in Washington, D.C., to discuss various problems and then briefed him and the senior personnel in the Navy in order to sensitize them. In December, 1970, he issued a Z-gram to all naval personnel which ordered them to maximize their efforts to improve the lot of minority service people and pointed out that the Navy should be one family without barriers of race, color, or religion. He then started a series of race relations seminars on every base and a vigorous campaign for recruiting black officers, including the establishment of naval ROTC programs in predominantly black colleges and universities. In April 1971, Captain Samuel L. Gravely, Jr., became the first black admiral in U.S. naval history. Then in 1974, Gerald E. Thomas was promoted to rear admiral. Blacks were placed in command of twelve of the Navy's vessels, and new ships were named in honor of outstanding blacks. A destroyer, for example, was named for Dorie Miller, the mess attendant at Pearl Harbor who won the Navy Cross in World War II.

As a result of the racial disturbances on the *Kitty Hawk*, *Hassayampa*, and *Constellation* in 1972, many Navy senior personnel criticized Admiral Zumwalt for permissive policies and creating too liberal a climate which led to a breakdown of discipline in the Navy. Zumwalt responded by calling more than 100 admirals and Marine Corps generals to Washington in November, 1972, and upbraiding them for not implementing the race relations programs he had ordered. The racial incidents were not the cause of racial pressures, he asserted, but rather "the manifestations of pressures unrelieved." The incidents, in his opinion, occurred because of the "failure of commands to implement these programs with a whole heart." Zumwalt stood his ground, but a year after the *Kitty Hawk* incident the Navy began quietly discharging thousands of those it considered misfits and malcontents, including large numbers of blacks, who were given general discharges under honorable conditions. The official certificates carried code numbers which many employers believed indicated that the discharged soldiers were undesirable and unsuitable for reenlistment. The policy was to weed out those people who were creating difficulties.

Black attitudes toward the military service were ambivalent by the mid-1970s. On the one hand, the depressed economic conditions in American society made the military service one place where poor blacks could get jobs. And with the black unemployment rate ever increasing and wages in the all-volunteer service very attractive, many blacks preferred enlistment. However, many of them expressed a reluctance to fight in order to oppress peoples of color in other countries who were engaged in wars of liberation. They also expressed ambivalence toward being the instruments for the ultimate enforcement of the law for what they regarded as essentially a racist state. White society and government seemed as inconsistent as they had appeared from the beginning of black military service. In time of war, blacks were a great manpower resource to be utilized by the Army, Navy, Air Force, and Marines, but white society in general still did not want to concede blacks equality. Whatever the future role of black Vietnam veterans, surely it remained obvious that they brought their hostility home with them. Gunnery Sergeant Paul Thomas predicted in Danang that if he returned from the war, he would know what to do about conditions at home: "I ain't comin' back playing 'Oh, say can you see.' I'm whistlin' 'Sweet Georgia Brown,' and I got the *band*." Another veteran put it more simply when asked whether he believed black veterans could become a dangerous force in American society: "What you learned over there you can apply here. Like when they teach you to blow up a bunker, man. . . . Like a concrete bunker is nothing but a concrete building, so if you can blow up a concrete bunker, you can do the same thing with a courthouse."

Blacks performed military service in every American war and, since the Civil War, during peacetime as well. Black soldiers, sailors, and Marines regarded military service as an obligation of citizenship and as a basis for claiming governmental protection of civil rights and the promotion of democracy and equality for blacks. Whites viewed black military service as necessary in an emergency or as a way of reducing the number of whites who had to serve, but they were extremely reluctant to reward that service by ending discrimination against blacks. Some blacks recognized the exploitation involved in the military use of blacks or resented the notion that blacks were at least more economically secure in the service than out of it, and avoided military service. The general pattern of black service from the colonial period to the 1970s was a refusal by whites to use blacks unless it was perceived as absolutely necessary to victory, minimum concessions toward favorable treatment during a crisis, and a retreat to outright oppression thereafter.

10

White Proscriptions and Black Protests

If you are never angry, then you are unborn.
Bassa proverb

There were several significant changes in the position of blacks after 1865. First, the decade of Reconstruction was marked by a dramatic improvement in the legal status of blacks; they were given the right to vote, the right to hold office, and a great deal of hope. In 1865 Congress passed legislation to repeal the 1810 law which had prevented blacks from being U.S. mail carriers, to make blacks eligible to be jurors in federal courts, and to ban discrimination on streetcars in the District of Columbia. A number of northern and western states moved toward a more egalitarian society. California repealed its laws prohibiting blacks from testifying against whites in 1863, followed three years later by Illinois and Indiana, which also repealed laws against blacks emigrating to their states. Some influential northern whites fought to protect the interests of southern blacks, and it appeared to some that nationally most discrimination against blacks would be prohibited.

PROTESTS DURING RECONSTRUCTION

Freed from the restraints of slavery, blacks led several successful attacks against discrimination during this period. George Downing, a wealthy black caterer in Newport, was able after a short campaign to bring about integrated schools in Rhode Island in 1866. From 1865 to 1871 blacks in Philadelphia, New Orleans, Savannah, Richmond, Charleston, and Louisville took part in sit-ins in streetcars reserved for whites, obstructed the tracks, shot into the cars, and generally created such havoc that the streetcars were finally integrated. Through their political influence, blacks were also able occasionally to get comprehensive public accommodations laws passed and enforced. This was especially true

342

in South Carolina and Louisiana, the two southern states where blacks gained some political power. Undoubtedly the high point in the blacks' drive for legal equality came in 1875 with the passage of a national civil rights law banning discrimination in places of public accommodations and in jury selection. The law, passed as a tribute to deceased Senator Charles Sumner, was, however, rarely enforced.

DISFRANCHISEMENT AND SEGREGATION, 1877–98

After 1875 blacks descended rapidly toward what historian Rayford Logan has described as their nadir, that low, rugged plateau in race relations which existed from about 1900 to 1920. The tombstones along the road to this valley of hell were numerous. The first killer of the dream of equality was the Republican party. By 1875 blacks had been driven from political influence everywhere except in South Carolina and Louisiana. After Rutherford B. Hayes' election as President in 1877, the Republican party tried to build up a lily-white southern wing, fought to reconcile the sections by taking a hands-off policy where blacks were concerned, and refused to use federal troops to enforce national laws that could protect black citizens. The enforcement acts of 1870 and 1871 and the Ku Klux Klan Act of 1870 became dead letters because the U.S. Attorney General refused to prosecute cases under their provisions.

The Republican betrayal of the southern blacks had a disastrous impact on them. Once southern whites found out that the North would not interfere with their internal affairs, they began systematically to curtail black political influence. Crude methods were used in the 1870s and 1880s. Most southern elections, except in Tennessee and North Carolina, were reigns of terror in which whites intimidated, physically abused, or killed blacks when they attempted to vote or cheated them when they managed to win elections. Such tactics led to the last national effort to defend the freedmen, the Lodge Force Bill of 1890, which would have provided for federal supervision of congressional elections. The bill was buried in a Senate committee. Congress' failure to pass the bill confirmed national abandonment of black welfare in the South.

In the 1880s, the southern conservatives were badly shaken when poor southern farmers, or Populists, began uniting with blacks to improve their economic condition. Tom Watson of Georgia, one of the most powerful Populists, appealed for political unity between white and black farmers. In spite of the conservatives' resort to racist demagoguery in the election of 1892, black and white Populists seized control of the North Carolina legislature in 1894. Unable to control the black vote, conservative Democrats raised the cry of white supremacy and began to push for constitutional disfranchisement of blacks. Characteristically, Mississippi led the way in this movement in 1890 by enacting a poll tax, by disfranchising a voter for committing petty crimes, and by requiring that voters be able to read and understand a section of the Constitution. Between 1890 and 1910 most southern states had disfranchised blacks, the most ingenious device being the grandfather clause in Louisiana. Legal disfranchisement was preceded by violence, gerrymandering, stuffing ballot boxes, secretly shifting polling places in black districts, extremely complicated ballots, and cumulative poll taxes. Southern whites made no bones about the methods they used to eliminate blacks from politics. Senator Ben Tillman of South Carolina boldly asserted: "We have done our best. . . . We have scratched our heads to find out how we could eliminate the last one of them. We stuffed ballot boxes. We shot them. We are not ashamed of it." In spite of all this, Congress consistently refused to use its authority to reduce southern representation in Congress because of the disfranchisement of blacks.

The second killer of the dream of equality was the Supreme Court. In practically every case concerning blacks after 1877, the Court ruled in favor of white supremacy. Adopting the specious sociology of William Graham Sumner that custom and not law determines mores, the Court changed from a friend to an enemy of blacks. In the case of *Hall* v. *Decuir* in 1878, the Court held that a Louisiana statute barring discrimination in transportation was unconstitutional. Similarly, the Court ruled in 1882 that the Ku Klux Klan Act of 1871 was void because the Fourteenth Amendment applied to deprivation of civil rights only by the state and therefore could not punish *individuals*. The Court delivered another blow in 1883 when it ruled that the public accommodations section of the Civil Rights Act of 1875 was unconstitutional. The Court concluded its infamous record in 1896 when it ruled in the case of *Plessy* v. *Ferguson* that a Louisiana statute segregating railroad passengers was constitutional as long as the separate accommodations were equal. Closely allied with the Court was the Interstate Commerce Commission, which ruled in several cases involving blacks from 1887 to 1910 that the separate-but-equal doctrine imposed no undue burden on black passengers in spite of the clearly unequal and filthy Jim Crow cars to which they were consigned.

The third killer of the dream was the communications media. Northern newspapers, magazines, and plays justified southern oppression of blacks, voiced approval of lynching, and generally showed that blacks were so stupid and morally degraded that they deserved an inferior place in society. White artists caricatured blacks in cartoons, paintings, advertisements, and post cards. With the possible exception of the Chinese, no other ethnic group was more frequently lampooned than blacks were between 1865 and 1900.

One of the most important contributors to the formulation of the white man's stereotype of blacks in the second half of the nineteenth century was the playwright. The black on the stage was irrepressibly happy, instinctively servile and loyal to whites, cowardly, debased, stupid, and given to drinking hard liquor, playing the "numbers," eating watermelons and chicken, and flashing razors. His entrance into politics was the signal for corruption and his migration to the city the beginning of degeneracy and riot.

Obviously, playwrights during this period wrote what they felt the public wanted. In this regard, they were doing what playwrights have always done: mirroring and molding public attitudes. The unanimity of their portrait of the black, however, is striking. Where the black was concerned, the playwright forsook both art and truth. In the very act of capitulating to the public fancy, he helped to rivet almost irrevocably in the mind of the white man two equally outrageous portraits of the black: the dangerous, lying, stealing, raping half-man on the one hand and the exasperating, obsequious, playful, loyal child on the other. The power the playwright exercised over the American mind was awesome, for it was he who created and reflected the attitudes of the opinion makers—businessmen, teachers, editors, and others. The portrait of the black on the stage—as devil incarnate or as fool—reinforced the insurmountable barriers to his equal participation in American life.

While the opinion leaders saw caricatures of blacks in the legitimate theater, the common folk flocked to minstrel shows, where whites in black face, painted lips, and outlandish costumes sang crude "coon songs" and portrayed the blacks' alleged laziness, licentiousness, ignorance, and dishonesty. Such minstrel troupes as Primrose and Dockstader, Bryant, and Duprez and Benedict toured the country from 1865 to the early years of the twentieth century, playing to enthusiastic crowds North and South. Music halls did a thriving business selling sheet music for such popular minstrel songs as "Old Zip Coon." The sheet music and playbills were illustrated with grotesque portraits of blacks.

Scientists joined with minstrels and playwrights in justifying the oppression of blacks at home and abroad. Charles Darwin's theory that in evolution only the fittest survive was taken out of context and applied to race relations. Since scientists argued that blacks were inferior, many whites felt that it was useless to try to uplift blacks, as they would lose out in competition with energetic Anglo-Saxons.

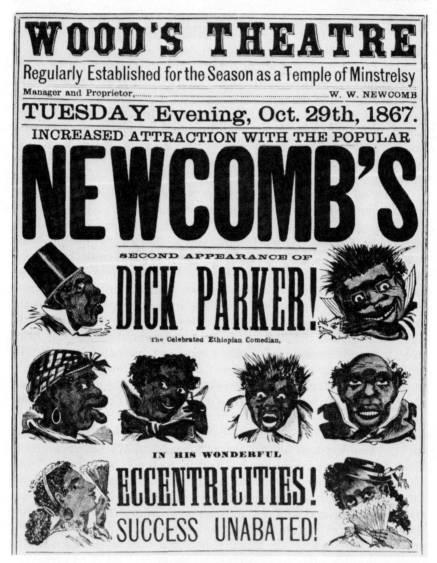

MINSTREL PLAYBILL

IMPERIALISM ABROAD RELATED TO RACISM AT HOME

Scientific theory provided an additional rationale for America's late nineteenth- and early twentieth-century imperialistic ventures. In 1867 the United States purchased Alaska, and in the 1870s President Ulysses S. Grant tried unsuccessfully to annex Santo Domingo. At the same time, the rapid European colonization of Africa was virtually completed when the continent was carved up by Europeans between 1884 and 1885. European successes in Africa encouraged Americans in their own imperialistic designs on lands close by. American businessmen overthrew the Hawaiian government in 1893, and the islands were annexed by the United States in 1898. Because of American investments in Cuba and desires for expansion, U.S. imperialists turned their attention to the American possessions of Spain. First, the United States supported the Cuban revolution in 1895 and used the destruction of the *Maine* in Havana harbor as a pretext for war on Spain in 1898. In the short war against Spain the United States added Cuba, Puerto Rico, and the Philippines to its colonies. From 1904 to 1944 the United States either intervened in the affairs of Haiti and the Dominican Republic or occupied them outright.

Between 1870 and 1920 the United States took up the white man's burden. All of the areas added or coveted during this period were inhabited by colored people. Believing that all nonwhites were backward, indolent, immoral, and unable to govern themselves, American whites insisted that Anglo-Saxons had to bring civilization to them. Whites often characterized such people as coons, mongrels, unwholesome, childlike, ignorant, lazy, savage, and superstitious. Lothrop Stoddard, a New England writer, summed up the general attitude of whites toward the capacity of colored people when he asserted in regard to Santo Domingo: "Complete incapacity for self-government is the most salient feature of the Dominican character. . . . The Political helplessness of the Dominican people is not merely the result of unfortunate circumstances; it springs from their very nature."

The relationship between America's manifest destiny to occupy the lands of allegedly backward colored people and the oppression of the American black was clear. If black or colored people in Haiti, Cuba, and the Philippines were too degraded to govern themselves, obviously, whites felt, American blacks, who were so similar to them, should not be given a chance to rule whites or to bring all of their corrupt practices into politics. American blacks deserved no protection, whites argued, because according to Charles Darwin, only the fit would survive. Reflecting on the domestic consequences of America's acquisition of colonies in the Spanish-American War, the *Atlantic Monthly* asked, "If the stronger and cleverer race is free to impose its will upon 'new-caught sullen peoples' on the other side of the globe, why not in South Carolina and Mississippi?" The New York *Times* concurred. It asserted in May, 1900, that "Northern men . . . no longer denounce the suppression of the Negro vote [in the South] as it used to be denounced in Reconstruction days. The necessity of it under the supreme law of self-preservation is candidly recognized." Another New York journal, the *Independent,* urged the United States in 1904 to annex Santo Domingo because "it would plant another star in the blue sky of the flag and plant the flag prophetically in the waters of the Caribbean. . . . If the United States has one 'mission' it is to propagate liberty under the direction of education and morality. . . . But it is said that annexation would be the ruin of a negro state. If so, so be it. . . . And if the Negroes or the white men of Santo Domingo, or of the South, under fair laws, cannot swim, they must sink, call it fate or law or what we will. It is best that the best should survive."

LYNCHING AND JIM CROW, 1890–1920

In the prevailing environment, white oppression of blacks reached its highest point between 1890 and 1920. Deprived of political power and the protection of law enforcement agencies, blacks faced a virtual reign of terror in the South during this period. For example, between 1882 and 1900 there were 3,011 lynchings in the United States. Most of them occurred in the South, and an overwhelming majority of the victims were black. Following the demise of the unification effort of the Populists in the early 1890s, the farmers who gained control of the southern state governments became the most virulent racist demagogues. They appealed to the basest emotions of their constituents. From 1890 to 1920 southern politicians subordinated almost all other issues to that of white supremacy. The black was pilloried in a virtual bacchanalia of racism. The most infamous of the degenerate crew were James K. Vardaman of Mississippi and Cole Blease and Ben Tillman of South Carolina. To such men and their cohorts, blacks were the scum of the earth. In 1908 Vardaman asserted that the very idea that the black was human and thus capable of improvement was "the most damnable and dangerous doctrine . . . in America." The even more despicable Blease argued, "In all Bible history and in all profane history, you will find that the superior race has ruled and controlled: and the white people of this country are going to rule it, and control it, if it be necessary, to wipe the black race off the face of the earth."

It is against this background that we must assess what historian C. Vann Woodward has called the "strange career of Jim Crow." Briefly stated, Woodward's thesis is that segregation in the South is a creation of the late nineteenth and early twentieth centuries. Arguing that the avalanche of Jim Crow laws started when poor white farmers came into power, Woodward believes that the old aristocratic white politicians were more paternalistic toward black people and frequently tried to protect them from the more racist poor whites. There were, of course, a few aristocratic white southerners who bravely fought to protect the black. But the majority of them did not believe segregation laws were necessary to protect their own preferred social and economic position. The most impressive evidence supporting this thesis is the history of the Jim Crow bills in aristocrat-dominated legislatures. The most striking thing is how long the southern whites were willing to live with the patterns established during Reconstruction. In South Carolina, for example, the public accommodations act of 1870 was not repealed until 1889. The most conclusive proof of Woodward's thesis, however, is how difficult it was to obtain passage of segregation bills in southern legislatures. In many of the states, segregation bills were defeated one or two times between 1877 and 1890. The South Carolina legislature defeated a bill providing for segregated trains six times between 1891 and 1898.

The difficulty in inaugurating the reign of Jim Crow is also revealed in the fact that none of the state legislatures passed a comprehensive segregation law. Instead, these laws generally emerged over a thirty- to fifty-year period. South Carolina segregated the races on trains in 1898, streetcars in 1905, at train depots and restaurants in 1906, in textile plants between 1915 and 1916, at circuses in 1917, in pool halls in 1924, and at beaches and recreation centers in 1934. The Georgia legislature segregated prisons and railroads in 1891, sleeping cars in 1899, and pool halls in 1925 but refused to segregate streetcars, parks, swimming pools, golf courses, and other places of public amusement between 1900 and 1954. It was only after the Supreme Court decision of 1954 (*Brown* v. *Topeka Board of Education*) that the legislature passed a whole bevy of segregation bills.

In the late nineteenth century, as Woodward has observed, a number of white southerners spoke out against Jim Crow customs and laws. The best example was a judge in Tennessee. In 1885 he asserted, "My observation has led me to conclude that those who are most horrified by the presence of the negro and find so much that is offensive in him have very often least to boast of in the way of birth, renown, or achievement. For the life of me, I cannot see what injury a neatly dressed well behaved colored person does me by riding in the same car."

With the exception of the few southerners such as George Washington Cable of Louisiana and Bishop Thomas Dudley of Kentucky, the southern aristocrat, even if he was interested in protecting the black, quickly capitulated to the racist farmers. Even the most paternalistic white aristocrat was a white supremacist. This was, for all practical purposes, true on a national scale. Northerners were often no better. For example, William Jennings Bryan, the Great Commoner and perennial presidential candidate, felt that white supremacy and the disfranchisement of the blacks were "absolutely essential to the welfare of the South." Under Woodward's schema, it seems fair to ask what the southern Progressives, a group of reformers acting from around 1900 to the First World War, ever did for blacks? If they were interested in helping the downtrodden and promoting democracy, it seems logical that they would have been concerned with the black. Yet they, the best example of Woodward's paternalistic whites, did practically nothing to halt the march of Jim Crow.

A primary element in the development of Jim Crow legislation was that segregation became national policy. Only one state, Tennessee, had segregated the races on the railroads before the Interstate Commerce Commission ruled in 1887 that separate but equal facilities were legal. As a direct result of this ruling, all but three southern states segregated the races on trains between 1887 and 1891. Those states which had no segregated travel arrangements received the green light from the Supreme Court in the *Plessy* case in 1896. The next important national approval of segregation was given by southern-born Woodrow Wilson. As president of Princeton University, Wilson had barred black students from the school. He took these ideas with him to the White House in 1913. Almost immediately a number of his cabinet officers, sometimes at the insistence of Mrs. Wilson, began segregating bathrooms and restaurants in federal offices. The Civil Service Commission began requiring that a photograph be submitted with every examination. Understandably, few blacks received federal appointments during Wilson's administration.

It must be remembered that segregation was not dependent solely on state legislation. First, many cities passed laws which were never even considered in the state legislatures. Between 1900 and 1920, Augusta, Savannah, Macon, and Atlanta, Georgia, required the segregation of blacks and whites on streetcars, in restaurants, in bars, and in barbershops. In the 1930s and 1940s they segregated taxis, parks, and movie houses. Between 1910 and 1924 several southern cities, including Baltimore, New Orleans, Richmond, and Atlanta, tried to enforce residential segregation. The laws generally forbade one race from moving to any street inhabited by more than 50 percent of the other race. Often when there was no state or local ordinance, segregation prevailed simply on the strength of local customs.

SCIENTIFIC "PROOF" OF BLACK INFERIORITY AFTER 1870

Throughout the nineteenth and twentieth centuries, scientists in England, the United States, and South Africa tried persistently to "prove" that blacks were intellectually inferior to whites. The English psychologist Francis Galton in his 1869 study, *Hereditary Genius,* contended that there was a large number of "half-witted men" among blacks who made "childish, stupid, and simpleton-like mistakes." Writing in the *South African Journal of Science* in 1929, Lawrence Fick declared that blacks demonstrated such "a marked inferiority" to Europeans that the number of Africans who could "benefit by education of the ordinary type beyond the rudimentary" was severely limited. While nineteenth-century scientists measured skulls to show that the brains of blacks weighed less than those of whites, during the twentieth century they turned their focus increasingly to genetics, because they had discovered that no one ever uses all of his brain. After the Frenchman Alfred Binet developed a test in 1905 which allegedly predicted success in school, Americans quickly adopted it as a measure of intelligence. Since the tests measured things native-born middle-class white children should know at given ages or after attending school, lower-class, undereducated blacks and the foreign-born predictably scored low on them. Almost immediately, the scientists contended that these groups were less intelligent. (Some politicians used the test scores to restrict the immigration of southern Europeans, Chinese, and Africans to America.) Racists pointed to the test results to establish the necessity for inferior segregated schools and limited employment opportunities for blacks. Lewis Terman of Stanford University, the creator of the most widely used test (Stanford-Binet—1916), asserted in 1926, "Indians, Mexicans, and Negroes . . . should be segregated in special classes [because] they cannot master abstractions. . . . they constitute a grave menace because of their unusually prolific breeding."

The most impressive "proof" of black inferiority was the results of tests given to men drafted in World War I. Analysts found in 1923 that black soldiers scored much lower than whites. Using this data and experiments (later discredited) with identical twins, they concluded that blacks were genetically inferior to whites in intelligence. More intensive studies later showed that northern blacks had scored higher than southern whites. Logically, this meant either that northern blacks were genetically superior to southern whites or had received a better education. Thrown into disarray by this dilemma (and horrified by Hitler's attempt to exterminate the "inferior" Jews), scientists between 1930 and 1950 placed less stress on black inferiority. During the 1950s Henry Garrett, Frank McGurk, and Audrey Shuey renewed the assault: Garrett claimed in 1961 that egalitarianism was "the scientific hoax of the century." The 1954 decision of the Supreme Court outlawing segregation in the public schools gave greater urgency to the campaign. The effort to enforce affirmative action in the 1970s made it essential to prove that blacks were naturally inferior and unqualified.

In the 1970s the old controversy attracted Arthur Jensen of the University of California at Berkeley and William Shockley of Stanford University. Using all the discredited studies of the past (even the World War I tests) and batteries of computers, Jensen, a psychologist, and Shockley, a Nobel prize-winning physicist, "proved" again that blacks were genetically inferior. Since popular magazines, newspapers, radio, and television disseminated the Shockley-Jensen thesis widely, many white Americans gave it some credence. If blacks were inferior genetically, any effort to enforce affirmative action had to be reverse discrimination against whites. Shockley became an especially effective proselytizer by arranging debates on television and at various colleges. When black and white students heckled or prevented him from speaking, Shockley became a *cause célèbre*. Although the genetics department at Stanford had contended that Shockley was not qualified to teach the subject, whites throughout the country listened avidly to him. As if contending that heredity determined intelligence were not enough, Shockley further argued that low-IQ persons, especially blacks, should be sterilized.

POPULATION CONTROL AND GOVERNMENTAL REPRESSION

Shockley's views about eugenics struck a responsive chord in federal agencies, foundations, and private groups interested in population control. After 1950 the major focus of many foundations was on limiting population growth in the Third World. Since the birth rate of blacks has consistently been higher than that of whites in America, advocates of abortion, sterilization, and family planning have concentrated an inordinate amount of their resources on Afro-Americans. Beginning in the 1960s, federal and local agencies supported such campaigns to eliminate black Americans. Birth control facilities were concentrated in counties, cities, and neighborhoods with heavy black populations. By the 1960s it was relatively easy for social planners to promote genocide as white Americans came increasingly to view blacks as "welfare loafers" and unproductive members of society. These stereotypes, added to a determination to limit the economic opportunities of blacks, led Sidney Wilhelm to write in *Who Needs the Negro?* (1971):

> The Negro is losing out because he is losing out in the technological development of American society; White America can, for the first time, easily bear the economic costs for implementing its racial values to the point of excluding the Negro race. More specifically, the developing

outcast position of the Negro is in keeping with the technological configuration of White America's economic interests. Just as the corporate industrialists supported the Negro's shift from slavery into serfdom as the minimum economic alteration to flow out of the Civil War, and segregation the maximum oppression to be tolerated from racist Americans following Reconstruction, so today, the economic values of White America allow for racism to shift once more to eliminate the Negro altogether.

Vehemently denying the charges of genocide, family planning advocates insisted they were simply trying to make the same services available to the poor as to wealthier classes. "Inevitably," the Population Reference Bureau admitted in 1971, "this has meant that official birth control centers have concentrated in poor communities, a disproportionate share of which are black." Kenneth Kammeyer, Norman Yetman, and McKee McClendon reported in a 1974 essay in *Social Problems* that the most important factor in the location of birth control centers was *race*, not poverty. Practices and policies in this area were considerably less than benign; coercion of black women on welfare had become widespread by the late 1960s. Occasionally white doctors sterilized black women without their knowledge or consent.

Although most historians have dismissed the claims of Afro-Americans that the United States had inaugurated a campaign of genocide against black people in the 1960s as unfounded "hysterical charges," the threat of genocide was real. It was roughly comparable to the threat faced by Jews in Germany in the 1930s. Hitler's sterilization program began with 56,000 operations per year and ended with the murder of more than 5 million Jews. By the 1970s, the Department of Health, Education, and Welfare was forcing 100,000 to 150,000 people to be sterilized annually. More than 90 percent of these people were black. In fiscal 1975 the federal government spent about $280 million on a birth control program for "low income persons." A North Carolina white, Eva Clayton, declared in 1973, "family planning, as it is now conceived, is directed mainly toward reducing population growth among the poor, and primarily the Black poor. The implication in this direction is genocide."

Another form of the federal government's efforts to repress blacks was its conspiracy against organizations and people challenging the status quo. Blacks have been primary targets. During the nineteenth century agents of the Army, the Postal Service, and the Justice Department kept most black organizations under close surveillance and threatened militant blacks with imprisonment for expressing "seditious" views. During the twentieth century the Federal Bureau of Investigation (FBI) led the federal government's efforts to limit black protest. For example, between 1961 and the 1970s the FBI systematically tried to prevent various groups from forming coalitions. In 1967 J. Edgar Hoover, head of the FBI, ordered his agents "to expose, disrupt, misdirect, discredit, or otherwise neutralize the activities of black nationalist, hate-type organizations and groupings, their leadership, spokesmen, membership, and supporters." Furthermore, Hoover wrote, the agents should "prevent the rise of a 'messiah' who could unify, and electrify, the militant black nationalist movement." By recording telephone conversations, planting false stories in newspapers, forging letters, planting spies to provoke physical confrontations, and smearing black leaders with charges of sexual improprieties and robbery, the FBI harassed black ministers, students, actors, and other outspoken Afro-Americans.

THE ROLE OF THE BLACK CREATIVE ARTIST IN ENCOURAGING PROTEST

Historians have generally ignored black reactions to white oppression in the nineteenth century. From most of their studies one gets the impression that blacks were passive agents in the process. Nothing could be further from the truth. Finding little in the way of mass-based, sustained protest on a national level, many historians concluded falsely that most blacks were accommodationists. Recorded protest in the nineteenth century was generally sporadic, localized, and short-lived, because repression was so systematic and blacks lacked that shared consciousness so necessary to group resistance. While systematic and violent oppression normally leads to individual acts of resistance, large numbers of individuals must learn that theirs is a shared oppression before they can act in unison.

The black artist played a significant role in creating the preconditions for large-scale protest movements among Afro-Americans. Creative artists reflected the thoughts, moods, and feelings of Afro-Americans and impelled them to action. They shaped and transformed the collective consciousness of blacks with their prophecies and presentiments of the future. At the same time, they helped whites to understand the black situation, elicited sympathy from them, and helped to discourage them from using violence against Afro-Americans. As among most groups, there was a long time lag between the artists' call for action and the beginning of effective protest movements.

Whatever their stated credos, many black creative artists have, in practice, subscribed to W. E. B. Du Bois' 1926 dictum: "all Art is propaganda and ever must be, despite the wailing of the purists. I stand in utter shamelessness and say that whatever art I have for writing has been used always for propaganda for gaining the right of black folk to love and enjoy. I do not care a damn for any art that is not used for propaganda." Implicitly or explicitly, many black poets have consistently protested the oppression of Afro-Americans. They enlisted in the antislavery crusade and spent much of the nineteenth century writing about heroes to be emulated by other blacks. Racial pride, solidarity, and uplift were the chief refrains in this poetry, equaled only by pleas for equality and justice. Heaping scorn on whites for their hypocrisy, the poets invoked the wrath of Jehovah, prayed for deliverance, and applauded the black's patience, hopes, dreams, Christian forgiveness, and loyalty.

BLACK PROTEST POEMS

A new note entered the poems in the 1880s. More of the poets applauded "manliness," courage, and heroic endurance, and urged blacks to break their fetters. Equating patience with cowardice, they complained bitterly of the "tyrant's heel." Characteristic of such sentiments was Albery Whitman's 1885 musings about the black:

> Ah! I abhor his protest and complaint!
> His pious looks and patience I despise!
> He can't evade the test, disguised as saint,
> The manly voice of freedom bids him rise,
> And shake himself before Philistine eyes!
> And, like a lion roused, no sooner than
> A foe dare come, play all his energies,
> And court the fray with fury if he can;
> For hell itself respects a fearless manly man!

Charles F. White's *Plea of the Negro Soldier* (1908), Edward S. Jones' *The Sylvan Cabin* (1911), Fenton Johnson's *Visions of the Dusk* (1915), George R. Margetson's *The Fledgling Bard* (1916), and other volumes elaborated on this theme.

There was only a short step from such views to advising violent resistance to oppression. After 1890 there was a persistent emphasis on the need to resort to violence in black poetry. The clearest early expression of this theme appeared in Frank B. Coffin's *Ajax's Ordeals* (1897): "There must be some blood shed by us,/ When Southern brutes begin to fuss,/ Some Brown and Turner've got to die, . . ." Richard E. S. Toomey joined Coffin in 1901 when he wrote that blacks should "not, as cowards, seek to fly; Our rights, maintain them, though we die." Stressing the black man's bitterness over injustice, Charles White contended in 1908 that when liberty awoke "there may be some rivers of red," because

> The heart of man oppressed and wronged
>   Yearns for vengeance, justice and right,
> And once it begins its angry course
>   It increases much fold in might.

Beginning in World War I, black poets issued more explicit calls for violence. In *The Harp of Ethiopia* (1914) Maurice N. Corbett invoked the spirit of Nat Turner and John Brown in "crushing out the tyrant's power" and calling for "martyrs to the cause" who would meet "death in gallant deeds." Most of the changes in man's lot had come through bloodshed:

> And blood the means will ever be,
> By which men gain their liberty.
> Not blood of some one in their stead
> But blood which they themselves have shed.

Maggie P. Johnson also urged blacks to "lose every drop of blood" fighting for freedom in *Thoughts for Idle Hours* (1915).

The black renaissance of the 1920s ushered in greater stress on resistance to oppression. The poets had greater pride in being black, viewed religion as less comforting, heaped more scorn on "white folk's niggers" and Booker T. Washington, and preached a fiercer hatred of whites than had their predecessors. Agitation, protest, and worship of the leaders of the Haitian revolution and Nat Turner were universal themes. Claude McKay set the tone in 1919 when he wrote:

> If we must die—let it not be like hogs
> Hunted and penned in an inglorious spot,
> While round us bark the mad and hungry dogs,
> Making their mock at our accursed lot,
> If we must die—oh, let us nobly die,
> So that our precious blood may not be shed
> In vain; then even the monsters we defy
> Shall be constrained to honor us though dead!
> Oh kinsmen! We must meet the common foe;
> Though far outnumbered, let us show us brave,
> And for their thousand blows deal one death blow!
> What though before us lies the open grave?
> Like men we'll face the murderous cowardly pack,
> Pressed to the wall, dying but fighting back!

The nineteenth-century poet's stress on patient endurance and humility receded into the background as the twentieth century progressed. The black poet muted his invocations to God for deliverance. His thirst for freedom became more acute; loud demands replaced supplications in the 1930s.

One of America's premier twentieth-century poets, Langston Hughes, typified the mood of the 1930s. Dedicated to using art to promote social change, Hughes presented his credo for the black writer in 1935: "There are certain practical things American Negro writers can do through their work. We can reveal to the Negro masses from which we come, our potential power to transform the now ugly face of the Southland. . . . Something has got to change in America—and change soon. We must help that change to come." The humility, patience, and contentment of blacks were anathema to Hughes. Writing of "Pride" in *Opportunity* magazine in 1930, he issued one of his many calls for action:

> *Let all who will*
> *Eat quietly the bread of shame.*
> *I cannot,*
> *Without complaining loud and long,*
> *Tasting its bitterness in my throat,*
> *And feeling to my very soul*
> *Its wrong.*
>
> *For honest work*
> *You proffer me poor pay.*
> *For honest dreams*
> *Your spit is in my face,*
> *And so my fist is clenched—*
> *Too weak I know—*
>
> *But longing to be strong*
> *To strike your face!*

Hughes was deeply committed to violent revolution. Many of the poems he published in the 1930s reflected this commitment. In "The Same," published in *The Negro Worker* in 1932, Hughes asserted that everywhere blacks were "exploited, beaten, robbed, shot and killed" and their blood turned into dollars by the exploiters:

> Better that my blood
> Runs into the deep channels of Revolution,
> Runs into the strong hands of Revolution,
> Stains all flags red, . . .

That same year, Hughes' "Good Morning, Revolution" appeared, in which he described revolution as "the very best friend I ever had." Hughes egged on the masses, who had been "bought and sold" by the white oppressor for "the last thousand years," in his 1934 poem "Revolution" and urged them to slit the exploiter's throat and "tear him limb from limb." Speaking often of "raising a black fist" as the best black response to the "iron heel" of oppression, ever-present police brutality, and piratical capitalistic exploitation, Hughes summed up many of his ideas in 1935 in "Air Raid Over Harlem":

> Bullets through Harlem
> And someday
> A sleeping giant waking
> To snatch bombs from the sky
> And push the sun up with a loud cry
> Off to hell with the cops on the corners at night
> Armed to the teeth under the light
> Lest Harlem see red.
> And suddenly sit on the edge of its bed
> And shake the whole world with a new dream
> As the squad cars come and the sirens scream
> And a big black giant snatches bombs from the sky
> And picks up a cop and lets him fly
> Into the dust of the Jimcrow past
> And laughs and hollers
> Kiss my
> ! x ! & !

From 1930 to 1960 black poets continued to write on the themes developed at the beginning of the black renaissance. They toned down the romanticism of the dialect poetry of Paul Laurence Dunbar and began to preach a religion of revolt. The meekness of Christ became the poet's metaphor for the black man's quiet acceptance of his oppression; the line "Christ is a Dixie Nigger" appeared frequently in poems written during this period. Frank Marshall Davis in *I am the American Negro* (1937) expressed this view when he advised blacks to

> Arm your Christ with a shotgun . . . hire six
> attorneys to work with Jehovah . . . teach your
> priests how to uppercut . . . if David had slung
> a prayer and a hymn Goliath would have chalked
> up another win.

> Sure, we all know there's one of you to nine of
> them so try to win sitting down . . . but if that
> won't work let 'em have it, buddy . . . you can't
> live forever anyhow!

Violent resistance was an underlying theme of a majority of the
volumes of poetry published by blacks between 1960 and 1975. The
poets called blacks to a "blood feast" where they would confront whites
and, in the words of Austin Black in *The Tornado in My Mouth* (1966),
"break their backs" and "kill the air they breathe." The poets penned
the obituary of the "white power structure," deified Malcolm X, glorified black hatred of white "worms," and sang paeans to revolutionaries.
Thomas (Ebon) Dooley's *Revolution* (1968) was typical of the new mood.
In "The Prophet's Warning, or Shoot to Kill," Dooley wrote that blacks
had seen whites "prospect for hate" in Afro-American communities:

> and we must Be that hate,
> coiled about their hearts,
> like a striking cobra!
> black poisons to fill their veins,
> bringing bullet holes
> and death
> and apple pie!

BLACK PROTEST PLAYS

The black playwright joined the poet in raising the consciousness,
uplifting, and encouraging the masses to protest. Since Broadway pro-
ducers refused to accept their plays, they read them in black churches,
produced them in black high schools and colleges, published them
in such journals as *Crisis, Opportunity, Saturday Evening Quill, Negro
Quarterly, Brownies Book, Ebony and Topaz,* and the *Negro History
Bulletin,* or organized their own theater groups.

From 1890 to 1950 the chief vehicle used by dramatists to encourage
protest was the historical play about Haitian revolutionaries, black rebels, and runaway slaves. They included William Easton's *Dessalines*
(1893) and *Christophe* (1911), Leslie P. Hill's *Toussaint L'Ouverture*
(1928), S. Randolph Edmonds' *Denmark Vesey* (1929) and *Nat Turner*
(1934), Georgia D. Johnson's *Frederick Douglass* (1935) and *William
and Ellen Craft* (1935), Langston Hughes' *Emperor of Haiti* (1936),
May Miller's *Christophe's Daughters* (1935), *Harriet Tubman* (1935),

and *Sojourner Truth* (1935), Owen Dodson's *Amistad* (1939), and Theodore Ward's *John Brown* (1950).

Black drama was a relatively underdeveloped area until the 1920s
and 1930s, when several black theater groups emerged in New York
and other cities. Reflecting the oppressive society in which they lived,
black dramatists portrayed blacks as noble, courageous, rebellious, and
proud. Slaves in these plays refuse to be flogged, Africans appear as
brave warriors, black is a standard of beauty, and men who die rather
than submit to oppression are idolized. Some of the best examples of
the earlier protest plays were the works of S. Randolph Edmonds. In
Bad Man (1934), Edmonds tells the story of a black saw mill worker
who, detesting cowards, refuses to run when threatened by a lynch
mob. Edmonds' *Nat Turner*, also published in 1934, portrays a leader
who uses religion to inspire blacks to rebel. The despicable characters
in both plays are Uncle Tom types who advise submission. Nat Turner
urges slaves to be fearless: "No real man ain' willing tuh be wurked
lak a mule in 'de field, whupped lak a dog, and tied tuh one farm
and master. . . . We mus' let dem know dat jes because our skins is
black we is not afraid tuh die." The most successful play produced
during the 1930s was Langston Hughes' *The Mulatto*. Since its publication in 1935 it has been translated into Italian, Spanish, French, Portuguese, and Japanese. A brilliant study of miscegenation and southern
racial practices, *The Mulatto* tells the story of a Negro who kills his
white father because the latter wants him to be submissive to whites.

Several important protest plays appeared in the 1940s. Theodore
Browne's *Natural Man* (1941), a drama based on the legendary giant
black man who raced a machine, shows the defiance of John Henry
in the face of white America. At one point, taunted by whites in his
jail cell, he speaks for all black men: John Henry says he feels "Like
a giant in a straight jacket! . . . Like a great king without a throne
to sit on! . . . You tallow-faced sissies might be sitting on the throne,
but that don't make you king cause you set there. Nossir! I built that
throne. Built roads so you could travel from place to place. And I
ain't asking you all to thank me for what I do. I ain't asking you to
be my friend. Ain't wishing to eat at the same table with you. . . .
All I ask is that you let me be." Theodore Ward wrote a revolutionary
black play which appeared on Broadway in 1947. *Big White Fog* was
about a black family in Chicago debating the ideas of Marcus Garvey.
While stressing racial pride and the plight of the black, the play ends
with a call for revolution. Ward also wrote another historical play,
Our Lan, in 1946. An accurate portrayal of black life during Reconstruction, *Our Lan* is the story of a group of former slaves, their religious
ideas, and their desire for education. They successfully raise a cotton

crop but are then denied title to their land. Rather than give up possession of their farms, all of the men are killed fighting Union troops sent to dislodge them.

Many plays during the 1950s mirrored that turbulent period. In 1951 a New Haven, Connecticut, native, William Branch, wrote a very controversial play, *A Medal for Willie*. The story of the reaction of a deep South city when a young black soldier is killed and receives a medal, the play gets at the heart of American hypocrisy. The eternal question it raises is, why should a black fight and die for America when he has no rights? Understandably, the day after Branch's play opened, he was inducted into the Army. While stationed in Germany, Branch wrote an even more explosive play, *In Splendid Error*. Examining the relationship between John Brown and Frederick Douglass, Branch tried to settle the question of whether violence or nonviolence is the road to freedom for blacks. In the end, he accepted both. Another play reflecting the times was written by Loften Mitchell in 1957. Entitled *A Land Beyond the River*, Mitchell's play is based on the true story of the blacks of Clarendon County, South Carolina, who filed one of the suits leading to the desegregation of schools. Again there is conflict between those who favor nonviolence and those who advocate violence.

After 1960 black drama began to emerge from its preoccupation with appeals to whites. Directed more clearly to black audiences, the plays became an important part of the socializing process. Black theater groups in Detroit, Philadelphia, New Orleans, Washington, D.C., San Francisco, New York, and Los Angeles produced the new plays. On stage the predominant images were cruel, murdering, castrating whites; armed confrontation between the colonized and the colonizer, the oppressed and the oppressor; revolutionary black armies; Black Muslims; slave revolts; brooding, violent black men; and armed defense against systematic police violence.

LeRoi Jones, arguing that "the Revolutionary Theatre should force change: it should be change," led the new movement. In such plays as *Dutchman* (1964), *The Slave* (1964), *Insurrection* (1968), and *The Slave Ship* (1969), he stressed the positive value of violence in the liberation struggle. Clay, speaking to a white woman in *Dutchman*, says at one point: "Just let me bleed you, you loud whore, and one poem vanished. A whole people neurotics, struggling to keep from being sane. And the only thing that would cure the neurosis would be your murder. Simple as that. I mean if I murdered you, then other white people would understand me. You understand? No. I guess not. If Bessie Smith had killed some white people she wouldn't needed that music. She could have talked very straight and plain about the world. Just straight two and two are four. Money. Power. Luxury. Like that. All of them. Crazy niggers turning their back on sanity. When all it needs is that simple act. Just murder. Would make us all sane." Ben Caldwell in *Family Portrait* (1967), Kingsley B. Bass in *We Righteous Bombers* (1968), N. R. Davidson in *El Hajj Malik* (1968), Herbert Stokes in *The Man Who Trusted the Devil Twice* (1969), Archie Shepp in *Junebug Graduates Tonight* (1971), and Ron Milner in *Who's Got His Own* (1971) joined Jones in calls for revolutionary violence.

Concentration camps, martial law, apartheid, and black guerrillas became commonplace in plays written by blacks after 1965. The white man was the embodiment of evil—cold, soulless, beastly, twisted, demonic, and vindictive. Integration was anathema. Although there were numerous portrayals of the strengths and weaknesses of the black family, invocations of racial pride, and realistic sketches of black culture, the predominant theme of these plays was violent struggle. Reflecting the influence of the black psychiatrist Frantz Fanon, the dramatists viewed violent retaliation for wrongs as redemptive. In Shepp's *Junebug Graduates Tonight* Sonja tells a white man: "I been so scared so long that now I'm a killer inside. If I had a rusty nail, I'd jam it in your eyes, your mouth, into your testicle. I'd like to kill you slow, Cowboy. The way you killed me." Almost always, it was the memory of the white man's systematic, violent crushing of black dreams that inspired the desire for and the act of vengeance. The children in Milner's *Who's Got His Own* hate their father for kowtowing to whites until their mother explains that he had witnessed the lynching of his own father when he was eight years old. At this point, the son responds: "Just one. At least one of 'em! If I could make just one of 'em know! Make 'em feel! . . . Hurt 'em. Rip their insides out!—Tear their guts!— Kill 'em! Kill 'em! Kill 'em!"

Dramatists continued to focus on the heroes of the past in their effort to encourage blacks to struggle against contemporary oppression. Nathan Barrett in *Engagement in San Dominque* (1964), Harry Dolan in *Nat Turner* (1966), and Charles Fuller in *Brother Marcus* (1967) were among those utilizing historical themes. Generally, however, dramatists in the 1960s concentrated on the future. The message was clear: if blacks in the audience did not try to break the chains of oppression, the future was bleak. The contours of that future were obvious in their present. Looking back from the future, the revolutionaries in Bass' *We Righteous Bombers* spoke of the 1960s as a period when whites "tried to turn all us Black children into white things in their schools," silenced the artists, "exterminated" the leaders, and then "in the following years walls of electrified barbed wire were put up around every Black community in America."

From the time William Wells Brown began reading his plays in antebellum churches in the 1850s until the 1970s, the black dramatists exhorted their people to work actively to free themselves from violent oppression. Whatever its form, they wanted action. Their objective was to raise the black's consciousness of his beauty, his strengths, his oppression, and his obligation to free himself. LeRoi Jones characterized the historic role of the black dramatist best when he wrote, "Our theatre will show victims so that their brothers in the audience will be better able to understand that they are the brothers of victims, and that they themselves are blood brothers. And what we show must cause the blood to rush, so that prerevolutionary temperaments will be bathed in this blood, and it will cause their deepest souls to move, and they will find themselves tensed and clenched, even ready to die, at what the soul has been taught."

THE BLACK PROTEST NOVEL

Primarily concerned with social criticism, the black novelist since the 1850s has condemned racism, called on black readers to resist oppression, and urged whites to "let my people go." While focusing on such universal themes as man's alienation from his society, conflict, love, oppression, and resistance, the novel constitutes one of the best measures of the black situation in America. The terrain covered by the black novelist is a white-controlled world devoid of justice and sanity where ordinary and heroic Afro-Americans face dehumanization. Outraged and embittered, the black characters assert their humanity and resist white cultural dominance. The black novel is an exposé of white oppression, violence, and economic and sexual exploitation. Although blacks wrote many kinds of fiction, their greatest artistic achievement was the protest novel.

The novelists urged blacks to take pride in their racial identity, folk customs, and the history of their past struggle against oppression. Charles W. Chesnutt in *The Conjure Woman* (1899), James Weldon Johnson in *The Autobiography of an Ex-Coloured Man* (1912), George W. Henderson in *Ollie Miss* (1935), and Zora Neale Hurston in *Jonah's Gourd Vine* (1934) and *Their Eyes Were Watching God* (1937) were among the early novelists who treated black folk religion, music, and customs sympathetically. After 1935 such fictional approaches to black folk culture were commonplace. Johnson and Chesnutt—in *The House Behind the Cedars* (1900)—also joined in the novelist's attempt to convince blacks to be loyal to their race by indicting the propensity of mulattoes to pass for white. Walter White in *Flight* (1926), Nella Larsen in *Quicksand* (1928) and *Passing* (1929), and Jessie Fauset in *Plum Bun*

(1929) and *Comedy American Style* (1933), emphasized the empty life and tragedy awaiting Afro-Americans who "passed."

History attracted a number of novelists interested in encouraging blacks to protest against discrimination. John H. Paynter in the *Fugitives of the Pearl* (1930) recounted the story of a group of slaves who tried to escape from Washington, D.C., while Arna Bontemps in *Black Thunder* (1936) described the unsuccessful 1800 slave revolt of Gabriel Prosser in Virginia. Three years later Bontemps treated Haitian revolutionaries in *Drums at Dusk* (1939). Marcus Garvey and calls for violent resistance to oppression appeared in Edmund Austin's *Black Challenge* (1958). In 1965 Alston Anderson traced the life of a freedom-loving, heroic black man through his bondage, escape, and service as a Union soldier during the Civil War in *All God's Children* (1965). Margaret Walker's *Jubilee* (1966) detailed the struggles of blacks during slavery and Reconstruction.

Between 1857 and 1970 blacks wrote more than 150 novels. A remarkable achievement for an oppressed people long denied the educational opportunities automatically available to whites, these works cover a wide range of topics, approaches, and attitudes. One of the underlying themes in them is violence; the white mob is omnipresent. Characteristically, flight (from the fugitive slave to the black revolutionary) is the only way to escape white oppression. Living in a world where whites resort to force to deny their freedom, the protagonists in black novels move inexorably to the advocacy of retaliatory violence.

While many novelists stressed the need for individual blacks to kill the whites oppressing them, Richard Wright and Chester Himes were most skillful in portraying the psychological dimensions of such acts. The earliest of these novels was George Lee's *River George* (1937), in which a black attempting to organize sharecroppers kills a white man. In 1938 Richard Wright's collection of short stories, *Uncle Tom's Children,* depicted southern blacks with a deep-seated hatred of whites, the killing of a white man by Big Boy and Bobo, the capture, burning, and mutilation of Bobo by a white mob, and the flight of Big Boy to the North. Wright published a fuller exploration of these themes in *Native Son* (1940).

One of the most influential novels of the twentieth century, *Native Son* depicts the devastating psychological impact of racial oppression and shows how blacks are outsiders and aliens in the land of their birth. Wright argues that individual acts of violence against whites flow inevitably from a racist, exploitive system and that such acts are psychologically liberating. Boris Max, the white lawyer for the protagonist, Bigger Thomas, sees his murder of a white as the symbol of the repressed rage and desire for revenge haunting every black. He informs the white jury judging Bigger, "Everytime he comes in contact with us he kills! It is a physiological and psychological reaction, embedded in his being. Every thought he thinks is potential murder. Excluded from, and unassimilated in our society, yet longing to gratify impulses akin to our own but denied the objects and channels evolved through long centuries of their socialized expression, every sunrise and sunset make him guilty of subversive actions. Every movement of his body is an unconscious protest. Every desire, every dream . . . is a plot or a conspiracy. Every hope is a plan for insurrection. Every glance of the eye is a threat. *His very existence is a crime against* the state!" Later, Max becomes prophetic: "Who knows when some slight shock, disturbing the delicate balance between the social order and thirsty aspiration, shall send the skyscrapers in our cities toppling?" After Wright, individual acts of violence against whites were common in such black novels as Chester Himes' *If He Hollers Let Him Go* (1945).

The first novel calling for organized protest was Sutton Griggs' *Imperium in Imperio* (1899), the story of a secret organization trying to form a separate black nation in Texas. W. E. B. Du Bois, in *The Quest of the Silver Fleece* (1911), portrayed the efforts of blacks to form a sharecroppers' union. The call for organized violence did not emerge as a persistent theme, however, until the 1940s. Carl Offord in *The White Face* (1943) tells the story of Chris Woods, a southern migrant in Harlem who joins a black nationalist organization dedicated to winning freedom by resorting to violence. At one point the leader of the organization tells Chris: "The black man's been brutalized. Every nigger you meet is a walking streak of vengeance. He's a walking killer. The white man made him that way and he's itching for a chance to get back at the white man."

The chief exponents of retaliatory violence in the 1950s were John O. Killens and William Gardner Smith. In Killens' *Youngblood* (1954) a group of Georgia blacks unite to fight a white mob and a black minister says, "look all around you at your brothers and sisters, thousands of them, and Great God Almighty, fighting mad, and we're going to make them pay one day soon, the ones that're responsible. There's going to be a reckoning one day right here in Georgia and we're going to help God hurry it up." While Killens shows angry blacks striking back at whites, Smith in *South Street* (1954) follows the Bowers brothers, whose father had been lynched, to Philadelphia. Michael organizes the Action Society to prevent police brutality. Convinced that force must be met by force, Michael tells the members of the society that whites "have told us, in their books, and in their schools, and in their newspapers, that the black man has made great and continual gains in a steady upward rise since the days of slavery; and they lie: for, all the years since Reconstruction, through depression, social revolution and two earthquaking wars, have been but a desperate striving, continually, and in pain, to reach again the human heights we occupied in the triumphal years immediately after the Civil War. So have we fought, and still we fight!"

Many novels stressing the need for violent resistance appeared in the 1960s. Killens spoke for many of the writers when he asked in 1965:

> How long America? How long, especially my friends of the liberal per-suasion, how long in the light of this violence against me, can you con-tinue to speak to me of non-violence? The chasm widens steadily. Soon it will no longer be possible for me to hear you.
>
> For your black brother is spoiling for a fight in affirmation of his manhood. This is the cold-blooded Gospel truth. The more violence perpetrated against him, with pious impunity, the more he becomes convinced that this thing cannot resolve itself non-violently, that only blood will wash away centuries of degradation. The burden is on White America to prove otherwise. But you had better get going in a hurry, for we are at the brink.

Guerrilla warfare, black revolutionary armies, systematic assassinations, bombings, and attacks on the police appeared in Julian Mayfield's *The Grand Parade* (1961), John O. Killens' *And Then We Heard the Thunder* (1962) and *'Sippi* (1967), Hari Rhodes' *A Chosen Few* (1965), Ronald L. Fair's *Many Thousands Gone* (1965), John A. Williams' *The Man Who Cried I Am* (1967) and *Sons of Darkness, Sons of Light* (1969), Sam Greenlee's *The Spook Who Sat By the Door* (1969), and James Baldwin's *Tell Me How Long the Train's Been Gone* (1968). One of the characters in Williams' *Sons of Darkness, Sons of Light* expressed the prevailing mood in these novels when he said he "wanted people to know that if they were willing to take black lives the way they had been, then they ought to know that they had to forfeit their own. Once everyone understood that, things would improve."

BLACK PROTEST MUSIC

Dramatists, poets, and novelists had their most important impact on such leaders in the black community as teachers and ministers. Their influence on the mass of black people was, consequently, often indirect. The less literate members of the black community heard similar calls for protest from black folk singers. In spirituals, work chants, prison songs, and the blues, freedom was a persistent theme from 1865 to the 1930s. A continuation of forms evolved during slavery, black folk songs were so subtle and contained so many hidden meanings that most of the early collectors missed the element of protest in them. Instead, they emphasized the self-pity, joy, hope, resignation, and sorrow most evident on the surface in the songs. Since the early singers could not speak openly, they often disguised their rebellious feelings to avoid the wrath of whites. Even so, under the biting irony of the songs is a call to action, a consciousness of injustice and oppression.

The folk song presents a panorama of the black world. Calls for endurance, defiance, and heroism in the face of white violence and exploitation were characteristic. Beneath the pathos, lamentation, and self-pity so frequently noted by collectors was bitterness, savage anger, ridicule of whites, complaints of wrongs that needed righting, and a pervasive desire for revenge. When the folklorist Alan Lomax asked a black singer the meaning of the blues, he replied: "The blues is mostly revenge." Naturally, white collectors rarely heard such songs because the singers noted:

> Got one mind for white folks to see,
> 'Nother for what I know is me;
> He don't know, he don't know my mind
> When he see me laughing
> Laughing just to keep from crying.

When they did not have to conceal their feelings from whites, black singers complained of being cheated out of their wages, of working long hours for little pay, and of systematic brutality. The desire for revenge against whites was pervasive:

> Well, you kicked and stomped and beat me,
> And you called that fun, and you called that fun.
> If I catch you in my home town,
> Gonna make you run, gonna make you run.

The most important protest symbol recurring in the folk song was the "bad man." Whatever his station in life, a black could identify with the exploits of Stagolee, Railroad Bill, or Eddie Jones, blacks so mean, so courageous that whites feared them. Defiant and boastful, the bad man defeated black and white alike:

> I got de blues, but too damn mean to cry.
> I was bohn in a mighty bad lan',
> For my name is Bad-lan' Stone;
> I want you all fer to understan'
> I'm a bad man wid my licker on.

Stagolee and Railroad Bill, the most popular of the folk heroes, are always laying whites on the floor with a forty-four or shooting all the buttons off the sheriff's coat.

Considerably more than harmless poetic boasting, the bad man songs indicated the widespread anger of blacks at the treatment meted out to them and the desire for retaliation. As they raised the consciousness of the masses about specific injustices, the folk singers generalized their anger, stressed their hope for a better future, and encouraged blacks to struggle actively against oppression:

> At night when the world, it seem most dark,
> I toss and moan the whole night long,
> 'Bout all the wrong,
> I can't do nothing but get mad.
>
> But when it come, the morning light,
> Then I just know the sun will pour
> On my back door,
> It come soon sweet day.

From the slave's spirituals and secular songs to blues, swing, bebop, rock and roll, soul, and jazz, black music has had a political content. Exploited themselves by whites, black professional musicians nurtured the undercurrent of protest in the black community from 1930 to the 1970s. The jazz musician replaced the blues singer as protest leader in the 1950s. Charles Mingus, Miles Davis, John Coltrane, Dizzy Gillespie, Archie Shepp, Charlie Parker, Thelonious Monk, Cecil Taylor, Sonnie Rollins, and others began in the 1950s and 1960s to encourage racial solidarity, pride, and a sense of kin with Africa, and to focus on the black man's historic struggle against oppression. Important elements of black folk culture appeared in such jazz albums as *Bronze Dance, The Sermon, Black Preacher*, and *Sermonette.* Jazz compositions with an African theme were a normal feature of the musical scene after 1954 (*Dakar, African Lady, Bantu, Dahomey Dance*, and *Uhuru*). Seeking to encourage organized protest, jazz musicians turned to black heroes and the stories of struggle against oppression in *Garvey's Ghost, Emancipation Blues, Freedom Dance, Afro-American Sketches*, and *Freedom Suite*. Liberation was the message and racial solidarity the way. Large numbers of jazz compositions with "Soul" in their titles appeared in the 1960s: *Soul Brother, Soul Station, Sack Full of Soul, Bowl of Soul*. From 1950 on, "Freedom Now" was a clear and persistent message in the jazz songs. Such titles as *Justice, Free, It's Time* (for liberation), *We Insist: The Freedom Now Suite*, and *Now's the Time* were typical.

United with other blacks under the heel of oppression, the musician expressed their desire for freedom, their anguish, defeats, and hopes. Paul Oliver's characterization of the blues is equally applicable to other black musical forms: "Blues is the wail of the forsaken, the cry for independence, the passion of the lusty, the anger of the frustrated and the laughter of the fatalist. It's the agony of indecision, the despair of the jobless, the anguish of the bereaved and the dry wit of the cynic." Since most forms of black music received little consideration from whites when they first emerged, the musicians could articulate an unadulterated call for freedom before segregated black audiences. More than any other creative artist, the black musician sang his song of protest to the black masses.

THE ROLE OF THE BLACK PRESS

While black artists worked persistently to raise the general consciousness of the masses, the major immediate catalyst for local and national protest was the black journalist. Since the first newspaper appeared in 1827, black journalists have led the drive for freedom and equality. They played a crucial role in the abolition movement and became the most essential leaders of the black community during Reconstruction. The only self-supporting black institution other than the church, the black press campaigned against lynching, disfranchisement, and American imperialism between 1880 and 1930. Complaining bitterly about the status quo, the press built and sustained black pride and self-esteem, played up interracial cooperation, stressed black history, recounted the deeds of black heroes, and gave legitimacy to black lifestyles. The press was, as the Swedish scholar Gunnar Myrdal asserted in *The American Dilemma*, "the greatest single power in the Negro race."

Although viewed by whites as the most radical black institution, the black press has traditionally spent most of its time preaching thrift, unity, social elevation, and education. This was especially true of journals located in the South. On a few occasions, however, the journals lived up to their "radical" label. During the 1870s and 1880s, for example, the Fort Scott, Kansas, *Colored Citizen*, the New York *Globe*, the Washington, D.C., *People's Advocate*, the Harrisburg, Pennsylvania, *State Journal*, the New Orleans *Weekly Pelican*, the Indianapolis *Freeman*, and the Washington, D.C., *Bee* called upon blacks to demand an eye for an eye and to answer white violence with violence. On November 24, 1883, the *People's Advocate* expressed sentiments characteristic of such journals:

We are shot down like dogs, let us shoot back. We are cheated out of our earnings, let us demand remuneration, and apply the torch when

"I'm durned sure gonna contact the NAACP if we get out a this, Bootsie. I *know* the white folks has engineered this whole thing!"

PROSCRIPTION

From Bootsie and Others *by Ollie Harrington. Copyright © 1958 The New Pittsburgh Courier Publishing Company. Reprinted by permission of the New Pittsburgh Courier Publishing Company.*

the demand is not acceded to, and the means of removing the subject of the contention. We can no longer afford to lie supinely upon our backs to be treaded upon by ruthless robbers.

If our homes are invaded, let the shotgun protect them. . . . ; if our rights are denied, let a navy six be their arbiter; if our property is destroyed, let the torch be applied until devastation, destruction, blood, tears, and misery and starvation serve to teach the whites that justice must be done.

One important aspect of black journalistic protest rarely noted by scholars was the cartoon. Subject to gross caricatures in cartoons, comic strips, and on post cards, blacks began in the 1880s to utilize comic illustrations of their own to protest their treatment in American society. Beginning with the Indianapolis *Freeman* in the nineteenth century, black newspapers and magazines employed artists who penned graphic exposés of American racism in the *Voice of the Negro*, the *Messenger Magazine*, the *Pittsburgh Courier*, *Ebony*, and other journals. One of the earliest artists, John Henry Adams, laid down the credo of the black cartoonist in 1906 when he wrote in the *Voice of the Negro*, "No people have felt the sting of the cartoon more than we. Almost in any direction can be seen great wide mouths, thick lips, flat noses, glaring white eyes, and to wind up the thing, there close beside the caricatured is the familiar chicken-coop and out beyond that is the rind of the 'dervastat'd watah million.' These cartoons have done no little toward increasing our persecutions and our enemies. The time has come when we must not only have artists to show up the best that is of us, but we must have real live cartoonists amongst us to make sentiment." The "real live cartoonists" of the twentieth century—Ollie Harrington, Brumsic Brandon, Charles R. Johnson, Morrie Turner, and John Henry Adams—produced biting social satire, crystallized the sentiments, and raised the consciousness of Afro-American readers.

INDIVIDUAL REACTION TO OPPRESSION AND DISCRIMINATION

Despite the efforts of journalists and creative artists, late nineteenth-century blacks encountered oppression at the hands of whites. Angry and despondent over the proscriptions they encountered, blacks developed several techniques to deal with racial discrimination. They held on tenaciously to any memory of cordial relations with whites, looked vainly for divine retribution, took up the martyr's mantle, dreamed of better days, became brutally realistic and self-reliant, and protested in every way they could against oppression. Assuming an attitude of moral superiority, they stressed the virtues of the race to prove their right to share all of the opportunities that other Americans had. They appealed to the conscience of white Americans and their sense of fair play. Proud of their race, they insisted that whites recognize the black's manhood. The burden of race rested heavily on the shoulders of most blacks. They described their travail in their autobiographies.

If they escaped the lyncher's rope or the torch, blacks still faced discrimination in almost every phase of their lives. They were generally barred from all except the most menial occupations, public schools, and places of public accommodation. Most of the autobiographers were humiliated at some point by being thrown out of white hotels and restaurants and off trains and streetcars. There was no respite from the galling humiliations. Thomas Fuller, the only black in the upper house of the North Carolina legislature in 1898, was forced to kiss the Bible last in the swearing-in ceremony and was refused a committee assignment. In spite of James Corrothers' ability, no white newspaper would hire him as a correspondent, and when he wrote an article on the black community in Chicago, a white reporter for the Chicago *Tribune* rewrote it, putting ludicrous dialect in the mouths of the blacks he interviewed.

The reaction of blacks to discrimination was more varied than before the Civil War. First of all, there was more hope in the black community after the war. Blacks were gratified at the public acceptance of and private support for black schools. They were buoyed up by southern pronouncements against lynchings. Booker T. Washington epitomized the hope and the belief in the future in the black community. In 1900, Washington declared: "there was never a time when I felt more hopeful than I do at present."

Paradoxically, there also appeared to be greater fear in the black community after the war. William Holtzclaw wrote that blacks in Mississippi were afraid to move around much, and he feared for his life and for the life of Booker T. Washington when he spoke in Utica. Miflin W. Gibbs' brother, fearing the Florida Ku Klux Klan, lived in his attic surrounded by his guns. During the North Carolina campaign to disfranchise blacks, Thomas Fuller discovered that the blacks "were in a state of dread and suspense."

If it is possible, the pain of discrimination was also greater after the war. Having cast off the incubus of slavery, blacks took a few joyful steps toward the promised land only to fall into the cesspool of American racial prejudice. The painful lamentations of the blacks over the oppression they faced appears everywhere in their autobiographies. M. L. Latta expressed this pain clearly when he wrote, "Oh! how strange it seemed to me to believe that a just God would make some races superior to others, and to stamp a seal of damnation upon a race eternally because their faces were black, and whatever they should undertake to do should fail! . . . My heart bled within me."

Frequently, strong black men were brought to the brink of despair. Booker T. Washington recalled that as a result of Ku Klux Klan outrages in his neighborhood in the 1870s, "it seemed to me . . . that there was no hope for our people in this country." The black's agony of spirit was revealed most often when he was refused accommodations. When whites were admitted to a northern hotel and M. L. Latta was turned away, he wrote that he "then went down the streets with tears

in my eyes, to think how I was treated just because my face was not
. . . white."

Many blacks felt better about the certainty of discrimination in
the South than the bewildering twists and turns in the color line in
the North. It was not that the South was a land of opportunity or
that race relations were better there than in the North. On the contrary, blacks preferred the South because below the Mason-Dixon line
they knew what to expect from whites. While in the North discrimination appeared in the most unexpected places and a black was never
sure of how to act, the very rigidity of southern customs relieved any
anxiety about the behavior expected in any situation. James D. Corrothers summarized this strange phenomenon perfectly in his 1916 autobiography:

> In the South one *knows* he is a Negro—if he is one—the moment he
> enters "Dixieland." Which is not to say that he is in *every* way worse
> treated than in the North, but rather that things are *different*—to a
> *Northern* Negro, shockingly different. In the North, he is often encour-
> aged to aspire to any height, though seldom permitted to attain it.
> The South makes him few promises beyond the boon of becoming ordi-
> narily useful, or of aspiring among his kind. The North promises what
> it *cannot* or *does* not fulfill; the South is not hypocritical, in this respect.
> In the North, an ambitious Negro bumps into the color line unexpect-
> edly, on the street cars, in hotels, theatres, parks, public buildings and
> schools, on trains, in pleasure resorts, or at the polls, and even in the
> Church of Christ. Yet he may go a week or a year, sometimes without
> meeting with any *unusually* humiliating experience. In the South he
> is given immediately and unmistakably to understand that he must get
> definitely on his side of the colour line, and *stay* there. In the North
> he understands that *legally* he may go where he pleases and run the
> risk of insult. In the South his status is plainly fixed by special legal
> enactments.

Surprisingly, in spite of all the discrimination they encountered,
blacks retained their loyalty to America and their feeling that it was
the best country in the world. While rejecting American practices in
race relations, the autobiographers were proud of American ideals.
At the same time, however, they insisted that the black was the most
patriotic American because he had no divided loyalties. America's
treatment of the black not only caused pain for individual autobiographers, it also caused them to fear for their country. Sam Aleckson
indicated this feeling clearly: "I for one, have no fear for the ultimate
fate of the Negro. My fears are for the American nation, for, I feel
as an American, and cannot feel otherwise."

The plans blacks suggested to improve their condition in America
were numerous and complex. It would be fruitless to characterize them

as "accommodationist" or "militant." Sometimes they were neither; often they included several complex and contradictory features, and many times one man represented all of the points on the compass from practical acceptance of discrimination to a thinly veiled call for violent resistance. Any attempt to categorize the blacks in simple dichotomies would be a serious distortion of their views.

A few blacks felt that the only solution to the American race problem was for blacks to emigrate to Africa, while another group placed their faith in the development of friendly cooperation between the races. Blacks and whites had to understand each other, to appreciate both the similarities and the differences in their character. Only in this way could harmony be promoted. Some of the autobiographers argued that the way to promote mutual respect and understanding and decrease hatred and fear was to organize integrated churches and schools. Segregated institutions, James Still contended in 1877, were an invitation to racial hatred, and if America did not integrate them, "our children may rise up in another generation to condemn us, claiming that they lived as they were trained, that revenge and hate were instilled in their tender minds, grown with their growth, and strengthened with their strength."

Exhibiting a remarkable faith in the American sense of fair play, many of the autobiographers argued that whites appreciated worth in any man, black or white. Afro-Americans had only to excel at their calling to be treated fairly by whites. Booker T. Washington was one of the most consistent exponents of this view. He contended in 1901: "My experience is that there is something in human nature which always makes an individual recognize and reward merit, no matter under what colour of skin merit is found. I have found, too, that it is the visible, the tangible, that goes a long ways in softening prejudices. . . . The individual who can do something that the world wants done will, in the end, make his way regardless of race."

Brutally realistic, the autobiographers did not think that blacks would rise automatically. Instead, realizing that the whites had all of the power and wealth, many of them appealed for a chance to work in the shadows, for patience. They could advance only as fast as the whites would permit them to do so. M. L. Latta expressed this view clearly in 1903:

> We are here among the predominant race. We must admit, in the first instance, that the Anglo-Saxon race owns everything in the Southern States. . . . We are but a few in number as a race. All I ask for as a member of the unfortunate race is the wasteland, and ask them to give me an opportunity to build up the waste places. I admit that the

Negro people, as a race, are ignorant; they want to go too speedily. . . .
We, as a race, are depending almost entirely upon the sympathetic
treatment of the predominant race that we live among.

While few of the autobiographers were as sycophantic as Latta,
many of them contended that blacks had to be patient. They argued
that blacks should cease agitating for their rights and seek instead to
promote industry, moral virtues, education, and thrift and obtain land,
wealth, and business skills. The black had to react sensibly to oppression, analyze his condition, and depend on the passage of time to correct the evil system under which he lived. The chief exponent of the
"go slow" policy was Booker T. Washington. Washington argued that
the black had to be modest in his claims. He asserted, "I believe it is
the duty of the Negro—as the greater part of the race is already doing—
to deport himself modestly in regard to political claims, depending
upon the slow but sure influences that proceed from the possession
of property, intelligence, and high character for the full recognition
of his political rights."

ORGANIZED PROTEST AGAINST SEGREGATION

Before and after Washington's rise to power, blacks rejected his advice
and protested against legal changes that maintained their subordination. They lambasted the Supreme Court for its 1883 decision declaring
the Civil Rights Act of 1875 unconstitutional. One black newspaper
felt that the decision proved that the American government "is a farce,
and a snare, and the sooner it is overthrown and an empire established
upon its ruins the better." Blacks immediately petitioned Congress
for a new civil rights bill to insure equality in public accommodations.
Failing in this, they began agitating for state civil rights laws in the
North. In the next few years California, Colorado, Connecticut, Illinois,
Indiana, Iowa, Kansas, Massachusetts, Michigan, Minnesota, Nebraska,
New Jersey, New York, Ohio, Pennsylvania, Rhode Island, Washington,
and Wisconsin passed or strengthened civil rights acts. The laws in
these fifteen states generally barred discrimination in places of public
amusement, travel, inns, and theaters. Nine states prohibited discrimination in advertising.

These laws were passed and enforced primarily because of black
political power. In Ohio, for example, where there were approximately
25,000 black voters, about 200 local equal rights leagues were organized
in 1883 after the Supreme Court decision. These blacks demanded
repeal of antimiscegenation laws, integration of schools, and a state
civil rights law. Since blacks held the balance of political power in

the state, the legislature enacted a state civil rights law in 1884. In most cases, however, the fines for violating the public accommodations laws were so low—generally not exceeding $100—that they were not effective documents. Courts generally levied token fines. While travel facilities were generally integrated, northern whites consistently refused to integrate recreational facilities, hotels, and restaurants. Even so, state civil rights acts were generally more effective than the federal law of 1875.

One of the most persistent campaigns of the blacks was against Jim Crow travel arrangements. They challenged state laws in the Supreme Court, and between 1887 and 1910 they brought six cases before the Interstate Commerce Commission. Both of these bodies were so hostile that blacks could obtain no redress. The black press damned the commission and the Court for accepting the legality of segregation. After a decision in 1907, the *Voice of the Negro* asserted that blacks were "appalled that a federal commission should give sanction to such a pernicious principle as is embodied in the Jim Crow car. They feel that it is inconsistent with the democratic professions of this country and subversive of our fundamental tenets. There is no justice in discriminating against people because of their race or color and no sense either." The Jim Crow car was so clearly unequal that blacks began to insist on equal treatment with the idea that it would be so expensive for the railroads to do this that they would be forced to drop segregated seating arrangements. The Hampton Negro Conference from 1904 to 1906 and the National Baptist Convention in 1908 urged blacks to sue the railroads on this point. Several black organizations spoke out against segregated travel arrangements.

At its Rochester convention in 1898 the Afro-American League called for a boycott of Jim Crow railroads by blacks. Later that year while meeting in Washington, D.C., the league resolved that the "separate car laws" were "so unjust, degrading and oppressive in their operations, that we deem it urgent to direct attention to them. . . . It is a principle of the common law that a man shall pay for what he wants and get what he pays for. . . . A contract valid in one state of the Republic should be valid in every state. With all citizens [other] than Afro-Americans, it is." In 1904 the Maryland Suffrage League began campaigning against the state's new Jim Crow law and supported a successful suit against it in regard to interstate travel in 1905. A year later, W. E. B. Du Bois and other black leaders asserted at the Niagara Conference, "we want discrimination in public accommodations to cease." Two hundred black members of the Georgia Equal Rights League met in 1905 and declared that they expected to be able "to travel in comfort and decency and to receive a just equivalent for our money, and yet we are the victims of the most unreasoning sort of caste legislation." The National Negro Conference took the same position in 1909 when it denounced "the ever-growing oppression" of blacks and the fact that they were "segregated by common carriers."

Many black leaders spoke out against segregated travel because they felt it was unchristian, inconvenient, tyrannical, and an attempt to fasten a badge of inferiority on blacks. Archibald Grimké told the members of Washington, D.C.'s American Negro Academy in 1905 that as citizens, blacks had a right to be admitted equally to all public places and that segregation "ought not to be permitted in a republic. It is inconsistent with citizenship. . . . It stands for a hostile public sentiment; it is part of a concerted plan which seeks to degrade us, to rob us of our rights, to deprive us of privileges enjoyed by other citizens, because of the color of our skin."

When Senator Joseph B. Foraker introduced an amendment to the Interstate Commerce Commission Act in 1906 providing that railroads "give equally good services to all persons paying the same compensation for interstate transportation of passengers," blacks throughout the country claimed that it represented national recognition of Jim Crow. The Rev. E. W. Moore of Philadelphia argued in 1909 that while every American citizen had a right to choose his associates in his own parlor, upon entering a public conveyance "he has no exclusive right to say that another citizen, tall or short, black or white, shall not be accorded the same civil treatment." Any other position was unchristian and "unreasonable." Jim Crow railroad laws represented a sad blot on America's republican banners, for "nowhere else on the globe, except in the United States are colored people subjected to insult and outrage on account of race. . . . we denounce it here as a disgrace to American civilization and American religion and as violative of the spirit and letter of the Constitution of the United States." Slightly different and more influential than other black leaders in his appeal was Booker T. Washington. In 1908, Washington tried unsuccessfully to get the Republican party to adopt, as part of its platform, a resolution approving President Theodore Roosevelt's efforts to "secure equal accommodations on railroads . . . for all citizens, whether white or black."

Blacks did more than talk. Their most effective protest was against segregation in streetcars. Most southern states or municipalities passed Jim Crow laws in this area between 1891 and 1909. At first, the most vocal opponents of these laws were the streetcar companies. Pointing to the added expense of such practices and fearful of losing their black customers, in some cases the companies were able to defeat such legislation. Eventually, however, they gave in to public pressure. When these laws were passed there was an immediate boycott by black passengers.

From 1892 to 1899, blacks in Atlanta, Augusta, and Savannah, Georgia, were so successful in their boycotts that the companies dropped the segregated seating arrangements. From 1901 to 1905 black boycotts were partially successful in Jacksonville and Pensacola, Florida, and in Montgomery and Mobile, Alabama. In addition to these cities, there were boycotts in Rome, Georgia; New Orleans and Shreveport, Louisiana; Little Rock, Arkansas; Columbia, South Carolina; Houston and San Antonio, Texas; Vicksburg and Natchez, Mississippi; Memphis, Nashville, Chattanooga, and Knoxville, Tennessee; Richmond, Danville, Lynchburg, Portsmouth, Norfolk, and Newport News, Virginia, between 1900 and 1907. Generally the boycotts were organized and led by black ministers and supported by black newspapers. Among the journals, the Savannah *Tribune* was characteristic. After the city council passed a segregation bill in 1906, the *Tribune* asserted, "Do not trample on our pride by being 'jim crowed.' Walk!" The whites were startled by the effectiveness of the boycotts in their early stages. So many blacks walked or created miniature transit companies of their own that many of the companies lost too many customers; they either ended Jim Crow practices or went out of business. In Richmond, Virginia, so many blacks walked for a whole year that the company went into bankruptcy. But splits among the black leaders, the harassment of officials of black transit companies, and fatigue ended most of the boycotts after several months, leaving Jim Crow still intact.

BARRIERS TO BLACK PROTEST ACTIVITIES

Facing unrelenting oppression, blacks searched continuously for effective ways to protest against the conditions under which they lived. Several things affected black protest: wars, emigration from the South, rates of urbanization, international developments, Supreme Court decisions, the political climate, the devotion of whites to violent repression, and the extent of black political power.

Before 1900 organized black protest was largely localized, with few effective national black organizations emerging after the Civil War. Pinning all of their hopes on political advancement, the only forum blacks had for voicing other concerns was the frequent national conventions they held between 1865 and the 1890s. These meetings were quickly dominated by black politicians and used largely as mechanisms for endorsing presidential candidates. During this period the most effective protest mechanisms were state and local organizations and the state annual conventions of blacks. The perennial concerns of these organizations were public accommodation laws, jobs, justice, and equal suffrage. Occasionally they raised money to challenge discriminatory local laws and launched boycotts of especially obnoxious merchants. In the absence of national protest organizations, many national black professional associations tried to halt the Afro-American's plunge to his nadir.

Hampered by an underdeveloped national black communications system, high rates of illiteracy, and poverty, blacks found it difficult to develop the unity and level of consciousness necessary to confront systematically the white forces arrayed against them. Fragmented into small rural communities, their leaders were manipulated and controlled by whites. The twentieth-century protest infrastructure was, however, created in the nineteenth century. It began in the 1860s when blacks founded the National Equal Rights League. By the 1870s the league had largely splintered into ineffective state organizations and political clubs. While blacks continued to meet periodically in national conventions after 1870, the 1890s witnessed the birth of a number of protest organizations. Between 1890 and 1900, the Afro-American League, the National Personal Liberty League, the National Colored Protective League, the Black Man's Burden Association, and numerous others vied for the allegiance of blacks.

As twentieth-century America became less isolationist, blacks would draw on the tradition of nineteenth-century protest organizations to launch a revolution in race relations. Among the preconditions for their successful revolt were the increase in black literacy, the establishment of such nationally read periodicals and newspapers as the Chicago *Defender*, the Pittsburgh *Courier, Crisis, Opportunity,* and *Ebony,* the steadily declining willingness of large numbers of whites to resort to violent oppression over long periods of time, and the migration of blacks to the North and to the cities. As a result of black migration the percentage of blacks living in the South declined from 90 percent in 1890 to 55 percent in 1960. Similarly, the percentage of urban dwellers in the black population rose from about 23 percent in 1900 to more than 70 percent in 1960. The cosmopolitan atmosphere of the city encouraged the growth of a black intelligentsia and provided a base for mass protest.

Another important factor affecting the character of twentieth-century black protest was the steady decline in the power of Booker T. Washington in the decade before his death in 1915. After 1900, Washington's black critics, led by Boston editor William Monroe Trotter and W. E. B. Du Bois, were numerous. In *The Souls of Black Folk* (1903) and several essays, Du Bois and his colleagues railed at Washington's gradualism. Writing in 1908, the editors of *Horizon,* Du Bois, L. M. Hershaw, and F. H. M. Murray, launched a typical attack on Booker T. Washington and his ideology. In contrast to Washington, Du Bois insisted that "to sin by silence when we should protest makes cowards of men. The human race has climbed on protest. Had no voice been raised against injustice, ignorance and lust, the inquisition yet would serve the law, and guillotines decide our least disputes. The few who dare must speak and speak again, to right the wrong of the many." Reading Washington's speeches and essays, Hershaw was outraged because it seemed that Washington was "always finding the advantage of disadvantage" and presenting a "noncensurable" case for southern whites to gain their support: "The White South knows Mr. Washington, it understands him, and it listens to him, not because he has a sincere purpose and upright character which compels public respect and confidence, but because he has given his assent to its policy of unequal schools, 'jim-crow' cars and disfranchising constitutions." Such attacks eroded Washington's strength in the black community.

Freed of the constricting tentacles of Washington's Tuskegee machine, with its control of black newspapers and Republican party patronage, black leaders were able to return to the unequivocal nineteenth-century stance of Frederick Douglass in the second decade of the twentieth century. According to Douglass, blacks needed the ballot box and the cartridge box to exert power, secure justice, and defend themselves against oppression. Douglass asserted that "if there is no struggle there is no progress—power concedes nothing without a demand." In his mind, it was no more logical to hope for progress without agitation than to hope for "crops without plowing." Consequently his advice to blacks was to agitate, agitate, agitate.

THE RISE OF THE NAACP

Douglass had a profound impact on early twentieth-century black leaders. His immediate heirs were William Monroe Trotter, editor of the Boston *Guardian,* and the indefatigable W. E. B. Du Bois. In 1905 Du Bois and Trotter founded the Niagara Movement in opposition to Booker T. Washington's emphasis on gradualism and his advice that blacks should eschew politics and protest. After a riot in Lincoln's hometown, Springfield, Illinois, in 1908, a number of white liberals decided in 1910 to form a national organization to fight for equal rights for blacks. Trotter, suspicious of white intentions, refused to join the newly formed National Association for the Advancement of Colored People (NAACP), because all of the officers except Du Bois were white. Booker T. Washington, on the other hand, fought against the NAACP because he thought it was too radical and cooperated instead with a more conservative organization, the Urban League, which was founded in 1911.

By the 1970s the NAACP had an entirely different image. It became fashionable to denounce it for seeking integration, being conservative, and directing its energies toward helping middle-class blacks. All of this was, of course, to some degree true. Placed in historical perspective, however, the objectives and accomplishments of the organization are impressive. Until the 1970s the NAACP was considered a "radical" organization. The primary objectives of the NAACP were, according to the founders, "to promote equality of rights and eradicate caste or race prejudice among the citizens of the United States . . . [and to assist blacks in] securing justice in the courts, education for their children, employment according to their ability, and complete equality before the law." By 1970, many blacks were questioning not the ends but the means of the NAACP. They accused the organization of seeking integration for the sake of integration. On the surface this may appear to be true, but the NAACP has always operated on the premise that as long as blacks are separated or treated differently from whites, they will be oppressed. In this regard, it is obvious that at least until the 1950s the NAACP articulated the demands of a majority of blacks.

During its first decades, the NAACP was dominated by whites. The surprising thing about this, however, is that such a large number of whites would join with blacks for organized protest against discrimination in 1910. Most of these whites were inheritors of the abolitionist tradition and generally were anti-imperialistic and sympathetic to all downtrodden groups. Whatever could be said against them, no one can doubt the sincerity of such whites as Oswald Garrison Villard, Mary White Ovington, and Moorfield Storey.

Storey, the famous lawyer and old Mugwump reformer who became the first president of the NAACP, was one of the more interesting of the white leaders. A graduate of the Harvard Law School and personal secretary for Charles Sumner during Reconstruction, Storey had accepted the abandonment of the Negro after 1876. The rise of Jim Crow and disfranchisement convinced him that this was a mistake, and during the 1890s he led the fight for civil equality for all minority groups and protested against American imperialism. He then began railing against historians for their biased treatment of the blacks during Reconstruction and social scientists who supported white supremacy. He also insisted that it was obvious that whites were not sure that the black was inferior. He asked some irrefutable questions: "If the Negro is so hopelessly inferior, why do the whites fear the effect of education? Why do they struggle against his progress upward?" He could only conclude, "The attempt to prevent him from rising, by violence or by adverse legislation, is a confession that the assumption of white superiority is unsafe." Storey gave more than rhetorical support to the concept of equality. From 1912 to 1919 he successfully fought against efforts to exclude blacks from the American Bar Association and in 1922 against the exclusion of blacks from dormitories at Harvard College.

Whatever the character of the white leaders, they were primarily responsible for directing the NAACP's actions toward the most conservative and stubborn pillar of the American caste system, law. One of the earliest of the slow and costly legal campaigns of the NAACP was against lynching. Beginning in 1916 the NAACP systematically collected statistics, circulated petitions, encouraged newspaper campaigns, supported conferences, and fought for a federal antilynching bill. In 1918 President Woodrow Wilson and the American Bar Association condemned lynching. This was also the year that Congressman Leonidas Dyer introduced a federal antilynching bill which was passed by the House in 1922 but defeated in the Senate by a southern filibuster. Again in 1937 and 1940 the lobbying of the NAACP was primarily responsible for House passage of antilynching laws. In each of these cases, however, the failure of President Franklin D. Roosevelt to take a positive stand in favor of the bills enabled southern Senators successfully to filibuster against them. Still the campaign was not wholly unsuccessful. As a result of the NAACP publicity and free radio broadcasts by NBC and CBS, there was a change in public opinion. In 1937 a Gallup poll showed that 70 percent of the people in the United States and 65 percent in the South favored a federal antilynching law.

The NAACP also joined with other black organizations in protesting against the portrayal of Afro-Americans in movies. Blacks were incensed when film maker D. W. Griffith and a sick North Carolina racist and sometime preacher, Thomas Dixon, began circulating the film *The Birth of a Nation* (1915). One of the most racist productions in the annals of American history, the film portrayed blacks as brutal savages who stalked the byways of the South raping angelic white women.

The NAACP immediately began efforts to have local censors cut the most objectionable parts of the movie. Dixon, however, largely nullified this effort by showing the film to President Wilson, who was enthusiastic about it. It was, Wilson asserted, "history written with lightning." The NAACP countered by instituting criminal proceedings against Griffith. Some northern white newspapers refused to advertise the film. In some cities, portions of the film were cut; blacks rioted in front of theaters or threw stink bombs into them; 6,000 people in Boston petitioned the Censorship Board to ban the film; Woodrow Wilson retracted his support; and the state of Illinois and the city of Wilmington, Delaware, banned the film. In spite of these actions, by the second half of 1915 the film could generally be seen throughout the United States. Defeated in their efforts to ban the film, black intellectuals called for a greater commitment to writing plays and movies more representative of black life. Lacking technical skills and money, however, the early black film makers made little headway. The NAACP kept up its campaign against Hollywood; by the 1950s many of the most unflattering stereotypes of blacks had begun to disappear from the movies.

PROTEST IN THE 1930s AND 1940s

In the 1930s blacks began to emphasize economic issues. They organized black cooperatives and boycotted stores and businesses which did not hire blacks. The most successful boycott occurred in Harlem in 1933. The intransigence of the white merchants, however, is indicated in the 1935 riot in Harlem, which resulted in the destruction and looting of several businesses. The Depression, plus the few benefits blacks received from Roosevelt's New Deal policies, diverted separatist demands, but blacks eagerly joined the mass demonstrations of the Communist party and especially rent strikes.

The thirties and forties also witnessed the emergence of the black pictorial magazines *Flash!* (1937–38), *Newspic* (1940–46), and *Eyes* (1946) to "give the Negro a new and better psychological outlook on life." While white journals refused to publish photographs of any blacks except criminals, black pictorial magazines presented alternative standards with photo essays on black beauty queens, soldiers, college students, athletes, judges, politicians, and scientists. They campaigned for better housing and public health facilities in the black community and against European imperialism in Africa, employment discrimination, disfranchisement, and segregation in the United States.

The Second World War led to increased militancy and readiness to protest against discrimination. This was symbolized by A. Philip Randolph in his threatened march on Washington in 1941. Arguing that "only power can effect the enforcement and adoption of a given policy," Randolph obtained a greater share of jobs and better treatment in the military for blacks. An all-black movement of 50,000 people, Randolph's march represented the beginning of mass protests and foreshadowed the tactics of the 1950s and 1960s. It is significant that during the war the NAACP became more of a mass-based organization. It grew from 40,000 members in 1940 to 450,000 in 1946. It was also during the war, in 1943, that the Congress of Racial Equality (CORE) was formed.

In their fight for equality, blacks also had to deal with the conservatism of whites. While blacks wanted complete equality and a revolution in race relations, a 1942 poll revealed that six out of ten whites felt that Afro-Americans were satisfied, that their status would not improve after the war, and that blacks were completely responsible for their own plight. Such diametrically opposed views set the stage for violent racial conflicts like the riot which occurred in Detroit in 1943. It left thirty-four blacks and whites dead and had to be quelled by the National Guard. In spite of the fact that riots occurred in 1946 in Tennessee, Alabama, and Pennsylvania, the foundation had been laid for the civil rights revolution.

THE CIVIL RIGHTS MOVEMENT IN THE 1950s AND 1960s

Beginning with CORE's first freedom ride in 1947, blacks became increasingly aggressive in their demands for integration after the Second World War. Joined by sympathetic young whites, drawing pride from the liberation of African peoples, and winning worldwide moral support from press coverage and the presence of the UN, blacks gained a number of victories. In 1956 the Rev. Martin Luther King, Jr., led a successful boycott against segregated buses in Montgomery, Alabama, and Tallahassee, Florida, blacks quickly followed suit. Four years later, a group of black students in North Carolina, adopting the tactics of Frederick Douglass, began the sit-in movement which led to the desegregation of facilities in 100 cities by 1962. The high points of the movement came with the march on Washington in August, 1963, and the passage of the Public Accommodations Law in 1965. The ideological position of most blacks during this period was the nonviolent resistance of Reverend King and his Southern Christian Leadership Conference (SCLC). Whites were prominent in the movement and joined with dedicated blacks to lay their bodies on the line to organize southern black communities and to fight against segregation.

When blacks began to take stock in the second half of the sixties, they discovered several things. First, Ghandian passive resistance was of limited usefulness in a society where the oppressed were not in a majority. Second, King's philosophy was based on the false premise that there was a large residue of Christian love in white America to which blacks could appeal. The deep-seated prejudice did not seem to decrease among whites, and the pace of integration was agonizingly slow. White resistance seemed to harden as the decade wore on. The trail of billy clubs, hoses, beatings, bombings, and murders was long. Citizen's councils in the South prevented the employment of blacks pushing for integration. A white mob attacked Autherine Lucy when she tried to register at the University of Alabama in 1956. In 1957 and 1962 federal forces had to be used to break up mobs in Little Rock, Arkansas, and at the University of Mississippi. Between 1946 and 1964 there were twenty white riots against blacks attempting to exercise their rights, twelve bombings, including five churches, and countless numbers of beatings and murders both North and South. At the same time, northern riots against integrated housing, growing de facto segregation, and the slow pace of southern school integration convinced many blacks of the intransigence of white racism and the folly of integration. Finally, in 1966 Medgar Evers, executive secretary of the state NAACP, was killed in Mississippi.

The Black Muslims played a key role in the expansion of the new mood among black Americans. In the face of all of the beatings and bombings, Malcolm X's voice seemed to be one of reason, while that of King, James Farmer of CORE, and Whitney Young of the Urban League appeared to be utopian. Youthful blacks were especially attracted by the proud defiance, sharp mind, and vision of manhood that Malcolm projected. The dedicated blacks in the Student Non-Violent Coordinating Committee (SNCC), which had been founded in 1960, fell under the spell of Malcolm as they contemplated their successes and failures. Beginning with the Mississippi Summer Project in 1963, SNCC started to emphasize political tactics. The Mississippi Freedom Democratic Party (MFDP), an integrated organization led by Aaron Henry, led to great disillusionment for young blacks. At its National Convention in 1964, the Democratic party turned back the voting challenge of the MFDP, refused to recognize it, and instead gave it two token seats. This act, more than anything else, convinced the young blacks that whites did not understand racism and were unwilling to deal with discrimination when it really mattered. After 1964, SNCC began to discourage the participation of whites and in 1965 Stokely Carmichael, head of SNCC, began an all-black political organization, the Black Panther party. Founded in Lowndes County, Alabama, where no blacks were registered to vote in spite of the fact that they represented four-fifths of the population, the party lost its election because of physical intimidation.

Guaranteed black political participation and equal access to public accommodations were accomplishments of the nonviolent civil rights movement. But unequal employment, housing, and educational opportunity remained beyond legal and political solutions. Poor blacks began to feel that the civil rights movement had benefited only middle-class blacks. In the late 1960s they began to look to nationalist organizations for leadership and to turn ever increasingly to violence.

THE DECLINE OF THE NONVIOLENT PROTEST MOVEMENT

The black masses engaged in riots and rebellions in major American cities, most often set off by instances of police brutality. In Los Angeles, Detroit, New York, and smaller cities throughout the country, rebellions became a significant form of protest. The assassination of Martin Luther King, Jr., in April, 1968, set off a series of rebellions over a three-day period in Baltimore, Washington, and other cities with large concentrations of blacks.

The black protest movement of the late 1960s took a violent separatist turn for many reasons. Nonviolent protest, blacks saw, was no more effective in solving basic social and economic problems than legal and political solutions had been. The federal and state governments determined that the violent protests were a threat to the national peace and took strong steps to suppress it; by 1971 the movement was bereft of leadership.

When the violent black protest movement was virtually destroyed, the NAACP, the Urban League, and democratic socialists like Bayard Rustin were still around to pick up the pieces. Remembering Malcolm X's admonition to think internationally, the new intellectual leadership of the revolutionary black movement turned its attention to Africa and the Caribbean, in the hope that real independence for black people elsewhere could be a means of exercising leverage against the U.S. government on behalf of blacks. Working with African leaders for the success of guerrilla movements to liberate Mozambique, Angola, South Africa, and Zimbabwe and to undermine neocolonialism in independent African countries became their goals.

By 1980, black protest organizations seemed largely ineffective and fragmented. Many of the militants of the 1960s had become the managers of capitalistic enterprises or politicians. There were no charismatic leaders like Martin Luther King, Jr., or Malcolm X to galvanize the masses, no rallying cries like "Freedom Now" or "Black Power." It was a period of quiescence reminiscent of earlier ones in the ebb and flow of black protest.

Most black Americans have always been more American than white Americans. They have protested against discrimination and segregation in the name of the Constitution and the Declaration of Independence. They have always demanded equal treatment with other citizens, coming slowly to understand that the actions of those who control the levers of power are more important than the words in documents and laws. Those who have power have not been concerned with moving to give blacks an equal share of power and economic benefits. They have made concessions only when they seemed necessary to maintain enough order to perpetuate the existing social and economic system.

When blacks were nearer to slavery and whites regarded Booker T. Washington's accommodationist philosophy as most appropriate, it seemed radical to whites and blacks for organizations like the NAACP to call for political and civil equality. After it became clear that paper civil and political equality did not address the basic socioeconomic conditions of life for the black masses, merely continuing to lobby for legislation and to litigate seemed conservative to blacks and safe to whites. When sit-ins, picketing, boycotts, and nonviolent direct action emerged nationwide, they seemed radical until they, too, produced no basic improvements in the lives of the black masses. Black power, violent action, militant stances, and black revolution seemed to be more appropriate radical tactics to blacks, while nonviolent direct action now seemed to whites very nonthreatening in comparison. When the black militant leaders were killed, arrested, or co-opted and their movements effectively suppressed, blacks of the 1970s, in order not to lose hope, turned full circle and, led by upper-class blacks, began lobbying for legislation and supporting court suits all over again. Black unemployment remained at an all-time high and military service seemed the only way out for many young blacks. Afro-Americans appeared to be poised for a new era of protest of uncertain duration, ideologies, and strategies.

11

Black Nationalism

Trying to be black and an American is such a complicated task, it's remarkable that so many of us have kept at it as long as we have.

Brown American Magazine, 1941

BLACK NATIONALISM DEFINED

Black nationalism is the belief that black people share a common culture and world view, have a common destiny, and have had a common experience: slavery, oppression, colonialism, and exploitation. Racial solidarity is perhaps the most basic form of black nationalism. Presuming no movement, program, or ideology, it is simply a feeling that black people, because of their common descent, color, and condition, should act in unison. A higher and different level of consciousness is cultural nationalism, the view that all black people share a common lifestyle, aesthetic, and world view, often expressed in a distinctively black idiom in literature, art, or music. Religious nationalism, a specific component of cultural nationalism, is the belief in a special black religious cosmology, including the idea that the deity is black. The highest expression and form of black nationalism is Pan-Africanism. In its broadest sense, Pan-Africanism is the belief that African peoples share a community of interests. Whether they are in Jamaica, Barbados, the United States, Uganda, Nigeria, Sweden, or Spain, blacks must unite in a common struggle for liberation. In a narrower sense, Pan-Africanism refers to the unity of African nations on the continent for mutual progress.

Whatever their ideology, nationalists seek to control their own destiny, to resist the destructive effects of white racial chauvinism, and to break the constricting tentacles of Anglo-American cultural hegemony. They stress group survival and positive self-concepts. Nationalists have a clearly defined consciousness that blacks differ from all other Americans. Community mindedness, feelings of spiritual affinity, a sense of a common destiny and responsibility, and a stress on brotherhood and mutual devotion have generally marked black nationalist thought.

NAMING THE RACE AS A MEANS OF DEVELOPING GROUP IDENTITY

Finding labels to distinguish "us" from "them" has always been crucial in developing a sense of group identity. For Africans brought to America and eventually stripped of the names identifying them with specific nations and ethnic groups (e.g., Ibo, Mendi, Yoruba) and renamed by their enslavers, it was even more important. Although historians have generally treated the debate over ethnic designations as inconsequential, Afro-Americans viewed the generic name applied to them as intimately related to their self-esteem and their place in American society. From the 1830s on, the descendants of Africans argued that the racial name was a symbol of unity, of shared suffering, a rallying point for developing pride, an indication of their separate identity. A black man contended in 1831 that Afro-Americans "should have a distinct appellation—we being the only people in America who feel all the accumulated injury which pride and prejudice can suggest." In 1837 the editors of the *Colored American* insisted on a special designation for the descendants of Africans, because "our circumstances require special action. We have in view objects peculiar to ourselves and in contradistinction from the mass. How, then, shall we be known and our interests presented but by some distinct specific name. . . . ?" Writing in 1906, journalist T. Thomas Fortune claimed, "It is of the highest importance that we get ourselves straightened out on this question of 'Who are We?' . . . Until we get this racial designation properly fixed in the language and literature of the country we shall be kicked and cuffed and sneered at. . . ."

USING THE NAME "AFRICAN"

The designation "African" or its variants ("Afro-American," "African-American," "Africo-American") has the longest history in the United States. In their earliest known letters, poems, pamphlets, and autobiographies, blacks consistently referred to themselves as "Africans" and added the prefix before the names of practically all their early schools, churches, lodges, and social organizations. Seeking to explain this in 1844, Reuben Simpson wrote in the *Liberator* that blacks retained "Africa" in the names of their organizations in an effort to "manifest that respect due to our fathers who begat us." Between 1827 and 1899,

CHANGE

From Black Humor *by Charles R. Johnson. Copyright © 1970 Johnson Publishing Co. Reprinted by permission of Johnson Publishing Co.*

"African" or one of its derivatives appeared in the titles of 36 percent of the newspapers and magazines published by and for blacks. The term dropped from first to third place among editors in the twentieth century; between 1900 and 1950, about 28 percent had "African" or "Afro-American" in their titles. Advocates for the term spoke out throughout the second half of the nineteenth and early years of the twentieth century. In 1896 J. C. Embry called for the universal adoption of "Afro-American"—"for the reason that it is euphonious, beautiful, true. . . . [The] descendants of our African forefathers should neither adopt nor recognize the intended stigma which European and American slaveholders invented for us . . . and if any man ask you why so, tell him she (Africa) is the land of our origin; and since she is, by the facts of history and ideology, mother of the oldest civilization, the oldest science, the oldest art, she is by eminent fitness placed first in the compound title, 'Afro-American.' " T. Thomas Fortune expressed similar views in 1906.

Most critics of "African" and its derivatives stressed their birth in the United States. Obviously, some of them, as W. E. B. Du Bois observed, "feared any coupling with Africa" because of the stereotypes about it current during the nineteenth and much of the twentieth century. An 1831 correspondent of the *Liberator* asserted that the term was "objectionable" and "no more correct than 'Englishman' would be to a native-born citizen of the United States." Many blacks continued to stress their American over their African identity during the twentieth century. Contending that the prefix "Afro" did "nothing but qualify us as a particular kind of citizen," the Pittsburgh *Courier* on May 10, 1924, insisted that the "Negro is as much American as he can be under any kind of circumstance. The 'Afro' is not to his credit, nor does it enlarge his citizenship."

USING THE NAME "COLORED"

Beginning in the 1830s persons of African descent started referring to themselves as "colored" and "colored Americans." Between 1827 and 1899 about 34 percent of all black magazines and newspapers containing a racial designation in their titles used the term "colored," and an overwhelming majority of all state and national conventions of people of African descent held in the nineteenth century used the same title. Between 1900 and 1950 about 32 percent of the black journals containing a racial term in their titles included the word "colored." Almost as soon as "colored" came into widespread usage, objections began. An Afro-American declared in the September 24, 1831 edition of the *Liberator,* "The term 'colored' is not a good one. Whenever used, it recalls to mind the offensive distinctions of color." T. Thomas Fortune contended in 1906 that the word was a vague misnomer and had "neither geographical nor political significance, as applied to a race. It may mean anything and it may mean nothing. . . . it is a cowardly subterfuge—an attempt of the person appropriating it, or to whom it is applied, to convey the impression that he has no race that he cares to acknowledge." In 1919 journalist W. A. Domingo used essentially the same arguments and concluded that the term "connotes shame and implies an insult." The term conjured up the vision of whites forcibly mixing with and leaving a progeny among blacks.

USING THE NAME "NEGRO"

When the Portuguese first met Africans they called them "os negros" for "blacks." By the middle of the fifteenth century "negros" had become synonymous with the Portuguese word for "slave," "escravos." Although "negro" appeared in the English language in the sixteenth century, American whites did not begin using the word extensively until the second half of the seventeenth century to replace such terms as "moor," "Ethiopian," and "blackamoor." Occasionally blacks used the appellation to describe themselves in the eighteenth century. But "Negro" vied for primacy with "colored" and "Afro-American" in the first three quarters of the nineteenth century. In black journals published between 1827 and 1899 only 17 percent included "Negro" in their titles. Even so, advocates for "Negro" appeared before the Civil War. In 1843 a black man wrote to the *Liberator* that the "term 'negro' is an honest, expressive and well-meaning one, and distinctive to the black race. . . . let there be no unmanly shrinking from the significant, straight forward, dyed-in-the-wool appellation which distinguishes it." As more blacks accepted "Negro" after the Civil War, they began to attack whites for spelling it with a small "n." Contending that whites spelled all other proper nouns and names of races with capital letters, they charged that whites used the small "n" to symbolize the inferiority of blacks. Almost every convention of black newspaper editors between 1870 and 1930 passed a resolution calling for spelling "Negro" with a capital "N," and Booker T. Washington, W. E. B. Du Bois, black poets, and scholars supported their campaign. The three most important victories for the advocates of the capital "N" came in 1913 when the Associated Press adopted it as the rule, on March 7, 1930, when the New York *Times* accepted it, and in 1933 when the Government Printing Office began capitalizing the word. Although there were some holdouts in the southern white press, most publishers had begun capitalizing "Negro" by 1950. The success of the capital "N" campaign contributed to the rapid adoption of "Negro"; between 1900 and 1950 the designation achieved first rank in the preference of Americans of African descent. During this period 36 percent of the black-owned journals included the word in their titles.

The first in a long and continuous line of protests against the word "Negro" came from the pen of David Walker in 1829. Walker objected to it because "white Americans have applied this term to Africans by way of reproach for our color, to aggravate and heighten our miseries, because they have their feet on our throats." When someone asked the former South Carolina slave Harry McMillan how blacks referred to themselves in 1863, he answered: "We call each other colored people, black people, but not negro because we used that word during secesh [antebellum] times." The Rev. J. C. Embry of Philadelphia called for the abolition of the use of "Negro" because it indicated color only, was too narrow to include both Africans and their descendants in America, and unlike the designations of the other "great races of men" had no geographical locus: "This title 'Negro' is . . . a device of our enemies, designed to make us contemptible in the eyes of the world." Throughout the nineteenth and twentieth centuries, blacks objected to the word because whites corrupted "Negro" into such derisive and contemptible terms as "nigger," "nigra," or "Negress" (a black woman). Stores often advertised "Nigger goods," and "nigger" appeared so frequently in textbooks that between 1911 and 1938 the *Negro Yearbook* annually included a list of protests by blacks against such practices.

After 1920 there was a steady increase in opposition to "Negro." A group of blacks in Philadelphia even organized a club in the 1930s "to outlaw 'Negro' as a device for humiliating the race." There were few changes in the arguments over the decades. "Negro" was debasing, opprobrious, inexact, and classified the black as an alien. Richard B. Moore's eighty-two-page pamphlet, *The Name "Negro": Its Origin and Evil Use* (1960), was one of the most significant attacks on the term. Moore summed up all of the objections to the word and contended that the inferior status of blacks was due primarily to the label applied to them: " 'Negro' is not the right name, because of its slave origin, its consequent degradation, and its still prevalent connection in the minds of people generally with prejudice, vileness, inferiority, and hostility, and further, because this name woefully fails to set forth the true, vital, and honorable connection of our people with ancestral or present land, history, and culture." Accepting Moore's call to "abolish the evil use of the oppressors' vicious smear name," in the 1960s the Nation of Islam (and especially Malcolm X) led the assault on the term and fastened it almost irrevocably to the idea of a name given by masters to their slaves, to docility, and to Uncle Tom. The poets quickly followed suit. In the introduction to his collection of poems *We Walk the Way of the New World* (1970), Don L. Lee wrote: "we used to be blackmen/women (or Africans); now we're known as *negroes*. That movement toward becoming an adjective was not accidental; but carefully planned and immaculately executed to completely rape a people of their culture. . . . most of us have become another man's fantasy, a nonentity, a filthy invention."

USING THE NAMES "BLACK" AND "AFRO-AMERICAN"

At first glance, the most elusive word in the racial lexicon is "black." In the eighteenth century it was second only to "African" as the preferred racial designation. Used interchangeably with other designations in the first decades of the nineteenth century, "black" had fallen into disfavor as a racial designation by 1900. Between 1827 and 1899 only 6 percent of the journals published by persons of African descent contained the word in their titles. In the first half of the twentieth century, editors used the word even less; between 1900 and 1950 only 3 percent of the journals included "black" in their titles. During this same period, however, poets used the term almost as often as any other. Charles R. Dinkins wrote in *Lyrics of Love* (1904):

> We must share the rights of others,
> Dwelling here as kin with kin;
> We are black, but we are brothers;
> We are black, but we are men.

And in 1934 Claude T. Eastmond wrote a long poem about a "Black God" in which he asserted that because the white man's "white" God taught murder and hatred,

> I shall seek my own God—a black God,
> Who can sympathize with black folks.

Theoretical discussions of the use of the word "black" were rare until the twentieth century. In 1926 George S. Grant insisted that it was the most logical term: "The argument for it begins with the fundamental assertion that we are not Negroes (niggers) or colored people (cullud fellahs) but . . . BLACK AMERICANS; . . . By voluntarily choosing the logical mark which distinguishes our group from the group of White Americans, we endow both it and ourselves with a dignity, which . . . will operate to dispel the fallacious ideas of white purity, white beauty, and white superiority." The Chicago *Whip* supported Grant's views in an editorial in 1931: "It is accepted the world over that we Americans of African lineage are members of the black race. It seems that we ought to learn to love our race. . . . We ought to be proud of the term 'black.' We are members of the black race and all other names mean little descriptively, historically or genetically." People who supported emigration to Africa, even when they used other terms, almost always had a preference for "black" as a racial appellation throughout the nineteenth and twentieth centuries.

Most opponents of the term "black" argued that it was an inaccurate description of a race kaleidoscopic in color. More than anything else, however, this attitude reflected the impact of white prejudice and propaganda on the psyche of the descendants of Africans. In white America they faced, as W. E. B. Du Bois wrote in *The Souls of Black Folk* (1903), "the all-pervading desire to inculcate disdain for everything black, from Toussaint to the devil." The descendants of Africans shrank from being called "black," Henry M. Turner declared in 1896, because "hundreds, if not thousands, of the terms employed by the white race in the English language are . . . degrading to the black man. Everything that is satanic, corrupt, base and infamous is denominated *black*, and all that constitutes virtue, purity, innocence, religion and that which is divine and heavenly, is represented as *white*." By the early years of the twentieth century many blacks unconsciously glorified whiteness. According to Du Bois, they did so "because the world had

**Jackson, when you find the time,
I'd like to see you in my office.**

NOMENCLATURE

From Black Humor *by Charles R. Johnson. Copyright* © *1970 Johnson Publishing Co. Reprinted by permission of Johnson Publishing Co.*

taught them to be ashamed of their color. Because for 500 years men had hated and despised and abused black folk. . . . The whites . . . have exhausted every ingenuity of trick, of ridicule and caricature on black folk. . . . We are instinctively and almost unconsciously ashamed of the caricatures done of our darker shades. Black *is* caricature in our half conscious thought." George Grant characterized the aversion to the use of "black" perfectly when he said it was based on "the false notion of white purity and black impurity."

By the mid-1960s racial nomenclature had returned to its status in the eighteenth century: "black" and "Afro-American" became the most popular terms. Poems and autobiographical works clearly reflected this trend. Between 1960 and 1973 "black" appeared in 82 percent of the autobiographical works containing a racial designation in their titles. At no other period did volumes of poetry use the word as many times as they did in the 1960s. James A. Emanuel's 1968 poem "Negritude," with each of its twenty-four lines beginning with the word "black," was characteristic of the new mood:

> Black is the first nail I ever stepped on;
> Black the hand that dried my tears.
> Black is the first old man I ever noticed;
> Black the burden of his years . . .
>
> Black is the sorrow-misted story;
> Black the brotherhood of pain . . .
> Black is Gabriel Prosser's knuckles;
> Black Sojourner's naked breast . . .
>
> Black is a burden bravely chanted:
> Black cross of sweat for a nation's rise.
> Black is a boy who knows his heroes;
> Black the way a hero dies.

GROUP SOLIDARITY IN SEPARATISM

Throughout history black nationalists have received a very bad press in the United States. Nowhere is this revealed more clearly than in the scholarly attitude toward emigration and separatism as manifestations of black nationalism. Ignoring the persistence of separatist movements and ideas, white scholars have argued that these are extreme solutions suggested only during times of increased frustration and racial discrimination, that they are pathological responses, escapist fantasies, and unrealistic dreams. They overlook the fact that there has always been a close relationship between the impact of external and internal forces in the generation of group solidarity. Furthermore, since blacks have been struggling for more than 350 years to be integrated into American society, it is doubtful whether integration is more realistic than separatism for the masses of black people. In their bias toward integration, many scholars ignore the duality of the black man's existence in white America.

Since blacks have not been assimilated into American society, they are often loyal to several groups. They may flatly deny their membership in the American nation, or they may be good citizens and rally to its cause in time of need. If the latter occurs, blacks may still retain their loyalty to their race because they have been integrated into the

American nation only to the extent of obeying the orders of a government too powerful to oppose.

Like Welshmen, Scotsmen, and Englishmen in Great Britain, or diverse groups in Switzerland and Belgium, blacks may continue to stress their special group cohesion, cultural peculiarities, and loyalty of race without necessarily abandoning their identification with the larger nation. W. E. B. Du Bois summed up the ambivalence, the most essential conflict in loyalties among black Americans, when he wrote that blacks always felt their twoness: "An American, a Negro, two souls, two thoughts, two unreconciled strivings; two warring ideals in one dark body, whose dogged strength alone keeps it from being torn asunder." As NAACP Executive Secretary James Weldon Johnson put it, there were times "when the most persistent integrationist becomes an isolationist, when he curses the white world and consigns it to hell." In many cases, racial solidarity and separatism have represented the only apparent alternative for blacks. Du Bois, after viewing the growth of Jim Crow and the economic strangulation of blacks, wrote that he reached the conclusion that "I was not an American; I was not a man; I was by long education and continued daily reminder, a colored man in a white world; and that white world often existed primarily, so far as I was concerned, to see with sleepless vigilance that I was kept within bounds, . . . that I was, and must be a thing apart."

As a result of their oppression, Afro-Americans came early to the realization that they were a separate people who had to unite for self-elevation and to fight oppression. This was one of the primary messages of Afro-American journalists and black conventions held between 1830 and 1900. The clearest expression of the idea of a separate black nationality came from Martin R. Delany in 1860; he contended that Afro-Americans were "a nation within a nation—as the Poles in Russia, the Hungarians in Austria; the Welsh, the Irish and Scotch in the British dominions." According to Delany, blacks had to develop "independently of anything pertaining to white men or nations." This feeling led practically all blacks to press for racial unity, uplift, and the development of a sense of solidarity. A national convention of blacks in 1848 asserted, "It is more than a mere figure of speech to say, that we are as a people, chained together. We are one people— one in general complexion, one in a common degradation, one in popular estimation.—As one rises, all must rise, and as one falls all must fall."

American blacks were just as consistent throughout the nineteenth century in their optimism about the future. David Walker expressed the typical view when he wrote in the 1820s that he had "the glorious anticipation of a not very distant period, when these things which now help to degrade us will no more be practised among the sons of Africa,—for, though this, and perhaps another, generation may not experience the promised blessings of Heaven, yet, the dejected, degraded, and now enslaved children of Africa will have, in spite of all their enemies, to take their place among the nations of the earth."

BLACK ATTITUDES TOWARD AFRICA

One of the most persistent and important aspects of the history and development of black nationalist consciousness has been attitudes of blacks toward Africa. Black Americans retained a strong sentimental and historical nostalgia for Africa. Even while black Americans took pride in the accomplishments of the ancient Egyptians and Ethiopians and insisted they were black, they recognized that the vast majority of Afro-Americans had been transported from the West African coast. They exulted in the black kingdoms of Songhay, Mali, and Ghana, which developed in the Sudan, and those of Benin and Zimbabwe, famous throughout the world for their metallurgical skill, statuettes, and masks. Trying to counteract charges of the inherent inferiority of Africans, they proudly pointed to the sophisticated agricultural development and well-organized governmental structures characteristic of these kingdoms before the arrival of European invaders. Black Americans were most interested, however, in survivals in their social and cultural habits and behavior, which could be attributed to their African origins. Although one can identify traces of African languages, religious activities, arts and crafts, and kinship attitudes in black American communities, that is less important than the re-creation of African ties.

BACK-TO-AFRICA MOVEMENTS

This search for roots was frequently manifested in back-to-Africa movements. Since economic deprivation and white oppression were constant realities for the mass of blacks, there was always great interest in separatist movements in the black community. In spite of this, only a few blacks migrated to Africa. Ill-conceived, poorly financed and organized, all back-to-Africa movements failed, primarily because blacks were simply too poverty-stricken to emigrate. Those blacks who were wealthy enough to support such schemes generally opposed them, because they would immediately diminish their own economic and political power. Powerful external forces also hampered emigration. As long as black labor was essential for profits, white capitalists strenuously opposed any mass emigration of Afro-Americans. European powers tried to prevent any American blacks from coming to the areas in Africa they controlled. State, local, and national officials erected as many roadblocks as they could to mass emigration movements.

PRE–CIVIL WAR INTEREST IN THE AMERICAN COLONIZATION SOCIETY

One segment of white opinion in the early Republic believed that democracy and Christianity required the deportation of blacks to Africa. This philosophy, espoused by Thomas Jefferson and others, was the basis for the founding of the American Colonization Society (ACS) in December 1816–January 1817 and the establishment of Liberia on the West Coast of Africa in 1822. Many free blacks denounced the ACS because they felt it viewed Afro-Americans as aliens and would forcibly transport them to Africa. One of the major objections to the society, even by blacks favoring emigration, was that whites controlled it. In 1855 the arch emigrationist Martin R. Delany asserted that "white men generally, and *American* white men in particular, are wholly inadequate to the important undertaking of the establishment of colonies, and the spread of the Gospel as missionaries among the colored races."

Most free black leaders rejected emigration and attacked the ACS because they considered themselves Americans and held on to the myth that they would one day receive equal treatment from whites. During his July 4, 1830, attack on the ACS, the Rev. Peter Williams of New York maintained, "We are Natives of this country, we ask only to be treated as well as Foreigners. Not a few of our fathers suffered and bled to purchase its independence; we ask only to be treated as well as those who fought against it." The Rev. Henry Highland Garnet, a former Maryland slave, expressed the characteristic sentiments of the free blacks in a speech in 1848:

> We must . . . cherish and maintain a national and patriotic sentiment and attachment. Some people of color say that they have no home, no country. I am not among that number. It is empty declamation. It is unwise. It is not logical—it is false. Of all the people in this wide earth, among the countless hordes of misery, there is not one so poor as to be without a home and a country. America is my home, my country, and I have no other. I love whatever good there may be in her institutions. I hate her sins. I loathe her slavery, and I pray Heaven that ere long she may wash away her guilt in tears of repentance. I love the green-hills which my eyes first beheld in my infancy. I love every inch of soil which my feet pressed in my youth, and I mourn because the accursed shade of slavery rests upon it. I love my country's flag, and I hope that soon it will be cleansed of its stains, and be hailed by all nations as the emblem of freedom and independence.

Because of their own predilections, historians have devoted much more attention to the opponents of the ACS than to its supporters. Given the poverty of antebellum blacks, it was a remarkable achievement for the ACS to send 147 ships with 18,959 emigrants to Liberia between 1817 and 1865. For every emigrant there were more than ten blacks who requested aid and did not receive it from the ACS. One of the most efficient antebellum propaganda agencies, the society stressed the discrimination American blacks suffered, offered them an opportunity to obtain real freedom in the land of their origin, and urged planters to liberate and send their slaves to Liberia. The propaganda of the society struck a responsive chord among some free blacks. Abraham Camp wrote from the Illinois Territory in 1818 that he and other blacks in the area were "all willing to leave America whenever the way shall be opened. We love this country and its liberties, if we could share an equal right in them; but our freedom is partial, and we have no hope that it ever will be otherwise here; therefore we had rather be gone, though we should suffer hunger and nakedness for years."

Although historians insist that there was little real interest in emigration before the passage of the Fugitive Slave Act of 1850, the thousands of letters in the files of the ACS suggest another story. Slaves and free blacks continually wrote to the society after 1817 expressing their desire to migrate to Liberia to escape discrimination, to establish a Christian outpost in Africa, to obtain the same kinds of opportunities in a new land as European immigrants had found in the United States, and to aid in crushing the African slave trade. Almost universally they viewed Liberia as the "land of promise" where they would enjoy liberty, equality, and self-government. Like the Pilgrims, the blacks wanted to establish "a city upon a hill." The semiliterate free black Peter Butler of Petersburg, Virginia, expressed the typical view when he wrote in 1848, "I wish to Go to Liberia So as I may teach Sinners the way of Salvation and also Educate my children and injoy the Right of a man[.] I have tride a great meny placess in these united state and I find that none of them is the home for the Culerd man and So I am Looking in my mind for a home and I find that Liberia is the onley place of injoyment for the Culerd man. . . ." Judging by the letters received by the society and those reprinted in a number of newspapers, about 20 percent of the free blacks supported emigration between 1817 and 1861. By 1849, even Garnet had abandoned his patriotic stance and asserted that he was "in favor of colonization . . . wherever it promises freedom and enfranchisement. In a word, we ought to go anywhere where we can better our condition."

BLACK-LED EMIGRATION EFFORTS BEFORE THE CIVIL WAR

Seeking to provide for their elevation through their own efforts, blacks began advocating emigration long before the founding of the ACS. In spite of all the formidable barriers, there was much interest among blacks in emigration from the era of the American Revolution to the 1970s. Although Africa was the primary focus, large numbers of American blacks felt that they should be "anyplace but here." The first indications of interest in migrating to Africa appeared in the eighteenth century. In 1773 a group of Massachusetts blacks petitioned the legislature, expressing their desire "to transport ourselves to some part of the coast of Africa," and in 1783 the Free African Society in Boston and Newport, Rhode Island, voiced similar sentiments. Four years later, the Methodist preacher Prince Hall and seventy-four other blacks petitioned the Massachusetts legislature for assistance in leaving the United States because they wanted "to return to Africa, our native country, . . . where we shall live among our equals and be more comfortable and happy, than we can be in our present situation." Newport and Providence blacks organized emigration societies and urged Boston and Philadelphia blacks to join them in the 1780s, petitioned the state legislature in the 1790s, sent an agent to inquire about land in Sierra Leone, and negotiated settlement rights with British authorities in 1795. Poverty and the machinations of British authorities defeated these early emigration schemes.

When Paul Cuffee, a black Massachusetts captain and shipbuilder, began calling for the establishment of a colony in Africa in 1808, many New England blacks supported him. After an exploratory trip to Sierra Leone in 1811, Cuffee contacted black leaders in Baltimore, Philadelphia, Boston, and New York and urged blacks to emigrate, to send missionaries to Africa, and to form a single organization to speak for the "African Nation" in America. Cuffee took 38 blacks to Sierra Leone at his own expense in 1815; when he died in 1817 he was planning another voyage and had a waiting list of 2,000 blacks who wanted to return. Interest in emigration continued after Cuffee's death.

Blacks formed branches of the Haytian Emigration Society in Philadelphia, Boston, New York, Baltimore, and Cincinnati in the 1820s, and more than 6,000 Afro-Americans migrated to Haiti, where President Jean Pierre Boyer provided travel stipends for them. Secretary-General Balthasar Igniac greeted a group of Haitian emigrants in 1824 and told them that since "the common blood of GREAT AFRICA makes unbreakable ties, all blacks are brothers regardless of language and religious distinctions."

In the 1830s and 1840s Lewis Woodson, a former Virginia slave, kept the emigration sentiment alive. A minister and teacher in Pittsburgh, Woodson stressed the need for racial solidarity, the development of a "national feeling" among the blacks constituting a separate caste in America, and called variously for the establishment of all-black communities ("Africanas") in the United States and for emigration. Woodson's most famous student was Martin R. Delany.

Although Woodson later abandoned his support of emigration, his newspaper essays in the 1840s helped to make emigrationists of Mary Ann Shadd, Henry Bibb, Henry Highland Garnet, Alexander Crummell, Samuel Ringgold Ward, James T. Holly, and others. Henry Bibb, a fugitive slave from Kentucky, went to Canada in 1850, began publication of its first black newspaper, the *Voice of the Fugitive*, in 1851, and in 1852 organized a Refugee Home Society to provide land to blacks fleeing from American bondage and discrimination. In September, 1851, Bibb presided over the North American Convention of Colored People, where the delegates urged blacks to leave the United States. Bibb also led in the formation of the short-lived American Continental and West Indies League to unite "the colored people of the North and South American continents . . . for the protection of the common rights of their brethren throughout the world." James T. Holly, a native of Washington, D.C., served as co-editor of the *Voice of the Fugitive* and urged the formation of one organization to "mould the destiny of the whole Afro-American race." From 1850 until the 1870s, Holly called at various times for emigration to Liberia, Canada, or the West Indies. Finally, he settled on Haiti, eventually making it his home.

The emigrationists held their own national conventions in 1854, 1855, and 1856. As the most practical site for colonization, some chose the Caribbean, Canada, Mexico, or Africa. These leaders generally insisted that blacks had contributed to world civilization in the past and could do so in the future if they went to Africa, destroyed the slave trade, and redeemed and christianized the continent.

Martin R. Delany, a journalist and physician who spent one year at the Harvard Medical School, had a long-standing interest in emigration. In 1854, Delany, who coined the phrase "Africa for the Africans," issued a call for a national emigration convention which met in August of that year in Cleveland. The convention considered a number of proposals for emigration, but none were adopted. Four years later, the convention board discussed emigration to Central America, Haiti, and West Africa. Delany was chosen a commissioner to explore Africa, and along with Robert Campbell led the Niger Valley Exploring Party. Sailing to Africa in May, 1859, Delany remained there for one year, negotiating for land and for the settlement of blacks. The advent of the Civil War and the hope that it would bring complete liberation led to a decrease in Delany's interest in emigration. After his return to the United States, he helped to recruit black troops, became a major in a black regiment, and later played a prominent role in South Carolina politics during Reconstruction.

POST–CIVIL WAR BLACK NATIONALIST MOVEMENTS, 1865–1903

Nationalist movements and ideological views, never completely suppressed during the Civil War, became much more obvious again soon thereafter. The masses of black people noted that the war ended in the abolition of slavery, but that despite Reconstruction, unequal treatment under the law, lynching, mob violence, and economic dependency and deprivation still haunted them. Freedom did not mean economic, political, or social equality. In an effort to insulate themselves from white oppression, blacks placed more and more emphasis on self-help, racial solidarity, emigration, separatism, and attempts to create all-black communities for self-protection and advancement of the race during and after the Reconstruction period. Illiterate Benjamin "Pap" Singleton, a former Tennessee slave who had escaped to Canada before the Civil War, began one of the first separatist movements. Returning to Tennessee after the war, Singleton urged blacks to abandon politics because they were being swindled. As a result of the stress on politics during Reconstruction, Singleton contended that "whites had the lands and the sense and the blacks had nothing but their freedom." In order to make this freedom real, Singleton organized a land company in 1869. After prices proved too high in Tennessee, he began urging blacks to acquire public lands in Kansas in 1871, and between 1873 and 1879 he took several groups of Tennessee and Kentucky blacks there. Southern blacks showed feverish interest in emigration between 1876 and 1881; thousands of Louisiana, Mississippi, and Arkansas blacks moved into Kansas during this period. They had purchased about 10,000 acres of public land by 1879. The emigrants were generally so destitute, however, that initially they had to obtain relief from Kansas whites. This led to an investigation of Singleton and the exodus by the U.S. Senate in 1880, the opposition of such black leaders as Frederick Douglass and P. B. S. Pinchback, and most important, increased discrimination in Kansas.

Singleton and his cohorts obviously wanted to create an independent and separate black enclave in Kansas. One of the most popular tunes at Singleton's rallies included this verse:

> In the midst of earth's dominion
> Christ has provided us a kingdom
> Not left to other nations
> And we've surely gained the day.

As their numbers increased and discrimination and segregation arose in Kansas, Singleton began urging blacks to emigrate to Canada or Liberia, and in 1885 he formed the United Trans-Atlantic Society to foster African colonization. Despairing of achieving manhood in the United States, the society argued that only in an African state with a separate national existence could blacks survive.

One of the first postwar emigration movements to achieve some limited success arose among blacks in South Carolina in the 1870s. With the support of Martin R. Delany, South Carolina blacks formed the Liberian Exodus and Joint Stock Steamship Company and acquired a boat, the *Azor.* After the first voyage in 1878 with 206 black passengers, the company went bankrupt. In 1885 S. H. Scott, an attorney in Fort Smith, Arkansas, attempted to encourage support for an all-black state. Edwin P. McCabe, once a state auditor in Kansas, began a similar movement in the Oklahoma Territory in 1889. Their efforts were short-lived.

Also coming into prominence during this period was the most controversial nineteenth-century emigrationist, Henry McNeal Turner. A former Union soldier and Georgia legislator, Turner was deeply affected by the continued discrimination against blacks during Reconstruction. Constantly reiterating his determination never to take up arms again in defense of the United States, Turner was the chief supporter of the back-to-Africa idea from the 1870s until World War I. A most bitter nationalist, Turner felt that no black American could logically be patriotic and asserted that a "man who loves a country that hates him is a human dog and not a man." As for himself, Turner once declared that he wished the United States nothing but misfortune and hoped that he would live to see it go down to ruin and its memory blotted from the pages of history. On another occasion, Turner described the U.S. Constitution as "a dirty rag, a cheat, a libel, and ought to be spit upon by every Negro in the land." Only in Africa, he argued, could a black person be and act like a man. Contending that white persecution of blacks would never end until they manned a government of their own, Turner looked to Africa as a place of refuge, as a means of increasing black self-respect, and as a powerful bulwark against white oppression. Young blacks would have no models for emulation so long as whites denied Afro-Americans access to places of honor and power. Turner asserted, "Till we have black men in the seats of power, respected, feared, hated, and reverenced, our young men will never rise for the reason they will never look up."

Africa was a place where the blacks could get a new start and be free of persecution. But instead of mass emigration, Turner hoped that 5,000 to 10,000 proud and resourceful blacks would return to their homeland annually. As a jibe at his numerous black opponents, Turner declared that none of "the riffraff of white-men worshippers, aimless, objectless, selfish, little-souled and would-be-white Negroes" of America should go to Africa because they "would be of no help to anyone anywhere." Contending that too many American blacks worshipped whiteness, Turner stressed black pride and argued that God himself was black. He felt it was just as reasonable to think that God was black as to think that he was white. Anticipating the theology of Marcus Garvey and the Nation of Islam, Turner insisted, "God is a Negro; Even the heathens in Africa believe that they were 'created in God's image.' But American Africans believe that they resemble the devil and hence the contempt they have for themselves and each other!" While Turner had no viable organizational base or economic means for sending blacks to Africa, some whites supported him. In 1894, with the backing of Alabama Senator John Morgan, Turner formed the International Migration Society and sent two boatloads of emigrants to Liberia by 1896. Turner inspired a black stockbroker, William Ellis, who led an expedition to Ethiopia in 1903. Harry Dean, a descendant of Paul Cuffee and a black ship captain, was another follower of Turner. He dreamed of establishing an African empire and obtained a territorial concession in Basutoland, but was swindled out of it.

DEMANDING REPARATIONS

Emigrationists consistently demanded that the U.S. government pay blacks reparations for all of their sufferings and unrequited toil while in bondage. At the Emigration Convention of 1854 the blacks insisted, "Nothing less than a national indemnity, indelibly fixed by virtue of our own sovereign potency, will satisfy us as a redress of our grievances for the unparalleled wrongs, undisguised impositions, and unmitigated oppression, which we have suffered at the hands of this American people. . . . For our own part, we spurn to treat for liberty on any other terms or conditions." Henry McNeal Turner also felt that blacks should receive reparations: "We have worked, enriched the country and helped give it a standing among the powers of the earth, . . . The way we figure it out, this country owes us forty billions of dollars." He wanted to use $100 million to pay for emigration to Africa. The Peace Movement of Ethiopia petitioned President Franklin D. Roosevelt and the Virginia legislature in the 1930s and supported the 1939 congressional bill introduced by Mississippi's racist Senator Theodore Bilbo for federally supported transportation of blacks to Africa. The African Nationalist Pioneer Movement (1964) and the African-American Repatriation Association (1969) petitioned the President for aid in resettling blacks in their "African homeland."

A few nonemigrationists also demanded reparations as a mechanism for gaining economic resources for blacks. Soon after the Civil War, Sojourner Truth led an unsuccessful petition campaign to obtain free public land for former slaves. During the 1890s another black woman, Callie House, organized the Ex-Slave Pension and Bounty Movement in Tennessee, filed lawsuits, and unsuccessfully petitioned Congress for reparations payments to former slaves. Although most black leaders opposed the movement, Frederick Douglass endorsed it. The most famous demand for reparations occurred in the twentieth century. Speaking in Detroit in 1969, James Forman, former executive director of SNCC, issued a Black Manifesto calling for "a revolutionary black vanguard" to take control of the U.S. government. To finance the revolution, Forman demanded $5 billion in reparations from the "white Christian churches and Jewish synagogues, which are part and parcel of the system of capitalism." Lambasted by most whites, Forman's manifesto received a respectful reading in such journals as *Commonweal, Christian Century,* and *World Outlook. Christian Century* typified such views: "We do not believe the idea of reparations is ridiculous. This generation of blacks continues to pay the price of earlier generations' slavery and subjugation; this generation of whites continues to enjoy the profits of racial exploitation." The churches responded to the manifesto by increasing their annual contributions to black organizations by $1 million.

THE PERSISTENCE OF PAN-AFRICANISM

One of the strongest elements running through nineteenth-century black nationalist thought was a nascent sense of Pan-Africanism. In 1854, Martin R. Delany and others claimed that the great issue which would decide the world's destiny "will be the question of black and white." They continued, "The black and colored races are four-sixths of all the population of the world; and these people are fast tending to a common cause with each other. . . . Shall the last vestige of an opportunity, outside of the continent of Africa, for the national development of our race, be permitted, in consequence of our slothfulness, to elude our grasp and fall into the possession of the whites? This, may Heaven forbid. May the sturdy, intelligent Africo-American sons of the Western Continent forbid." The clergyman James T. Holly expressed the Pan-African ideal even more clearly in an 1857 pamphlet on Haiti. Describing Haiti as "the vanguard of the race," Holly called upon American blacks "to contribute to the continued advancement of this negro nationality of the New world until its glory and renown shall overspread and cover the whole earth, and redeem and regenerate by its influence in the future, the benighted Fatherland of the race in Africa." Holly also believed that in Haiti, "this black nationality of the New World . . . is . . . the lever that must be exerted, to regenerate and disenthrall the oppression and ignorance of the race, throughout the world."

There were, of course, many black missionaries who preached the responsibility of American blacks to uplift their African brethren. When Garnet and others organized the African Civilization Society in 1858, they said its first objective was "the civilization and christianization of Africa, and of the descendants of African ancestors in any portion of the earth, wherever dispersed." The most important nineteenth-century exponent of Pan-Africanism was the New York-born Liberian missionary Alexander Crummell. In 1860 he stressed the duties American blacks and their Latin American brothers had to Africa. According to Crummell, there was "a natural call upon the children of Africa in foreign lands to come and participate in the opening treasures of the land of their fathers." This had to be done to prevent Europeans from raping Africa. Crummell asserted that since

> *all* men hold some relation to the land of their fathers, I wish to call the attention of the sons of Africa in America to their "RELATIONS AND DUTY TO THE LAND OF THEIR FATHERS."
>
> You should learn willingly to give, even of your best, to save, and regenerate, and build up the RACE in distant quarters. You should study to rise above the niggard spirit which grudgingly and pettishly yields its grasp upon a fellow laborer. You should claim in regard to this continent that "THIS IS OUR AFRICA," in all her gifts, and in her budding grace and glory.

Beginning in the 1880s Afro-American newspapers and magazines increased their coverage of African affairs, and by the 1920s many of them had regular African correspondents. Always, they saw a glorious future for the continent. T. Thomas Fortune's 1887 assertion in the New York *Freeman* was typical: "It is written on the wall that there will one day be an African Empire whose extent and power will be inferior to that of no government now denominated as a first class power." It was also during this period that black scholars began advocating Pan-Africanism in their research and writing. The Rev. T. McCants Stewart in *Liberia: The Americo-African Republic* (1886), stressed the American blacks' kinship to Africa and advised them "to put our ships upon the sea. . . . We must have our own vessels carrying our African workers, our civilization, and our wares back to the 'Fatherland,' and bringing back its riches." Like Fortune, Stewart envisioned a great empire in Africa's future where "there will arise a stable and powerful Government of Africans, for Africans, and by Africans, which shall be an inestimable blessing to all mankind."

When Bishop Henry M. Turner visited South Africa in 1898, he extolled the virtues of African civilization, said the South Africans were descendants of the Ethiopians, and predicted that they would eventually throw off the yoke of the white man. Black churches, especially the AME, paid for the education of several African leaders in the United States. Booker T. Washington, while cooperating with the colonial powers in the early years of the twentieth century, tried to attract African students to Tuskegee Institute, sent some of his graduates to provide technical assistance to the Africans, and encouraged American blacks to study their African past in his 1909 book, *The Story of the American Negro,* and in the 1912 conference on Africa he convened at Tuskegee.

The early systematic development of twentieth-century Pan-African ideas was also due largely to the efforts of American blacks. The first Pan-African Congress (held in 1900) was chiefly the work of an AME bishop, Alexander Walters, and American blacks dominated all of the early congresses. Black Americans assumed the early leadership in the Pan-African movement because they had more opportunities for research into the African past and because they could speak out on the issue, while Africans were constrained by the yoke of European imperialism. One of the earliest Pan-Africanists was the New York journalist John Edward Bruce, who from 1911 to 1914 joined with several other New Yorkers to foster the study of African history and was one of the first men to push the concept of "an African personality." Carter G. Woodson's organization of the Association for the Study of Negro Life and History in 1915 was one of the most important forces in creating an interest in African history in the United States. In his lifetime many African nationalists corresponded with Woodson.

Around the time of the deaths of Bishop Henry M. Turner and Booker T. Washington in 1915, Ghanaian Alfred Sam started an emigration movement in Oklahoma. Blacks had attempted to turn the Oklahoma Territory into an all-black state during the 1890s. The result was twenty-five black towns, including Boley and Langston. These communities proudly considered themselves as examples of what blacks could accomplish through mobilization on the basis of race pride and solidarity. Continuing racial oppression, combined with the cotton depression of 1913, led to disenchantment of many of the blacks in Oklahoma. This, along with the strong desire of the blacks to avoid contact with whites, allowed Chief Sam, who said he was an African chief, to sell stock in his Akim Trading Company and to form several emigration groups. Sam did take a group of blacks to Ghana, but the English colonial officials defrauded him of his ship and he soon disappeared.

Because of the continued refusal of whites to integrate American society or to assimilate blacks and revived emphasis on race pride and solidarity in the early twentieth century, many Afro-Americans advocated and supported the development of separate institutions. Some blacks felt that separate schools were better for black children than mixed ones because they would not be discriminated against or subjected to the prejudice of white schoolmates and teachers, and would have black models in teachers and principals to inspire them. A special problem was control of black colleges; most of them were in the hands of white boards, professors, and presidents. There was a general movement to replace them with black professors, administrators, and boards in the early twentieth century.

MARCUS GARVEY'S MOVEMENT

As blacks crowded into the North in the 1920s and were more free to follow their own inclinations in their segregated black communities, a variety of black nationalist organizations and movements developed. One of the most important was that of Marcus Moziah Garvey. Born in Jamaica in 1887, the grandson of an African slave, Garvey migrated to London, where he lived for several years working at his trade as a printer. He became acquainted with native Africans, from whom he learned about the exploitation and immense potential of Africa. When he returned to Jamaica, he led an unsuccessful printer's strike which cost him his job. He then shifted his emphasis to the establishment of a school, read Booker T. Washington's *Up from Slavery*, wrote to the Tuskegean, and received an encouraging offer to come to the United States. But before he arrived in 1916, Washington died. Garvey came to America anyway and established the Universal Negro Improvement Association (UNIA). Garvey found the initial base for his association among the West Indian immigrants in Harlem. A commanding, charismatic figure, Garvey insisted on Africa for the Africans and tried to build a sense of pride and racial solidarity through elaborate ceremonies, uniforms, parades, and titles. He urged blacks to support black businesses, and the UNIA itself organized a chain of groceries, restaurants, laundries, a hotel, a factory to make black dolls, and a printing plant. Thousands of blacks bought stock in the UNIA's Black Star Steamship Line, organized to establish a commercial link among the United States, the West Indies, and Africa. Tens of thousands of blacks swelled with pride at parades of the mass units of the African Legion in blue and red uniforms and the white-attired contingent of the Black Cross Nurses. Its followers proudly waved the black, green, and red association flag: black for the skin, green for the hopes, and red for the blood. They sang the UNIA anthem, "Ethiopia, the Land of Our Fathers." Garvey, aware of the religious aspirations of the masses, formed the Negro Orthodox Church, with a black as bishop. He gloried in the African past and taught that God and Christ were black.

Naming himself the provisional President of Africa in 1922, Garvey petitioned the League of Nations to turn over the former German colonies in Africa to the UNIA. His charisma led at least 1 million and perhaps as many as 4 million blacks to adhere to his movement. A strong element of his appeal was the militant stance he inspired. For example, one of his chief lieutenants, Hubert Harrison, who was for a time associate editor of the *Negro World,* urged blacks to demand an eye for an eye in their struggles against discrimination and mob violence: "If white men are to kill unoffending Negroes, Negroes must kill white men in defense of their lives and property."

Garvey's movement had an impact not only upon blacks in America and the Caribbean, but also in Africa. Four branches of the UNIA were established by South African blacks in 1921, and one of them argued that as a result of the Garvey movement, American blacks would soon liberate South Africa. The oppression of the dominant white minority in South Africa, the circulation of Garvey's *Negro World,* and widespread reprinting of his speeches led to thinly veiled calls for violent resistance by Africans in the 1930s. In 1933, a South African nationalist wrote to Garvey that "the red, the black and the green are the colors talked about by the young men and women of Africa. It shall bury many and redeem millions. Today in Africa, the only hope of our race is the gospel the U.N.I.A. has sung—it is sung and said as during the period of the French Revolution."

Many nationalists in West Africa also seriously studied Garveyism. President Kwame Nkrumah of Ghana once said that Garvey had more impact on the development of his nationalist ideas than anyone else, and in 1958 he asserted that many Afro-Americans had "made no small contribution to the cause of African freedom. Names which spring immediately to mind are those of Marcus Garvey and W. E. B. Du Bois. Long before many of us were conscious of our own degradation, these men fought for African national and racial equality." A branch of the UNIA was formed in Lagos, Nigeria, in 1920, and the Nigerians were especially interested in Garvey's steamship line and bought some shares of stock in it.

Garvey's influence on the Africans, both potential and real, was great enough to cause nightmares for the colonizing powers. The fear was not unfounded. For example, although there were no branches of the UNIA in the French colonies, some of the French West Africans did attend its meetings, and one devotee of Garvey tried unsuccessfully to liberate his country in 1925. Also Jomo Kenyatta of Kenya, like Kwame Nkrumah of Ghana, was influenced by his ideas. As a result of Garvey's movement, the colonial administrators in Senegal, Gambia, and Sierra Leone passed laws to restrict the immigration of American blacks. The British banned the circulation of Garvey's *Negro World* and refused in 1923 to give Garvey a visa to travel in British-controlled areas in Africa. The British Colonial Office refused the visa because it felt the object of his visit was "to stir up trouble and to incite sedition in Africa."

Garvey had enemies not only among the European colonial powers, but also among a number of black American leaders. Since he criticized the light-skinned integrationists and middle- and upper-class blacks active in the NAACP for being ashamed of their ancestry, established black leaders resented and feared him. (W. E. B. Du Bois and A. Philip Randolph were especially bitter in their attacks on Garvey.) Several of them called the attention of the U.S. government to irregularities in the management of the Black Star Steamship Line and demanded Garvey's arrest. Garvey was jailed and then deported on charges of using the mail to defraud; his movement collapsed.

W. E. B. DU BOIS AND PAN-AFRICANISM

The period of Garvey's ascendancy was also the period of development of Pan-Africanism by W. E. B. Du Bois. Du Bois is universally considered the intellectual godfather of Pan-Africanism. He attended the first Pan-African conference in 1900 and organized five meetings between 1919 and 1945. Four meetings took place between 1919 and 1927. Throughout Du Bois' career the Pan-African theme was central in his writings. Whether it was cultural nationalism as expressed in his early 1897 paper "The Conservation of the Races," the idea that Afro-Americans should have a special attachment to Africa, or an emphasis on the political redemption of the continent through Pan-African conferences, he was always in the vanguard of black intellectuals in the development of Pan-African ideas. Primarily through his influence, the NAACP pushed for partial self-determination for European colonies in Africa at the Versailles Peace Conference in 1919. The NAACP also paid most of the expenses of the Pan-African Congress which met that year in Paris and was influential in the creation of the mandate system of the League of Nations.

A prolific writer and pamphleteer, Du Bois was a determined propagandist, a great theorist, and a popularizer of African interests; he wrote almost constantly about Africa from the 1890s until his death in 1963. He encouraged American blacks to recognize their brotherhood with Africans and insisted that the struggle for equality in America was tied irrevocably to the fight for African independence. Agitating for an early end to European imperialism, Du Bois argued that racial solidarity and economic independence would lead to self-government in Africa and the regeneration of all blacks. In the first Pan-African congresses, Du Bois took the position that black Americans would lead the struggle for Africa's liberation. But by the 1950s he was conceding that the Africans themselves would lead the fight.

Eventually Du Bois contended that all the colored peoples of the world had to unite against white oppression. Throughout his life he stressed the importance of economic independence in all of the African world. For example, in 1933 he wrote, "It is therefore imperative that the colored peoples of the world, and first all those of Negro descent, should begin to concentrate upon this problem of their economic survival, the best of their brains and education. Pan-Africa means intellectual understanding and cooperation among groups of Negro descent in order to bring about at the earliest possible time, the industrial and spiritual emancipation of the Negro peoples."

CULTURAL NATIONALISM, 1890–1930

The 1920s were the heyday of cultural nationalism. Howard University's William Leo Hansberry began his pioneering research into African history and Negritude, Monroe Work of Tuskegee published *A Bibliography of the Negro in Africa and America* (1929), and Pan-Africanism emerged as a central literary theme for black writers during this period. Africa was not, however, a new topic for black poets.

Between 1890 and 1920, black poets occasionally wrote romantic epics containing blurred images of the continent they had never seen and emphasizing their hopes for its regeneration. In his 1893 poem the "Song of the Slave," James T. Franklin wrote:

> Oh, send me home to Africa,
> Back across the sea,

> From America's cruel shores
> To my own country.

Aaron B. Thompson, in *Echoes of Spring* (1901), wrote "A Song to Ethiopia" and in 1914 Maurice N. Corbett painted word pictures of "Black Kingdoms of the Future":

> Kingdoms and empires will they form
> In Afric's fertile bosom warm;
> Liberia will important grow;
> An empire great will be Congo;
> Ashantee's greatness will return;
> The Zulus, great distinction earn;
> Proud Abyssinia's lurid skies
> To leading kingdom will arise.

After 1920, black poets described Africa as the "sun of rising hope," the cradle of civilization, the land of kings, "liberty loving people," powerful gods, "men of noble blood," justice, truth, and light. A rhythmic continent of sacred dances, balmy shores, mosaics of colors, Africa was symbolic of glory, strength, wisdom, Eden, and the "place where traders shaped my father's pain." It was, as Langston Hughes wrote, the unifying bond between black people everywhere:

> We are related—you and I
> You from the West Indies
> I from Kentucky
> We are related—you and I
> You from Africa
> I from these States
> We are brothers—you and I.

The poets expressed the sentiments of most blacks when they treated Africa as a shared symbol of Afro-American group consciousness, unity, and loyalty. The African past was a major concern of the poets and novelists active in the 1920s and 1930s, such as Langston Hughes, Claude McKay, Lucian B. Watkins, Horatio Warrick, Hugh Gloster, and Frank Marshall Davis. Among the most famous of these poems was Countee Cullen's 1925 work "Heritage":

> What is Africa to me:
> Copper sun or scarlet sea,
> Jungle star or jungle track,

Strong bronzed men, or regal black
Women from whose loins I sprang
When the birds of Eden sang?
One three centuries removed
From the scenes his fathers loved,
Spicy grove, cinnamon tree,
What is Africa to me?

Africa would remain as a major theme in the works of black poets. Similarly, from the 1920s on, Afro-American intellectuals would continually call for the creation of a distinctive black literature that would reflect the soul and aspirations of the race. Black artists believed their creations should mirror the unique racial tradition and distinctive world of black people.

W. E. B. DU BOIS' SEPARATIST IDEOLOGY

During the 1930s, the Depression, the influx of Communists into the black community, and events in Africa all helped to foster nationalist ideas. The most important theoretician of a new separatist ideology was W. E. B. Du Bois. In 1934 Du Bois broke with the NAACP because it refused to support his demand for the creation of a "Negro nation within a Nation."

Du Bois argued in 1935 that the concentration of blacks—with more intelligence, labor skills, and purchasing power than many independent nations—gave them a chance to break the circle of poverty formed by discriminatory labor unions, exploitive capitalists, and an unfeeling public. He described his dream in these words:

> For a nation with this start in culture and efficiency to sit down and await the salvation of a white God is idiotic. With the use of their political power, their power as consumers, and their brain power, added to that chance of personal appeal which proximity and neighborhood always give to human beings, Negroes can develop in the United States an economic nation within a nation, able to work through inter-cooperation, to found its own institutions, to educate its genius, and at the same time, without mob violence or extremes of race hatred, to keep in helpful touch and cooperate with the mass of the nation. This has happened more often than most people realize, in the case of groups not so obviously separated from the mass of people as are American Negroes. It must happen in our case, or there is no hope for the Negro in America. . . .
>
> There exists today a chance for the Negroes to organize a cooperative State within their own group. By letting Negro farmers feed Negro

artisans, and Negro technicians guide Negro home industries, and Negro thinkers plan this integration of cooperation, while Negro artists drama-tize and beautify the struggle, economic independence can be achieved. To doubt that this is possible is to doubt the essential humanity and the quality of brains of the American Negro.

Du Bois contended that the problems of the black masses could not be solved by the integration of, and opportunities given to, edu-cated and wealthy blacks. Instead, the black bourgeoisie had to uplift the black proletariat for its own salvation by fostering economic solidar-ity. To those who accused him of advocating self-segregation, Du Bois answered that a separate black nation already existed in separate black churches and schools and the concentration of blacks into self-support-ing economic units. The only way to advance the black toward equality, he asserted, was through deliberate self-segregation. It was obvious, according to Du Bois, that

if the economic and cultural salvation of the American Negro calls for an increase in segregation and prejudice, then that must come. Ameri-can Negroes must plan for the economic future and the social survival of their fellows in the firm belief that this means in a real sense the survival of colored folk in the world and the building of a full humanity instead of a petty white tyranny. Control of their own education, which is the logical and inevitable end of separate schools, would not be an unmixed ill; it might prove a supreme good. Negro schools once meant poor schools. They need not today; they must not tomorrow. Separate Negro sections will increase race antagonism, but they will also increase economic cooperation, organized self-defense and necessary self-confi-dence.

PAN-AFRICANISM AND SEPARATISM IN THE 1930s

Africa loomed large in the consciousness of Afro-Americans, whether separatists or integrationists, in the 1930s. Blacks rallied to the cause of Liberia when its European creditors and charges of forced labor threatened it with extinction. It was Du Bois who led this campaign, and in 1935 he asserted that Liberia's chief crime was that it was a symbol of black self-government. "She lacks training, experience, and thrift. But her chief crime is to be black and poor in a rich, white world; and in precisely that portion of the world where color is ruth-lessly exploited as a foundation for American and European wealth. The success of Liberia as a Negro republic would be a blow to the whole colonial slave system." The Ethiopian peace movement formed in Chicago in 1932 also represented Afro-Americans' sense of kin with

Africa. Extremely proud of the oldest black self-governing nation in the world, Ethiopia, American blacks sprang into action when the ancient African kingdom was overrun by Italian armies between 1935 and 1936. The Italian invasion became the symbol of white oppression and exploitation of dark peoples. American blacks immediately began raising funds, organizing clubs, and holding mass meetings to recruit volunteers to defend Ethiopia. Two black pilots joined, and one of them, Herbert Julian, headed the Ethiopian air force. A small Garvey Club in New York distributed the following prayer to be read in black churches: "Great God, grant that no Ethiopian soldier misses when he fires and that every Italian bullet goes astray."

A number of black nationalist organizations evolved in the 1930s, including the National Movement for the Establishment of a Forty-Ninth State, founded in Chicago in 1934 by Oscar Brown, Sr., and Bindley C. Cyrus; Nobel Drew Ali's Moorish American Science Temple, founded in Newark, New Jersey, in 1931; and the Nation of Islam, established in 1930 by W. D. Fard, leader of one faction of the Moorish Temple. Many ex-Garveyites found their way into the Nation of Islam.

Blacks found the greatest theoretical support for their nationalistic aspirations in the Communist party, and especially in the writings of Lenin. Insisting on the right of subjugated peoples to self-determination, Lenin urged all Communist parties to render "direct aid to all the revolutionary movements among the dependent and underprivileged nations (for example, Ireland, the American Negroes, etc.) and in the colonies." Lenin also felt that subjugated peoples had a right to separate from their oppressors and "to create autonomous areas, however small, towards which members of the respective nationalities scattered all over the country, or even all over the world, could gravitate and with which they could enter into relations and free associations of every kind." In the 1930s the Communist party, applying the Soviet nationality theory to black America, proposed the formation of a black republic in the southern part of the United States under the slogan "Self-determination in the black belt."

BLACK SEPARATISM, 1940s–60s

Even though integration seemed to be the overwhelmingly dominant ideology among blacks from the 1940s through the early 1960s, there were still various manifestations of black separatism. The Black Muslims and various groups that succeeded Garvey's UNIA, such as the African Nationalist Pioneer Movement in Harlem, still existed, and a dramatic increase in the black American's sense of identification with Africa became more apparent. This occurred for several reasons; the most obvious was the increase in the number of independent African states, beginning with Ghana in 1957. The emergence of a more truthful picture of Africa by contemporary scholars and an emphasis on precolonial history and culture in schools both added fuel to the fires of black American interest in Africa after 1940. The symbolic and real importance of Africa for blacks during this period cannot be exaggerated. In 1957 the famous black singer Paul Robeson asserted:

> I think a good deal in terms of the power of black people in the world. . . . That's why Africa means so much to me. As an American Negro, I'm as proud of Africa as one of those West Coast Chinese is proud of China.
>
> Now that doesn't mean that I'm going back to Africa, but spiritually I've been a part of Africa for a long time.
>
> Yes, this black power moves me. Look at Jamaica. In a few years the white minority will be there on the sufferance of black men. If they're nice, decent fellows they can stay.
>
> Yes, I look at Senator Eastland [of Mississippi] and say, "So you think you are powerful here? If only I could get you across the border."
>
> Although I may stay here the rest of my life, spiritually I'll always be a part of that world where black men can say to these crackers, "Get the hell out of here by morning."
>
> If I could get a passport, I'd just like to go to Ghana or Jamaica just to sit there for a few days and observe this black power.

Even though blacks were told by whites that Africans would not regard them as brothers, many Afro-American travelers discovered a sense of union and solidarity throughout the continent. As novelist John O. Killens said after a visit, "Everywhere I went people called me brother. . . . 'Welcome American brother.' It was a good feeling for me to be in Africa. To walk in a land for the first time in your entire life knowing within yourself that your color would not be held against you. No black man ever knows this in America." W. E. B. Du Bois' move to Ghana in 1961 was a return to the motherland for Afro-America's leading intellectual and a symbol of the place of Africa in the thinking of many other blacks.

Malcolm X and Frantz Fanon emerged as the key philosophers of the black nationalists in the 1960s in their espousal of the use of violence. Viewing the nonviolent campaign led by Martin Luther King, Jr., as emasculating, Malcolm X insisted, "Revolution is never based on begging somebody for an integrated cup of coffee. Revolutions are never fought by turning the other cheek. . . . And revolutions are never waged singing 'We Shall Overcome.' Revolutions are based upon bloodshed. . . . Revolutions overturn systems." Frantz Fanon, in his books *Black Skin, White Masks* (1952), *The Wretched of the Earth* (1961), and *Toward the African Revolution* (1964), provided the ideological justification for resort to violence by the oppressed. A psychiatrist in Algeria, Fanon described the imperatives of African liberation from Europeans. But many Afro-Americans accepted his compelling logic: "It is the intuition of the colonized masses that their liberation must, and can only, be achieved by force. . . . for the colonized people this violence, because it constitutes their only work, invests their characters with positive and creative qualities. . . . The armed struggle mobilizes the people; it throws them in one way and in one direction. The mobilization of the masses, when it arises out of the war of liberation, introduces into each man's consciousness the ideas of a common cause, of a national destiny, and of a collective history . . . violence unifies the people. . . . At the level of individuals, violence is a cleansing force. It frees the native from his inferiority complex and from his despair and inaction; it makes him fearless and restores his self-respect."

During nonviolent integration campaigns characteristic of the 1950s and 1960s, Robert F. Williams, leader of the NAACP chapter in Monroe, North Carolina, began advocating armed retaliation by blacks against violent attacks by whites in his newspaper, *The Crusader*. After being falsely charged with kidnapping a white couple during a riot, Williams fled first to Cuba and then to China, where he continued to publish his newspaper from exile. In 1964 he asserted, "The new concept of revolution . . . is lightning campaigns conducted in highly sensitive urban communities with the paralysis reaching the small communities and spreading to the farm areas." His philosophy of revolutionary nationalism and armed struggle inspired such groups as the Revolutionary Action Movement and the Republic of New Africa in the 1960s. The violence greeting the nonviolent integration struggle, and fears that whites were beginning to dominate nominally black organizations, produced a resurgence of black nationalism in the 1960s. Idealistic civil rights activists, disillusioned by the battles in the South fought by SNCC or CORE, soon became separatists and black nationalists. The obvious manifestation of their views was the black power movement so prominent after 1966.

THE BLACK POWER MOVEMENT IN THE 1960s

During James Meredith's march for freedom from fear in Mississippi in June, 1966, someone heard Willie Ricks yell "black power"—black power as the antithesis of white power and the strength to make the white man deal with blacks as people rather than as problems. Stokely Carmichael, the best known leader around Ricks, soon found the slogan attributed to him; reporters asked him to define it. Carmichael and Charles Hamilton, a black political scientist at Columbia University, asserted that black power meant that blacks would control their own destiny and would no longer depend solely on integration as a way of achieving their objectives. Integration had been opposed by whites generally, and integration between unequals would be a farce anyway. Another black power advocate, LeRoi Jones (later Imamu Amiri Baraka), wrote, "We want power to control our lives as separate from what Americans, white and white oriented people want to do with their lives. That simple, we ain't with y'all. Black power cannot exist within white power. One or the other, they might exist side by side as separate entities, but never in the same space, never. They are mutually exclusive."

Although novelist Richard Wright, New York Congressman Adam Clayton Powell, Jr., and others had called for the acquisition of black power before, Carmichael, Hamilton, and Jones were more nationalistic in their orientation. Black power in the second half of the 1960s meant rejection of the white man's images of fun, beauty, profit, and virtue, replacing them with black images. It was cultural, political, social, religious, and economic. According to Vincent Harding, head of the Institute of the Black World, black power was young blacks saying, "We're glad to be black, we rejoice in the darkness of our skin, we celebrate the natural texture of our hair, we extol the rhythm and vigor of our songs and shouts and dances." Denying charges that he was encouraging a black version of the Ku Klux Klan, Carmichael insisted that black power was not antiwhite. The black man, he argued, "wants to build something of his own, and that is not anti-white. When you build your own house, it doesn't mean you tear down the house across the street. Black people do not want to take over this country, they don't want to get whitey, they just want to get him off their backs."

Essentially, Carmichael was returning to some of the ideas expressed by Frederick Douglass in the 1850s, stressing black pride and unity while urging whites to wipe out racism in their own communities and form a coalition with blacks to end capitalistic exploitation. Carmichael also affirmed the right of black people everywhere to defend themselves when threatened or attacked. He hoped that programs could be implemented that would make violence unnecessary. Vincent Harding was more radical; he argued that blacks had to acquire justice by the only power white America respects: votes, money, and violent retaliation. The advocates of black power, he contended, rejected the killing of men abroad to protect America's wealth; instead they said, "If we must fight, let it be on the streets where we have been humiliated. If we must burn down houses, let them be the homes and stores of our exploiters. If we must kill, let it be the fat, pious white Christians who guard their lawns and their daughters while engineering slow death for us. If we must die, let it be for a real cause, a cause of black men's freedom as black men define it."

RIOTS AND REBELLIONS IN THE 1960s

Increased consciousness of the origins of oppression caused blacks to destroy the property of whites in black neighborhoods. Riots and rebellions (usually precipitated by police brutality against blacks) accompanied the resurgence of black nationalism in the 1960s. Black rebellions occurred in New York, Watts, Detroit, and numerous other cities between 1964 and 1967. When a white southerner, James Earl Ray, assassinated the Rev. Martin Luther King, Jr., in April, 1968, many blacks felt that their last hope for a nonviolent end to their oppression had died. In the 1960s large numbers of blacks began seriously considering violent revolution. *Black America*, the organ of the Revolutionary Action Movement, in 1965 declared that its purpose was "to bring clarity and direction in revolutionary struggle. To help build revolutionary nationalist leadership. To present a revolutionary program of national liberation and self-determination for the African captives enslaved in the racist United States of America. To forge a revolutionary unity among peoples of African descent and to give a new international spirit to Pan-Africanism. To fight for the liberation of oppressed peoples everywhere."

CULTURAL AND RELIGIOUS NATIONALISM IN THE 1960s

Black artistic expression enjoyed a renaissance greater than that of the 1920s. More than twenty new magazines (including *Black Scholar, Renaissance II, Journal of Black Poetry, Black Theater, Soulbook,* and *Black Lines*) appeared; black playwrights such as Baraka and Ed Bullins started emphasizing the necessity for violent revolution and the internal strengths of the black community. In its first issue in 1968, *Black Theater* called upon black artists to use drama as "a tool for raising the consciousness of black people and guiding them on the right path to national liberation." *Black Dialogue* pointed to the essential nationalistic imperatives for black intellectuals in a 1966 editorial:

Afro-American literature must be based on a thorough assessment of our cultural heritage and our present position in the U.S. society. Moreover, it must be directed toward the establishment of a viable and distinct cultural base. In line with this objective it should (1) stress things like the strong feelings of spiritual kinship and brotherhood which draw our people together; (2) extract objects and symbols from our already-existing culture, especially those which increase our sense of pride and self respect; and (3) point out conditions, such as economic exploitation and discrimination, which give us cause for our unified action. Finally, it must make a conscious effort to promote attitudes and values which when put into practice will either correct or completely destroy all the oppressive conditions confronting us in this society.

The poet, novelist, and playwright LeRoi Jones became a major spokesman of cultural nationalism. Jones changed his name to Imamu Amiri Baraka, and his Spirit House Movers in Newark and the Chicago-based Organization of Black Culture became two of the best-known cultural organizations. In 1964 he declared, "The Black Artist's role in America is to aid in the destruction of America as he knows it. His role is to report and reflect so precisely the nature of the society, and of himself in that society, that other men will be moved by the exactness of his rendering and, if they are black men, grow strong . . . and if they are white men, tremble, curse, and go mad because they will be drenched with the filth of their evil."

Religious nationalism was expressed not only by Elijah Muhammad in his message to the black man but by the Rev. Albert Cleage, in *The Black Messiah*, published in 1969. Reverend Cleage changed the name of his church in Detroit to the Shrine of the Black Madonna and insisted, in the tradition of Marcus Garvey's church, that God and the Madonna were black.

THE BLACK PANTHER PARTY

The Black Panther party, founded in 1966 by two Oakland, California, blacks, Huey Newton and Bobby Seale, seemed at first to be a black nationalist organization. Newton and Seale drew on the writings of Frantz Fanon and Malcolm X as the basis of their program:

1. We want freedom. We want power to determine the destiny of our Black Community.
2. We want full employment for our people.
3. We want an end to the robbery by the capitalists of our Black Community.
4. We want decent housing, fit for shelter of human beings.
5. We want education for people that exposes the true nature of this decadent American society. We want education that

teaches us our true history and our role in the present-day society.

6. We want all black men to be exempt from military service.
7. We want an immediate end to POLICE BRUTALITY and MURDER of black people.
8. We want freedom for all black men held in federal, state, county and city prisons and jails.
9. We want all black people when brought to trial to be tried in court by a jury of their peer group or people from their black communities, as defined by the Constitution of the United States.
10. We want land, bread, housing, education, clothing, justice, and peace. And as our major political objective, a United Nations-supervised plebiscite to be held throughout the black colony in which only black colonial subjects will be allowed to participate, for the purpose of determining the will of black people as to their national destiny.

The party's major initial objective was organization of the black community against police brutality and harassment; armed Black Panthers followed police cars patrolling Oakland's black districts and took pictures of every arrest. Another disciple of Malcolm X, former prisoner and senior editor of *Ramparts* magazine, Eldridge Cleaver, joined the party in 1967. Cleaver, author of the popular *Soul on Ice* (1962), became the party's major theoretician. Constantly referring to the police as "pigs," the Panthers called upon black colonials in America to join with white revolutionaries to overthrow the American government. By 1969 they had adopted Marxist-Leninism.

AFRICA AND BLACK NATIONALISTS

Most of the nationalistic movements during this period evinced some interest in Africa. Malcolm X called on African states in 1964 to protest the treatment of black Americans in the United Nations and asserted that spiritually and culturally black Americans had to return to Africa. Blacks formed the American Negro Leadership Conference on Africa in 1962 to force the United States into an anticolonial stance on imperialism in Africa. The director of the conference, Theodore Brown, tried unsuccessfully in 1967 to end the civil war in Nigeria. And in the same year, the Rev. Floyd McKissick, head of CORE, called on Congress to train black Americans to provide technical skills for African nations. A year later, blacks in East Palo Alto, California, tried to change the name of the town to Nairobi, and soon there was the emergence of Charles Kenyata's Harlem Mau Mau, New York's Yoruba Temple, Ron

Karenga's U.S., and Stokely Carmichael's Pan Africanism. On college campuses, militant black student groups became commonplace. They insisted on courses in black studies, admission of more black students, employment of more black faculty and staff, and separate living and extracurricular facilities on some campuses.

By 1970 whites had begun to feel that black nationalist organizations (and especially the Black Panthers) were dangerous and subversive. The police and FBI systematically attacked and killed members of the Black Panther party, harassed the Black Muslims, and increased surveillance, wiretapping, and infiltration of other groups. The concerted effort to destroy the effectiveness of these organizations was successful. The major casualty of the campaign was the Black Panther party. By 1975 its chief spokesmen, Eldridge Cleaver, Bobby Seale, and Huey Newton, were either in exile, immersed in traditional politics, or had turned to creative writing.

As black nationalist organizations were cut down by police, by surveillance, and by leaders being forced into exile, despair set in in the black community. Black intellectuals began to search for a new ideological direction and a new base from which to operate. By 1974, Angela Davis, Imamu Amiri Baraka, Ron Karenga, S. E. Anderson, and Howard Fuller (Owusu Sadawki) were espousing Marxist-Leninist philosophy and accusing traditional black nationalists of being unscientific in neglecting the primary causes of black oppression—economic and class exploitation.

When the sixth Pan-African Congress convened in Tanzania in the summer of 1974, most speakers argued that the way to liberate black people was the adoption of the philosophy of scientific socialism. American black Marxist-Leninists contended that Afro-Americans would be liberated only when white workers united with them in overthrowing the capitalist system and that black capitalists are as bad as white capitalists. Other black nationalists agreed that a socialist revolution was necessary but despaired of overcoming the racism of white workers. They insisted that black people could be liberated only by their own efforts.

Increasingly the liberation of southern Africa dominated black nationalist thought. Afro-Americans celebrated the victory of freedom fighters in Mozambique and Angola when guerrillas defeated the American-supported Portuguese army and the independence of Zimbabwe in 1980. Then they began arranging a spate of marches, demonstrations and conferences in support of their oppressed brothers and sisters in South Africa and Namibia. Though few Afro-Americans joined guerrillas fighting in Namibia and South Africa, they clearly viewed African liberation as the next assignment in their historic mission to the land of their mothers and fathers.

Bibliography

In addition to the materials in the bibliographies for each chapter, there are several reference tools in black history available. James M. McPherson et al., *Blacks in America: Bibliographical Essays* (Garden City, 1971); Dorothy B. Porter, *The Negro in the United States: A Selected Bibliography* (Cambridge, 1966) are useful, in addition to Monroe N. Work, *A Bibliography of the Negro in Africa and America* (New York, 1928). For those interested in narrative versions of Afro-American history, John Hope Franklin, *From Slavery to Freedom* (New York, 1979); August Meier and Elliott Rudwick, *From Plantation to Ghetto* (New York, 1966); Benjamin Quarles, *The Negro in the Making of America* (New York, 1964); Lerone Bennett, *Before the Mayflower* (New York, 1969), and Philip Foner, *A History of Black Americans* (Westport, Conn., 1975) are readily available and contain bibliographies.

Students wishing to explore literary and cultural history should consult: Theresa G. Rush et al., *The Black Writers Past and Present* (Metuchen, N.J., 1975); Geraldine O. Matthews, *Black American Writers, 1773–1949: A Bibliography and Union List* (Boston, 1975); Anne Powers, *Blacks in American Movies: A Selected Bibliography* (Metuchen, N.J., 1974); Abby A. Johnson and Ronald M. Johnson, *Propaganda and Aesthetics: The Literary Politics of Afro-American Magazines In the Twentieth Century* (Amherst, Mass., 1979); Edward Margolies and David Bakish, *Afro-American Fiction, 1853–1976: A Guide to Information Sources* (Detroit, 1979); William French et al., *Afro-American Poetry and Drama, 1760–1975: A Guide to Information Sources* (Detroit, 1979); and Jessamine S. Kallenbach, *Index to Black American Literary Anthologies* (Boston, 1979). Although there are no adequate bibliographies or location guides for black magazines and newspapers, many of the journals consulted for this book can be found in Armistead Pride, "A Register and History of Negro Newspapers in the United States: 1827–1950" (Ph.D. dissertation, Northwestern University, 1950) and Warren Brown, *Checklist of Negro Newspapers in the United States (1827–1946)* (Jefferson City, Mo., 1946).

1. AFRICA, SLAVERY, AND THE SHAPING OF BLACK CULTURE

Albanese, Anthony G. *The Plantation School.* New York, 1976.

Aptheker, Herbert. *American Negro Slave Revolts.* New York, 1943.

Argyle, W. J. *The Fon of Dahomey.* Oxford, 1966.

Berry, Mary Frances. *Black Resistance/White Law: A History of Constitutional Racism in America.* New York, 1971.

Berry, J. *Spoken Art in West Africa.* London, 1961.

Blassingame, John W. *The Slave Community: Plantation Life in the Ante-Bellum South.* New York, 1979.

———, ed. *Slave Testimony: Letters, Speeches, Interviews, and Autobiographies, 1736–1938.* Baton Rouge, La., 1977.

Brewer, J. Mason, ed. *American Negro Folklore.* Chicago, 1968.

Christensen, A. M. H. *Afro-American Folklore.* Boston, 1892.

Courlander, Harold. *Negro Folk Music, U.S.A.* New York, 1963.

Curtin, Philip D. *The Atlantic Slave Trade: A Census.* Madison, Wis., 1969.

Davis, David B. *The Problem of Slavery in Western Culture.* Ithaca, N.Y., 1966.

Debrunner, H. *Witchcraft in Ghana.* Kumasi, 1959.

Degler, Carl. *Neither Black Nor White.* New York, 1971.

Dorson, Richard M. *American Negro Folktales.* New York, 1967.

———, ed. *Negro Folktales in Michigan.* Cambridge, Mass., 1956.

Dundes, Alan, ed. *Mother Wit from the Laughing Barrel.* Englewood Cliffs, N.J., 1973.

Elkins, Stanley. *Slavery: A Problem in American Institutional and Intellectual Life.* Chicago, 1959.

Ellis, Alfred Burdon. *The Tshi Speaking People of the Gold Coast.* London, 1887.

Fogel, Robert W., and Engerman, Stanley L. *Time on the Cross; the Economics of American Negro Slavery.* Boston, 1974.

Fortier, Alcée, collector and ed. *Louisiana Folk-Tales in French Dialect and English Translation.* Boston, 1895.

Freyre, Gilberto. *The Masters and the Slaves.* New York, 1946.

Genovese, Eugene. *Roll, Jordan, Roll: The World the Slaves Made.* New York, 1974.

———. *From Rebellion to Revolution: Afro-American Slave Revolts in the Making of the Modern World.* Baton Rouge, 1979.

Gerber, A. "Uncle Remus Traced to the Old World." *Journal of American Folklore* 6 (October–December, 1893):245–57.

Georgia Writers Program. *Drums and Shadows: Survival Studies Among the Georgia Coastal Negroes.* Athens, Ga., 1940.

Goldin, Claudia Dale. *Urban Slavery in the American South, 1820–1860: A Quantitative History.* Chicago, 1976.

Hall, Gwendolyn M. *Social Control in Slave Plantation Societies.* Boston, 1971.

Harris, Joel Chandler. *Nights with Uncle Remus.* Boston, 1883.

———. *Mingo and Other Sketches in Black and White.* Boston, 1884.

———. *Uncle Remus: His Songs and Sayings.* Boston, 1892.

———. *Uncle Remus and His Friends.* Boston, 1899.

Harris, Joseph E. *Africans and Their History.* New York, 1972.

Herskovits, Melville. *The Myth of the Negro Past.* New York, 1941.

Herzog, George. *Jabo Proverbs from Liberia.* London, 1936.

Huggins, Nathan. *Black Odyssey: The Afro-American Ordeal in Slavery.* New York, 1977.

Jablow, Alta. *An Anthology of West African Folklore.* London, 1961.

Johnston, H. A. S., comp. *A Selection of Hausa Stories.* Oxford, 1966.

Jones, Charles C., Jr. *Negro Myths of the Georgia Coast.* Boston, 1881.

Junod, Henry Philippe, and Alexandre A. Jacques. *The Wisdom of the Tonga-Shangaan People.* Pretoria, 1936.

Knight, Franklin W. *Slave Society in Cuba During the Nineteenth Century.* Madison, Wis., 1970.

Lewis, Ronald L. *Coal, Iron, and Slaves: Industrial Slavery in Maryland and Virginia, 1715–1865.* Westport, Conn., 1979.

Little, Kenneth. *The Mende of Sierra Leone.* London, 1951.

Meaders, Daniel E. "South Carolina Fugitives as Viewed Through Local Colonial Newspapers with Emphasis on Runaway Notices, 1732–1801." *Journal of Negro History* 60 (April, 1975):288–319.

Meek, Charles K. *The Northern Tribes of Nigeria.* 2 vols. London, 1925.

Mullin, Gerald. *Flight and Rebellion: Slave Resistance in Eighteenth Century Virginia.* New York, 1972.

Mullin, Michael G., ed. *American Negro Slavery: A Documentary History.* Columbia, S.C., 1976.

Nichols, Charles H. *Many Thousand Gone.* Leiden, 1963.

Nyembezi, C. L. *Zulu Proverbs.* Johannesburg, 1963.

Owen, William, "Folklore of the Southern Negro." *Lippincott's Magazine* 20 (December, 1877):748–55.

Owens, Leslie H. *This Species of Property.* New York, 1976.

Phillips, Ulrich B. *American Negro Slavery.* New York, 1918.

Rattray, R. S. *Ashanti Law and Constitution.* Oxford, 1929.

Rawick, George. *From Sundown to Sunup.* Westport, Conn., 1972.

Sheridan, Richard H. *Sugar and Slavery: An Economic History of the British West Indies, 1623–1775.* Baltimore, 1973.

Sobel, Mechal. *Trabelin On: The Slave Journey to an Afro-Baptist Faith.* Westport, Conn., 1979.

Stampp, Kenneth. *The Peculiar Institution.* New York, 1956.

Stein, Stanley. *Vassouras.* Cambridge, 1957.

Talbot, P. Amaury. *Tribes of the Niger Delta.* London, 1932.

Tannenbaum, Frank. *Slave and Citizen.* New York, 1947.

Thomas, Northcote. *Anthropological Report of the Edo-Speaking People of Nigeria.* London, 1910.

———. *Law and Custom of the Ibo.* London, 1914.

———. *Law and Custom of the Timne and Other Tribes.* London, 1916.

Thorpe, Earl E. *The Old South: A Psychohistory.* Durham, N.C., 1972.

Van Deburg, William L. *The Slave Drivers: Black Agricultural Labor Supervisors in the Antebellum South.* Westport, Conn., 1979.

Wade, Richard. *Slavery in the Cities: The South, 1820–1860.* New York, 1964.

Webber, Thomas L. *Deep Like the Rivers: Education in the Slave Quarter Community, 1831–1865.* New York, 1978.

Williams, Chancellor. *The Destruction of Black Civilization: Great Issues of a Race from 4500 B.C. to 2000 A.D.* Chicago, 1974.

Wood, Peter. *Black Majority: Negroes in Colonial South Carolina from 1670 Through the Stono Rebellion.* New York, 1974.

Woodson, Carter G. *Free Negro Heads of Families in the United States in*

1830, Together with a Brief Treatment of the Free Negro. Washington, D.C., 1925.

2. AN UNSECURE PEOPLE: FREE NEGROES IN AMERICA

Asher, Jeremiah. *An Autobiography.* Philadelphia, 1862.
Bartlett, Irving H. *From Slave to Citizen: The Story of the Negro in Rhode Island.* Providence, R.I., 1954.
Bell, Howard H. "Negroes in California, 1849–1859." *Phylon* 28 (Summer, 1967):151–60.
————, ed. *Minutes of the Proceedings of the National Negro Conventions, 1830–1864.* New York, 1969.
Berlin, Ira. *Slaves Without Masters: The Free Negro in the Antebellum South.* New York, 1974.
Berwanger, Eugene H. "The 'Black Law' Question in Ante-Bellum California." *Journal of the West* 6 (April, 1967):205–20.
Birnie, C. W. "The Education of the Negro in Charleston, South Carolina, Before the Civil War." *Journal of Negro History* 12 (January, 1927):13–21.
Bracey, John H., et al., eds. *Free Blacks in America, 1800–1860.* Belmont, Calif., 1971.
Brown, William Wells. *Clotel; or, the President's Daughter: A Narrative of Slave Life in the United States.* London, 1853.
Brown, William Wells. *The Escape; or, A Leap for Freedom.* Boston, 1858.
Coppin, Levi J. *Unwritten History.* New York, 1916.
Cuffee, Paul. *Narrative of the Life and Adventure of Paul Cuffee.* Vernon, Mass., 1839.
Delany, Martin R. *Blake; or, the Huts of America.* Boston, 1970.
Dick, Robert. *Black Protest: Issues and Tactics.* Westport, Conn., 1974.
Fischer, Roger A. "Racial Segregation in Ante Bellum New Orleans." *American Historical Review* 84 (February, 1969):926–37.
Foote, Julia A. J. *A Brand Plucked from the Fire.* Cleveland, 1879.
Fox, Dixan R. "The Negro Vote in Old New York." *Political Science Quarterly* 32 (June, 1917):252–75.
Freeman, Rhoda G. "The Free Negro in New York City in the Era Before the Civil War." Ph.D. dissertation, Columbia University, 1968.
Garnet, Henry Highland. *An Address to the Slaves of the United States.* Buffalo, 1843.
Garvin, Russell. "The Free Negro in Florida Before the Civil War." *Florida Historical Quarterly* 46 (July, 1967):1–17.
Gibbs, Miflin W. *Shadow and Light.* New York, 1902.
Green, John P. *Fact Stranger than Fiction.* Cleveland, 1920.
Harrison, Samuel. *Rev. Samuel Harrison: His Life Story.* Pittsfield, Mass., 1899.
Huggins, Nathan I. *Slave and Citizen: The Life of Frederick Douglass.* Boston, 1980.
Jackson, Luther P. "Free Negroes of Petersburg, Virginia." *Journal of Negro History* 12 (July, 1927):365–88.
Jacobs, Donald M. "A History of the Boston Negro from the Revolution to the Civil War." Ph.D. dissertation, Boston University, 1968.
Kennicott, Patrick C. "Negro Antislavery Speakers in America." Ph.D. dissertation, Florida State University, Tallahassee, 1967.

————. "Black Persuaders in the Antislavery Movement." *Speech Monographs* 27 (March, 1970):15–24.

Langston, John Mercer. *From the Virginia Plantation to the National Capital.* Hartford, Conn., 1894.

Lapp, Rudolph M. *Blacks in Gold Rush California.* New Haven, Conn., 1977.

Levesque, George A. "Black Abolitionists in the Age of Jackson: Catalysts in the Radicalization of American Abolitionism." *Journal of Black Studies* 1 (December, 1970):187–202.

Levy, John. *The Life and Adventures of John Levy.* Lawrence, Mass., 1871.

Lindsay, Arnett G. "The Economic Condition of the Negroes of New York Prior to 1861." *Journal of Negro History* 6 (April, 1921):190–99.

Litwack, Leon F. *North of Slavery: The Negro in the Free States, 1790–1860.* Chicago, 1961.

Magee, J. H. *The Night of Affliction and Morning of Recovery.* Cincinnati, 1873.

Malvin, John. *North Into Freedom: The Autobiography of John Malvin, Free Negro, 1795–1880.* Cleveland, 1966.

Marrant, John. *A Narrative of the Lord's Wonderful Dealings with John Marrant, a Black.* London, 1802.

Mix, Mrs. Edward. *In Memory of Departed Worth.* Torrington, Conn., 1884.

Offley, G. W. *A Narrative of the Life and Labors of the Rev. G. W. Offley, a Colored Man.* Hartford, Conn., 1860.

Payne, Daniel A. *Recollections of Seventy Years.* Nashville, 1888.

Pease, Jane, and William H. Pease. *They Who Would be Free: Blacks' Search for Freedom.* New York, 1974

Peterson, Daniel H. *The Looking Glass.* New York, 1854.

Prince, Nancy. *A Narrative of the Life and Times of Mrs. Nancy Prince.* Boston, 1850.

Quarles, Benjamin. *Frederick Douglass.* Washington, D.C., 1948.

————. *Black Abolitionists.* New York, 1969.

Russell, John H. "Colored Freemen as Slave Owners in Virginia." *Journal of Negro History* 1 (July, 1916):233–42.

Smith, Amanda. *An Autobiography.* Chicago, 1893.

Still, James. *Early Recollections and Early Life of Dr. James Still.* Philadelphia, 1877.

Sydnor, Charles S. "The Free Negro in Mississippi Before the Civil War." *American Historical Review* 23 (July, 1927):769–88.

Thornbrough, Emma Lou. *The Negro in Indiana: A Study of a Minority.* Indianapolis, 1957.

Wade, Richard. "The Negro in Cincinnati, 1800–1830." *Journal of Negro History* 39 (January, 1954):43–57.

Walker, David. *Walker's Appeal, in Four Articles, Together with a Preamble to the Colored Citizens of the World, But in Particular, and Very Expressly to Those of the United States of America. Written in Boston, in the State of Massachusetts, Sept. 28th, 1829.* Boston, 1829.

Walker, Peter. *Moral Choices: Memory, Desire, and Imagination in Nineteenth-Century American Abolition.* Baton Rouge, 1978.

Ward, Samuel Ringgold. *Autobiography of a Fugitive Negro.* London, 1855.

Wesley, Charles H. "The Negro's Struggle for Freedom in Its Birthplace." *Journal of Negro History* 30 (January, 1945):62–81.

————. "Negro Suffrage in the Period of Constitution-Making." *Journal of Negro History* 28 (April, 1947):143–68.

Wilson, Calvin D. "Black Masters: A Side Light on Slavery." *North American Review* 181 (November, 1905):685–98.

Woodson, Carter G. "The Negroes of Cincinnati Prior to the Civil War." *Journal of Negro History* 1 (July, 1916):1–22.

————, ed. *The Mind of the Negro as Reflected in Letters Written During the Crisis, 1800–1860.* Washington, D.C., 1926.

Woolfolk, George R. "Turner's Safety-Valve and Free Negro Westward Migration." *Journal of Negro History* 50 (July, 1965):185–97.

3. FAMILY AND CHURCH: ENDURING INSTITUTIONS

Baker, Thomas Nelson. "The Negro Woman." *Alexander's Magazine* 3 (December, 1906):71–85.

Barrett, Leonard F. *Soul-Force.* Garden City, N.Y., 1974.

Bell, Robert R. "Lower Class Negro Mothers' Aspirations for Their Children." *Social Forces* 43 (May, 1965):493–500.

Bernard, Jessie. *Marriage and Family Life Among Negroes.* Englewood Cliffs, N.J., 1966.

Billingsley, Andrew. *Black Families in White America.* Englewood Cliffs, N.J., 1966.

"The Black Family." *The Black Scholar* 5 (June, 1974): whole issue.

"The Black Woman, 1975." *The Black Scholar* 6 (March, 1975): whole issue.

Blassingame, John W. *Black New Orleans, 1860–1880.* Chicago, 1973.

Brink, William J., and Harris, Louis. *The Negro Revolution in America; What Negroes Want, Why and How They are Fighting, Whom They Support, What Whites Think of Them and Their Demands.* New York, 1963.

Bruce, Philip A. *The Plantation Negro as a Freeman; Observations on His Character, Condition, and Prospects in Virginia.* New York, 1889.

Burkett, Randall. *Black Redemption: Churchmen Speak for the Garvey Movement.* Philadelphia, 1978.

Carson, Josephine. *Silent Voices; the Southern Negro Woman Today.* New York, 1969.

Childs, John Brown. *The Political Black Minister: A Study in Afro-American Politics and Religion.* Boston, 1980.

"The Colson Family." *Negro History Bulletin* 10 (October, 1946):3–9.

"The Cook Family in History." *Negro History Bulletin* 9 (June, 1946):195–96, 213–15.

Daniel, Constance E. H. "Two North Carolina Families—The Harrises and the Richardsons." *Negro History Bulletin* 13 (October, 1949):3–12, 14, 23.

Davis, Arthur P. "William Roscoe Davis and His Descendants." *Negro History Bulletin* 13 (January, 1950):75–89, 95.

De Rachervity, Boris. *Black Eros.* New York, 1964.

Douglass, Fannie H. "The David T. Howard Family." *Negro History Bulletin* 17 (December, 1953):51–55.

Du Bois, William Edward Burghardt. *The Philadelphia Negro.* Philadelphia, 1899.

————. *The Negro American Family.* Atlanta, Ga., 1909.

"The Family of Porter William Phillips, Sr." *Negro History Bulletin* 27 (January, 1964):81–84.

Fauset, Arthur Huff. *Black Gods of the Metropolis.* Philadelphia, 1944.

Fordham, Monroe. *Major Themes in Northern Black Religious Thought, 1800–1860.* Hicksville, N.Y., 1975.

"The Forten Family." *Negro History Bulletin* 10 (January, 1947):75–78, 95.

Frazier, E. F. "Three Scourges of the Negro Family." *Opportunity* 4 (July, 1926):210–13, 234.

———. "Family Disorganization Among Negroes." *Opportunity* 9 (July, 1931):204–7.

———. *The Negro Family in Chicago.* Chicago, 1932.

———. *The Negro Family in the United States.* Chicago, 1939.

Gaines, Ernest J. *The Autobiography of Miss Jane Pittman.* New York, 1971.

Genovese, Eugene D. *Roll, Jordan, Roll: The World the Slaves Made.* New York, 1974.

Graham, Irene. "The Negro Family in a Northern City." *Opportunity* 8 (February, 1930):48–51.

Gutman, Herbert G. *The Black Family in Slavery and Freedom, 1750–1925.* New York, 1976.

Harley, Sharon, and Rosalyn Terborg-Penn, eds. *The Afro-American Woman: Struggles and Images.* Port Washington, N.Y., 1978.

Hays, William, and Mendel, Charles H. "Extended Kinship Relations in Black and White Families." *Journal of Marriage and the Family* 35 (February, 1973):51–57.

Henri, Florette. *Black Migration: Movement North, 1900–1920.* Garden City, N.Y., 1975.

Hilton, Bruce. *The Delta Ministry.* London, 1969.

Insley-Casper, R. "The Negro Unmarried Mother in New York." *Opportunity* 12 (June, 1934):172–73.

Jackson, Luther P. "The Daniel Family of Virginia." *Negro History Bulletin* 11 (December, 1947):51–58.

Johnson, Everett. "A Study of the Negro Families in the Pinewood Avenue District of Toledo, Ohio." *Opportunity* 7 (August, 1929):243–45.

Johnson, Willa D., and Green, Thomas L., eds. *Perspectives on Afro-American Women.* Washington, D.C., 1975.

"The Johnson Family." *Negro History Bulletin* 12 (November, 1948):27–28.

Killens, John O. *Youngblood.* New York, 1954.

King, Earl. "A Comparison of Negro and White Family Power Structure in Low-Income Families." *Child and Family* 6 (Spring, 1967):65–74.

———. "Adolescent Perception of Power Structure in the Negro Family." *Journal of Marriage and the Family.* 31 (November, 1969):751–55.

Kiser, Clyde V. "Diminishing Family Income in Harlem." *Opportunity* 13 (June, 1935):171–73.

Kuyk, Betty M. "Seeking Family Relationships." *Negro History Bulletin* 42 (July–September, 1979):60.

Ladner, Joyce. *Tomorrow's Tomorrow: The Black Woman.* Garden City, N.Y., 1971.

Lantz, Herman R., et al. "The American Family in the Preindustrial Period: From Base Lines in History to Change." *American Sociological Review* 40 (February, 1975):21–36.

"The Leary Family." *Negro History Bulletin* 10 (November, 1946):27–34, 47.

"The Lees from Gouldtown." *Negro History Bulletin* 10 (February, 1947):99–100, 108, 119.

"The Loguen Family." *Negro History Bulletin* 10 (May, 1947):171–74, 191.

Mercer, Daniel A. "The Lovetts of Harpers Ferry, West Virginia." *Negro History Bulletin* 32 (February, 1969):14–19.

Miller, M. Sammye. "Portrait of A Black Urban Family." *Negro History Bulletin* 42 (April–June, 1979):50–51.

"More About the Tanner Family." *Negro History Bulletin* 10 (May, 1947):175–76, 189.

Moynihan, Daniel P. *The Negro Family: The Case for National Action.* Washington, D.C., 1965.

Mulligan, William H., Jr. "The Pressure of Uncertain Freedom: A Documentary Note on the Antebellum Black Family." *Negro History Bulletin* 42 (December, 1979):107.

Nelson, Hart M., and Nelson, Anne K. *Black Church in the Sixties.* Lexington, Ky., 1975.

Palosaari, Ronald G. "The Image of the Black Minister in the Black Novel from Dunbar to Baldwin." Ph.D. dissertation, University of Minnesota, 1970.

Paris, Peter J. *Black Leaders in Conflict: Joseph H. Jackson, Martin Luther King, Jr., Malcolm X, Adam Clayton Powell, Jr.* New York, 1978.

Parker, Seymour, and Kleiner, Robert J. "Characteristics of Negro Mothers in Single-Headed Households." *Journal of Marriage and the Family* 28 (November, 1966):507–13.

——. "Social and Psychological Dimensions of the Family Role Performance of the Negro Male." *Journal of Marriage and the Family* 31 (August, 1969):500–506.

Pope, Hallowell. "Unwed Mothers and Their Sex Partners." *Journal of Marriage and the Family* 29 (August, 1967):187–93.

Radin, Norma, and Kamii, Constance K. "The Child-Rearing Attitudes of Disadvantaged Negro Mothers and Some Educational Implications." *Journal of Negro Education* 34 (Spring, 1965):138–46.

Rainwater, Lee. "Crucible of Identity: The Negro Lower-Class Family." *Daedalus* 95 (Winter, 1968):258–64.

Reiss, Ira. *The Social Context of Premarital Sexual Permissiveness.* New York, 1967.

Robinson, Henry S. "The Descendants of Daniel and Hannah Bruce." *Negro History Bulletin* 24 (November, 1960):37–41.

Schulz, David. *Coming up Black: Patterns of Ghetto Socialization.* Englewood Cliffs, N.J., 1969.

Sheeler, J. Reuben. "The Nabrit Family." *Negro History Bulletin* 20 (October, 1956):3–9.

Staples, Robert, ed. *The Black Family: Essays and Studies.* Belmont, Calif., 1971.

"The Tanner Family." *Negro History Bulletin* 10 (April, 1947):147–54, 167.

TenHouten, Warren. "The Black Family: Myth and Reality." *Psychiatry* 33 (May, 1970):145–73.

Tucker, David M. *Black Pastors and Leaders: Memphis, 1819–1972.* Memphis, Tenn., 1975.

Turner, Lucie Mae. "The Family of Nat Turner, 1831 to 1954." *Negro History Bulletin* 18 (March, April, 1955):127–32, 145, 155–58.

Turner, Lucie Mae, and Fannie V. Turner. "The Story of Nat Turner's Descendants." *Negro History Bulletin* 10 (April, 1947):155, 164–65.

Vacheenas, Jean, and Betty Volk. "Born in Bondage: History of a Slave Family."
    Negro History Bulletin 36 (May, 1973):101–106.
Willie, Charles V. *A New Look at Black Families*. Bayside, N.Y., 1976.
Wilmore, Gayraud S. *Black Religion and Black Radicalism*. Garden City, N.Y.,
    1972.
Wilson, Dwight H. "John H. Burrus and His Family." *Negro History Bulletin*
    12 (October, 1948):3, 15, 23.
Woodson, Carter G. "The Record of the Clements." *Negro History Bulletin*
    9 (June, 1946):197–200.
———. "The Gibbs Family." *Negro History Bulletin* 11 (October, 1947):3–
    12, 22.
———. "Robert Smalls and His Descendants." *Negro History Bulletin* 11 (No-
    vember, 1947):27–33, 46.
———. "The Wormley Family." *Negro History Bulletin* 11 (January, 1948):
    75–84.
———. "The Waring Family." *Negro History Bulletin* 11 (February, 1948):99–
    107.
———. "The Cuney Family." *Negro History Bulletin* 11 (March, 1948):123–25,
    143.
———. "Alice Victoria Weston and Her Family." *Negro History Bulletin* 11
    (June, 1948):195–98.
Wright, Richard. *Black Boy; a Record of Childhood and Youth*. (New York
    and London, 1945).
———. *Uncle Tom's Children*. New York, 1938.

4. SEX AND RACISM

Allen, William G. *The American Prejudice Against Color*. London, 1853.
"Are Interracial Homes Bad for Children?" *Ebony* 18 (March, 1963):131–38.
Benedict, Steve. "Dark Are My Roots." *Negro Digest* 9 (November, 1950):
    44–49.
Bennett, Lerone. "Miscegenation in America." *Ebony* 17 (October, 1962):94–
    104.
Bernard, Jesse. "Note on Homogany in Negro-White and White-Negro Mar-
    riages." *Journal of Marriage and the Family* 28 (August, 1966):274–76.
Berry, Brewton. "Mestizos of South Carolina: White-Indian-Negro Hybrids."
    American Journal of Sociology 51 (July, 1945):34–41.
Booker, Simeon. "A Challenge for the Guy Smiths." *Ebony* 23 (December,
    1967):146–50.
Bourne, George. *Slavery Illustrated in Its Effects Upon Women and Domestic
    Society*. Boston, 1837.
Britt, May. "Why I Married Sammy Davis, Jr." *Ebony* 16 (January, 1961):97–
    102.
Brown, Letitia W. *Free Negroes in the District of Columbia, 1790–1846*. New
    York, 1972.
Burma, John H. "The Measurement of Negro Passing." *American Journal of
    Sociology* 52 (July, 1942):18–22.
———. "Research Note on the Measurement of Interracial Marriage." *Ameri-
    can Journal of Sociology* 57 (May, 1952):587–89.
———. "Interethnic Marriage in Los Angeles, 1948–1959." *Social Forces* 42
    (December, 1963):156–65.

Burroughs, Nannie H. "Not Color But Character." *Voice of the Negro* 1 (July, 1904):277–79.

Cain, Rheba. "Dark Lover." *Crisis* 36 (April, 1929):137–38.

Campbell, Jeanne. "This Is My Daughter." *Negro Digest* 14 (June, 1965): 83–85.

Campbell, John. *Negro-Mania: Being an Examination of the Falsely Assumed Equality of the Various Races of Men.* Philadelphia, 1851.

Cannon, Poppy. "Can Interracial Marriage Work?" *Ebony* 7 (June, 1952): 25–40.

——. "How We Erased Two Color Lines." *Ebony* 7 (July, 1952):47–58.

Carse, James P. "Interracial Marriage: A Christian View." *Christian Century* 84 (June 14, 1967):779–92.

Cash, Eugene. "A Study of Negro-White Marriages in the Philadelphia Area." Ph.D. dissertation, Temple University, 1956.

Cash, Wilbur J. *The Mind of the South.* New York, 1941.

Chenault, Lee. "How I Face the World With My Negro Child." *Ebony* 16 (December, 1960):54–64.

Cox, Earnest S. *White America.* Richmond, Va., 1923.

Davis, Sammy. "Is My Mixed Marriage Mixing Up My Kids?" *Ebony* 21 (October, 1966):124–32.

Day, Caroline Bond. *A Study of Some Negro-White Families in the United States.* Cambridge, Mass., 1932.

"Detroit's Most-Discussed Mixed Marriage." *Ebony* 8 (April, 1953):97–103.

Dollard, John. *Caste and Class in a Southern Town.* New Haven, 1937.

Du Bois, W. E. B. "Intermarriage." *Crisis* 5 (February, 1913):180–81.

Fortune, T. Thomas. "Intermarriage and Natural Selection." *Colored American Magazine* 16 (June, 1909):380–81.

Golden, Joseph. "Characteristics of the Negro-White Intermarried in Philadelphia." *American Sociological Review* 18 (April, 1953):177–83.

——. "Patterns of Negro-White Intermarriage." *American Sociological Review* 19 (April, 1954):144–47.

——. "Facilitating Factors in Negro-White Intermarriage." *Phylon* 20 (Fall, 1959):273–84.

——. "Social Control of Negro-White Intermarriage." *Social Forces* 36 (March, 1958):267–69.

Goosey, Margret May, and Johnson, Thomas Henry. "Till Law Us Do Part." *Newsweek* 31 (January 19, 1948):25–26.

Halsell, Grace. *Black-White Sex.* New York, 1972.

Harrisburg (Pa.) *State Journal* 15, 22 December, 1883; 5 January, 22 March, 26 April, 10 May, 28 June, 26 July, 13 September, 1884.

Heer, David M. "Negro-White Marriage in the United States." *Journal of Marriage and the Family* 28 (August, 1966):262–73.

Helper, Morris K. "Negroes and Crime in New Orleans, 1850–1861." M.A. thesis, Tulane University, 1960.

Heim, Oskar. "Why I Want a Negro Wife." *Negro Digest* 9 (July, 1951): 54–68.

Hernton, Calvin. *Sex and Racism in America.* Garden City, N.Y., 1965.

Holm, John J. *Holm's Race Assimilation.* Atlanta, Ga., 1901.

"Intermarriage and the Race Problem." *U.S. News and World Report* 55 (November 18, 1963):84–93.

"Interracial College Marriages." *Ebony* 9 (July, 1954):89–94.

Johnson, Caleb. "Crossing the Color Line." *Outlook* 158 (August 26, 1931): 526–43.
Johnson, Jack. "Does Interracial Marriage Succeed?" *Negro Digest* 3 (May, 1945):3–5.
Johnson, James Weldon. *The Autobiography of an Ex-colored Man*. Boston, 1912.
Johnston, James Hugo. *Race Relations in Virginia and Miscegenation in the South, 1776–1860*. Amherst, Mass., 1970.
Kennedy, Ruby J. "Single or Triple Melting Pot." *American Journal of Sociology* 49 (January, 1944):331–39.
Keyser, Charles S. *Minden Armais*. Philadelphia, 1892.
Kornhauser, Eberhard, and Kornhauser, Phyllis. *Pornography and the Law*. New York, 1964.
Larsson, Clotye M., ed. *Marriage Across the Color Line*. Chicago, 1965.
Lee, Reba, pseud. *I Passed for White*. New York, 1955.
Lewis, Anthony. "Race, Sex and the Supreme Court." *New York Times Magazine*, November 22, 1964, pp. 30, 130–34.
Lewis, Frank G. "The Demand for Race Integrity." *Voice of the Negro* 3 (December, 1906):564–74.
Lewis, Sinclair. *Kingsblood Royal*. New York, 1947.
"The Love that Never Died." *Ebony* 12 (January, 1957):17–22.
Lynn, Annella. "Some Aspects of Interracial Marriage in Washington, D.C." *Journal of Negro Education* 25 (Fall, 1956):380–91.
Massaquoi, Hans J. "Would You Want Your Daughter To Marry One?" *Ebony* 20 (August, 1965):82–90.
Mencke, John G. *Mulattoes and Race Mixture: American Attitudes and Images, 1865–1918*. Ann Arbor, Mich., 1979.
Murray, Daniel E. "Color Problem in the United States." *Colored American Magazine* 7 (December, 1904):719–24.
———. "Race Integrity—How To Preserve It in the South." *Colored American Magazine* 11 (December, 1906):369–77.
Musgrave, Marian E. "Triangles in Black and White: Interracial Hostility in Black Literature." *CLA Journal* 14 (June, 1971):444–51.
"My Daughter Married a Negro." *Harpers* 203 (July, 1951):36–40.
Myrdal, Gunnar. *An American Dilemma; the Negro Problem and Modern Democracy*. New York, 1944.
Pavela, Todd. "An Exploratory Study of Negro-White Intermarriage in Indiana." *Journal of Marriage and the Family* 26 (May, 1964):209–11.
Phillips, Cyrus E. "Miscegenation: The Courts and the Constitution." *William and Mary Law Review* 8 (Fall, 1966):133–42.
Porterfield, Ernest. "Mixed Marriage." *Psychology Today* 6 (January, 1973): 71–78.
Potter, Eliza. *A Hairdresser's Experience in High Life*. Cincinnati, 1859.
Rabinowitz, Howard N. *Race Relations in the Urban South, 1865–1890*. New York, 1978.
Rankin, John. *Letters on American Slavery Addressed to Mr. Thomas Rankin, Merchant of Augusta County, Virginia*. Newburyport, Mass., 1836.
Reuter, Edward B. *Race Mixture*. New York, 1931.
Robertson, Y. A. "Color Lines Among the Colored People." *Literary Digest* 72 (March 18, 1922):42–44.
Rogers, Joel A. *As Nature Leads*. Chicago, 1919.

———. *Sex and Race*. New York,. 1940.

Ross, Michelle. "Is Mixed Marriage Jinxed?" *Ebony* 18 (August, 1963):34–38.

Ruchames, Louis. "Race, Marriage and Abolition in Massachusetts." *Journal of Negro History* 40 (July, 1955):250–75.

Sampson, J. Milton. "The French and Racial Intermarriage." *The Messenger* 2 (October, 1920):111.

Scarborough, William S. "Race Integrity." *Voice of the Negro* 4 (May, 1907):197–202.

"School Integration Leads to Intermarriage." *The White Sentinel* 8 (September, 1958):1–2.

Schuhmann, George. "Miscegenation: An Example of Judicial Recidivism." *Journal of Family Law* 69 (Spring, 1968):69–78.

Schuyler, George. *Racial Intermarriage in the United States*. Girard, Kan., 1929.

Schuyler, Josephine. "17 Years of Mixed Marriage." *Negro Digest* 4 (July, 1946):61–65.

Seaman, L. *What Miscegenation Is: And What We Are To Expect Now that Mr. Lincoln Is Re-elected*. New York, 1864.

Shadrach, J. Shirley. "Black or White—Which Should Be the Young Afro-American's Choice in Marriage?" *Colored American Magazine* 6 (March, 1903): 348–52.

Shaffer, Helen B. "Mixed Marriage." *Editorial Research Reports* 1 (May 24, 1961):381–98.

"Shall We All Be Mulattoes?" *Literary Digest* 84 (March 7, 1925):23–24.

Shufeldt, Robert William. *The Negro, a Menace to American Civilization*. Boston, 1907.

———. *America's Greatest Problem, the Negro*. Philadelphia, 1915.

Stampp, Kenneth M. *The Peculiar Institution: Slavery in the Ante-bellum South*. New York, 1956.

Stuart, Irving R., and Abt, Lawrence E., eds. *Interracial Marriage: Expectations and Realities*. New York, 1973.

Teicher, Joseph D. "Some Observations on Identity Problems in Children of Negro-White Marriages." *Journal of Nervous and Mental Diseases* 146 (March, 1968):249–56.

"The Trials of an Interracial Couple." *Ebony* 20 (October, 1965):66–75.

Wade, Richard C. *Slavery in the Cities; the South, 1820–1860*. New York, 1964.

"Wanted: Negro Husbands and Wives." *Ebony* 6 (March, 1951):65–69.

Washington, Joseph R. *Marriage in Black and White*. Boston, 1970.

Weinberger, Andrew D. "Interracial Marriage in the U.S.A." *Crisis* 74 (March, 1967):68–71.

"Where Mixed Couples Live." *Ebony* 10 (May, 1955):61–66.

"A White Man's Daughter." *Crisis* 39 (March, 1932):89, 105.

Wood, Clement. *Sexual Relations in the Southern States*. Girard, Kan., 1929.

Woodson, Carter G. "The Beginnings of Miscegenation of Whites and Blacks." *Journal of Negro History* 3 (October, 1918):335–53.

5. BLACKS AND THE POLITICS OF REDEMPTION

"A Negro Millionaire's Advice to His Race." *U.S. News and World Report* (September 4, 1967):68–69.

Banfield, Edward C., and Wilson, James Q. *City Politics*. Cambridge, Mass., 1963.

Baron, Harold. "Black Powerlessness in Chicago." *Transaction* 6 (November, 1968):27–33.

Bartley, Numan V. "Atlanta Elections and Georgia Political Trends." *New South*, 25 (Winter, 1970):22–30.

Bartley, Numan V., and Graham, Hugh D. *Southern Politics and the Second Reconstruction*. Baltimore, 1975.

Bennett, Lerone, Jr. "The Politics of the Outsider."*Negro Digest* (July, 1968).

———. "Passion: A Certain Dark Joy." *Ebony* 24 (December, 1968):43–53.

"Black Voting Percentage Drops Lower than Whites." *Jet* 45 (December 13, 1973):26.

Boesel, David, et al. "White Institutions and Black Rage." *Transaction* 6 (March, 1969):24–31.

Booker, Simeon. "The New, New, New Negro, Esq." *Vital Speeches* 31 (November 1, 1964):53–55.

Brauer, Carl M. *John F. Kennedy and the Second Reconstruction*. New York, 1977.

Cartwright, David. "Political Futures and the Negro," *Crisis* 44 (June, 1937): 171–72.

Chambers, Ernest W. "We Have Marched, We Have Cried, We Have Prayed." *Ebony* 23 (April, 1968):29–36.

Church, Annette E., and Church, Roberta. *The Robert R. Churches of Memphis: A Father and Son Who Achieved in Spite of Race*. Ann Arbor, Mich., 1974.

Cornwell, Elmer E. "Bosses, Machines, and Ethic Groups." *Annals of the American Academy of Political and Social Sciences* 353 (May, 1964):27–39.

Cutler, John Henry. *Ed Brooke: Biography of a Senator*. New York, 1972.

Drake, St. Clair, and Clayton, Horace. *Black Metropolis: A Study of Negro Life in a Northern City*. New York, 1970.

Du Bois, W. E. B. *The Souls of Black Folk*. Chicago, 1903.

———. "Politics." *Crisis* 4 (August, 1912):180–81.

———. "How Shall We Vote?" *Crisis* 20 (September, 1920):213.

———. "Political Rebirth and the Office Seeker." *Crisis* 21 (January, 1921):104.

Foner, Eric. *Politics and Ideology in the Age of the Civil War*. New York, 1980.

Fortune, T. Thomas. "The Afro-American Political Giant With the Strength of a Child," *Colored American Magazine* 9 (December, 1905):675–79.

Frye, Hardy T. *Black Parties and Political Power: A Case Study*. Boston, 1980.

Gaither, Gerald H. *Blacks and the Populist Revolt: Ballots and Bigotry in the "New South."* University, Ala., 1977.

Garrow, David J. *Protest at Selma: Martin Luther King, Jr., and the Voting Rights Act of 1965*. New Haven, 1978.

Gillette, William. *Retreat From Reconstruction, 1869–1879*. Baton Rouge, 1979.

Gilliam, Reginald E. *Black Political Development: An Advocacy Analysis*. Port Washington, N.Y., 1975.

Glantz, Oscar. "Recent Negro Ballots in Philadelphia." *Journal of Negro Education* 28 (Fall, 1959):430–38.

———. "The Negro Voter in Northern Industrial Cities." *Western Political Quarterly* 13 (December, 1960):999–1010.

Gosnell, Harold F. *Negro Politicians*. Chicago, 1935.

Grossman, Lawrence. *The Democratic Party and the Negro: Northern and National Politics, 1868–92*. Urbana, Ill., 1976.

Hadden, Jeffrey K., et al. "The Making of the Negro Mayors, 1967." *Transaction* 5 (January–February, 1968):21–30.

Harris, William C. *The Day of the Carpetbagger: Republican Reconstruction in Mississippi*. Baton Rouge, 1979.

Harvey, James C. *Black Civil Rights During the Johnson Administration*. Jackson, Miss., 1973.

Hatcher, Richard G. "The Black Role in Urban Politics." *Current History* 57 (November, 1969):287–89, 306–7.

Haywood, Harry. *Black Bolshevik: Autobiography of an Afro-American Communist*. Chicago, 1978.

Hine, Darlene C. *Black Victory: The Rise and Fall of the White Primary in Texas*. Millwood, N.Y., 1979.

Holloway, Harry. "Negro Political Strategy: Coalition or Independent Power Politics?" *Social Science Quarterly* 49 (December, 1968):534–47.

Holt, Michael F. *The Political Crisis of the 1850s*. New York, 1978.

Holt, Thomas. *Black Over White: Negro Political Leadership in South Carolina during Reconstruction*. Urbana, Ill., 1977.

Johnson, James Weldon. "A Negro Looks at Politics." *American Mercury* 18 (September, 1929):88–94.

Jones, Eugene Kinkle. "The Negro and Civil Rights." *Opportunity* 2 (February, 1924):43.

Kilson, Martin. "From Civil Rights to Party Politics: The Black Political Transition." *Current History* 67 (November, 1974):193–99.

Kirby, John B. *Black Americans in the Roosevelt Era: Liberalism and Race*. Knoxville, Tenn., 1980.

Klingman, Peter D. *Josiah Walls: Florida's Black Congressman of Reconstruction*. Gainesville, Fla., 1976.

Lamon, Lester C. *Black Tennesseans, 1900–1930*. Knoxville, Tenn., 1977.

Lawson, Steven F. *Black Ballots: Voting Rights in the South, 1944–1969*. New York, 1976.

McLemore, Leslie B. "Toward a Theory of Black Politics—The Black and Ethnic Models Revisited." *Journal of Black Studies* 2 (March, 1972):323–31.

Meier, August. *Negro Thought in America, 1880–1915*. Ann Arbor, 1963.

Patterson, Beeman C. "Political Action of Negroes in Los Angeles: A Case Study in the Attainment of Councilmanic Representation." *Phylon* 30 (Summer, 1969):170–83.

Porter, Dorothy, ed. *Negro Protest Pamphlets, Early Negro Writing*. New York, 1969.

Riddleberger, Patrick W. *1866: The Critical Year Revisited*. Carbondale, Ill., 1979.

Schweninger, Loren. *James T. Rapier and Reconstruction*. Chicago, 1978.

Sears, David O. "Black Attitudes Toward the Political System in the Aftermath of the Watts Insurrection." *Midwest Journal of Political Science* 13 (November, 1969):515–44.

Sewell, Richard H. *Ballots for Freedom: Antislavery Politics in the United States, 1837–1860*. New York, 1976.

Shofner, Jerrell H. *Nor Is It Over Yet: Florida in the Era of Reconstruction, 1863–1877*. Gainesville, Fla., 1974.

"Southern Mayors Deal with Realities." *Jet* 45 (December 6, 1973):20–24.

Stone, Chuck. *Black Political Power in America.* New York, 1970.

Straker, D. Augustus. "No Negro Problem." *Colored American* 6 (May, 1903):413–21.

"Strictly Personal White Folks Are Easy to Please." *Saturday Review of Literature* 27 (November 25, 1944):12–13.

Tabb, William K. *The Political Economy of the Ghetto.* New York, 1970.

Tucker, David M. *Memphis Since Crump: Bossism, Blacks, and Civil Reformers, 1948–1968.* Knoxville, Tenn., 1980.

Walton, Hanes, Jr. *Black Political Parties.* New York, 1972.

———. *Black Politics.* Philadelphia, 1972.

Wilson, James Q. *Negro Politics.* Glencoe, Ill., 1960.

———. "Two Negro Politicians: An Interpretation." *Midwest Journal of Political Science* 4 (November, 1960):346–69.

Wolseley, Ronald E. *The Black Press, U.S.A.* Ames, Iowa, 1971.

Young, Richard. "The Impact of Protest Leadership on Negro Politicians in San Francisco." *Western Political Quarterly* 22 (March, 1969):94–111.

6. THE ECONOMICS OF HOPE AND DESPAIR

Abrams, Elliott. "Black Capitalism and Black Banks." *New Leader* 52 (March 17, 1969):14–16.

"Agrarian Work." *Party Organizer* 6 (August–September, 1933):80–82.

Aldridge, Dan. "Politics in Command of Economics." *Monthly Review* 21 (November, 1969):14–27.

Allen, Robert L. *Black Awakening in Capitalist America.* Garden City, N.Y., 1969.

America, Richard F. "What Do You People Want?" *Harvard Business Review* 47 (March–April, 1969):103–12.

Bates, Timothy M. *Black Capitalism: A Quantitative Analysis.* New York, 1973.

Becker, Gary S. *The Economics of Discrimination.* Chicago, 1957.

Block, Herman D. *The Circle of Discrimination.* New York, 1969.

Bluestone, Barry. "Black Capitalism: The Path to Black Liberation?" *Review of Radical Political Economics* 1 (May, 1969):36–55.

Boggs, James. *Racism and the Class Struggle.* New York, 1970.

Brimmer, Andrew F. "The Black Revolution and the Economic Future of Negroes in the United States." *American Scholar* 38 (Autumn, 1969): 629–42.

———. "Economic Integration and the Progress of the Black Community." *Ebony* 25 (August, 1970):118–21.

Burrell, W. P. "History of the Business of Colored Richmond." *Voice of the Negro* 1 (August, 1904):317–22.

"C. I. Resolution on Negro Question in U.S." *The Communist* 9 (January, 1930):48–55.

Crosswaith, Frank R. "The Trade Union Committee for Organizing Negroes." *The Messenger* 7 (August, 1925):296–97.

Daniel, Pete. *The Shadow of Slavery: Peonage in the South, 1901–1969.* Urbana, Ill., 1972.

DeCanio, Stephen J. *Agriculture in the Postbellum South: The Economics of Production and Supply.* Cambridge, Mass., 1974.

Denison, Edward F. *The Sources of Economic Growth in the United States and the Alternative Before Us.* Washington, 1962.

Domingo, W. A. "Socialism, the Negroes' Hope." *The Messenger* 2 (July, 1919):22.

————. "Private Property as a Pillar of Prejudice." *The Messenger* 2 (April–May, August, 1920):9–10, 69–71.

————. "A New Negro and a New Day." *The Messenger* 2 (November, 1920):144–45.

Du Bois, W. E. B. *The Souls of Black Folk.* Chicago, 1903.

————, ed. *The Negro in Business.* Atlanta, Ga., 1899.

Fein, Rashi. "An Economic and Social Profile of the Negro American." *Daedalus* 94 (Fall, 1965):815–46.

Foley, Eugene P. *The Achieving Ghetto.* Washington, 1968.

Foner, Philip S. *American Socialism and Black Americans: From the Age of Jackson to World War II.* Westport, Conn., 1977.

Ford, James W. "The Negro and the Struggle Against Imperialism." *The Communist* 9 (January, 1930):22–34.

Fortune, Timothy Thomas. *Black and White: Land, Labor, and Politics in the South.* New York, 1884.

Gallaway, Lowell E. "The Negro and Poverty." *Journal of Business* 40 (January, 1967):27–35.

Ginsberg, Eli. "Segregation and Manpower Waste." *Phylon* 21 (Winter, 1960): 311–16.

Gould, William B. *Black Workers in White Unions: Job Discrimination in the United States.* Ithaca, N.Y., 1977.

Haddad, William, and Pugh, C. Douglass, eds. *"Black Economic Development.* Englewood Cliffs, N.J., 1969.

Harrington, Michael. *The Other America: Poverty in the United States.* New York, 1962.

Haynes, Marion. "A Century of Change: Negroes in the U.S. Economy 1860–1960." *Monthly Labor Review* 85 (December, 1962):1359–65.

Henderson, Vivian W. *The Economic Status of Negroes: In the Nation and in the South.* Atlanta, Ga., 1963.

Holsey, Albion. "Seventy-five Years of Negro Business." *Crisis* 45 (July, 1938): 201, 241–42.

Huiswood, Otto E. "World Aspects of the Negro Question." *The Communist* 9 (February, 1930):132–47.

Hunt, Linda. "Nixon's Guaranteed Annual Poverty." *Ramparts* 8 (December, 1969):64–70.

"Is Socialism the Negro's Hope?" *Colored American Magazine* 9 (August, 1905):425–29.

Jackson, Jesse L. "Resurrection City: The Dream, The Accomplishments." *Ebony* 23 (October, 1968):65–69, 72–74.

Johnson, Charles S. "Negroes at Work in Baltimore, Md." *Opportunity* 1 (June, 1923):12–19.

————. "Negro Workers in Los Angeles Industries." *Opportunity* 6 (August, 1928):234–40.

Jones, Eugene K. "The Negro in Industry and in Urban Life." *Opportunity* 12 (May, 1934):141–44.

Kain, John F., ed. *Race and Poverty: The Economics of Discrimination.* Englewood Cliffs, N.J., 1969.

Kosa, J., and Nunn, C. Z. "Race, Deprivation, and Attitude Toward Communism." *Phylon* 25 (Winter, 1964):337–46.

Lane, R. E. "The Fear of Equality." *American Political Science Review* 53 (March, 1959):33–51.

Levitan, Sar A., Johnston, William B., and Taggert, Robert. *Still a Dream: The Changing Status of Blacks Since 1960.* Cambridge, Mass., 1975.

McLaurin, Melton A. *The Knights of Labor in the South.* Westport, Conn., 1978.

Magdol, Edward. *A Right to the Land: Essays on the Freedmen's Community.* Westport, Conn., 1977.

Malone, T. H. "Peonage—Its Works and Features." *Voice of the Negro* 3 (February, 1906):114–16.

Mandle, Jay R. *The Roots of Black Poverty: The Southern Plantation Economy After the Civil War.* Durham, N.C., 1978.

Marshall, Ray, and Christian, Virgil L., Jr., eds. *Employment of Blacks in the South: A Perspective on the 1960s.* Austin, Texas, 1978.

Miller, Herman Phillip. *Rich Man, Poor Man.* New York, 1964.

Minor, Robert. "The First Negro Workers' Congress." *The Communist* 5 (December, 1925):68–73.

"The Negro and the Social Order." *Voice of the Negro* 2 (February, 1905): 697–98.

"Negro Sharecroppers Building Their Union." *Party Organizer* 6 (January, 1933):14–16.

"Negroes Organizing in Socialist Party." *The Messenger* 2 (July, 1918):8–9.

Novak, Daniel. *The Wheel of Servitude: Black Forced Labor After Slavery.* Lexington, Ky., 1978.

Osthaus, Carl R. *Freedmen, Philanthropy and Fraud: A History of the Freedman's Savings Bank.* Urbana, Ill., 1976.

Oubre, Claude F. *Forty Acres and a Mule: The Freedmen's Bureau and Black Land Ownership.* Baton Rouge, 1978.

Owen, Chandler. "White Supremacy in Organized Labor." *The Messenger* 5 (September, 1923):810–11, 819.

Perlo, Victor. "Trends in the Economic Status of the Negro People." *Science and Society* 16 (Spring, 1952):115–50.

———. *Economics of Racism, USA: Roots of Black Inequality.* New York, 1975.

Ponder, Henry. "An Example of the Alternative Cost Doctrine Applied to Racial Discrimination." *Journal of Negro Education* 35 (Winter, 1966): 42–47.

Powdermaker, Hortense. "Education and Occupation Among New Haven Negroes." *Journal of Negro History* 23 (April, 1938):200–15.

Ransom, Reverdy C. "Socialism and the Negro." *Alexander's Magazine* 1 (May 15, 1905):15–16.

Ransom, Roger L., and Sutch, Richard. *One Kind of Freedom: The Economic Consequences of Emancipation.* Cambridge, Eng., 1977.

"Resolution on the Negro Question in the United States." *The Communist* 10 (February, 1931):153–67.

Ross, Arthur M., and Hill, Herbert, eds. *Employment, Race and Poverty.* New York, 1967.

Rustin, Bayard. "The Lessons of the Long Hot Summer." *Commentary* 44 (October, 1967):39–45.

Sawyer, Broadus. E. "An Examination of Race as a Factor in Negro-White Consumption Patterns." *Review of Economics and Statistics* 44 (May, 1962):217–20.

Schwartz, Michael. *Radical Protest and Social Structures: The Southern Farmers' Alliance and Cotton Tenancy, 1880–1890.* New York, 1976.

Siegel, Paul M. "On the Cost of Being a Negro." *Sociological Review* 35 (Winter, 1965):41–57.

Sommers, Montrose, and Bruce, Gladys D. "Blacks, Whites, and Products: Relative Deprivation and Reference Group Behavior." *Social Science Quarterly* 49 (December, 1968):631–42.

Sowell, Thomas. *Race and Economics.* New York, 1975.

Spaulding, C. C. "Business in Negro Durham." *Southern Workman* 66 (December, 1937):364–68.

Street, David, and Leggett, John C. "Economic Deprivation and Extremism: A Study of Unemployed Negroes." *American Journal of Sociology* 67 (July, 1961):53–57.

Sturdivant, Frederick D., and Wilhelm, Walter T. "Poverty, Minorities, and Consumer Exploitation." *Social Science Quarterly* 49 (December, 1968):642–50.

"A Trade Union Program of Action for Negro Workers." *The Communist* 9 (January, 1930):42–47.

"Why Is Socialism Necessary?" *Colored American Magazine* 9 (November, 1905):623–27.

"Why Negroes Should be Socialists." *The Messenger* 2 (October, 1919):15–16 and 2 (December, 1919):13–15.

Williams, Henry. *Black Response to the American Left, 1917–1919.* Princeton, N.J., 1973.

Willits, Joseph H. "Some Impacts of the Depression Upon the Negro in Philadelphia." *Opportunity* 11 (July, 1933):200–4.

Work, M. C. "Winning the Negroes in the Struggle Against Unemployment." *Party Organizer* 7 (April, 1934):4–7.

———. "A 'Turn to the Masses' in our Section Convention." *Party Organizer* 10 (September, 1937):22–25.

Wright, Gavin. *The Political Economy of the Cotton South: Households, Markets, and Wealth in the Nineteenth Century.* New York, 1978.

Wright, Nathan. "The Economics of Race." *American Journal of Economics and Sociology* 26 (January, 1967):1–12.

Wright, R. R. "Home Ownership and Savings among the Negroes of Philadelphia." *Southern Workman* 36 (December, 1907):665–76.

———. "Negroes in Business in the North." *Southern Workman* 38 (January, 1909):36–44.

———. The Negro Skilled Mechanic in the North." *Southern Workman* 38 (March, 1909):155–68.

———. "The Negro in the Professions in the North." *Southern Workman* 38 (April, 1909):237–45.

———. "The Economic Condition of Negroes in the North." *Southern Workman* 40 (December, 1911):700–9.

7. AMERICAN ARCHIPELAGO: BLACKS AND CRIMINAL JUSTICE

Alex, Nicholas. *Black in Blue: A Study of the Negro Policeman.* New York, 1969.

Alexander, Raymond Pace. "The Negro Lawyer and His Responsibility in the Urban Crisis." *Pennsylvania Bar Association Quarterly* 40 (June, 1969):585–92.

Alschuler, Albert W. "The Prosecutor's Role in Plea Bargaining." *University of Chicago Law Review* 36 (Fall, 1968):50–112.

"Arrest Records as a Racially Discriminatory Employment Criteria." *Harvard Civil Rights and Civil Liberties Law Review* 6 (December, 1970):165–78.

Attica: The Official Report of the New York State Special Commission on Attica. New York, 1972.

Baldwin, James. *Nobody Knows My Name; More Notes of a Native Son.* New York, 1961.

Bayley, David H., and Mendelsohn, Harold. *Minorities and the Police: Confrontation in America.* New York, 1969.

Bell, Derrick A., Jr. "Racism in American Courts: Cause for Black Disruption or Despair?" *California Law Review* 61 (January, 1973):165–203.

———. *Race, Racism, and American Law.* Boston, 1973.

Berry, Mary Frances. *Black Resistance/White Law: A History of Constitutional Racism in America.* New York, 1971.

Blackburn, Sara, ed. *White Justice: Black Experience Today in America's Courtrooms.* New York, 1971.

"Black Cop." *Newsweek,* August 4, 1969, p. 54.

"Blacks and the U.S. Criminal Justice System." *Journal of Afro-American Issues* (May, 1974).

Blakley, Robert Dwain. "Prisoner Rights." *American Journal of Criminal Law* 1 (Fall, 1972):104–8.

Bogle, Donald. "Black and Proud Behind Bars: Swahili and Soul Programs at Colorado Prison." *Ebony* 24 (August, 1969):64–66.

Broeder, Dale W. "Negro in Court." *Duke Law Journal* 1965 (Winter, 1965): 19–31.

Brown, Dulcey A. "Black Muslims in Prisons and Religious Discrimination: The Developing Criteria for Judicial Review." *George Washington Law Review* 32 (June, 1964):1124–40.

Brown, Lee P. "Crime, Criminal Justice, and the Black Community." *Journal of Afro-American Issues* 2 (May, 1974):219–30.

Carl, Earl L., and Callahan, Kenneth R. "Negroes and the Law." *Journal of Legal Education* 17 (1965):250–71.

———. "The Shortage of Negro Lawyers: Pluralistic Legal Education and Legal Services for the Poor." *Journal of Legal Education* 20 (1967):21–32.

"Case for Black Juries." *Yale Law Journal* 79 (January, 1970):531–50.

"The Challenge of Crime in a Free Society." A Report by the President's Commission on Law Enforcement and Administration of Justice. Washington, D.C., 1967.

Chevigny, Paul. *Cops and Rebels: A Study of Provocation.* New York, 1972.

Chrisman, Robert. "Black Prisoners—White Law." *The Black Scholar* 1 (April–May, 1971):45.

Coles, R. "The Question of Negro Crime." *Harper's* 228 (April, 1964):134–36.

Crockett, G. W., Jr. "Black Judges and the Black Judicial Experience." *Wayne Law Review* 19 (November, 1972):61.

Cross, Cranville J. "Negro, Prejudice, and the Police." *Journal of Criminal Law* 55 (September, 1964):405–11.

Davis, Angela Y. *If They Come in the Morning—Voices of Resistance.* New York, 1971.

"The Death Penalty for Rape." *The Nation.* 200 (February 15, 1965):156–57.

Douglas, Carlyle C. "How Justice Shortchanges Blacks." *Ebony* 29 (October, 1974):76–84.

Epstein, Jack. *Trials of Resistance.* New York, 1970.

Feldman, Glenn M. "The Legal Rights of Prisoners." *Journal of Missouri Bar* 28 (June, 1972):293–306.

Foner, Philip S., ed. *The Black Panthers Speak.* Philadelphia, 1970.

Forys, Major Conrad W. "Constitutional Rights of Prisoners." *Military Law Review* 55 (January, 1972):1–38.

Fox, Vernon. "Why Prisoners Riot." *Federal Probation* 35 (March, 1971):9–14.

————."Prisons: Reform or Rebellion?" in Charles E. Reasons (ed.), *The Criminologist: Crime and the Criminal.* Pacific Palisades, Calif., 1974.

Frankline, Steven P. "Manacles and the Messenger: A Short Study in Religious Freedom in the Prison." *Catholic University Law Review* 14 (1965):30–66.

Fursland, Morris A. "A Comparison of Negro and White Crime Rates." *Journal of Criminal Law, Criminology, and Police Science* 61 (June, 1970):214–17.

Gellhorn, E. "Law Schools and the Negro." *Duke Law Journal* 1968 (December, 1968):1069–97.

Gerard, Jules B., and Ferry, T. Rankin, Jr. "Discrimination Against Negroes in the Administration of Criminal Law in Missouri." *Washington University Law Quarterly* 1970 (Fall, 1970):415–38.

Gitelman, Morton. "The Relative Performance of Appointed and Retained Counsel in Arkansas Felony Cases—An Empirical Study." *Arkansas Law Review* 24 (Winter, 1971):442–52.

Goodell, Charles. *Political Prisoners in America.* New York, 1973.

Gossett, W. T. "Bar Must Encourage More Negro Lawyers." *Trial* 4 (April–May, 1968):22–27.

Graham, Fred P. "Black Crime: The Lawless Image." *Harper's* 241 (September, 1970):64–71.

Halstead, Fred. *Harlem Stirs.* New York, 1966.

Higginbotham, A. Leon, Jr. "Racism and the Early American Legal Process, 1619–1896." *Annals of the American Academy of Political and Social Science* 407 (May, 1973):1–17.

————. *In the Matter of Color: Race and the American Legal Process: The Colonial Period.* New York, 1978.

Hirschkop, Philip J., and Milleman, Michael A. "The Unconstitutionality of Prison Life." *Virginia Law Review* 55 (June, 1969):795–839.

Jackson, George. *Soledad Brother.* New York, 1970.

Kellor, Frances A. "Criminal Negro." *Arena* 20 (January–May, 1901):59–68; 190–97; 308–16; 419–28; 510–20.

Kenne, Bill. "Who Is a Political Prisoner?" *Hilltop* (April 5, 1973):8.

Knight, Etheridge. *Black Voices from Prison.* New York, 1970.

Levy, Burton. "Cops in the Ghetto: A Problem of the Police System." *Behavioral Scientist* (March–April, 1968):31–34.

Martin, Charles H. *The Angelo Herndon Case and Southern Justice.* Baton Rouge, 1976.

Martinson, Robert. "Planning for Public Safety." *New Republic* 166 (April 15, 1972):17–18.

————. "The Meaning of Attica." *New Republic* 166 (April 15, 1972):17–18.

————. "Collective Behavior at Attica." *Federal Probation* 36 (September, 1972):3–7.

McGee, H. W., Jr. "Minority Students in Law School: Black Lawyers and the Struggle for Racial Justice in the American Social Order." *Buffalo Law Review* 20 (Winter, 1971): 423–69.

———. "Blacks, Due Process, and Efficiency in the Clash of Values as the Supreme Court Moves to the Right." *Black Law Journal* 2 (Winter, 1972):220.

McNickles, Roma K. *Differences that Make a Difference: Papers Presented at a Seminar on the Implications of Cultural Differences for Corrections.* College Park, Md., 1970.

Minton, Robert, and Rice, Stephen. "Using Racism at San Quentin," in Frank Browning (ed.), *Prison Life: A Study of the Explosive Conditions in America's Prisons,* pp. 104–17. New York, 1972.

Moore, Howard, Jr., and Moore, Jane Bond. "Some Reflections on the Criminal Justice System, Prisons, and Repressions." *Howard Law Journal* 17 (1973):831–43.

Moore, Winston E. "My Cure for Prison Riots: End Prison Racism." *Ebony* 27 (December, 1971):84–90; 94–95.

National Advisory Commission on Criminal Justice Standards and Goals, *Task Force on Corrections.* Washington, D.C., 1973.

National Advisory Commission on Criminal Justice Standards and Goals, *Task Force on Courts.* Washington, D.C., 1973.

"The Negro Crime Rate: A Failure in Integration." *Time* 71 (April 21, 1958):16.

Oswald, Russell S. *Attica—My Story.* Garden City, N.Y., 1972.

"Pre-Trial Detention in the N.Y. City Jails." *Columbia Journal of Law and Social Problems* 7 (Spring, 1971):350–80.

"Race Distinctions and the Courts." *Survey* 38 (August, 1917): 509.

Reasons, Charles E. "Racism, Prisons and Prisoners' Rights." *Issues in Criminology* 9 (Fall, 1974):3–20.

——— and Kuykendall, Jack L. *Race, Crime, and Justice.* Pacific Palisades, Calif., 1972.

Reid, Herbert O., Sr. "The Administration of Justice in the Minority Communities." *Howard Law Journal* 17 (1972):266–325.

Report of the National Advisory Commission on Civil Disorders. Washington, D.C., 1968

Report of the Philadelphia Bar Association Special Committee on Pennsylvania Bar Administration Procedures—Racial Discrimination in the Administration of the Pennsylvania Bar Exam. (Liacouras, Dandridge, Green, Jackson, Ruthrauff). *Temple Law Quarterly* 44 (Winter, 1971):143–258.

"Report on Prisons." *Outlook* 157 (January 7, 1931):8–9.

Rogers, Cornish. "Black Liberation and the Prisons." *Christian Century* 88 (December 15, 1972):1462.

Rubin, Sol. "Developments in Correctional Law." *Crime and Delinquency* 19 (April, 1973):251–52.

Ryan, William. *Blaming the Victim.* New York, 1971.

Samuels, G. "Justice in the Court Room: Can the Poor Get It? Public Defender System." *Saturday Review* 49 (January 29, 1966):25–28.

Savitz, Leonard. "Black Crime," in Kent Miller and Ralph Dreger (eds.), *Comparative Studies of Blacks and Whites in the United States,* pp. 484–87. New York, 1973.

Seale, Bobby. *Seize the Time.* New York, 1968.

Shufeldt, Robert W. "Crime Among Washington Negroes." *Science* 18 (August, 1891):94–95.

Silberman, Charles. *Criminal Violence, Criminal Justice.* New York, 1978.

Skolnick, Jerome H. *Justice Without Trial: Law Enforcement in Democratic Society.* New York, 1960.

Special Society Report. "The Black Judge in America: A Statistical Profile." *Judicature* 57 (June/July, 1973):18–21.

Sutherland, Edwin H. *White Collar Crime.* Dryden, N.Y., 1949.

Swett, Daniel. "Cultural Bias in the American Legal System." *Law and Society Review* 5 (August, 1969):79–110.

Symposium: Disadvantaged Students and Legal Education—Programs for Affirmative Action. *University of Toledo Law Review* 1970 (Spring–Summer, 1970):277.

Thorstein, Sellin. "The Negro Criminal: A Statistical Note." *Annals of the American Academy of Political and Social Sciences* 140 (November, 1928):52–64.

"To Judge Murtagh: From the Panther 21," in Philip Foner (ed.), *The Black Panthers Speak,* p. 204. Philadelphia, 1970.

"The Unconstitutionality of Plea Bargaining." *Harvard Law Review* 83 (April, 1970):1387–1455.

U.S. Commission on Civil Rights. *Justice.* Washington, D.C., 1961.

Wald, Patricia. "Poverty and Criminal Justice," in Norman Johnston, Leonard Savits, and Marvin E. Wolfgang (eds.), *The Sociology of Punishment and Corrections.* New York, 1970.

Wambridge, Eleanor Rowland. "Negroes in Custody." *American Mercury* 21 (September, 1930):76–83.

The White Problem in America by the editors of *Ebony.* Chicago, 1966.

Wolfgang, Marvin, and Cohen, Bernard. *Crime and Race: Conceptions and Misconceptions.* New York, 1970.

Work, Monroe N. "Crime Among Negroes of Chicago." *American Journal of Sociology* 6 (September, 1900):204–23.

———. "Negro Criminality in the South." *Annals of the American Academy of Political and Social Sciences* 49 (September, 1913):74–80.

Yee, Min S. *Melancholy History of Soledad Prison.* New York, 1973.

8. THE BATTLE FOR EDUCATION

Ahmad, Muhammed. "On the Black Student Movement, 1960–1970." *Black Scholar* 9 (May–June, 1978):2–11.

Aptheker, Herbert, ed. *W. E. B. Du Bois: The Education of Black People.* Amherst, Mass., 1973.

Atwood, R. B., et al. "Negro Teachers in Northern Colleges and Universities in the United States." *Journal of Negro Education* 18 (Fall, 1949):564–67.

Bacote, Clarence A. *The Story of Atlanta University: A Century of Service, 1865–1965.* Atlanta, Ga., 1969.

Ballard, Allen B. *The Education of Black Folk.* New York, 1973.

Belles, A. Gilbert. "Negroes Are Few on College Faculties." *Southern Education Report* 4 (July–August, 1963):23–25.

Blassingame, John W., ed. *New Perspectives on Black Studies.* Urbana, Ill., 1971.

Bond, Horace Mann. *The Education of the Negro in the American Social Order.* New York, 1934.

———. *Black American Scholars: A Study of Their Beginnings.* Detroit, 1972.

Bullock, Henry A. *A History of Negro Education in the South.* Cambridge, Mass., 1967.

Campbell, Robert F. "Community Control." *Southern Education Report* 4 (July–August, 1968):10–13.

Crossland, Fred E. *Minority Access to College.* New York, 1971.

Du Bois, W. E. B., ed. *The Negro Common School.* Atlanta, Ga., 1901.

Edwards, G. Franklin. *The Negro Professional Class.* Glencoe, Ill., 1959.

Engs, Robert F. *Freedom's First Generation: Black Hampton, Virginia, 1861–1890.* Philadelphia, 1979.

Forman, James. *The Making of Black Revolutionaries; a Personal Account.* New York, 1972.

Fortune, T. Thomas. "False Theory of Education Cause of Race Demoralization." *Colored American Magazine* 7 (July, 1904):473–78.

Franklin, John Hope. "Jim Crow Goes to School." *South Atlantic Quarterly* 58 (Spring, 1959):225–35.

Franklin, Vincent P., and Anderson, James D., eds. *New Perspectives on Black Educational History.* Boston, 1978.

Graglia, Lino A. *Disaster by Decree: The Supreme Court Decisions on Race and the Schools.* Ithaca, N.Y., 1976.

Graham, Hugh D. "Desegregation in Nashville: The Dynamics of Compliance." *Tennessee Historical Quarterly* 25 (Summer, 1966):135–54.

Harlan, Louis R. *Separate and Unequal: Public School Campaigns and Racism in the Southern Seaboard States, 1901–1915.* New York, 1958.

———. *Booker T. Washington: The Making of a Black Leader, 1856–1901.* New York, 1972.

Johnson, Roosevelt. *Black Scholars on Higher Education in the 70s.* Columbus, Ohio, 1974.

Knoll, Erwin. "The Truth About Desegregation in the Washington, D.C. Public Schools." *Journal of Negro Education* 28 (Spring, 1959):92–113.

———. "Colleges: An Imprint Already." *Southern Education Report* 4 (July–August, 1968):14–20.

Lander, Ernest M., and Calhoun, Richard J., eds. *Two Decades of Change: The South Since the Supreme Court Desegregation Decision.* Columbia, S.C., 1975.

Logan, Rayford W. *Howard University, the First Hundred Years, 1867–1967.* New York, 1968.

McGee, Reece J. *Academic Janus.* San Francisco, 1971.

McGrath Earl J. *The Predominantly Negro Colleges and Universities in Transition.* New York, 1965.

Morais, Herbert M. *The History of the Negro in Medicine.* New York, 1969.

Moss, James A. "Negro Teachers in Predominantly White Colleges." *Journal of Negro Education* 27 (Fall, 1958):451–62.

Nanorato, Michael V., ed. *Have We Overcome? Race Relations Since Brown.* Jackson, Miss., 1979.

Payton, James Warren. "Some Experiences and Customs at Yale." *Colored American Magazine* 1 (June, 1900):80–87.

Pickens, William. "Southern Negroes in Northern University." *Voice of the Negro* 2 (April, 1905):234–36.

Plault, Richard L. "Racial Integration in Public Higher Education in the North." *Journal of Negro Education* 23 (Summer, 1954):310–16.

Poindexter, C. C. "Some Student Experiences." *Voice of the Negro* 3 (May, 1906):335–38.
Queen, Hallie E. "I am a College Negro Problem." *Colored American Magazine* 17 (July, 1909):30–33.
Read, Frank T., and McGough, Lucy S. *Let Them Be Judged: The Judicial Integration of the Deep South.* Metuchen, N.J., 1978.
Rist, Ray C. *The Urban School: A Factory for Failure.* Cambridge, Mass., 1973.
———. *The Invisible Children: School Integration in American Society.* Cambridge, Mass., 1978.
Robinson, Armistead L., ed. *Black Studies in the University.* New York, 1968.
Sherer, Robert G. *Subordination or Liberation? The Development and Conflicting Theories of Black Education in Nineteenth Century Alabama.* University, Ala., 1977.
Vaughn, William Preston. *Schools for All: Blacks and Public Education in the South, 1865–1877.* Lexington, Ky., 1974.
Washington, Booker T. *Up From Slavery.* New York, 1901.
Weinberg, Meyer. *A Chance to Learn.* New York, 1977.
Wilkinson, J. Harvie. *From Brown to Bakke: The Supreme Court and School Integration: 1954–1978.* New York, 1979.
Willie, Charles V., and McCord, Arline S. *Black Students at White Colleges.* New York, 1972.
Winston, Michael R. "Through the Back Door: Academic Racism and the Negro Scholar in Historical Perspective." *Daedalus* 100 (Summer, 1971):678–720.
Wolters, Raymond. *The New Negro on Campus: Black College Rebellions of the 1920s.* Princeton, N.J., 1975.
Woodson, Carter G. *The Miseducation of the Negro.* Washington, D.C., 1933.

9. MILITARY SERVICE AND THE PARADOX OF LOYALTY

Aptheker, Herbert. "The Negro in the Union Navy." *Journal of Negro History* 32 (April, 1947):169–200.
Banks, Samuel L. "The Korean Conflict." *Negro History Bulletin* 36 (October, 1973):131–32.
Barbeau, Arthur Edward, and Henri, Florette. *The Unknown Soldiers: Black American Troops in World War I.* Philadelphia, 1974.
Berry, Mary Frances. *Black Resistance/White Law: A History of Constitutional Racism in America.* New York, 1971.
———. *Military Necessity and Civil Rights Policy: Black Citizenship and the Constitution, 1861–1868.* Port Washington, N.Y., 1977.
"Blacks Win Class Election at the U.S. Naval Academy." *Ebony* 28 (January, 1973):100–4.
Bond, Horace Mann. "The Negro in the Armed Forces of the United States Prior to World War I." *Journal of Negro Education* 12 (Summer, 1943):268–87.
Bonsal, Stephen. "The Negro Soldier in War and Peace." *North American Review* 185 (June 7, 1907):320–27.
Brewer, James H. *The Confederate Negro.* Durham, N.C., 1969.
Brown, Williams Wells. *The Negro in the American Revolution.* Boston, 1855.
Buchanan, Russell. *Black Americans in World War II.* Santa Barbara, Cal., 1977.

Campbell, Nicholas H. "The Negro in the Navy." *Colored American Magazine* 6 (May, 1903):406–13.

Dalfiume, Richard M. *Desegregation of the U.S. Armed Forces: Fighting on Two Fronts, 1939–1953.* Columbia, Miss., 1969.

Du Bois, W. E. B. *The Gift of Black Folk; the Negroes in the Making of America.* Boston, 1924.

Emilio, Luis A. *Brave Black Regiment: A History of the 54th Massachusetts.* Boston, 1891.

Fletcher, Marvin E. *The Black Soldier and Officer in the United States Army, 1891–1917.* Columbia, Miss., 1975.

Flipper, Henry O. *The Colored Cadet at West Point.* New York, 1878; reprint ed., New York, 1969.

Foner, Jack D. *Blacks and the Military in American History.* New York, 1974.

Forten, James. *A Series of Letters by a Man of Color.* Philadelphia, 1813.

Garrison, William Lloyd. "The Loyalty and Devotion of Colored Americans in the Revolution and War of 1812," in *The Negro Soldier.* Boston, 1861; reprint ed., 1970.

Gatewood, Willard. *Smoked Yankees and the Struggle for Empire: Letters from Negro Soldiers, 1898–1902.* Urbana, Ill., 1971.

Gropman, Alan L. *The Air Force Integrates: 1945–1964.* Washington, D.C., 1978.

Hartgrove, W. B. "The Negro Soldier in the American Revolution." *Journal of Negro History* 1 (April, 1916):110–31.

"Jim Crow in the Army Camps," by a Negro soldier. *Crisis* 49 (December, 1940):385.

Johnson, Thomas A. "Negroes in 'The Nam.'" *Ebony* 23 (August, 1968):31–39.

Kenworthy, E. W. "Taps for Jim Crow." *New York Times Magazine* (June 11, 1950):12, 34–37.

Lane, Ann J. *The Brownsville Affair: National Crisis and Black Reaction.* Port Washington, N.Y., 1971.

Leckie, William H. *The Buffalo Soldiers: A Narrative of the Negro Cavalry in the West.* Norman, Okla., 1967.

Lee, Ulysses G., Jr. *The United States Army in World War II. Special Studies. The Employment of Negro Troops.* Washington, 1966.

Llorens, David. "Why Negroes Re-Enlist." *Ebony* 23 (August, 1968):80–90.

Long, Howard H. "The Negro Soldier in the Army of the United States." *Journal of Negro Education* 12 (Summer, 1973):307–15.

McConnell, Roland C. *Negro Troops of Antebellum Louisiana.* Baton Rouge, La., 1968.

Marshall, Thurgood. "Summary Justice: The Negro GI in Korea." *Crisis* 58 (May, 1951):297–304.

Milne, Lucille B. "Jim Crow in the Army." *New Republic* 110 (March 13, 1944):339–42.

Moore, George Henry. *Historical Notes on the Employment of Negroes in the American Army of the Revolution.* New York, 1862.

Moton, Robert Russa. "The American Negro and the World War." *World's Work* 36 (May, 1918):74–77.

Mullen, Robert W. *Black Speeches on the Vietnam War.* Cranbury, N.J., 1976.

National Archives. *The Negro in the Military Services of the United States. A Compilation of Official Records, State Papers, Historical Records, 1639–1865.*

"A Negro in the Army." *New Republic* (June 26, 1944):851.

Nell, William C. *The Colored Patriots of the American Revolution*. Boston, 1855.

———. *Colored Americans in the Wars of 1776 and 1812*. Philadelphia, 1902.

Osur, Alan M. *Blacks in the Army Air Forces During World War II: The Problem of Race Relations*. Washington, D.C., 1977.

"Our Men in Vietnam," section in each issue of *Sepia*, 18–19 (1969–70).

Quarles, Benjamin. *The Negro in the American Revolution*. Chapel Hill, N.C., 1940.

———. *The Negro in the Civil War*. Boston, 1958.

Rackleff, Robert B. "The Black Soldier in Popular American Magazines, 1900–1971." *Negro History Bulletin* 34 (December, 1971):185–89.

Reddick, Lawrence D. "The Negro in the United States Navy During World War II." *Journal of Negro History* 32 (April, 1947):201–19.

———. "The Negro Policy of the American Army Since World War II." *Journal of Negro History* 38 (April, 1953):196–215.

Scott, Emmett J. *American Negro in the World War*. Chicago, 1919.

Singletary, Otis, *Negro Militia and Reconstruction*. Austin, Tex., 1957.

Steele, Matthew F. "The 'Color Line' in the Army." *North American Review* 184 (December 21, 1906):1285–88.

Storey, Moorfield, "Athens and Brownsville." *Crisis* 1 (November, 1910):13.

Taylor, Clyde Comp. *Vietnam and Black America: An Anthology of Protest and Resistance*. Garden City, N.Y., 1976.

Terry, Wallace. *The Bloods*. New York, 1973.

"The Search for Military Justice." *Report of an NAACP Inquiry into the Problems of Negro Servicemen in West Germany*. New York, 1971.

"Voices from Vietnam," each issue of *Sepia*, 20–23 (1971–January, 1973).

Weaver, John D. *The Brownsville Raid*. New York, 1970.

White, Milton. "Malcolm X in the Military." *The Black Scholar* 1 (May, 1970):31–35.

White, Walter. "What the Negro Thinks of the Army." *Annals of the American Academy of Political and Social Sciences*. 223 (September, 1942):67–71.

Wiley, Bell. *Southern Negroes, 1861–1865*. New Haven, Conn., 1938.

Wilson, Joseph T. *The Black Phalanx*. Hartford, Conn., 1888.

Williams, George Washington. *A History of the Negro Troops in the War of the Rebellion*. New York, 1888.

Wynne, Lewis N. "Brownsville: The Reaction of the Negro Press." *Phylon* 33 (Summer, 1972):153–60.

10. WHITE PROSCRIPTIONS AND BLACK PROTESTS

Abramson, Doris E. *Negro Playwrights in the American Theatre, 1925–1959*. New York, 1969.

Adams, George R. "Black Militant Drama." *American Image* 28 (Summer, 1971):121–28.

Adams, John H. "Rough Sketches." *Voice of the Negro* 1 (August, 1904):323–26.

Aleckson, Sam. *Before the War, and After the Union*. Boston, 1929.

Anderson, Alston. *All God's Children*. Indianapolis, Ind., 1965.

Austin, Edmund. *Black Challenge*. New York, 1958.

Baldwin, James. *Tell Me How Long the Train's Been Gone*. New York, 1968.

Beardsley, H. C. "Black Psychology, 1975." *Black Scholar* 6 (July–August, 1975): whole issue.

Berry, Faith, ed. *Good Morning Revolution: Uncollected Social Protest Writings of Langston Hughes*. New York, 1973.

Black, Austin. *The Tornado in My Mouth*. New York, 1966.

Blasi, Anthony J. *Segregationist Violence and the Civil Rights Movement in Tuscaloosa*. Washington, D.C., 1980.

Blassingame, John W. "The Press and American Intervention in Haiti and the Dominican Republic, 1904–1920." *Caribbean Studies* 9 (July, 1969):27–43.

Bontemps, Arna. *Black Thunder*. New York, 1936.

———. *Drums at Dusk*. New York, 1939.

Brisbane, Robert. *The Black Vanguard*. Valley Forge, Pa., 1970.

———. *Black Activism: Racial Revolution in the United States, 1954–1970*. Valley Forge, Pa., 1974.

Buckner, George W. "St. Louis Revives the Segregation Issue." *Opportunity* 1 (August, 1923):238–39.

Bullins, Ed, ed. *New Plays from the Black Theatre*. New York, 1969.

———. *The New Lafayette Theatre Presents*. Garden City, N.Y., 1974.

Burke, William M. "Modern Black Fiction and the Literature of Oppression." Ph.D. dissertation, University of Oregon, 1971.

Burkhart, J. Austin. "Yonder Sits the Rocking Chair." *Crisis* 59 (December, 1952):619–24.

Button, James W. *Black Violence: Political Impact of the 1960s Riots*. Princeton, N.J., 1978.

Cantor, Norman F. *The Age of Protest: Dissent and Rebellion in the Twentieth Century*. San Francisco, 1969.

Capeci, Dominic J. *The Harlem Riot of 1943*. Philadelphia, 1977.

Carter, Wilmoth A. "Negro Main Street as a Symbol of Discrimination." *Phylon* 21 (Fall, 1960):234–42.

Cartwight, Joseph H. *The Triumph of Jim Crow: Tennessee Race Relations in the 1880s*. Knoxville, Tenn., 1976.

Chafe, William H. *Civilities and Civil Rights: Greensboro, North Carolina, and the Black Struggle for Freedom*. New York, 1980.

Chapman, Abraham, ed. *New Black Voices: An Anthology of Contemporary Afro-American Literature*. New York, 1972.

Chesnutt, Charles W. *The House Behind the Cedars*. Boston, 1900.

Coffin, Frank B. *Coffin's Poems with Ajax's Ordeal*. Little Rock, Ark., 1897.

Cook, Mercer, and Henderson, Stephen. *The Militant Black Writer in Africa and the United States*. Madison, Wis., 1969.

Corbett, Maurice N. *The Harp of Ethiopia*. Nashville, Tenn., 1914.

Corrothers, James D. *In Spite of the Handicap; an Autobiography*. New York, 1916.

Couch, William, ed. *New Black Playwrights*. Baton Rouge, La., 1968.

Cripps, Thomas. *Slow Fade to Black: The Negro in American Film, 1900–1942*. New York, 1977.

Davis, Benjamin J. "Build the United Negro People's Movement." *Political Affairs* 26 (November, 1947):996–1006.

———. "The Negro People's Liberation Movement." *Political Affairs* 27 (August, 1948):880–98.

Davis, Frank Marshall. *I Am the American Negro*. Chicago, 1937.

Dodson, Owen. *Six Plays for a Negro Theatre*. Boston, 1934.

Dooley, Thomas. *Revolution*. Chicago, 1968.

Du Bois, W. E. B. *The Souls of Black Folk*. Chicago, 1903.

————. *The Quest of the Silver Fleece*. Chicago, 1911.

Dyer, Thomas G. *Theodore Roosevelt and the Idea of Race*. Baton Rouge, 1980.

Easton, William E. *Dessalines, A Dramatic Tale; A Single Chapter from Haiti's History*. Galveston, Tex., 1893.

————. *Christophe; A Tragedy in Prose of Imperial Haiti*. Los Angeles, 1911.

Echeruo, M. J. C. "American Negro Poetry." *Phylon* 24 (Spring, 1963):62–68.

Ehrmann, Jacques Comp, ed., *Literature and Revolution*. Boston, 1967.

Ellison, Curtis W. "Black Adam: The Adamic Assertion and the Afro-American Novelist." Ph.D. dissertation, University of Minnesota, 1970.

Ellison, Ralph. *Shadow and Act*. New York, 1964.

Engle, Gary D., ed. *This Grotesque Essence: Plays from the American Minstrel Stage*. Baton Rouge, La., 1978.

Fair, Ronald L. *Many Thousand Gone*. New York, 1965.

Fauset, Jessie. *Plum Bun*. New York, 1929.

————. *Comedy, American Style*. New York, 1933.

Ferris, William. *Blues from the Delta*. New York, 1978.

Fischer, Roger A. "A Pioneer Protest: The New Orleans Street-Car Controversy of 1867." *Journal of Negro History* 53 (July, 1968):219–33.

————. *The Segregation Struggle in Louisiana, 1862–77*. Urbana, Ill., 1974.

Ford, James W. "The Communist Party: Champion Fighter for Negro Rights." *Political Affairs* 28 (June, 1949):38–50.

Ford, Nick A. *The Contemporary Negro Novel*. Boston, 1936.

Fuller, Thomas O. *Twenty Years In Public Life, 1890–1910, North Carolina-Tennessee*. Nashville, 1910.

Galton, Francis. *Hereditary Genius; An Inquiry Into Its Laws and Consequences*. London, 1869.

Gerber, David A. *Black Ohio and the Color Line, 1860–1915*. Urbana, Ill., 1976.

Gloster, Hugh. *Negro Voices in American Fiction*. Chapel Hill, N.C., 1948.

Graham, James D. "Group Tactics and Ideals." *Messenger* 8 (December, 1926):361, 383; 9 (January, 1927):11–14, 29, 31; 9 (April, 1927):110, 114; 9 (October, 1927):308–9, 313.

————. "Negro Protest in America, 1900–1955: A Bibliographical Guide." *South Atlantic Quarterly* 67 (Winter, 1968):94–107.

Greenlee, Sam. *The Spook Who Sat by the Door*. New York, 1969.

Griggs, Sutton. *Imperim in Imperio*. Cincinnati, 1899.

Hair, William I. *Carnival of Fury: Robert Charles and the New Orleans Race Riot of 1900*. Baton Rouge, La., 1976.

Hare, Nathan. "Integrated Southern Town: How a Small Southern Town Makes Integration Work." *Phylon* 22 (Summer, 1961):180–87.

Hatch, James V., ed. *Black Theater, USA*. New York, 1974.

Hawkins, W. Asbie. "A Year of Segregation in Baltimore." *Crisis* 3 (November, 1911):27–30.

Henderson, George W. *Ollie Miss*. New York, 1935.

Hill, Leslie P. *Toussaint L'Ouverture*. Boston, 1928.

Himes, Chester. *If He Hollers Let Him Go*. Garden City, N.Y., 1945.

Holtzclaw, William H. *The Black Man's Burden.* New York, 1915.
Hughes, Langston. "My Adventures as a Social Poet." *Phylon* 8 (Fall, 1947):205–12.
Hurston, Zora Neale *Jonah's Gourd Vine.* Philadelphia, 1934.
Johnson, Abby A. and Johnson, Ronald M. *Propaganda and Aesthetics: The Literary Politics of Afro-American Magazines in the Twentieth Century.* Amherst, Mass., 1979.
Johnson, Fenton *Visions of the Dusk.* New York, 1915.
Johnson, James W. *The Autobiography of an Ex-Colored Man.* Boston, 1912.
Johnson, Maggie P. *Thoughts for Idle Hours.* Roanoke, Va., 1915.
Jones, Edward S. *The Sylvan Cabin.* Boston, 1911.
Kaiser, Ernest. "Recent Literature on Black Liberation Struggles and the Ghetto Crisis." *Science and Society* 33 (Spring, 1969):168–96.
Killens, John O. *Youngblood.* New York, 1954.
———. *And Then We Heard the Thunder.* New York, 1962.
———. *Sippi.* New York, 1967.
King, Woodie, and Milner, Ron, eds. *Black Drama Anthology.* New York, 1971.
Kirwan, Albert D. *Revolt of the Rednecks: Mississippi Politics, 1876–1925.* New York, 1951.
Klotman, Phyllis Rauch. *Another Man Gone: The Black Runner in Contemporary Afro-American Literature.* Port Washington, N.Y., 1977.
Kofsky, Frank. *Black Nationalism and the Revolution in Music.* New York, 1970.
Larsen, Nella. *Quicksand.* New York, 1928.
———. *Passing.* New York, 1929.
Latta, Morgan London. *The History of My Life and Work. Autobiography.* Raleigh, N.C., 1903.
Lee, George. *River George.* New York, 1937.
Lenin, V. I. *On Literature and Art.* Moscow, 1967.
Lomax, Alan. "I Got the Blues." *Common Ground* 8 (Summer, 1948):38–52.
Margetson, George R. *The Fledgling Bard and the Poetry Society.* Boston, 1916.
Mars, Florence. *Witness in Philadelphia.* Baton Rouge, 1977.
Mayfield, Julian. *The Grand Parade.* New York, 1961.
McDaniel, Paul A., and Babchuk, Nicholas. "Negro Conceptions of White People in a Northeastern City." *Phylon* 21 (Spring, 1960):7–19.
McPherson, James M. *The Abolitionist Legacy: From Reconstruction to the NAACP.* Princeton, N.J., 1975.
Meier, August, Plant, Thomas S., and Smothers, Curtis. "Case Study in Nonviolent Direct Action." *Crisis* 71 (November, 1964):573–78.
——— and Rudwick, Elliott. *Along the Color Line.* Urbana, Ill., 1976.
Miller, Kelly. "A Reply to Tom Watson." *Voice of the Negro.* 2 (August, 1905):536–43.
Mitchell, Loften. *A Land Beyond the River.* Cady, Wyo., 1963.
———. *Black Drama.* New York, 1967.
"Nashville's Revolt Against Jimcrowism." *Voice of the Negro* 2 (December, 1905):827–30.
Nielson, David Gordon. *Black Ethos: Northern Urban Negro Life and Thought, 1890–1930.* Westport, Conn., 1977.
Norris, Marjorie M. "An Early Instance of Nonviolence: The Louisville Demon-

strations of 1870–1871." *Journal of Southern History* 32 (November, 1966):487–504.
Odum, Howard W. *The Negro and His Songs.* Chapel Hill, N.C., 1925.
Offord, Carl. *The White Face.* New York, 1943.
Oliver, Paul. *The Story of the Blues.* Philadelphia, 1969.
Patterson, Lindsay, ed. *Black Theater.* New York, 1971.
Paynter, John H. *Fugitives of the Pearl.* Washington, D.C., 1930.
Phillips, W. M. "The Boycott: A Negro Community in Conflict." *Phylon* 22 (Spring, 1961):24–30.
Quillin, Franklin U. "Race Prejudice in a Northern Town." *Independent* 59 (July, 1905):139–42.
Rhodes, Hari. *A Chosen Few.* New York, 1965.
Richardson, Willis, and May Miller, eds. *Negro History in Thirteen Plays.* Washington, D.C., 1935.
Rowe, Kenneth T. *A Theater in Your Head.* New York, 1960.
Rustin, Bayard. *Strategies for Freedom: The Changing Patterns of Black Protest.* New York, 1976.
Scarborough, Dorothy. "The 'Blues' as Folk Song." *Publications of the Texas Folklore Society* 2 (1917):52–66.
Schraufnagel, Noel C. "The Negro Novel: 1940–1970." Ph.D. dissertation, University of Nebraska, 1971.
Smalley, Webster, ed. *Five Plays by Langston Hughes.* Bloomington, Ind., 1963.
Smith, William Gardner. *South Street.* New York, 1954.
Sosna, Morton. *In Search of the Silent South: Southern Liberals and the Race Issue.* New York, 1977.
Still, James. *Early Recollections and Life of Dr. James Still.* Philadelphia, 1877.
Sumpter, Clyde G. "Militating for Change: The Black Revolutionary Theatre Movement in the United States." Ph.D. dissertation, University of Kansas, 1970.
Takaki, Ronald T. *Iron Cages: Race and Culture in Nineteenth-Century America.* New York, 1979.
Toll, Robert C. *Blacking Up: The Minstrel Show in Nineteenth Century America.* New York, 1974.
Trotsky, Leon. *Literature and Revolution.* New York, 1957.
Walker, Margaret. *Jubilee.* Boston, 1966.
Washington, Booker T. *Up from Slavery.* New York, 1901.
Weiss, Nancy J. *The National Urban League, 1910–1940.* New York, 1974.
White, Charles F. *Plea of the Negro Soldier and a Hundred Other Poems.* Easthampton, Mass., 1908.
White, Newman I. *American Negro Folk-Songs.* Cambridge, England, 1928.
White, Walter. *Flight.* New York, 1926.
Whitman, Albery A. *Twatsinas Seminoles; or the Rape of Florida.* St. Louis, 1885.
Wilhelm, Sidney W. *Who Needs the Negro?* Cambridge, Mass., 1970.
Williams, John A. *The Man Who Cried I Am.* Boston, 1967.
———. *Sons of Darkness, Sons of Light.* Boston, 1969.
Williams, Raymond. *Marxism and Literature.* New York, 1977.
Wright, Richard *Uncle Tom's Children.* New York, 1938.
———. *Native Son.* New York, 1940.

11. BLACK NATIONALISM

African Repository, 1825–1892. Washington, D.C.

Athearn, Robert G. *In Search of Canaan: Black Migration to Kansas, 1879–80.* Lawrence, Kans., 1978.

Bennett, Lerone. "Negro vs. Afro-American vs. Black." *Ebony* 23 (November, 1967):46–54.

Bittle, William E., and Geis, Gilbert. *The Longest Way Home: Chief Alfred C. Sam's Back-to-Africa Movement.* Detroit, 1964.

Bowen, J. W. E. "Who Are We? Africans, Afro-Americans, Colored People, Negroes or American Negroes?" *Voice of the Negro* 3 (January, 1906):30–36.

Briggs, Cyril. "The Decline of the Garvey Movement." *The Communist* 10 (June, 1931):547–52.

Cleage, Albert B. *The Black Messiah.* New York, 1968.

Cleaver, Eldridge. *Soul On Ice.* New York, 1967.

———. "The Land Question." *Ramparts* 6 (May, 1968):51–53.

Corbett, Maurice N. *The Harp of Ethiopia.* Nashville, Tenn., 1914.

Crockett, Norman L. *The Black Towns.* Lawrence, Kan., 1979.

Crummell, Alexander. *Africa and America—Addresses and Discourses.* Springfield, Mass., 1891.

Cruse, Harold. "Revolutionary Nationalism and the Afro-American." *Studies on the Left* 2 (1962):12–25.

Cullen, Countee. *Color.* New York, 1925.

Curtis, Irene. "Emigration and Assimilation." *Colored American Magazine* 12 (March, 1907):176.

Davis, Benjamin J. "Build the United Negro People's Movement." *Political Affairs* 26 (November, 1947):996–1006.

Delany, Martin R. *The Condition, Elevation, Emigration, and Destiny of the Colored People of the United States Politically Considered.* Philadelphia, 1852.

Dinkins, Charles R. *Lyrics of Love.* Columbia, S.C., 1904.

Du Bois, W. E. B. "That Capital 'N.' " *Crisis* 11 (February, 1916):184.

———. "In Black." *Crisis* 20 (October, 1920):263–66.

———. "The Name 'Negro.' " *Crisis* 35 (March, 1928):96–97.

———. "On Being Ashamed of Oneself." *Crisis* 40 (September, 1933):199–200.

———. "A Negro Nation within a Nation." *Current History* 42 (June, 1935):265–70.

Eastmond, Claude T. *Light and Shadows.* Boston, 1934.

Emanuel, James A. *The Treehouse and Other Poems.* Detroit, 1968.

Essien-Udom, E. U. *Black Nationalism: A Search for Identity in America.* Chicago, 1962.

Fanon, Frantz. *The Wretched of the Earth,* tr. Constance Farrington. New York, 1963.

———. *Black Skin, White Masks,* tr. Charles Lam Markham. New York, 1967.

———. *Toward the African Revolution,* tr. Haakon Chevalier. New York, 1967.

Ford, James W. "The Communist Party: Champion Fighter for Negro Rights." *Political Affairs* 28 (June, 1949):38–50.

Fortune, T. Thomas. "Who Are We? Afro-Americans, Colored People, or Negroes?" *Voice of the Negro* 3 (March, 1906):194–98.

Franklin, James T. *Mid-Day Gleanings.* Memphis, 1893.

Garvey, Amy Jacques, ed. *The Philosophy and Opinions of Marcus Garvey.* London, 1967.

Geiss, Imanuel. *The Pan-African Movement.* London, 1974.

Grant, George S. "What Are We?" *Messenger* 8 (October, 1926):300.

Gregory, A. J. "Black Nationalism." *Science and Society* 27 (Fall, 1963):415–32.

Haywood, Harry. "The Crisis of the Jim Crow Nationalism of the Negro Bourgeoisie." *The Communist* 10 (April, 1931):330–38.

———. "The Theoretical Defenders of White Chauvinism in the Labor Movement." *The Communist* 10 (June, 1931):497–508.

Henriksen, Thomas H. "Black Is Beautiful, an Old Idea." *Negro History Bulletin* 34 (November, 1971):150–52.

Hill, Adelaide Cromwell, and Kilson, Martin, eds. *Apropos of Africa: Sentiments of Negro American Leaders on Africa from the 1800's to the 1950's.* London, 1969.

Hite, Roger W. "The Search for an Alternative: The Rhetoric of Black Separatism, 1850–1860." Ph.D. dissertation, University of Oregon, 1971.

———. "Voice of a Fugitive: Henry Bibb and Ante-bellum Black Separatism." *Journal of Black Studies* 4 (March, 1974):269–84.

Kiely, Pat. "A Cry for Black Nun Power." *Commonweal* 89 (September 21, 1968):167.

Langley, Jabez A., "Garveyism and African Nationalism." *Race* 11 (October, 1969):157–72.

Lee, Don L. *We Walk the Way of the New World.* Detroit, 1979.

Llorens, David. "Natural Hair, New Symbol of Race Pride." *Ebony* 23 (December, 1967):139–44.

———. "Black Separatism in Perspective." *Ebony* 23 (September, 1968):34–36.

Lynch, Hollis. *Edward Wilmot Blyden: Pan Negro Patriot, 1832–1912.* London, 1967.

———, ed. *Black Spokesman—Selected Published Writings of Edward Wilmot Blyden.* New York, 1971.

Martin, Tony. *Race First: The Ideological and Organizational Struggles of Marcus Garvey and the Universal Negro Improvement Association.* Westport, Conn., 1976.

Matheurin, Owen C. *Henry Sylvester Williams and the Origins of the Pan-African Movement, 1869–1911.* Westport, Conn., 1976.

Mbadinuju, C. Chinwoke. "Black Separatism." *Current History* 67 (November, 1974):206–13.

Miller, Floyd J. *The Search for a Black Nationality: Black Colonization and Emigration, 1787–1863.* Urbana, Ill., 1975.

Moore, Richard B. *The Name "Negro," Its Origin and Evil Use.* New York, 1960.

Morsell, J. A. "Black Nationalism." *Journal of Intergroup Relations* 3 (Winter, 1961–1962):5–11.

Moses, Wilson J. *The Golden Age of Black Nationalism, 1850–1925.* Hamden, Conn., 1978.

Padmore, George. *Pan-Africanism or Communism: The Coming Struggle for Africa.* London, 1956.

Pinkney, Alphonso. *Red, Black and Green: Black Nationalism in the United States.* Cambridge, Eng., 1976.

Redkey, Edwin S. *Black Exodus: Black Nationalist and Back-to-Africa Movements, 1890–1910.* New Haven, 1969.
———, ed. *Respect Black: The Writings and Speeches of Henry MacNeal Turner.* New York, 1971.
Rogers, Joel A. "What Are We, Negroes or Americans?" *The Messenger* 8 (August, 1926):237–38, 255.
Scothron, Samuel R. "New York African Society for Mutual Relief—Ninety-Seventh Anniversary." *Colored American Magazine* 9 (December, 1905):685–90.
Shepperson, George. "Notes on Negro American Influences on the Emergence of African Nationalism." *Journal of African History* 1 (1960):299–312.
———, and Price, Thomas. *Independent Africa: John Chilembwe and the Origins, Setting and Significance of the Nyasaland Native Rising of 1915.* Edinburgh, Scotland, 1958.
Spurgeon, James Robert. "New York and Liberia Steamship Company." *Colored American Magazine* 7 (December, 1904):734–42.
Standing, T. G. "Nationalism in Negro Leadership." *American Journal of Sociology* 40 (September, 1934):180–92.
Stewart, Thomas McCants. *Liberia: The Americo-African Republic.* New York, 1886.
Sweet, Leonard I. *Black Images of America, 1784–1870.* New York, 1976.
"The Terms Defined." *Ebony* 25 (August, 1970):34–44.
Thompson, Aaron B. *Echoes of Spring.* Rossmoyne, Ohio, 1901.
Tracy, R. Archer. "Negro Immigration: Unsound, Impractical, and Retrogressive." *Colored American Magazine* 12 (January, 1907):17–25.
Uya, Okon Edet, ed. *Black Brotherhood: Afro-Americans and Africa.* Lexington, Mass., 1971.
Vass, S. N. "Emigration as a Means of Improving the Condition of the Negro Race." *Colored American Magazine* 12 (January, 1907):44–48.
Walden, Daniel, and Wylie, Kenneth. "W. E. B. Du Bois: Pan Africanism's Intellectual Father." *Journal of Human Relations* 14 (First Quarter, 1966):28–41.
Washington, Booker T. *The Story of the Negro, the Rise of the Race from Slavery.* New York, 1909.
Weisbord, Robert G. "The Back to Africa Idea." *History Today* 18 (January, 1968):30–37.
———. "Africa, Africans and the Afro-American: Images and Identities in Transition." *Race* 10 (January, 1969):305–21.
Williams, Oscar, ed. "Afro-American vs. Negro: A 19th Century Essay Against the Use of the Term 'Negro.'" *Negro History Bulletin* 32 (March, 1969):18.

Some Significant Dates
in Black American History

1502   First Africans arrive in the New World.

1619   Twenty Africans arrive on Dutch man-of-war at Jamestown, Va.

1619–   Legal slave trade: 400,000 to 1 million of the 10 to 50
1803   million Africans forcibly transported to America arrive. Others smuggled in illegally until 1860.

1662   Virginia enacts a statute making slavery hereditary, following the status of the mother.

1770   Crispus Attucks, first of five men killed in the Boston Massacre.

1787   Richard Allen and Absalom Jones found the Free African Society, precursor of the Bethel AME Church, founded in 1794.

1800   Gabriel Prosser, a Virginia slave, hanged together with a number of his followers, for plotting to lead a slave attack on Richmond, Va.

1815   Free Negro battalion fights in the Battle of New Orleans against the British.

1815   Paul Cuffee carries thirty-eight Negro immigrants to Africa at his own expense.

1817–   Blacks and Indians fight against federal troops in the
1842   First and Second Seminole wars.

1816–   American Colonization Society organized by Bushrod
1817   Washington, Henry Clay, and other whites to take blacks to Africa.

1820   Missouri Compromise enacted prohibiting slavery north of Missouri.

1822   Denmark Vesey's slave conspiracy takes place in Charleston, S.C.

1827   Samuel E. Cornish and John Russwurm found *Freedom's Journal* in New York.

1829	David Walker publishes *Walker's Appeal*, a militant antislavery pamphlet.
1831	William Lloyd Garrison founds the *Liberator*.
1831	Nat Turner's slave rebellion takes place in Southhampton County, Va.
1833	Free Negroes and whites found the American Anti-Slavery Society, which meets in Philadelphia.
1834	Prudence Crandall's School for Negroes attacked by citizens and closed by local authorities in Canterbury, Conn.
1838	*Mirror of Liberty*, the first black magazine, begins publication in New York City.
1849	Benjamin Roberts loses court challenge to segregation in Boston schools.
1852	Publication of Harriet Beecher Stowe's *Uncle Tom's Cabin*.
1853	Publication of *Clotel*, the first novel by a black American, William Wells Brown.
1857	The Supreme Court decides *Dred Scott* v. *Sanford*.
1858	William Wells Brown publishes the first American black-authored play, *The Escape*.
1859	Martin R. Delany and Robert Campbell lead the Niger Valley exploring party to explore possible settlements of American blacks in Africa.
Oct. 1859	John Brown's raid on Harpers Ferry.
Jan. 1863	Lincoln issues the Emancipation Proclamation.
Mar. 1863	First National Draft Act passed; does not exclude blacks.
Mar. 1865	Freedman's Bureau Act, including provision for land for the freedmen, passed.
Apr. 1865	Opening of the government-chartered Freedmen's Bank; goes bankrupt after being milked by directors in June, 1874.
Dec. 1865	Ratification of the Thirteenth Amendment abolishing slavery.
Apr. 1866	Civil Rights Act passed by Congress, giving black citizens civil rights equal to those of whites.
Mar. 1867	Reconstruction Act, including voting rights for blacks, passed by Congress.

July 1868	Ratification of the Fourteenth Amendment protecting civil rights from state interference.
1869	First of twenty blacks to serve in the House of Representatives during Reconstruction seated.
1870	Hiram Revels elected to the Senate from Mississippi.
Mar. 1870	Ratification of the Fifteenth Amendment prohibiting denial of the right to vote on the grounds of race or previous condition of servitude.
1873–1879	Exodus of blacks from the South to Kansas.
1874	Blanche K. Bruce elected to the Senate from Mississippi, the only black elected to a full term until 1966.
1875	Civil Rights Act providing equal public accommodations passed by Congress.
1877	Reconstruction ends with withdrawal of the last federal troops from the South.
1881	Booker T. Washington founds Tuskegee Institute.
1883	Civil Rights Act of 1875 declared unconstitutional by the Supreme Court.
1895	Booker T. Washington's Atlanta University speech.
1895	Frederick Douglass dies February 20.
1896	*Plessy* v. *Ferguson* decided by the Supreme Court, approving separate but equal facilities.
June 1898	Ninth and Tenth Cavalry, two of four black regiments in the Regular Army, and Theodore Roosevelt's Rough Riders at San Juan Hill during the Spanish-American War.
1900	Booker T. Washington founds the National Negro Business League.
1903	W. E. B. Du Bois publishes *The Souls of Black Folk*.
1905	W. E. B. Du Bois, Monroe Trotter, and others found the Niagara Movement to fight for civil rights.
1906	Brownsville, Texas, shooting incident involving black troops.
1909	Springfield, Ill., lynching and subsequent white attacks in black neighborhoods leads to founding of the National Association for the Advancement of Colored People.

1910   W. E. B. Du Bois starts *Crisis* as the official NAACP publication.

1915   NAACP wins *Guinn* v. *U.S.*, finding use of the grandfather clause to qualify voters unconstitutional.

1915   Booker T. Washington dies in Tuskegee, Ala.

1915   Ghanaian Alfred Sam leads black emigration movement to Africa from black towns organized earlier in Oklahoma.

1916   Marcus Garvey arrives in New York from Jamaica and founds the Universal Negro Improvement Association.

1917   Houston, Texas, shooting incident involving black troops.

1919–   Five Pan-African Congresses organized by W. E. B. Du
1945   Bois.

1925   A. Philip Randolph organizes the Brotherhood of Sleeping Car Porters and Maids.

1928   Oscar DePriest elected to Congress, the first black since the term of George White of North Carolina ended in 1901.

1930   Black Muslims founded by W. D. Fard, succeeded by Elijah Muhammad in 1934.

1935   National Council of Negro Women founded with Mary McLeod Bethune as president.

1941   A. Philip Randolph's threat of a march on Washington leads Roosevelt to issue Executive Order 8802.

1946   *Ebony* magazine started by John Johnson.

1949   Secretary of Defense Lewis Johnson issues orders to desegregate opportunities in the military service.

1950   Ralph Bunche becomes the first black man to receive Nobel Peace Prize.

1954   *Brown* v. *Board of Education* decided by Supreme Court.

1955   Court order requiring desegregation with all deliberate speed issued in the Brown case by the Supreme Court.

1956   Montgomery, Ala., bus boycott led by Martin Luther King, Jr.

1956	Autherine Lucy expelled from the University of Alabama.
1957	Eisenhower orders use of troops in enforcing Little Rock, Ark., school desegregation.
1957	Congress passes the Civil Rights Act creating the U.S. Commission on Civil Rights and a Civil Rights Division in the Justice Department.
1960	Sit-ins at lunch counters in Greensboro, N.C.
1961	W. E. B. Du Bois joins the Communist party, renounces his U.S. citizenship, and moves to Ghana.
1961	CORE Freedom Rides in interstate transportation.
1962	Mississippi officials attempt to keep James Meredith out of the University of Mississippi; leads to violence.
1963	Assassination of Medgar Evers, leader of the NAACP in Mississippi.
Aug. 1963	March on Washington for jobs and freedom.
Sept. 1963	Four black children killed in bombing of a black church in Birmingham, Ala.
1964	Civil Rights Act creating the Equal Employment Opportunity Commission and ending discrimination in public accommodations, passed by Congress.
July 1964	Lemuel Penn shot by the Ku Klux Klan while driving along a road in Georgia.
Aug. 1964	Three civil rights workers—James Chaney, Michael Schwerner, and Andrew Goodman—murdered in Mississippi; bodies found.
Oct. 1964	Martin Luther King, Jr., receives the Nobel Peace Prize.
Feb. 1965	Malcolm X murdered.
Mar. 1965	Civil rights march from Selma to Montgomery, Ala., leads to passage of the Voting Rights Act.
Aug. 1965	Riot set off by police arrest in Watts, Los Angeles, Calif.
1965	Robert C. Weaver appointed Secretary of Housing and Urban Development, the first black cabinet officer.
June 1966	On the march for freedom from fear led by James Meredith in Mississippi, "Black Power" slogan attributed to Stokely Carmichael, head of the Student Non-Violent Coordinating Committee.

1966	Edward Brooke of Massachusetts elected to the Senate, the first black elected since Reconstruction.
1966	Founding of the Black Panther party by Huey Newton and Bobby Seale in Oakland, Calif.
June 1967	Muhammad Ali convicted for draft evasion and his heavyweight boxing title taken away. After he wins on appeal, he has to fight George Foreman three years later to win back the title.
1967	In *Loving* v. *Virginia* Supreme Court declares illegal the ban on interracial marriage.
1967	Thurgood Marshall appointed first black Supreme Court Justice.
Apr. 4, 1968	Martin Luther King, Jr., assassinated.
1971	Jesse Jackson founds Operation PUSH.
1972	Gary National Black Political Convention.
1974	Sixth Pan-African Congress convened in Tanzania.
1978	*Bakke* v. *University of California* decided by Supreme Court. Racial quotas cannot be used in university admissions decisions, but race may be taken into account.
1979	*Weber* v. *Kaiser Aluminum* decided by Supreme Court. Voluntary agreements to give preferential training opportunities to blacks in an industry are legal.
1980	*Fullilove et al.* v. *Klutznick, Secretary of Commerce et al.* decided by Supreme Court approves minority fund set-aside in public works act included in an amendment proposed by Congressman Parren Mitchell.
May 17, 1980	March for Jobs, Peace, and Justice in Washington, D.C. led by Rev. Jesse Jackson.

Index